THE POLITICS
OF
ENGLISH JACOBINISM

WRITINGS OF JOHN THELWALL

Edited with an Introduction and Notes
by
Gregory Claeys

THE PENNSYLVANIA STATE UNIVERSITY PRESS
UNIVERSITY PARK, PENNSYLVANIA

Library of Congress Cataloging-in-Publication Data

Thelwall, John, 1764–1834.
    The politics of English Jacobinism : writings of John Thelwall / edited with an introduction and notes by Gregory Claeys.

        p.   cm.
    Includes bibliographical references and index.
    ISBN 0-271-01347-8 (cloth)
    ISBN 0-271-01348-6 (paper)
    1. Jacobins—Great Britain.   2. Great Britain—Politics and Government—1789–1820.   3. Radicalism—Great Britain—History—18th century.   I. Claeys, Gregory.
II. Title.
DA520.T37   1995
320.5'12'09033—dc20   94-20695
                                                                                                                    CIP

It is the policy of The Pennsylvania State University Press to use acid-free paper for the first printing of all clothbound books. Publications on uncoated stock satisfy the minimum requirements of American National Standard for Information Sciences—Permanence of Paper for Printed Library Materials, ANSI Z39.48–1984.

FRONTISPIECE: John Thelwall. Engraving, c. 1794. Copyright British Museum.

Contents

Acknowledgments   xi

Introduction   xiii

    Thelwall's Life and Times   xiii

    Thelwall's Intellectual Development and Significance   xxxv

    The Writings of John Thelwall   lvi

Further Reading   lix

A Note on the Texts   lxi

The Natural and Constitutional Right of Britons to Annual Parliaments,
Universal Suffrage, and the Freedom of Popular Association (1795)   3

The Tribune (1795–96), Selections   65

    From Volume 1:

    On the Means of Redressing the Calamities of the Nation.   66

    On the Exhausted State of Our National Resources, and the
    Consequent Condition of Our Labourers and Manufacturers.   74

    The Duty and Interest of the People to Enquire into the
    Causes and Conduct of Wars, in the Guilt of Which They
    Are Involved, by Contributing to Their Support. — From the
    Second Lecture on War.   80

    On the Moral and Political Influence of the Prospective
    Principle of Virtue.   88

The Second Lecture on the Moral and Political Influence of
the Prospective Principle of Virtue.   102

On the Humanity and Benevolence of the Dutch Revolution,
and the Causes of the Excesses in France. The Third Lecture
on the Moral and Political Influence of the Prospective
Principle of Virtue. With a Parallel Between the Character
of Pitt and Robespierre.   116

From Volume 2:

The Present War a Principal Cause of the Starving Condition
of the People.—The First Lecture "On the Causes of the
Dearness and Scarcity of Provisions."   138

The Second Lecture on the Causes of the Present Dearness
and Scarcity of Provisions.   162

Consequences of Depriving the Mass of the People of Their
Share in the Representation. The Third Lecture "On the
Causes of the Present Dearness and Scarcity of Provisions."   181

Report on the State of Popular Opinion, and the Causes of the
Rapid Diffusion of Democratic Principles. Part the Second.
Including Definitions of Democracy, Aristocracy, and
Monarchy. Original Meaning of the Word King —
Consequences of Ministerial Ambition, &c.   209

Report on the State of Popular Opinion, and Causes of the
Increase of Democratic Principles. Part the Fifth. Including
Sketches of the Affairs of Scotland and Ireland, with a History
of the Progress of Defenderism, and Reflections on the Fate
and Deportment of O'Connor.   232

On the Causes of the Calamities and Disturbances That
Afflict the Nation. Part the Second — Including a Vindication
of the Moral Character of the Laborious Poor, Against the
Insulting Calumnies of Their Oppressors; with Sketches of the
Starving Misery of the British Peasantry.   245

From Volume 3:

The Connection Between the Calamities of the Present
Reign, and the System of Borough-Mongering Corruption —
Lecture the Second — Including Sketches of the Connection
Between the Growth of Taxation and Corruption, and the
Increasing Miseries of the Industrious Poor; and Reflections
on the Metaphysical Sophistries of Windham, and the Pious
Ravings of Burke.   267

The Connection Between the Calamities of the Present
Reign, and the System of Borough-Mongering Corruption —
Lecture the Third. — The Connection Between Parliamentary
Corruption and Commercial Monopoly: With Strictures on the
West-India Subscription, &c.   284

The Second Lecture on the Unfortunate Restoration of the
House of Stuart, with Strictures on the Differences Between
the English Revolution 1649, and That of France, in 1792,
and the Impossibility of Restoring Royalty in the Latter
Country: Including a Delineation of the Character of
Cromwell.   298

A Warning Voice to the Violent of All Parties; with
Reflections on the Events of the First Day of the Present
Session of Parliament; and an Enquiry Whether Conciliatory
or Coercive Measures Are Best Calculated to Allay Popular
Ferments.   314

*Sober Reflections on the Seditious and Inflammatory Letter of the
Rt. Hon. Edmund Burke to a Noble Lord* (1796)   329

The Rights of Nature, Against the Usurpations of Establishments
(1796)   389

Editor's Notes to the Texts   501

Index   526

Acknowledgments

I am grateful to Donna Andrews, John Barrell, Iain Hampsher-Monk, and E. P. Thompson for comments and references, and to the following institutions: the Guildhall Library; the library of Regent's Park College, Oxford; The Library Company of Philadelphia; the Library of Canterbury Cathedral; the Library of Royal Holloway and Bedford New College, University of London; the Goldsmiths' Library, University of London; the staff of The British Library, Great Russell Street, London; the National Library, Canberra; the History of Ideas Unit, Australian National University; Rice University Library.

The frontispiece, an engraving c. 1794, is reproduced courtesy of the Department of Prints and Engravings, The British Museum.

In Memoriam
E. P. Thompson
(1924–1993)

Introduction

Thelwall's Life and Times

The name John Thelwall is inextricably linked with the explosive debate the French Revolution triggered in Britain and with the contemporaneous emergence of the British working-class movement. Though the bulwark of church and state would hold firm, few decades in modern British history have witnessed such a tempestuous coincidence of political ferment, war, and economic change as the 1790s. For many hundreds of thousands, the existing social and political system had exhausted its legitimacy and seemed to be held together merely by force—and solely to serve a privileged and rapacious minority. To these, especially in the first years of the revolution, the example of France was not "a warning to Britain," as loyalists, such as the agricultural writer Arthur Young, insisted in 1793, but a beacon heralding democratic reform, lower taxes and food prices, and the humbling of an arrogant ruling class.[1] To become the prophet of these prospects was the peculiar fortune of John Thelwall—political lecturer, poet, and writer.

Yet, although Thelwall emerged by the mid-1790s as the chief orator, strategist, and theoretician of the largest radical organization of the period—the London Corresponding Society—he has not been well served by historians. His pivotal role as "one of the boldest political writers, speakers, and lecturers of his time" is usually acknowledged,[2] but his part even as a man of action has been overshadowed by a more famous contemporary, Thomas Paine, who was forced to flee to France in 1792. Moreover, Thelwall's great originality has gone largely unappreciated, despite his novel focus on wage labor, and his attempts to explain the origins of poverty and

1. Arthur Young, *The Example of France, a Warning to Britain* (1793).
2. John Binns, *Recollections of the Life of John Binns* (1854), p. 44. See, e.g., E. P. Thompson, *The Making of the English Working Class* (Harmondsworth: Penguin Books, 1968), esp. pp. 156–60.

to analyze the implications of economic development for the democratic movement.[3] More than any other reformer of the 1790s, in fact, his work heralds the interest in economic conditions that was to define nineteenth-century radicalism by contrast with the more predominantly constitutionalist concerns of the past.

John Thelwall was born on 27 July 1764 in Covent Garden, a descendant of an ancient Saxon family that took refuge in North Wales during the Norman invasion. ("The pride of ancient descent," his widow reported, Thelwall "never ceased to ridicule.")[4] His grandfather was a naval surgeon, and his father, Joseph Thelwall, was a London silk-mercer who died when John was nine. Early marked by his energy, studiousness, and cheerful disposition, the boy received some education at various London schools, especially at Highgate, where, Thelwall later recalled, a young clergyman named Harvey "sowed in the mind of his pupil the seeds of literary ambition." But his youth was exceedingly difficult. Life at home was marred by the dissipation and violence of Thelwall's older brother, whose tyranny over him instilled a lifelong revulsion against corporal punishment. His mother's efforts to keep up the family business faltered, and at age thirteen John was installed behind the shop counter to help. But while he served there three years, Thelwall was already lost to a private world of study and poetry writing. Apprenticed briefly thereafter to a tailor, he remained obstinately distracted. Carrying a candle in his pocket, he stole moments to read even while walking at night. (This greatly amused his friends, but nearly proved fatal when he was robbed one night near Lambeth by the light of his own taper.) When his brother-in-law helped him to become articled to an attorney of the Inner Temple, Thelwall showed greater promise and remained three-and-a-half years (c. 1782–86). But even there he devoted more hours to poets and philosophers than to cases and reports. And this career too was soon imperiled by the realization that the attractiveness of the fee often outweighed the dictates of justice. Thelwall was also overly sensitive toward the law's victims; required to serve a writ upon a cottager at Norwood, he fled without doing so, mumbling an

---

3. Recent studies of Thelwall include Günther Lottes, *Politische Aufklärung und plebeisches Publikum: Zur Theorie und Praxis des englischen Radikalismus im späten 18. Jahrhundert* (Munich: R. Oldenbourg, 1979), esp. pp. 267–99, 327–34; Geoffrey Gallop, "Ideology and the English Jacobins: The Case of John Thelwall," *Enlightenment and Dissent* 5 (1986), 3–20; and Iain Hampsher-Monk, "John Thelwall and the Eighteenth-Century Radical Response to Political Economy," *Historical Journal* 34 (1991), 1–20.

4. C. Boyle Thelwall, *The Life of John Thelwall* (1837), p. 3.

embarrassed excuse in his fear of its consequences for the man's family. On one occasion he donated his last shilling to aid a poor client. "Lawyers," he would later exclaim, had "spread more devastation through the moral world than the Goths and Vandals, who overthrew the Roman Empire." Though his legal drudgery would eventually serve him well, it was, he later reflected, the most miserable period of his existence.[5]

Turning now to painting—the career his father had proposed—and then to acting and playwriting, Thelwall also published two volumes entitled *Poems on Various Subjects* in 1787.[6] These were praised as indicating "an original and bold imagination," and they introduced Thelwall to London literary circles. For a time, he edited and wrote for *The Biographical and Imperial Magazine*. But these efforts brought in less than £50 a year, from which he had to help maintain both his mother and his brother.[7] Despite weak lungs and a slight, initial speech impediment that led some to nickname him "the lisping orator," Thelwall now also began to join public debating societies. There he upheld High Church politics and declaimed against "fanatics and republicans." (He was later described as "a complete Church-and-King man" in late adolescence.) But Thelwall's humanitarian feelings were beginning to redefine his politics. It has been claimed that his early writings, bearing mostly on the Gothic mystery, adventure, and romantic pastoralism popular in the day, evince no special concern for the lowly and dispossessed, "or any desire for reform," despite their condemnation of the slave trade and the fate of seduced women.[8] Nonetheless, even Thelwall's youthful poetry clearly betrays the powerful sense of injustice that would remain his dominant passion: "Is this the land where liberal feelings glow?" he demanded regarding imprisonment for debt in 1786.[9] And while his biography of the prison reformer John Howard, which ap-

5. John Thelwall, *The Natural and Constitutional Right of Britons* (1795), p. 29 (infra, p. 22); *Register of the Times; or, Political Museum* 2, suppl. (1794), 354.

6. A further work by Thelwall, *Orlando and Almeyda: A Legendary Tale in the Manner of Dr. Goldsmith* (1787), has not been rediscovered.

7. *State Trials for High Treason, Part Third, Containing the Trial of Mr. John Thelwall* (1795), p. 72.

8. Charles Cestre, *John Thelwall: A Pioneer of Democracy and Social Reform in England During the French Revolution* (London: Swan Sonnenschein, 1906), p. 25; C. Boyle Thelwall, *Life of John Thelwall*, pp. 46–47; John Thelwall, *Poems on Various Subjects* (1787), pp. 83–108.

9. John Thelwall, *Poems Chiefly Written in Retirement*, 2nd ed. (1801), pp. vi, ix, xix, 100; C. Boyle Thelwall, *Life of John Thelwall*, pp. 4–10, 15, 22, 40, 45. For evidence of Thelwall's oppositional sympathies in 1789, see, e.g., his comments on Charles James Fox in *Biographical and Imperial Magazine* 2 (1789), 43–44. Thelwall never renounced his belief in the moral and intellectual effects of scenery on the character. See *The Poetical Recreations of the Champion* (1822), pp. 73–77.

peared in 1790, praised the uses of religion in reforming convicts, it also hailed "the rights of humanity."[10]

Thus, in the late 1780s Thelwall grew steadily more disillusioned with the factional struggles of both great parties. He still considered the influence of the Crown as the best counterweight against oligarchical tendencies in the Commons, and in addition sympathized deeply with George III's mental derangement. When he discovered that rural life for many meant drudgery and a poor reward, however, his romantic sensibilities were rudely disturbed.[11] But it was the French Revolution that finally pushed Thelwall away from ministerial politics and toward radicalism. His first political publication proper was "Ode on the Destruction of the Bastille."[12] At least initially, however, what politicized Thelwall was more the British establishment's reaction to the revolution; "it was not *Tom Paine* but *Edmund Burke* that made me so zealous a reformer, and convinced me of the necessity of annual Parliaments and universal suffrage," he later emphasized.[13] But he was clearly also radicalized by renewed debates over the slave trade and by the Dissenters' efforts, in 1788–90, to have the Test Act and the Corporation Act repealed, which led him to regret some of his own Anglican prejudices against them.

But radicalism did not yet provide a career for Thelwall. He completed another romance, *The Rock of Modrec* (1792), set in ancient Britain and bursting with knightly valor, enslaved damsels, enchantment and necromancy, dark forests, and fire-breathing serpents. On 27 July 1791 he married seventeen-year-old Susan Vellum. He continued his private studies, making good headway with Latin under the tutelage of a friend. His time was also much occupied with scientific interests. An early poem, *Ode to Science* (1791), praised its contribution to "social Joys and Reason's calm controul."[14] Thelwall also attended anatomy and physiology lectures at Guy's and St. Thomas's hospitals between 1791 and 1793 to widen his knowledge of such subjects, and soon he was highly regarded by fellow students. (Four renowned surgeons bore witness to his character during his 1794 trial.) These concerns blossomed into a well-received talk to the

10. [John Thelwall], *Sketch of the Life of John Howard* (1790), pp. 21, 75.

11. See his account in *The Tribune* (1795–96, 3 vols.), 2:33–34 (infra, pp. 151–52).

12. *Biographical and Imperial Magazine* 2 (1789), 313–15, reprinted in *The Tribune* 1 (1795), 21–24. Cestre nonetheless exaggerates the impact of the revolution itself on Thelwall's development (*John Thelwall*, p. 25).

13. *The Tribune* 3 (1796), 95.

14. John Thelwall, *Ode to Science* (1791), p. 3.

Physical Society at Guy's Hospital on 26 January 1793 that was discussed for six successive evenings and published as *An Essay Towards a Definition of Animal Vitality* (1793). Here Thelwall, taking "the simple principles of materialism" as his point of departure, argued the controversial point that there was no "vital principle" of life separate from the fact of existence itself, which he admitted implied there was no separate "soul" in human beings.[15] Clearly he was taking his leave of religious orthodoxy fairly quickly.

It was in the much-contested Westminster election of July 1790 that Thelwall's growing political concerns first assumed a practical form. He must, about now, have become much more aware of how thoroughly the aristocracy dominated and manipulated political life, and how much of even the parliamentary process was under direct control of the government's ability corruptly to engineer majorities at elections with relative impunity. Even the few who could vote, therefore, had little power or voice through their representatives, compared with the large numbers of MPs nominated directly by great landlords and often controlled by the party in power. Volunteering to assist the independent reformer John Horne Tooke, who sought to extend the suffrage and to purify the electoral process, Thelwall formed thereby an enduring friendship with the elder radical. Soon they were dining together once a week and calling each other "Citizen." Tooke even offered to send his "political son" to Cambridge to read theology in place of his own boy, who showed no aptitude for study. In late 1790, however, the reformers' cause suffered a setback. Sympathy for the French Revolution had hitherto been fairly widespread, for most Britons were flattered to think that the French desired a constitutional monarchy like their own. In November, however, appeared Edmund Burke's *Reflections on the Revolution in France*, which denounced the revolutionaries as bloodthirsty enthusiasts greedily plotting to subvert the entire ancient order of Europe, and their British supporters as dupes who would overturn Church, King, and sound morals. Responses poured from the reformers' presses. First came Mary Wollstonecraft's *Vindication of the Rights of Men*, which appeared a mere month later. As the political atmosphere became increasingly heated, several dozen other works followed, of which by far the most important was Paine's *Rights of Man* (1791–92). Within a few months, every other topic of debate was suspended.

The burgeoning controversy took place against a background of growing

---

15. John Thelwall, *An Essay Towards a Definition of Animal Vitality* (1793), pp. 7–9, 13.

popular radicalism whose appeal astonished friend and foe alike. Reform groups sprang up in most parts of the country, but especially in the capital, where the London Corresponding Society was founded by shoemaker Thomas Hardy in early 1792; in the Midlands; and in Scotland. Their opponents, for whom the very limited franchise (one in twenty adult males) already adequately reflected the interests of the nation, were as quick to muster, however. By late 1792, the country resounded with the promises, denunciations, slogans, and threats, veiled or otherwise, of both parties. Loyalist violence quickly set the tone of the official reaction. When Birmingham reformers celebrated the second anniversary of the revolution in July 1791, a drunken mob burned the house and laboratory of the liberal dissenter Joseph Priestley to the ground. Everywhere civil authority connived with bribery and intimidation to deny the reformers meeting places and opportunities for publicity. Heralded by a royal proclamation against sedition, an official stamp of approval seemed to be placed on every form of repression short of murder. Freedom of speech was disappearing; in November 1792, Thelwall saw the Society of Free Debate, which he helped to manage, suppressed after existing nearly half a century.[16]

Now swept up by the unrelenting radical tide, Thelwall by late 1792 found himself unable to rent a room for political discussion anywhere in London, though on a large, widely posted handbill he offered the exceedingly generous sum of twenty guineas for the privilege. He was by now beginning to acquire a reputation; after a lecture at Canterbury, soldiers were marched into the town in case order broke down.[17] Earlier in the year, he had joined the Southwark branch of the Society of the Friends of the People, founded in April by Major John Cartwright. Some of its members called for annual parliaments and universal suffrage, goals with which Thelwall himself only finally concurred while in the Tower in 1794. The Society also raised funds for various causes—for example, to assist the cause of Polish independence against Russia.[18] When it was virtually crushed by government pressure, Thelwall shifted his allegiance on 21 October 1793 to the essentially plebeian and much larger London Corresponding Society, whose objects were similar but whose social caste made

---

16. John Thelwall, *Political Lectures, Volume the First* (1795), p. v.

17. Ibid., pp. vi, viii.

18. See *Southwark Society of the Friends of the People* (1792); and Iain Hampsher-Monk, "Civic Humanism and Parliamentary Reform: The Case of the Society of Friends of the People," *Journal of British Studies* 18 (1979), 68–86.

it a very different kind of organization. Elected a delegate of Division 25 in late October, Thelwall by November was diligently collecting signatures and subscriptions with the printer and land-nationalization advocate Thomas Spence, the physician and radical Painite William Hodgson, Thomas Hardy, and others.[19] With a foot in both camps, Thelwall also helped to bridge the widening gap between the Society and other more genteel organizations, such as the Society for Constitutional Information, to which he was deputed in April 1794.[20]

In this environment, Thelwall's talents as an orator shone most brightly. Speaking frequently, he rapidly acquired a reputation as the most compelling rhetorician in the reformers' camp. To a paranoid government, his more acute remarks often verged on sedition. At one gathering in November, he related an encounter in a farmer's yard with a tyrannical gamecock, King Chanticleer, which resulted in the rooster being beheaded for tyranny. The radical publisher Daniel Isaac Eaton found the story so pointedly amusing that he printed it, evidently with certain embellishments. Eaton was then charged with sedition (by a government, Thelwall pointed out, which assumed that every mention of tyranny must refer to George III). But he was acquitted after three months' imprisonment.[21]

Such measures only heralded even greater repression. In November 1793, delegates from many reform groups assembled in Edinburgh at a "Convention" to clarify their principles, to define the mechanisms by which popular sovereignty was to be expressed in future, and to focus popular support. Well aware that the French Revolution was now embodied in a similarly named assembly, the government arrested a number of its delegates and, after show trials (which were easier to stage in Scotland), sentenced several to fourteen years' transportation at Botany Bay. Thelwall responded by hiring lecture halls at Southwark, Soho, and elsewhere, to raise funds to defend the imprisoned delegates. Ready to pounce, the police scrutinized his movements carefully. But a first lecture, "On the Moral Tendency of a System of Spies and Informers," took place without inci-

19. Public Record Office (PRO), Treasury Solicitor's Papers, TS11/955; *The London Corresponding Society Addresses the Friends of Peace and Reform* (broadsheet, 1793). The best source for Thelwall's activities in this period, and for the Society generally, is Mary Thale, ed., *Selections from the Papers of the London Corresponding Society, 1792–1799* (Cambridge: Cambridge University Press, 1983).

20. PRO, TS11/962.

21. For the prose story, which appears to have been taken verbatim, see *Politics for the People* 8 (1793), 102–7. Thelwall reprinted a poetic version of the tale as *John Gilpin's Ghost; or, The Warning Voice of King Chanticleer* (1795) and discusses it briefly in *The Tribune* 1:165.

dent, and others followed for some three months. Irritated that Thelwall was insufficiently seditious, the government attempted to disrupt other meetings. On one occasion, loyalists and police armed with bludgeons hid in an adjacent room, awaiting a pretext to invade the hall.[22] On another, the exasperated authorities hired two coalheavers, accompanied by police officers, to start a riot. But the laborers, after first singing rude songs, were apparently soon converted by Thelwall's arguments "and departed from the room with denunciations against those who had attempted to delude them, and to inflame their minds against those who, instead of enemies, they found to be their best friends."[23]

Nonetheless, Thelwall sensibly grew increasingly paranoid. Government spies were everywhere. Police hecklers shouted "God save Great George Our King" in lectures, and magistrates themselves egged loyalist rioters on to destroy Thelwall's lectern at one meeting. His handbills were torn down as soon as they went up. Landlords were threatened with the loss of their licenses when they rented him premises. Gangs of loyalist thugs shadowed his footsteps awaiting an opportunity to strike, and Thelwall, it was said, took to walking only in the middle of the street, taking "special care never to go down back streets, for fear of assassins."[24] Some of his relatives were turned out of their farm by Lord Winchelsea for reading his publications. Even his scientific associates were rattled. When he attempted to present a second paper, "On the Origin of Sensation," to the Physical Society in late 1793 or early 1794, an uproar occurred, and when the paper was finally read it was "voted out of the Society," from which Thelwall and several friends then withdrew.[25]

Thelwall obstinately refused to succumb to pressure. Instead, he commenced, in a small room at 3 New Compton Street, Soho, a series of lectures that became a focal point of London radicalism in 1794–96. At first, a scant eleven persons huddled together in a room capable of holding sixty, though Division 2 of the Corresponding Society also met at the address. But soon Thelwall attracted several hundred, and with the aid of a Smithfield leather-seller, George Williams, who put the lease in his own name, moved to a larger lecture hall at No. 2 Beaufort Buildings, Strand,

22. Thelwall, *Political Lectures, Volume the First*, p. xi.
23. *The Tribune* 2:283.
24. Binns, *Recollections*, p. 44; *State Trials for High Treason, Part Third*, p. 21; C. Boyle Thelwall, *Life of John Thelwall*, p. 144.
25. Thelwall, *Poems in Retirement*, pp. xxii–xxiii.

on the right side at the end of a cul-de-sac. This occupied the site of five previous houses and included living quarters upstairs.[26] Here his "bold and decided manner" soon drew an average audience of between 400 and 500, rising to 800, with nearly twice as many sometimes turned away.[27] At the rear of the hall, a fourteen-year-old boy named Henry Eaton (the son of the radical publisher) sold admission tickets and pamphlets as well as Thelwall's exceedingly popular songs.[28]

Outdoors, Thelwall reached even larger numbers. At several great meetings in early 1794, some with five "tribunes," or stages, from which speakers could address 50,000 listeners, with Thelwall drafting many of its resolutions, the London Corresponding Society set forth its view of the debasement of British liberties and the prospects for reform.[29] In his speeches, Thelwall steered a narrow course, aiming at once to reinforce the good cause, to mollify his more intemperate fellow reformers by insisting that the pen was superior to the sword, and to taunt the agents-provocateurs the police had smuggled into the organization, whom he claimed sought "from our meetings and assemblies to pick out pretences for introducing that system of military despotism which they hope to establish over us."[30] Some found his oratory almost captivating, but as one listener later recalled, Thelwall also succeeded in remaining "select and cautious in his phraseology."[31]

But the government failed to appreciate such restraint, and several times it attempted to get a Grand Jury to indict Thelwall for sedition.[32] In spring

26. Thomas Rees, *Reminiscences of Literary London from 1779 to 1853* (1896), p. 138; PRO, TS11/957. See also Mary Thale, "London Debating Societies in the 1790s," *Historical Journal* 32 (1989), 57–86. The buildings were demolished c. 1869. The site is presently occupied by the Savoy Theatre, Savoy Court. Many lecture notes from the Compton Street and Beaufort Buildings series are preserved in PRO, TS11/953 and TS11/955.

27. *The Tribune* 2:vi; Joseph Farington, *The Farington Diary* (London: Alan Hutchinson, 1923), 1:123; *Public Characters of 1800–1801* (1801), p. 125.

28. *The Trial of Thomas Hardy, for High Treason*, 4 vols. (1795), 3:311. These songs are reprinted in *The Tribune* 1:166–68, 190–92, 338–40; and in C. Boyle Thelwall, *Life of John Thelwall*, pp. 445–51. When interviewed by the Privy Council, Eaton attacked one of its members for "increasing the national debt, . . . causing unnecessary wars; and taxing the people to an enormous extent" (*The Tribune* 1:119, 187).

29. John Thelwall, *The Speech of John Thelwall at the Second Meeting, called by the London Corresponding Society, 12th November 1795* (1795), p. 1. This is reprinted in my *Political Writings of the 1790s*, 8 vols. (London: Pickering & Chatto, 1995), vol. 4.

30. *Account of the Proceedings of a Meeting of the London Corresponding Society . . . October 26, 1795* (1795), p. 15; *The Tribune* 1:188.

31. John Britton, *The Autobiography of John Britton*, 2 vols. (1850), 1:182.

32. See *The Tribune* 1:296–98.

1794, finally, seizing as a pretext a second planned convention that the London Corresponding Society proposed (and that Thelwall later claimed to have argued against),[33] the government imprisoned him and eleven other leading reformers on a charge of high treason. Thelwall was arrested on Tuesday, 13 May, though rumors that warrants would be issued had reached him the previous Friday. All of his books and papers were confiscated (most were never returned), and Thelwall was interrogated by the Privy Council, with the Prime Minister, Pitt, the Attorney General, Sir John Scott, and the Home Secretary, Dundas, present in person. Refusing to be intimidated, Thelwall, who later admitted to feeling "a little sulky" at the time, confessed to nothing more than being "bold in the consciousness of innocence." Declining to answer most of their inquiries, he finally put a finger to his lips when they persisted, and began to examine a watercolor drawing of a ship hanging over the fireplace.[34] His obstinate silence did nothing to allay the government's fears, and shortly thereafter, on 23 May, habeas corpus was suspended, permitting nearly any number of "preventive" confinements. As the screws tightened outside, Thelwall endured five months of solitary confinement (for a time, two armed guards watched him day and night) in his own "bastille," a small room (once occupied by Mary Queen of Scots) next to Thomas Hardy and near John Horne Tooke above the western gate of the Tower of London. He then suffered seven more weeks in the "dead-hole" in Newgate, a room with little light and no air, where the corpses of prisoners who had died of diseases were dumped. Outside, *The Times* satirized him as "President Citizen Telwell," the future head of an arbitrary, bloodthirsty British Convention.[35] Meanwhile, prosecutors scoured his papers in vain for solid evidence of real treason against the King. With some difficulty, they concocted a case against him, doubtless expecting that a loyalist jury would overlook legal niceties in order to make an example of Thelwall. On 25 October 1794, he and eleven supposed co-conspirators were arraigned at the Old Bailey for "conspiring to overturn the Government and perpetrate the King's death."[36]

In order to prove this charge and to secure a general condemnation of the reformers, and especially of the London Corresponding Society, the

---

33. See Thale, *Selections*, p. 132n, on Thelwall's proposals in this regard.

34. See *The Tribune* 1:85–95.

35. Ibid., p. 306; *The Times*, 6 September 1794, appendix: *The New Times* of 1 January 1800. Thelwall's account of his imprisonment is in *The Tribune* 1:301–27.

36. For a comprehensive account of these trials, see John Barrell, *Imagining the King's Death* (Oxford: Oxford University Press, forthcoming); and "Imaginary Treason, Imaginary Law: The State Trials of

government aimed, on the one hand, to establish the threat of violent action, particularly the "overt act" of conspiracy to overturn Parliament, and, on the other hand, to prove connections to revolutionary France. Intemperate language was easy to find. Symbolic acts of rebelliousness were plentiful. (A spy reported that Thelwall once cut the froth from a pint of porter and wished a similar fate on monarchs.)[37] And not only did the Edinburgh Convention have certain parallels to the French National Convention; various organizations had issued congratulatory addresses to the new republic since then. Worse still, Thelwall himself had scribbled, "in a moment of warmth," an inflammatory letter to a friend in America that went well beyond his published and spoken protests against the existing order.[38] This aligned him, as "a Republican and a true Sans-Culotte," with the "men of the Mountain" (Jacobins) in France, and denounced America for having "too great a veneration for property, too much *religion*, and too much *law*."[39] And as another letter from this period indicates, Thelwall did indeed feel, after long wavering between the Brissotines and the Jacobins, that during the previous year "the Mountain were the men most fitted for the helm of affairs in the stormy, and at that time of the struggle, the critical and alarming situation of France."[40]

But despite its successes in 1793, the efforts of its agents-provocateurs, and its attempt to tar all republicans as subversives, the government in the 1794 trials failed singularly to prove that the radicals were guilty of treason, or that Thelwall, whom it termed "one of the most active members," even "the leader" of the London Corresponding Society, actually aimed to overthrow the government instead of to reform Parliament.[41] Despite the flimsiness of its case, there is no doubt that the government would have hung Thelwall if it had secured a conviction. But his prosecutors overplayed

1794," in John Barrell, *The Birth of Pandora and the Division of Knowledge* (London: Macmillan, 1992), pp. 119–42.

37. Thale, *Selections*, p. 140. See *The Tribune* 1:119, 188.

38. *Trials for High Treason, Containing the Whole of the Proceedings at the Old Bailey, from October 28, to December 5, 1794*, 2nd ed. (1795), p. 392. Thelwall further discusses the evidence introduced at his trial in *Register of the Times; or, Political Museum* 2:263–64; and this letter, in *The Tribune* 1:91–92, 321–24. The letter itself is preserved in PRO, TS11/953.

39. *State Trials for High Treason, Part Third*, p. 21; PRO, TS11/953. See Thelwall's comments on the incompetence of the Brissotines to govern (infra, p. 120).

40. PRO, TS11/953. Thelwall's extraordinary lecture comparing the characters of Pitt and Robespierre shows his admiration of the Jacobins most clearly. See infra, pp. 116–37.

41. *The Second Report from the Committee of Secrecy*, 4th ed. (1794), p. 23; *State Trials for High Treason, Part Third*, p. 364.

their hand, and instead of trying Thelwall on the lesser and more nebulous charge of sedition, they aimed to take his life with the far more potent but considerably more strictly defined charge of high treason. By the time he was tried, on 1 December, Hardy and Horne Tooke had been acquitted and the case for a general conspiracy had virtually collapsed. But worries persisted that the evidence to be introduced against Thelwall would be more incriminating than that deployed against his associates.[42] Thelwall had vowed to defend himself during the three-day trial, and he prepared for the jury an elaborate speech replete with precedents, which set his own ordeal in the context of the reform struggle. But his lawyer, Thomas Erskine, deterred him from giving it and warned him he would be hung if he tried. (It was printed as The Natural and Constitutional Right of Britons; infra, pp. 3–63.) Thousands jostled outside the courtroom, awaiting the result. At his acquittal on 5 December, Thelwall addressed the court and insisted that he sought change "by peaceable means, by reason alone."[43] When he left the courtroom a free man, the crowd unharnessed the horses from his carriage, in the traditional manner of celebration, and drew him the half-mile from Newgate Street to Bloomsbury. Burke and others quickly condemned the acquittal as improper, and the death of his mother soon after Thelwall's release made it clear that the government had drawn his blood anyway.[44] But, as a consequence of this great victory, one member later recalled, the London Corresponding Society, whose General Committee had met above Thelwall's lecture hall since the day after it opened, "increased with great rapidity," at least for a short period of time.[45] The anniversary of the acquittal would be celebrated in London for at least forty-one years to come.[46]

Taking advantage of his now vastly augmented popularity, Thelwall commenced, on 6 February 1795, a new set of lectures at the Beaufort Buildings. Held twice weekly on Wednesday and Friday evenings, admission sixpence, the series began appropriately with a discourse "Upon the Moral and Political Importance of the Liberty of Speech." Over the next months, the atmosphere outside grew increasingly tense. As the war be-

---

42. Francis Plowden, A Short History of the British Empire During the Year 1794 (1795), p. 335.

43. The Politician, 27 December 1794, p. 19. An account of Thelwall's trial was also printed in Register of the Times; or, Political Museum 2 (1794), 225–46.

44. The Correspondence of Edmund Burke (Cambridge: Cambridge University Press, 1969), 8:423.

45. Thale, Selections, p. 145n; Francis Place, The Autobiography of Francis Place, ed. Mary Thale (Cambridge: Cambridge University Press, 1972), p. 132.

46. British Library, Add. MSS 27817:145.

came more unpopular, harvests failed, and food prices rose alarmingly, audiences often exceeded the capacity of 700. After his ordeal, Thelwall cut a brave, even heroic, figure. Some, with a sense of the social occasion, ventured forth just to see the man, whom one described as "small, compact, muscular—with a head denoting indomitable resolution, and features deeply furrowed by the ardent workings of his mind."[47] Others came to admire the power and intelligence with which the opposition case could be put in this most trying of times, with few of its sympathizers still willing to enter the fray so publicly despite the failure of the latest treason trials. (Some 80,000, Thelwall thought, had emigrated to America in the summer of 1794 alone.)[48] Even members of the nobility attended. The lectures not only showed Thelwall's renowned oratorical power at its peak. They were also pioneering in their combination of historical depth, statistical rigor, economic investigation, and a deep sympathy for and knowledge of the poor. In order to demonstrate the depths to which the working classes had sunk, Thelwall used many older texts to demonstrate the fall in wages, and had himself even gone from farm to farm—the habit of rural roaming ingrained from his earlier delight in nature—now turning to the human world, and gathering evidence about wages in order to support his views against the pervasive prejudices of those who did not know the real character of the working population. Many of the lectures were published in his weekly periodical, *The Tribune*, which appeared from March 1795 until the government suppressed it in April 1796.

Nonetheless, the danger of persecution was far from past. For several months, Thelwall withdrew from the London Corresponding Society in order to avoid having his opinions identified further with it, with the defense that standing alone "adhering to the cause of truth, I stand upon a rock which they cannot shake." Apparently he felt that he could either remain in the Society or conduct his lectures and the *Tribune*, but not both. He also acknowledged the grave strain prosecution had placed on his family, which had resulted, he feared, both in his mother's premature death and in his wife's subsequent miscarriage.[49] (Hardy's wife had miscarried and died shortly after his arrest.) But he rejoined again in the autumn, having decided only the night before to address an immense meeting, then probably the largest of its kind ever held, of perhaps 150,000 or even more

47. T. N. Talfourd, *Memoirs of Charles Lamb* (1892), p. 178.
48. *The Tribune* 1:3–4.
49. *Citizen Thelwall: Fraternity and Unanimity* (1795), p. 2; *The Tribune* 1:329–37.

people at Copenhagen Fields on 26 October 1795. (London's population was about one million at this time.) Here Thelwall again stressed that his own goal was "to diffuse amongst you the love of humanity, the love of peace, and the love of order." The day passed uneventfully.[50] But when stones struck the King's carriage—early rumors described them as bullets—at the opening of Parliament on 29 October, the alarm was raised again. The government responded by introducing new legislation regarding treason and sedition, and, in a clause evidently aimed at Thelwall himself (who was named several times during the parliamentary debates), proposed to make even rendering the government and constitution contemptible a serious crime.[51] As the risk of confrontation neared, another and possibly even larger meeting was called for 12 November. His voice nearing exhaustion, Thelwall again spoke at length. Every evening the bills were debated in Parliament; moreover, he lectured "on the Occurrences, Projects and *Conspiracies* of the present MOMENTOUS CRISIS," warning his would-be listeners that "BRITONS, who wish for information . . . be expeditious, for in a Fortnight hence it may be High Treason to sell a political pamphlet."[52] On 7 December, the London Corresponding Society again marshaled the friends of reform at Marylebone Fields, where an unsympathetic observer described Thelwall as "a little, and very mean looking man; of a sickly sallow complexion, and black, lank hair" who appeared "covered with a large, thick, loose great coat." (A more charitable onlooker acknowledged that he seemed "emaciated, and labouring under severe indisposition.")[53] But on 18 December the Two Acts, as they were soon termed, received royal assent. Large-scale political meetings were now virtually proscribed. Though it did not disband, the Society was forced to climb down. Thelwall's livelihood and principles alike were also directly threatened, for lectures "on the Laws, Constitution, Government, and Polity of these kingdoms" were now entirely prohibited, with a penalty of £100

50. John Thelwall, *The Speech of John Thelwall, at the General Meeting of the Friends of Parliamentary Reform Called by the London Corresponding Society, 26th October 1795* (1795), pp. iii, 3–4.

51. C. Boyle Thelwall, *Life of John Thelwall*, p. 391. The bills were "A Bill for the More Effectually Preventing Seditious Meetings and Assemblies" and "A Bill for the Safety and Preservation of His Majesty's Person Against Treasonable Practices and Attempts." The final versions are printed in *The History of Two Acts* (1796), pp. 772–80.

52. *Every Evening, During the Discussion of Lord Grenville's Bill . . .* (broadsheet, 1795). During the debate in the Lords, the Marquis of Lansdowne remarked he had heard that Thelwall had said the opposition was just as bad as the ministry, which was anathema to the old Whig reformers (*History of Two Acts*, p. 679).

53. John Thelwall, *Speech, 12th November 1795*, p. i; Farington, *Diary* 1:118; *History of Two Acts*, p. 649.

for each violation. Thus, as William Cobbett later recalled, "was stifled, for that time, the great cause of Parliamentary Reform."[54]

Thelwall nonetheless sought to evade the restrictions of the Acts by shifting the focus of his lectures to classical history, and particularly the abuses of monarchy and aristocracy in ancient Rome. This hoisted the banner of civic virtue once again while avoiding overt sedition; "*Locke, Sydney*, and *Harrington* are put to silence, and *Barlow*, *Paine*, and *Callendar* it may be almost High Treason to consult," Thelwall proclaimed, "but *Socrates* and *Plato*, *Tully* and *Demosthenes*, may be eloquent in the same cause."[55] Spies and two reporters paid by the government were in attendance, and several attempts were made to disrupt the proceedings. But finally, dwindling numbers forced Thelwall to end these talks as well in mid-April 1796, after about twenty lectures had been delivered.[56] In keeping with his new persona, Thelwall in 1796 also edited the seventeenth-century republican Walter Moyle's *Essay on the Constitution and Government of the Roman State*, giving it a new and somewhat unsuitable title, *Democracy Vindicated* (for Moyle had been no democrat) and billing himself on the title page as a "Lecturer on Classical History." He still retained at least a few middle-class admirers. For example, the radical writer and scholar Joseph Ritson commented on the reformers, "I really think that Thelwall is the best of them," but acknowledged "I find myself pretty singular in my good opinion of him."[57] Several of Thelwall's wealthier liberal patrons, in fact, now withdrew their subsidy toward the rent of the Beaufort Buildings.[58] When booksellers now refused to accept *The Tribune* any longer, he lost a considerable sum. A further exposition of his views, *The Rights of Nature*, which was to become his most important theoretical work, also had to be concluded prematurely.

An additional and in many ways more bitter blow was Thelwall's abandonment, in 1795, by the man he regarded as his "philosophical father," the former Dissenting clergyman and novelist William Godwin.[59] The lat-

---

54. *The Tribune* 3:261; *Cobbett's Weekly Political Register*, 19 June 1811, cols. 1505–7.
55. John Thelwall, *Prospectus of a Course of Lectures* (1796), pp. 7–8, 18–19.
56. For their subjects, see *The Tribune* 3:325–27.
57. Joseph Ritson, *Letters of Joseph Ritson*, 2 vols. (1833), 2:117.
58. See *The Rights of Nature*, ltr. 3, pp. 123–24 (infra, pp. 499–500). On Thelwall's patrons, see E. P. Thompson, "John Thelwall" (forthcoming).
59. On their relations, see B. Sprague Allen, "William Godwin's Influence upon John Thelwall," *Publications of the Modern Language Association of America* 37 (1922), 662–82. Nonetheless, Allen's claim that "the substance of Thelwall's thought is derived from *Political Justice*" is an exaggeration that pays too little heed to the developments in *The Rights of Nature* in particular.

ter's *Enquiry Concerning Political Justice* (1793) had a profound impact on many more educated and youthful reformers. Thelwall had praised it as commending "the most extensive plan of freedom and innovation ever discussed by any writer in the English language."[60] Both men shared a great faith in the inevitable progress of reason in human affairs, in its role in the gradual diffusion of "universal benevolence," and in the superiority of the latter over merely limited love of country.[61] Both believed that violence rarely assisted the cause of reform, though Thelwall also insisted (in 1793) that, despite the excesses of the French Revolution, every despotic government was "stained with crimes of blacker horror."[62] Both also shared no small nostalgia for a simpler society of greater independence and virtue. Thelwall had done much to popularize Godwin's ideas to plebeian audiences, reading from *Political Justice* (his copy of which was seized by the police on his arrest) on coercion and punishment to the London Corresponding Society in early 1794, for example, and at the Three Kings Tavern in the Minories.[63] He also gave at least five lectures on a favored Godwinian theme—the abuse of the professions, especially law.[64] He was even quoted (or possibly misquoted) as asserting at a London Corresponding Society meeting that eventually there would be no need for laws, a conclusion with whose antinomian, anarchistical implications Godwin alone is usually associated at this time.[65] Thelwall was criticized, similarly,

---

60. *The Tribune* 2:vii.

61. "Patriotism, or the love of our country," Thelwall wrote, "is after all but a narrow sectarian principle; the source very often, it must be confessed, of splendid actions, but the parent at the same time of much illiberality and injustice, of contentions, massacres, and devastations. The true activating principle of virtue, is the love of the human race, the benevolent sentiment which enfolds the world in one large embrace, and sanctifies the universal equality of rights" (Walter Moyle, *Democracy Vindicated*, ed. John Thelwall [1796], p. 7). See also *The Tribune* 1:132–33, 147–63, 226–27). Elsewhere he described virtue as "the happiness and welfare of the human race" (John Thelwall, *Citizen Thelwall* [1795], p. 3) and contended, "I advocate the cause of the human race, the rights of the universe, the happiness of ages yet unborn" (Cestre, *John Thelwall*, p. 39).

62. John Thelwall, *The Peripatetic; or, Sketches of the Heart, of Nature and Society*, 3 vols. (1793), 2:10. And Thelwall too would later reflect on the revolt of the poor that "the deeper we have sunk in misery, the less capable we are of emerging from it" (*The Daughter of Adoption*, 4 vols. [1801], 2:6). This seems more pessimistic about the prospects for reform than Thelwall had been during the mid-1790s. See also *The Tribune* 1:51–52.

63. PRO, TS11/955/3499; *The Tribune* 1:91; *State Trials for High Treason, Part Third*, p. 35. Coleridge in fact objected to Thelwall's popularizing of Godwin, and in Bristol he gave a theological lecture whose target was probably Godwin. See Nicholas Roe, *Wordsworth and Coleridge: The Radical Years* (Oxford: Clarendon Press, 1988), p. 117.

64. PRO, TS11/955/3500.

65. PRO, TS11/956/3501 (18 February 1794). It is usually argued that Thelwall did not follow Godwin in this respect (e.g., Allen, "William Godwin's Influence," 678).

for holding to the peculiarly Godwinian doctrine that gratitude was no virtue because individuals ought always to act according to the dictates of social duty, without expecting any reward.[66]

But if Thelwall was much the most prominent of Godwin's admirers, "the philosopher," as friends often called him, was extremely critical of his role in the London Corresponding Society, whose proceedings, Godwin feared, posed a considerable threat to social order. In his anonymously published *Considerations on Lord Grenville's and Mr. Pitt's Bills* (1795), Godwin finally upbraided Thelwall publicly. The *Critical Review* observed that Thelwall would "scarcely have been treated in such a manner by his greatest enemy," and Thelwall himself later reflected that "the bitterest of my enemies has never used me so ill as this friend has done."[67] But Godwin was preeminently cautious and Whiggish in his practical politics. He was deeply concerned that the calm voice of rational argument was in danger of being shouted down by mob oratory. He had even reinforced this point in the second edition of *Political Justice*, doubtless with Thelwall, whose lectures he had twice attended, in mind.[68] The latter, he fretted, was precisely the man of the hour, possessed of considerable talents, and not prejudiced like most Whigs against popular involvement in politics, who could sway the volatile sentiments of the crowd. Godwin had already castigated Thelwall, evidently with some success, when the latter was in prison, for manifesting "a spirit of resentment" against his persecutors, where, Godwin believed, equanimity and benignity ought to reign.[69] Now the *Considerations* condemned "the system of political lecturing" as "a hot-bed, perhaps too well adapted to ripen men for purposes, more or less similar to those of the Jacobin Society of Paris."[70] Recognizing the style, Thelwall confronted Godwin. He also denied publicly that his lectures bore "evidences of that character which the perusal of the pamphlet in question is calculated to suggest." If anything, he retorted quite justly, it was Godwin's own far more utopian speculations on property that were imprudent, given the un-

---

66. William Belcher, *Holcroft's Folly* (n.d.), p. 8. See *The Tribune* 1:229–32.

67. *Critical Review* 15 (1796), 451; John Thelwall, *Sober Reflections on the Seditious and Inflammatory Letter of the Rt. Hon. Edmund Burke* (1796), p. 105 (infra, p. 382).

68. William Godwin, *Enquiry Concerning Political Justice*, 2nd ed. (1796), bk. 4, chaps. 1–2.

69. Quoted in Cestre, *John Thelwall*, p. 202. See Thelwall's acknowledgment, in June 1795, that "some erroneous passions and feelings" had sometimes "perverted my feelings, and which tho' they had never seduced me into the approbation of violence, had mixed perhaps too much of asperity and personal resentment, where all ought to have been philosophy and benevolent enquiry" (*The Tribune* 1:331).

70. [William Godwin], *Considerations on Lord Grenville's and Mr. Pitt's Bills* (1795), p. 22.

enlightened state of public opinion on the subject.[71] But Godwin was unrepentant.[72]

With the *Tribune* halted, and his lecturing prospects reduced to nil in London, Thelwall now set out for the provinces, to Norwich, Wisbech, Lynn, Yarmouth, Derby, and elsewhere, to rally support and recoup some of his losses. Unfortunately his movements here, too, were monitored closely by local "anti-Jacobins." In May 1796, he delivered twenty-two warmly received lectures to audiences of 4,000 to 5,000 people in sympathetic Norwich, where he was hailed as "a most powerful speaker."[73] Here he felt that "the prejudices so artfully excited against me, were regularly diminished in proportion as my real sentiments and feelings became more generally known."[74] But there were few further opportunities to exonerate himself, and elsewhere he was given a warm reception of a different kind. In at least four towns, Thelwall was physically attacked, usually with the connivance of the local authorities. At Ashby de la Zouch, a small mob of soldiers and rabble assaulted him. At Yarmouth, in August, a crowd of some ninety persons rioted on his arrival, and a large group of sailors, led by Captain Roberts of the warship *L'Espiegle*, and assisted by several clergymen, seemed bent on carrying him off into forced naval service. (This was no idle threat in an era of frequent naval impressments. Kamchatka was the rumored destination.) Here Thelwall rescued himself only by putting a pistol to the head of his most resolute pursuer and exclaiming, "Offer the least violence, and you're a dead man!" But the books on which he was to lecture, including such notoriously seditious works as Plutarch's *Lives* and Dionysius of Halicarnassus's *Roman Antiquities*, were either torn to pieces or carried off as trophies. At Lynn, loyalists smashed the windows of his hall and threw brickbats and stones at his audience. At Wisbech a similar scene was repeated. Riots provoked by soldiers also led to the gutting of two public houses when Thelwall returned to Norwich to lecture again at the end of May 1797. In the Midlands, at Derby, on 23 March 1797, he faced an angry loyalist mob with a pistol in his hand, declaring that he "would

71. *The Tribune* 2:vii–xviii, 3:101–5; Thelwall, *Sober Reflections*, p. 17.

72. It was reported that the pair were reconciled at William Taylor's house in Norwich, though, as E. P. Thompson points out, Godwin still kept his distance from the reformers. See Thompson, "Hunting the Jacobin Fox," *Past and Present* 142 (1994), 94–140.

73. C. B. Jewson, *The Jacobin City: A Portrait of Norwich in Its Reaction to the French Revolution, 1788–1802* (Glasgow: Blackie, 1975), pp. 72, 81; John Thelwall, *An Appeal to Popular Opinion* (1796), pp. 20, 24, 55, 64–66.

74. Thelwall, *Appeal to Popular Opinion*, p. 13.

shoot any person who molested him," and again escaped without injury.[75]
But here too he found some sympathizers, and at Stockport in 1797 Thelwall discussed "agrarian laws, the expediency of property in land, the impossibility of equalising property, the necessity for a law to discountenance
accumulation," with a man named Owen, possibly the later founder of
British socialism, Robert Owen.[76]

Though he made every effort to retain an unyielding moral stance in the
face of such persecution, even helping an emigré French priest find employment, Thelwall's reputation as a firebrand now preceded him everywhere.[77] Helping greatly to foster this image were several widely circulated
anti-Jacobin novels that grotesquely caricatured Thelwall's behavior and
motives. He was ridiculed as an "indefatigable incendiary and missionary of
the French propaganda, . . . the Beaufort Buildings political philosopher,
. . . John Bawlwell." He was accused, at least metaphorically, of cheating
by gambling with loaded dice and of pandering to the "worthless" sons and
husbands of the London Corresponding Society.[78] In George Walker's anti-
Godwinian potboiler, The Vagabond (1799), he is unmistakably the political lecturer Citizen Ego, who jests at human follies, makes good money
haranguing the public, and vows to rule the nation through the political
clubs "upon the backs of the people, superior to law or human control."[79]
In Isaac Disraeli's Vaurien; or, Sketches of the Times (1797), he is simply Mr.
Rant, orator to the masses.[80] Since radical fiction had nearly dried up completely,[81] these efforts helped to foster the grossly unfair view that Thelwall
was some sort of madman intoxicated with a lust for power and willing to
sacrifice anything and anyone to his aims. Presenting the case for Thelwall's perverseness, the Critical Review observed, for example, in 1803:

> Whatever may be allowed to be his motives, his conduct is so truly
> singular, his mind of a mould so uncommon, so little adapted to the

75. Annual Register for the Year 1797, "Chronicle," p. 16. But at least at Yarmouth twenty-two citizens also put up £50 each to prosecute the mayor for his connivance in the riot (Thale, Selections, p. 365).

76. Quoted in Cestre, John Thelwall, p. 195.

77. E.g., The Anti-Jacobin; or, Weekly Examiner, 5 March 1798, p. 135.

78. Thomas Mathias, The Pursuits of Literature: A Satirical Poem in Four Dialogues, 13th ed. (1805), p. 372; Robert Bisset, Douglas; or, The Highlander, A Novel, 4 vols. (1800), 2:170, 3:180–88.

79. George Walker, The Vagabond: A Novel, 3rd ed., 2 vols. (1799), 1:81, 84–85, 90–96.

80. Isaac Disraeli, Vaurien; or, Sketches of the Times, 2 vols. (1797), 1:50.

81. Some of Thomas Northmore's Memoirs of Planetes (1795) may be loosely based on Thelwall's activities. See my edition of the text in Utopias of the British Enlightenment (Cambridge: Cambridge University Press, 1994), pp. 169–71.

arrangements of this aera, that, to carry his ideas into execution, would lead to the anarchy which we have so often deplored in other countries. Even in early youth, with respect to his own prospects in life, the same unsteadiness seems to have prevailed; and, were democracy established, we might expect to see him the advocate of monarchy.[82]

In the face of this onslaught, Thelwall found solace in the friendship of another (brief) disciple of Godwin, Samuel Taylor Coleridge.[83] The latter had first written in late 1796 approving Thelwall's ideas on "the origin of property & the mode of removing its evils" and mentioning that he had collected nearly all of Thelwall's works.[84] "Though personally unknown," Coleridge boldly declared before they had met, "I really love you, and I count but few human beings whose hand I would welcome with a more hearty grasp of friendship. . . . *You* uplift the torch dreadlessly, and show to mankind the face of that idol which they have worshipped in darkness."[85] Commenting later that "energetic activity of mind and heart is his master feature," Coleridge at their meeting found Thelwall to be "a very warm hearted man, . . . intrepid, eloquent, and honest—perhaps the only acting democrat that is honest."[86] He praised Thelwall's poetry as well as the style of *The Rights of Nature Against the Usurpations of Establishments* (1796), which had just appeared. And he confided his plans for a "pantisocracy," or community of shared interests and communal labor, which was to be established in America with the help of William Wordsworth and Thomas Poole. (This plan, we shall see, Thelwall might have accepted as practicable for a small group, but never for a nation.)[87] Coleridge, however, disagreed vehemently with Thelwall's condemnation of Christianity as "a

82. *Critical Review* 38 (1803), 83.

83. On their relationship, see, generally, Roe, *Wordsworth and Coleridge*, pp. 16, 145–98; and Nicholas Roe, "Coleridge and John Thelwall: The Road to Nether Stowey," in *The Coleridge Connection*, ed. Richard Gravil and Molly Lefebure (London: Macmillan, 1990), pp. 60–80. See also Burton Pollin, "John Thelwall's Marginalia in a Copy of Coleridge's *Biographia Literaria*," *Bulletin of the New York Public Library* 74 (1970), 73–94.

84. H. J. Jackson, ed., *Samuel Taylor Coleridge: Selected Letters* (Oxford: Clarendon Press, 1987), p. 30; John Morrow, *Coleridge's Political Thought: Property, Morality, and the Limits of Traditional Discourse* (London: Macmillan, 1990), p. 37.

85. Mrs. H. Stanford, *Thomas Poole and His Friends*, 2 vols. (1888), 1:205; letter of 17 December 1796, quoted in Cestre, *John Thelwall*, p. 142.

86. Mrs. Stanford, *Thomas Poole and His Friends*, 1:234.

87. Thelwall later termed Robert Owen's plans for cooperative communities "benevolent" and noted that they might be "highly useful to mankind." He stressed, however, that attaining universal suffrage

mean religion," and defended his own beliefs at length.[88] In July 1797, Thelwall came to visit him in the small village of Nether Stowey, where he found "delightful" the company of both Coleridge and Wordsworth, who described him as "a man of extraordinary talent."[89] But here too, alas, he met with hostility from the local inhabitants. Nor could such a visit be prolonged sufficiently to compensate for his reception elsewhere, and it seems that spies dogged his steps nearly everywhere he went.

With nowhere else to turn, Thelwall finally retired from politics late in 1797.[90] Assisted by a few friends, and after a four-month search on foot for a suitable location, he withdrew like his ancestors before the Norman invaders to a thirty-five-acre farm overlooking the Wye Valley near the village of Llyswen, Breconshire, Wales, chosen for its unrivaled scenery. Here Thelwall dug trenches, carted dung, and confessed of his "simple and frugal" life that he was "not only reconciled [but] even more enamoured of it than is wise." But persecution was unavoidable even here, and in any case Thelwall's isolation seems to have been far from total; not only did he receive a number of visitors, he was reported as sneaking fortnightly over to Hereford to meet furtively with local "Jacobins." He was even linked to nearby food riots.[91] Thelwall soon found himself condemned from the pulpit by local clergymen. Superstitious locals murmured that he communed with evil spirits on his solitary walks. A neighbor hit him with a pick-axe as he was opening up his watercourse (though a dispute over property seems to have been the pretext). Even in exile too, his correspondence (which appears to have been considerable) was still tampered with. Nor was nature sympathetic; his eldest, six-year-old daughter died suddenly, and Thelwall was deeply distraught. Then one of the century's worst harvests in 1799 left him with scarcely a subsistence.[92] Though he claimed in 1798 that he had "no appetite for writing," Thelwall nonetheless published a further volume of poems in 1801 and contributed several pieces to

---

was a preferable goal (*The Champion*, 1 August 1819, p. 482). He similarly protested against "Spencean agrarianism" that Roman agrarian laws had not touched any man's legitimate property, being concerned only with conquered lands and public property (*The Champion*, 20 May 1820, p. 328).

88. Jackson, *Coleridge, Selected Letters*, pp. 41–48.

89. *Wordsworth's Poetical Works*, ed. W. Knight, 2 vols. (1896), 1:234; Mrs. Stanford, *Thomas Poole and His Friends*, 1:233.

90. On this period in Thelwall's life, see Edward Thompson's "Hunting the Jacobin Fox," *Past and Present* 142 (1994), 94–140.

91. Letter of 16 January 1798, quoted in P. J. Corfield and Chris Evans, "John Thelwall in Wales: New Documentary Evidence," *Bulletin of the Institute of Historical Research* 59 (1986), 235–37.

92. *Public Characters of 1800–1801* (1801), p. 218; *Mr. Thelwall's Reply to the Calumnies* (1804), p. 26.

the *Monthly Magazine* to make ends meet. He also produced, under the transparent pseudonym of John Beaufort, a novel, *The Daughter of Adoption* (1801), which he bore to London by foot to deliver to his publisher.[93] This paid heed to the "new philosophy's dictum that the few should not be allowed to accumulate all while the many were left wretched," but in a cautious, Godwinian vein also adverted to the dangers of revolt by those who were "too frantic with revenge and too blind with ignorance, to know how to secure the liberty" they desired.[94]

After three years, edged out by his landlord, Thelwall moved again. By now he was deeply disillusioned with the "sordid ignorance" of the area's "boorish inhabitants," who doubtless had also had their fill of this strange interloper. Whatever virtues solitude had elicted from Thelwall had seemingly been greatly outweighed by the inconveniences of the life, and the sheer bad luck he had endured.[95] But this rural interlude was clearly a turning point in his life. Compared to the 1790s, the next thirty years were relatively quiet. From 1801, he lived mainly by lecturing on elocutionary technique, for some time assisted by his wife at a school at No. 40 Bedford Place, London, and working in particular, with remarkable success by all accounts, on methods of curing stammering. He was not reclusive; his parties included Godwin (the old wounds now apparently healed), Thomas Holcroft, Major John Cartwright, Charles Lamb (who remembered him as "a thoroughly honest man in both thought and morals"), William Frend, George Dyer, and other notables.[96] Nor was he completely unpolitical. Some of his later poems took up topical themes. *The Trident of Albion*, published in 1805, for example, celebrated Nelson's Trafalgar victory and bemoaned the admiral's death, while a similar tribute was offered to Charles James Fox on his demise in 1806. In 1808, he also delivered an ode on Spanish liberty at the Freemasons' Tavern. His new career was Thelwall's primary concern, however. In 1809, he moved to Lincoln's Inn Fields in order to supervise his patients more closely. Here he also lectured on literature and gave "dramatical" recitations. Later he moved again to Brixton. In 1814, he visited Paris with Henry Crabb Robinson and others.

---

93. The Godwinian components of the novel are discussed in Allen, "William Godwin's Influence upon John Thelwall," pp. 680–82.

94. [Thelwall], *The Daughter of Adoption*, 2:4–5.

95. P. J. Corfield and Chris Evans, "John Thelwall in Wales: New Documentary Evidence," *Bulletin of the Institute of Historical Research* 59 (1986), 239. See, generally, Thompson, "Jacobin Fox."

96. Britton, *Autobiography*, 1:185; Talfourd, *Memoirs of Charles Lamb*, p. 176; Henry Crabb Robinson, *Diary, Reminiscences, and Correspondence*, 3 vols. (1869), 1:373.

In the following year, the long revolutionary wars finally came to an end. Though he had always opposed Bonaparte's imperial ambitions, writing even that these had "destroyed, perhaps for ever all my glorious speculations of the improvability of man," Thelwall nonetheless lamented the prospects of an imminent restoration.[97] His wife died in 1816, leaving two sons (who became ministers) and two daughters. He remarried in 1817 to a girl barely twenty years old. In 1818, as the radical cause gathered momentum once again, Thelwall took over a newspaper, *The Champion*, in what proved to be a faltering and expensive effort to reenter political life despite twenty-one years' absence from the public arena. During his editorship, which lasted until 1821, Thelwall pressed the goal of universal suffrage as his "great object." His new interests, however, included such issues as currency reform. He now frequently appeared at political meetings with Henry Hunt, John Cartwright, and other radicals, supporting Queen Caroline and other causes.[98] He lived to witness the first Reform Act, instigated by some, at least, who had known his writings in the 1790s. Indeed, when Thelwall tried to raise a subscription for his old age, he wondered why the older generation of democrats had such shallow pockets, given his "sufferings and sacrifices in the political cause."[99] As late as 1833, he was still lecturing (at the London Mechanics' Institute). In his declining years, Thomas Hardy noted, Thelwall was "highly and deservedly respected by a greater number of his countrymen" and was remembered as "of a mild and amiable disposition, domestic habits, open-hearted and generous, of high moral feeling, and of inflexible integrity."[100] He died on 17 February 1834.

Thelwall's Intellectual Development and Significance

This volume reprints three of Thelwall's main political works, which coincide with the peak of his political career during the mid-1790s: *The Natural and Constitutional Right of Britons to Annual Parliaments, Universal Suffrage,*

97. Thompson, "Jacobin Fox"; Robinson, *Diary, Reminiscences, and Correspondence*, 1:491.
98. *The Champion*, 4 July 1819, p. 413; 22 November 1818, p. 740; 6 December 1818, pp. 769–71; 11 January 1819, p. 32.
99. British Library, Add. MSS 37950:131. Sir Francis Burdett in particular seems to have been unwilling to help (37949:291).
100. Thomas Hardy, *Memoirs of Thomas Hardy* (1832), p. 48; *The Penny Cyclopaedia*, 23 (1842), 307; Britton, *Autobiography*, 1:186.

and the Freedom of Popular Association (1795), *The Rights of Nature Against the Usurpations of Establishments* (1796), *Sober Reflections on the Seditious and Inflammatory Letter of the Rt. Hon. Edmund Burke to a Noble Lord* (1796); and substantial excerpts from his political lectures, published as *The Tribune* (3 vols., 1795–96). These writings tell us much about the debate over reform, the growth of political persecution, the process and effects of the treason trials, and the reshaping of radical aims in response to rapidly changing social, political, and economic developments in this period. They show that Thelwall was one of the most perceptive and innovative thinkers among the reformers, probing into many areas untouched by his more renowned contemporary, Thomas Paine; fighting with panache and bravery against his far more powerful opponents; and restating with great conviction the virtues of the English republican tradition against the inhumanity of aristocratic cabals.

Without doubt, however, Thelwall's main contribution to radical thought during the 1790s, and the issue I want to concentrate on here, lay in his approach to property and commerce at a crucial turning point in modern social and political thinking.[101] For it was now that the language of politics began inexorably to shift toward that focus on economic factors, especially the nature of a competitive market and the problem of poverty, which, with claims for extending the franchise, would become increasingly prominent in political thinking during the following century.

The beginnings of this shift can be discerned in the early years of the revolutionary debate. By the autumn of 1792, radicals and loyalists alike were increasingly concerned with property rights and with the implications of "leveling" the property of the rich, which the reformers were widely accused of seeking under the guise of demanding a broader franchise.[102] But more than anything else, it was poverty that altered the framework of political debate. By 1795, and for much of the next decade, near-famine conditions and rising food prices generated a growing number of disturbances aimed at preventing speculators from withholding grain from the market until prices rose. As the burden of the poor rates grew heavier,

---

101. An incisive treatment of Thelwall's thought, particularly valuable for its analysis of rights doctrines, is Hampsher-Monk's "John Thelwall and the Eighteenth-Century Radical Response to Political Economy." A comparative treatment of Thelwall's thought is offered in my "Republicanism and Commerce in Britain, 1796–1805," *Journal of Modern History* 66 (1994), 249–90, on which the present account draws.

102. This theme is explored in my *Thomas Paine: Social and Political Thought* (London: Unwin Hyman, 1989), pp. 110–76.

landlords complained bitterly that they were forced to shoulder this considerable tax by themselves. Merchants, meanwhile, contended that famine could be forestalled only by leaving the market alone, for even if speculators did profit by hoarding grain, their actions at least ensured that some food was always held in reserve. (This view was succinctly expressed in Burke's *Thoughts and Details on Scarcity*, 1795.)[103]

To these circumstances, the radicals responded with their own more careful scrutiny of the question of property rights, notably in Thomas Paine's *Agrarian Justice* (1796), which also entered into parallel debates in France; in the works of the agrarian reformer Thomas Spence; and in Thelwall's chief writings.[104] What was novel in their views was not a concern with property per se. Earlier eighteenth-century "commonwealthmen" and republicans had often evoked Machiavellian and Harringtonian worries over the dangers of social inequality for a free people. They also conjectured that political power tended to follow the balance of property in any nation.[105] In this sense, a concern with grave inequality was central to republican thought. But few republicans had been much concerned with *improving* the condition of the laboring classes, for few desired to alter the system of ranks itself. Both Paine and Thelwall, however, favored greater social equality and insisted that increasing indigence demanded a more generous safety net than the existing poor laws provided. With this aim in mind, Paine had proposed a redistributive taxation scheme in the final section of the *Rights of Man*, part two (1792). By 1796, however, both he and Thelwall put forward the new and startling argument that the laboring poor should be ensured a *proportionate* right to the increasing wealth of society as a whole—a right, in other words, to growing affluence, rather than merely relief from distress. The key problem was how to define and secure this right, and the subsequent development of democratic republicanism in Britain was defined by its strategy vis-à-vis this rights question.

103. On "moral economy" debates in this period, see E. P. Thompson, "The Moral Economy of the English Crowd in the Eighteenth Century," *Past and Present* 50 (1971), 76–136; my *Machinery, Money, and the Millennium: From Moral Economy to Socialism, 1815–1860* (Princeton: Princeton University Press, 1987), pp. 21–33; and J. R. Poynter, *Society and Pauperism: English Ideas on Poor Relief, 1795–1834* (London: Routledge and Kegan Paul, 1969), pp. 45–106.

104. On Spence's ideas and influence in this period, see Malcolm Chase, *The People's Farm: English Agrarian Radicalism, 1775–1840* (Oxford: Oxford University Press, 1988); and Iain McCalman, *Radical Underworld: Prophets, Revolutionaries, and Pornographers in London, 1795–1840* (Oxford: Oxford University Press, 1988).

105. See, generally, Caroline Robbins, *The Eighteenth-Century Commonwealthman* (Cambridge: Harvard University Press, 1959); and J.G.A. Pocock, *The Machiavellian Moment* (Princeton: Princeton University Press, 1975).

This claim, moreover, constituted a significant shift toward that focus upon economic rights, and especially the right to the products of one's labor, which was to be central to socialism (though this was not the direction in which Thelwall wanted to move).[106] Though Thelwall still lamented the burden that taxes imposed upon the laboring classes,[107] his was a profoundly different, and in some respects contradictory, emphasis compared with the concerns with historical, political, and constitutional rights that had dominated the reform movement up to the mid-1790s. His thought, indeed, points to a paradigmatic restructuring within radical thought, though this much-abused terminology refers to an intellectual development, a process of gradual displacement, not a pattern in mass thinking or any necessary "victory" of one set of ideas over another.

Nor does this imply that many other traditional radical themes were not also Thelwall's concern. What the French Revolution presented, Thelwall early concluded, was an opportunity to purge corrupt British morals and politics and to renew both civic and private virtue through moral and political reform. By 1794, Thelwall was wholeheartedly committed to the pursuit of universal suffrage and annual parliaments. (In 1795, he criticized the new French constitution for restricting the franchise.)[108] In much he happily followed Paine, whose works, a spy reported, he once said "alone contained the true principles of government."[109] Like Paine, he considered that pure democracy was practicable only in small states. A modern republic meant "a government so constituted and organised that the whole body of the people may convey their will to the heart and centre of government, and by means of representatives and properly appointed officers, conduct the business of the country according to the general voice of the people."[110] Politically, Thelwall remained devoted to

> one grand principle, namely, that the people are the fountain of all power, honour, trust and distinction—that they have the absolute

106. Yet it is still misleading to argue that Thelwall believed that "any attack on private property would produce complete anarchy and a more intolerable tyranny than any yet experienced," for Thelwall's opposition was to leveling and equality, not a more just distribution (H. T. Dickinson, *British Radicalism and the French Revolution, 1789–1815* [London: Blackwell, 1985], p. 17).

107. In *The Tribune* (1:39) he estimated that the total burden of taxation was twice as great as the entire wages of the laboring poor.

108. John Thelwall, *Peaceful Discussion, and Not Tumultuary Violence, the Means of Redressing National Grievances* (1795), pp. 12–13.

109. PRO, TS11/956.

110. *The Tribune* 2:210–11, 3:196.

right of choosing the representatives that are to make their laws, and of cashiering not only those representatives whenever they have forfeited their confidence, but all such officers and magistrates, also, as by their arbitrary proceedings or corrupt practices impede the due execution of those laws. A principle like this, if followed through all its conclusions, must shortly annihilate all party. It is not possible, if you admit so broad a principle, for any combination of families, however great or powerful, . . . to grasp and monopolize all power in their hands, as they now do.

"The quick rotation of magistracy and subjection" was thus "the very soul of the republican system."[111] Thelwall's political agenda also included the creation of a civic militia instead of a standing army; the abolition of the slave trade; the reduction of the national debt and reform of the funding system; and the ending of all unfair forms of taxation. Only by such reforms could good institutions be constructed and civic virtue be reinforced, for "liberty and good laws" alone made "good men."[112] Consistent with much previous eighteenth-century British radical thought, these views were also leavened by certain French influences, notably a burning "sans-culotte" desire for social equality. (This so-called "Jacobin" element in Thelwall's thinking emerged most clearly in the letter introduced as evidence during his trial. But he also considered that at a critical period in the revolution the Jacobins were better equipped to govern than any other group.)[113]

But it was no longer solely the domain of citizenship and the reform of political corruption that interested Thelwall by the mid-1790s. Increasingly, he also considered relations between employer and employee in the sphere of civil society as crucial to any examination of the issue of wealth and poverty. Thelwall remained anxious about the economic burdens that the "inordinate taxation" of a corrupt state imposed upon the poor, and even estimated that four-fifths of the laborer's product went toward "the support of placemen, pensioners, and other tools of corruption."[114] But by 1796, he began to see the profits of rapacious employers as a key cause of poverty, and to conceive of justice increasingly in terms of fair wages rather than solely the accession of political rights.[115]

111. Ibid., 1:197; Walter Moyle, Democracy Vindicated, ed. John Thelwall (1796), pp. 39–40.

112. Cestre, John Thelwall, p. 58.

113. See The Tribune 1:246 (infra, p. 120). Given his attitude toward violence, Thelwall is, despite such reservations, perhaps best associated with the Girondins, whom Paine also supported.

114. The Tribune 3:115–16.

115. Ibid., p. 5.

Central to this shift in Thelwall's perceptions was the rapid extension of commerce and trade at the end of the eighteenth century, and the growth in luxury and inequality that followed it. Reacting against this trend, one school of radicals harkened back to what they took to be classical Greek and Roman republican notions of political virtue and a relative economic equality among citizens. Deeply concerned that expanding commerce merely fueled political corruption, fostered luxury, and forced labor away from farming and into manufacturing, republicans such as James Burgh proposed restrictions upon trade with the aim of returning to a simpler, chiefly agricultural society.[116] By the 1790s, however, and despite the efforts of Godwin in particular, such views appeared to be in retreat (at least temporarily, for they would reemerge in early socialism). Much the most influential radical of this period, Thomas Paine was himself a consciously "modern" republican who not only saw little threat to political virtue or stability in the growth of trade, but also stressed that free commerce could bring far greater international cooperation and peace by rendering nations more interdependent.[117] Yet there remained the crucial, and growing, objection that whatever promise the commercial system ultimately held out, the poor during the 1790s—a period of considerable economic expansion—were nonetheless evidently growing poorer, while the rich seemed to be doing better than ever. Both Paine and Thelwall responded, therefore, by claiming that the poor had a right not only to subsistence but to the *increasing* wealth of society as well.

Thelwall's contribution to this shift was in many respects more substantial than Paine's. The latter had said little about class in relation to the means of production as opposed to constitutional arrangements, and was concerned with inequality of landownership rather than that generated by trade, to which he had given little thought. Until the mid-1790s, however, Thelwall's own views show scant interest in anything but the negative effects of commerce, and instead reflect a deeply rural and pastoral, as well as classical, orientation. The growth of commerce and luxury, that "opiate of the soul," as he put it in 1794, with the increasing selfishness and rapacity of the rich, had debased political institutions and manners, weakened the national fiber, and lessened that love of liberty which alone protected a free nation.[118] His hand never far from a history of ancient

---

116. See Burgh's *Account . . . of the Cessares*, reprinted in my *Utopias of the British Enlightenment* (Cambridge: Cambridge University Press, 1994), pp. 71–136.

117. Thomas Paine, *Rights of Man*, ed. G. Claeys (Indianapolis, Ind.: Hackett Publishing Company, 1992), pp. 127–31.

118. John Thelwall, *Poems Written in Close Confinement in the Tower and Newgate* (1795), p. 3.

Greece or Rome, Thelwall in the early 1790s in particular often harkened back to the simple manners and staunch patriotism of their heroic ages. But the republican virtue of the ancients might, he hoped, be wedded to the more cosmopolitan and peaceable vision that the phrase "universal benevolence" conjured up for many reformers in this period.

Until about 1795, Thelwall's ideas about commerce were thus certainly closer to the neoclassical republicanism of Burgh, and to the Rousseauist pastoralism of Godwin and his followers, than to Paine. In the three volumes of his poetry and narrative published as *The Peripatetic* in 1793, Thelwall adopted the device of a ramble through London and elsewhere to comment on social conditions. He warned that commerce was a "doubtful" and "partial" good that often fostered war, spread "the poison'd stream of luxury," and "fatten'st a few upon the toils of all." He lamented that amid "Grandeur and Opulence," the poor man was ignored, and too often driven from "his cottage, from his little garden, and his bubbling spring, to seek, perhaps, a miserable habitat in the smoky confines of some increasing town." How could a country like Britain be termed "wealthy," he demanded, when the majority of its inhabitants could afford meat barely once a week? Thelwall regretted that the concentration of landed wealth had curtailed the rental of small allotments. Once master and laborer had been "near enough to a level to sympathise in each other's misfortunes; and the reciprocity of kindness might rationally be expected." Now "the system" threw "every advantage into the hands of the wealthy few, at the expence of the entire depression of the many."[119]

Some of this hostility to commerce Thelwall retained well into the mid-1790s. In a poem entitled "To Luxury," written in 1794, he condemned its "noxious weeds." In "To Simplicity of Manners," he praised "those ancient Manners—simple and severe," which Sparta in particular had cherished.[120] These alone, Thelwall believed, upheld that political virtue without which no free state could long survive. And they were compatible solely with a far more egalitarian society than nearly any that had existed in Europe since the rise of feudalism. Individual reformation of manners, he hoped, would commence a new era of self-restraint. In his London lectures of 1795–96, Thelwall thus urged his listeners to

> labour to abolish luxury. . . . Let us in our own houses, at our own
> tables, by our exhortations to our friends, by our admonitions to our

119. Thelwall, *The Peripatetic*, 1:38–39, 134–35, 145–46, 173–74. Excerpts from the *Peripatetic* appeared in Daniel Isaac Eaton's *Politics for the People* (1794), pp. 48–50, 73–76, 118–21, 212–17.

120. Reprinted in John Thelwall, *The Poetical Recreations of the Champion* (1822), pp. 169–70.

enemies, persuade mankind to discard those tinsel ornaments and ridiculous superfluities which enfeeble our minds, and entail voluptuous diseases on the affluent, while diseases of a still more calamitous description overwhelm the oppressed orders of society, from the scarcity resulting from this extravagance. Thus let us administer to the relief of those who, having the same powers of enjoyment with ourselves, have a right to, at least, an equal participation of all the necessaries of life, which are the product of their labour.[121]

He also reminded the London Corresponding Society that "a love of *virtuous poverty*" was among the indispensable prerequisites of a people "desiring to obtain or to preserve the blessings of liberty."[122]

This potent, somewhat romantic mixture of classical republicanism and nostalgic pastoralism portrayed the good life as virtually incompatible with an advanced commercial society. Indeed, it was doubtful whether any of the supposed advantages of civilization should be retained, if all were secured only at the cost of oppressing the multitude. Nonetheless, in 1795–96, Thelwall began to accept commerce to a much greater degree than formerly. He now began to plead for an end to scarcity by establishing universal freedom of trade in surplus produce. At the same time, his attitudes toward trade and luxury became markedly more sophisticated. Any reversion toward "simplicity," in particular, Thelwall now began to see as neither possible nor necessary. Against a scheme strongly reminiscent of Godwin's position in the first edition of his *Enquiry Concerning Political Justice*, for reducing human labor to half an hour daily by abolishing luxuries and producing only necessities, thus, Thelwall now conceded that buildings, books, paintings, and the like were advantageous, provided they did not grind the poor down. Though he still feared its effect on manners, Thelwall now saw the crucial problem of luxury as lying less in its tendency to engender moral and political corruption than in its exacerbation of social inequality. (There is some evidence that Godwin was edging toward a similar stance at about the same time.) "Commerce," he now submitted, "uncorrupted by monopolizing speculation," was "one of the greatest advantages that result from social union." When conducted "on liberal and equal principles," it could help eradicate narrow patriotic chauvinism "and convince us that we ought to extend the narrow sphere of our affections."

121. *The Tribune* 1:13 (infra, p. 67).
122. *Moral and Political Magazine of the London Corresponding Society*, June 1796, p. 26.

Commerce had been vital in breaking the stranglehold of feudal tyranny and could do much to secure future peace. Thelwall's shift in concerns, thus, was toward the monopolistic results of commerce and away from the moral effects of luxury.[123] Hence he now began to scrutinize carefully the origins and nature of modern trade and to grapple with the problem of poverty from an urban, political, and economic perspective, more than from a narrowly moral perspective.

Though it clearly had other causes, including a probable rereading of Paine's *Rights of Man*, this new sophistication in Thelwall's views, and his manifest optimism about commerce, certainly resulted in part from his close scrutiny of the *Wealth of Nations* at this time. He now paid greater heed to the categories of political economy, and notably the all-important language of "productive and unproductive labour," than any other radical in this period.[124] Examining in several lectures the causes of the dearness and scarcity of provisions in 1795, a near-famine year, Thelwall agreed with Smith that "real wealth" consisted only in "the quantum of real necessaries and comforts." He praised "the fair, the just, and rational system of commerce" that exported a surplus only after home demands had been met, and whose advantage was that it helped "prevent excessive want and scarcity." "My idea of the first and genuine principles of just government, with respect to agriculture," he proposed, was "to produce the largest quantity of the necessaries of life, and to promote the most equal distribution of those articles." This implied that the interest of the domestic consumer should be placed above profits from foreign trade in food. The object of agriculture ought not "to be *commerce*, but the comfort and accommodation of the people," which were being disregarded by "monied speculators." This would help to avoid the extreme inequality that characterized the present commercial system. Instead, society should be linked by "imperceptible gradations of rank, where step rises above step by slow degrees" until all were "connected together by inseparable interests." This gentle hierarchy was superior even to any "golden age of absolute equality." But such an ideal was unattainable where monopoly existed. Speculation, "the over eager pursuit of opulence among one class of the people," had eradicated the moral advantages of a "fair and equitable process of exchange."[125] But leveling the existing system of ranks was no answer either, and the community

123. *The Tribune* 2:8; 3:38, 44.
124. E.g., ibid., 1:36, 130. Some called Smith "the high priest of democracy" at this time (R. Dinmore Jr., *An Exposition of the Principles of the English Jacobins* [1796], p. 20).
125. *The Tribune* 1:13; 2:38, 46, 59, 66–67, 150; 3:38–39.

of goods he elsewhere referred to as "a wild and absurd scheme" that was impracticable on a large scale.[126] Thelwall told a huge crowd in late 1795:

> Equality of property . . . is totally impossible in the present state of the human intellect and industry, and if one of you once could be reduced to attempt a system so wild and extravagant, you could only give to rascals and cut-throats an opportunity, by general pillage and assassination, of transferring all property into their own hands, and establishing a tyranny more intolerable than anything of which you now complain.[127]

Instead, Thelwall insisted, what he sought was an equality of rights, "the equality which protects the poor against the insults and oppressions of the rich, as well as the rich against the insults and invasions of the poor."[128]

This embracing of "fair" commerce entailed a new look at luxury. Referring in October 1795 to a plan by an African colonization projector, the Swedenborgian C. B. Wadstrom, which proposed supplying individuals only according to their real rather than their "artificial" wants, Thelwall agreed—and his readiness to pose the question in these terms is notable—that this addresssed "the important dilemma of simplicity or luxury." But it is clear that his sympathy toward simplicity was undergoing a vital shift. Taking a very different tack from his position in 1793, he argued at length that commercial luxury did not inevitably corrupt any nation. Athenian republicanism, for example, sprang from a "generous and magnanimous virtue" that a commercial nation (for Athens had also gained much by trade) might also possess. But it could do so only where greater independence resulted from individuals reaping "the profits of their individual exertions." This alone aided "the general happiness and welfare," and might therefore be derived from trade as well as landownership. The chief flaw in modern commerce was thus that the necessaries of life, especially grain, had become objects "not of *open* traffic, but of commercial speculation." True freedom of trade would lower prices to the point where only "a living profit" would be attained, which was in the general interest. But commercial freedom in a republic also required civil and political liberty, which in

---

126. *Rights of Nature*, ltr. 1, p. 65 (infra, p. 422).

127. Thelwall, *Speech, 26th October 1795* (1795), p. 14. But Thelwall praised as just and moderate the agrarian laws of ancient Rome (Walter Moyle, *Democracy Vindicated*, ed. John Thelwall [1796], p. 20).

128. Thelwall, *Speech, 26th October 1795*, p. 14.

turn rested on "a simplicity of manners, a fortitude of character, and a pure and generous system of morality." These, Thelwall confessed, were more often found at present in largely agricultural countries like Switzerland. Earlier republics, like ancient Greece, had possessed them only because commerce had increased the independence of all by being

> made to produce equal advantage to every citizen of the community. Every man participated not only in the labour, but in the profit. . . . When the rich merchant, the great landed proprietor, and higher classes of society, are enabled to enjoy more luxuries, and live in great pomp, the tendency of the laws and institutions of society ought to be such, that the labourer also will have his proportion of the advantage, eat with more comfort, sleep in a better cabin, and be enabled to give his offspring a better education, and a better knowledge of their rights and duties.[129]

The problem was how to accomplish this in a vastly more unequal modern society. It was in *The Rights of Nature Against the Usurpations of Establishments* (1796), a work of which he was justly proud and that included a rousing defense of liberty of thought, that Thelwall most clearly outlined how the majority might share in the advantages of commerce. Though the two were likely unaware of each other's tracts, Thelwall like Paine now thought that demands for both greater social equality and increasing opulence could be reconciled by enriching the laboring classes.[130] In his 1795 lectures, and at one of the great London Corresponding Society meetings that year, Thelwall stressed that the standard of living of the poor, but also of tradesmen, shopkeepers, plowmen, and mechanics, had been falling steadily. The cause lay in "the corruption that has poisoned the government and constitution of this country" with "the luxury and splendour of political plunderers" coming from the oppression of the so-called lower or-

---

129. *The Tribune* 3:43, 46, 248 (infra, pp. 289–90); Thelwall, *Speech, 26th October 1795*, pp. 9, 20. This vision of the best commerce being that which furnished the greatest employment to all, and nourished the health and strength of the inhabitants, as well as being "most certain," was also shared by such writers as Capel Lofft (*Elements of Universal Law* [1779], pp. 120–21). But Lofft also opposed luxury and insisted that "Luxury in a *commonwealth* is either extinct the instant it springs up, or the *commonwealth*" (ibid., p. 106).

130. *Agrarian Justice* was written in the winter of 1795–96 and published in early 1796 in Paris. A London edition appeared in 1797. One copy of *The Tribune* survives (in the Cambridge University Library) and is inscribed to "Citizen Thomas Paine, with the respect and sincere admiration of the author," though there is no way of knowing when or even whether Paine received it.

ders, which allowed greedy monopolizers and forestallers to thrive. Thelwall's chief concern here was to tie economic discontent to the necessity for political reform. "If you had not a system of borough-mongering corruption—that is to say, a system of political monopoly," he insisted, "there could be no monopoly of trade, much less of the necessaries of life; and above all, the price of labour would keep pace with the price of these necessaries." In *The Rights of Nature*, his central premise was that every man and woman had

> a sacred and inviolable claim, growing out of the fundamental maxim, upon which alone all property is supported, to some comforts and enjoyments, in addition to the necessaries of life, and to some "tolerable leisure for such discussion, and some means of such information," as may lead to an understanding of their *rights*; without which they can never understand their *duties*.

Thelwall's aim here was to give the poor and laboring classes greater independence. But, while Paine's redistributive plans assumed an essentially static economy and focused on taxing landed wealth, Thelwall's own ideal was more dynamic and commercially oriented. Society had the duty "not merely to *protect*, but to *improve* [emphasis added] the physical, the moral, and intellectual enjoyments . . . of the whole population of the state. It ought to expand the faculties, encrease the sympathies, harmonize the passions, and promote the general welfare."[131]

This claim was defended in *The Rights of Nature* in four ways. First, Thelwall proposed that "man has naturally an equal claim to the elements of nature," of which light, air, and water in particular remained in common. ("Naturally" here meant man taken as an "abstraction," devoid of social and political ties, with natural rights being determined by a person's wants, faculties, and means.) This implied that each person also possessed

---

131. *Rights of Nature*, ltr. 1, p. 16, ltr. 2, p. 46 (infra, pp. 398–99, 461). In short, it ought actively to promote the ends of "society" as writers like Pufendorf had used the term, and as Paine had also concluded at the end of his *Rights of Man*, part two; or to follow the obligation to improve both body and soul, as Hutcheson phrased it, as well as the "talents," as Sharp had insisted (Francis Hutcheson, *A System of Moral Philosophy*, 2 vols. [1755], 2:111–12; Granville Sharp, *A Tract on the Law of Nature* [1777], p. 23). Cestre thus misleads in asserting that Thelwall "chiefly aimed at reducing the excessive consumption of luxuries by the few, in order to increase the share of necessaries for the many," and saw commerce as at best only a doubtful good. This was true for the early 1790s, but far less so after 1795 (Cestre, *John Thelwall*, pp. 59, 61).

"*a right to exercise his faculties upon those powers and elements, so as to render them subservient to his wants, and conducive to his enjoyments.*" Since all rights entailed a reciprocal duty to secure the identical rights of others, those who monopolized the means of support violated such rights.[132] Thelwall's first rights claim was thus that because this natural inheritance was shared by all in the state of savagery, society must compensate for its subsequent loss.[133] This parallels a similar argument by Paine in *Agrarian Justice*.[134] It also echoed, though here in a quite secular form, the familiar natural law doctrine concerning the Creation and God's intention that the earth be used for the support of all its inhabitants.

Thelwall's conclusion regarding common property rights was reached by reviewing the progress of society through the savage, pastoral, and agricultural stages. He concurred with the widespread view that property in herds alone had existed in the pastoral state, with land having been appropriated only after agriculture had made considerable headway.[135] Thereafter, Thelwall stressed, property ought always to be the "*fruit of useful industry; but the means of being usefully industrious are the common right of all.*" This clearly implied a right to labor and to receive a reasonable reward therefrom.[136] The state of cultivation was admittedly an immense improvement upon the ruder stage. But the appropriation of land by "moral and political expediency," not merely by occupancy or a right derived from labor, ended the relatively equal distribution of property that had long prevailed.[137] Afterward, the invention of primogeniture and government protection of privilege and wealth further divided society into proprietor and laborer, with the few monopolizing the benefits of the majority's labor. (Broadly speaking, Thelwall here followed a Harringtonian view of the primacy of property ownership in the evolution of society, though he warned against applying it too rigidly.)[138] Reinstating an equality of landed property was to

132. *Rights of Nature*, ltr. 2, pp. 39–42 (infra, pp. 457–59). Natural law writers agreed that the chief obligation of property was not to hinder the rights of others to enjoy their own. On this obligation, see, e.g., Thomas Rutherforth, *Institutes of Natural Law*, 2 vols. (1754), 1:138–39.

133. *Rights of Nature*, ltr. 2, pp. 27, 38–39 (infra, pp. 452, 457–58).

134. Thomas Paine, *Agrarian Justice* (1796), p. 6.

135. Adam Smith, *Wealth of Nations* (1776), bk. 3, chap. 1. See, generally, Ronald Meek, *Social Science and the Ignoble Savage* (Cambridge: Cambridge University Press, 1976).

136. *Rights of Nature*, ltr. 2, pp. 54–55 (infra, pp. 464–65). Thelwall may here have followed Blackstone's account of the evolution of property (*Commentaries on the Laws of England*, 5th ed. [1773], 2:1–9).

137. *Rights of Nature*, ltr. 2, p. 62 (infra, pp. 468–69).

138. He wrote, "If *Polybius, Machiavel*, etc, have placed too much stress upon the moral causes, *Harrington, Moyle*, and other English writers have erred still more in referring everything to 'the balance

Thelwall clearly impossible. The question, therefore, was what rights prop-ertyless laborers now possessed. And these, he contended, rested on "the triple basis of *nature*, of *implied contract*, and *the principles of civil association*."[139]

Naturally, laborers were "men," and as such heirs to "the common boun-ties of nature." But at birth each found "his inheritance is alienated, and his common right appropriated." Individuals of course retained the right to the "advantages" of their industry when employed on the common ele-ments of nature, but such opportunities were now rare. Most of the time, proprietor and laborer were far from equal, and society was thus "responsi-ble . . . for an equivalent for that which society has taken away." The permanent possession of land was rooted in mere expediency, especially the generally acknowledged tendency of private ownership to stimulate produc-tion. But, Thelwall argued, the laborer had (on the basis of an unexplored principle of reciprocity) the right to receive as much in return as he or she had given to society, as well as to employ his or her faculties beneficially. Any unjust agreement "extorted by the power of an oppressor" for inade-quate wages was thus morally and politically void, the genuine basis of property being labor alone.[140]

So far, we have seen, Thelwall proposed a redistribution of property, first on the basis of compensation for the loss of natural inheritance, and sec-ond with reference to a reciprocal reward all laborers merited through their contribution to society. Thelwall's third argument for redistribution rested on the notion of an "implied compact" tacitly entered into by all upon leaving the state of nature, but now relevant to any agreement between laborer and employer.[141] This is an interesting use of a social contract argument usually applied only to the problem of consent and political legit-

---

of property,'" adding, "The progress of intellect, the balance of property, and the insolence of oppression have their respective influences in the production of great revolutions" (Walter Moyle, *Democracy Vindicated*, ed. John Thelwall [1796], p. 21).

139. *Rights of Nature*, ltr. 2, pp. 77–86 (infra, pp. 476–80).

140. Ibid., pp. 54–79 (infra, p. 477). This extended the natural law view that contracts that tended to ruin the community were no longer binding (e.g., Hugo Grotius, *De Jure Belli et Pacis*, 3 vols. [Cambridge: Cambridge University Press, 1853], 2:125; Francis Hutcheson, *A Short Introduction to Moral Philosophy*, 2nd ed. [1753], p. 168). Thelwall later recalled having suffered under a "surfeit . . . of the glossing and barbarous jargon of the law" during his studies of the subject. Here, while mentioning Grotius and Pufendorf and quoting frequently from Blackstone, he disgustedly dismisses "Sir W. Blackstone, and the fraternity of Lincoln's Inn" for their slavish devotion to ancient custom (*Rights of Nature*, ltr. 2, p. 24; ltr. 3, p. 110) (infra, pp. 451, 492).

141. On the background of the concept of "implied contract," see Peter Birks and Grant MacLeod, "The Implied Contract Theory of Quasi-Contract: Civilian Opinion Current in the Century Before Blackstone," *Oxford Journal of Legal Studies* 6 (1986), 46–85.

imacy, and it demonstrates how important political models are in explaining economic oppression in this period. An original agreement of this type, Thelwall claimed in his most striking argument, conceded to the laborer the right to the products of his or her employer *proportionate* to the latter's profit. This contract was "implied in the very distinction of labourer and employer . . . by the reason of the thing, and the rules of moral justice," specifically because capital could not be productive without labor, or vice versa. Moreover, its general ground was further supported by the widely accepted notion that civil association was constituted for the general good, for mankind had abandoned natural society for "the comforts and abundance of all," rather than for individual advantage. Agricultural cultivation also occurred by common labor alone. Tyranny by the wealthy few, therefore, was "not a compact of civil association, but a wicked and lawless anarchy" that violated "the very nature" of the tenure of the property holder by substituting usurpation and plunder for legitimate possession. To Thelwall, moreover, the laborer had the right not merely to maintenance but to the education of his family, and to have them participate in "all the sweets of polished society." Natural rights, crucially, were thus not fixed in Thelwall's view but could encompass the greater needs that social evolution fueled. Consequently, "natural" entitlements had expanded and now included the produce of commerce and manufacturing as well as agriculture.[142] And the recognition of such rights alone legitimated any further expansion of a capitalist economic system.[143]

We see here how important for Thelwall, as well as for other natural law writers, a claim to recall the original intention of the founders of civil society was. To Grotius, for example, the defense of rights of necessity, in other words of the poor facing starvation, assumed that this was what the first persons to appropriate property *would themselves have* intended. This hypothetical intention indeed obviated the need for firmer discussions of any original contract. For Samuel Pufendorf, too, a "tacit compact" accompanied the introduction of private property. For Locke, such a contract recognized the original mixing of labor with raw materials that founded property.[144] As Istvan Hont has emphasized, the more "negative commu-

---

142. *Rights of Nature*, ltr. 2, pp. 80–82, 45, 76 (infra, pp. 477–78, 461, 475). For Blackstone on implied contracts, see the *Commentaries*, 3:159–67.

143. E.g., Albert Goodwin, *The Friends of Liberty: The English Democratic Movement in the Age of the French Revolution* (London: Alan Hutchinson, 1979), p. 473.

144. Grotius, *De Jure Belli et Pacis*, 1:238–39; Samuel Pufendorf, *The Whole Duty of Man According to the Law of Nature*, 5th ed. (1735), pp. 135–36; Hutcheson, *System of Moral Philosophy*, 1:330; John

nity" theorists (who believed individual appropriation was consistent with an original community of property) stressed a gradual and historical emergence of private property, the less likely was any reliance upon a contract. (Hutcheson, for example, denied the need to assume such a compact.)[145] But for Thelwall, the "implied contract" that supported a proportionate right to profits played a crucial role and established that the relation of capital to labor was as important as the rules of civil association.

Thelwall's first two arguments clearly parallel the principles of both "progress" and "social duty" that Paine defended in *Agrarian Justice*.[146] Thelwall too made much of the idea that compensation for the loss of a natural inheritance justified greater equality of property. What was particularly distinctive to *The Rights of Nature*, however, and what most clearly yoked it to the cause of commercial progress, was the claim that the laborer possessed a right to a *proportion* of the employer's profits because society rested upon common labor. Here Paine, while agreeing that "personal property is the effect of society," instead proposed that a fixed sum be paid to all as restitution for their loss of land.[147] Appropriately, given his greater stress on the labor basis of property, Thelwall through the rule of proportionate advantage instead considered the problem of how to cope with wages generally. This represented a critical shift away from previous republican treatments of the limitation of landed property by an agrarian law, and toward a focus on commercially generated forms of inequality. Now Thelwall felt it possible to insist—quite dramatically, given his earlier, more stoic views—that he "would extend civilization: I would increase refinement" while meeting the demands of social justice.[148]

Given its importance to his argument, Thelwall's rule of proportionate advantage merits closer examination. In keeping with his dictum that society should not merely protect but also improve the welfare of all, Thel-

---

Locke, *Locke's Two Treatises of Government* (Cambridge: Cambridge University Press, 1970), p. 317. Rutherforth follows the doctrine of tacit consent by occupation (*Institutes*, 1:48, 81), emphasizing that this would have been seen as "for the convenience of all," while rejecting Locke's theory that labor contributed to property (p. 56).

145. See Istvan Hont, "From Pufendorf to Adam Smith: Sociability, Commercial Society, and the Four Stages Theory," in *The Languages of Political Theory in Early-Modern Europe*, ed. Anthony Pagden (Cambridge: Cambridge University Press, 1987), p. 270. On Grotius and the introduction of a contract in the transition from common property, see Richard Tuck, *Natural Rights Theories* (Cambridge: Cambridge University Press, 1979), p. 77.

146. Paine, *Agrarian Justice* (1796), pp. 5–8.

147. Ibid., p. 13.

148. *Rights of Nature*, ltr. 3, pp. 83–84 (infra, p. 479).

wall's juristic strategy can be understood as seeking to *socialize* existing theories of property rights by construing all property relationships as occurring between consenting *equals*, albeit possessing unequal property, rather than between master or servant.[149] This invoked a familiar natural law concern for the interdependence of all ranks, and the duties of the wealthy toward the poor. But we can also term Thelwall's emphasis here a radical republican interpretation of jurisprudential discussions of contract—an extension of "politics" into "society"—and a strategy that was impossible without both the demand for political equality and a Lockean and Smithian stress on the role of labor in production.

Thelwall's account thus relied heavily upon a reinterpretation of the nature of contractual relations. His claim that all property was essentially social in nature, and specifically that all cultivation rested on social labor, can be construed as a reworking of the early-eighteenth-century natural law truism that the chief advantage of society lay, as Hutcheson put it, in the division of labor and the increasing expertise and production it encouraged.[150] And this was also one basis of Smith's commercial sociability.[151] But Thelwall applied the idea of sociability rather differently in *The Rights of Nature*. Most important was that, by adverting to the equal contributions of both capital and labor, he clearly conceived of the relationship of master to servant (the core of most previous descriptions of wage relations) not solely in terms of a contractual *compromise* of interests. This implied—as Burke, for example, contended—that once a wage had been settled no further conflict of interests remained between employer and employee.[152] Instead, while Thelwall remained enough of an individualist to insist that "whatever can be done by an individual is always better done single-handed, than when the same thing is attempted by several persons combined together,"[153] he evidently concluded here that all labor relations should be understood in terms of the law of partnership and the pursuit of common gain. This he presumed to be the part of the "implied contract" that justified proportionate advantage in dividing profits. This also involved the restitution of what Thelwall took to be natural equity, whose protection Grotius and others had also described as one of the goals of the original

149. Grotius, e.g., distinguishes between societies of equals, such as brothers, and those of unequals, such as masters and servants (*De Jure Belli et Pacis*, 1:4).
150. Hutcheson, *System of Moral Philosophy*, 1:288.
151. Smith, *Wealth of Nations*, bk. 1, chap. 2.
152. Edmund Burke, "Thoughts and Details on Scarcity" (1795); *Works*, 5 (1887), 139.
153. *The Tribune* 2:113.

establishment of private property.[154] Wage labor, therefore, was no longer to be defined solely by the market—that is, by the usefulness of the labor and the number of laborers, as Grotius's disciples (such as Thomas Rutherforth) insisted. This premise permitted the payment of mere subsistence wages—indeed even less, if charity supplemented wages, as it commonly did. Instead, wage labor embodied not merely a "contract for mutual benefit" (to use Rutherforth's phrasing), as the hire of labor had been construed previously, but a *full partnership* governed by the rules of "comparative share" or proportionate gain. This for Thelwall was the only form of contractual relationship fully compatible with the general obligation to mutual advantage of the social compact (which such writers as Rutherforth admitted should not be violated in such contracts).[155] This was the meaning of the assertion that the "implied contract" rested on the principles of civil association generally, for the state of nature was left only for common, not particular, advantage.[156] And this was clearly the only construction of economic activity compatible with republicanism, in Thelwall's view.

The key problem here was the question of what right we have to use the "property" (which for Thelwall crucially included labor) of others for our own profit. In Pufendorf, for example, probably the best-known natural law writer in eighteenth-century Britain, we find a plea both for a "just equality" in contractual relationships and, more specifically, the injunction that in partnerships "when any Labour is bestow'd in the *Improvement* of any Commodity, which is put in by another, he is suppos'd to have such a Share in the Thing it Self, as is proportionable to the *Improvement* it has received." But Pufendorf admitted that many types of "accessional advantages" added value to commodities, which nonetheless belonged to the property owner and not to the laborer. And this, of course, was the usual understanding of wage labor.[157] But partners, the natural law writers agreed, were entitled to a return from any enterprise proportionate to their contribution, whether this be in labor or capital.[158]

What Thelwall evidently did, in his search for greater equality between laborer and employer, was to envision every employment contract in these

154. Grotius, *De Jure Belli et Pacis*, 1:237. The best contemporary account of partnership was William Watson, *A Treatise of the Law of Partnership* (1794); on partnerships between labor and capital, see ibid., pp. 135–37.

155. Rutherforth, *Institutes*, 1:231, 214, 276; 2:255.

156. *Rights of Nature*, ltr. 3, p. 80 (infra, pp. 477–78).

157. Pufendorf, *Whole Duty of Man*, pp. 162–63, 169, 140–41.

158. A position followed by, e.g., William Paley, "Principles of Moral and Political Philosophy," in *The Works of William Paley* (1831), p. 37.

terms and thus to extend the rule of proportionate advantage to all. While agreeing that the genuine basis of property was labor, however, he put forward no claim for "the whole produce of labour." (Charles Hall would take this up a few years later.)[159] Instead, he argued for reciprocal, proportionate rights based upon the constitution of society for the benefit of all. These rested, as we have seen, on common rights to both a reasonable reward for labor and "the means of being usefully industrious," as well as equivalency rights based upon the implicit contract and the constitution of society as a collective enterprise.[160] Thelwall did not, therefore, merely echo jurisprudential discussions of the poor's right to subsistence. Virtually every natural law commentator had conceded that the poor had the right to be supported through their labor and to some share of the social surplus in times of necessity.[161] But while such writers as William Ogilvie acknowledged a claim to the improvements of landed property, the natural law tradition recognized a right to a proportionate return of *all* property to be generated not in a relationship of servitude but only as a consequence of partnership. A key example was where one individual lent money to another to profit from, and was thereby entitled to a share of the profit.[162] Nor did Thelwall therefore attempt to revive a "moral economy" of just prices and fair wages, since wages were now to be proportionate to profit, not to the cost of living. Instead he proposed a new vision of economic justice that assumed an expanding economy, centered on the contractual relations

159. See my "Republicanism and Commerce in Britain, 1796–1805," *Journal of Modern History* 66 (1994), 249–90.

160. This solved the Lockean problem of the right to the produce of others' labor outside of the common materials of nature. For Locke, though the mixing of labor with common property created private property in the natural state, "my servant's turfs" belonged to me in later social stages, even if he or she had cut and stacked them—nay, even if they were cut on common land. For Thelwall, no servant Mought ever to labor at such a disadvantage. See *Locke's Two Treatises of Government*, pp. 306–7. Blackstone merely acknowledged that in return for work a servant was entitled to wages (*Commentaries*, 1:428).

161. For Hutcheson, e.g., "the indigent must be supported by the compensations they get" for their labor (*System of Moral Philosophy*, 2:1). Grotius had insisted that the poor had the right to purchase necessities at a fair price (*De Jure Belli et Pacis*, 1:252). Pufendorf reiterated cases where extreme necessity superseded existing rights (*Whole Duty of Man*, pp. 87–88). Cumberland agreed that no right of dominion permitted the removal of necessities from the innocent (Richard Cumberland, *A Treatise of the Law of Nature* [1727], p. 68). William Paley too recognized the imperfect right of the poor to relief by the rich on the basis of original divine intention ("Principles of Moral and Political Philosophy," pp. 20, 50). See also Thomas Horne, *Property Rights and Poverty: Political Argument in Britain, 1605–1834* (Chapel Hill: University of North Carolina Press, 1990), pp. 123–41.

162. Ogilvie, *An Essay*, p. 12. For treatments of partnership, see, e.g., Hutcheson, *System of Moral Philosophy*, 2:71; Pufendorf, *Whole Duty of Man*, pp. 168–69.

between worker and employer, and did not merely expect economic grievances to be removed by the alleviation of unduly heavy taxation.[163]

The Rights of Nature thus heralded that ideal of cooperative partnership
between labor and capital that some socialists believed was an attractive
alternative to both capitalism and communism in the following century,
and that even such a dedicated *laissez-faire* liberal as John Stuart Mill,
finally, was to settle upon as the most satisfactory solution to the problem
of class inequality and the degenerate, selfish character that he conceded
commercial society almost universally created.[164] Its central themes fore-
shadow that emphasis on "fair exchange" within a socialist market system
which some of Owen's followers, notably William Thompson, found appealing.[165] Thelwall's assessment of the results of machinery, especially its
tendency "to furnish a cheaper substitute for manual labour" and to "accelerate the progress of accumulation" in the hands of the capitalist, strikingly
anticipates the central themes of Owenite economic thought, the most
sophisticated analysis put forward by the early socialists. So too does his
growing sense that the laboring classes were becoming ever more "subject
to the whole *Corporation* of *Employers*, instead of an individual proprietor,"
and that the increasing concentration of wealth was creating a three-class
system of "monied speculators," "drones" (the aristocracy), and "the poor
hard-working drudges" (the laboring classes).[166] This account of wage labor
in an industrial economy shows how far the discourse on political rights of
the early 1790s could be shifted toward an economic focus. Thelwall's observations were intended to be extended in further lectures on the mercantile, manufacturing, and funding systems that unfortunately were never

163. But unlike the later Owenite socialist view, for which it clearly laid the foundations by
concentrating on the contractual relationship between laborer and employer, Thelwall's theory did not
enjoin the exact exchange of equal amounts of labor in contracts in order for justice to be fulfilled. In
Grotian terms, Thelwall demanded beneficial contracts, with a limited degree of equality; Owenism
demanded commutational contracts, where complete equality was guaranteed. See Grotius, *De Jure
Belli et Pacis*, 2:65. On the relations between early British socialism and natural jurisprudence, and the
notion of the ideal of partnership and "cooperation" as a new form of sociability, see my *Citizens and
Saints: Politics and Anti-Politics in Early British Socialism* (Cambridge: Cambridge University Press, 1989),
pp. 23–62.

164. See my "Justice, Independence, and Industrial Democracy: The Development of John Stuart
Mill's Views on Socialism," *Journal of Politics* 49 (1987), 122–47. There is some evidence that Thelwall
was interested in the development of consumer cooperation in the postwar period. In 1832, for example,
he wrote proposing a visit to Dr. William King of Brighton, who had established a well-known
cooperative store (letter of 3 November 1832, Seligman Collection, Columbia University Library).

165. See my *Machinery, Money, and the Millennium*, pp. 99–109.

166. *Rights of Nature*, ltr. 4, p. 90 (infra, p. 483); *The Tribune* 2:67 (infra, p. 194). See my *Machinery,
Money, and the Millennium*, esp. pp. 34–67.

given. Nor, with his retirement from politics, did Thelwall build upon the prescient comments he made on the cotton industry in Manchester in 1797, when, gathering details on the new manufactories, he noted, "Machinery that brings a multitude to labour in one spot, bad. *Regulations possible.*"[167]

Thelwall's last major contribution to the debates of the 1790s was, appropriately enough, an attack upon Edmund Burke's final tirade against the revolution, *A Letter to a Noble Lord* (1796), before his death the following year. Here Burke, in a virulent assault upon the aristocratic reformers, actually mentioned Thelwall's lectures, expressing the hope that no lord would attempt to augment his education there.[168] Thelwall's response, *Sober Reflections on the Seditious and Inflammatory Letter of the Rt. Hon. Edmund Burke to a Noble Lord* (1796), linked the ferocity of Burke's reaction to the reformers to his receipt of aristocratic patronage and a government pension. Burke himself, Thelwall asserted, was a mere "high-toned aristocrat" willing to manipulate any cause to serve his own ends, and not therefore inconsistent in his seeming sympathy for the American Revolution and opposition to the French. Such rancor as Burke manifested against those nobles who sympathized with reform, warned Thelwall, threatened finally to undermine all respect for "rank, fortune, and hereditary station." It might indeed bring about a far more complete social revolution than even most of the reformers sought. For Burke, in impugning the origins of the title from which the Duke of Bedford's estate originated, had also recalled the massacres, murders, venality, and corruption that paved the way for the ennoblement of many an ambitious commoner. Thelwall then turned to the causes of the war; to Burke's role in fomenting the reaction against reform; to the inevitably of the Terror in France; and to the role of "philosophy" in fomenting the revolution. Thelwall's defense here of the revolution's central principles, "equal rights and equal laws," was, he insisted, unrelated to what "a few ruffians" had perpetrated by dictatorial means. We thus can see clearly here the distance between Thelwall and Robespierre, despite the former's momentary sympathy for the Jacobins, and how far the causes of the Terror lay for him in the rapine, oppression, and tyranny of "the old despotism" rather than the principles of the revolu-

---

167. Quoted in Cestre, *John Thelwall*, p. 164. In *Rights of Nature*, Thelwall noted that "every large workshop and manufactory is a sort of political society" (ltr. 1, pp. 20–21) (infra, pp. 400–401). See also his comments on the dangers to common-use rights of a "pestilential manufactory" (ltr. 2, p. 28; infra, p. 452).

168. Edmund Burke, *A Letter from the Rt. Hon. Edmund Burke to a Noble Lord* (1796), p. 35.

tion itself.[169] This was Thelwall's final substantial critique of "the oligarchy of the rotten borough-mongers." It is a stalwart defense of the principles from whose profession he was finally forced to retreat but that he would reassert with renewed vigor when public sympathy for political reform revived some twenty years later.

The Writings of John Thelwall

All works cited below and in the notes were published in London unless otherwise noted.

An Address to the Inhabitants of Yarmouth, on the Violent Outrage Lately Committed in Their Town (Yarmouth, 1796).

An Appeal to Popular Opinion Against Kidnapping and Murder, Including a Narrative of the Late Atrocious Proceedings at Yarmouth (1796).

The Black Bowl, February 3, 1208; or, Tears of Eboracum (York, 1802).

Britain's Glory; or, The Blessings of a Good Constitution (1795).

Citizen Thelwall: Fraternity and Unanimity to the Friends of Freedom (1795).

The Daughter of Adoption (1801).

Elocution and Oratory: General Plan and Outline of Mr. Thelwall's Course of Lectures (Manchester, 1803).

An Essay Towards a Definition of Animal Vitality (1793).

Introductory Discourse on the Nature and Objects of Elocutionary Science (Pontefract, 1805).

John Gilpin's Ghost; or, The Warning Voice of King Chanticleer (1795).

A Letter to Francis Jeffray, Esq., on Certain Calumnies and Misrepresentations in the Edinburgh Review (1804).

A Letter to Henry Cline, Esq., on Imperfect Development of the Faculties (1810).

A Monody Occasioned by the Death of the Rt. Hon. Charles James Fox (1806).

Moyle, Walter. *Democracy Vindicated: An Essay on the Constitution and Government of the Roman State*, ed. John Thelwall (Norwich, 1796).

---

169. Robespierre's "wanton and revengeful cruelties" and "scenes of blood and cruelty" are condemned in *The Tribune* 1:155, 114. See also *The Tribune* 1:249–54 (infra, pp. 119–24), and the comparison of Pitt's and Robespierre's characters at the end of this lecture (*The Tribune* 1:255–60).

Mr. Thelwall's Introductory Discourse on the Nature and Objects of Elocutionary Science (Pontefract, 1805).

Mr. Thelwall's Ode Addressed to the Energies of Britain in Behalf of the Spanish Patriots (1808).

Mr. Thelwall's Plan and Terms of Tuition, Etc.: Institution for the Cure of Impediments of Speech, Instruction of Foreigners, Cultivation of Oratory, English Composition and Polite Literature, and the Preparation of Youth for the More Liberal Departments of Active Life (1808).

Mr. Thelwall's Reply to the Calumnies, Misrepresentations, and Literary Forgeries, Contained in the Anonymous Observations on His Letter to the Editor of the Edinburgh Review (Glasgow, 1804).

The Natural and Constitutional Right of Britons to Annual Parliaments, Universal Suffrage, and the Freedom of Popular Association (1795).

News from Toulon; or, The Man of Gotham's Expedition (1795).

Ode for the Summer Anniversary of the Sols (1790).

Ode to Science (1791).

Orlando and Almeyda: A Legendary Tale in the Manner of Dr. Goldsmith (1787).

A Particular Account of the Late Outrages at Lynn and Wisbeach (1796).

Peaceful Discussion, and Not Tumultuary Violence the Means of Redressing National Grievances (1795).

The Peripatetic; or, Sketches of the Heart, of Nature and Society, 3 vols. (1793).

Poem and Oration on the Death of Lord Nelson (1805).

Poems Chiefly Written in Retirement (1801).

Poems on Various Subjects (1787).

Poems Written in Close Confinement in the Tower and Newgate (1795).

The Poetical Recreations of the Champion (1822).

Political Lectures (No. 1): On the Moral Tendency of a System of Spies and Informers (1794).

Political Lectures (No. 2): Sketches of the History of Prosecutions for Political Opinion (1794).

Political Lectures, Volume the First, Part the First: Containing the Lecture on Spies and Informers, and the First Lecture on Prosecutions for Political Opinion (1795).

Political Miscellanies (c. 1796).

Prospectus of a Course of Lectures, to Be Delivered Every Monday, Wednesday, and Friday, in Strict Conformity with the Restrictions of Mr. Pitt's Convention Act (1796).

Results of Experience in the Treatment of Cases of Defective Utterance (1814).

The Rights of Nature, Against the Usurpations of Establishments (1796).

The Rock of Modrec; or, The Legend of Sir Eltram, an Ethical Romance, 2 vols. (1792).

Selections and Original Articles, for Mr. Thelwall's Lectures on the Science and Practice of Elocution (1802).

Selections for the Illustration of a Course of Instruction on the Rhythms and Utterance of the English Language (1812).

A Sheepsheering Song (1795).

Sketch of the Life of John Howard (1790).

Sober Reflections on the Seditious and Inflammatory Letter of the Rt. Hon. Edmund Burke to a Noble Lord (1796).

The Speeches of John Thelwall, at the General Meetings of the London Corresponding Society (1795).

A Speech in Rhime, on the Assertion of the Marchioness of Lambert, That Love Improves the Virtuous Soul (1788).

The Speech of John Thelwall at the General Meeting of the Friends of Parliamentary Reform, called by the London Corresponding Society, 26th October 1795 (1795).

The Speech of John Thelwall, at the Second Meeting, called by the London Corresponding Society, 12th November 1795 (1795).

Spies and Informers: On Wednesday, Feb. 5, 1794, J. Thelwall Will Begin a Course of Lectures on Political Morality (broadsheet) (1794).

Strike! But Hear (1796).

To My Muse Give Attention (1795).

The Trial at Large of John Thelwall: For High Treason (1795).

Trials for High Treason, Containing the Whole of the Proceedings at the Old Bailey, from October 28 to December 5, 1794 (1795).

The Tribune (1795–96).

The Trident of Albion (1805).

The Vestibule of Eloquence (1810).

Vindication of the Liberty of Speech (1793?).

A Warning Voice to the Violent of All Parties (1795).

NOTE: *Thelwall's Vindication of His Political Conduct* (1795) (*National Union Catalogue* 589:236) is in fact *The Natural and Constitutional Right of Britons*.

Further Reading

There have been two biographies of John Thelwall. C. Boyle Thelwall's *The Life of John Thelwall* (1837) was planned as two volumes, but only one was published and the account ends in 1795. Charles Cestre, *John Thelwall: A Pioneer of Democracy and Social Reform in England During the French Revolution* (London: Swan Sonnenschein, 1906) is now much dated, but Cestre used a six-manuscript-volume set of Thelwall's writings, including letters, which he purchased at an auction in 1904 and which have since disappeared. See also Geoffrey Gallop, "Ideology and the English Jacobins: The Case of John Thelwall," *Enlightenment and Dissent* 5 (1986), 3–20; and Iain Hampsher-Monk, "John Thelwall and the Eighteenth-Century Radical Response to Political Economy," *Historical Journal* 34 (1991), 1–20. Reprints of primary sources from the 1790s include Edmund Burke's *Reflections on the Revolution in France*, ed. J.G.A. Pocock (Indianapolis, Ind.: Hackett Publishing Company, 1987), and *The Writings and Speeches of Edmund Burke* (Oxford: Oxford University Press, 1981–); Thomas Paine, *Rights of Man*, ed. G. Claeys (Indianapolis, Ind.: Hackett Publishing Company, 1992); William Godwin's *Enquiry Concerning Political Justice* (Harmondsworth: Penguin, 1976), and, in a scholarly edition, ed. Mark Philp (London: Pickering & Chatto, 1993); Mary Thale, ed., *Selections from the Papers of the London Corresponding Society, 1792–1799* (Cambridge: Cambridge University Press, 1983). A large collection of pamphlets from the period is reprinted in my *Political Writings of the 1790s*, 8 vols. (London: Pickering & Chatto, 1995). Studies of the period and its main figures include Conor Cruise O'Brien, *The Great Melody: A Thematic Biography of Edmund Burke* (London: Sinclair-Stevenson, 1992); Stanley Ayling, *Edmund Burke* (London: John Murray, 1988); Mark Philp, *Paine* (Oxford: Oxford University Press, 1989); Ian Small and Ceri Crossley, eds., *The French Revolution and*

British Culture (Oxford: Oxford University Press, 1989); H. T. Dickinson, ed., Britain and the French Revolution, 1789–1815 (London: Macmillan, 1989); Seamus Deane, The French Revolution and Enlightenment in England, 1789–1832 (Cambridge: Harvard University Press, 1988); H. T. Dickinson, British Radicalism and the French Revolution, 1789–1815 (Oxford: Blackwell Publishers, 1985); Gregory Claeys, Thomas Paine: Social and Political Thought (London: Unwin Hyman, 1989); Albert Goodwin, The Friends of Liberty: The English Democratic Movement in the Age of the French Revolution (London: Alan Hutchinson, 1979); E. P. Thompson, The Making of the English Working Class (Harmondsworth: Penguin, 1968); Nicholas Roe, Wordsworth and Coleridge: The Radical Years (Oxford: Clarendon Press, 1988); Mark Philp, ed., The French Revolution and British Popular Politics (Cambridge: Cambridge University Press, 1991); J. A. Hone, For the Cause of Truth: Radicalism in London, 1796–1821 (Oxford: Oxford University Press, 1982).

A Note on the Texts

The Natural and Constitutional Right of Britons to Annual Parliaments, Universal Suffrage, and the Freedom of Popular Association (1795): Additions and corrections taken from Thelwall's own copy (British Library 12270:4[2]). The text was first given as three lectures in early 1795.

The Tribune (1795–96): vol. 1 (340 pp.); vol. 2 (388 pp.); vol. 3 (333 pp.). Selections from vol. 1, pp. 12–19, 34–41, 62–70, 147–63, 222–36, 237–54; from vol. 2, pp. 1–82, 209–35, 281–95, 321–42; from vol. 3, pp. 17–52, 183–200, 263–77. Additions and corrections taken from Thelwall's own copy (British Library 12270:6). The lectures were taken down in shorthand by a W. Ramsey and corrected by Thelwall.

The Rights of Nature Against the Usurpations of Establishments (1796): Additions and corrections from Thelwall's copy of the third edition in the British Library, 12270:5(1). Three editions of Letter One appeared. The first and second editions (British Library E. 2066/4 and 1572/791) were virtually identical, but the third edition, reproduced here, introduced a number of minor stylistic changes, mostly in the first half of the text (pp. 46–88 of the second edition are nearly identical to pp. 44–86 of the third).

Sober Reflections on the Seditious and Inflammatory Letter of the Rt. Hon. Edmund Burke to a Noble Lord (1796): Additions and corrections taken from Thelwall's own copy of the second edition in the British Library, 12270:4(1). Two editions were published.

The spelling and punctuation of the original, even where inconsistent, have been retained here. Like much else, language and style were in considerable flux during the 1790s, and many eighteenth-century usages ("shew," "cloath") were giving place to modern and sometimes American variants, with both being used in the text here.

Additions or corrections to the text by Thelwall himself have been marked here with asterisks and explained in footnotes.

Writings of John Thelwall

THE
NATURAL AND CONSTITUTIONAL
RIGHT OF BRITONS
To Annual Parliaments, Univerſal Suffrage,

AND THE

FREEDOM OF POPULAR ASSOCIATION:

BEING A

VINDICATION

OF THE

MOTIVES AND POLITICAL CONDUCT

OF

JOHN THELWALL,

AND OF THE

LONDON CORRESPONDING SOCIETY,
IN GENERAL.

Intended to have been delivered at the Bar of the OLD
BAILEY, in confutation of the late
Charges of High Treaſon.

This is the fatal Engine ſo often employed by corrupt and wicked
Miniſters againſt the nobleſt and braveſt patriots, whoſe laudable oppo-
ſition to their pernicious ſchemes, thoſe Miniſters are very ready to con-
ſtrue into Treaſon and Rebellion againſt the Prince; thereby confounding
their own and the Prince's intereſt together, as if the one could not be
oppoſed without the other. 1

PREF. STATE TRIALS.

LONDON:

PRINTED FOR THE AUTHOR,

AND SOLD BY SYMONDS, PATERNOSTER-ROW; RIDGEWAY,
YORK-STREET, ST. JAMES'S; EATON, NEWGATE-STREET;
AND AT THE LECTURE ROOM, BEAUFORT BUILDINGS.
AND BY R. PHILLIPS, LEICESTER.

1795.

ADVERTISEMENT.

THE ensuing pamphlet contains only the least important part, of that statement for which I stand pledged to the public. But the great number of facts which it is necessary to ascertain, the complication of matter, and the chaos of iniquitous proceedings, which it is necessary to reduce, not only into form, but into some reasonable compass, rendering delay inevitable as to the "Narrative of the proceedings of Government", I send the Vindication, separately, before the tribunal of the public; that the investigation of the *principles* upon which we have acted may prepare them to appreciate with greater justice the *practices* by which our persecutors have aimed at our destruction.

The present publication, as will be evident, from the form it has assumed, is the Defence intended to have been delivered on the trial; if I had not been persuaded, by persons whose integrity and experience gave weight to their advice,[2] that in a cause of such serious importance, not only to myself, but to all who were implicated in the charge, and indeed to the nation in general, I ought to resign myself entirely into the hands of those whose talents and professional knowledge rendered them more adequate to the task of combating the host of Crown lawyers that were embattled against us. The habitual warmth of my temper was well known; and it was obvious that the cruelty, the injustice, and, in many respects, the absurdity of the proceedings relative to these prosecutions, must have aggravated, rather than softened the contempt and indignation I had long entertained against the men in power. It was supposed, therefore, that I might not only advance doctrines which, though not criminal, might be hostile to the prejudices of the Court, but might fall into such expressions of my feelings as might be offensive to some whom it was my interest to conciliate.

These arguments, if I had stood alone, would not have been satisfactory to my mind: for life was not all that I was anxious about. I was desirous also of vindicating the principles upon which myself and the Society had acted, and of convincing the people how infamously they have been plundered of their *rights* by the pretended champions of their *Constitution*. But as the stake was not individual, I did not consider myself at liberty to rely entirely upon my individual judgment. I resigned my defence therefore entirely into the hands of Messrs. Erskine and Gibbs;[3] and I did it the more cheerfully because I felt a thorough conviction that such talents, such legal knowledge, and such integrity have rarely been united at the English bar.

But whatever reasons might be suggested against my defending myself at the Old Bailey, they can have no weight against my standing in my own person at the bar of the public, whose right to the fullest investigation of every circumstance and every character in which they can be, by any means, interested, I have always maintained to the most unqualified extent. The substance of this Defence has, therefore, been delivered at the commencement of my present course of Lectures;[4] and it is now submitted, through the medium of the press, to that still more general investigation from which I can have no wish that any part of my conduct or sentiments should be protected.

DEFENCE, &c.

Gentlemen of the Jury,
IT may appear like affectation in me to declare, however truly, that though I have been seven months in close confinement, have heard the indictment in which I am charged by name as a Traitor, have been arraigned at this bar, and am now come to plead for my life before you, yet that I cannot, even now, (so far as relates to my feelings) persuade myself that these proceedings are serious, or that in reality I lie under the imputation of any crime. Every thing appears like the incoherency of a dream; and when I compare my conduct with my situation, judgment would impell me to pronounce that all is delusion.

When I look upon these solemn preparations, and behold the crowded anxiety of the audience, it is true, I cannot but recollect that I am in a Court of Justice, and that a cause of momentous concern is at issue. But when I strip the charges brought against me of the calumnious epithets and far-strained innuendoes with which they are encumbered, I am compelled to conclude, either that I am not in Britain, or that what surrounds me is nothing but a theatrical pageantry.

If I look back upon so much as I can remember of the thirty years during which I have inhabited this world, I behold, it is true, some of those little follies and intemperances which youth is heir to; but not one—I am bold to say it—not one of those actions which in the catalogue of Reason are marked as crimes—or which, from moral considerations, I could anxiously wish undone. I have drank of the cup of adversity, even to the dregs, without once swerving from the dictates of integrity; and have had the good fortune to challenge the respect and friendship of persons whose situation in life placed them above me, and of others whose learning and talents will render them the admiration of ages, by the conspicuous rectitude of my conduct. Yet here I stand, pleading at the Bar of the Old Bailey for my life; occupying the place so frequently polluted by the most atrocious guilt; and holding up my hand like the vilest ruffian and murderer.

But no ruffian, however practised,—no murderer, however atrocious, ever came to this Bar, with such a load of calumny and prejudication upon his head, as during six months of close confinement has been industriously accumulated upon mine.—Inflammatory speeches in the House of Commons, and hasty resolutions, rushed into in the moment of artfully-excited alarm; calumniating pamphlets, and the most direct and horrible accusations in the public papers—nay the most unqualified prejudications from the lips of persons in authority, have been incessantly employed to poison the public mind against myself and my fellow-sufferers, during a season when it was impossible for us to administer any sort of antidote. Every private feeling has been belied; and every fact misrepresented; and the individual who for years has been remarked, by *all who knew him*, for carrying the principles of humanity to an extent which the world in general is disposed to consider as romantic—with whom the life of the meanest insect, not immediately hostile to the existence or comfort of man, is regarded as sacred and inviolable, has been publicly upheld, by name, (that he might be deprived of all chance of an impartial trial) as a ruffian insatiable of blood, and to whom every crime was indifferent that might lead to the gratification of his ambition.

And what are the foundations—what are the reasons for this monstrous accumulation of hired calumny—and this jeopardy in which our lives are so ignominiously placed?—What but the activity we have displayed—the pains we have taken to convince the people (groaning under their miseries but unacquainted with the causes of their oppression) of the innumerable evils that result from their total exclusion, by a few monopolizing Borough-mongers, from all share in the *Representation*, as it is insultingly called, of their Country? This is our crime—for a crime it is in the eyes of those interested individuals who think the right of legislating for seven millions and an half of human beings a part of their property; and the very paroxism of our Treason is only that anxious to know how far the general desire of reformation had extended, we consulted in the year ninety-four upon the propriety of doing that which in the year eighty-two, many of his Majesty's present ministers actually did.[5]

Gentlemen, if my life alone were implicated in this question, I would not deign to answer the charge that is brought against me: for that life is not worth preserving which can be brought in question, at the nod of a minister upon such pretences. But the stake is deeper. These trials, if they mean any thing, are the prelude only to a dreadful tragedy of despotism and oppression, at the representation of which, if not prevented, Britain must groan even to dissolution. I shall, therefore, enter into the examination of the charge with an earnestness of which it is not intrinsically worthy.

The crime I am accused of is High Treason—a crime the most penal in our sanguinary calendar: and which not only condemns the criminal to a savage and tormenting death, but extends the vindictive spirit of the Law to his innocent and helpless family. The Statue I am indicted under is the 25 Edward III.—one of those plain, simple, and concise specimens of the jurisprudence of our ancestors which it is *impossible for any honest man to doubt over*, or misunderstand. It bears its whole meaning evident upon its surface: no explanation can make it more obvious; nor is it possible to bring any one case fairly within the reach of any of its clauses that would not occur to the plainest capacity on the first perusal. As that great Oracle of the Law, Lord Coke, observes—Every thing must be so plain, so obvious, and so direct as not to admit the possibility of defence, or it is no treason.[6]

The particular branch of that statute within the verge of which it has been thought most practicable to *drag* the projects and exertions in which I am accused of participating, is that of compassing and imagining the King's death:—that is to say, designing to put the King to death; and concerting means to carry that design into execution.

All other treasons, and all other criminal intentions must be absolutely *acted upon* to constitute the offence. But in consideration of the scenes of bloodshed, which an attempt to cut off the chief magistrate, is likely to produce, and the horrible baseness and treachery of assassination, by which such projects are generally carried into execution, the legislature, in this single instance, has thought fit to declare the *proven* intention (the compassing and imagining) equal to the act itself; and to punish it accordingly. But then it is also prudently provided that such intention shall be *positively and clearly proved*, by *open deed*: not by ambiguous or suspicious circumstances; but by clear, direct, and undeniable evidence; capable of no explanation, and standing in need of neither commentary nor innuendo.

It is necessary, therefore, that an overt act, an *open deed*, should be charged in every indictment for compassing and imagining the death of the King, and indeed for every species of High Treason whatever.

But what is *an Overt Act?* This the learned President has told us, in his

Charge to the Grand Jury, it is impossible to define.[7] And this is true. But the same learned authority has not assigned the reason. Permit therefore, a plain, unlearned man to supply the deficiency. An *overt act*, or *open deed* is a phrase that cannot be defined, because it wants no definition. It is com-posed of the simplest elements of language. Every body understands the whole meaning of the word *open*, nor is any one at a loss to conceive the meaning of the word *act* or *deed*. It is, therefore, evident, that an overt act can be nothing else than an act wilfully, palpably, and directly tending to the accomplishment of the treasonable design imputed.

I do not mean that there must have been an absolute attempt to stab, to shoot, or poison the King, to constitute an open act of compassing and imagining his death: but I do contend, that there must have been a posi-tive conspiracy, the avowed or *evident* object of which was the death of the King: or there must have been steps taken by the individual accused which obviously and wilfully tended to the accomplishment of that criminal in-tention.—The late infamous and ridiculous assassination plot[8] (for exam-ple) so wickedly *fabricated*, so *critically divulged*, and so *politically believed* by a certain circle, notwithstanding its monstrous absurdity and impractica-bility, would, if there had been any truth in it, have been as clear and evident an open act of treason, from the steps said to have been taken, as if the dart had been positively buried in the breast of the Sovereign; for though it is true (and though, in all other cases, the Laws of England have admitted this as a sufficient plea) that a man may repent before the deed is done, and that fear, or the conviction of the impracticability of his under-taking may persuade him to desist; yet there ought to be no door left open for monsters who could meditate so diabolical a project; nor ought the life of the chief magistrate in any country to be so loosely guarded that the dagger must be absolutely lifted before the law is at liberty to interpose its shield. No, Gentlemen; guard the life of the Sovereign as jealously as you please. Let the fences of the law be thick and strong around him. Such jealousy has my applause; and were I conscious of having ever attempted (even in the precipitancy of intemperate passion) to overleap these fences, instead of standing thus bold and confident before you, crest fallen and mute I would await your sentence, and pay, without a murmur, the heavy but just penalty due to the violated laws and endangered peace of my coun-try. For, whatever speculative opinions I may entertain, no *speculation* was ever yet presented to my mind which I would attempt to advance by crimes and violence. I respect the peace—I respect the happiness of society—that peace without which virtue can never flourish—that happiness without which Liberty itself would be but an empty name. And I call upon this tribunal, I call upon my country at large, I call upon that posterity whose impartiality will do justice to my memory, to search with scrutinizing exactness into the evidence of my motives and conduct, and see whether the promotion of that peace and happiness has not been the principal, if not the sole motive of that conduct the cruel and wicked misrepresentation of which has brought me here.

But the absurd and inexplicable doctrine of constructive treason is so far from being an additional shield to the Royal Person, that British history informs us that not one of those sovereigns whose wicked ministers have broached this detestable doctrine have reigned in peace and happiness among their subjects; and that a majority of them, in consequence of these doctrines, have come to an untimely end. I appeal, among other instances, to the histories of the turbulent and disastrous reigns of Richard II. Edward II. Richard III. Henry VIII. Charles I. and II. and James II.[9] during all which the discontent and violence of the people rose in exact proportion to the violent and irrational principles of criminal jurisprudence which the evil Counsellors of those Princes successively adopted. Nor were the fatal consequences confined to the deluded Sovereigns. The Ministers who counselled, and the Judges who conducted these unjust and cruel prosecutions were, most of them, the victims also of their mistaken policy; being either banished, executed, or torn to pieces by the rage of an injured people, whose oppressions became in time too heavy to be endured.

O deluded and impolitic rulers of the earth, when will ye open your ears to the warning voice of experience?—When will ye have the prudence to regulate your conduct by a perpetual remembrance of this incontrovertible axiom—That there is no stability for power—no security for grandeur but in a temperate and inflexible adherence to the immutable principles of Truth and Justice?

It is by an administration of the known laws of the country, by these immutable principles alone—not by the underhanded tyranny of *ex post facto* interpretations, the inexplicable theories of constructive treason, the vague and unmeaning cant of existing circumstances, and the endless train of "Doctrines fashioned to the varying hour", that the safety of the King, and indeed of every individual throughout the country, can be upheld. For if every intelligible distinction is thus to be broken down—if every difference of political opinion—every steady and conscientious opposition to the views and interests of a minister is to bring the individual, dragged like a felon to this bar—If the conscientious Associator (however mistaken in his principle) merely for disseminating his opinions, and endeavouring to collect the sentiments of the nation on the subject of Reform, is to be indicted for this unheard of treason—"Conspiring to subvert the Monarchy", and placed in the same situation of disgrace and peril as the most vile and execrable assassin, what must be the consequence?—Who does not perceive that the great shield by which the life, not only of the Sovereign, but of all human society is protected—the shield of moral discrimination, is hewn away? and that we must presently be exposed to that horrid state of society—or rather *anarchy*, which even now prevails in some despotic states of Europe, in which it is safer to *stab* than to *reason*; because the former can be practised with greater *secrecy*, and therefore, with greater *impunity* than the latter?

In order to give some colour to proceedings thus fraught with moral and political calamity, you have been told by the Crown Lawyers, in language equally ambiguous and sophistical, that "He who does an act, meaning to do it, which *may endanger* the King's life, compasses and imagines the death of the King."[10] This assertion, though apparently suggested by the language of the Lord President, that "*Overt Acts* are all the *possible* means which *may* be used in prosecution of the end proposed",[11] I shall take the liberty to examine: because upon this sophism depends the whole pernicious doctrine of Constructive Treason in general, and all that is serious in this indictment in particular.

If this doctrine went no farther than to assert, that every step proved to have been taken by the accused party for the purpose of producing the King's death, is in such party an overt act of this species of treason, no one would attempt to controvert it. It would be self evident: and the very statement would be superfluous. But if nothing more had been intended, neither myself nor my colleagues could have been placed at this bar: for the substantive project charged in the indictment is one in which our accusers themselves have formerly co-operated: nor could human intellect conceive, however blinded by prejudice or misled by passion, that a few idle speeches and ridiculous toasts (the forgeries chiefly of those professional spies whose audacious perjuries have insulted the justice and degraded the character of their country) were sufficient to fix a treasonous intention upon actions otherwise innocent—much less to extend that criminality to every individual with whom the persons they were alledged against might happen to be politically connected.

It was evidently the intention of the Crown Lawyers, that the fullest latitude of interpretation should be given to the ambiguous axiom. For taking for granted, in the first instance (what their own witnesses have sufficiently disproved) that the proposed Convention[12] was to assume the supreme authority, we are led, step by step, into the very centre of the inextricable labyrinth of Constructions: and at last we are gravely told, that although "it had been intended to retain the name and office of King in the person of the present King, creating, however, a new legislature, to act with him",—"still such a conspiracy is an overt act in the true construction of law, and high treason in compassing the King's death."[13]

As the suggested purpose of assuming any degree of sovereign or legislative authority, has been contradicted by the most unequivocal testimony, I shall not now contend that the necessity of appealing to arguments so futile and absurd is itself a sufficient proof that the pretended treason of *subverting the Monarchy*, as it is called, is no treason at all by the law of England. It is more to my purpose to shew you the precipice to the brink of which these legal sophisters have conducted you: for if it be true, that to seek to alter or ameliorate the laws and constitution of your country is high treason, because the people may *possibly* become unreasonable in their demands, and the government may *possibly* oppose their wishes, and a contest may *possibly* ensue, in which the King may *possibly* be deposed or slain, then farewell at once to every boasted exercise of reason!—farewell to political improvement!—farewell even to the hope of regenerating the venerable institutions of our ancestors, or preserving the mouldering fragments that yet remain!—If it is high treason for the people to lift up their voices when they conceive themselves oppressed by partial and arbitrary laws—If it is high treason to seek for political amelioration by impressing the legislature with an aweful sense of the collective wishes of the people, in what but in name consists the difference between the *free-born Briton* and the *Asiatic slave?* And if he who does an act, "meaning to do that act" (though without any proven intention as to the consequence) "which may" (ultimately or collaterally) "*endanger* the King's life", is to be hanged, drawn and quartered,[14] by virtue of a legal quibble, which he never heard of, as having "compassed and imagined the death of the King",[15] what valuable life can be secure? CONVENTION is at present the *war whoop* of the tribe in power. But should they succeed in their sanguinary purpose, who can answer for the cry that may next be raised, or the victims that may be hunted down?—For mark their chain of reasoning, and tell me where is the individual of active mind—(and it is only by the coalition of active minds that society ever was, or ever can be benefited?)—Where is the individual of active mind who has never been engaged in some project that might, by the circuitous sophistry of Crown Lawyers, be tortured into a charge of treason, as plausible as that upon which you are now to decide?

A Convention in France, you are told, overthrew the Constitution, and brought the King to the scaffold.—This by the way is not true. The Constitution of France was totally overthrown before the National Convention was called; and the doom of the unfortunate Louis[16] was sealed inevitably by the battle of the Thuilleries;[17] if indeed it was not sealed, at an earlier period, by his own rash hand; when, by written instrument, he declared himself a hypocrite and a perjurer.[18]

Let us, however, for a moment, grant the premises. "A Convention in France", we are told overthrew the Constitution and brought the King to the scaffold; therefore a Convention *might possibly* overthrow the constitution of this country: and when the constitution was once overthrown, the King *might possibly* be brought to the scaffold, and Anarchy and Massacre *might possibly* stalk thro' our streets; and as it is *possible* that these events *might* follow, it is *possible* these men, when they consulted about assembling a Convention, *might* have these treasonable objects in contemplation; "therefore it is a case of no difficulty: It is the clearest act of compassing the King's death!"[19]

Immortal memory of our brave and simple ancestors! do I stand here to defend my life, upon a charge of High Treason, against this monstrous train of possibilities, constructions and improbable contingencies?—and am I still in Britain?

But even this reasoning, strained and remote as it is, will not answer the purpose of our prosecutors. The parallel will not hold. For granting (which I never can—for I can trace them to another source) that all the excesses in France resulted from calling the Convention, the conclusion does not follow. The cases are essentially different; the consequences, therefore, never could have been the same: nor is there a man, I am confident, in the whole list of proclaimed conspirators who was mad enough to expect, or to wish that they should.

The Convention in France was a thronged representation of the aggregate power and population of the country: it had in its bosom several of the most powerful and wealthy individuals remaining in the nation: the influence of these was considered encreased by the base and cowardly conduct of the great body of the aristocracy, who after having, by their evil councils, plunged the King in inextricable difficulties, and brought upon him the general indignation of the people, ran away, and left the victim to his fate.

Such was the National Convention of France!—a Convention chosen in the very ferment of popular rage and apprehension: when all the constituted authorities of the country were dissolved; when anarchy was already introduced; and when the pressure of external danger, and the intrigues of internal factions, had produced such a delerium of the public mind, as could be satisfied with nothing but the most violent measures, and was therefore likely to fix its election on men of the most violent character.

Gentlemen,—If I were a man disposed to conceal my real sentiments, it is not in my power. The arm of authority—pardon me if I say the *ruffian* arm, has broke into the most secret recesses of my meditations. The private correspondence, the labours, and the reflections of my life have been exposed to the examination of my persecutors. Out of that mass of evidence which to them must have revealed the real sentiments and feelings of my heart, every thing that could disprove this monstrous charge, refute their calumnies and impress you with a favourable opinion has been industriously suppressed; and every thing that might appear injurious to my character as industriously brought before you. From part of this evidence it appears, and I do not wish to deny, that there have been moments when credulity has fluctuated as to the truth of those dreadful narratives which have been repeated in this country with such insidious exultation, the extent of the exaggerated cruelties, and the provocations and necessities under which they were committed. But whatever speculations I may have indulged upon this subject (and I am yet to learn that to speculate on foreign occurrences, is a crime) I have always admitted—I have always insisted (and I call upon every individual who is at all acquainted with my character and sentiments to stamp the broad seal of infamy upon my forehead if I speak not truly) I have always insisted that many actions have been perpetrated in France, that no good mind can contemplate without horror. But it was not the Convention of France that begot the anarchy in France; but the anarchy that begot the convention: nor could such a set of men as the leaders of *one party* in that convention, have concentrated the suffrages of the people in any possible state of society but that in which the country was plunged at the time of their election.—They were men whose ferocious passions could have been engendered only by the licentious barbarity of the old despotism, and hatched in the ferment of an unprecedented revolution. Such, however, as they were they seem to have been calculated for the desperation of the times; and were hailed, like thunder storms and convulsions of nature, which men gaze and tremble at, but whose explosion is necessary to clear the clouded and infectious atmosphere.

These men have "stalked their hour upon the stage."[20] They have performed their part in the most eventful drama ever exhibited on the theatre
of the world; and their exit has been such as is little calculated to encourage imitation: for, thanks to the workings of Eternal Justice, Demogogue by
the hand of Demogogue, they have fallen—the unpitied victims of their
own violent councels; and have yielded their power and their popularity to
leaders of more humane principles;[21] who will, in their turn, I hope and
trust, as the popular ferment more and more subsides, and the danger of
foreign interference retreats to still greater distance from their doors, be
peaceably succeeded by others still more conspicuous for the mildness of
their sentiments and the humanity of their measures.

If this outline of the history and composition of the French Convention
is just (which I believe it is)—if the causes of its excesses are accurately
traced (and I have laboured to do it with an impartial hand) I shall be
justified in concluding, and you Gentlemen of the Jury, will be compelled
to join in the conclusion—that even if the meeting in question had been
intended to be a National Convention, yet no decision or presumption as
to its eventual conduct could be drawn from what has occurred on the
Continent. It is not the word Convention that constitutes either the crime
or the power. These, in the instance we have witnessed, resulted from
local circumstances peculiar to the French nation; and, in such assemblies,
always must depend upon the state of society, and the weight and current
of popular opinion, at the season of their formation.

But this is an argument totally superfluous on the present occasion.—
The meeting premeditated, but never determined upon in England, has
been distinctly proved to *have been, in its very proportion*[22] a mere
convention of Delegates from the different patriotic societies, for the purpose of comparing their sentiments upon the necessity of Reform, and giving weight, by their co-operation, to any applications that might be made
to Parliament or the Throne.

The idea that it was to act either as a National Convention, or a Constituent Assembly was never started in our deliberations; nor is the least
trace of it to be discovered in the evidence before you.

Compare then the gigantic fabric I have already delineated with the
pigmy structure likely to be moulded by the hands of a few powerless societies of tradesmen and mechanics, associated with two or three gentlemen
of private fortune, whose whole estates would scarcely furnish the luxuries
of a Prime Minister's table, and then tell me whether it is possible that any
body could be so mad as to meditate or apprehend similar effects from
means so immeasurably disproportionate.

Gentlemen, I have not been in the habit of estimating people by their rank and fortune; nor shall I, in this situation, so far depart from the independency of my feelings. Such men have as much right to meet, confer, and enquire as the greatest and richest monopolists in the country. But that a little knot of individuals like these should be objects of jealousy to government, any farther than as their association might provoke enquiry, and lead to the detection of abuses which those who reap the profit may wish to cover with a veil of mystery, is a phenomenon unparalleled in British History. That fifty or sixty such men assembled in convention (even if such convention had positively been determined upon and called) should be regarded as engines formidable enough, in defiance of the whole wealth, power, constituted authorities, and military establishments of the country, "to pull down and to subvert from its very foundations, the glorious fabric of the British monarchy",[23] annihilate a rich and powerful nobility, overthrow the charters, institutions, and labours of ages, and bring the sovereign to the scaffold, is an absurdity so monstrous, that if it ever did enter the brain of any one of the supposed conspirators, not the strong holds of the Tower, nor the cells of Newgate, ought to be his punishment, but the straw and regimen of Bedlam, where he might meditate at leisure over his moonstruck fancies; and indulge his frantic speculations without injury to mankind.

And yet the principal overt act charged in this indictment, and that out of which the rest in a manner grow, is conspiring to call such convention, for the purpose of overthrowing the monarchy and constitution of the country.

How then is this to be solved? By what clue shall we unravel this political mystery?—Were our prosecutors totally unacquainted with the favourable circumstances that have come out in evidence? Certainly not. Had I access to the mass of papers which I know they have been in possession of, I could produce from them demonstrations far more unequivocal (if more unequivocal can be) that the objects of the purposed Convention were no other than I have expounded.—I could produce from them letters explicitly announcing these objects; and one, in particular, from a Society in Scotland, offering to send a Delegate, but informing us that other Societies in the same town declined, *because the object of the Convention* WAS *to petition Parliament*: a measure they did not approve.

But it should appear that our prosecutors are of opinion that their popularity will appear greater, so long as public opinion can be repressed, than when the general voice is permitted to give notoriety to the feelings of the people. A false popularity was therefore to be supported at the expence of every thing dear to liberty and morals. Political heresy was to be hunted down by a herd of spies and inquisitors; and all who presumed to differ from the orthodox faith of the cabinet, were to be terrified by birds-eye prospects of proscriptions and *auto-de-fees*.[24] The spirit of the nation was to be insulted by the most partial administration of justice; and while libels the most scurrilous, and the utmost rancour of personal abuse were not only tolerated, but publicly patronised, in those who poured forth their venom against the friends of liberty; even argument and enquiry, when directed against established abuses, have been persecuted with the most rancorous avidity. Every liberal speculation has been branded and punished as a crime; nor is it safe to vent an opinion, even upon transactions in a neighbouring country, unless to exaggerate the wild excesses of emancipated slaves, and lament the fallen glories of the ancient despotism. And now as the final consummation of this system of terror and imposition, men who consulted together on the propriety of eliminating, by a Convention or meeting of Delegates from different societies, the extent to which the desire of parliamentary reform had extended are indicted for High Treason.

Such are the sanguinary extremities to the brink of which this harrassed nation is conducted by the mistaken principles and selfish passions of a few ambitious men, who finding the suppression of public opinion essential to the preservation of their power, and the perpetuity of profitable abuses, have contrived to render even those who have an interest in the truth, participators in their alarm at the progress of investigation. From *prosecution for libel*, they have proceeded to *transportation for sedition*;[25] and now, as the grand climax of political expediency, sixteen or eighteen innocent and virtuous men are to be hanged, drawn and quartered, to ascertain, by the *experiment*, whether or not it is High Treason to endeavour to collect the opinions of the people, or oppose, in any manner, their destructive measures.

But it was obvious to the prosecutors that the mere circumstance of calling, or consulting whether it would be proper to call a Convention, could not by any possible construction be considered as an overt act of Treason. They could not but recollect that, in Ireland, they had very lately caused an act of parliament to be passed to prevent a convention from assembling there;[26] and that consequently that which required an express act of parliament to make it treasonable in Ireland could not be treason in England, whose laws and constitution are the same, without a similar interference of the legislature. Neither could they be blind to the absurdity of supposing it High Treason in England merely to consult and meditate upon the expediency of a measure, which it was only sedition to carry into actual effect in Scotland. It is likely also that our persecutors had not quite forgot (tho' the Right Honourable Chancellor of the Exchequer[27] found some difficulty in remembering it) that, about twelve or thirteen years ago, several of themselves actually attended a Convention, or meeting of Delegates, without ever dreaming of indictments for High Treason.[28]

It is true the learned judge has demanded—Suppose we should be of opinion that the proceedings in 1782, were treasonable—what advantage would you derive from the precedent? To this I answer—None: I am afraid. We could lament, indeed, the verification of an old and trite observation, "That laws are cobwebs which ensnare small flies to their destruction, but let wasps and hornets through":[29] but this would be poor consolation. This supposition, however, never suggested itself in the first stages of these proceedings; and the plain matter of fact not being sufficient, it was necessary (for the *first time*, and in direct violation of every principle and explicit regulation of English law) in an indictment for High Treason to insert an innuendo.—I say an innuendo, for what is it but an innuendo to affirm a concealed and improbable purpose as the object of any measure, when an avowed, notorious, and practicable object presents itself at once to the mind.

Observe, Gentlemen, the curious mode of reasoning by which this innuendo is supported. The charge against us is compassing and imagining the King's death: the principal overt act is conspiring to call a Convention: but, in order to make this an *open* act of High Treason, it was necessary to take for granted a *secret* intention "a purpose hidden under the veil"[30] of deposing the King, and bringing him to death and destruction, by means of this Convention: although it does not appear that any such design or purpose was ever declared, insinuated, or hinted, at any meeting or consultation of these tremendous Conspirators whatever.—Even taking it for granted, which no man, considering the characters of the witnesses, can be credulous enough to do, that all which has been sworn is fact, yet nothing like a single treasonous expression, *spoken in prosecution or furtherance of any design, or in relation to any design*, (which are the indispensable requisites to make words admissable evidence in cases of Treason) appears against any one of the supposed conspirators: notwithstanding that the total want of caution in the generality of them, appears to have been the most criminal trait in their characters. A violent word in the moment of irritation and debate;—a ridiculous toast, perhaps suggested by these spies themselves, and repeated in the hour of conviviality, without thought or meaning—

these are the only pretences for fixing criminality of intention upon associations and projects in themselves of the most innocent—I believe of the most laudable nature.

Thus then an hypothesis is first assumed, and a fact is afterwards asserted in support of that hypothesis; but before the fact itself can be applied to the subject in debate, it is necessary to take for granted, as already proved, the very conclusion as a foundation for which the fact was itself asserted.

If this mode of proceeding is countenanced; if this retrograde and inexplicable reasoning is adopted, it would save trouble hereafter if his Majesty's ministers would hang up, without ceremony, all persons who presume to censure or oppose them, and then set their Attorney General to discover, and *their* judges to explain, the crimes for which they suffered. This would be quite as consistent with reason and justice as upon mere *ex parte* evidence (and even before the examination of that was concluded) to pronounce a solemn *extra judicial sentence* of High Treason against eighteen or twenty men, and then, after five or six months deliberation, indite them for a conspiracy to kill the King, for no other reason than because they could find nothing else to charge against them.

Does not this—I ask you seriously gentlemen—does not this look as if Ministers having predetermined to hang us, had reasoned the matter thus?—

These men certainly have not levied war against the King; neither have they defiled his bed; we cannot find that they have adhered to his enemies within, or held treasonable correspondence with those without the realm; there is but one description more in the statute of Treason; let us indite them therefore, without further enquiry, for compassing and imagining the King's death.

Let me conjure to you, Gentlemen, by all that is dear to Britons, reflect what must be our situation, if juries can be induced to countenance such practices! Think not that it is me you are trying; you are sitting in judgment upon the liberties of your country. The whole present generation is interested—Posterity is interested in your verdict; and the blood of your children, and your children's children may lay upon your heads, if party prejudice, the bias of interest, or the delusions of political partiality draw you from the strait line of duty.—Remember that the question you have to try is whether I have conspired to kill the King: for that is the treason I am charged with. If you are convinced by the evidence that such was the object of our conspiracy in general, and of myself in particular, pronounce your verdict; and may your consciences never be troubled at the recollection. But if no such detestable design is proved; then whether you are convinced that we meant to call a convention, or whether you are not; whether you approve our political speculations or detest them, are circumstances not to be weighed for a moment. The crime charged against me is not proved; and you must pronounce—NOT GUILTY.

Treason, Gentlemen!—A meeting of delegates from different societies to consult on the propriety and means of Parliamentary Reform, High Treason? Never was such a charge built upon such foundations; nor upon such foundations can it now be supported unless we are indeed sunk into that *abyss* of slavery that the mere application of the word traiterously from the lips of a Minister, or an Attorney General to things which never before were Treason, shall be admitted to metamorphose them into that highest of all political offenses.

But the very maintenance of such a doctrine is an act of the Highest Treason against the common understanding of mankind; and to sanction it by the verdict of a jury were a sacrilege against the sacred Temple of our Freedom which no temptation could excuse, no repentance could wash away. It were indeed an assassination of that constitution you are empannelled to defend—of that liberty which our ancestors (like the pelican) have nourished from their own bleeding bosoms. As Lord Treasurer Danby[31] formerly exclaimed, defending himself against a frivolous charge of accumulative and constructive treason—"If after so many heats and disputes which our ancestors had had with the Crown about their liberties, this doctrine should be admitted for law, we would seem to endeavour, as much as in us lies, to be our own *Felo's de se.*" (*St. Tr.* vol. 2. p. 741.)[32]—Yes, Gentlemen, you, the Jurors of Britain, are the soul—the vital spirit of what yet remains of British Liberty. And should you (overawed by power, or misled by prejudice) be rendered instrumental to this encroaching system of terror and oppression it were indeed a *suicide* of the worst description.—But it cannot be. Your eyes are not closed against the consequences. You cannot but foresee the ruin and desolation that must inevitably follow if Ministers and Crown Lawyers are suffered to alter the law of treason at their pleasure, by newfangled constructions and circuitous inferences. As the same Lord Treasurer observes, "If it should be found that this will hold water, and should be maintained for good doctrine; truly I think there would need no other arbitrary power to make men quit this country. For, as to any man's liberty, it might be equal to him whether he lived under the French government, or under the Grand Signior's government, as under a government so arbitrary as this doctrine alone would make ours." *Ib.* 752.[33] What monstrous extent is there to which it may not spread?—How effectually will all the barriers erected by our ancestors for the security of our lives and liberties be thrown down? and how absolutely will it be in the power of ministers to destroy every virtuous individual who shall be obnoxious to their caprice, or a bar to their ambition?

Let me then impress upon your minds the duty and the necessity that you should both discern the truth of the evidence, and distinguish truly what the actions *are* (if proved) and not what they are *called* by the intemperance of our accusers.

For this reason it was that our ancestors—keeping a jealous eye upon prosecutions for High Treason, and well knowing them to be "the fatal engines so often employed by corrupt and wicked ministers against the noblest and bravest patriots, whose laudable opposition to their pernicious schemes those ministers are very ready to construe into treason and rebellion against the Prince." (*Pref. St. Tr.* p. 4.)[34] For this reason it was that our ancestors, by a variety of judicious regulations, and particularly by that excellent (though perverted and evaded) act, the 25 Edward III. took particular care to provide that the *special matter*—the *overt act* should be laid before the jury, "as the end they may be satisfied *whether the charge have its right determination.* Otherwise it were to no purpose to desire special matter, unless it were right to see whether the special matter alledged be what it is called. As for example, if a man were accused of having traiterously passed the river in a pair of oars; this is special matter and stiled treason, by inserting the word traiterously"; (*St. Tr.* vol. 2. p. 730)[35] yet, though the fact should be established beyond contradiction, you would not, therefore, by finding the verdict of guilty, subject the prisoner to all the penalties of High Treason for passing the river in a boat. And yet I can shew as many acts of Parliament and maxims of our Common Law and Constitution declaring it High Treason to pass the river with a pair of oars, as the Crown Lawyers, with all their laborious erudition can produce declaring it High Treason to conspire to assemble a Convention.

I have quoted this part of my argument principally in the words of the Lord Treasurer Danby, because it gives me an opportunity of observing how that nobleman, after having (like all the successive ministers of Charles II.) done whatever lay in his power to injure the cause of Liberty, and pollute the stream of Justice, for the purpose of arbitrary usurpation, was himself obliged to struggle with the injustice he had connived at, and appeal to those strong and original principles of liberty which his own administration had so much discoutenanced—

"For in these cases
We still have judgment here; that we but teach
Bloody instructions, which, being taught, return
To plague the inventors: this evenhanded Justice
Commends the ingredients of our poison'd chalice
To our own lips."[36]

But what are the pretences for concluding that the Convention was to have brought the King to the scaffold? Why, truly, one of the reasons for this monstrous conclusion is that a committee had been appointed as a preliminary step to *watch* the proceedings of the Parliament and Administration. And yet, till the publication of the reports of the Secret Committee,[37] this circumstance was universally considered, and must have been considered by every individual at all acquainted with the Laws and Constitution of the country, to be as innocent an act as ever entered into the imagination of man.

If this is denied, shew me the act of Parliament that makes it criminal— that commands the people of Britain to shut their eyes against the political transactions of their country; and declares it high treason to scrutinise the conduct of their public servants and representatives. Turn me to the article in the Magna Charta—to the page in the Bill of Rights—to the maxim of the Common Law (that still surviving fragment of the free and glorious Constitution of our Saxon ancestors!)—Turn me, I say, to the article, the page, the maxim which prohibits the native of this island from watching with jealous circumspection the proceedings of those functionaries whose conduct, in proportion as it is regulated by virtue, or influenced by corruption, may produce the happiness, or the misery of every individual in the state.

Gentlemen—There is no such article, no such maxim, no such passage in any of the constitutional authorities of this country. Those brave ancestors who bled so freely for the liberties of Britain, have not left it now to be disputed, whether we have a right to investigate those measures for the support of which our purses must be drained and our veins exhausted. The universal right of political investigation was ratified when representation was established. The question now before you is whether you will repeal those sacred decrees of liberty and justice, sealed by the blood of our ancestors, and erect again the golden calf of passive obedience, which after repeated struggles for the establishment of such an absurd idolatry, was at last bruised to pieces by the strong mace of the Revolution in 1688, and scattered over that ocean which happily *separated* the country from the exiled race of the *Stewarts*.[38]

But mark, Gentlemen, I pray you, the *steps* by which these oracles of the law, are artfully conducting us to that *abyss* of slavery, where every thing is to be treason that the minister chuses to call so. The 25 Edward III. in plain and inflexible terms, lays it down that it shall be High Treason to compass and imagine the King's death; but provides that the design to levy war, must be carried into execution to constitute the treason. The reason for this distinction is obvious. Our blunt ancestors had some regard to discrimination. They could not bear to put the bold and open warrior, even though engaged in rebellion, upon a level with the sly and dastardly assassin, who aimed by secret plots and conspiracies at the Sovereign's life. They knew also (by experience) that rebellions, even when successful, do not inevitably tend to the King's destruction; that they have sometimes placed him even in a more respectable and happy situation: nay, that it had sometimes even been necessary for the subject to take arms to redeem him from the tyranny and usurpation of a minister, who, by filling all the posts of trust and authority with his immediate dependents, had rendered himself alike despotic master of the people and the prince. It was, therefore, that a line of just distinction was drawn between the assassin and the rebel, and that even the intention was punished in the one, while nothing short of absolute action could drag down the penalty upon the head of the other.

Lawyers, however (a race of man who have spread more devastation through the moral world than the Goths and Vandals, who overthrew the Roman empire!)—soon began to aspire to favour by extending the narrow limits of the law of treason. It was declared that a conspiracy to depose the King, to seize his person, or to put him under bodily restraint was compassing and imagining his death: for say they, "Experience has taught us that the distance is generally small between the prisons of princes and their graves."[39]

This was certainly some violation of the simple meaning of the statute, and evinced a palpable disregard to the reasons which dictated the distinction. Nevertheless, as the reasoning is plausible, and the authorities that support it are respectable, it has met with general acquiescence. But the door of construction thus opened, the next step was to declare every *conspiracy* to levy war for any purpose of *general concern* (as to remove evil counsellors, or to alter whatever the government for the time being chose to consider as fundamental laws) an act of High Treason. Such conspiracy could not, it is true, be made an overt act under the clause of levying war—the jealous caution of our ancestors having provided that the war must be actually levied to constitute the Treason. But the ingenuity of Judges and Attorney-Generals over-leaped the difficulty, and discovered that a conspiracy relative to one distinctive species of treason, though not an overt act of that treason, was an overt act of another distinct species.

Common sense revolted at this: but the general and just abhorrence of tumult and violence interposed; and the friends of peace and order connived at the absurdity.—Fatal delusion;—If the simple provisions of the 25 Edward III. were not sufficient—if the altered state of society had done away the reasons for the ancient distinction, and rendered it necessary that lurking assassination and open resistance should be treated with equal severity, some law for that purpose ought to have been provided: for the country that tolerates constructive treason, makes its judges its legislators—puts the power of altering the laws at will into their hands, and establishes a tyranny against which no virtue, no prudence, no degree of knowledge is a sufficient shield. Rome fell into despotism when the legislative and judicial power were united; Athens bowed to the dust, when the same individuals were her judges and her rulers; nor am I certain that I am not, at this moment, performing the funeral obsequies of British Liberty. For mark the step that now is taken—An alledged conspiracy for the purpose not of deposing the King;—not of imprisoning the King—not of putting bodily restraint or coercion upon him—but for the purpose of over-aweing parliament (as it is ambiguously called) and so, by assumed consequence, laying the *mind* of the King under bias or restraint, is offered to you as an overt act of compassing or imagining the King's death. "A force upon the Parliament", you are told, "must be immediately directed against the King, who is an integral part of it; it must reach the King, or it can have no effect at all."[40]

But what was to reach the King?—Not the point of the dagger; nor the bayonets, nor the fear of the bayonets, of the soldiers of insurrection:—No—but the "Power", or, as it is afterwards called the "Force", of opinion, collected and concentrated by 50 or 60 individuals, without fortune, rank, or connection, assembled for three or four weeks in convention, and delivering their opinions on Parliamentary Reform. This forsooth, from the possibility (if possible it was) that it should occasion Parliament to reform itself contrary to its own free will, and thereby eventually occasion the King, contrary to his own free will, to consent to such reform:—this is to be considered now as an overt act of compassing the King's death.

But let not the lives of Men and Britons be trapped in the ambiguity of words: nor let it be supposed—(for if you consult the authorities referred to, you cannot suppose) that by restraining and putting a force upon the King was ever meant that gentle coercion which aggregate and concentrated opinion may produce. If it was, then would every attempt of any body of the people to express their opinion, upon any political subject whatever, be an open act of High Treason: for every such aggregate expression must mean, if it means any thing, to restrain and direct, in some measure, the future conduct of Government. Nay, at this rate, I will be bound to prove that every motion in Parliament for censuring the measures, or enquiring into the conduct of ministers, nay, every new bill, of a public nature, not absolutely originating in the Cabinet, is an act of High Treason in the framers and agitators of such bill or motion. For it must pass through the two Houses of Parliament, before it is presented for the Royal assent. And does it not then come with a *power or force of opinion* likely to *restrain* the free judgment of the Sovereign? And do not historians agree that several princes have positively yielded an unwilling assent to such bills and motions, in consequence of the *power or force* of opinion thus put upon them?

As for the position itself of the unity and indivisibility of the King and Parliament, and the consequent inference, upon which so much stress has been laid by the Crown lawyers, that to put a restraint upon the Parliament is to put a restraint upon the King; this is so far from being true, that instances are not wanting in history where their interests were in diametrical opposition; and where every friend to the sovereign was called upon to shew his zeal for his service by the most open resistance to the usurping Oligarchy that tyrannized in the House of Commons. How then is a force upon Parliament (particularly a force of voices and opinions) of necessity immediately directed against the King?

You have been told, it is true, with some attempt at plausibility, that the King, being by his coronation oath the guardian of the laws, is bound to resist any *extra-parliamentary* attempt to alter those laws; and that as, by that resistance, his life may be endangered, such *extra-parliamentary* attempt is an *overt act* of High Treason. But in this statement there are two palpable fallacies. In the first place, the Coronation Oath does not pledge the King to resist all alterations of existing laws (for then would the Laws of Britain, like those of the Meads and Persians, or the fiats of a fabled Jupiter,[41] be irrevocable) but only to conform to those laws so long as they remain unaltered. And as it is the duty and practice of Parliament (*when there is a Parliament!*) to influence the Crown, by its voice and councils, in the improvement and alteration of those laws; so it is the right and bounden duty of the people to influence, by their voice and opinions, the conduct of their representatives in Parliament, relative to such alterations. In the next place there is still more gross abuse of common sense in the ambiguous use of the word *resistance*. For, whatever designs may be attributed to us, as to the amelioration of our laws and institutions, yet the very witnessses for the prosecution, (the perjured spies alone excepted) have uniformly declared that force and violence were entirely out of the question. With respect to myself in particular it has been distinctly sworn that "I was a zealous advocate for universal peace; and that I deemed all violence hostile to the object we had in view";[a]—"That I always upheld, both in public and in private, that truth and reason ought to be the only weapons of the friends of liberty;—and that speculative opinions ought never to be enforced by violence."[b] That "in the committee of the society a rash individual, an agent perhaps of gentlemen, high in office, having talked of resisting peace officers, if they came to disturb the meeting, my answer was "By no means. *Submit to the laws and the laws will justify you*", and that my doctrine uniformly was "*The pen is the only artillery, and ink the only ammunition that the London Corresponding Society must ever use.*"[c] Nay, Lynam[42] himself, that prevaricating, professional spy—whose evidence is one tissue of malicious misrepresentation, has been compelled, *reluctantly*, to acknowledge that "a proposition being made to publish a list of persons who had given evidence against the patriots, it was unanimously rejected, upon my representing that such a measure might inflame the public mind, and lead to massacres."[43]

If then the peaceful, the spirited remonstrances of the people, were to be resisted only by the peaceful rejection of their wishes, where was the danger to the Royal person? And if, on the contrary, we are to understand that Reason is to be silenced by execution, and remonstrance repelled at the point of the bayonet;—if peaceful assemblies of the people are to be dispersed by the sabres of armed associators; and their leaders to be hanged, drawn, and quartered, for pointing out the necessity of reform;—and it is argued, as it may be with too much truth, that the probable consequences of such measures must be universal uproar and rebellion, who, I ask, are

[a]Testimony of Stewart Kyd.
[b]J. S. Taylor of Norwich, Surgeon: witness for the Crown.
[c]R. Davidson: witness for the Crown.

the traitors?—who are the conspirators against the King and Constitution? the formentors of anarchy? and the imitators of French violence and massacre?—Who, I say, in such case, ought to be placed at the Bar of the Old Bailey—the persecuted associator for reform, or the ministers who could advise such unheard of tyranny?

But it is time to analyse, more particularly, the idea of *overawing Parliament:* for this is, at last, the new fangled treason we are charged with. Let us see what in reality it means: for words of ambiguous import beget a confusion in the mind eminently injurious to the cause of justice.

This overawing of Parliament, then, must be effected in one of these two ways—either

By levying an armed force for the purpose of intimidating, and becoming master of its deliberations—or

By concentrating such a number of suffrages and opinions as might command the respect and attention of that assembly; and thus induce them, however unwillingly, to turn their serious attention to the subject of reform.

How foreign from our system the former of these projects is, has already been shewn; as also, the extreme absurdity of supposing that such men, so totally destitute of all requisite resources, should embark upon this Quixotic adventure, and without sword or lance (for contemptible as the nonsense about pikes and bayonets has proved, no part, even of this attaches to me or my immediate associates) should attempt to over throw, not the wind mill of ministerial intrigue, but the enchanted castle of the British Constitution itself.—It has also been fully proved, both by my witnesses and the witnesses for the Crown, that the Society in general, and myself in particular, have always regarded bloodshed and violence with the utmost detestation; and exerted every faculty to preserve the order so essential to the diffusion of political truth.—I shall not, therefore, consume your time with further reasoning upon this part of the subject. Nay, Gentlemen, if this evidence had not been given, yet no satisfactory evidence, under that head, having been adduced on the part of the crown, you would have been bound to put such suggestion entirely out of the question: for it is a maxim of justice, and one of the avowed principles of English law (without which, indeed, no innocence could be unspotted, no virtue secure) that when any action is capable of two interpretations, that which is most favourable must be adopted.

This maxim, it is true, in the tumult of factious assemblies, in the ebullition of political passion is sometimes forgotten: but what must be the con-

dition of mankind if these passions—if this factious intolerance gets footing
in a court of Justice?—Woe indeed upon that Nation whose Judgment Seat
is polluted by party—whose Magistrates are the servile echoes of a Court,
or a Minister—or whose Juries are biassed by the declamations of men
whose passions are inflamed by the struggle for emoluments and distinctions!

To the latter only of these charges then I am called to reply; namely,
That a conspiracy was formed to call a Convention to disseminate the
principles of annual election and universal suffrage, and increase the associations for that purpose, till such a general sentiment should be evinced,
as might challenge the respect of Parliament, and induce that assembly to
comply with the popular wish.

Now, Gentlemen, the first question is, whether even this is proved?

The next is to enquire, if proved, how far it is to be considered as criminal?

The first of these I leave where the Gentlemen of the Long Robe have
left it: as for the other I shall not scruple to declare that this charge, if
properly understood, instead of placing us at this bar, ought to enrol our
names among the benefactors of mankind. For what does the charge
amount to? Simply to this: that we attempted so to organize the public
opinion that it might be made known to the representative, and Ministers,
if that opinion really is in favour of Reform, might have no pretence for
refusing our just desire.

If this is a crime, Representation is itself High Treason; and to talk of
the Commons of Great Britain in Parliament assembled, is mockery and
absurdity. If, as has been asserted, even by the enemies of Reform, the
Members of the House of Commons, though *chosen by a few*, *virtually represent the whole* of the people; then have the *whole* of the people a right to
direct those representatives, whenever the general opinion can clearly and
peaceably be collected; and it follows of course, that if the collective voice
of the people has a right to be heard, devising means to ascertain that
voice, cannot be a crime: much less the enormous crime of High Treason.

The Members of the Commons House of Parliament ought, indeed, to
deliberate upon the means of advancing the general happiness; but they are
no longer representatives, either *positive* or *virtual*, if the people have not a
right to instruct them as to particular objects of deliberation.

But this right of the public to declare its congregated will does not rest
upon the sandy foundations of what has been *fantastically* called *virtual representation*. It is built upon the basis of eternal truth; it is supported by the

pillars of common sense and general expediency; and its "Corinthian capital"[44] is that splendid display of intellect and public virtue it is calculated to produce, and which *should never fail*[45] to be conspicuous beneath its spacious porch.

If words have any meaning, representation must be a trust—and all trusts, says Lord Somers[46] (a constitutional writer of allowed authority, and once Lord Chancellor of this country), "all trusts, by their nature, import that those to whom they are given are accountable, though no such condition be specified",[a]—"There must be", continues he, "in every government a power to preserve itself, not only against force from without, but against violence and every thing else that is destructive from within. As a man preserves his person from diseases, as well as defends it against violence. He cannot renounce this power, because self-preservation is, and will always be a duty; neither can a people"—Mark, I pray you the language of this writer, whom as a constitutional authority no one will call in question—"*Neither can the people*, united in society, renounce the power of maintaining that society or government, the instrument of their safety and preservation; for the condition of all subjects would be alike, whether under absolute or limited government, if it were not lawful to maintain and preserve those limitations: since will and pleasure, and not law, would be, alike in both, the measures of obedience—For to have liberties and privileges, unless they may be defended, or to have none at all, is the same thing, as to be governed by mere will and pleasure, or by laws subject to will and pleasure." *Ib.* p. 24.[48]

Thus then that representatives are accountable to the people represented, and that the *people not only* have a *right*, but are bound in *duty* to watch over and defend their liberties, are principles, founded in unalterable justice, and ratified by the British constitution. But how is this account to be called for? How are these liberties to be asserted? How—but by collecting the aggregate voice of the nation, and reminding those whom power is apt to seduce into forgetfulness of the true sources of their authority?

In short—frequently and peaceably to collect in a clear and audible manner, this aggregate opinion of a nation, is the best way of securing general happiness, fortifying the virtue, and expanding the intellects of mankind: and he *who devises* the method of collecting this opinion with

[a]*Judgment of Nations*, p. 23.[47]

the greatest purity (that is to say with the greatest freedom from influence, fear, or corruption) will confer the greatest possible benefit upon the human race. It is from the want of this that mankind still continue to be but half humanized—to be divided into casts and factions, rendered hostile by opposing interests, and irritated by reciprocal jealousies. Who is the man? What is his country? his class? his condition? To what sect or society does he belong? are the enquiries we are constantly making—not what are his merits, his capacities or his virtues?

Such being the maxims upon which this Convention was to have been formed, if it had assembled, it would have commanded respect in proportion only to the numbers represented, and the wisdom, firmness, and moderation of its measures. But that it ever could assume, or ever meant to assume any legislative authority of its own, or meditate the collection of any *power* or *force* for the purpose of restraining (in any common acceptation of the term) the deliberations of Parliament or the functions of the executive power, is an absurdity so monstrous that I will not libel the understandings of my prosecutors by supposing they ever gave it one moment's belief.

But Gentlemen, during these proceedings it has been sometimes insinuated, and sometimes openly avowed that the professed objects of some of the societies, namely, *Universal Suffrage* and *Annual Parliaments*, were of themselves High Treason; inasmuchas the establishment of them would be a subversion of the constitution. This assertion, however necessary to the support of the charge you are to decide upon, is the most unfortunate that could be made by the professed advocates of ancient institutions. For what is our boasted Constitution, if the moment you realize it, it must crumble into atoms? and what politician familiar with the history of that constitution, does not know that it is only by encroachments and innovation that we have been robbed of these invaluable privileges.

With respect to *Annual Parliaments*, to say nothing of the innumerable passages in the works of our best constitutional writers in which the right is positively affirmed, it cannot be forgotten that during the agitation of this question in 1780,[49] it was demonstrated by authentic documents, not only to have been the acknowledged right, but, for a considerable period the absolute practice of Englishmen to elect representatives for every session (G. *Sharp, Def.* &c.).[50] And as for *Universal Suffrage*, if this be not a part of the genuine constitution, what is the meaning of that maxim so frequently reiterated by Blackstone, Sommers, and a variety of constitutional writers, that every British freeman should be governed by laws of his own making? For the distinctions of vassalage are now no more; and no one will have the audacity to deny that by "every British freeman" is explicitly to be understood "every native inhabitant of Britain." What also is the meaning of the following quotation from Blackstone? "No subject of England", says he, "can be constrained to pay any aids or taxes"—and be it remembered that for every morsel of bread that goes into the labourer's mouth taxes have been levied in a variety of forms. "No subject of England can be constrained to pay aids or taxes, even for the defence of the realm or the support of government, but such as are imposed by *his own consent,* or that of his representatives in Parliament"! In support of which he quotes a variety of acts of Parliament, particularly "34 E. I.st. 4, c.1, which enacts that no talliage or aids shall be taken without the assent of the archbishops, bishops, earls, barons, knights, burgesses, and *other freemen* of the land." *Book,* 1, *cap.* 1, *p.* 140.[51] Is this not an ample acknowledgment of the right of universal suffrage? Is it not an express declaration that *every individual debarred the right of suffrage is in reality a slave?*

But let us meet the question upon broader grounds—the grounds of expediency and justice.

It is *just* that every individual should enjoy the full benefit of his own faculties. It is expedient, that every inducement should be held out for the exertion of those faculties; because it is only by such exertion that either the individual or the public can reap advantage. The best way to stimulate these exertions is to secure to every one the fruits of his assiduity: and this can only be done by *equal laws.* But equal laws must proceed from equal weight and influence: for if representation is confined to particular classes, Benevolence may exert her energies in vain. Man will still be man; the few will continue to be favoured; and the mass will be inevitably oppressed.

Why is it that factors, merchants, wholesale-dealers and opulent manufacturers enter into combinations with impunity? monopolize as they please? and fix, in their conventions, the price of commodities at discretion? while labourers and mechanics who enter into associations to appreciate their own labour are sentenced, like felons, to a gaol?[52] Why has commerce, by which the opulence, the pleasures, the luxuries of the higher orders are so eminently increased, sunk the industrious poor into still more abject misery? Why is the labourer taken from his plough, or the manufacturer from his loom to bleed in foreign contests? while those who riot in luxurious indolence enjoy the glory of his scars at home? Why?—Because only the opulent and powerful are represented in Parliament; and therefore the opulent and powerful alone are they whose interest the representatives find it necessary to consult. If once in every year the poor man's vote were as important as his employer's, the poor could not be forgotten.

But it is *property*, we are told, that ought to be represented, because by property government is supported. What!—does property man the navy? Does property fill the ranks of armies? O! that this cruel contest, which is desolating Europe, were indeed but a war of property! that government required no support but from the funds of opulence! and that the blood of our fellow beings might stream no more!

Let us not deceive ourselves!—Property is nothing but human labour. The most inestimable of all property is the sweat of the poor man's brow:— the property from which all other is derived, and without which grandeur must starve in the midst of supposed abundance. And shall they who possess this inestimable property be told that they have no rights, because they have *nothing* to defend? Shall those who toil for our subsistence, and bleed for our protection, be excluded from all importance in the scale of humanity, because they have so toiled and bled? No: man and not moveables is the object of just legislation. All, therefore, ought to be consulted where all are concerned: for what less than the whole ought to decide the fate of the whole. And if a few are to be the *ultimate* organ of that decision, what medium is there between *suffrage* and *usurpation*? Those who are entitled to this suffrage are the only free men. The rest are Helotes, bondsmen, slaves! The former are, in fact, the proprietors of the liberties, lives and properties of the latter; and, even if corruption were entirely out of the question, their votes could but give taskmasters and tyrants to the disfranchised multitude. As it is, the unjust distinction renders the few it pretends to favour still more abject slaves.

If you wish that representation should be productive of real advantage, let that representation itself be real. The evils that result from it are the consequences of its partiality. If you wish that representation should be any thing more than the vehicle of corruption, extend the rights of suffrage till no one can have the means to corrupt. Realize the Constitution if you expect us to admire it. And before you boast again of the mingled advantages of monarchy, aristocracy and democracy, redeem the democratic branch, the most valuable of the three, from the hands of the venal oligarchy, (the ONE HUNDRED AND SIXTY-TWO PROPRIETORS)[53] who have usurped it; and let the Commons House of Parliament be in reality a House of Commons.

In short, if you wish the people to be content, restore to them the means of being happy.—If you wish that wisdom and virtue should take place of intrigue and venality, restore to the people at large their right of legislating for themselves.

Vox populi vox Dei.—For what is the voice of God but the general voice of Nature? And, with respect to political regulations, what oracle can you consult, what part of nature can you render vocal but man, for whose benefit alone political institutions exist.

But we are told by our opponents that the judgments of men are so fallible, and so liable to be misled by passion and prejudice, that to suffer them to be in any degree their own masters is to devote them to destruction. To this I need only answer, that those who make the objection are men themselves, and do not pretend to the knowledge of any accessible being to whose *more infallible* judgment we might appeal.

The question then is—Whether mankind should be subjected entirely to a few self-constituted arbitrators, who not only are liable, like themselves, to all the delusions of passion and prejudice, but who always *may conceive*, and sometimes *positively have* a separate interest hostile to the happiness of the whole?—or whether the aggregate body of the people should appoint their own representatives, and revise occasionally the limits of their delegated authority?

This question does not require an answer. In short, as Montesquieu observes, "The people *ought* to do for themselves whatever conveniently they *can*; what they themselves cannot rightly perform they must do by their agents: and the agents are not properly their's, nor can expect their confidence, unless they have the nomination of them." (*Sp. L. B. 2 c. 2*)[54]

Nor is it any objection that this is quoted from a chapter professedly treating of democracy. It is the democratic part of the Constitution I am defending: it is that only with which it is my present business to interfere: it is that which it is the interest and the *duty* of the people, at this time, to defend; and if they do not defend it with intrepidity, they are lost for ever: swallowed up in the vortex of new-created peerages, and buried beneath the rubbish of rotten boroughs.

The *right* then of the people to a voice in the government by which their lives, their properties, their labour is disposed of, is so well established, that the practical expediency—that is to say, the capability of the mass of mankind to exercise this right, is all that remains in dispute.

But what ground of objection can there be in this point of view? If the mass of mankind appear at present to be lost in ignorance, what is this but the consequence of their degradation? Restore them to their rights and they will of necessity learn their duties. Shew them that they are of some importance in society, and they will enquire into the means of promoting its happiness. It is from the want of this importance and this enquiry that passions are so frequently generated destructive to the public peace. For if you will treat us only like beasts of burthen, what wonder if we sometimes break the yoke and become beasts of prey! If you wish the people to be humanized, restore them to the privileges of humanity—restore to every individual that liberty without which he may sometimes be a spaniel and sometimes a tyger, but never can be a man.

Besides, can any thing be so absurd as the objection of ignorance?—Are not many of those who constitute at this time, the electing body, persons (if situation could disqualify men for the enjoyment of their most simple rights) least capable of exercising these exclusive functions? Is the pot-wallopper[55] (whose sole qualification is dressing his dinner once in seven years in an open street) a fit person to vote for a representative in parliament? and is there yet a human being of adult years, not incapacitated by crimes or insanity, to whom it would be dangerous to extend the privilege? Nay, what are the requisites for exercising this right? "They have only to be determined by things to which they cannot be strangers—by facts that are obvious to sense."[56] Is not the meanest peasant capable of knowing who is a kind and indulgent master to his dependents, and a benefactor to the surrounding neighbourhood? who is careful of his own property, and enjoys it to the credit of his family, and the happiness of his fellow creatures? And if so are they not capable of electing those who are to be entrusted with their protection and their prosperity.—"These", as Montesquieu observes, "are *facts of which they can have better information in a public forum, than a Monarch in his palace.*" Book 2, Chap. 2.[57]

"Should we doubt", continues this Philosopher, "of the people's natural ability in respect to the discernment of merit, we need only cast an eye on the continual series of surprising elections made by the Athenians and Romans; which no one surely will attribute to hazard."[58] And in his chapter on the Constitution of England, speaking of the right of suffrage in the composition of the House of Commons, he expressly says—"Though few can tell the exact degree of men's capacities, yet there are *none* but are capable of knowing, in general, whether the person they chuse is better qualified that most of his neighbours." *Book* 11, c. 6.[59]

Thus then we see that philosophy and experience are united in this testimony—that there are certain important functions which the aggregate body of the people are not only *capable of discharging*, but which *they ought always to discharge*, because they are more capable of discharging them with propriety and effect than any individual, corporation or privileged order whatever.

The more intricate parts of government I acknowledge the multitude are not capable of managing themselves. They are not qualified to find out and make proper use of places, occasions, moments. This is beyond their capacity. And if these things were not beyond their capacity, representation would be useless: government itself would be useless; and the aggregate body of the people, without subjection and without expence, might conduct the whole affairs of the nation. It was then because the people themselves are capable of performing only those more general and obvious functions, which require nothing but common honesty, and common experience for their due discharge, that our ancestors consented to part with a proportion of the produce of their labour, to support the expences of government; and reposed the more difficult and intricate parts of public administration in the hands of those whose talents they had experienced, and in whose integrity they had reason to confide. But as power is too apt to intoxicate its possessors, and from long enjoyment and gradual usurpation, from having been accepted as a trust, to be considered as a property, it not only results as a *right*, but as a *necessary duty* that the people should associate whenever they feel themselves oppressed by unusual burthens, to enquire into the nature and causes of their grievances, to see whether those burthens are not unnecessarily augmented by exhorbitant salaries and unmerited pensions; and to see, in short, whether their *delegates*, in various departments, have, or have not violated their compact; and whether any, and what additional barriers are necessary for the security of their rights, and the promotion of general happiness. This, I repeat, if representation has any meaning—must not only be a right, but a bounden duty: since the very circumstance of electing representatives proves the right of the electors to do that which those representatives are delegated to perform. They who appoint another to discharge for them any particular function, must of necessity have a right to see that such function is duly and faithfully discharged.

But it is urged, in aggravation of our supposed offence, that numerous meetings were called, and strong resolutions passed, marking, in *intemperate language*, the most decided disapprobation of *certain measures in contemplation of the legislature*.

In this accusation there are two points which require very different answers. There is something to justify, and something to apologise for; but there is no Treason: and those who place me at this bar, when conscience presses the question home to them, must acknowledge that they knew there was none. For, admitting, for a moment, all the aggravated colourings of the public prosecutor, the acts charged upon these meetings amount to nothing more than *what is called sedition*, and repeated decisions, judicial and parliamentary, have declared that no possible number of actions not in themselves distinct overt acts of treason, can, by accumulation, amount to that crime.

But I shall not drop the question there. It is not enough for me to shew you, that I and my companions ought not to be hanged, drawn, and quartered; and our families reduced to hopeless beggary. The liberty of my country is attacked at the very vitals; and it is necessary I should assert the genuine principles of that liberty, that, as far as depends upon my individual exertions, it may descend, uninjured, to posterity. With respect to these meetings themselves, then, I contend that it results from the premises already established, that in them there is no criminality whatever. Peaceably to meet in such assemblies, and compare their sentiments on the proceedings of Government is, I contend, an absolute right of the people, and every part of the people of this country—the *constitutional right* of nonelectors as well as constituents—of those who have no particular representatives as well as those who have. "For every member of Parliament", says Blackstone, "though chosen for one particular district, when elected and returned, *serves for the* WHOLE *realm.* The end of his coming is not particular, but general; not barely to advantage his constituents, but the *Commonwealth*." (B. 1. c. 2 f. 159.)[60] Every part, therefore, of that *Commonwealth* must have a right to investigate the conduct of such representatives, to express their sentiments of the proceedings of the representative body, and discuss, when they feel occasion, those interests to which it is the duty of that body to attend. It is a right inherent in the frame and constitution of all free societies, and which has hitherto been enjoyed without question or interruption.

If this is not true, why was the universal right of petitioning declared at the Revolution? and how is that right to be exercised? Why has the Minister so frequently sought to bolster up the reputation of his measures by tavern meetings, Reevite clubs,[61] and parochial associations?—Is the boasted liberty of Britons a liberty only of servility and adulation?—Is it constitutional to call numerous meetings to applaud the sanguinary and ruinous projects of men in power? and High Treason to do the same thing for purposes of remonstrance and reprobation?

In short, as has been before demonstrated, the right of popular representation includes the right of popular opinion, and popular opinion can only
be collected by popular assemblies. Provided therefore such popular assemblies proceed to no attempts of violence, they must be lawful. Nor can
their resolutions, however indecorous in point of language, amount to treason, even admitting the utmost latitude of construction contended for by
any of the authorities, unless they contain direct incitements to the death
or deposition of the King. Much less can they be brought under the penalty
of that crime when, as in the instances before us, they are directed, not in
any shape against the person or authority of the sovereign, but against the
misconduct and usurpations of his ministers.

"It is the last stage of intolerable despotism", says Gibbon, tracing with
philosophical hand the progress of Roman degeneracy, "when offences
against the ministers of the prince are confounded with those against his
person."[62] Yet such is the case in the present prosecution. For what are the
addresses and resolutions of the meetings under consideration, but bold,
sincere, and (*sometimes*[63] I admit) intemperate attacks on the proceedings of what they call "the faction in power"?

And here let me ask you, Gentlemen, if the direct and open appeals
which I have been in the habit of making against the folly and wickedness
of the present administration were not the *real* crime for which *they conspire*
my destruction, how happens it, that out of this huge mass of evidence,
notwithstanding my alledged activity in the society, so little should be
produced for which I am personally accountable?

Out of all the transactions of the society there are only three papers
originating in me, which they have thought proper to select. 1. A letter to
Norwich, dated Nov. 23, 1793, calling upon the society there for "the
most active exertions in *every constitutional measure* that can be devised for
the *recovery of our rights*, and the complete *renovation* of the liberties and
happiness which, as men, we are entitled to, and, as Britons, we have been
taught to expect." (*Rep. Sec. Com.* p. 150 *Jordan's edit.*)[64] 2. The circular
letter, falsely attributed to the Committee of Co-operation, but in reality
the sole act of that temporary Committee of Secrecy which has been the
subject of so much confused and absurd misrepresentation: a letter in
which you will remember the different societies are invited to "co-operate
in the only *peaceable* measure presenting itself with any prospect of success"
(*Rep. Sec. Com.* p. 22.) and 3. The resolutions adopted at Chalk Farm.[65]

With respect to the meeting at the Globe, it has been proved to you
that *two* papers were read and adopted. Of one of these I am proved to

have been the *publisher*. But the other (a circumstance much more conclusive as to my particular motives and sentiments) was *written* by me. If I am
the dangerous traitor—the man of *peculiar violence*—the *Maratist*[66]—the
Anarchist I have been represented by the unprincipled agents of my prosecutors, why were not more of my personal acts, and this paper in particular, brought forward, instead of rummaging my closet for unfinished letters,
and breaking open the houses of my nearest relations for the secrets of my
familiar correspondence?[67]

The fact is, these documents could have proved nothing but a heart
bleeding for the miseries of the lower orders of the community, and burning with indignation against the oppressive corruption from which those
miseries proceed. But these facts, however, calculated to inflame their hatred, were likely to inspire in an English Jury but little of that sort of
sympathy which might suit the purpose of the prosecutors. Every thing was
therefore suppressed that might reveal in naked deformity, the real motives
of this sanguinary prosecution: and the scanty materials selected by their
discretion were to be parceled out with collateral forgeries; and all the
rancorous prejudices which calumny could accumulate.

O miserable country! O degenerate Britain! whose liberties can be suspended, and whose sons, after languishing seven months in Bastiles and
noxious dungeons, can be arraigned for their lives by a junto who dare not
give in evidence the *real* causes of the prosecution!

But what are the transactions they *have* given in evidence? Are not
these, also, statements of grievances produced by the maladministration of
our accusers? What are the *intemperances* upon which so much stress is laid,
but expressions of indignation against the ruinous measures of "that corrupt
and overbearing faction which tramples on the rights and liberties of the
people." (*Circular Letter*, Rep. 1, p. 22.)[68]

"We must have redress from *our own laws*", says the address from the
Globe Tavern,—and this is the part upon which particular stress is laid:
"We must have redress from our own laws, not from the laws of our *plun-
derers, enemies and oppressors*."[69]

Now this "corrupt and overbearing faction:—these "plunderers, enemies, and oppressors", say the prosecutors, "are the legislature of the country—the King, Lords, and Commons of Great Britain."[70] But does the
context say so? No—Candid interpretation applies these expressions
(harsh and intemperate, I acknowledge—but not treasonous) in one instance to the administration only; and in the other, to that administration,
in conjunction with the borough proprietors, and other instruments of cor-

ruption, who command, and while the present miserable state of representation continues, must inevitably command the property, lives, and liberties of the people.

These are, at present, the makers of the laws. But these are not the
constitutional authorities. Nor do I know where to look for the act of parliament that defines the limits of treason against placemen, pensioners, and
proprietors of rotten boroughs. These are the sovereigns against whom the
conspiracy ought to have been charged—if *conspiracy* had existed—which
it did not—for our transactions were *public*; and to *conspire* is to *breathe* or
whisper together in *private*.

But, say the prosecutors, "what are we to understand by 'redress from *our
own laws*'? Is not this an open avowal of the intention of these societies to
seize the government into their own hands, and, by *their* Convention,
make new laws for themselves?"[71]—No. The Society is speaking to the
people at large—Is speaking of the common cause and common oppressions of the people, of which they are a part; and speaks, therefore, as usual
in such cases, in the name of the whole—"*We* must have redress from *our*
own laws": and if the people at large have not a right to be governed by
their own laws, what do Judge Blackstone and other constitutional writers
mean by affirming, that "in a free state, every man who is considered as a
free agent, ought to be in some measure *his own governor*; and therefore a
branch, *at least*, of the legislative power should reside in *the whole body of
the people*"? (B. 1, c. 2, p. 158)[72] What is the meaning, also, of that provision already quoted of 34 E. 1. which so expressly declares taxation without
representation a public robbery? Why does the constitution call the House
of Commons "The *Commons of Great Britain* in Parliament assembled"?
Are the burgage-holders[73] of Bramber, East Grinstead, Downton, Old
Sarum, and the like, the Commons of Great Britain? and are the myriads
of inhabitants in Manchester, Birmingham, the suburbs of London and
Westminster, and all these populous portions of the island, to whom not
even the shadow of representation is extended, nothing but beasts of burthen?[74] Are the *thirty-two* electors of Bath, and *sixty* or *seventy non-residents*
of Winchester, the Commons of those populous cities? and are the *thousands* of disfranchised inhabitants nothing? In short, do corporate bodies
alone partake of the nature and privileges of human beings? and are the
rest of the people only chattels and lumber?

It is then from "the Commons of Great Britain", by real and adequate
representation, "in Parliament assembled", that the London Corresponding
Society expressly tell you they expect redress. "There is no redress", say

they, "for a nation circumstanced as we are, but"—from what? From a partial Convention of Delegates, representing a few societies—a small portion only of the people? No. These were only to deliberate, as the letter of the 27th of March explicitly declares on "the means of obtaining in a legal and constitutional method such a representation as might redress the grievances under which we labour." (*Rep.* 1, p. 20.) The redress itself you are expressly told could never be expected, but from "a *fair, free,* and *full* representation of the people." (*Rep.* 1, p. 16.)[75]

Thus, then, it appears from the context, that the language and conduct of the society go no further than this—"Such are the grievances under which we labour from the prosecution of an unjust and ruinous war, from the oppressive usurpations of a Minister", from unequal laws, and the partial administration of justice. But these are consequences only of the corrupt and vicious state of our representation. It is in vain therefore to seek redress of these grievances till the representation is reformed. "We must have redress from our own laws": that is, from laws made by "a fair, free and full representation of the people." But how is this to be obtained? We have been petitioning, in separate bodies for 30 or 40 years, and are none the nearer. Our petitions have been rejected with indignant contempt, or swept away in mouldy silence from the table. Let us try what can be done by the force of collective opinion. Let us meet in general Convention, that we may repeat our petitions with one loud and united voice; or determine upon any other *peaceable* method, not prohibited by the constitution or law of the country, that may best promote so desireable an end. And if we can once obtain this fair, free, and full representation, never doubt but that our grievances will all be redressed."[76]

This I contend is the fair and full construction of the evidence. This is the only manner in which we expected our Convention to be instrumental in "securing us from future illegal and scandalous prosecutions, preventing a repetition of wicked and unjust sentences, and recalling those wise and wholesome laws that have been wrested from us." (*Rep.* 1, p. 21.)[77]

I do not vindicate the intemperate language in which some of these resolutions are expressed. Intemperance, though in some degree excusable, when the provocations have been great, is never, I believe the best friend of Truth and Liberty. But the members of the London Corresponding Society, like those whose corruption they complain of, are but men. Nor is it strange, after the monstrous calumnies and abuse which the latter had heaped upon them—after the manner in which their most virtuous members had been vilified, and their most able and upright leaders persecuted

and oppressed—after they had seen their "respectable and beloved associates cast fettered into dungeons among felons in the hulks", and transported to Botany Bay, "while no one pretended to identify the law which
they had broken."—It is not, I say, surprising that after all these aggravations, their minds should become heated, and that they should sometimes
express their feelings in language which their cooler reflections would not
justify. In the midst, however, of their indignation and intemperance, no
shadow of violence, or disposition to treason or rebellion ever made its
appearance. Sedition, that *new fangled, anomalous* crime, which no statute
ever defined, and whose limits no lawyer professes to comprehend, is the
utmost that by any possible construction could ever have been thought
chargeable against them.

These remarks are equally applicable to the Resolutions passed at Chalk
Farm.[78] They are attacks, not upon the person or government of the King,
but upon the mad and desperate measures of Ministers and their dependant
majority. They are solemn admonitions to those Ministers to beware how
they betray their master into situations of the utmost peril and calamity, by
audaciously repeating those very measures by which the successive Ministers of the House of Stewart dragged down the vengeance of the nation on
that unhappy family. They are solemn warnings to the people to be upon
their guard against the introduction of foreign mercenaries; and the most
obnoxious of them all is not an attack upon the constitution, but an appeal
to its principles—an aweful assertion of the inviolability of that most sacred of all its barriers—the barrier of trial by jury. It is a protest against an
alarming threat held out—not by the sovereign—not by the legislature—
but by Mr. Secretary Dundas[79]—He alone it was who had the audacity to
threaten the violation and subversion of those yet remaining *laws* that
guarantee to Englishmen an impartial trial by a jury of their country; and
to substitute, in their place, the arbitrary and tyrannical *practices* of the
Court of Justiciary in Scotland.[80] It is a declaration that this violation and
subversion would affect the vitals of British Liberty; would dissolve the
constitution of the country.

Mark the very words of that resolution, Gentlemen, "That any attempt
to violate those yet remaining laws"—Is this an attack upon the existence
of law and social order, or a vindication of their purity and importance?—
"Any attempt to violate those yet remaining laws, intended for the security
of Englishmen against the tyranny of Courts and Ministers, and the corruption of dependant Judges"—(and does any body believe that Courts and
Ministers would not tyrannize if the laws made for the protection of the

subject were trampled down)—to attempt this "by vesting in such Judges a legislative or arbitrary power (such as lately has been exercised by the Court of Justiciary in Scotland) ought to be considered as dissolving the social compact between the English nation and their governors; and driving them to an immediate appeal to that incontrovertible maxim of eternal justice, that *the safety of the people is the* SUPREME, *and in cases of necessity the* ONLY LAW."[81]

And is not the safety of the people the supreme law? Has it not been so acknowledged by every country where Liberty and Civilization have reared their heads? And must not the law which is supreme, in all cases of the last necessity be appealed to as the only law?—If this be treason, what is become of the boasted "Majesty of the People"? What is the meaning of that phrase which, in the opinion of continental philosophers, "is sufficient, of itself, to immortalize the British language"? (*Raynal, Hist. Philos. & Pol* . &c.)[82] And is not the trial by fair and impartial jury the sheet anchor of this safety? What hope, despight of conscious innocence, could I have in this storm of persecuting power, this hurricane of faction—what hope could those have had, who have already "braved the beating of this pittiless storm",[83] to escape shipwreck, but form this anchor alone? And will you suffer it to be torn away, and the vessel of personal safety to be left to the mercy of these savage elements? Will you, an impartial English jury!—I believe an honourable and impartial jury!—notwithstanding the arts and machinations of our persecutors—Would you, even though you were trying me for sedition only, instead of sitting in judgment on my life, sanction by your verdict the practices of the Court of Justiciary, and thereby pave the way, by a sort of tacit consent, to the introduction of similar practices among yourselves? Would you, an English jury, be instrumental to the violation of every principle upon which the excellence of English juries, and the most valuable part of the criminal jurisprudence of England has for centuries depended? Would you consent that the pannel of jurors should be *packed* in the first instance by the public prosecutor himself, and afterwards *picked* by the judges before whom the cause was to be tried? and thus unite, as it were, in the same hands, the power of accusation, adjudication, and punishment.

Would you, I say, by your solemn verdict, acknowledge that such doctrines may be held with impunity in an English Court of Justice as have been laid down in the Court of Justiciary in Scotland?—Doctrines that invest the Courts of Law with legislative authority—annihilate the very idea of settled and impartial justice! and, by usurping the sanctions of the legislature, render that important branch of government a cumbrous nullity.

For remember what these doctrines are. Recal to mind the trials of *Skirving, Margarot,* and *Gerrald;* of *Muir* and *Palmer.*[84] Recollect the speeches of *Lord Justice Clerk,*[85] *Lord Henderland,*[86] and the other Judges of that Court, and you will find them solemnly promulgating as legal doctrine that "the judgment of a Privy Council is to be quoted as authority in a Court of Law, because pronounced by Judges who were sitting (no doubt most of them) in Parliament." (*Trial of Gerrald,* p. 112.)[87] You will find them affirming, avowedly upon no better authority, that "they have a right to inflict the punishment of banishment *by transportation*", (that is to say, to inflict the greater punishment where the act of Parliament prescribes the less) because—why?—because there is some law authorising them so to do? No—but "because there is no law restraining them from so doing!" *Ib.*—So that, instead of it being lawful for the people to do whatever the law has not forbidden—instead of it being unlawful for the Judge to inflict any punishment but what the law has commanded, he is to be at liberty to punish every thing, and in every manner which the law has not positively declared shall not so be punished. If this is what the Court of Justiciary means by British Liberty, let them keep it at least on the other side the Tweed.

You will find the *Lord Justice Clerk* also declaring on the trial of *Skirving,* and *Lord Henderland* echoing on that of *Gerrald,* that there are laws, carrying with them the enormous and unconstitutional punishment of transportation, which no act of Parliament has declared, and which it requires no usage to establish. "The law of Scotland", says the former of these *judicial legislators,* (*Skirving's Trial,* p. 55)[88] "is founded on *many grounds* besides that of acts of Parliament; there are many things in it which are established by usage" (that is to say, Gentlemen, what we call Common Law—the fragments of institutions whose origins we cannot trace, but which have been sanctioned by universal assent, "time whereof the memory of man reacheth not to the contrary!")—"by the laws of God"—(which of those laws, I should wish to know, have denounced transportation against reformers for writing and declaiming against the vices and corruptions of government?—If such a law had really existed among what are called the laws of God, what would have become of the prophets? and particularly of the sublimest of those who are considered as inspired writers?—Must not they have been treated like felons upon charges of Sedition, as Christ and his apostles afterwards were, when those laws were violated and trampled down?) These laws, however, be they what they will, are no laws in this country, any further than as they have been expressly recognized by the legislature.[89] But the most extraordinary passage is yet to come—"there are many things", says this same *Lord Justice Clerk*, "in the law of Scotland, which are established" (independent of acts of Parliament—independent of ancient and immemorial usage—independent of the laws of God!) "by *the dictates of the conscience of men!*" That is to say, "whatever the consciences (such as they generally are) of the party in power, and the Judges (who are generally dependent upon them) may consider as crimes, are, by the laws of Scotland, to be punished at discretion, by the whipping-post, by transportation, or the gibbet, because there is no express law prohibiting these exertions of arbitrary authority!"[90]

Do you not tremble, Gentlemen, when you hear these doctrines? Do you not shudder with indignation and horror?

The same maxims, are, however, re-echoed on the trial of *Gerrald*—"It *requires no statute*", says Lord Henderland, "*it requires no usage*, it follows from the nature of the thing, that to *impugn*" (*that is to say, to* controvert, or assail by argument) "the *authority of Parliament* is a crime".—(*Ger. Tr. p.* 104.)[91] In other words, to discuss the measures of government—to remonstrate against any of the proceedings of the legislature—to controvert the doctrines that influence the Parliament (no matter how unanswerable your arguments—nay, it should seem the more unanswerable they are the more they are criminal!)—this, though prohibited by no statute, though condemned by no established usage, "is a crime—is the crime of Sedition", (*ib.*) and is to be punished at the discretion of the Court.[92]

Is not the direct interpretation of all this, "That the Judges of Scotland, like the Bashaws of Turkey, and the despots of the Roman Empire are to promulgate their arbitrary will as law; are to punish, by *ex-post-facto* regulations, whatever they chuse to consider as *impugning the authority of Parliament*, and dispose of life and liberty as their own caprice, or that of their employers may chance to dictate!"

Why talk we of star chambers?[93] of the tyranny of Laud?[94] or the execrated ministers of the House of Stewart? Which of these had ever the audacity to publish such doctrines? They wantoned, indeed, in the excesss of arbitrary authority—though even they did not venture to transport, like the vilest felons, the advocates of toleration and reform. They trampled, it is true, on the laws and liberties of the people—But these would establish despotism as a principle—a despotism which no one could hope to elude because no one could determine where the shaft would next be aimed. Yet such are the doctrines we are persecuted for exposing—Such are the practices it is high treason to determine to resist, if ever they should be substituted in the place of our constitutional provisions—our established laws and trial by impartial Jury.

Thus then the principle of this resolution is both just and constitutional. Neither is the mode of expressing it indecorous or unprecedented. It is almost a literal transcript from one of those speeches, which, on account of the constitutional doctrines they contain, have been collected together since the Revolution, and inserted among the State Trials.

"These Judges", says Lord Falkland, alluding to the case of Hampden, "have delivered an opinion such as came not within their cognizance; they being Judges, and *neither philosophers, nor politicians*. In which when that is absolute and evident, *the Law of the land ceases*; and of *general reason and equity, by which particular laws were at first framed*, returns to his throne and government, where *Salus Populi* becomes not only *suprema*, but *sola lex*." (*St. Tr. Vol. I. p. 676.*)[95]

I do not stand here to vindicate myself against a charge of sedition; and it would be an insult to your understanding to suppose that you can consider, for a moment, these resolutions as an overt act of compassing the King's death; else it would be easy to apply these arguments to the remaining articles; and to prove that, so far from treason—so far from aggravated sedition, there is not, in this whole paper any thing that can be considered as criminal in any degree whatever—unless, indeed, we are so sunk in abject servility that a few sarcastic and intemperate expressions can subject the once free and manly inhabitants of Britain to the penalties of criminality.

But you are told, in aggravation of the supposed offence, that these resolutions were entered into at a time when the maxims and measures they oppose were in contemplation of the Legislature.—What, Gentlemen! Did I hear the Crown Lawyers rightly? Was it really in the contemplation of the Legislature not only to suspend the Habeas Corpus Act[96] (which they have since suspended) and pass a Convention bill (which, it seems, they afterwards supposed they could hang men fast enough without)—not only "to levy unconstitutional contributions, under pretence of benevolences", "to arm one party of the people against the other", and "train and discipline in the country bands of foreign emigrants, driven from their homes for their known attachment to an infamous despotism?"—but was it also in the contemplation of the Legislature "to people our barracks with foreign mercenaries", "to proclaim martial law" and "to substitute the *arbitrary practices* of a Scottish Court of Justiciary, in place of the *English Law* of

trial, by statutes previously announced, and Juries impartially selected?"[97]—
and, was it not time for Britons to rouse from their lethargy, and enter
their serious protest against innovations so tyrannical, and encroachments
so decisive?

O miserable country, indeed, if thy legislature could meditate so many
fatal stabs! and thy sons can be arraigned for treason for crying to the
parricides to forbear!

O miserable country! whose rulers not only demand obedience to their
laws, but implicit reverence also to the crude conceptions of their brains—
their hints—their threats—their contemplations—the shapeless embrios
of their legislative imaginations!

Is it not enough to enforce obedience to existing laws? but must we be
indicted for irreverence to those which are about to be adopted? If so, what
oracle shall we consult for our safety? What less than second sight can
insure us from the penalties of High Treason?

But what is the meaning of these terms "Contemplation of the Legislature"? Is Mr. Dundas the Legislature of this country? for he, and he only
had the boldness to utter the threat which was the object of this obnoxious
resolution!

Are Mr. Pitt and his ministerial coadjutors the Legislature of this country? for they, and they only had hinted at any of the unconstitutional
measures these resolutions were intended to avert. The utmost, therefore,
that can be said in aggravation of these proceedings is, that the measures
they reprobate were then in contemplation of the MINISTRY: And degraded beyond conception is the character of this country, if a jury can be
found to pronounce it treason to reprobate, in whatever language, the intended measures of a Cabinet—however implicitly obeyed by the supposed
representatives of the people!

If then the public accuser himself rests the supposed guilt of the supposed
determination of calling a Convention (for this Treason is made up of
nothing but suppositions!) upon the hypothetical foundation that we either
intended to bring about a revolution by force, or to effect our purpose, by
disseminating our principles, and concentrating the public opinion, till it
was no longer decent for the legislature to resist the wishes of the people;—and if not only the state of the evidence, but the acknowledged
maxims of Justice call upon you to adopt the most favourable construction,
I think myself entitled to conclude, not only that no criminality attaches
to this part of the charge; but that we are entitled to applause as guardians
of public liberty. And I trust you will unanimously agree, that if peaceful

assemblies of the people for the purposes of political investigation are pro-hibited, it will be impossible for a mixed constitution to exist. For as the Royal Power is concentrated in a single person, girt and surrounded by Ministers of his own appointment; and as the aristocratic body is also inti-mately encorporated, if the people are not permitted to associate and knit themselves together for the vindication of their rights, how shall they frus-trate attempts which will inevitably be made against their liberties? The scattered million, however unanimous in feeling, is but chaff in the whirl-wind. It must be pressed together to have any weight. Deny them the right of association, and a handful of powerful individuals, united by the com-mon ties of interest, and grasping the wealth of the Nation, may easily perservere in projects hostile to the wishes, and ruinous to the interests of mankind; and in the very midst of this execrated career, exult in apparent popularity.

But political combination, among a people of bold and decided character cannot be prevented; and when *public association* is suppressed it only drives them to those *private cabals*, in which projects ten thousand times more dangerous are frequently hatched than any thing, which, in a society as-sembling in the broad eye of day, could be suggested or devised. It is then, from being forbidden to reason, that men become gloomy, violent, and ferocious. Brooding over thoughts they dare not utter, a sullen and impa-tient watchfulness is generated, prompt to continue, and eager to seize the most desperate opportunities of emancipation and revenge.

And will an English jury lend their hand to produce a state of society so dangerous and so degraded? Will they not assist in the annihilation of all that is manly in the human character? and meet from henceforth, in our streets, the haggard eye of the coward, and the down-cast gloomy counte-nance of the assassin. This you do consent to—this you do assist, if, by the verdict of this day, you render it no longer safe for Englishmen to associate, and seek redress of grievances.

What do you suppose produced the manly character of this country?—Our sea-girt shores and soggy atmosphere?—Idle suggestion!—If you would trace the real sources of National Character, seek them in the institutions and political maxims of the country.

The political freedom of the people—their habits of public intercourse, and voluntary association, have hitherto been the root of all the blessings, and all the virtues they could ever boast. If you love the fruit, lay not the axe to the vital fibres. Pause before you strike (for the arm is lifted) and remember the aweful admonition of the president Montesquieu—"The English have much reason to be jealous of their liberty; for were they ever so unhappy as to lose it, they would be the most servile nation upon earth." (*Sp. I.. B. 2. c. 4.*)[98] And lose it they will where juries lose their independence and discernment and suffer themselves to be biassed by the declamations of a Crown Lawyer, or overawed by the authoritative sophistry of a Judge. This is all that is left to us. The representation in Parliament is already gone—the appointment of sheriffs is wrested from us[99]—the Habeas Corpus Act is no more and the provisions of Magna Charta have mouldered imperceptibly away. Juries are the only reliques that remain of the temple of our ancient freedom; and when these shall cease to afford their jealous protection to the people, the ground-plot of liberty may still remain, but buried in the rank weeds of tyranny the beauties of the edifice will be traced no more.

The assertion of the necessity, and constitutional right of political association having led me thus far into the written evidence, I shall throw together all the observations I have to make upon that part of the proceedings.

Of the correspondence with the Jacobins and Convention of France I shall take little notice: not one of the addresses being produced in evidence being either prepared by me, or adopted by any society of which I was a member at the time of their adoption. Certainly, however, had it fallen in my way to be consulted upon the subject, while we were at peace with that country, I should have suspected no criminality in lending either my assent, or my assistance. Nay, I will even acknowledge that before the appearances of hostility, an address to the Convention was prepared by me from the Borough Society.[100] But in consequence of the proclamation of November ninety-two,[101] the Society dispersed, and the address was never sent.

In the same manner I shall pass over the works of Paine and Barlowe;[102] none of which were ever distributed by the Society after I became a member. And as for the work of the latter author, it is one of those books of which I have never read one single sentence. The Crown Lawyers, therefore, among other wonderful and original elucidations of the various shades and degrees of constructive treason, have to define to you the exact portion of criminality which attaches to a man in consequence of another person having published a book which *he* has never seen.

These observations equally apply to more than four-fifths of the written and printed evidence which has been piled before you. Of whatever bears date prior to the 21st October 1793, it is impossible I should have had any

knowledge; and of the subsequent transactions little, in proportion, is produced.

These papers (such as they are) have been twice produced in evidence
against persons concerned in their composition and circulation; and have
been twice pronounced insufficient for their crimination; and I make no
doubt but that you participate in the indignation of my eloquent and
learned Council, at seeing them dragged forward a *third time* to criminate
an individual no more concerned in them than yourselves. For though the
Lord Chief Justice lays it down as a maxim that a man may be criminated
by acts committed in the prosecution of a conspiracy before he became a
party in such conspiracy, how I can be more deeply implicated in act of
which I never had not could have any knowledge whatever, than the persons by whom they were prompted, is beyond my comprehension.

The original declaration of the Southwark Society applies somewhat
more directly.[103] It is true I was present when it was adopted. It is not,
however true, that I was one of the original founders of that Society. Of
the first meeting, in which the Committee was appointed that brought
forward this declaration, I had no sort of knowledge. The second meeting
was called by public advertisement; and I attended, and spoke, and in all
probability voted for the declaration, as others did, without critically an-
alyzing every word in the composition. You have been told by the only
witness called by the prosecutors to this part of the charge, that he is not
sure whether the cause of my attendance was not his calling at my house,
informing me that a meeting of friends to parliamentary reform was to be
held that evening, and inviting me to accompany him. This was in reality
the fact. He tells you also, that the speech I there delivered was a strong
recommendation of peace and order in the proceedings of the friends of
liberty; and such as evidently proved me to have no other object in view
than a reform in the Commons House of Parliament. And yet the Crown
lawyers would not only persuade you that I was the original framer of that
Society but from the heedless insertion of one ambiguous word (*representative government*) would charge the declaration to my account as an *Overt
Act* of High Treason.

It is true, indeed, I was, at a subsequent meeting, nominated one of the
general committee; it is true also that, some weeks before the dispersion of
the society, I was regularly enrolled in one of the divisions: but the circumstances I mentioned in cross examination are nevertheless true: that I was
not concerned in drawing the declaration; and that I was only an accidental visitor when it passed: Circumstances which it is no further necessary to
detail, than as they are connected with the vindication of that veracity for

the violation of which the situation I am placed in could furnish no satis-factory apology.—Individuals may perish; and others may supply their places; and the public cause receive but little injury. But he who is influ-enced by fear, to violate the sacred principles of truth, stabs at the vitals of public virtue; and commits an irreparable injury.

But if this part of the proceedings of my prosecutors, bear such strong marks of personal animosity and misrepresentation what must we say to those circumstances I am about to mention?—What must we say to the attempt to criminate me, not only by every act of every individual con-nected with any political society in any part of the nation!—no matter whether I had ever seen, or heard of such individual in my life!—but to criminate me also by acts never adopted by any political society, and which had been absolutely rejected by means of the opposition they had met with from myself and other active members included in this indictment. The injustice of this proceeding is in some respects so barefaced as hardly to require a comment: particularly the circumstance of producing in evidence against me a paper purporting to be resolutions intended for the meeting at Chalk Farm: a paper which the very evidence for the prosecution proves that the Committee of which I was a member never approved. For in the first place it has been proved to be in the hand writing of a person who was not a member of that Committee; and in the next it is proved that their resolutions never were proposed, and that others were actually adopted. The fact is, these resolutions were *unanimously* rejected by the Commit-tee—not because they were supposed treasonable—(for how can it be trea-sonable to quote the words of that Coronation Oath, upon which the pros-ecutors have laid so much stress in the course of these trials?)—not because they were supposed seditious—(for how can it be seditious to quote an historical fact?—to remind the people of an alteration which the three estates of the country thought fit to make in that Coronation oath at the period of the Revolution?—For surely that alteration would never have been made if the words struck out had not been considered as containing a vicious principle—And I am yet to learn that it can be a crime to warn the people against the adoption of a principle, which a solemn act of the Legis-lature has declared to be vicious!)[a] (The fact is these words were ordered to be struck out of the Oath of Allegiance, by the Convention parliament, at

---

[a]It may be necessary to inform those who have not read the trials that the following is the obnoxious resolution particularly alluded to—"Resolved, That it is the right and bounden duty of the people to punish all traitors against the nation; and that the following parts are not now a part of the oath of allegiance", to wit—"*I declare it is not lawful, upon any pretence whatever, to take arms against the King*"! (See 2 Rep. Sec. Com. H. C. p. 22).[104]

the epoch of that Revolution which placed the present family on the Throne; it being considered as a maxim that lead to inevitable despotism.)—No: it was rejected because it was not consistent with the plans of the Society—because the sort of Convention it alluded to was such as it was neither in the power nor inclination of the Society to assemble!

Before I quit this subject, I shall single out another instance from the heap that presents itself of the flagrant injustice of these proceedings. A Report of a Committee of Constitution has been presented upon which considerable stress has been laid as shewing the views and objects of the Society, and of the persons charged in this Indictment in particular: although the *faithful* spies of the prosecutors must have informed them that this report was rejected by the Society, in consequence of the determined opposition of Baxter[105] and myself, and other false traitors, against whom they are now made charges of criminality; and another Committee was appointed to draw up, and actually did draw up and print, another report essentially different.

The Constitution thus proposed to supersede the one which our prosecutors consider as so treasonable, and which was notoriously, in a considerable degree, the production of Baxter and myself, never was mentioned during the whole of the trials, although printed copies of this must have been found in the possession of most of the apprehended persons. So that no criminality being found in our own acts, we were to be tried for crimes, (as they are called) which we prevented others from committing.

These and a mass of similar circumstances, which prove the candour with which these prosecutions have been conducted, I leave to speak for themselves. They are the inevitable consequences of the system of accumulative and constructive treason. Prosecutions for which must inevitably depend for their success, not upon the principles of justice and rational conviction; but upon laborious attempts to confound the prisoner, and bewilder the understandings of the Jury.

But there are other circumstances in this prosecution for the monstrous injustice of which not even this weak apology can be made. I mean the manner in which the papers produced in evidence were seized, and the whole conduct of the messengers and Bow-Street officers relative to the execution of their arbitrary warrants.

I say nothing of the indignities offered to my person; which was searched and rummaged by common thief-takers, as if I had been a house-breaker or a high-way robber. The facts I particularly allude to, are of much more serious importance.

During the despotism of Charles the second, when the wicked measures of the Cabinet drove the best and noblest patriots to form associations for the purpose of reforming the Government, and when the persecution of opinion had driven them from *open investigation* to the necessity of *private cabal*, it cannot be forgotten that the Government then, as now, attempted to take away the lives of virtuous men, not for actions only, but for the private and unpublished sentiments with which they had amused themselves in their closets. Warrants were accordingly granted for the seizure of their papers; and their *speculative opinions* were produced in evidence against them. Yet even in those times the most despotic cabinet that had ever disgraced the annals of Britain did not leave the victims of their tyranny to the mercy of their meanest retainers: nor resign every thing to the discretion of a few ignorant runners, whose *blunders*, or whose *forgeries* might be equally fatal to those with whose security they were entrusted. The papers, as may be seen in the trial of Sidney,[106] were sealed in the presence of the persons apprehended; and they were permitted, if they pleased, for security against insidious practices, to put their own seals upon them; that they might be opened in their presence, at the time of their examination. But had we the same attention? Far from it. It was in vain that I remonstrated that I had a right to know what they took, and to see that they did not exceed their authority. I was hurried away by one of the messengers as soon as he had conveyed a few insignificant scraps of paper out of my pocket into his own; the papers were bundled away without any precaution whatever; and were scattered in the utmost disorder, about the Privy Council and adjoining offices, where I afterwards saw them, mingled with others with which I had no acquaintance.

The consequences have been such as might have been expected. A letter, the direction of which has been torn away, (by what *accident*, or by what *design* it is not easy to conceive) is sworn to have been found in my pocket by the Messenger *Tims*:[107]—a letter which for any evidence to the contrary, may have been written to himself, or may be a mere forgery of some underling in office:—a letter, which at any rate, I never saw; which is written from a person I never heard of, and a country where I never had a correspondent.[108] In the meanwhile another letter, *or commencement of a letter, for it was never finished and unlikely to have been either printed or sent*,[109] which certainly never was out of my possession, till seized by the Messengers, is sworn to have been found upon Richter,[110] by whom it was never seen. Nay what is more extraordinary, the Messenger, Tims, who swears that he found this last paper upon Richter, *was not the person by whom it could have been found at all*: for it was in my study, in the back house, where Tims never went; he having (in spite of my remonstrance) hurried me away before the search of that house began.

Visionary, indeed, is the boasted security of Britons, if, upon any pretence whatever, papers can be seized, and brought in evidence against them in such a manner, under circumstances so ambiguous; thus open to forgeries and practices of the basest kind; and to blunders, which may be equally fatal.

Nor can I take my farewell of these Gentlemen Messengers—these despotic retainers of the Cabinet, without some observations on a species of testimony, which, under a virtuous modification of Government, never could be tolerated, because while it is so, no degree of innocence can be secure. I allude particularly to the testimony of Tims, who, after having declared in his first examination, that my conduct was the very reverse from shewing any desire of resistance or escape, comes forward a second time to despose that, although he had previously warned me, that whatever I said would be repeated to the Privy Council, and brought forward against me, yet I had made him so far my confidant, as to tell him that "if I had been fourteen days longer at liberty, I should have been surrounded with so many friends, that it would have been difficult to apprehend me."[111]

So absurd a forgery is unworthy of serious disavowal; but if such testimony is admissable, which however false, can never be contradicted, upon what sort of tenure does every Briton hold his life, should the *ingenuity* of these servile dependants be commensurate with their *zeal*?

The man who is at liberty, can select his society; and if he trusts himself alone with a stranger of ambiguous character, or subjects himself to the misrepresentations of a perjured dependant, he must abide the consequences. But Discretion is as impotent as Innocence, to guard against the *inventive* malice of the being, who, armed with the warrant of a Privy Council, drags the victim from his home, and excluding him from all choice of society, and all guardianship of disinterested witnesses, can afterwards come forward in a Court of Justice, and deprive him of his life by swearing to circumstances, which, though they never occurred, are incapable of contradiction.

But it is vain to cavil about particulars. If loose conversations are once permitted as evidences of Treason, pretences can never be found wanting to destroy the most innocent and virtuous of mankind!

Yet to the disgrace of an English Court of Justice—to the scandal of the British character—to the indelible reproach of that Constitution, which those who have violated every principle of it, continue so extravagantly to applaud—at the close of the eighteenth century, in a prosecution for Treason, is the feeble mass of accumulative and constructive charges, bolstered by evidence of this contemptible nature.

For this purpose every tavern and coffee-house has been haunted, into which (rare visitant as I have been to places of that description) I may occasionally have put my head. My hours of conviviality have been attended by spies and sycophants, my doors beset with evedroppers, my private chambers haunted by the familiar spirits of an infernal Inquisition, and my confidential friends stretched on the rack of interrogatory, in order to extort from them the conversation which in the unsuspecting hours of social hilarity may have been uttered at my own table.

But it will not be believed—posterity will not credit the monstrous tale—that, unsatisfied with former arts—despairing of success, yet eager in the scent of blood, four or five days only before my trial, the agents of this wicked prosecution should have sent, in the name of the Privy Council, for a person known to be one of my most familiar friends—known to be one of the witnesses subpoena'd on my behalf—known, also, to have been entrusted confidentially by my family, and my Solicitor in the management of my defence; and after clapping a Testament to his lips (let Mr. White or Mr. Ford contradict me if this is false!)[112] should interrogate him on the mode of my intended defence, on the evidence I had to contradict particular charges, and the subjects of those private conversations which, in the unsuspecting confidence of our souls, we had frequently indulged together.[113]

O Sejanus and abhorred Rufinus, yet tyrannic scourges of the Roman world![114] why are ye handed down in the page of infamy as monsters of the human race?—why boils our blood with indignation, at the recital of your base artifices? Britain has, also, its Sejanus in the present day—Its base Rufinus and his herd of perjured spies and inquisitors; and in this degenerate country, as in the Roman empire, the blood-hounds of power can hunt the devoted patriot from the banquet to the closet, from the closet to the public theatre, and from the public theatre to the retreat of private friendship, to drag forth the secrets of his heart, and the levities of his imagination and pervert them to his destruction.

O Britain! Britain! while thy pimps and perjurers, Old Bailey Solicitors, and the sweepings of the stews, boast of the confidence of thy Gentlemen High in Office! while innocence and virtue stand trembling for their lives before them, what must be the feelings of thy once generous sons?—and how must their tongues henceforward faulter when they talk of their liberties and their charters?

But the inquisition has not stopped even here.—Unpublished letters are dragged forth, from the corners of my study, where they had mouldered in forgetfulness. The watchword has been transmitted to distant counties; and pious priests, pettifogging lawyers, and illiterate apothecaries, the pigmy gentry of obscure towns and villages, have been associated for months in dark conspiracy against a friendless, powerless, unconnected individual; have intercepted his private correspondence, and broke into the houses of his nearest relations for the letters of confidence written by him to a brother-in-law, and by his wife to her own brother.

Yet see the pitiful figure which, after all this inquisitorial industry, the evidence for the prosecution makes. The indecorous expressions charged against me upon Hardy's trial[115] the prosecutors have been obliged to abandon, because they knew we could disprove them; and a new batch of forgeries, still more improbable, are brought forward, that they might attack me in quarters where they supposed me to be less prepared. These forgeries excepted (which scarcely deserve reply) what does the whole amount to? I am convicted, it is true, of having used the word Citizen, of boasting of the rapid circulation of three songs,[116] which the prosecutors have talked a great deal about, but from which they have not thought fit, on any of the trials, to quote one single line: though the Counsel for the prisoners have called upon them to do so. They have proved me also, to be desirous that an honest countryman, my brother-in-law, should lay aside his distant respect, speak his mind openly, and behave towards me upon the footing of "equality and perfect freedom."

They have proved also, by an unpublished letter, upon which Mr. Serjeant Adair[117] has laid particular stress, that I had opinions about the state of parties in Paris very different from those which are propagated by the agents of Government; and that though I abhorred the dagger of the Maratists, I believed the Mountain[118] to be the party best calculated to manage the helm in that storm by which France was on every side assailed; and that I even had not quite so bad an opinion even of Marat, as many people had, and as I had once entertained myself. They also, perhaps have proved, that I am, in private speculations, a *Republican*. But if you put this together with the evidence that has been distinctly given of my sentiments and conduct in the society, and my invariable maxims that "truth and reason were the only weapons of the friends of liberty"—and that "speculative opinions ought never to be enforced by Violence",[119] I do not see what tendency such private opinion can have to support the charge of treason.

I do not vindicate the whole of that letter. There are parts of it which prove at once the irritation and the aggravations under which it was written: parts which my cooler judgment does not approve. But who expects to answer at the bar of the Old Bailey for every intemperate expression he may utter, nay, every crude imagination that in the revolution of opinions may pass across his brain But as for the passage upon which Mr. Adair has laid such peculiar emphasis, I both disavow, and approve it. I do believe that the people of America—in many parts, at least, have "too much veneration for property—too much religion—and too much law."[120] I think it is having too much law to be encumbered with one fourth of the intricacy, complication, and uncertainty in which the law of this country, for example, is involved. And in many of the provinces of America, I understand, they are encumbered with more than half. I think there is too much religion in a country, when a man taking a ride on a Sunday afternoon is to have the hue and cry raised to bring him back, as a prophaner of the Lord's day; and when a husband can be made to do pennance in a white sheet, for saluting his wife on the street, upon meeting her after a seven years absence. Yet such is the religion of some of the American provinces. And as for the other member of the sentence, I believe all veneration for property, in the sense in which I have used the phrase, is vice—is destructive to the morals and intellects of Society—is the source of all that oppressive rapacity and unfeeling avarice which produce so many vices in one description of men, and so much misery in another.

But when I say this let me be understood. The person I was writing to knew my heart, and would have required no commentator. By veneration for property I meant that habit, much too prevalent in all countries—and, if I have been rightly informed, particularly prevalent in America, of respecting mankind in proportion to their property—looking up to *affluence* as an honourable distinction, instead of proportioning our esteem to the talents and virtues of mankind. This you have been distinctly told, by one of the witnesses, is the interpretation (from the doctrines he knew me to be in the constant habit of upholding) his mind would have afforded; nor can malevolence itself, after the evidence that has been given, put any other construction upon the sentence. For call to mind my whole conduct, in and out of the Society, such as it appears from the uniform testimony of all but the spies by profession, and see what part of it can justify the malignant and outrageous comments of the Crown lawyers?—Call to mind the testimony of those respectable characters who having known me the most intimately, are most likely to be acquainted with my real sentiments and feelings. Remember the colours in which they have described my character—the history they have given of my life! and then ask your own hearts,

Is this the composition—are these the sentiments—the qualifications of an incendiary?—an apostle of plunder, and its inevitable concomitant massacre?—Ask your own hearts also—What innocence, what virtue can be unimpeached if it is to be tried, as the Crown lawyers would have you try me and my coadjutors, by the partial selection of a few ambiguous phrases? Where is the man whose conversation and sentiments never lay open to misrepresentation? Where is the man who never, in the gaiety of youthful passion, gave utterance to an idle expression, or drank a ridiculous toast, which if gravely repeated, with the colourings of a malignant commentator, might not be tortured into evidence of intentions from which his soul would have revolted? And where is the man (can any one who hears me answer to the description?) who never in confidential correspondence, to a friend who knew him too well to be capable of misunderstanding him, expressed himself in terms which if read in a court of Justice with the malicious interpretations of a public prosecutor, might not convey a meaning very different from what he intended?

These observations will equally apply to another passage in which I avow myself a "Sans Culotte": a phrase which Mr. Serjeant Adair has thought fit to define in terms the most gross and monstrous that the imagination even of an assassin could have suggested.[121] To what authority he referred for this definition he has not informed us: but as the term had been defined by myself, in the Lecture, which is published, "on the Moral Tendency of a system of spies and informers", it would have been, at least, candid to have quoted this passage to shew the real sense in which I was in the habit of using it. The definition then is as follows:—"I am a SANS CULOTTE!—one of those who think the happiness of millions of more consequence than the aggrandisement of any party junto! or, in other words, an advocate for the rights and happiness of those who are languishing in *want* and *nakedness*! for this is my interpretation of a *sans culotte*:—*the thing in REAL-ITY which Whigs pretend to be!*" (P. 34. Ed. 3. p. 20. Ed. 4.)[122]

I have dwelt upon this subject with some anxiety, not because it does in reality form any substantial part (for substantial part there is none) of the charge exhibited against me; but because acquittal would afford me no satisfaction; if those who dismissed me from this bar, freed from the suspicion of treason, did not dismiss me, also, freed, in their minds, from the imputation of feelings and sentiments that would rank me with the plunderer and the ruffian.—Death in the cause of liberty and virtue I flatter myself, I am prepared to encounter; but I am not prepared for the still heavier calamity of supporting existence under that accumulation of calumny and misrepresentation which has been heaped upon me by the authors and conductors of this prosecution.

One word upon the subject of my Lectures; and I have done. Though the whole testimony of the solitary witness, out of the thousands that attended, who has been brought forward, might have been contradicted by the most respectable testimonies, if the clear detection of this wretch in two distinct perjuries, and an attempt at subornation of perjury, had not rendered it superfluous, yet I am convinced the *crime* of giving political lectures is in reality my principal offence. There was, it is true, *no treason* in these Lectures, but there was that which was infinitely more offensive to the men in power—a bold and open investigation of those measures by which they are plunging the country in irretrievable destruction.

When they crushed the societies for political debate, I was the only individual who openly resisted that arbitrary measure. I was the only individual who for two years openly struggled for the restoration of that free discussion so essential to the preservation of liberty, but so dangerous to a corrupt and vicious Administration; and when I found it impossible to communicate my own resolution to the minds of others, I stepped forward to supply the deficiency to the utmost of my power, and to revive, in another shape, that investigation which others had so timidly abandoned. This is the reason why they seek my destruction—this is the crime I have committed.

Of the manner in which this crime, as it is called, has been perpetrated, you have heard much on the part of the prosecutors; and much might be said in reply. It is not necessary, however, that you should depend either upon their representations, or upon mine. Some of the Lectures are in print; and many quotations might be made to prove their general object and tendency to be the very reverse of what the prosecutors and their perjured spy have represented. I shall content myself however with one.

It is from the first lecture, in which, after dwelling for some time on the necessity of investigating with temper and moderation the grievances under which we labour, I thus proceed—

"There is also another—better motive than that of prudence, to prompt us to this moderation in our deportment—Benevolence!—the kind and candid feelings of the heart! without which a pure and enlightened freedom never can be enjoyed, never can be understood. Anarchy may rage where asperity of soul triumphs in all its bitterness, but where personal hatred, and the burning desire of vengeance usurp dominion over the hearts of men, genuine liberty, and the tranquil happiness which liberty ought to secure to us, never can be hoped. Reason and the pure spirit of philosophy, are essential requisites to this state of social independence, and these will teach us to consider, that every action, however hostile to the sacred cause we are pursuing, is the unhappy consequence of errors result-ing from the circumstances by which the actor has been surrounded; and that, consequently, instead of stirring up the gloomy passions of the soul, we ought to pity the instrument while we redress the evil." (*Lect. Spies & Informers. p.* 15. 3d *Edit.* p. 12 of 4th)[123]

Such are the sentiments which in the *opinion* (or rather the *language*) of our prosecutors are "calculated from their very extravagance to catch the attention of the audience—inflame their minds, alienate them from the laws and constitution of their country, and habituate them to principles of sedition and rebellion." (*Rep. Sec. Com.* p. 22.)[124]

In short the whole of this *collateral* Charge, resolves itself into the simple fact of having assembled people together for the purpose of discussing be-fore them the principles of Government and the measures of the Adminis-tration. But I trust I have already proved, in a former part of this defence, not only that it is, at all times a right, but that, in particular situations, it is the bounden duty of the people to assemble for the purpose of such discussion.

If this be admitted (and I should be glad to hear the arguments by which it can be confuted) who will venture to affirm that this is not a time for the exercise of this right?

I will not dwell upon the calamities of the starving multitude. They are written too legibly in the countenances of friendless widows and orphans in every manufacturing town in the nation—The men, it is true, have met with a *milder fate*—They have escaped the last extremities of domestic misery, by laying down the intolerable load of existence among the marshes of Flanders, and the dykes of Holland.

I shall dwell only upon that flagrant departure from the letter and spirit of our Constitution, and the genuine principles of political Justice by which these calamities have been produced. This is of itself sufficient to prove not only the duty—but the *present necessity* of political enquiry. And upon this foundation alone my vindication might have been rested; unless, indeed, as the conduct of our prosecutors seems most openly to affirm, *loyalty* (that is to say *respect for the laws*) consists only in attachment to the regal and aristocratical branches of the Constitution, and all vindication of the genuine principles of the Democratic branch (which has hitherto been regarded as *the most valuable of the three*) is to be branded as rebellion and High Treason.

For, alas! to what a miserable shade, or shadow of a shade is the representation of seven millions and a half of human beings reduced, when out of 513 members of the Democratic assembly as it is called, 306, that is to say a decided majority of 99, are returned by the patronage of the Treasury and 162 individuals; out of which to aggravate this outrageous insult, 167 are absolutely nominated by 71 Peers, who by the Constitutional jealousy of our ancestors, and the annual resolution of the House of Commons, are precluded from "any right to vote in the election of any member to serve in Parliament", and are declared guilty of "a high infringement upon the liberties and privileges of the Commons of Great Britain, if they concern themselves in the Elections of Members to serve for the Commons in Parliament." (*Petition of the friends of the people*, p. 8.)[125]

I have stated the number of patronised members from the pamphlet published by the Society of the Friends of the People—but it must immediately occur to you that the evil has been considerably increased since that publication. Even while I have been shut up in rigorous confinement for the horrible High Treason of associating for Parliamentary Reform, and delivering lectures on the corruptions and abuses of our Constitution, a fresh batch of Borough proprietors has been decorated in the *borrowed plumage* of nobility, that they might increase the *fixed* majority of the Minister, by their *votes*, in the house of Peers, and by their *influence*, in the House of Commons.[126]

Such, then, is the state of *what is called representation* in this country, that if it should suit the views and interests of 162 rich and powerful individuals to unite their influence they *might*, without a struggle—nay, without even a perceptible alteration in the semblance of our Government, overturn the Constitution, establish a perfect oligarchy, and render themselves completely masters at once of the prerogatives of the Crown, and the property, lives, and liberties of their fellow citizens. And is this the Constitution of England?—Is this the triple balance, the boasted equipoise of King, Lords, and Commons?—Is this a time when enquiry ought to be crushed, and English juries to be called upon to punish like the vilest ruffians those who shall labour to enlighten their fellow citizens, and rouse them to a sense of their situation?

Remember, Gentlemen, the aweful—the prophetic words of that philosopher I have so often quoted—"As all human things have an end", says he, "the state we are speaking of will lose its liberty. It will perish. Have not Rome, Sparta, and Carthage perished?"—Let it be remembered, that Rome and Sparta still preserved the *exterior form* of their free constitutions, (particularly the former), even while groaning beneath the most abject despotism.—"Have not Rome, Sparta, and Carthage perished? It will perish"—When, Gentlemen? When the door is opened for universal suffrage?—When meetings of delegates, from a few popular societies, attempt to "*overawe* the legislature" by publishing their sentiments on Parliamentary Reform?—When Lectures and Debating Societies are opened to discuss the measures of government? No. But "it will perish when the legislative power shall be more corrupt than the executive." (B. *xi. c.* 6.)[127]

Gentlemen—Mine is not a situation to hazard bold propositions.—To provoke one prejudice—to inflame one ungentle passion, may be fatal, perhaps, to an individual, whose brain is yet working for the welfare of mankind, and whose heart [is] vibrating for all that is dear in social life!—But truth and conviction are struggling at my heart, and I must acknowledge—Such to me appears the melancholy condition of Britain at this hour. The fulfillment of the fatal prophecy seems fast approaching; and I own I have contemplated the prospect with a degree of anguish, which, from the warmth I have expressed it with, and the activity with which I have laboured to avert the catastrophe, seems at once to have marked me as a victim to the rage of my oppressors, and laid me open to the *misrepresentations* of their perjured agents. But that I ever conspired, or connived at any conspiracy for the purposes of violence, plunder, or insurrection, is a calumny so black and infamous as could have entered the imagination of none but the most practised assassin.

Such, Gentlemen, are the *real motives* for this prosecution—and such are the *pretences* upon which I have been locked up in close confinement, excluded from every intercourse of friendship and affection; and for a part of that time prohibited even the use of pen and ink, and the amusement of books:—such are the pretences upon which, for five dismal weeks, I have been destined to the vilest dungeon of Newgate—a miserable hole almost impervious to a ray of light; and in which a few diurnal sprinklings of vinegar supplied the total absence of circulating air—a charnel house, whose ragged walls, and old hereditary filth might persuade the wretched inhabitant that he was already buried; and which was indeed, till I was thrown into it, the common receptacle for the putrid carcases of felons, who died beneath their load of fetters. Such also are the pretences for which every tender relative and connection has been stretched, month after month, upon the lingering rack of terror and apprehension; and for which the family that used to subsist in comfort by my labours, has been doomed to moisten with their tears the precarious bread of charity.

From the fangs, however, of this prosecution, I am at last permitted to call upon you—and I do call upon you with confidence, to emancipate me by your verdict. I call upon you in the aweful name of Justice, to restore me to the sphere of my active usefulness—to my public and private duties—to my relatives—to my friends—to the aged mother who has been so long deprived of her only protector—to the wife who stretches forth her arms to receive her slandered husband, and the infant yet unconscious of my un-merited sufferings. To these I call upon you, by the sacred love of Justice to restore me; and by your verdict to proclaim to the world the honest convic-tion of your minds, that though my conduct may sometimes have been marked by the levity or the intemperance of youth, my heart is untainted by any crime!

END OF THE DEFENCE.

Address to the Court after the Verdict; with the Reply of the Lord Chief Baron, from the short-hand Notes of Mr. Ramsey.

J. THELWALL. "My Lord and Gentlemen of the Jury, if any thing could increase the affection I bear to my country, it certainly must be the circum-stance of this acquittal. If a plain, simple, unconnected man, with neither rank, fortune nor connections to recommend him, after having laboured twelve months under all the calumny which a particular set of party writers could pour upon his head—after having felt all the irritation of mind, and committed many of the imprudences which have resulted from those aggra-vating circumstances—after lying seven months in prison, without any op-portunity to vindicate himself, and whose friends could not dare to vindi-cate him, for fear of falling under similar predicaments themselves—if under all these circumstances, after the diligent collections of this mass of evidence, (a great part of which, I own, appeared to me not connected with my case—but I submitted to the Judgment, of the Court)—if under all these circumstances, the accumulated weight and pressure laid upon me was not sufficient to bear down and crush so insolated and unprotected a man, there must be something in the dispositions of the people of Great Britain—something eminently virtuous in this country, which every Briton must reflect upon with pride, and which must render every individual still more anxious to promote its happiness and prosperity.

My Lord and Gentlemen of the Jury, I will confess to you that part of the charge so candidly delivered by the Court, which says that there are some circumstances in my conduct that may require explanation, is founded in truth: though I protest in the sight of my country, and call upon that posterity whose applause I hope to obtain, and whose happiness I have anxiously laboured to procure, to bear witness for me that I never was actuated by one vicious motive in any part of my political conduct, however provoked by the insults and indignities that may have stimulated a too irritable disposition. I call upon that country, and upon that posterity, to regard either with detestation or affection my memory hereafter, as what I now say shall be found true or false—that no part of my political conduct has ever had any actuating motive but a desire to promote the welfare and happiness of my fellow creatures, by peaceable means, by reason alone; and that there stands not an individual in this Court, there exists not an individual in this country, or in the universe, who has blended so much activity with so anxious a desire to prevent all violence. Not only have I forborne all personal concern with violence, or plans of violence myself; but a great part of that activity which I have so pompously and so ridiculously held out in a very foolish and very incoherent letter, (which I never sent, which I never read after I had written it; and which, I am sure, though there be an intemperate moment in my life when I wrote it, I never should have read without committing to the flames)—a great part of that activity, which I have there described in bombastic language, has been exerted in preventing the Society with which I have been connected, from being led by spies and informers (by the Taylors[128] and the Lynams who had insinuated themselves into it for purposes of the blackest treachery) into schemes of rashness and violence—in preventing them from being seduced by such beings into the ridiculous project of procuring arms, and exchanging the artillery (*holding up a pen*) which you have been told in evidence is the only artillery I ever meant to make use of, for pikes and guns, and all those instruments of destruction, which I hope, one time or other, and anxiously believe, will be entirely thrown aside, and no longer be permitted to make the wife a mourning widow, and the orphan babe an outcast from society. To enter into particulars of explanation would be improper in this place, I shall seize, therefore, an early opportunity of submitting to the public a full explanation of my conduct—"

Lord Chief Baron MACDONALD. "Mr. Thelwall, I must remind you, that in the case of Mr. Holcroft[129] the Court were of opinion that it was not proper to hear any such declaration, at the same time a little warmth of temper having been ascribed to you in evidence, I felt a great reluctance to stop you; I am sure you will not trespass upon the indulgence."

J. THELWALL. "My Lord, I was just speaking the last sentence I meant to deliver, and declaring that I should seize another opportunity of submitting (*temperately*, I hope, I am sure *truly*) to the public, a justification of my conduct. At present it would be impertinent; and therefore I take leave of the Court and Jury, returning them my most sincere thanks for the anxious attention they have paid to this trial."

Lord Chief Baron MACDONALD—"It perhaps never happened before, in any judicial proceedings, that Juries were called upon to exercise so severe a service; and, therefore, that great attention must be a great satisfaction to you and to the public. And permit me to say, now you are *acquitted in that most reputable of manners*, by the verdict of an attentive Jury, I wish you, I give it to you as a piece of advice, to avoid rashness, even in the pursuit of objects that may appear to you to be good; and that you would profit by what has now passed, and leave the Constitution of the country whole and well as it stands at present. Before you take any measures, however good they may appear to you, and before you enter into combinations with others, I think you may derive a useful lesson from it: and I hope that appeal you have now made, will not be made in vain, to the whole context of your future conduct."

———◆———

I have reprinted this Address and Reply for the purpose of marking the very different light in which the same facts may be viewed by the leaders of factious assemblies and even the moderate and considerate part of their own agents. The Lord Chief Baron tells us, "we are acquitted in the *most respectable of manners*"; but the ministerial leaders in the House of Commons say we are "*white-washed felons!*"[130] and their echoes in the House of Lords declare that the verdicts of "attentive Juries" cannot free us from "the imputation of *moral guilt*"![131]

Before the trial by Jury had been thus wantonly insulted, would it not have been well for the conspicuous members of the legislature to have considered whether they were likely to increase the public respect for their own functions, by outraging, in such a manner, that dearest and most sacred of all the institutions in this Country?

THE

TRIBUNE,

A PERIODICAL PUBLICATION,

CONSISTING CHIEFLY OF THE

POLITICAL LECTURES

OF

J. THELWALL.

TAKEN IN SHORT-HAND BY W. RAMSEY, AND REVISED BY
THE LECTURER.

To paint the voice, and fix the fleeting found.
HAYLEY.

LONDON:

PRINTED FOR THE AUTHOR,

AND SOLD BY THE FOLLOWING BOOKSELLERS :

D. I. EATON, Newgate-Street; SMITH, Portfmouth-Street, Lincoln's-Inn-
Fields; and BURKS, Crifpin-Street, Spitalfields.

1795.

[Selections from Volume 1]

On the means of redressing the Calamities of the Nation.[1]

WHAT then are the means of redress for which the calamities of the nation call? For redress of political calamities let us apply ourselves to correct the vices, the errors, the delusive ambition, which have led to those calamities. And if the present situation of the country, with respect to policy, results from the quixotic imagination that a handful of Britons could subdue the enthusiastic myriads of France—If we have attempted to trample their infant liberty in the dust, without considering with what gigantic energy that infancy was endued—If we have madly supposed that the pigmy efforts of a *Pitt*, a *Dundas*, a *Loughborough*,[2] a *Jenkinson*,[3] and a *Colonel Mack*,[4] could subdue this gigantic energy, and reduce a mighty nation once more to the tramels of despotism;—and if this has been the political source of our calamities, let us acknowledge that we see our error, that we see the folly of our attempt; and ere it be too late, consider how we can save our own country from that very *famine* and destruction with which we threatened to depopulate the streets of Paris. This also would lead to the remedy of those internal calamities that have fallen upon us, by calling forth the resources of nature and energies of a well directed industry. And as for those heavier calamities which may threaten to assail us at our own door—If Britons, as perhaps may be the case, are speedily to be called upon to defend their own habitations and their own families from those hostile aggressions with which they so unjustly and so absurdly threatened the enemy they have thus provoked, let our governors appeal in time to those popular concessions, those conciliating acts of justice which have been so long and so intemperately refused; but without which, I fear, that unanimity and energy can never be expected which circumstances so alarming may require.

To restore us to our vigour, let them restore us to our rights; let them convince us that it is for ourselves, and ourselves alone, that we are struggling; nor suffer us to suspect, for a moment, that we are contending for our own chains, for the security of our oppressors, and the perpetuity of our oppressions.

Remove the possibility of this suspicion, and then shall it be found that the British character has not lost its energy; but that we are still as capable of vindicating our own cause as ever we were in the most brilliant periods of our history. Then shall it appear in the eyes of Europe that Britons still retain that resolute and unanimous affection for the real interests of their country which can alone secure its protection or improve its happiness.

For the alleviation of calamities of another description, let us also labour to abolish luxury: and every man may do much towards this reformation. Let us in our own houses, at our own tables, by our exhortations to our friends, by our admonitions to our enemies, persuade mankind to discard those tinsel ornaments and ridiculous superfluities which enfeeble our minds, and entail voluptuous diseases on the affluent, while diseases of a still more calamitous description overwhelm the oppressed orders of society from the scarcity resulting from this extravagance. Thus let us administer to the relief of those who having the same powers of enjoyment with ourselves have a right to, at least, an equal participation of all the necessaries of life, which are the product of their labour. Let us seek also to restore the freedom of commerce. Let us consider that while the ports of nations are open, scarcity can never exist to any alarming degree. Every country, if not prevented by political impediments, will send its surplus productions to the best market.

The best market is always the country which is most in want, and, therefore, those who have most of any particular commodity will carry it to the port where its scarcity is most notorious: So that the effects of that scarcity will hardly be perceptible to the community at large. Let us consider what the real utility of commerce is: not that it may swell, as at present, the opulence of a few individuals; give the luxuries of the globe to the great man's table, and thus inflate his pride with the imagination, that he is a being of superior species to those by whose toil his appetites are pampered. No: the real advantage of commerce is, that the surplus resources of one nation exchanged for the surplus resources of another, may prevent excessive want and scarcity from being felt by any individual portion of the universe.

Let us consider then for one moment what are the real causes of the political and natural calamities of the country; and we cannot be long before we find redress.

The greater part of our calamities result from a ridiculous, an unjust, and therefore, an unnecessary war; and that state of corruption into which the democratic branch of our constitution has so unfortunately fallen. It is from those that the political distresses of the great body of the people arise. And let it be remembered that even the physical calamities, those which originated in the severities of the season, may also be removed by the same species of redress which may remove the other calamities. In the first place then let us consider how we can put a period to the present disastrous war. Let us see how we can conciliate the affections of the irritated republic of France, and how we can convert again into our dearest friends those people whom our unjust interference with their internal concerns has compelled to be our bitterest foes: or, to speak more correctly, the bitterest foes of our ministerial directors. Let us remember that however a few desperate individuals may have stained with crimes the revolution of that country, and however we may deplore the excesses into which the aspiring disposition of some individuals may have plunged a mighty nation; yet, on the other hand, we see, in the virtues they have exhibited, a character so great and glorious, that nothing but the delusive cant of political corruption could have induced us, for a moment, to brand them with those epithets, so liberally, and so impoliticly, bestowed.

Let us apply ourselves assiduously to compose the differences and restore the peace and cordial intercourse of Europe: and let us recollect that if this intercourse, this peace and affection can be restored, whatever calamities the elements may chance to inflict upon an individual country will be presently removed, even by that interested, but yet in its effects *philanthropic* spirit which induces mankind so universally to barter those commodities they can spare with other nations that stand in need of them.

Citizens, let us also, seeking for a more immediate redress, consider what our natural resources are. Let us consider that this is a country watered by innumerable streams, not only imparting fresh verdure to the fields they flow through; but teeming also with that food which, but from the unjust monopoly with which it is incumbered, might supply the necessities of all our industrious poor. For proof of this we need only appeal to facts. One of those fish which is certainly among the most luxurious of the finny tribe, the salmon was so abundant in this country, before the streams were made the property of individuals, that it was necessary in many parts of the country to insert a clause in the indentures of poor boys from the parish, to prevent their being fed upon this delicious dainty more than three times in a week. I refer you to the indentures of the city of Winchester particularly, where the clause is still retained, thought it is diffcult now in that town to get a morsel of that fish without paying two and sixpence or three shillings per pound for it.

Circumstances also of equal impolicy and injustice have produced an artificial scarcity of salt water fish: and a red herring which some years ago might be bought for a half-penny, is now to be had for less than threehalf-pence or twopence. What then is the cause of this? Will any man make me believe that the fishes are infected also with the rage of emigration?—Will you tell me that they also have drank the poisonous doctrines of jacobinism, and become discontented with the *glorious constitution*, under which for so many centuries they have so happily been eaten; and that, therefore, the herrings have fled from the coasts of Scotland, and the salmon deserted our rivers, and, together with the other factious inhabitants of our streams and shores, have fled, with atheistical abhorrence of all *regular government*, to the coasts and rivers of French anarchy, or the distant and happy shores of America, that they might enjoy the pleasure of being eaten without alloy from the consideration that they were put in the mouths of what they rebelliously consider as bondmen and slaves? No, Citizens, it is the infernal spirit of monopoly, that cruel and wasteful demon that has rendered poverty, want, and distress the portion of the mass of the people of this country; that has produced in the midst of abundance this cruel, artificial scarcity.

Citizens, is it not enough that men should have a property in that which has been procured by the labours of their ancestors? Is it not enough that the soil, which from time immemorial has been worked by a herd of men who were to receive a scanty portion only of its produce should be the property of a few wealthy and privileged individuals? Is it not enough that the birds of the air should be monopolised by these men?

Must the wild inhabitants of the very waves, must all the common bounties of nature, be also considered as articles of monopolising accumulation? Shall one or two men grasp to themselves the whole product of our rivers;

and then make an agreement with a fishmonger to waste and destroy whatever cannot be sold at an extravagant price, rather than suffer the swinish multitude to feast upon luxuries with which the tables of the great ought to be exclusively furnished; and thus produce an artificial scarcity into the country, so ruinous to the population, so detestable in its principles, so alarming in its effects.

Citizens, the harvests of our waves, if I may use the metaphor, if once relieved from this intolerable exercise, might always be reaped in abundance; and when plenty smiled not in our valleys, it would still sparkle in our streams, and in the neighbourhood of our shores, whose finny produce might compensate, in some degree for the accidental scarcity of the field.

The surplus production also, of those streams and shores might produce, by the exchange of a liberal commerce, abundance of the necessary supplies of which the country might stand in need. Look to the coasts of Scotland, look to the little islands, the Hebrides and the Orkneys. Behold how populous the surrounding waves! See the whole ocean one animated mass, as it were; one thronged association of little beings who offer themselves as the food of man.

Consider, that in the neighbourhood of one island, even upon a very moderate calculation, more than one hundred thousand millions of the finest herrings are devoured annually, by one species of wild fowl only, the solan goose, that frequents the rocky shores. Consider also, that the bays of that country are frequented by such huge quantities of them, that the whales (which might be caught there, also, instead of sending to Greenland for them) may be seen eating their way through the innumerable shoals that throng every part of the shores. Why is it then that they do not come to our markets in such quantities as to render superfluity, not want, the lot of man? Why is it that the superfluous produce of this fishery is not imported by the inhabitants of these coasts and islands, in such quantities as to produce in return an abundant supply of those necessaries and conforts of which those barren fragments of our isle stand so much in need?—Why is this fishery neglected, and resigned to the more politic and industrious Dutch, who almost engross the exclusive advantages of that trade, and thus sell to us, at an increased price, the produce of our own coasts and bays? Why stamp this shameful indignity on the British character? for it is, in reality, a much more shameful indignity than any of the offensive decrees of the French Convention, against which aristocrats and alarmists have so querulously declaimed!

I will tell you, Citizens—The flagrant policy of government is the sole cause of this scarcity and this insult. It is this that has brought the country into a situation like that of Tantalus,[5] where the waves rise to our lips and yet we cannot drink; and the food hangs down to our very mouths, and yet we cannot eat. To this situations are we reduced by those who (constantly engaged in the intrigues of party—in the coalitions of faction—in the management, as it is called, of majorities in the House of Commons—in adjusting the interests of proprietors of rotten boroughs—in disposing, I had like to have said like cattle, of those people whom they ought to preserve are too busy to attend to the insignificant consideration of providing for the comfortable sustenance of millions.

But it is not only by their neglect that we suffer; we are equally injured by their impolitic regulations: their excises, their partialities, their gabelles on salt, and their restrictions of the free spirit of trade and barter. I shall read from *Buchanan's* General View of the British Fishery, what he says upon this subject, as it is highly interesting. "What added greatly to the hurt of the fishing trade in Scotland in these latter times, appears to have arisen from the regulations and heavy restrictions respecting foreign and home-made salt. These are particularly hurtful to the isles, without storehouses to supply them with salt in their neighbourhood; and the poor inhabitants, or fishers, are incapable of procuring it, from its extravagant price when sold by merchants, and its immense distance to purchase that article at first hand, where it may be had at a moderate price.

This circumstance deserves serious consideration.

All herrings cured for home sale are subject to a duty of one shilling per barrel, if used in Scotland, and only three-pence or fourpence if used in England; which heavy duty must greatly retard the fisheries, and is too glaring an imposition to pass long without amendment.

The custom-house fees in Scotland are become a nuisance to the adventurers, so heavy as to absorb the greatest part of the bounty, especially on small vessels.

A man of respectability, named Macbride, and now in London, declares that he saw eighteen barrels of fresh herrings given for one barrel of salt, to the master of a smack; and three barrels for one shilling sterling:—The owners judging this trifle better than to allow them to rot without salt, as has been the case before.

An intelligent minister on Skye told the author, that he had seen heaps upon heaps rotting on the shore; and until carried off to dung the ground, no man durst pass by on the leeward of them, for the rotten offensive effluvia emitted from the fish."[6]

Is it not better then to turn our attention to the redress of these evils, than to be engaged in ridiculous crusades to restore a fallen despotism, and reinstate a superstitious priesthood, in a country where they have been torn from their pedestals, and trampled down, by the enlightened energy of the people.

Citizens, it will be asked, what should be the first step towards the general reform that seems so requisite?—The first step, perhaps I shall be expected to say, is the restoration of peace. But, alas! that cannot be restored till other steps have been taken. So long as those men now at the helm remain in power, no more, I fear, must the olive-branch of peace wave over this devoted country: never more, I fear, must that tranquillity and happiness be restored to Europe, for which we have so long and so ardently wished.

The first step, I believe, toward the redress of our national calamities, must be taken by the people—by manly and spirited, but peaceable remonstrances—by the unanimous voice of the friends of liberty throughout the country: and I believe in that description I include, at this time, by far the greatest part of the nation. The unanimous voice of the friends of liberty must be uplifted against the abuses and corruptions which have crept into the administration of the country. With these boldly, but peaceably, we must endeavour to hurl those men from the fate of ill-gotten power, who, Jehu like,[7] are driving us to destruction. We must seek for the redress of our grievances, by depriving of the power of future injury those men to whom our present injuries are to be attributed.

Yes Citizens, I believe it is necessary to shew our indignation, our detestation, our abhorrence of the mad, the frantic and destructive measures which the present administration are pursuing.

But let me be understood.—When I say, we ought to shew our indignation, I mean not violence—I mean that we ought to show that benevolent feeling which disdains to see the miseries of our fellow creatures, without attempting to obtain redress. I do not mean that frantic impetuosity you should plunge the devoted country into desolation. I hope I have a heart that *really* shudders at the idea of civil discord, as much as the aristocratic hypocrites and cowardly alarmists of the day *pretend*; and which would never consent to uplift the arm of violence but in absolute self-defence— when it is palpably necessary to the preservation of that life, or that liberty, which every individual undoubtedly has a right, and which it is his duty, to vindicate; because, without vindicating that, he can never have the power to discharging any other duty to himself, or his fellow beings.

By manly exertions then,   and by *manly* I mean *benevolent* and *peaceable*; for fury and devastation, though sometimes those fiends have inhabited the forms of men,—fury and devastation are not the passions of human beings. Humanity is lost, when we appeal to desolating violence. By manly and spirited *remonstrances* then, I would have you seek redress! And your courage, and your fortitude I would have you display—by shewing what you are ready to suffer in the cause of reason and of man—not what you are ready to inflict on the deluded and therefore selfish, antagonist of this cause. This is the sort of energy I wish the human character to display; this is the sort of argument I wish to enforce—the energy of mind, not the energies of the dagger—the logic of assassination.

But think not, Citizens, if you should accomplish the fall of a particular faction, that your work is done.

You may, if you please, like the fox in the fable, drive away the infatiable swarm of gnats that are now molesting you; but, when they are driven away, another swarm, still more hungry, may come upon you, and the devouring system still go on.

You must show that it is *principles*, not *men* you contend for; that you are indifferent to the name of a *Pitt* or a *Fox*;[8] that you scorn alike all party distinctions, and all party prejudices; that you venerate nothing but the virtuous principle of liberty, and are attached to no man any farther than as he may be the organ of this principle—the instrument by which its energies may operate for the public good.

If therefore a change of men should take place, think not that all is done: resign not yourselves to supineness:—remember you must show that your spirits are teeming with the love of liberty; that you are seeking the reformation of those abuses in the Commons House of Parliament—which if you had obtained before, you never could have laboured under your present calamities. And therefore treat with equal indignation *every administration* that does not, by active exertions, shew its zealous attachment to these principles of liberty.—Never lose sight of this grand political truth, that "there is no redress for a nation, situated as we are, but in a fair, full, and free representation of the people in the Commons House of Parliament."

On the EXHAUSTED STATE of our NATIONAL RESOURCES, and the consequent CONDITION *of our* LABOURERS and MANUFACTURERS. From the same.[9]

CITIZENS—If merchants and monied men, in the fury of unfounded alarm, are determined to rush into bankruptcy to preserve their property; they certainly have a right to do so, according to the present organisation of society. Every individual has also a right to show them the precipice upon which they are treading: of the real condition of the mass of the people in the midst of our boasted prosperity, some sketches have been given already; and I shall have frequent opportunities to review the subject.

But, Citizens, what can be so absurd, in speculation, as well as in experience, as to talk of the flourishing state and the happiness of a country that is loaded with such an enormous mill-stone of debt as hangs round the neck of this.

If the subject is not too dry for your attention, let us call to recollection the real state of our revenues and finances. Let us, in the first place, pay a little attention to few facts relative to the *National Debt*, with which we are incumbered by the *Providence*, the *virtue*, and the *enlightened politics* of those ancestors to whose institutions we are called upon to bow down with implicit veneration.

In January 1793, before we engaged in the present *wise* and *necessary* war, by which so great a part of the debt was doubtless intended to be paid, the nation was already involved in a debt of £260,000,000, the interest of which, together with the expenses of collection, may be estimated at near ten millions.

Such, then, was the annual deduction to be made from the gross product of the labour and our industrious peasants and manufacturers, simply to defray the interest of debts contracted without their consent, and from the expenditure of which they never reaped any individual advantage whatever.

I say, from the labours of our peasants and manufacturers; for it should be remembered, Citizens, that the real sources of all revenue, and, indeed, all the enjoyments and necessaries of life, are the labours of those classes of society, whom we treated with so much contempt; but to whom, if we were just, we should acknowledge the greatest of all possible obligations.

It is upon the shoulders then of the industrious poor that the enormous weight of this burden is laid. For it is they who must produce those articles which are given in exchange for the specie which defrays, not only the interest of this debt, but the whole expenses of the government.

Let us consider then, how very considerable a damp must necessarily be produced upon the spirit of industry, upon the ingenious inventions and labours of mankind by this enormous burthen. Let us remember, that the poor labourers and manufacturers have, in the first instance, to produce not only that which is necessary for the support of their own existence and that of their families, not only that which is necessary to produce a large profit to their immediate employers, not only that which is necessary to pay the enormous expenses of the government under which they live, but annually also very nearly ten millions of specie for defraying the interest of those debts which their ancestors contracted, by which they never were benefited, and which have no other influence than to strengthen the hands of their rulers, and to increase the price of provisions, and every individual article by which the accommodations of life can be supplied.

To these are to be added also the burden which is laid upon their shoulders by tythes, by parochial assessments, by rates of innumerable kinds, and which amount to an extent never yet fairly and faithfully calculated. Let us add, then, to this, ten millions of annual interest, seven millions more for the annual ordinary expenses of the country, and thus we shall find (independent of the expenses of the religious establishments, independent of the expenses of the inferior governments of parishes and districts) the enormous sum of seventeen annual millions, even in years of peace, to be produced out of the labours of the lower orders of society—that is to say, a sum almost equal to the whole annual receipts of one million of peasants, mechanics, and manufacturers, taking the average price of labour at seven shillings per week, which, after the accidental, but inevitable deductions, from the sickness, vacation, &c. is as much as it can be rated at. So that if we calculate the really productive inhabitants (that is to say the laborious orders of the community) at one million two hundred thousand effective men (which is a large calculation considering that the whole number capable of bearing arms, of all ranks and denominations whatever, have never been estimated at more than a million and a half) we shall find that nearly one half is necessarily deducted from the price of their labour for this part of the national burthens alone, even when the nation is at peace.—In other words: But for these burthens and incumberances (the price of commodities remaining as they are) every labourer and mechanic might receive twice the wages that he now receives, without deducting in the least from the profit of his employers, or the convenience of the consumers. And if to this we add the great number of unproductive hands now employed in the collection assessment, and regulations of the various and intricate branches of revenue by which this enormous demand is provided for, who would otherwise be employed in productive exertion, it is impossible to calculate the advantages that might have resulted to every class of people, placemen, pensioners, and contractors alone excepted, had this fatal system of funding credit (the consequences of our eternal wars) never been adopted. Nor can we suppose that any thing now produced by the efforts of the nation bears the smallest proportion to what might be produced by a just and liberal spirit of the government that regarded the real welfare of every order of society instead of being engaged in that squabble for places and pensions, the contention for the monopoly of power and the aggravation of revenue which constitutes the whole history of the INS and OUTS, the factions, the cabals, and the contentions of this country.

There are other calculations I know which make the interest of the National Debt amount to near twelve millions, and the expences of government to five million *only*; however it is of small consequence whether the expences of government are seven and the interest of ten millions, or whether the interest of the National Debt is twelve millions and the expences of the government five. If a burden of seventeen millions is heaped upon the annual industry of the people, it is scarcely worth investigation upon which side two or three millions of it are in reality laid. That which it is most important to remember is, that in consequence of this burden every individual in the country has been compelled for many years to undergo double the fatigues he need to have undergone for the same earnings he now enjoys; he might have twice as much comfort at his table; twice as comfortable a cottage to live in; twice as comfortable cloathing; and twice the quanity of enjoyments for himself and his family, that he had even before the commencement of the present war.

But, Citizens, if this was the condition of the country when were were first engaged in this war, what must we think of frenzy, what must we think of the Quixotism of that man, who under such circumstances, plunged into so mad, so extravagant, so ridiculous a crusade as the present? Let us remember how rapidly this debt has always accumulated during the continuance of war: however successful that war might be, however powerful and faithful the allies with whom we were engaged, and however small the power with which we had to contend.

War is always a losing trade. All that the victor can boast is, that he had received a smaller number of honourable scars than the enemy he has vanquished: he perhaps having only lost a leg and an arm while the other had lost both legs and arms together. At any rate the most important members of the nation must be lopped off; and therefore, if there were not some strange delusion among the people propagated by men whose interests were hostile to the general good, not one war could have taken place where fifty have defiled the page of history.

But the present war has not only been particularly disgraceful, it has not only been marked by treachery and by crimes which never before sullied the name of Britain, it has also with respect to pecuniary calculations been extraordinarily fatal, for when was there a period in which two campaigns had plunged any nation into the enormous accumulated debt of seventy millions of money. Yet in the pamphlet lately published by Mr. Walker of Manchester (Review of Political Events, p. 160)[10] it is proved that seventy millions have already been expended in this *just* and *necessary* war.

Add then those seventy millions to the two hundred and sixty which you had before, and you have a debt of three hundred and thirty millions with which you are at this time burdened; and the increase of which, that is to say upwards of twelve millions sterling, is every year to be wrung from the toil of the peasant and manufacturer; to be subtracted from those comforts of life which ought to be the fruits of industry. It is to be collected by drawing from their purses not only all the means of indulgence, but even of information, as to the cause of the oppression: for the poverty of the people would have no charms in the eyes of certain individuals, if they did not believe that the consequence of that poverty would be ignorance; and the consequence of that ignorance implicit subjection to their *wills*.

Therefore it is, that duty upon duty is to be laid upon newspapers and pamphlets; that every bit of paper that can be used through the medium of the press to convey intelligence to the people is to be made an object of excessive taxation, not so much for the purpose of revenue as of preventing the progress of information.[11]

Thus it is that the fine gilt paper upon which lords and ladies write their amorous billets, and their little invitations of compliment, are to be burdened with a less degree of taxation than the clumsy coarse paper which may chance to convey intelligence to the *swinish multitude*.

Now, Citizens, there is another part of this subject which must be stated to you, namely, the increased expence of the operation of government.

It might formerly be disputed by those who were inclined to amuse themselves with those calculations, whether the expences of government were something more than five millions or something less than seven. But this dispute would now be vain and idle indeed. It might be something whether you were paying five millions or seven towards a particular object; but when it is doubled, trebled, and quadrupled, what signifies contesting about trifles? what signifies arguing in what manner the animal has been cut up? whether a little more went to the loin? or a little more to the haunch? the whole animal almost is gone, and it is of little importance to poor John Bull in what particular portions he has been disposed of.

From six or seven millions annually, the expences of government are now extended to twenty millions and a half. Such is the difference between the expence with which men may live in some degree of peace and happiness, and in which they may live disturbed by those hostile passions which are disgraceful to the human character; and whose only fruit is mutual butchery: Man rioting in the blood of man, and nation in the blood of nation, till whole oceans are insufficient to wash the guilt from those who occasioned the fierce contention.

So that an annual deduction is to be made from the fruits of industry of *thirty-two millions and a half* for national burdens; which together with *three millions and a half* of poors rates, and *five millions*, to state it at the lowest, tythes and other parochial assessments, amounts altogether to *forty-one millions*. And, therefore, as the whole amount of the annual wages actually paid to all the labourers and working manufacturers in the nation (estimating them, as I have, at so high a calculation as one million, two hundred thousand men—and averaging their pay, after all incidental deductions, at seven shillings per week), amounts to no more than twenty-one millions, nine hundred thousand pounds, it follows that THE MONEY PAID IN TAXES, is, in reality, near TWICE AS MUCH AS THAT WHICH IS PAID TO ALL THE LABOURING POOR.

Citizens, I do not mean to contend, that a country can subsist without taxation; but the experiment ought to be how little it can do with, not how much it can bear. I do not contend, that you can have government and not support the expence of that government: it is the degree, not the thing I complain of. When I endeavour to shew you the whole magnitude of the evil, it does not therefore follow that I think the whole ought to be swept away. Certainly not. But I mean to draw this inference, that every thing superfluous in that system ought to be retrenched; because in proportion as you retrench these superfluities, you increase the happiness of mankind.

The evil has already spread to a great extent, you ought therefore to be the more careful how you increase it; and not like desperate traders on the eve of bankruptcy, carelessly to rush deeper still into ruin, because you are so deep already. You ought to forbear the cruel, ruinous system of war which has brought you into that debt. You ought to retrench (as if you were faithfully represented you might by the notes of your representatives retrench) the extravagant expences of government (I mean the expences of corruption), not those expences which are necessary for the regular government of the country; for the promotion of internal happiness and protection against hostile invasion.

But chiefly, the men of property ought to be aware how they heap mischief upon mischief, for the supposed preservation of that property. I would I could see them half as careful of that property as the friends of liberty are. I wish I could convince them of the danger of stretching the cord till it breaks: for if it should break, miserable to them must be the consequence. And break it must if it be not relaxed. If the government thus go on, adding war to war, campaign to campaign, million upon million, and seventy million upon seventy million, they must in time exhaust the resources of the country to such a degree that the country can no longer bear the weight of the interest even. And when this is the case, what is to become of the capital? For remember your capital is but moonshine: a bubble! You have the name of it. You have the entries on the books: but shew me the bullion that can realize it!

Bank notes and Exchequer bills may supply the place of currency, while the credit of the nation is supported:—that is to say, while the people are able and willing to pay the interest: but when the bubble bursts, you may tie them on strings to make tails for kites; for their value will be only their weight in paper. If the bubble should burst, and burst, I repeat it, it must, if the blast of war continues thus to swell it beyond all proportion; woe unto the rulers who have been the causes of its bursting. The frenzy of those who are ruined by the explosion will fall, I fear, with a heavy hand.—They will forget what willing tools they have been to their own destruction; and consider themselves as inhumanly betrayed. Yet this war, at least, so big with destruction, is, in reality, all their own:—the war of the monied alarmists: of the meeting at Merchant Taylor's Hall.[12]

Infatuated monopolists? whither are you running?—hastening to inevitable ruin over the trampled rights of your fellow men! If you would preserve your property (the real king of your thoughts! the only God of your adoration!) urge not your country down the precipice of bankruptcy by which your own property must be destroyed. If you love your own security, consider how that security may be preserved. If national credit is no more, as the word indicates, than the bubble of confidence, remember that the bubble must burst when inflated beyond its bounds. Half—two thirds of the produce of human labour may be seized by the hand of power, to pay the interest which supports this bubble of annihilated capital; nay perhaps the people may be so sluggish that three fourths may be taken with impunity. But another such campaign or two as the last; another such budget or two as the present, and three fourths will no longer do. But beware how you go beyond. Should the people once demur to the claims of the tax-gatherer, the richest stockholder is from that day a beggar.

Those, then, are the enemies of property who continue this mad and ruinous war; not they who cry aloud for peace. Those are the enemies of law and order, who heap burthen upon burthen without remorse; not those who say to you "alleviate the sufferings of your fellow citizens; enable them to be happy, or they will not be contented: it is not in the nature of man. Enable them to receive an honest competency for their labours; let your policy and your institutions contribute to their happy subsistence; and you will retain your situation in tranquillity."

These are not the doctrines of anarchy. The real promoters of commotion and anarchy are those who would silence complaint by chastisement; who would check the progress of reason by barbarous coercion; who would make truth sedition and argument high treason. These are the enemies of order; because these are driving their fellow beings to desperation: And who shall answer for the conduct of man when desperation has taken possession of his mind.

The DUTY and INTEREST of the PEOPLE to enquire into the Causes and Conduct of WARS, in the GUILT of which they are involved, by contributing to their Support. —From the second Lecture on War. [13]

IN my former Lecture on this subject I seriously recommended you to consider no individual as infallible, to look up with veneration to no man's opinions; to estimate all opinions and all sentiments in proportion to the conviction they bring to your own minds, and not the partial attachments you may have for the persons who submit them to you. I endeavoured to shew you that all instruction, all reading, all eloquence are no further useful than as they cultivate the seeds of enquiry in the minds of those who listen or peruse; and as they furnish them with materials wherewith to work for themselves in those grand enquiries in which it is the happiness and interest of man to be engaged. I advised you seriously to consider for yourselves how far this system of war is good or bad in itself; how far the pretences for it have been realized; and, if realized, how far they were worth the price that was paid for them.

I shall now endeavour to shew you, that it is equally your duty and your interest; and that a considerable degree of moral turpitude attaches to that individual who, by his personal services, or by his property, contributes to the prosecution of any war, the justice of whose principle he has not investigated; of the probability of whose success he has not formed some estimate; and whose objects he has not properly weighed.

Citizens, let us consider that the morals, the happiness, and the prosperity of every individual are involved in every war in which the country may be engaged: let us consider that we all have every thing at stake; that not only the comforts of life, not only that liberty and independence which we so much prize, but the very existence of every individual may be involved in the event. However securely we may sit at home; however carelessly we may read the Gazettes which announce the slaughter of thousands; let us recollect, that in the giddy changes of the wheel of fortune, the war which is now at a distance may come home to us; slaughter and devastation may confront us at our own doors; and those who have so madly and so franticly engaged to carry desolation through the streets of Paris, may fly through the streets of London before the face of those very Parisians, whose habitations they so madly threatened with conflagration, and whose sires and relatives with slaughter.

If, then, the lives and happiness of every individual are at stake, surely all ought to give themselves some pains to calculate the chances of cards, and endeavour to discover the rules of the desperate game they are playing.

"War", says Citizen Gerrald in his excellent pamphet, [a Convention the only means of saving us from ruin] "though declared by the government must be supported by the people. Parliament imposes taxes but you pay them. The King declares war, but it is the blood of the peasant and manufacturer which flows in the battle, it is the purse of the tradesman and the artificer which is emptied in the contest."[14] Let us recollect also, that not only in the catastrophe but in the guilt we are participators. Whatever turpitude may attach itself to the war in general, so far as it depends upon our exertions or our sluggishness, lays at our doors.

Comparison between the Guilt of a COMMON MURDERER, and the DELIBERATE PROJECTOR OF UNNECESSARY WAR. From the same.

AS war can only be just in one of the parties, it follows, of course, that in the other it must be murder! Nay, I believe that in nine wars out of ten it has not been just either on the one side nor on the other. If, however, it appears in any particular contest that the individuals who compose one government, have made use of every exertion to produce negociation, instead of slaughter; if they have sent ambassador after ambassador to treat with the cabinet of the threatening country, and that country, with insolent disdain, with scorn, with contempt, with ill-founded confidence, and a degree of arrogance which nothing but ignorance could produce, has rejected all those overtures of peace and negociation, I am terribly afraid we shall be compelled, in spite of national vanity, in spite of national prejudice, to justify the party that would have negociated, even though that party should be contending against ourselves.

I have said, Citizens, that war, on one side or the other, must be murder—but the epithet is feeble. There is no term in language that can describe the crime with justice and energy.—Murder which stands so prominent in the catalogue of moral vices, bears but a trifling proportion to the political guilt of those who plunge two nations, nay, not content with that, who plunge almost the whole habitable globe in scenes of slaughter and desolation, to gratify their caprice or exalt their ambition.

Perhaps the murderer, whom we so justly execrate, might find many circumstances to plead in alleviation of his guilt, which it would be difficult to apply to the other. Want, misery, the persecuting insolence of monopolizing power, the hard griping hand of famine may drive a miserable individual to acts of depredation, which afterwards, from a mistaken sense of personal security, or in the moment of unexpected contest may provoke him to plunge into guilt he never meditated. Hasty revenge, intemperate rage, the boiling passion of the moment may have inflicted the fatal blow. But the political murderer proceeds by system. He plans, he deliberates, he meditates, in the calm recesses of the closet, those scenes of fury and desolation which his hired assassins are to perpetrate, as soon as his cold blooded ambition shall have formed by mathematical lines and calculations the plans upon which they are to act. He, also, strikes, not at the life of an individual. He strikes at thousands. He murders by wholesale;

and exults over the catalogue of his atrocities. He kills in safety also—shuns the danger; but perpetrates the guilt. He breathes the pestilential mandate, and myriads perish; but, bathed in the true thieve's vinegar of office, he strips the dead without partaking the infection.

How much more atrocious this than the crimes which excite so much indignation in our hearts! and which, because they are rare, because they come before us in individual instances, and present the real picture to the mind, we contemplate with indignation; while we remain indifferent to the other.

Citizens, then let us consider how important it is (since every individual is, some how or other, concerned in what are called the acts of the nation) that every individual should seriously investigate the justice or the injustice of the wars in which he may be plunged: because, though the principle of self preservation may justify the individual who draws his sword on the defensive side, the soldiers who march into the field in support of an unjust cause, are only the hired assassins (however unconscious they may be of the guilt) of the persons who planned the war.

NO WAR JUST *but a War of* SELF DEFENCE.
From the Same.

CITIZENS, A war of absolute defence is the only war that can be justified: What criminality then must attach to those who are engaged in a war of directly opposite nature. "If the life of one man is not to be taken away but on a principle of self defence, or on the previous conviction of his guilt by a calm and sober appeal to reason, how much more does it become us scrupulously to weigh in the balance of the sanctuary the causes for which we embark in a complicated war, in which the kindred blood of thousands of our fellow creatures is poured out like water by the unfeeling arm of a mercenary soldier."—*Gerrald.*[15]

Citizens—I do not mean to confine my animadversions to the war in which we are at present engaged. Principles and not men should be the objects of attention—the general system, not the individual instance, matters little that you should put a period to the present war, if you are not convinced of the madness and turpitude of war in general, and determined to diffuse those benevolent and generous principles of peace and amity which may prevent fresh calamities of this description, from falling again immediately upon your heads.

No war can be just that is not politic, and by politic I mean promotive of the happiness of the people; for how can that be good which does not secure the general happiness of mankind. No war can be politic but that which is engaged in for the real and actual defence of the Parent State; because, though it is good and right to exert all the energies with which we are endued, for the preservation of the individual, or the community, all wars for frivolous pretences (and I call all the ambitious schemes of courts and cabinets frivolous) however successful or triumphant, must cost more than they are worth; and the sole glory and triumph that you obtain is to see so many mutilated beings stalking through your streets, or filling up your hospitals, and reminding you of the thousands and tens of thousands of your fellow men, who have been slain in battle, but who might have been increasing the prosperity and real wealth of the state, if they had been employed in producing the comforts of life, instead of destroying each other in a ridiculous contest.

Consequences of our NATIONAL GLORY and PROSPERITY, to the great body of the PEOPLE. —From the same.

LET us look at the mass of mankind. Do we not find them still doomed to eternal drudgery! Still plunged in ignorance and servitude? Is not their bitter lot (even when they can obtain subsistence at this rate) to go from the hard pallet to their different occupations, from their occupations to the scanty meal, from the scanty meal to labour, and from labour again to repose? as if the bulk of the human species, existed for nothing, were fit for nothing, were capable of nothing but to drudge eternally for the luxuries of a few, to eat, to drink, to propagate, and rot.

However, Citizens, these advantages, even if they could be proved, which are supposed to result from conquest and victory, are advantages of which this country has for some time almost entirely lost sight. It is true, at the commencement of the present war, his Royal Highness took Valenciennes[16] in the name of the Emperor of Germany;[17] and he ran away from

Dunkirk[18] in the name of his Royal Father. Let the widows and orphans of those who were slaughtered in these glorious exploits, tell me, if they can, which of them was the most advantageous to the country? which of them afforded the largest proportion of comfort to themselves, or alleviated best the wants and anguish of their expiring relatives?

Extreme difference between the INTERESTS OF MINISTERS, and the INTERESTS OF THE PEOPLE, with respect to Peace and War. From the same.

Patronage.

BUT we must admit, whatever may be the effect to the people at large, as our governors are men of discernment, men of considerable learning and intelligence, that they are playing a game not quite so losing, that they at least know what they are about. The fact is, they may have an interest while we have not. "The great source of the evil is here, the people of Europe in general, have no more connection with their respective governments, except indeed as they are made the objects of plunder and taxation, than they have with the governments of China and Japan." It may then be good for them to pursue a system which is destructive to us. "All war, as it multiplies places, and increases the receipts of government, at least while the war endures, extends of course the power and patronage of the minister though it loads the people with additional taxes." [Ger.] "As long as war lasts", continues Citizen Gerrald, "government has immense sums to dispose of; and as revenue has hitherto been the object of governments, the hope of making conquests will induce them to carry on the system of war as long as the people will submit to it. Every addition of territory furnishes a new field for the collection of more taxes, every conquered district is considered a new farm; and the people who cultivate it being regarded as sheep, are annually brought up to be shorn of their fleeces."[19]

Thus every minister, while affairs are situated as they are, has an interest in plunging the country into war; because in consequence of that war a great variety of fresh places are created, and great patronage thrown into his hands, he has the power of appointing Contractors, Colonels, Ensigns,

and Officers of various descriptions, which increases his power and patronage, secures him in his situation, and gratifies his avarice or his ambition. These facts need but to be mentioned, and every one will feel conviction immediately.

Ministerial Prerogative.

THERE is another circumstance of considerable importance why the interests of the people and of ministers should be considered, in a very eminent degree, diametrically opposite to each other with respect to war.
Those persons who are at the helm during a time of war, have a pretence
for vesting themselves with discretionary powers; for increasing their own
arbitrary authority; for trampling down the liberties of the people; and putting them under restrictions which, in times of peace, there could be no
pretence for doing; and, consequently, we find one of the blessed harvests
of the present war (to say nothing of the discretionary powers vested, by
the bill for manning the navy and other late acts of Parliament, in the
Privy Council)[20] is the happy suspension of the Jacobinical Habeas Corpus
Act.[21]

It is an argument to which every driveller can appeal: "The country is in
a state of external *threat*;[22] you must, therefore, take care of turbulent
spirits within"; by which phrase (turbulent spirits) is always meant every
man who dares to speak against the mad and foolish projects of ministers.
The fences of authority are, therefore, doubled: the personal protection of
the individual members of the state suspended and annihilated.

Where is the man who will pretend that, in times of peace, such acts
could have been quietly thrust down the people's throats as the *Alien Act*,[23]
the *Bill*, so nobly disputed in the House of Commons, by those persons
who, according to the calculation of some, are enemies to the Laws and
Constitution of the country, because they dared to shew that the ministers
were violating that Constitution. To these [we][24] may add the *suspension of
the Habeas Corpus Act*, after the persons were taken into custody whom
that suspension was meant to affect; thus making the laws a sort of trap, to
ensnare us with an appearance of security; and when the harpies of power
have drawn the victims into their toils, the laws are suspended; down goes
the trap; and Britons, when most in need of British privileges, find they are

Britons no more. No, Citizens: in times of peace, in times of national tranquillity such strides cannot be made: and it is a fact standing upon the records of all the histories of Europe—it is a fact proved by thousands of instances, that war after war has been produced, nation after nation, has been plunged into ruin and desolation, and whole continents have been embroiled, for no other purpose whatever than to given an opportunity to the ministers and cabinets of those countries to extend their own arbitrary power, and lay prostrate, at their feet, the lives and liberties of their fellow-citizens.

It is then not from ministry that we are to expect a proper exposition of the system of war; it is not from Court expectants in opposition, who, however distinguished they may be by their talents or boasted principles of liberty, still have their eyes fixed on a succession to places of soul-corrupting power and aggrandisement. I say it is not from one or other of these classes of politicians that you ought to expect a *thorough* investigation of that system of war which for more than a century has continued to depopulate Europe. No: Every individual knows how powerfully self-love and interest operate upon the judgment. Like a thick film before the eye it obscures the lines and confuses the colours of the political landscape. Views of personal interest pervert the judgment and prevent us from seeing those evils from which at one time or other we may expect advantage. It is, therefore, from the virtuous energies of the public mind, from the bold and manly spirit of general investigation, from the spirit and good sense of the people that we are to expect a thorough exposition of the horrors of war.

Oh, what but ambition, what but the wild passions of interested individuals could so long have kept up that system of delusion which has depopulated the ancient, and continues to depopulate the modern world? Is it not strange, does not imagination sicken, does not reason stagger when we conjure up the picture fairly and justly before us? What can be the reason that so many thousands of human beings rush into the field of battle with no provocation of malice; no one real interest to direct them? How astonishing is it that age after age, generation after generation, country after country should have beheld this phenomenon of man destroying man— intellectual beings rushing forward frequently to inevitable destruction; with a mad and fierce enthusiasm, courting the stroke of death, as it were a blessing!

Citizens—The picture is too astonishing to have been believed, if we had nothing but records of history to attest it.

Lecture—On the MORAL and POLITICAL Influence of the Prospective Principle of Virtue.[25]

CITIZENS, neither the forms of the world, nor my own feelings permitted me to address you on the last Friday evening; and I would, if I could have devised any effectual means, have prevented on that evening any assembly in this place. But as I found that impracticable, or rather, as my mind was not in a state to seek for expedients, I thought the best way to prevent any disturbance, which might have arisen from a multitude of persons assembling, who could not gain admittance, was to get a friend to take this situation for me. I did accordingly procure a Citizen of whose understanding and excellent principles I have the highest opinion, and who, I am sure, is well qualified to utter those truths to which it is worth the while of any individual to listen.

Citizens, the subject of this evening's lectures is "The Prospective Principle of Virtue"; or, in other words, "That all Virtues consist in so directing our exertions, and regulating our passions that we may be constantly promoting the future good of mankind."[26] This is a principle, Citizens, in itself, so consistent with reason that it, almost at the very first blush, presents itself to us as unanswerable and self-evident. And yet, Citizens, when we come seriously to investigate this principle, when we come to follow it through all the mazes of practice, into which it will lead us, perhaps there are few of us who have not some prejudices, some habits of mind which will be shocked, some dispositions and principles long imbibed which will be found to be very deeply and materially wounded by this principle.

It is our duty, however, in the first instance, seriously and maturely to deliberate upon the principles of human action; and when we have brought them to the test of reason and argument, and are thoroughly convinced of their truth and authenticity, we must not be terrified at any particular conclusions that may result. Particular conclusions are only the branches of the tree; frequently only the leaves at the extremities of those branches. If the root, therefore, is good, for principles are the root—the stamina of moral excellence! we must not take it into our heads, that we are at liberty to root them up—to fell them to the earth, because there are particular conclusions resulting from them, which are hostile to our passions, or inconsistent with our habitual mode of thinking. I am, however, aware that liberal as the auditory I have so frequently the honour of meeting here has generally been, notwithstanding their habits of free enquiry, that, yet, I may, perhaps, in the progress of this investigation, advance some doctrines, so new and unexpected that their minds may, in the first instance, revolt from them. Let it be remembered, however, Citizens, that novelty is of itself no proof of falsehood, that the opinions of six moments and of six thousand years, if such an opinion should be found, stands precisely upon the same basis, the basis of reason and argument; and, therefore, must be brought to the same test of experimental investigation, or else must be permitted to fall at once, and be abandoned as unworthy our adoption.

Citizens, though I shall speak my opinions with that firmness which results from the conviction of my own mind, yet I warn you again—I have warned you frequently, but I cannot too often, that I do not deliver opinions from this place, for you to adopt them without examination. I advance them for your serious investigation, and I warn you again and again, to beware of that prejudice which, from having formed attachments to individuals, leads us to take for granted all they say. I most seriously recommend you to be as averse to a Pope in Beaufort Buildings[27] as to a Pope at Rome.

Citizens, giving you this warning, I shall proceed without remorse or fear to cut up wide and deep rooted prejudices, with all the power and energy I am master of. Those things which appear to be prejudices to me, may perhaps upon better examination appear to others well founded truths. My opinions (though the results, I believe, of very *dispassionate*, and I am sure of very *anxious* enquiry) may, also, upon more mature deliberation, appear even to myself to have been taken up too hastily, and I shall never be ashamed publicly to change my opinions as often as I am convinced they are wrong. We live to improve, if we are wise; and if we are virtuous, we live not only to improve ourselves but to improve our fellow beings, by encouraging free and liberal enquiry, and submitting, with candour and sincerity, to their investigation, the sentiments which we believe important to their felicity and virtue: and if we treat with detestation the wretch who hoards his gilded counters in a box; with how much more contempt ought we to look upon that individual who locks up in secrecy the more invaluable treasures of the human mind, the discoveries (be they small or be they great) which he has either made, or supposes he has made in the progress of his enquiries. The widow's mite, we are told, was an acceptable offering; the mite of science is an acceptable offering also; and be it remembered that with knowledge, as with coin, we must divide it into small parts before we can diffuse it through the general circle of society, and fit it for the accommodations and uses of life.

If, Citizens, virtue consists in promoting the happiness of mankind—if virtue, in reality, means neither more nor less than intentionally doing that which is best for general happiness and welfare, it results, I conceive, as an inevitable consequence, that all virtue must be of an *active*, not of a *passive* nature; and, therefore, that it is the duty of every individual to keep his eye steadily fixed upon that which is before him, and to lose none of the powers and energies of intellect in unavailing glances upon what is past, and never can return. Citizens, this argument will lead us to many conclusions hostile to the general sentiments of mankind. Superstition, with her hood and cowl, presents herself before us at every step, with her doctrines of repentance, contrition, retaliation, and retributive justice, and points us back again to the dark and gloomy paths of error, which we, and which others may have passed; and bids us, in sackcloth and ashes, consume our faculties in unavailing lamentations, which can never undo the acts that are past, but which have but too powerful an influence to unfit us for what is to come. We shall find, also, that many of the institutions and habits of society are equally unfriendly to a steady and consistent perseverance in this prospective principle: and hence the general disposition of mankind to brood over the past; to hatch in sullen silence the gloomy passions of despondency and revenge;—hence also the sullen traits of misanthropy which deform the human character and reduce it almost to the brute. Nay, strange to say, the wisdom of ages has conspired to assist this malignant retrospective principle; and the administration of civil justice almost every where recals to our minds the evils which, because they are irremediable ought to be forgotten, and plunges us, thereby, but too frequently, in others that might have been avoided. You have been told, it is true, in this country, that punishments (such is the cant and theory of law!) are inflicted, not because particular acts of criminality have been done, but because they should not be repeated. But look at the general practice of mankind, mark the arguments with which they maintain their systems, and then tell me whether another principle, the sullen principle of revenge, is not the legitimate offspring of the system; and frequently, and evidently, the prompting motive even with the legislature itself.

Citizens, the retrospective system, the system of brooding over the past, instead of looking forward to the future, has also another tendency of a most fatal description. It frequently sinks the first and greatest characters into despondency and lethargy. We have found, by a gloomy interference of superstition, man unnerved of the energies of his nature; we have seen characters whose powers of mind might have darted like lightning from one extremity of the universe to another sunk by this enfeebling principle into sullen misanthropic monks, and devoting their lives to melancholy sighs and unavailing regrets for the errors (superstitious or real) into which in the vigour of intemperate youth they had been betrayed: and monarchs, and great commanders have shut themselves in their closets to beat their breasts, and rend their souls in repentance for past transgressions, while the cruel, but less infatuated invader, routed their armies and desolated their country.

Citizens, whatever may have been our errors, let us recollect, that there is a nobler path for man to tread. Whatever wrongs he may have committed, whatever errors he may have fallen into, while energy remains, there may be reparation to society. Virtue and beneficence are still attainable; and the same energies which, under the delusions of error, made him criminal, guided by the light of truth, might produce such qualities and such effects as would make full compensation to the world.

Charles VI,[28] after desolating whole nations, and plunging into all the crimes which conquerors (and none but conquerors, and would be conquerors) can perpetrate, retired within the walls of a monastry to whitewash his soul with prayers and repentance, and brood over the remembrance of his inhuman guilt. But if, instead of this he had exercised those powers and faculties of mind which he possessed, and used in a proper manner the advantages of his elevated situation, he might have rendered the latter period of his life as beneficial to the cause of truth and virtue as the former part had been inimical to the happiness of the human race.

Citizens, I do not mean to condemn that retrospective glance which surveys the vices and errors of the past, with a view to enable us to avoid them for the future; or which contemplates the virtues of former times, to increase the useful energies of mind. Certainly not. If the page of history ought to be explored, it is still more important that the history of our own private conduct should be searched with critical severity. But for what purpose? That we may afterwards lose our time in repentance—that we may exclude ourselves from the society of those fellow beings who have a just claim upon our exertions in the promotion of the general happiness? No: These are not the objects we are to have in view; and if we are to study with real views of wisdom and benevolence, the history of the human mind, we shall find that every moment of our existence has its duties, that every power and energy has its correspondent obligations, and that, therefore, not one moment, not one thought can virtuously be cast away in any other employment but that of seeking to promote the present and future happiness of mankind, with whose happiness our own is incorporated; and without the promotion of which no generous mind can itself receive the smallest particle of consolation.

But, Citizens, the contrary conduct so frequently preached and enforced by all the artifices which could be invented, has its charms for a particular class of people; and we cannot be surprized that there have been men who found it their interest to encourage the desponding, listless, melancholy misanthropy of the retrospective principle.

Yes, Citizens, there is a particular class of jugglers in the world, to whom truth is by no means acceptable; who cannot digest—(though, in some respects, they seem to have the digestion of an ostrich, and no stone is too big, no iron bar too hard or too rusty for their stomachs); notwithstanding this, they are not capable of digesting so plain, simple, wholesome, and alimentary a maxim as that "the only thing a man can do in this world that entitles him to respect and veneration, is prompting the happiness and welfare of his fellow citizens."—*Fellow Citizens of the world*, I mean! Not Citizens of a town or district.

These men, therefore, finding it their interest to support a different sentiment, have chosen to oppose a system so beneficial to the human race, and teach those who have the misfortune to fall under their tuition, that melancholy and repentance, are the proper feelings with which the lamp of life should be consumed; because they know very well, that such dispositions unnerving the energies of the human mind, filling the soul with images of terror and apprehension, though the most unfriendly to human happiness and virtue, are very well calculated to make the poor slave of their ridiculous artifices, obedient to their exactions, and subservient to their ambition. If they can make terror, in this manner, the *order of the day*, they know very well that, in consequence of the bugbears which the melancholy imagination is too apt to realize, they can make the poor victims come to them with their laps full of those good things, which might, according to my opinion, be better distributed among the industrious orders of the community. But they, right wisely, no doubt, think otherwise. Their inspiration teaches them—and who shall contend with the inspirations of the spirit, that these good things are more fit for the luxurious accommodation of their tables than to be thrown to a poor, despicable, grunting, swinish multitude, who, as they have no fleece to be shorn certainly cannot expect to be considered as part of their flock!

Thus, then, Citizens, this retrospective system which has such a tendency to unnerve the character of man, to annihilate those active virtues by which only the human race can be benefited, and to reduce him to the sole dominion of melancholy, terror, and dejection, are principles which we must expect will continue to be propagated so long as one class of mankind are paid for deluding the rest.

Is it not evident then, Citizens, that the only energy of character likely to be produced by this retrospective principle, is the feeling of revenge: a passion, indeed, active enough in its operation, and productive of many and many a tale over which the eye will pour with anxious avidity, but which no friend to human happiness will wish to see encouraged.

This has hitherto been the common principle of action between nation and nation. Hence is the page of history deformed with continued tales of slaughter and devastation. Hence imaginary insults, which the flag, or the *flag-staff* of one country (for I see no difference between the gaudy rags and toys of national vanity and the sticks that carry them), may receive from the flag or flag-staff of another. Hence the slightest injury offered to Courts and Princes, has plunged the world in scenes of horror and desolation. Hence it stands recorded on the page of history, that the favourite of one great man bidding against the favourite of another great man for a ring, at a common auction, plunged the Roman empire, that is to say, almost the whole of the then known world into a destructive civil war, which ended in the tyrannous usurpation of Augustus Caesar, and the total overthrow of the profligate Mark Anthony.[29]

Citizens, whether this last anecdote is accurately true or not, is not worth our investigation. We have witnessed of late, a quarrel almost as ridiculous. We have seen two great nations on the eve of being plunged into a chaos of mutual slaughter and desolation for a few cat skins.[30] It is very true, the agitation of this question might have been encouraged by a bird's eye prospect of a better ground of quarrel; and the two nations that pretended to be about to *clapper-de-claw*[31] one another about the insult offered to these said cat-skins, might, perhaps, have had their eyes upon a sweeter piece of vengeance; and while they were pretending to quarrel, were, perhaps agreeing to divide the robe of which they thought to strip the insolent, Jacobinical nation of France, which had dared to provoke the just revenge of all *regular governments*, by talking of rights and liberties.

Not only between nation and nation, has this spirit of revenge, the first fruit of the system of retrospective *virtue*, as it is called, been plunged in war and desolation; but party has whetted the dagger against party, and faction uplifted the axe against the head of faction from the same detestable cause. Thus we find in almost all the histories of the universe, that one party seldom prevails over another, but the scaffold streams with the blood of the vanquished, and scenes of horror present themselves on every hand, from the contention of principles and struggles of intellect, which might have been productive, but for these revengeful principles, of the greatest portion of happiness and instruction to mankind.

See, Citizens, from this principle of revenge what dreadful consequences have taken place in France! The most noble, the most virtuous, the most magnificent principles that ever were broached by man, have produced effects which tyranny itself can hardly surpass. We have seen from the seeds of freedom, a harvest of desolation. We have seen party struggling with party, stimulated at first, perhaps, by the private feelings of ambition, or the more destructive, though at the same time, in some degree, more excuseable principle of universal suspicion, but embittered by opposition, rising to a horrid enthusiasm of revenge which the soul of benevolence trembles to contemplate. The profligacy of manners and the inflexible rage of vengeance, which the cruelty of the Court and the superstition of the Church had conspired to engender in that country, bursting forth in the ferment of the revolution, laid for awhile in the dust the bleeding limbs of that freedom which the revolution was effected to promote: though, happily for mankind, physicians have been found to stanch the wounds and restore her again to the universe.

Citizens, I had hopes that the excesses and cruelties of the system of revenge in that country were entirely at an end. I did believe that the benign principles of benevolence and liberty had completely triumphed; that the scaffolds were to stream with the victims of vengeance no more; but that peace and universal philanthropy were to twine their myrtles together with that laurel which triumphant energy has reaped in the fields of victory; but alas! I cannot read without regret one part of the present transaction in that country. Perhaps while I am speaking, four individuals who, whatever may be their vices, certainly shine conspicuous in the ranks of intellectual energy, have fallen by the guillotine of vengeance, victims to the party that now prevails in France.[32]

Citizens, this is not the howl of apostacy, this is not the lamentation of a man who wishes for a pretence to desert his principles. I adore—I care not what danger there may be in the declaration! I will not exist longer than I can speak the truths that I believe to be useful to my fellow Citizens!—I will proclaim my principles, because I am sure if mankind would but act candidly and fairly, and avow the genuine feelings of their hearts, that system of terror and tyranny which has so long subjugated the nations of Europe, must fade and shrink away without a struggle—without an individual victim.—I glory in the *principles of the French Revolution!* I exult in the *triumphs of reason!* I am an advocate for the *rights of man!* nor will I desert my principles, without a better reason than the example that other men have acted inconsistently with theirs. But daggers and guillotines are not principles. The disordered imagination of a Burke,[33] the metaphysical phrenzy of a Windham,[34] or the artful and studied harangues of that great arithmetician Pitt, may confound things together as opposite as darkness to light, or as their darling measures to the interests of humanity and justice; but we will not be so deceived. Daggers and guillotines are not principles; massacres and executions are not arguments; the principles of truth still continue to be true, though those men who have them most frequently on their lips, should happen, in some instances, to have them least frequently in their hearts. It is not the men of France, that I glory in; it is not the execution of the King—I am an enemy to all executions! it is not the fall of the Bastille,[35] for a Bastille, a Luxembourg,[36] or a Newgate[37] are to me indifferent; it is not for names, it is for principles that I am anxious—it is to principles, not to unprincipled actions, that I am wedded; and the wanton and revengeful cruelties of Robespierre[38] and his party can no more prove the principles of the French revolution to be wrong, than the sanguinary attempts of a faction in this country, who, with all their vices without any of their virtues, should attempt to establish the same system of terror without the energy to support it, would prove that the new fangled inquisitorial system of spies and informers, which has supplanted the constitution of Britain, is right.

That which I glory in, in the revolution of France is this, That it has been upheld and propagated as a principle of that revolution, that ancient abuses are not, by their antiquity, converted into virtues; that it has been affirmed and established that man has rights which no statutes or usages can take away; that intellectual beings are entitled to the use of their intellects; that the object of society is the promotion of that happiness of mankind; that thought ought to be free, and that the propagation of thought is the duty of every individual; that one order of society has no right, how many years soever they have been guilty of the pillage, to plunder and oppress the other parts of the community, whose persons are entitled to equal respect, and whose exertions have been much more beneficial to mankind.

These are the principles that I admire, and that cause me, notwithstanding all its excesses, to exult in the French Revolution. But I do not believe that violence and cruelty, I do not believe that scenes of carnage and execution, can either be the promoters, or the consequences of principles like these. No: the excesses and violences in France have not been the consequences of the new doctrines of the Revolution; but of the old leaven of revenge, corruption and suspicion which was generated by the systematic cruelties of the old despotism.

Citizens, I am still the unaltered friend of liberty. But if liberty has not a tendency to promote the feelings of benevolence, to promote the happiness of mankind, and to make us better members of society, and more happy in our individual capacity, take your liberty, for I will have none of it.

I am convinced, however, that liberty has all these tendencies. I am convinced also, notwithstanding the excesses which have taken place in France, that the struggle in that country will be eventually beneficial, not only to that country but to the human race. I believe it was good that such a despotism as existed in France should not perpetuate itself from generation to generation; and all that I lament is that a few turbulent and ambitious spirits should have stained with their excesses the annals of the most glorious era in the history of man. Let us, however, be just to this great nation. They have received obloquy and abuse enough; they have received threats and injuries enough; let us not dwell only on the gloomy side of the picture; let us not be fond of recapitulating their vices and their errors only; let us speak, also, of those more amiable traits of character, which they have discovered; and which, even at this time, are gaining so considerable an ascendancy. Let us not forget the magnanimity with which they spurned, in some very striking instances, this gloomy retrospective principle of revenge which I am so anxious to see exterminated from the human character. See how they treated their prostrate enemies; let us remember that they present the first picture ever exhibited in the world of a conquering army imparting freedom and felicity to the people over whom they had triumphed. Think of Holland—exalted by being vanquished![39] Think of the generosity with which they spurned the idea of insulting the weakness of the little prostrate state of Tuscany.[40] Think of the generous maxims which, in the midst of all the exultation of unparalleled victory, they have laid down as principles with respect to hostile and half vanquished nations. Let us remember also that in their present conduct with respect to interior policy there are strong symptoms of the final overthrow of the system of terror and revenge. They have, it is true, and I am sorry they have hung over the heads of Barrere, of Billaud Varennes, Collot d'Herbois,[41] and

Vadiere,[42] the sword of the law.—O! that I could once see law and justice without a sword; with scales in one hand and the olive of peace in the other;—the weapon of destruction buried deep in the bowels of the earth! I do not mean to vindicate the conduct of these individuals. I am convinced, that if it had not been for the tyranny of Robespierre and the assistance lent to that tyranny by these men, the cause of liberty throughout Europe would have been in a very different situation at this moment. I am sure, that if the practice of France had been as good as the theory of France, the irresistible light of reason, the torrent of benevolent humanity that would have swelled the hearts of Englishmen—of all mankind, would have left us, by this time, no abuses to redress. For it is not forms, it is not particular fabrics, that are worth contending for.—You may be happy in a cottage, you may be happy in a palace; you may be happy in a Corinthian dome, you may be happy though your mansion should be ornamented only with the simple, republican, doric pillar; nay, you may be happy though you should happen to reside under a venerable pile of Gothic architecture, provided you have but good security that the disjointed stones are not ready to fall about your ears.

It is not, then, the external structure of government that I find fault with—I may like the simple doric best perhaps—but we will not quarrel about the external shell. It is the furniture, the accommodations, the security, and convenience that I am anxious about—It is in short the principle that actuates the government, and if this is sufficiently pure to secure the happiness of the people, perish the wretch who would breed contention for forms. Shew me the principles of peace, benevolence, and universal affection, of equal rights and equal laws, I will hail and venerate that country as my own, and rejoice in the establishment of such principles, whatever may be the exterior incumbrances, with which accident, or choice, may happen to have surrounded it.

Cititzens, I cannot quit this subject without wishing that the party now triumphant in France, and every party who, in the political struggles that convulse the universe, may happen to triumph, could feel how ungenerous it is first to draw the sting and then to bruise the head of the serpent.—O! for a great lesson to the world, that they would argue thus—"This animal has a glossy many coloured skin, whose beauties, if we had never felt its venom, would have delighted our imaginations. Well—why should we not forget?—We have drawn away the sting;—the venomed tooth is gone; it can bite no more. Why should we still retain our horror? and remembering the evil that is past prevent the good that yet might come? Revenge!—

where is the benefit of thy backward glance? Magnanimity!—how great are the advantages of thy prospective virtues!" Could they but apply this to the various energies of genius, that adorn the minds of these men, and of Barrere in particular, "We have felt your tyranny, they might say, we know that you have brought an odium on our good and holy cause in the eyes of Europe; but France is enlightened, and you can repeat your crimes no more. Go: we have drawn out your sting: we know there are graces and energies of genius in you which can be useful and beneficial to mankind. Having disarmed you of your power to wrong us go where you will. You can no longer be Citizens of France, because the sight of you might awaken indignation, and be assistant to the revival of that system of terror of which you were once the supporters and might be too soon the victims. But go where you will: the Republic of France has too much magnanimity to punish a prostrate enemy. It has magnanimously forgiven Holland; it has magnanimously forgiven the injuries assisted by the weak arm of Tuscany. It has still the same warm benevolence for its children. Go. It has drawn a veil over the rebellions of La Vendee;[43] and it will forget, in its Old Committee of Public Safety,[44] every thing but its victories, and its energy. Employ, for the future, those talents to the benefit of society which have too often been applied to the destruction of the human race."

O! could I see this benevolent and magnanimous feeling thus triumphant, I should be sure that the sun of liberty had risen indeed, and I should know that my own cottage sooner or later must be illuminated by its cheering light. The clouds of prejudice would then disperse, the fears, the terrors of mankind would vanish before the strong ray of truth and reason, and the night of ignorance would no longer be invoked to shelter the errors of ambition and the interested projects of a few individuals, who call themselves the nation though they are the nation's scourge.

Citizens, the retrospective principle, which has hitherto excited the gloomy passions and resentful dispositions of mankind, is, I am afraid, but too prevalent in this country also. We have light; but I am afraid our light is not entirely of the right description. The common people feel that they are aggrieved; they feel that the hand of famine is fastening upon them. They begin to perceive that all this mischief proceeds from this mad ridiculous crusade for restoring the fallen despotism of France, and from the errors and oppressions of government. But I cannot persuade myself that, hitherto the best mode has been adopted for enlightening them as to the proper means of redress. We have taught them the sources of their grievances, and we have talked of denunciations and impeachments, and retribution and revenge: but I am afraid we have not yet been anxious to trace the principles of liberty to their real sources. Let us then unite our energies to diffuse the genuine principles of freedom among mankind. Let us teach them to seek redress, indeed, but to seek it by the means least injurious to public tranquillity and individual happiness. Let us tell them—You are full of commotion;—you talk of the prices of the necessaries of life; you talk of the monopoly among the dealers in these commodities. Silly men! restrain your indignation. The objects of your rage are innocent, are injured, like yourselves. A few rotten principles have found their way into the general system of government under which you live. Corruption has reared its head on high. Let us oppose that corruption. Let us say to our governors, we ask you not for power; we ask you not for slaughter; we ask you not for the banners of conquered enemies, even if you had banners of conquered enemies to give; we ask not for the French West India Islands, by conquering which you will inevitably lose your own; we ask not a bead-roll of appendages and colonies in this part of the world, and that part of the world, and in the other; we ask you for that generous, that just, that peaceful administration which will restore to us the opportunity of earning a *comfortable subsistence by moderate labour*; this is according to our opinions the only useful object of government. We will not contend with you for form, *if you will grant us this*. But this we must have—this we will. We are enlightened—we shall soon be unanimous; for we are determined to speak our minds, and such plain truths as we utter must make their way to every heart; and when this unanimity takes place (if you do not give us our rights, now, while you have power to give) you must sink, without a struggle, sink into nothingness; and justice must triumph.

By such spirit, by such reason, by a proper detestation of violence, stilling the fears which have been so artfully excited, peaceful redress might be obtained: and no one can say that temperate redress and progressive improvement are not better than violence and confusion.

Citizens, I wish you to remember, that revenge is always vice—that violence is never to be appealed to but in self-defence. It is true, every individual has a right to defend himself, every community has a right to defend itself also; and I will give you the best authority in a case of this kind, the authority of Judge Foster[45] upon the subject. You shall hear that he lays it down as a constitutional principle, that *the people have a right to resist oppression*. "I am not at present concerned (says he, speaking of the deposition of one of our kings) to enquire whether the charge brought against Edward II. was or was not well founded; but admitting that it was, the Parliament proceeded upon a principle, which in the case of individuals is perfectly understood and universally assented to. I mean the right of self-defence in cases of great and urgent necessity, and where no other remedy is at hand, a right which the law of nature giveth, and no law of society hath taken away". And he might have added, which no law of society can take away. "If this be true in the case of individuals, it will be equally so in the case of nations, under the like circumstances of necessity. For all the rights and powers for defence and preservation belonging to society are nothing more than the natural rights and powers of individuals transferred to and concentering in the body for the preservation of the whole. And from the law of self-preservation resulteth the well-known maxim *Salus populi suprema Lex.*"[46]

Citizens, will you not hear with astonishment, that this very maxim, laid down by Judge Foster, in his Crown Law, was one of the maxims for reprinting which, we were accused of High Treason, kept seven months in close confinement (which you are told was no punishment at all) and afterwards tried for our lives at the Bar of the Old Bailey? "I think" continues Judge Foster "the principles here laid down must be admitted; unless any one will chuse to say, that individuals in a community are, in certain cases, under the protection of *the primitive law of self-preservation*, but communities, composed of the same individuals, are, in the like cases, excluded. Or that when the enemy is at the gate every single soldier may and ought to stand to his arms; but the garrison must surrender at discretion."[47] Such are the sentiments of this learned Judge, that the people, in cases of the last dire necessity have a right, upon principles of self-defence, to preserve themselves from ruin and destruction. I do not wish to root out from your hearts the conviction of this truth, but I wish to plant by the side of it another truth, that the redress obtained by headlong violence can never be as effectual as that which is obtained by benevolent means. Thus we see the Republic of France, after having rushed through violence after violence, and finding only change of tyranny, is at last obliged to resort to the principles of benevolence and humanity; and before her work can be completed she must call into action a still larger proportion of these generous principles.

Citizens, It is necessary that we consider a little what are the limits of self-defence. We lay it down as a principle; but before we act upon any principle we ought to understand it. The very term defence supposes it to be the only means you have of redress. If an assassin meets me at the corner of the street, and aims a poniard at my breast, if I have no other means of preservation, I have a right to poniard him. But if I have the power to arrest his hand, and take from him the weapon of destruction, it would be murder in me to prefer the use of the poniard. If the same assassin, struggling in my gripe, resisting my benevolent intention to preserve his life, falls prostrate at my feet, however provoked I may have been in the quarrel, whatever stripes or injuries, whatever wounds I may have received, if I strike my prostrate enemy to the heart, the principle of prospective justice or virtue is abandoned, the retrospective passion of revenge triumphs—he is the injured man and I become, myself, the assassin.

Let us consider then that nothing but the last extremity can justify an appeal to violence. Let us not listen to that sanguinary enthusiasm which breathes revenge—which talks of force and violence. There is no force like truth; there is no omnipotency but reason. Let this force, this omnipotency be the objects of your constant attention; and do not fear, Citizens, but that the condition of mankind will be ameliorated. All amelioration must be gradual; no society ever rushed at once from absolute tyranny to perfect freedom; no person ever rose from raging disease to florid health in an instant. We may change one sort of misery for another, but change is not always redress.

Citizens, this prospective system, which is to lead by steps to political amelioration, ought to actuate you not only in your public but in your private feelings. Never forget that virtue is a uniform principle; that the same principle that makes a man virtuous in public life, would, if applied to private affairs, make him virtuous there also. There is but one principle of virtue—the principle of benevolence; and the only way to promote this benevolence is to keep our attention fixed upon the circumstances that surround us, and to be constantly considering how we can ameliorate or improve the condition of mankind. To this all our faculties ought to be directed; nor let it be forgotten, that in whatever notions or prejudices we have been brought up, we are practically vicious whenever we consume the energies of our minds by fixing our eyes upon that which is past and irretrievable, and resigning ourselves to the retrospective emotions of revenge, repentance, or regret.

Citizens, in this respect, I come before you (such as it is) with my example as well as my precept. I have recently passed through one of the severest struggles which human nature can experience. I have lost, since I saw you last, a parent by whose aged side, year after year, I have toiled through many a scene of trial and calamity.[48] With her I have met, unappalled the grim countenance of disaster—almost of want; and I have beheld in her age, the same fortitude, the same undrooping resolution that buoyed up myself. This aged partner has been torn from my side. I will not dwell upon her virtues; for what are the virtues of an obscure individual to mankind? I will tell you, however, that she fell a victim to the public spirit of her son. Already bowed down with years and infirmities, the blast of ministerial oppression aimed at this head, though powerless to bend the young oak against which it was directed, struck, in its passage, the aged plant, whose sap could no longer resist its influence.

She broke.—I beheld, when I came from the jaws of my miserable dungeon, the characters of death upon her countenance. I saw that she was not long for this world. My conviction was too prophetic. She is gone. I have soothed her last moments; I have caught her expiring breath; and these hands have sealed her eyes.

What can I more?

Society lives; and it is to the living, and to them alone, that benefit can be imparted.

Be gone, ye idle, melancholy sensations; ye feelings that can produce no fruit.—I call upon *Roman energy*—I call upon *Spartan fortitude*, which characterised the pure and virtuous republicans of the ancient world;—upon these I call to steel my heart with firmness. Let me, so long as I exist, impart (such as it is) my advice, my little knowledge, my best assistance to my fellow citizens; and let me not, by unavailing regrets, and retrospective views, consume the energies to which I have no exclusive right—which are your's—which are the property of my country—of all mankind. For I am not a solitary individual. I stand not upon a world where I behold no inhabitant but myself. I am but a part—a little, little member of the great animal of human society—a palpillary nerve upon one of the extremities! and I must do that duty to the whole, for which by my structure and organization I am adapted.

The Second Lecture *On the Moral and Political Influence of the Prospective Principle of Virtue.* (For the First see Tribune No. VII.)[49]

CITIZENS, The subject of this evening's Lecture is *the Prospective Principle of Virtue*. It will be remembered that some evenings ago, the first time I had the pleasure of meeting you after a melancholy circumstance had taken place in my family, I delivered a Lecture upon this subject, a subject to the choice of which I was led, in a considerable degree, by the state of my feelings. I was conscious of the duty of struggling with those sentiments of regret which we cannot wholly avoid when deprived of those who are dear to us, and I recollect that one of the most pleasing and efficacious methods of rivetting instruction in our own minds, is to endeavour to impart it to others; and I, therefore, upon that evening, undertook to prove that virtue is a prospective, not a retrospective principle, that it regards always those things we are to look forward upon, not those to which we may look back.

Citizens, I had no sooner determined to treat upon this subject, than I found the extreme importance of considering it with accuracy, and giving it an extensive investigation; it will not, however, be surprising to you that I should feel myself, under such circumstances, incompetent to give that methodical and orderly arrangement to which the subject is entitled: for, notwithstanding all our boasts, fortitude itself is a struggle, and when we are struggling against powerful passions our thoughts may occasionally flow, perhaps, with considerable energy, but they will generally be uttered in a loose and unconnected way. I found, accordingly, after I had concluded, that I had very imperfectly performed the task I had undertaken, that many important topics had not been touched at all, and particularly one important branch of my subject, which, perhaps, I was called upon to investigate with some degree of boldness and accuracy; because I had shocked, in a considerable degree, the prejudices of some of my hearers by having promised to attempt to prove that gratitude is in reality no virtue.[50]

I have been induced, therefore, to consider the subject again, and to bring before you those parts of the argument into which I did not sufficiently enter; and though this subject may, in the first view, appear considerably metaphysical, and though many persons may expect that the investigation will not be sufficiently political, I believe this suspicion will be found only to originate from not having sufficiently considered the nature of the subject.

The fact is, that the great question whether virtue is or is not always a prospective principle, is one of those which takes in an almost boundless range of investigation. Perhaps no question, in morals or politics, can possibly be started which has not some degree of reference to it; and I hope I shall be able to prove, that the proper understanding of the subject is of equal importance to practical utility, as to the accurate arrangement of ideas comprehended in the investigation. I think I shall be able to shew, that the prospective principle of virtue, that is to say, that principle which looks forward always to the advantages and benefits that are to be attained—which thinks of nothing but promoting the present and future happiness of society, is a principle the most magnificent, extensive and generous in its influence upon the human character of any that can be devised.

Citizens, If we could but persuade ourselves, not only in theory, but in practice, to keep our eyes thus constantly before us, I have no doubt but we should be able to produce a harvest of felicity of which mankind, as yet, entertain no conception; that we should be stimulated to a degree of energy that would expand the human intellect, enlarge the political powers of man, and produce a universal triumph of happiness throughout the universe;—that we should convert all the passions, powers, and energies of man, now so frequently wasted in profligacy, revenge, or apathy, into powerful engines to promote the general happiness, and to enlarge the capacities of our species!

Citizens, This proposition might, in a considerable degree be illustrated from what all of us must have observed in the intercourses of private life. If we regard the human character, such as we find it, we cannot but reflect, upon the considerable degree of force and activity which the youthful character displays, in proportion as it is inspired by the energies of hope, in preference to that tendency to regret and melancholy which frequently distinguishes the later period of life: for what is this hope but an enthusiastic ardour of the mind that keeps the eye constantly fixed on things that are before. Hence not only the human intellect unfolds to a degree which could not otherwise be accomplished, but we also find the youthful character struggling with, and frequently surmounting dangers and difficulties which, but for this prospective principle, would sink them listless to the earth, and consign them to hopeless desperation. We find them also frequently springing forward to the full attainment of objects which to the cold eye of censure appear unattainable, and which occasion the soi-disant moralists of the day to ridicule and censure their daring enthusiasm.

Citizens, Could we carry this principle into the political world—could we persuade mankind to consider the universe, as in reality it is, one continuous system of animated being, and could we persuade the individual to think himself only a part, a portion of that great, and, as far as we can perceive, immortal existence, think how those energies would be prolonged, and reflect what must be the beneficient consequences! For why does age droop into despondency? Why is the vigour, the ardour of youthful character suppressed by the chilling hand of experience? Is it because we have found that hope and exertion are of no avail? No—It cannot be. Let any individual who has once felt this enthusiastic ardor consider what he has attained by its means, and it is impossible that he should conclude that ardor and enthusiasm are fruitless.

What is the reason then that the energies of the human character are of such short duration? Citizens the reason is this, man when considerably advanced in life thinks he has but little to look forward to, and therefore slides imperceptibly into the retrospective, dwells on that which is past, seeks his pleasures and his gratifications from the remembrance of what is no more, and thence drops too often into regret, repining melancholy, and dissatisfaction, from reflecting upon those parts of his past history which he cannot approve, or which, if he does approve, are accompanied with the melancholy conviction that they can return no more.

These are the consequences of the selfish system. That man who considers himself as an isolated individual, who believes that all his exertions ought to be made for his individual benefit, soon has reason to relax in his exertions. He finds that he is approaching towards the catastrophe he wishes to avoid; that there is little for him to hope for; little for him to wish; his anxiety for the future is only a gloomy consideration of his approaching dissolution; and he therefore resigns that energetic character which in youth had been the source of his delight and prosperity, and sinks into that disposition to regret and melancholy which is equally barren to himself and injurious, or at least unproductive, to society.

But if we extend our view a little further; if we consider that man lives not for himself alone, but that every existing being, each individual that participates the feelings and sensations of which he himself is conscious— all that have the same common faculties with himself, are entitled to the same enjoyments and the same rights; that year after year, generation after generation, ages after ages, and myriads of ages after myriads, may pass away, and still society exist to reap the benefit of our exertions; then our energy becomes as it were immortal, and the desire, the hope, the anxiety to labor for human happiness, can only terminate with existence, because there only can terminate that satisfaction which the virtuous mind conceives from the consciousness of laboring to promote the general felicity, from the conviction that unborn ages may taste the harvest which his virtue is cultivating.

Citizens, Such, I conceive, with respect to the energies of the human character, are the effects that must result from considering virtue as a prospective principle. It creates to man a sort of eternal interest, in the advancement of virtue and happiness: it enlarges every day, in proportion as his knowledge enlarges the sphere of his activity; and consequently it is likely to be productive of effects to society which nothing but such a principle can possibly produce.

But it may be said, what avails to me the felicity that is to be enjoyed by unborn ages? Why should I exert myself for happiness that is to be tasted an hundred thousand years to come? Citizens, this way of arguing may look like philosophy, but it partakes very little of benevolence, and still less of a thorough knowledge of the sources of human happiness. It is true we may not live to realize a very large portion of the happiness we are laboring to produce. Some of it certainly we must behold; because if our labours in the cause of general happiness are continual, the harvest will be springing up day after day. But this proportion, you say, is small.—True, this proportion, if you consider this only, may be small. But is this all that man enjoys? Those atoms which compose the individuals that surround me, some few years hence may perhaps be winnowed in the gale; in the eternal revolutions of matter they may be transmuted into various forms, flow in the wave, mount with the element of fire, or mingle with their parent dust: but have we therefore no interests in the enjoyments of posterity?—Yes, we have. In contemplation we enjoy them; in the noble and sublime satisfaction which springs from the consciousness of laboring, from the most disinterested principles, in the promotion of the grandest cause in which the faculties of man can be employed. And though you may not live to see the whole of those benefits you are toiling to produce, if you cannot anticipate them and enjoy them, in prospect, while you are toiling, I pity the coldness and sordidness of your imaginations.

The principle of retrospective virtue, if such a contradiction may be permitted, is however of a very different description. The passions it engenders are almost uniformly the very reverse of benevolence. Instead of imparting energy, it begets listlessness; instead of permanent happiness, it produces a sensual disposition to the gratification of the moment; and instead of ardent labor to promote the welfare of mankind, it generates the gloom of hatred, the rancour revenge, and the eternal brooding of malignant passions that disturb the universe and deform the character of man.

The most conspicuous of the pretended virtues of this system—for there is hardly any passion, however vile or base, which has not, in some country or some age, been dignified with the name of virtue.

The most conspicuous of the pretended virtues of this retrospective system, may be classed under a very few heads.

The first I shall hold out to your observation is Nationality. A certain indigenous set of romance writers called English Historians, having, time after time, told you very pompous stories of Frenchmen cut into fritters by English valour, of mountains of Spaniards looked to death by the terrors of the British eye, you are taught, by these fine stories, to contract an affection and veneration for the exploits of these glorious proficients in the science of human butchery, and hence you are taught to consider, of course, that as the persons who tell all these great exploits bore the name of Englishmen, you ought to love the character of Englishmen better than any other, and to hold all other beings in contempt: without enquiring whether they do not possess the same powers of mind, nay, whether the romance writers of other countries, that is to say, their historians, have not, in return, made those Spaniards and Frenchmen cut myriads of English Dogs into fritters in the same miraculous manner. In short, you are to love Englishmen because they are descended from those Englishmen who, as you are told, murdered the natives of France in inconceivable numbers, and you are to hate all Frenchmen (run away emigrants *now* excepted) because they are descended from the Frenchmen so murdered. Hence, Citizens, that perpetual animosity between nation and nation. What!—am I who are descended from Britons who have so frequently scourged those dogs of France—am I to suffer a Frenchman to consider himself my equal? Shall I, who pretend to be so proud of liberty, suffer a Frenchman to think of liberty for himself?—No, it is an insult to the sacred records of British history; and, remembering the cut-throat virtues of my ancestors, I must be sure to carry on the same trade of cutting throats in my time also.

Another species of this kind of partiality, is the spirit of party, proceeding also from the retrospective notion of virtues derived from ancestors—I have known gout, stone, and gravel to be derived from ancestors, but no one ever yet found the power of transmuting virtue, intellect, or learning from father to child. But, in remembrance of virtuous acts, forsooth, which the heroes of particular houses have accomplished, we are to bow down in veneration to those particular houses, we are to love the *Whigs*, because some of their ancestors stole the name from the *Scotch Sans Culottes*, who stood about 150 years ago so boldly and conspicuously forward in vindication of the rights of man.[51]

We are to revere sects in politics and religion also, because our ancestors were brought up in those political and religious notions; and as we have looked back for the example, it follows, of course, that the example must be right, and it would be almost atheism itself to think we could make any sort of improvement.

Another of the virtues which spring from the retrospective principle, is the system of *proscription*; that is to say, if any man, at any former period of his life, happens to have been guilty of any imprudence, or to have fallen into any vice, we are to take a resolute determination that he shall never have an opportunity of being virtuous again: we are never to think what the man is. The capacities and energies of his mind may be of the most useful nature, his virtues, private and public, may be most eminently conspicuous; we may look forward, also, to the prospect of his being beneficial to society: all this is very good till you happen to hear, some how or other, that at some former period of his life, he had committed some faux pas, or was accused of something of that kind, and then, forsooth, all your veneration and respect is to terminate, and you are to push him back into the paths of vice from which his enlightened intellect had rescued him.

Citizens, can any thing be more opposite to the great interests of mankind, to the desirable object of promoting universal happiness, diffusing felicity to those who are at present around us, and cultivating those virtues that may tend to the felicity of posterity than this retrospective principle of proscription, which so ridiculously and inhumanly says to the unfortunate man struggling to regain his place in society, you may make what efforts you will, and struggle to be virtuous to the last degree, but, if we can prove that you have once been vicious, we will forget your present exertions, we will shut the doors of future virtue against you, and drive you back, whether you will or not, to that situation from which the energies of your intellect had redeemed you.

Two other of the vices which the retrospective principle cultivates are *sorrow* and *regret*,—weaknesses, which it is no further necessary for me to dwell upon, than as they have frequently not only been cherished, but hypocritically assumed, that the individual who might challenge the praise of sensibility. Sensibility! what is it? Sensibility means nothing more than acuteness of feeling; and if there is any particular honor in having a more acute sense of pain than other people, the sickest valetudinarian has more virtue to boast than robust health and vigorous and useful activity can ever aspire to. In the same degree the feeble, sickly mind, in which there is not energy or virtue enough to do one virtuous action, frequently bears off the palm which ought to be conferred only upon the man glowing with a generous and extensive love of his fellow creatures, but which is, in general, conferred upon that debility into which persons sink from contemplating nothing but their own sensations, and supposing that to those sensations the world and its happiness ought to be rendered subservient.

Another of the virtues of the retrospective system is *repentance*. This is one of the virtues I shall touch upon very delicately, because I would not wish to offend the fine sensations of those reverend Gentlemen who may, perhaps, be anxious not to lose that hold which it gives them of the consciences and consequently the purses of their followers.

But the most conspicuous and energetic of all the *virtues* resulting from the retrospective principle is *revenge*: a passion that has done more towards deforming the face of human society, and plunging nation after nation, and generation after generation into all the horrors the mind can conceive, than all the other vices in the catalogue of human errors. Of this principle I shall not enter particularly into the investigation at this time, having spoken of it at length in my former Lecture. I shall, therefore, proceed to the consideration of a more plausible part of the retrospective system; I mean the supposed virtue of Gratitude. These two passions I shall compare together, and endeavour to shew that, however different in appearance, they both proceed from the same selfish principle.

Citizens, as this passion or sentiment of Gratitude is the only one generated by the retrospective system which has any plausible pretence to virtue, and as it has been long revered by the most amiable characters as the germ of every virtue, I am well aware that I have a delicate task to perform. Few, perhaps, who hear me ever questioned that gratitude was a virtue of the first description. A chain of serious reasoning has induced me to consider it as a vice. It will be necessary, therefore, for me to state the question to you with great precision, so that I may be thoroughly understood, and you may perceive the foundations upon which my conclusion is built. It is a doctrine, I believe, which no one has been hardy enough to broach in this country, till it was advanced by a celebrated author of the present day (Godwin) in his "Enquiry concerning Political justice";[52] and the odium it has drawn upon his head is little calculated to induce others to tread the same path. I am not afraid, however, of popularising those ideas which I believe to be true, because the persons who first propagated them have encountered reproach. If gratitude is a virtue—if it has a tendency to expand the heart, and promote the line of conduct most conducive to general happiness, let it be proved, and I shall be happy to retract. If gratitude, on the contrary, has a tendency to draw the human mind from the consideration of the whole, and to fix it, from a principle of self love, upon a few individuals,[53] then I shall be obliged to conclude that gratitude is no virtue, but that, on the contrary, it is an enemy to that great fountain of all virtue—Justice!—which commands us, without favor or regard to personal feelings, to cultivate felicity in every bosom capable of receiving its impression, and remove sorrow and affliction from every sentient being, wherever the opportunity is presented.

Citizens, let us enquire, in the first instance, what is the principle of gratitude, and what is justice. If justice consists in nothing more, according to the ideas of Lombard-street,[54] than merely paying your debts that you may neither injure your credit, nor be sent to prison, why then justice is not the sole foundation of all virtue. But if justice consists, as I suppose, in doing, in all possible cases, all the good we possibly can for our fellow beings, then I must conclude that every thing that is not just is criminal, that nothing that militates against this justice can be a virtue.

Well, then, what do you mean by gratitude? Either it means something, or it means nothing. If it means something, it must mean either something more or something less than justice; or else justice and gratitude are convertible terms:—a position that will never be allowed. If justice, then, is a supreme virtue, if justice embraces the whole universe, if it is the elementary principle of justice that you should do all the good to human beings that you have the power of doing, and never neglect any opportunity of doing good to any individual, unless by doing that good you are likely to do more injury to another individual, or, to society at large—If these are the principles of justice, and if gratitude means something more or something less than this, it must be injustice, and consequently is no virtue. It is mistaking a part for the whole, and confining our exertions to a few particular individuals, merely because they have done more for us than we were entitled to, and thereby neglecting that great scale of justice which would lead us to do all the good in our power to all existing beings.

Gratitude is generally understood to be a return of benefits. Now let us consider what are the benefits which ought to be returned.

You must never lose sight, in this enquiry, of the first principle, namely, that justice includes doing all the good you can for all human beings. Now then what is returning favors? The obligation, as it is called, either was a favour which the individual did or did not deserve. If not deserved, then it was an act of injustice; for no man has power to do more than he ought to an individual, without doing less than his duty to the whole; the fact being, that he owes to the whole every power and faculty he possesses, and is bound to lay out those powers and faculties to the general advantage. If therefore he does more to any individual than that individual deserves, he is reduced to the necessity of doing less to other individuals than they deserve; consequently he has done injustice, he has done an ill act. If injustice then has been done in your favour, ought you to do a kindness to another because you have received the benefit of his injustice? Certainly not.

Grant, on the other hand, that what your benefactor did was no more than just and due; that it was beneficial to the human race that the kindness should be done, would you not be bound in the same manner to respect and reverence that human being, whose virtue had led him to do the best for his fellow beings, just the same whether that benefit was conferred upon another individual or yourself? If not, what makes the difference but your own self-love?

Thus then it resolves itself into the principle of justice. But if you lay it down as a principle of gratitude, that if you do me a kindness, I am to do you a kindness again, what is it but a barter? What is it but a traffic? a compact between parties?—Do more for me to day than I deserve, and I will do more for you tomorrow than you deserve!—or, in other words, you having done injustice to mankind, that you might heap unmerited favours upon my head; I will do injustice to mankind, for ever after, that I may heap favors upon your head of which you are not worthy.

Citizens, It is not often that I enter upon any subject in this dry and abstract manner: but I wish you to see, as it is a part of that great system I wish to impress upon your minds, that the conclusion I draw from this is not a conclusion unfriendly to doing kind and beneficent actions. It is not an argument against doing as many generous actions as you would otherwise do; on the contrary it is a stimulus to do more: for the conclusion is, that all the good you can do to all existing beings, you ought to do; and that the only standard by which you ought to regulate the proportions of good you are to administer, is the standard of effective right of the individual: that is to say, the capacity and the inclination of that individual to do good in his turn to other human beings whom it may be in his power afterwards to serve: and the only reason why you ought to give him that preference is, that by so doing, you throw your seed into a soil where it will be sure to be cultivated and bring forth a more abundant produce—not for your particular advantage, the paltry gratification of your contracted senses: no, but for the general diffusion of happiness and virtue through the whole of that great family of human beings every one of which, whatever be his name, his colour, or his country, is the brother of all the rest, and ought to enjoy with them a community of rights and happiness.

It matters not whether the individual has done me a kindness or an injury. A virtuous individual, supposing me to be vicious, may have done me wrong! This virtuous individual has the power and inclination to do benefit to all mankind. Now suppose this individual who has thus injured me unintentionally—or suppose he had intentionally wronged me (being then a vicious, tho' now a virtuous man)—This man who has wronged me languishes in want. Those powers, those faculties, those virtues, by which nations and generations might be blessed, are perishing before me. On the other hand lies some worthless individual whom nature may have made my relation, who may have heaped, in profligacy and idle intoxication, perhaps, unmerited favours upon my head: I have the power of serving but one: Who does gratitude call upon me to serve? The worthless being by whose exertions society will never be benefited, or him whose relief confers an essential benefit upon mankind? Gratitude says, relieve the worthless, and let the important sufferer perish. But who does justice, who does virtue, who does the love of my fellow man call upon me to serve? The man whose conduct, perhaps, was once a scorpion to my breast; who, if I relieve his necessities, if I triumph over the selfish narrow principles corroding my heart, may become a blessing to the universe and diffuse felicity through a wide sphere of human population.

Citizens, it may appear paradoxical, but I shall endeavour to prove how nearly gratitude and revenge are allied. I might argue this point by dogmatism, and inference from fact. I might appeal to observation, and remind you that grateful men are generally revengeful, and that revengeful men are generally grateful; and even hence, perhaps, it would be no great presumption to conclude that the revengeful and grateful man act from the same selfish spring of motion, that is to say, the recollection of the benefits or injuries heaped upon himself, and the hatred or love he feels towards the individuals. I shall not however take advantage of this general association, but shall proceed to examine the question upon the open ground of argument. For this purpose, Citizens, I will refer to a recent circumstance, because it will give me an opportunity of meeting the arguments of my opponents on their strongest ground.

You all of you know that, together with other Citizens, I have lately been in circumstances of a very extraordinary nature: that the iron hand of oppression was stretched over me to crush me to atoms, that every species of persecution was made use of to destroy at once my person and my character. Well, how came I through this perilous storm? Citizens, TWELVE GOOD MARINERS and THREE EXCELLENT PILOTS conducted my vessel in safety into the harbour of peace. Twelve honest Jurors disdained the sophistry of an host of Crown Lawyers.—*Erskine*, with an imagination

all on fire, with a soul full of that energy which nothing but virtuous feelings could inspire, *Erskine* stepped forward with manly eloquence, and asserted the cause of truth and justice to the very teeth of that judge who, in
his charge to the Grand Jury, propagated doctrines to which I will not give
a descriptive epithet:—posterity will do them justice. *Erskine* stood up in
the face of power; he vindicated the rights and liberties of Englishmen, and
as he already stood unrivalled for forensic talents, determined to prove that
the qualities of his head were not superior to those of his heart.—*Gibbs*,
whose soul, unbiassed by party, never yet was plunged into political disputes, felt a correspondent ardour. Burning with honest conviction, elevated with a noble fortitude, conscious that the men who pretended to
reverence the law and constitution were trampling law and constitution
under foot, and endeavouring to mark every footstep of their tyrannic career with British blood;—*Gibbs*, not curious, perhaps, of those abstract and
speculative truths which form the basis of the character of the philosophical politician, but fired with that Constitutional enthusiasm, that zeal for
the faithful interpretation of the laws which has occasionally, though not
frequently, adorned the English Bar—*Gibbs* stood by his side, like the
younger *Ajax* by the side of *Telemon*,[55] seconded his strokes, and enforced
his advantages. Nor must we forget the labours of *Foulkes*,[56] who in a situation less conspicuous, but equally arduous, united the diligence of the solicitor with the disinterestedness of the philanthropist, and the ardour of the
patriot.

Such were our champions. They fought, they conquered, and Britain
escaped the chains that were forging for it.

Well, Citizens, I feel—I know all this: I acknowledge, I avow, I proclaim (for *justice* calls upon me to do so) that but for these honest jurors,
these honest advocates, and this honest solicitor, I had not been here. I
am not a man to deny the good offices I have received. That is no part of
the system I am upholding. The good actions of mankind ought to be
publicly proclaimed, nor ought the light of benevolence to be hid under a
bushel. But can I suppose, or, if I were so infatuated, could any body else
believe that the merit of these men is in any way increased because I was
the individual who was snatched by their exertions from the jaws of oppression, and restored to my sphere of public and private usefulness. Can I,
unless egotism has usurped the seat of justice in my mind, believe that
more affection is due to these men, more esteem for snatching me from the
meditated destruction than for snatching the veteran Tooke,[57] for example, from the same fate? or Hardy,[58] that gallant and disinterested leader of

the van of liberty? Certainly not. The *principle* and the *utility* of the action are the real foundations of the esteem we owe the actors, and not the individual object. They would be equally entitled to respect and veneration had they exercised the same energies of mind in behalf of any other individuals equally innocent and equally useful to mankind.

Nay, Citizens, I will go a step further, I say that the respect and veneration which we owe and which society owes to these men, does not arise from the circumstance of past exertions. No, those exertions ought only to be considered as proofs of energetic virtues calculated to produce the happiness of mankind; as land marks, if I may so express myself, on the shore of morals, pointing out to mankind, whenever their happiness and felicity shall need such a shelter of intellect, and legal knowledge, where they may seek that shelter with confidence.

In short, Citizens, it is not this or that good action which individuals have done, but their general usefulness, their power and inclination to benefit society, that ought to stamp their estimation with the thinking part of mankind.

Now, Citizens, I will contrast this by another circumstance. It is not likely that in mentioning these prosecutions I should forget the sanguinary ambition of a *Pitt*, the aristocratic enthusiasm of a *Burke*, the metaphysical frenzy of a *Wyndham*, or the apostacy of your *Portlands*,[59] your *Spencers*,[60] and the would-be Viceroy *Fitzwilliam*;[61] yet, Citizens, because we recollect the vices of these men, are our souls to fester with revenge? Are we, like harpies and furies, with lips quivering with rage and indignation (such lips as I beheld in the Privy Council when I was examined!)—Are we, I say, as if we were ready to lap the blood of these men because their principles and conduct are offensive to us, to brood over the gloomy feelings of resentment and revenge? No: Perish the wretch the fire of whose patriotism must be fed by the destroying fires of vengeance! Perish the wretch who, remembering only his own petty wrongs, forgets the great interests of humanity!

However contemptible their conduct may have been, or however conspicuous their sanguinary hatred and disposition to oppress, those individuals certainly are no worse members of society than they would have been if they had never persecuted me. If their persecution had fell upon other heads, ought I not to have the same abhorrence for their principles and practices which is justifiable now? Certainly this makes no difference in the great scale. If I am merely an isolated individual, if I am to be acting merely for myself, if I am to consider that I am all, and society nothing, then of course I must hate these men in proportion to the injury they have done me. But, admitting the benevolent principle, can any individual have a right to stake the happiness and prosperity of society, the welfare, the peace, the tranquillity of a whole generation, that he may satisfy his particular feelings of rage, of hatred, of resentment? No: such a right, reason, humanity, justice, all disclaim. I know this is not the popular sentiment. I know how strong a tendency there is in the human character to egotism and resentment; and I therefore warn you when you yourselves are wronged think twice—always think seriously before you suffer yourselves to feel indignation against any individual; but when yourselves are wronged think twice,—think how common a thing it is to over-rate ourselves, and consequently to over-rate the injuries we have received,—and learn that the principles of virtue are principles of general utility, not of particular feeling.

But, Citizens, there is one circumstance more relative to this gratitude, to which I shall allude, namely, the mischievous consequences it frequently produces in the most noble and capacious minds, fettering them to individuals when they were born for the universe, and extinguishing the great principles of general justice in their hearts. How is it that the Demosthenes of our senate, Fox, a man whose soul is occupied by magnificent virtues,—how comes it that this man shrinks as he does from the path of public duty at this period? What is the reason that he should affirm in the Senate, that elementary principles are not to be talked of, that you must not discuss general abstract rules,—you must only consider the particular motives and objects of the present day?[62]—In other words, you may make as many disputes as you please to get yourselves into power, but never discuss what are the rights of the People, the duties of Ministers, or the objects of Government! No: this would lead you to enquiry equally destructive to all parties, and the Outs have as much to tremble for during the investigation as the Ins. But can we believe that this great character is blind to the importance of first principles? Can we believe that his mind cannot see beyond the narrow line of conduct now chalked out?—It is impossible to think so meanly of his mind; but the harpy Gratitude has taken possession of him: recollecting that much of the felicity, much of the ease, the splendour, the consequence of his life, has been derived from a few aristocratic families, from a great combination of Whigs, as they call themselves, he therefore supposes that he is bound in gratitude never to desert this party, though, one after another, they have shewn little remorse in deserting him. Thus is this great, this powerful, in many respects this virtuous and energetic mind, trammeled by the fetters of Aristocracy, and society is robbed of those glorious advantages which might be reaped from the free and generous exertions of capacities so gigantic and immeasurable?

THE TRIBUNE, No. XI.
Saturday, 23d May, 1795.
On the humanity and benevolence of the Dutch Revolution, and the causes of the excesses in France. The Third Lecture On the Moral and Political Influence of the Prospective Principle of Virtue. With a Parallel between the Character of PITT and ROBESPIERRE.

CITIZENS, it will frequently happen, from the extempore manner in which these Lectures are delivered, that I shall be considerably mistaken in my calculations as to the extent of matter to be embraced by a single Lecture. On the last evening I intended to have closed the subject of the prospective principle of virtue, and to have entered largely into the *political* considerations that depend upon it; particularly that branch of the subject which relates to the revolutions of nations. I found, however, when the evening was considerably advanced that it would be impossible to accomplish this, or, indeed, to enter at any considerable length into that which forms the most important branch of the subject, namely, the application to the leading characters and events of this important aera, without considerably trespassing upon my usual limits. And as the state of my health was precarious, I thought it not right either to expose myself to hazard, or you to inconvenience by protracting that Lecture to an unusual length. I am glad I made use of this precaution, because, when I came to review my subject again, I found a vast variety of important matter entirely untouched. I recollected also that while I had the honor of residing in the Tower, I had perused, with a considerable degree of attention, the works of an author sometimes very much praised, and sometimes more abused,

> "Now hail'd with joy as true to Virtue's side;
> Now view'd with horror as the assassin's guide"[63]

I mean *Machiavel*,[64] who appeared, in a considerable degree, to furnish a clue to the events which have recently taken place in Europe; and from whom many important reflections might be adduced: An author, whatever might be his object—whether to instruct the tyrant, or expose the tyr-

anny, whose work is replete with political erudition and, therefore, worthy
of the most serious attention. I found in a review of the present subject,
that many of his reflections would apply to that branch I am now going to
enter upon, and I shall occasionally, therefore, make some quotations from
him. It may be necessary, however, to premise that this author is perpetu-
ally speaking of princes and of tyrants, whereas I shall have to apply his
reflections to leaders of revolutions by which princes and tyrannies have
been overthrown. You will see, however, that the reasoning applies just
the same, and that in one instance in particular the only irrelevant circumstance is the use of the word prince, a title to which the individual animadverted upon never attained, nor ever, perhaps, aspired.

Having premised this much, I shall proceed to remind you that in two
former lectures I have dilated very considerably upon that principle of virtue which looks forward to benefits to be procured, in opposition to that
which looks backward upon injuries already done. You will remember that
I dwelt upon the tendency of the passion of revenge to disappoint the aims
of those who use that engine to promote the principle of liberty; the very
essence of which is philanthropic virtue. I attempted also to shew you that
the deviations from the great principles of political virtue which, according
to my conceptions, are observable in that illustrious character, the Demosthenes of the British senate, are to be traced also from the delusive
principle of gratitude, a branch as I endeavoured to shew you, of the retrospective system.

I come now to the most important branch of my subject: namely, the
influence of the two principles in the grand revolutions which frequently
convulse, sometimes destroy, and sometimes improve great communities.
And here, Citizens, I shall dwell, in the first instance, not upon the
gloomy, but upon the benignant picture. I am sure no man who has a heart
can have read the proceedings of the revolution in Holland,[65] without
feeling that heart dilated, and finding himself a better member of society
from the grand sentiments of justice and benevolence upon which that
revolution has been conducted. Remember particularly the doctrines they
lay down, how they discard the principle of vengeance, and all those effusions of retrospective fury which have produced such miserable consequences
in the world. Think of that proclamation in which they declare their independence, and avow their determination of forming a government upon
the broad basis of liberty and equality. Having been required, with more
zeal than discretion, to satiate vengeance upon some of their late oppressive rulers, the provisional representatives, the leaders of the revolution,
publish a proclamation, equally admirable for its energy of sentiment, its

wisdom, and its humanity. "The Dutch", say they, "from the very moment when they first broke their chains, gave to astonished Europe too grand an example of generosity and humanity to let us believe that they would sully that glory in the moments of tranquillity, by avenging themselves upon a set of humbled despots, deprived of all strength."[66] This magnanimity will appear very conspicuous, when you consider what has been the conduct of the man who was once the chief magistrate of that country; when you reflect that during the American war, while Holland was at war with England, there are strong reasons to suspect that he sold the fleet of his own country to the cabinet of St. James's (I mean at the battle of the Dogger Bank)[67]—when you reflect, also, upon his conduct to the people, of whose constitution, be it remembered, the Stadtholderate was never an integral part—it was only a provisional office set up by the temporary will of the nation, and liable to be put down again whenever the nation so willed.

The Stadtholderate, I say, and the history of that country bears me out in the assertion, was no integral part of the constitution of the Batavian states; yet you will remember that when the Batavian people thought it their duty—and who shall venture to dispute the right of a people when they do so think, to ameliorate the government, they were prevented by the Stadtholder from so doing. How? By a larger portion of the people declaring against the patriots? No: but by the menacing of a British fleet that threatened their ports, and by troops of Prussians poured into the nation to thrust the Stadtholderate down the people's throats, with an increase of power, and additional prerogatives.[68]

But they forgot all this—generously and gloriously forgot it, and remembered the true principles of virtue and policy; as you will hear, "He deserves not to triumph", continue these philosophic patriots, "who basely abuses his victory; he alone can promise himself the constant and happy fruits of victory who makes his vanquished foes blush by his justice and generosity; and convinces them that they are the persons who have chosen the worst cause to defend. Citizens, generosity and justice carry with them irresistible force, nothing can save our country but a constant adherence to those virtues. The exercise of revenge may afford a transitory pleasure in the moments of passion and delirium, but its consequences are commonly sad and fatal; while the exercise of equity and generosity leaves nothing but agreeable sensations."

They then go on to declare that their great end is to establish a government upon the foundation of the genuine principles of freedom and equality; perceiving (as all men will sooner or later perceive) that all governments that are not founded upon this basis, that is to say, upon the basis of equal rights, equal laws, and equal means of obtaining justice, are in reality nothing but usurpations, how many hundred, or how many thousand years soever they may happen to have been established. "But", continues the proclamation, "how to attain this end? No method more likely than to shew, on the one hand, grandeur and generosity with respect to the past; on the other, to be severe and inexorable to all attempts against freedom and the supremacy of the people."[69]

Citizens, I am not sure whether to be severe and inexorable is ever right. You are always to exercise justice,—you are to preserve liberty; but take care, that, while you pretend to make distinctions, you do not ultimately fall into an undistinguishing system of terror and revenge. However, Citizens, there can be no doubt that, in the agitation of passions that must prevail in such a revolution as that in France, and that in Holland, there must be a considerable degree of ferment,—a necessity for a considerable degree of energetic exertion, which at other periods cannot be justified. In a moment of crisis, all the terrors, in the regular course of things, being on one side, it is necessary, perhaps, to create a salutary and counteracting terror, that persons who have no side, no sentiment, no principle but that of self-security, (a description which always includes a large proportion of every people) may not suppose that they have every thing to fear from the triumph of one party, and nothing from the other. If therefore there is any excuse for this language, it is from that consideration. Self-preservation is a right of nature which belongs as much to the friends of liberty as to courts and ministers.

Citizens, I mark this discrimination the more particularly, that I may shew you that there is no more foundation for the calumny which describes me, on the one hand, as a friend to passive obedience and non-resistance, than the calumny which represents me, on the other, as an agitator of violence and massacre. I love humanity, I love my fellow-beings, to whatever party they may belong; and I would no sooner wound or afflict my bitterest enemy than my dearest friend. Either the one or the other I would resist, if I met him in the prosecution of schemes destructive of the rights and interests of man; but I would resist him, which ever it might be, in the mildest and most benevolent manner, from which I could have any prospect of success. This is my land-mark—my boundary between Quakerism and violence; and here I think every man ought to stand to his post, and, when attacked, defend himself and his principles; and if ever the dire necessity should arrive, which I hope never will, I trust I shall be as willing to shed my blood, as spend my breath, in the defence of the rights and liberties of man. But not one blow for vengeance! No: that which is past, is past. I would prevent the future evil; I would remove the present; but when, instead of prevention, we talk of punishment, we may disguise it to ourselves what pompous languge we will, but we have departed from the genuine principles of liberty and justice, and plunged into the cruel system by which all the tyrannies of the ancient and modern world have been supported.

Unhappily, citizens, this great political truth has not been understood in all the stages of the French revolution; unhappily we do but too frequently observe, instead of the prospective principle of amelioration, the retrospective glances and passions of revenge, in the struggles of parties which, one after the other, have succeeded in that great, that glorious, though in some respects unhappy country.

Citizens, perhaps in the first instance every one of the factions which have alternately prevailed in that country acted from virtuous principles. I cannot, I own, call back to my mind the glorious sentiments, the godlike reasonings, the generous eloquence, which has so frequently resounded within the walls of the French assemblies, without being convinced that, in many of those leaders who have at last fallen victims to their own ambition, there were pure and enlightened principles of liberty and truth, which perhaps never shone before with equal lustre in the world. But, citizens, one of the first misfortunes of France was, that the leading characters of that country formed themselves into factions, (into parties as they are called here!) compacts and associations, which have an inevitable tendency to produce a selfishness of character, a sort of *esprit du corps,* and to banish from the mind those broad and generous principles, without a resolute adherence to which nothing like genuine liberty ever can be produced.

These parties soon became inflamed by suspicions, and aggravated by threat of vengeance. Yes, I say by threats of vengeance, for I believe the threats held out by the feeble Brissotines[70] were the first cause of the sanguinary proceedings which the Mountain afterwards adopted. When suspicions are generated, when denunciations are springing from every quarter, there is but too necessary a tendency in such proceedings to stir up the gloomy spirit of revenge. Opposition becomes inflamed by mutual hatred, and mutual fear, till nothing but the destruction of one party can satisfy the frantic ravings of those who began in delusion, but end in rancorous animosity. Let it be remembered however, citizens, that I do not attribute the whole of the mischiefs that have taken place in France to the revengeful dispositions of the particular leaders of the revolution. The time is near at hand when it will no longer be virtue to slander France. The time is near at hand when it will be no longer High Treason to do justice to the real character and virtues of that nation. Prussia has already, from a professing friend, become a professing enemy to this country.[71] Prussia already, from the foe of France, has become her ally; and, with very few grains of penetration, I think we may discover that part of the alliance, yet behind the curtain, is, that the arms of Prussia and France shall combine to drive the British forces from Germany. Spain and Sardinia, there is good reason to believe, have submitted already, or are upon the eve of submission.[72] The King of Prussia[73] is nominated, as it were, patron of a large portion of Germany; and, in all probability, under his wing peace will be procured from the French republic for those distracted and half-ruined states. Yet still we sleep supine: we lift not the manly voice for change of men and measures, though the period, I believe, is not very distant, when we must either discard our ministers to make a peace, or submit to a conquering foe, whose revenge we have stimulated by injustice and opprobrium, and whose generosity we have treated with ingratitude and contempt. I believe therefore, in such a posture of affairs, that it is not improper to prepare the public mind for amity, by removing a part of that odium unjustly thrown upon the French character; and I believe, if we consider the whole history of the revolution, we shall find that the excesses of that revolution have not, in general, proceeded principally from the character of the individual leaders, but still less from the principles which that revolution has promulgated. The revengeful character, the depravity of morals, which stained some stages of the revolution resulted from the old despotism. While every species of cruelty and licentiousness practiced by the court, during whose tyranny no poor miserable *sans culotte* could walk the bridges at night, without expecting that some great man's lackey might chuck him into the river, conscious that he would never be enquired after; while the monstrous cruelties practiced by the nobility, and gentry, as they called themselves, against the industrious order of people; while these things were fresh in the memory of the people, it is a circumstance to be lamented, but not to be wondered at, that a profligate spirit of revenge should have stimulated a part of the revolutionists also. Consider likewise the corruption introduced into that country by the court, nothing but splendor and power was treated with respect; and, therefore, splendor and power has but too frequently been grasped at by vices so detestable that no being would have had the audacity to perpetrate them, if he had not known that titles and gold would hide the deformity from the public eye, and his character be smoothed and polished over by the gold leaf of privilege and distinction.

To this I am sorry to add,—that I believe we must also attribute a considerable part of the intrigues and excesses in France to the cabals and artifices of the British cabinet. Do I say I believe? they have stood up in the houses of Parliament and avowed it. They have said that they sent the money of Britain into France to create internal commotions there. [*Interruption.*] The Citizen groans, but he will groan a little more when he remembers that Lord Stanhope[74] made a motion in reprobation of that avowal.[75] The motion was scouted, and the sentiment remained unretracted, to the disgrace of humanity, which could not but rise in indignation at the idea that any set of men could stand forward and say, we are employing the property of this country, taken from the hard earnings of industry, to spread treachery and crimes through the country of that enemy whom we wish to destroy though we have not the energy to conquer.

Citizens, you will consider, also, the situation in which France was plunged at that period: you will consider the barbarous manifesto of the Duke of *Brunswick*.[76] I mention not his name to give any wound to an unhappy female, who is torn from every connection to reside (such are the cruel mandates of state policy) at the mercy (for mercy, under such circumstances, it must be) of strangers whom, perhaps, she may love, but to whom, perhaps, she never can reconcile herself.[77] I have heard, and I am much disposed to believe,—for I am much inclined to think the Duke of Brunswick one, among the sovereigns of Europe, who possesses a larger share of intellect than belongs to most of them: our own blessed sovereign excepted. (*Reiterated applause.*)—

I am very happy to hear, Citizens, that you are so loyal; and that you will not suffer a just compliment to be passed upon our benign sovereign, without taking the notice of it that it merits!

I say this piece of Bobadil bravado[78] has been reported not to be the composition of the Duke of Brunswick. It was smuggled into the world, however, under his name: and I am sorry it should so frequently be the misfortune of Princes that their names should give the sanction of authority to measures of which they are totally ignorant, till the mischief has been disseminated through the world.

However, certain it is that this barbarous manifesto, whoever penned it, was one of the causes of the violences in France. Pressed with intrigues within, which were fomented and supported by cabals without, pressed by armies of invading despots, menaced on every side, provoked by every insult, injustice, and indignity, their enthusiasm and apprehensions arose to frenzy, and they did acts which I shall not attempt to justify—which I should wish could be blotted for ever from the page of history, if I were not sure that it is good for the future happiness of mankind that every historical fact should be fairly and publicly handed down.

Citizens, we are to remember, also, that, at the time when the country was driven to the last extremity, when arms could not be procured fast enough to be put into the hands of those brave defenders of liberty who were rushing forward to meet the foreign foe; at that time in the prisons, crammed with suspected persons, counter-revolutionists who had never been committed, were found to be concealed, in every part of Paris, and arms were found concealed in those places, evidently for purposes of the most detestable treachery. When we consider these circumstances, we must attribute to an unfortunate concurrence of events, those excesses which have been so frequently related with aggravation upon aggravation, as stains upon the character of the French people. We have, also, to consider that the situation in which they were placed rendered measures of considerable energy requisite. I am sorry they mistook the real character of energy: but the fears of a populace trembling for their new-born liberty, and driven to despair by such a combination of disastrous circumstances, can never be brought forward as a stain upon the general character of a nation, but by persons whose own understandings are either perverted, or who are determined to pervert the understandings of others.

If, however, we should admit, that there are some excuses for the excesses that took place in that country, we must, also, admit that there were men whose gloomy dispositions perpetuated those excesses when there could be no excuse for them whatever: for as Machiavel has well observed: "Cruelty, if ever it can be palliated, can only be so when it is committed but once, out of necessity, and for self-preservation, and never repeated afterwards, but converted, as much as possible, to the benefit of the subject."[79] I know that in the vague manner in which this is worded it might be made use of to justify the horrible massacres of St. Bartholomews, or even the still more horrible and atrocious massacre committed by that French aristocrat M. de Memmay,[80] and which all aristocrats are so willing to bury in oblivion. But I quote not the author's words because I mean to admit their full latitude, but because they give me an opportunity of shewing that even the advocates for cruelty and tyranny do not justify that reiterated fury and vengeance into which it is but too common for men to plunge in the fury of political contention. "Cruelty is ill applied", continues he, "when it is but little at first, and is afterwards rather increased than abated.—Those whose cruelty lingers and comes on by degrees, cannot possibly subsist long".[81] The event has shewn how truly this author was acquainted with the springs and influences of political action. It must, however, be admitted that few characters in the world ever had energy enough to do those things which were requisite in such a situation as France was plunged into, without, at the same time, indulging some disposition for revenge and cruelty.

"All new governments", says this same Machiavel, "are exposed to so many dangers, that it is impossible for a new Prince", and such, it cannnot be dissembled, at the latter part of his life, was Robespierre, though I believe, at the beginning, he was actuated by the true and genuine principles of republicanism. It is impossible, he says, for a new Prince, that is an usurper, "to avoid the scandal of being cruel."[82]

Citizens, as I believe the characters of great actors in the political world furnish the most important of the facts upon which the human mind expatiates, I shall next enter into some consideration of the character of Robespierre: by which I shall be able to shew you that he had not a constitution calculated to form an exception from this general rule. I admit, and I think I shall by and by prove, that there were in the character of Robespierre many as great qualities, as magnificent virtues as ever adorned a human being; unfortunately, however, none of those great qualities and virtues were of that description that led to moderation. He had no philosophy, he had no social affections, he had none of those tender sympathies which soften the rugged character of the politician, and reconcile the great and sublime powers of the human mind to the general endearments of humanity—that affection and general attachment to his species, which are necessary to constitute the truly excellent character: and without which no character, however splendid, can either command or deserve the general admiration of mankind. His virtues were of the severe and gloomy cast; his vices were those most favourable to cruelty and revenge; he was tainted, nay, he was saturated, if I may so express myself, with the monstrous vice of suspicion; a narrow selfish fiend, which, when it enters into the human character, debauches all the great qualities of the soul, and perverts the energies which might otherwise have been ornamental and beneficial to the human race. He was also, unfortunately a slave to personal cowardice. He had, it is true, political intrepidity; but the history of his proceedings show, that like *Marat* (though not to so great a degree) he had a heart that trembled for his personal security, and that, therefore, was disposed to raise fences and protections round him, which he thought necessary to cement with blood. He had also a political impetuosity that could brook no restraint; that must dash forward at once to its object, that could not go step by step to the attainment of that political amelioration at which, at first, he aimed, and which, therefore, hurried him from the path of patriotism to that of individual ambition. He had also a fanaticism gloomy and inveterate; and that fanaticism whetted the axe of the guillotine against the man who had long been his firmest and most useful friend; because, forsooth, (such was the popular pretence at least) this man denied some doctrines, of which he thought fit to make himself the champion.

I wish not to contend on this occasion, whether the atheism of Danton[83] were a vice or not; but I am convinced of this, that if it were a vice, it was of that description that man had nothing to do with; and the individual who once supposes he has a right to shed the blood of his fellow Citizens for differences in speculative opinion, knows not where he may stop. He may cut off this man's head to-day for being an atheist; he may cut off, the next day, another man's head for being a deist, and, the next, send flocks of people to the guillotine, because they receive the sacrament standing, when he takes it kneeling. In short, unless you suffer a man to enjoy the utmost freedom of opinion; unless you lay it down that speculative notions are not objects of punishment, and that punishment, if justifiable at all, is only useful when used to prevent destructive exertions of the powers and faculties of man, for the annihilation of life, or the overthrow of happiness,—Unless you admit these maxims, whatever your religious opinions may be, you are a fanatic. Whether you go to mass with Robespierre at one period, or at another bow down with this high-priest to his new-fangled allegorical religion,[84] whether you go to the conventicle, to the church, the chapel, or the plain meeting of the Quakers, it matters not; unless you uphold that every man has a right to his opinion, you cannot be a friend to genuine liberty and justice; you are hostile to human intellect: for though you think you are right, the man in direct opposition thinks he is right also, and if you want no other judgment than your own opinion to justify coercion, universal massacre must ensue, society must be unhinged, chaos return, and "darkness be the burier of the dead."[85]

The generality of these qualities, it is true, fitted Robespierre for the times he had to act in: and we may, indeed, observe a tendency in all times and postures of society, to create those characters which are necessary for them.

It is certain that the Brissotines were incompetent to the task of the salvation of France. They had virtue—they had philosophy; but they had no energy: and we may observe, from this, the reason why, in great revolutions, the first movers seldom steer through the whole. It is ridiculous, therefore, to suppose that any man, acquainted with the history of the universe, is anxious to produce revolutions. Revolutions are always produced by the folly and wickedness of the rulers, not by the projects of individuals. Whoever puts the first hand to the work, in all human probability will be one of the first that loses his head, in the progress of it; for the fact is, that the character of man only fits him for acting in that particular sphere where he finds a similar character in the posture of society. Hence what is called fortune. We say that this man is fortunate, and that man is unfortunate; for both have pursued their way with equal wisdom, and one has succeeded and the other fallen. But it is not fortune, but the times, and the victory of the one, and the fall of the other must result from one of these causes; either the individual who falls was not keen-sighted enough to see what the real state of society was, and what the proper mode of acting in that state of society, or else, seeing what it was, the habits of his character did not permit him to act in the particular way required.

Thus we find the Brissotines, at one period of the revolution, were characters best calculated to help it on. Their deliberate, progressive, cautious movements led forward the people and the country to a particular state, to which it, perhaps, never would have arrived but for those moderate exertions. But then came the daemon of foreign power, then came calamities, then came a posture of society for which their deliberate measures were no longer fitted. They could not assume the energy requisite for the moment; and the reins of power fell from their feeble hands. They were seized by the energetic gripe of the leaders of the mountain: men born to live among the storms of nature; and "rule them at their wildest."

The different dispositions requisite at different periods, are excellently animadverted upon by the author whom I have quoted to you before: "He whose manner of proceeding agrees with the times is happy, and he unhappy who cannot accommodate his conduct to them. Hence it is not rare to see a leader happy and flourishing one day, and ruined the next, without observing the least change in his disposition or conduct."[86] The fact is, the cause of his ruin is that he is incapable of that change. "For men, to arrive at the end which they propose, take very different courses; and if these different courses were accommodated to the characters and dispositions of the times, all might succeed. One acts with moderation, another with impetuosity; one with violence, another with art; one with patience, another with fury, and yet they may all arrive at the same end. We see, likewise, that of two persons, equally moderate, one succeeds, the other miscarries; and that two persons of different turns, one moderate, the other impetuous, are equally successful. This proceeds from nothing but the nature of the times, which either suits or disagrees with their manner of proceeding.—Upon this also depends the vicissitudes of good; for when a man acts always with moderation and patience, if the times and affairs turn so favourably as to suit his conduct, he prospers; but if the face of affairs and the times change, he is undone, because he does not change likewise."[87]

The whole of this reasoning, which Machiavel continues to a considerable extent, and which is certainly very just, is applied by him to Princes; but it is equally applicable to the leaders of revolutions: as I have in some degree shown you, from what I have observed relative to the Brissotines. The moment the crisis came they were incompetent to the task, and another faction of more power and energy stept forward, and seized the helm: otherwise, I believe, though France was too far enlightened eventually to have fallen, she would have experienced much greater calamities and difficulties, and been for the present, perhaps, disappointed of her object; a portion of her country would have perhaps been lost; and the real object of the allies, namely, a partition, and perhaps to a considerable degree, might have taken place.

But, however necessary the exertions of the Mountain for the moment might have been, cruel and unjustifiable beyond description, was the manner in which the triumph was enjoyed. Did they maintain such language as I have read to you from the proclamation of the friends of liberty in Holland? Did they with magnanimity turn round, forget the past, and enjoy the triumph without sullying it with vengeance? No: the retrospective principle had sunk too deep in their minds: the remembrance of the examples of cruelty so frequently set by the despotism from which they had so recently been emancipated, had contaminated their hearts; and the crimes of the French monarch survived, while the monarchy itself was broken in fragments.

Thus, Citizens, Europe was witness to the murder of the deputies; after that to the murder of the friends of those deputies; who were sent to the scaffold for fear they should revenge their blood; these were followed by their friends, and those by their's. And Robespierre, like Macbeth, soon found himself "so far gone in blood", that he thought it "harder to turn back than to go o'er":[88] Thus from suspicion and revenge he was driven to cruelty, and from cruelty to the necessity of ambitious usurpation; and this usurpation was to be fortified again by blood. Danton was to be sacrificed—Camille Desmolines[89]—Hebert[90]—all accused of counter-revolutionary crimes, though the real crimes I believe, of some of them were, that they were dangerous rivals to the ambitious Dictator; and the crimes of others, that they wished to restore to France that free representation, which was in some degree usurped by the plausible pretences under which the Convention contrived to procrastinate their power.

But whatever were the causes of the cruelty, the practice continued when the temper of the times could no longer endure it: And we find that not only justice was trampled upon, but discretion also—for though it may perhaps sometimes be true, as my Italian author has observed, "That it is of the two better to be impetuous than cautious; because fortune is a woman, with whom it is impossible to succeed without some degree of violence"; and that "it appears by experience that she more easily submits to those who are fierce and boisterous, than to such as are cool and deliberate."[91]— Though this may be true, yet certain it is, that such violent measures never can be of long duration. Fortunately for the universe, such crimes and such atrocities have a tendency to their own cure: accordingly we find that Robespierre fell by the machinations of his own violence; because he, no more than the party he had displaced, was capable of changing his character with the necessities of the times, but continued to act with violence when moderation and philosophy were requisite to heal the wounds which the struggle had given to the bosom of his country. This circumstance, I own, appeared to me so inevitable, from the perusal of the author I have so frequently quoted, that, when I read the following passage, I could not but consider it as a prophecy of the fall of Robespierre; though, at the time I read it, he appeared to be at the zenith of his power.—"Pope Julius II." (for Catholic Popes, as well as allegorical Popes, can be sometimes destroyers of the human race.) "Pope Julius II." says Machiavel, "in all his enterprizes acted with passion and vehemence; and the times and circumstances of affairs were so suitable to his manner of proceeding, that he always came off with success; and, by his violent and impetuous measures, succeeded in an enterprize which no other Pope, with all the wisdom of man", and he might had said, with all the infallibility of holiness "could ever have effected."—"But the shortness of his reign saved him from any reverse of fortune; for had he lived to see such times as made it necessary to proceed with caution and moderation, he would have certainly been ruined, because he could never have departed from his natural impetuosity. I conclude therefore, that, as Fortune is changeable, he who always persists in the same measures succeeds as long as the times fall in with them, but is sure to miscarry when the times alter."[92]

Citizens, it must also be observed from the first entrance of Robespierre upon the stage of the French revolution, we have strong traits of the ferocity of his disposition. He was the first man who lifted up his voice in justification of the wanton excesses of the people. So early as the 27th July, 1789, when a proclamation was proposed by M. *Lally de Tollendall*[93] to restrain the excesses and violences of the people, he says, "What has happened, after all, from this revolt of Paris? The public liberty."—So far he says true. The public liberty did arise from the revolt of Paris; and if Paris had not revolted as it did, Broglio[94] would have been upon their backs, with his train of mercenary assassins, to destroy every friend of Liberty in the country. But mark how he goes on!—"What has happened, after all, from this revolt of Paris? The public liberty: very little bloodshed, a few heads struck off", says he: "no doubt,—but guilty heads."[95]

This is the way in which that man, in the senate of his country, sported with the disastrous circumstance of the populace having taken vengeance into their own hands, and polluted the streets of Paris with streams of blood; shed in the spirit of wantonness and revenge.—"Very little bloodshed! A few heads struck off, no doubt; but guilty heads.—Ah! sir, it is to this commotion that the nation owes its liberty—that we are now sitting in this place."

Citizens, it is worth while to remark this passage, because it shows you how, from step to step, when a man begins a vindictive system, he goes to the utmost atrocity. This was the first justification, in the assembly, of the excesses of the people.

After the 10th of August 1792, the cry of vengeance was heard again. Some call the events of that day a massacre: I consider them as a glorious victory. The Royalists were conspiring to overthrow the constitution, and restore despotism; the Jacobins were endeavouring to overthrow the constitution, and set up republicanism. This is the bare statement of the fact: they met at the double crisis, each unconscious how near the plot of the other was to maturity: they met, and the battle was fought out bravely.— He who shall call that a massacre, must suffer me to pity the perversion of his understanding, if afterwards, he calls any battle by any other name. It was not a mere battle of mercenaries, contending for they knew not what, at the nod of a Court or a Cabinet; it was two parties of men, feeling conviction that their principles were their country; each knew, each felt, that without the downfall of the other they could have no security; and they struggled (in a situation where it was impossible for them longer to live in peace) by one decisive effort which should be the conqueror, the republican or the despot. The conflict began by treachery, gross, unpardonable, abominable treachery, on the part of the Royalists, who, upon seeing their King safe within the walls of the assembly, fired upon the populace, having previously told them that they were all friends, and would all hold together in the same cause. But though they began in treachery, they fought with courage; and, if the conqueror had been truly generous, they would have drawn a veil over the transaction; they would have said, We have conquered,—we are satisfied. But no: the man of blood went to the bar of the assembly, at the head of the sections of Paris, and called for punishment, upon the heads of the Royalists.—Punishment! for what? For having been beaten? for having been overthrown?—Revenge! punishment! retribution!—What, was it not enough to triumph over a party? And can you not then, with generous magnanimity, even applaud the courage of a vanquished foe; but must you yelp for vengeance.

Pardon me! I cannot restrain my indignation. Though I love the principles upon which the French revolution is founded, I cannot but lament that men, conspicuous for their talents, powers, and virtues, should sully so good and holy a cause by the wolfish and hellish yell of vengeance and slaughter.

This deputation went to the bar of the assembly on the 15th of August 1792. I shall draw a veil over the massacres that took place on the 2d and 3d of September.[96] They have been dwelt upon frequently enough already; and the aggravated colours in which they have been painted, and the care that has been taken to conceal all the palliating circumstances with which they were attended, prove that the Aristocrats of this country rather exult in them than deplore them. I shall mention, however, another massacre, which took place at an earlier stage of the revolution, and which the Aristocrats have not been so fond of dwelling upon, or pretended to regard with so much horror. It will shew, however, that the doctrines of Robespierre were in some degree countenanced by the transactions of some of the aristocracy at that time, and that, if the populace of Paris have plunged into cruel excesses of vengeance against their oppressors, they have only practised upon those tyrants a part of that inhumanity which the practices of those tyrants had learned them. During the beginning of the struggle in France, some time about the beginning of August, or latter end of July, 1789, one M. *de Memmay*,[97] who had always sided with the aristocracy, pretended to his tenants, and other inhabitants around his chateau, that he was in reality attached to the cause of liberty, and invited every person attached to that cause to come and join in a civic feast, and exult in the overthrow of despotism. They came (poor unsuspecting individuals!) from every part of the surrounding country. With hearts filled with gratitude and affection, they flocked to his castle, resounding the praises of the man who was thus about to sacrifice his oppressive privileges to the general happiness and welfare of his country. They were entertained with every semblance of hospitality: music, feast and dance went on chearfully and alternately round, and all was joy and unsuspecting felicity. But what was the catastrophe? The whole company, thus assembled, was led to a particular spot, by this infernal aristocrat, to vary their diversions, and he departed, under pretence that he would not damp their mirth by any restraint which his presence might put up on them. But no sooner was he withdrawn to a secure distance, than a match was applied to the fatal train; a mine was sprung, and, in one instant, the whole assembled multitude (men, women, and children) were scattered through the air, and their mangled carcasses were found by their patriotic friends weltering in blood,—a spectacle of horror which no tongue can describe, nor heart can scarcely conceive.

Citizens, we are told of the massacres of the 2d and 3d of September: the conflict of the 10th of August is called a massacre, that it may throw reproach and odium upon the friends of Liberty. But which of our senators (though this appeared in all the papers at the time) repeats the tale of this horrid massacre of aristocratic tyranny; this abandoned treachery, which taught the people to be cruel, by convincing them they had nothing but cruelty, nothing but tyranny to expect, if those privileged assassins, who had so long been tramping out human existence in the desolated realm of France, were restored to their irrational and soul-corrupting power.

Citizens, I shall now proceed to the last part of the lecture of this evening, namely, a comparison between the character of Robespierre and the immaculate minister of this country. I know well, citizens, what dangerous ground I tread upon: I know very well that though treason *once* meant *compassing and imagining the death of the King*, it now means telling truth to the shame and confusion of Ministers. I know also, "'Twere better pluck the master by the beard, then hurt the favorite's heel." I have no doubt, either, that there are persons here of various opinions: some of them, perhaps, good pious men, who, when they say their prayers, forget the name of God, and whisper Pitt. Let such, however, perform the bidding of their purblind deity. I invite them—I wish them to note every word I say. Let them call upon me to repeat any part they think good ground of prosecution: I will repeat it; for I can support, by historical facts, the opinion that I give; and if the country is so far lost in degeneracy that a jury can be *bought* to deprive an Englishman of his liberty, for saying the truth, this is no longer Britain, and I am desirous of being no longer in it. Send me with my beloved compatriot Gerrald—with him let me try the inhospitable climate of New Holland, herd among felons, or escape to the abodes of savages.[98]

Let us compare, then, the usurper Robespierre with the boasted Minister of this country:—a Minister who has been constantly imitating, for a long time, the worst parts of every oppressive measure of the French dictator and his faction, at the very moment when he was calumniating and abusing those measures: that Minister who, without the energy of Robespierre, has all his dictatorial ambition; who, without the provocations which Robespierre and his faction experienced, has endeavoured, vainly endeavoured, to carry into execution the same system of massacre for opinion, of sanguinary prosecution for proclaiming truth, of making argument High Treason, and destroying every individual who dared to expose his conduct, or oppose his ambitious views. Does this appear too strong a censure? It is only so, because the sanguinary malice of the English Minister has been as impotent as it was malignant;—because he and his faction had not energy enough, and British juries had too much honesty, to crown his malice with success. But if you want proofs of the views and objects of the man, peruse the facts relative to the late prosecutions, and particularly the trials, and the documents upon which those trials were founded.—If you find, from beginning to end, one single attempt, one single act, that *leans* towards what the law of this country calls treason—if you find any one act of violence, or attempt at violence, proved against any of the persons tried— if you do not find that the witnesses for the Crown (I should say for the *Minister*, for it is he, I must believe, and not the Crown, that stained the annals of the country with these prosecutions)—if it is not proved, even by the witnesses for the prosecution, that several of the men prosecuted for High Treason were most determinately hostile to all systems of violence; that they had opposed regularly and consistently every thing that looked like violence; that they had always contended that truth and reason were to be their only weapons—if you do not find these things as I now state them, brand me in the forehead, let me be marked with contempt and odium; let me (what can be worse) let me be baptized a *William*, and nicknamed a *Pitt!*

If it should be proved, and I have the documents to prove,—that is to say, I have them lodged where those who have an interest in suppressing the truth shall not be able to seize them till they are printed, and then they may get the printed copies.—If it should be proved also, that those men had all this in evidence before them in the Privy Council, from the witnesses they examined, what will you say, but that *Terror* was to have been *the order of the day* here also; that all argument was to be treason, and opinion felony; and that men for the future were to be afraid to open their lips to a friend at the table, or to encore a speech at the playhouse, for fear of being hanged, drawn and quartered, for High Treason?—I think, when you consider these facts, you can have no doubt what the disposition of this man was: what the inclination, however deficient he might be in energy, to imitate the tyranny of Robespierre.—If you recollect, also, as it is pretty well agreed, that 800 warrants for high treason were signed and sealed, ready to be executed upon the conviction of Hardy: of which they entertained no doubt: not recollecting that *English Juries are not Scotch Juries*, nor always ready to obey the nod of a minister, you will start with horror at the recollection of the precipice from which you have escaped.

But let us pursue the parallel.

Both of them have proved themselves to be men equally destitute of philosophy, and of those social affections, and tender sympathies that smooth the rugged temper of the politician, and make gentleness and energy go hand in hand. They have both, also shewn themselves to be sanguinary and revengeful, prone to suspicion, and exhibiting a strange mixture of personal cowardice and political impetuosity.

Robespierre and his faction ravaged France, it is true, for the destruction of royalty. Pitt and his faction have depopulated Europe, and spread a general famine through this quarter of the universe, for the annihilation of liberty.

Robespierre adopted a *fair* and *impartial requisition*, for the defence of the liberties of his country: (I say a fair and impartial requisition, for what is so just, and so impartial, if you are to have war, as to compel every man, whatever be his fortune, to partake of the hardships and perils of that war? to suffer no man, by procuring a substitute, to put the life of a human being who happens to be in a different state of society in competition with his paltry pittance of property, however it may be acquired?) *Pitt*, on the contrary, has adopted a *partial requisition*, by which the poor are submitted to the absolute controul, without appeal, of any justice of the peace, who chooses to pronounce that they have no visible means of subsistence; and in which the lower orders of society are to be compelled, exclusively, to bleed for the promotion and aggrandizement of the great.

Both have had their parties and their partialities.

Robespierre unjustly oppressed the rich, that he might support his popularity among the poor. *Pitt* has neglected, and by his wars and consequent taxes, oppressed the poor, to secure his popularity among the rich.

Robespierre, in order to preserve a plentiful circulation of the necessaries of life, punished combinations (cruelly and unjustly punished them!—for severity and cruelty are always unjust!) among the merchants and monopolists, that he might shew his partiality for the laborious part of the community. Under the administration of Pitt, punishments still continue to be awarded against the labourers who combine to increase their wages, while monopoly is connived at and encouraged, among the wealthy, upon whom alone administration chuse to rest their confidence.

Both have made use of extraordinary means for filling the ranks of their armies, and manning their fleets.

Pitt has tolerated crimps,[99] kidnappers, and press-gangs. *Robespierre* took care that, whatever might be the condition of the other members of society, the army and navy should be well clothed, well fed, and well paid.

Robespierre set up a free constitution, and tyrannized in direct opposition to it. *Pitt* praises another *free* constitution, and tramples all its provisions under foot.

One effected his purpose by a dependent *Committee of Public Safety*. The other by a packed majority of borough-mongers and white slave-merchants: for such we must consider them, if the assertion of Mr. *Alderman Newnham* is true, that the common people of this country, *of whom they dispose*, are in the condition of West-India slaves.[100]

Both pretended to reverence *Trial by Jury*: and both endeavoured to undermine it as fast as they could. *Robespierre* by erecting a Revolutionary Tribunal, which had a perpetual jury, of his own appointment; and *Pitt* by fabricating innumerable acts, which vest the trial of Englishmen (especially the poor, dependent, classes of Englishmen) in the arbitrary discretion of Justices of the Peace.

Robespierre is accused of keeping a set of witnesses to swear whatever he chose, and of calling them his lambs. I don't know whether *Pitt* may be called the *good shepherd*, but he also has as fine a flock as ever grazed on the bounty of his rival: he has his *Groves's*, his *Taylors*, his *Walshes*, his *Alexanders*, his *Lynams*, his *Uptons*,[101] and a long list of gentlemen, equally respectable, equally valuable. *I don't say with himself*, but with each other; and whom we will dignify, if you please with the titles of *Knights of the honorable order of Confidants, or retainers of gentlemen high in office*.

Pitt has, however, escaped the odium of part of this parallel; for *Robes-*

pierre has been accused of *actually sacrificing*, by these means, a monstrous number of people—A much greater number than he has been charged with destroying, than in reality have fallen; for I remember having read of one man's being guillotined six times, who was afterwards killed in a massacre, which never took place, and after that had the honour of sitting in the Convention: and to add to the pathos, he was a man 70 years old, and had nine children—*Santerre*[102] was guillotined twice, and had afterwards the honors of the sitting in the Convention. General *Miranda*[103] was guillotined several times, also; and *Kellerman*,[104] who has now the command of one of the armies. Undoubtedly however he did, under the pretence of law, commit a monstrous train of massacres.—But I will ask you, what might have been the situation of this country, if the late prosecutions had succeeded? Consider that there were many thousand members of the London Corresponding Society—and that a part of the doctrine was, that every member, whether present at their objectionable deliberations or not, was answerable for the whole acts of the sociey, and for every political act of every individual connected with it.

But, suppose they meant to go no farther than the destruction of those whom they had marked as their first victims—though I am credibly informed that a noble Lord was heard to say, that he believed they must hang a third part of the Constitutional Society,[105] and perhaps that might be enough. Now, as it was admitted that the Constitutional Society was not so bad as the London Corresponding Society, we may conclude that one half of the Members of the latter were to be hanged also; and that might have been enough for them. But who knows, when you once begin a system of massacre, and especially *legal* massacre, for opinion, where can you stop? I do not believe that *Robespierre* meditated, in the first instance, those scenes of carnage into which he at last was plunged. But fear of revenge, and the brooding malice of suspicion, hurried him from act to act of accumulating horror, till nothing but his own destruction could retrieve the country. And I have strong suspicions in my mind, that, if they had touched the life of an individual who stood at the bar of the Old Bailey, the gaols of London (and we all know we have abundance) would have been as crammed as ever the prisons of Paris were, even in the very dog-days of the tyranny of Robespierre.

Both these men also have a happy knack of sacrificing their friends, whenever they find it convenient to get rid of them. Thus we find a *Danton* and a *Hebert* have been cut off by *Robespierre*, as soon as they had answered his purpose. *Pitt* has also abandoned a *Jackson*, a *Fitzwilliam*, and a *Robert Watt*.[106]

But here, Citizens, the parallel ends. For, though *Pitt* has the dictatorial ambition, he can never be accused of the energy or virtues of *Robespierre*.

Pitt is the tool of an oligarchic faction, over whom he appears to tyrannize, but who can make him, when they please, their slave. *Robespierre* has made every thing subservient to his own views, and the greatness of his own mind.

The one was firm, steady, and constant; the first in the original assembly of France who declared himself hostile to royalty; and he never departed from his text—Whether that text was right or wrong I am not now enquiring. The other, on the contrary, throughout his whole conduct, has been shuffling, treacherous, and evasive. The most anxious advocate for parliamentary reform, associated with the first modern projectors of the plan of universal suffrage and annual parliaments; he has since been the bitterest enemy to reformation, and has even thirsted for the blood of every individual who would not be as great an apostate as himself.

He has, indeed, pretended to be consistent with respect to the slave trade; but it was only, I am afraid, consistent hypocrisy. He can command a majority for places and pensions: but he cannot command a vote for the interests of humanity.

Robespierre had a soul capacious, an imagination various, a judgment commanding, penetrating, severe. Fertile of resources, he foresaw, created, and turned to his advantage all the events that could possibly tend to the accomplishment of his designs. The mind of *Pitt* is barren and inflated, his projects are crude, and his views short sighted.

One was always politically intrepid and unmoved; his means always adequate to the end, and always perservered in with steadiness and consistency. The other, indecisive, fluctuating, and capricious, adopts a project to-day, and abandons it to-morrow; issues an order from the Privy Council in the morning, and countermands it at night. His calculations (which do not depend upon the rule of three)[107] have always been erroneous and deceitful; and his consequent blunders have been such as nothing but his smooth verbosity could cover.

One possessed the key of the passions and understood how to estimate their influences, and command the various operations of the human mind. The whole knowledge of the other is confined to his numeration table. Figures he can command, but in events he has always been so mistaken that he has attempted no one thing without effecting the very contrary.— Anxious to suppress Jacobinism in France, he adopted the very measures calculated to make "the banner of Jacobinism triumph without a struggle."[108]

The projector of the seizure of the French West India Islands, the means he has employed there have been so inadequate to the object, that the event in all probability, must be, after being flattered with a transient gleam of success, the total loss of all our possessions in that part of the world. [109]

The one, though dreaded was respected; he was revered while he was abhorred. The energy of his mind commanded success; victory attended upon the arms he directed, partly, it is true, from the energy of the country; but partly, from the energy, also, of his directing mind; which planned, which formed, which pervaded the whole system; saw all the parts, and knew to which in particular, it was necessary for him to direct his powers. Every one of his plans were conducted to its accomplishment except the last he undertook, and in which he was disappointed because France was too much enlightened, after having shaken off the chains of one tyrant, to yield to those of another. We find attendant upon the heels of his rival—on the contrary—not victory and triumph, but disgrace and defeat: disgraces so innumerable that nothing but the muddy imaginations of the inventors could possibly have occasioned them all: defeats so continued that scorn, instead of lamentation, followed at their heels.

Add to this that *Robespierre* had a mind too great to be debauched by any thing but ambition. He grasped at no accumulation of places and emoluments; he neither enriched himself nor his family; he indulged in no voluptuous pleasures; he was incorruptible; severe in simplicity to the last; and we cannot do greater justice to his memory than by closing this lecture by a quotation from the works of one of his bitterest enemies, *Montgaillard*: —"He possesses a character of incorruptibility", says he, "which hath preserved his influences against all the attacks of the Brissotines, and of the Commune of Paris. Solely confined in appearance to his functions of Member of the Committee of Public Safety and of Jacobin, Robespierre shews every appearance of the most unaffected man. This modesty of triumph, this oeconomy of person, and the obscurity of his private life, have so long secured him the popular favour: he lives as he did in 1790, neither altering his manners, nor his taste, and always changeless." [110]

Having reviewed these facts, it is impossible to doubt which of these characters we must prefer.

[Selections from Volume 2]

THE TRIBUNE, No. XVI

The PRESENT WAR *a principal cause of the* STARVING CONDITION *of the* PEOPLE.—The first Lecture "On the causes of the Dearness and Scarcity of Provisions"; *delivered by* J. Thelwall, *Wednesday, April 29th,* 1795.[1]

CITIZENS,

MY feelings are peculiarly gratified to find so thronged an attendance when a subject like the present is held out for investigation; because at the first view it must appear to be one of those which do not promise as large a proportion of amusement, as many other topics might lead you to expect. Your attendance therefore shews the deep anxiety you feel for the attainment of information; and I am sure a subject equally important with the present cannot frequently be selected for your attention. I know hardly any interest of humanity that is not involved in the enquiry. I know hardly any branch of political knowledge that is not necessary for the complete and thorough investigation; nor any individual subject that would require so large a proportion of time and attention to do it justice; or so much ingenuity and precision to place the facts it involves in a proper point of view; and it is[2] not the ostentation of false modesty, which compels me to say, that I am well assured, I do not come before you properly qualified to do it justice. If I should, however, in some degree awaken the attention of the audience, and through their means of the country at large, to the serious consideration of the subject, and a fearless enquiry into the *real* sources of the calamity, I shall have effected a very grand part of my object. And I am convinced that it is the duty of every individual, as far as lies within his power, to labour for the benefit of the human species, by dragging forth to public view every fact which industry and opportunity can put him in possession of, relative to circumstances which embrace so large a proportion of their happiness and prosperity.

There will arise considerable difficulties, however, in the investigation. If I should confine myself simply to facts and arguments, I am aware that a large portion of my audience would not only be disappointed, but from not being in the habits of abstract speculation, would fail of receiving that information which, as far as I have the power, I wish to give them. I am aware, also, on the other hand, that if I run too much into popular declamation, or give the reins too much to fancy, the great object which stimulates me to enter into the enquiry would be lost. Facts would not be brought to your minds with sufficient interest and simplicity; and instead of giving you that light which should guide to happiness, I might only produce that heat which by leading to turbulence, would be injurious to society.

I shall attempt, however, as much as I can, to steer a middle course, and without disdaining to rouse attention by occasional appeals to your feelings and imagination, I shall endeavour by the closest reasoning which hasty preparation enables me to command, to force my way to the conviction of your better judgments. By such a combination *I believe* the best effects are to be produced: But *I am sure* of this—that if I should be able to accomplish this purpose to the utmost of my wishes, I should do the most dangerous thing for my own personal security and peace that any individual, barring projects of violence and commotion, could undertake. For the facts involved in this enquiry are so monstrous, the abuses of government, and those who have the administration of government, so enormous, the scandalous practices and proceedings with which the understandings of mankind have so long been imposed upon, while so large a portion of the people have been reduced to beggary, are so dreadful, that a man who should successfully state them to the public, will be in eternal danger—from those men at whose interests he must strike; and if he escapes the traps and pitfalls of perverted law, he ought to wear a helmet on his head and a coat of mail upon his breast, to preserve him from assassination.

I am however too far pledged to the public to retreat from the path of public duty. After the situations in which I have stood, after the malice that has been directed against me, I cannot retire from the theatre of public action without betraying and injuring the cause I am embarked in, more than I have yet been able to do it good. I shall therefore put aside all personal considerations, and proceed to the investigation of my subject: nor shall I be prevented by any considerations from doing all the justice in my power, to the truths which I mean to bring before you.

I warn you however before hand, that small indeed will be the proportion of light which I can throw upon the subject, compared to what might be thrown upon it, by proper time and attention. Yet though I can do but little, it will be no excuse for me if I neglect doing the little that I can.

The enormous increase of the price of provisions must be so evident to the most casual observer, that it is not necessary to enter into any declamation upon the simple circumstance of that increase. If however we take into consideration the facts of former history, and compare together the state of human society, in this country, in former periods and at the present time, the increase will come swelling upon our view in a proportion so monstrous, that credulity will be staggered; and I should not venture to state the facts to you, if I had not *aristocratic authority* upon which those facts can be established.

When we learn that, 230 years ago, *a chicken was sold for a penny*, and *a hen for two-pence*, and that now a fowl is not to be purchased in the London market for less than five shillings, we are struck with wonder, and are led immediately to enquire how comes this monstrous increase in the price of provisions?

The philosopher perhaps will immediately appeal to theoretical reasoning, and tell you of the immense increase of the quantity of circulating specie—he tells you, and he tells you truly, that the mines of Peru have been constantly working; that the bowels of the earth have been rent in every quarter of the globe, in order to drag the hidden stores to the eye of day; and that hence results a rapid decrease of the value of money. He tells you, also, that in this country, in particular, the pompous use of furniture made of precious metals has very much declined, that this furniture has, also, got into circulation, and that hence arises another decrease of the value of money. He tells you, also, that the state of society is such that the circulating medium passes with greater facility from hand to hand, and that in consequence of that quick circulation he can adduce an additional reason for the increased price of the necessaries and luxuries of life—or in other words for the decreased value of money.

All this is true. But let us see *how far* this will carry us. It will show us, it is true, that a pound in money now is not as much as a pound in money formerly was. And perhaps, if we trace the matter farther back, we shall find another reason, for the increase of the *nominal value* of commodities;

namely, that the weight of that coin which bears the same nominal value, at this time, is not so great as it was at the periods when that nominal value was fixed.

From the first of the Norman Sovereigns of this country to the present times, we may trace a gradual diminution of the value of money: I mean to say in the weight of it. Originally a pound weight of silver was coined into no more than 20 shillings; and hence 20 shillings are called a pound at this very day; although we know very well that 20 shillings are not a pound weight of silver, at this time, but that, on the contrary, 60s. are now coined out of that quantity. This makes however nothing to my present argument, as by far the larger proportion, and if Bishop Fleetwood may be considered as an authority, the whole of this decrease in the weight of money had taken place before the reign of Queen Elizabeth, from whom I date the calculations I am about to make. For that Prelate in his very precise and laborious chronology of fluctuations in the standard and value of money, makes the sterling coin of Queen Elizabeth, correspondent with the standard of the present day.[3]

Let us see then how far these facts will account for the increased price of provisions: for if it is really true, that the sole causes of this increased price are the increase of circulating cash, and the variations in the standard of money, then the condition of the lower orders of society, and of all orders, ought to be precisely the same as before: because, it being the money that has declined, and not the articles of consumption that have advanced in value, the consequence is, that no other difference has actually taken place, than an increased incumbrance in the quantity of money that you are to take to market with you to purchase the articles you want.

A little enquiry, however, will teach us how very small a proportion of the swollen price of provisions is to be attributed to these causes—for at the very time of which I have been speaking to you, while depicting the very moderate price of several articles of consumption, the common price of manual labour was 8d. a day. You will therefore immediately see that there is no sort of proportion between the increase of the price of manual labour and the increase of the price of provisions, during that 230 years which has thus passed away, sweeping, if I may so express myself, in their flight, every comfort and enjoyment from the cheerless tables of the industrious poor.

As I told you before, I have aristocratic authority for these facts. Mr. *Hume*[4] has never yet been suspected of Jacobinism; yet Mr. *Hume*, in the 3d Appendix to his History of England, (*vol. 8, page 346, of Cadell's small edition*,[5] for I think it right to be very particular in my quotations) states it as a fact, upon the authority of an ancient author, that between 1550 and 1560 "a pig or a goose was sold for 4d. a good capon was sold for 3d. a chicken for 1d. and a hen for 2d.: and yet", continues this author, who wrote at the very period relative to which he speaks, "at this time the wages of a common labourer was 8d. per day." Now supposing that the prices of other things were equally low, according to the present ratio, we find that *the wages of a single day would have bought the poor labourer a fat pig, a loaf of bread, and some good ale to drink for himself and his family.* But consider, I pray you, how many days a poor labourer must work before he must touch either ale or fat pig in the present situation of affairs. For my own part, I do not see why a poor labourer (without whom, by the way, we should have none of us either ale, nor pigs, nor bread, nor any thing else) should not occasionally have his pig to banquet upon, and his pot of ale after it to refresh himself. But alas! these things are now entirely out of the question; and if a man has three or four children, his ordinary wages will not even buy a sufficiency of bread alone: for what is the present price of wages? I believe we may estimate them at about sixteen pence per day throughout the country; and I am in possession of facts enough to prove, that for ordinary labour, that is to say, for eleven months out of twelve, this is the outside. Now the price of a half peck loaf, which for such a family is not too much, is twenty-pence. Such are the blessings of our Constitution in Church and State as now administered.

But suppose we take the estimate from London, where the price of labour is considerably higher. The great part of labouring men employed in this capital receive from twenty-pence to two shillings a day. (Some particular trades, among whom combination is easy, have by a sort of insurrection and violence, extorted more!) But what is the price of a pig or a goose now? I never go to market, Citizens, and therefore am obliged to report these circumstances at second-hand; but I am told that a good pig or goose at this time will cost about *seven shillings*, instead of *four-pence*; that a capon instead of *three-pence* is *six shillings*; and that fowls, instead of a penny and two-pence, are about four shillings and six-pence, at the lowest.

Now taking the average of the increase from these facts; supposing, for the present, that the increase of other articles has been proportionate, the present price of provisions is about twenty-two times—Mark the fact, Citizens—the price of provisions is multiplied by about twenty-two, from what it was at the period I have been speaking of. Well, are the wages of the labouring poor increased in a proportion of 22 to one? If instead of this, they are scarcely doubled, let us mark in what a very different situation the lower orders of society are placed, from what they were in the golden days of Queen Bess as they are called.—(Golden they might be, to the poor, in this respect: but I cannot help putting in my caveat as to the general praise bestowed upon the reign of that despotic termagant.)

If the price of labour had kept pace with the growing price of pigs and of poultry, the wages of a labouring man would have been at this time not less than *fifteen shillings per day*.

Now Citizens, if these are facts, and if it is also true that no master could possibly afford to give his labourers fifteen shillings per day, I am entitled to draw this conclusion—that the increase of the price of provisions does not principally result from the decrease of the value of money, from the larger quantity of circulating specie, or from any of those causes which mock philosophers have appealed to, in order to gratify the tyrants who paid them for varnishing over their oppressions, and deluding the people who listened to their fallacious arguments.

Citizens this is not all. I have some reason to believe that, at the time I am now speaking of, the usual day's labour of a working man, instead of twelve or fourteen hours, was but eight.[6] I will tell you my reason for supposing this. I know it to be the fact, that, in a particular part of the country, it was but eight hours at that time; and you will judge how far it is likely that this was an exclusive privilege.

About three years ago, being on the coast of Kent, and taking up my habitation at a friend's house, at Dinchurch wall, which keeps out the sea from Romney Marsh; and being at the house of one of the principal members of the corporation by which that district has the misfortune to be governed, I had an opportunity of learning some particulars relative to their regulations. By the charter of this corporation, which was granted, I understand, about the time I have been speaking of, the price of the day's labour, for a man working upon the wall, which stands in need of constant repair, is fixed at a shilling.

This will shew you that at that period 8d. per diem was the average price, and not the maximum of the price paid for labour, for the price of a day's labour, upon Dinchurch wall, for keeping out the sea from Romney Marsh, was fixed by charter at 1s. Being fixed by charter, it remains the same at this time, and the Corporation itself has not the power of altering it. But the day's labour upon this wall being originally only eight hours, the poor labourers, finding themselves no longer able to live twenty-four hours upon one day's work, perform regularly a day and an half's work every day: that is to say, they toil twelve hours for which they receive 1s. 6d. for the support of themselves and families.

This is only an individual instance I grant; and therefore does not authorize a very positive conclusion; but as it has led me to suspect, that the day's labour was anciently no more than eight hours, I state the foundation upon which the suspicion rests, in hopes that others may think it worth while to enquire further into the subject. It is certainly worth enquiry; and for my own part, whether it was the general practice or not, I am thoroughly convinced that it is more than enough for the interests and happiness of society; and more than enough to be put upon the individual. Nor can I give unqualified praise to the laws of any country, that does not enable a poor man to maintain his family in decency by the diurnal labour of eight hours.

Nay Citizens, if—which I believe never can be the case, and therefore I don't wish to enforce it upon you as a thing practicable—but if an equal division of labour among all the inhabitants of this island, and if the luxuries, the follies, and fopperies of life were banished, even one hour per diem to each individual would be labour enough for the comfortable subsistence of all. Nay I am informed, that Mr. *Nicholson*,[7] a chymist and philosopher, whose very name commands our reverence, has absolutely calculated, that the whole labour employed in producing the absolute necessaries of life, when divided equally among the whole population of the country, is not more than *half an hour* in the day.

Now though I think it a very good thing, that some of the *embellishments*, as well as the NECESSARIES of life, should be attended to, though I think it a very good thing that a country should be adorned with splendid edifices, magnificent paintings, books to inform the mind, and diversions and indulgences to relax and soften it—that we should have articles of ease and gratification, as well as the bare accommodations of life; yet I do not think it right to grind the faces of the poor upon the mill-stone of oppression, that a few worthless individuals may arrogate to themselves the individual possession of all those comforts and advantages.

Citizens, when I am thoroughly aware of the applications that may be made of what I am saying, which I could wish always to be, and how far the inferences will go which I attempt to draw from the facts I am stating, I am very desirous that I should never appear to draw a conclusion beyond that point in which the facts, fairly and candidly stated, will bear me out. I ought therefore to observe, that, with respect to the former conclusion upon the prices of provisions, there is some degree of fallacy, and that when this fallacy is fairly stated, it must be admitted to operate as a drawback in some degree, with respect to the disproportion between the prices of provision and of labour; and consequently that the depression of the lower orders of society is *not quite so extravagant* as it might, in the first instance, appear. I wish to put you in possession of all the facts that I am master of; and I shall not therefore be very much afraid of appearing to contradict in one part of my lecture what I advance in another.

I leave ungenerous advantages to the wrong side of the question. Our cause stands not in need of them. I wish to submit the whole of the reasonings, pro and con, fairly and candidly, that you may see how much and how little the facts I bring before you bear upon the conclusions I wish to adduce.

Some abatement then is to be made from the calculation drawn from poultry and other articles of that description, because the fact is, that it was not, originally, so much as it is now, the practice of a few particular individuals of the privileged and opulent orders of society to monopolize to themselves a particular species of food. Luxuries did not always bear a price so disproportionate to the necessities of life as they do now. There was a time when salmon (for example) and all luxurious fish were so plentiful and abundant, that the poorest individual in society as well as the richest, could have them upon their tables, and banquet upon them to satiety.

I had an opportunity to mention to you once before, that it was found necessary, at Winchester, to insert a clause in the indentures of poor boys apprenticed from the parish, to prevent them from being fed more than three times a week upon salmon. But means have since been taken to preclude the necessity of such clauses. It was known by the great and mighty potentates who dance before us in the puppet show of state, adorned with stars and garters—it was known (I was going to say by these mountebanks but I mean by these *right honourable gentlemen*), that luxuries were adopted to pamper their appetites, and fill them with the sinful lusts of the flesh, and thereby corrupt their morals and render them but little disposed to go to church, and still less disposed to listen to every thing that the gentleman in the black gown should say to them, and finally to render them unfit for labour, and destroy their constitutions. These *Right Honourable Gentlemen*, therefore, with respect to many of those articles, were willing to engross the dangerous enjoyment to themselves, knowing very well that their own morals could not be made much worse, and that if they did eat and drink themselves to death, it was matter of very little consequence to society. Salmon was therefore contracted for by their agents of luxury, the great fishmongers; and agreements were notoriously made that only a given number should be brought to market, and the rest, let them be as plentiful as they would, should serve to manure the earth. Other practices (particularly the breaking up of small farms) have tended to increase the price of pigs and poultry: it being found improper for the swinish multitude to have such food—there being something monstrous in the idea of one pig eating another.

These circumstances have caused a great disproportion between the prices of those articles and of the articles of common food: much greater within the remembrance of some persons perhaps to whom I am now speaking, than it used to be. But suppose we take the general difference in the price of provisions at the most moderate calculation possible: suppose we should admit, for the present, that the price of these articles was no more at the period I am speaking of than the price of common butcher's meat: suppose for example at the same time that a chicken was to be bought for a penny, meat was a penny per pound; what shall we then find the proportion to be? Meat a penny a pound, and labour eightpence per day. *The price of a day's labour, then, at that period,* at the lowest computation, *was equal to the price of eight pounds of butcher's meat.* Is that the case now?

If this is the lowest calculation that can be admitted, then, certainly, whatever the result is, as to the difference between the proportionate prices of labour and provisions then, and the proportionate prices of labour and provisions now, we shall be compelled to admit that such difference does now exist between the condition of the laborious part of the community then and now.

Well then to make the price of labour at this period equal in point of real advantage to the price of labour at that period,—that is to say, to enable a man for the same quantum of labour to get the same quantity of comforts and accommodations, the average price of labour ought to be 5s. 4d. per diem throughout the country.

Let me be understood accurately. I do not mean to set myself up as the arbitrary judge of what ought to be, and what ought not to be, the price of labour. This is not what I am aiming at. I want to convince you of the nature and causes of the evil; and then let the good sense and understanding of the country seek for its remedy. Whether the proper remedy is to remove the causes of the extravagant price of provisions, or to raise the wages of labour, or whether both ought in some degree to be done, I do not at present decide: But I think I am entitled from this statement to draw this conclusion—that there is a monstrous advance upon the prices of the necessaries and accommodations of life; the whole of which cannot be attributed to the decrease of the real value of money by which these articles are bought. I think I am entitled, also, to conclude—that either one or other of these circumstances is the fact—either the quantity of money has been constantly increasing, and the prices of provisions have consequently kept equal pace with that increase, while the higher orders of society have monopolized the increasing money and all the consequent advantages to themselves, so that the lower orders of society, by whom the whole was produced, have not been proportionately rewarded; or else there is an increase in the price of the articles of consumption, disproportionate to an extravagant degree, with the increase of the specie by which those provisions is to be purchased.

I believe, Citizens, both these statements are true. I believe, from causes which I shall afterwards investigate, that the price of the necessaries of life has increased beyond the increase of the circulating medium: I mean the *general circulating medium*. I shall speak of *that swindling bubble called paper credit*, at another part of these Lectures. I believe, also, that there has been a neglect of the lower orders of society; and that the increase of their wages has not borne any sort of proportion with the *real increase of the quantity*, and consequent *decrease of the value* of money.

But let us bring the comparison a little nearer to us. Let us take facts of more recent date: and see what we are enabled to conclude from them.

I shall now proceed to statements to the accuracy of which (if they are accurate) a great proportion of you will be able to bear testimony; of the fallacy of which (if they are false) you will readily detect:—facts relative to the prices of provisions within the last twenty-five years. I shall then compare these prices with the increase of the price of labour; and see how far the lower orders of the people have been benefited even during that period, for a great part of which the growth of wealth, commerce and prosperity has been so frequently boasted, by that treacherous individual, who has all the while had his dagger at the heart of every blessing, and every comfort and accommodation of the country.

Twenty years ago bread was four-pence per quartern, now it is nine-pence farthing. (*I understand that in London it has since risen to a shilling.*)

Nay this increase, monstrous as it is, has another aggravating circumstance—namely, that many of those vegetables which used to decrease the consumption of bread, are now scarcely to be got at any price whatever. Potatoes which, since I have been a housekeeper, used commonly to be sold at five pounds for two-pence, are now three half-pence per pound. This circumstance may appear trifling and ridiculous to some of us: but it is no trifle, it is no ridicule to the poor individual who has five or six children to support; and who hitherto has been able to give them but little sustenance, but what was derived from these potatoes, sopped in a little of that chalk and water which in London we call milk.

But these are not the only articles which have thus increased in their price. We talk of famine in France. We have a worse famine at home. They have had no scarcity but of bread alone. We, it seems, have a scarcity of every thing. No kind of *meat*, in any part of that country, has ever been more than four-pence per pound. What is the case with us? Boiling beef, twenty or twenty-five years ago, might be bought at from two-pence to two-pence halfpenny: now from six-pence to six-pence halfpenny; roasting ditto at four-pence now at eight-pence; pork and veal at four-pence halfpenny, now at eight-pence halfpenny; mutton three-pence halfpenny and four-pence now eight-pence; for good salt butter that use to be bought at five-pence we now pay eleven-pence; loaf sugar, (good aristocratic loaf sugar) such as you must now pay thirteen or fourteen-pence per pound for, was then sold at sixpence; as for the cheap sort of loaf sugar, as it is called, for which you pay eleven-pence or a shilling, at this time, it is such coarse democratic stuff as no individual, at the period I am speaking of, would have bought at any price whatever. Moist sugar (a very important article to poor people, who wish to keep their children in health by regaling them frequently with a fruit pudding) used to be two-pence halfpenny per pound, it is now nine-pence. Coals, till within these seven years, were scarcely ever so high as a shilling per bushel. They have been three shillings and three shillings and sixpence, during the late inclement season; and twenty-pence was no uncommon price the winter before. What is the result of all this?—That coals have increased their price threefold, common sugar almost fourfold, butter and bread considerably more than double; some meats have increased threefold in their price, and the average of all animal food is considerably more than double the price now that it was twenty or twenty-five years ago. Now then supposing we could admit that all this increase of price resulted from the increase of gold and silver, from the wealth, and grandeur, and splendour, and prosperity of the country—and Mr. *Dundas* having told you that *general bankruptcy is a proof of the prosperity of the country*, may perhaps be able to prove to you, that the increased price of provisions is a proof of the grandeur, prosperity, and happiness of the country: But, if this be true, what justice has been done to those millions of our fellow citizens, from whose labour, from whose industry, from the sweat of whose brow, all that wealth and prosperity has been reaped? Ought not this wealth, grandeur, and prosperity, to have enabled the labourer who procured them, at least to eat as well, drink as well, cloath himself as well, lay on as good a bed, and be sheltered by as good a roof as formerly?

For the accomplishment of this, the price of labour ought to be considerably more than doubled. It has not, however, upon an average, from one end of the country to the other, been increased during that period one fourth. In some places it has scarcely been increased at all; and, in many, not one sixth. Mark then the blessed effects of the martial administrations of *North*[8] and *Pitt*; two characters that will go hand in hand down to infamy; the one for the sordid and pusillanimous cowardice with which he suffered himself to be made the chief tool and instrument of a war he never approved, the other for his savage propensity to the destruction of the human race, and the unfeeling duplicity with which he has pursued his ambitious views. But why do I put epithets to the word? Hypocrisy itself includes every thing that is detestable and abhorred; and wherever you find that scowling countenance, that shuffling gait, that lopsided arrogance of deportment which marks the political maypole of this devoted country, set down the being thus stamped by the broad seal of nature, for all that the catalogue of guilt contains, from solitary intoxication to debauchery, to the ravage of nations and the depopulation of continents, and the most inveterate hatred to the liberties and happiness of mankind.

Thus, then, we find that the labourers of this country, at this time possess considerably less than half the necessaries, comforts, and accommodations, which they were able to obtain twenty or twenty-five years ago, and less than a third of what recompensed the same or a less degree of labour in the middle of last century: while at the same time, the pensions, places, and luxuries of our rulers have been extravagantly increased. The wealth, the power, the insolence of successive administrations, have kept pace with the growing misery of the people; and while one are stripped of half their necessaries, the others are insulting common sense and common decency, with the pompous display of more than twice their former opulence and wasteful grandeur. Yet *aristocrats* have the shameless audacity to tell us, that if the price of the necessaries of life has increased, the price of labour has increased also.

It is a courtly virtue to lie with the words of truth; and therefore I give them credit for their consistency. The price of labour has indeed increased from eight-pence to a shilling, and from a shilling to fifteen-pence, while the necessaries of life have risen at a proportion of from eight-pence to two shillings, and from two shillings to five.

Such then are the facts with respect to the usual articles of common accommodation. But there are other articles which, though not immediately consumed by man, have also a tendency to increase his misery, when they are increased in their price. Hay, for example, and indeed every individual article that bears any price whatever. What then are the facts relative to those articles? Have they increased in price, or have they not? Within five years, from the year 1790, oats have increased 75 per cent. in price.

I believe I state this fact from such authority, that I do not stand in danger of any contradiction. I am not myself an adept in the market price of these articles, or in the commerce that is carried on relative to them: but I believe I can state from the best authority, that since the year 1790, the price of oats has increased 75 per cent. while hay, every article of pulse, and a great variety of those articles which contribute, in a second hand way, to the comforts of life, have kept pace with this increase.

What then shall we say to all these facts?—Is it necessary, or is it not, that the causes should be enquired into? I believe it is necessary: for whatever may be the case with respect to theological matters, with respect to political concerns, I believe it is virtue to know good from evil. I believe, that we ought to pluck the apple of science whenever it hangs within our reach. I am sure, also, that if it is good to enquire, it is necessary that the people should make the enquiry for themselves: for I do not believe the ministry will be inclined to make it for them. At this period indeed they have better employment abroad. Their wits and faculties are too much engaged in showing how consistent it is for them to talk of the faithlessness of republicans, by persuading the Royalists of La Vendee to break thro' all the oaths and engagements they have made with the republic of France. They are too busy in sending their 50,000 stand of arms, with their scoundrel run-away emigrant officers, to excite fresh insurrections—fresh scenes of blood and massacre, among the ignorant priest ridden peasants of Poictou; in arming afresh the Chouan banditti—the midnight murderers of Brittanny,[9] that they may have the pretence of something like a shadow of a shadow of the shadow of a probability of success, upon the strength of which, to persuade the people of Britain to be gulled, once more to spend another forty millions in a fresh campaign; and to have the honour of finding themselves in a worse situation at the end than ever.

However this gives me no uneasiness: for things at the worst must surely mend; and our rulers seem determined that it shall not be long before they drive matters to the very worst that human nature is capable of bearing. But say these *virtuous men*, and their *most sapient advocates*, it is not right to enter into enquiries of this kind, at this time. Consider the state of the public mind. It will lead to commotion. Such is the trick and cheat which they have been putting upon our understandings, and perhaps upon their own, for centuries; such have been always the pretences of the individuals who have walked the same infamous round before them, and such always will be the pretences of those who follow in the same routine. The *delinquents* will always think it is not a proper time to enquire into the state of their delinquency. But the fact is, that commotions spring from ignorance, and not from knowledge. He who is wise knows how to redress the grievances he labours under. He who is ignorant feels the sting of disaster: but, instead of taking the path of amelioration, plunges headlong into violence. Men ignorant and uninstructed become mad and frantic with their wrongs: for what is madness? What is phrenzy; but the want of knowledge and capacity to understand right from wrong, truth from falsehood, and to perceive which is the way to accomplish those designs which wisdom, justice, and virtue would dictate.

I wish to allay, not to increase fermentation. I wish I knew how to give you a *Spartan determination of soul*, together with the benevolence and philanthropy with which a few speculative philosophers of the present day have endeavoured to inspire mankind.[10] I would make you hard as rocks, against the assaults of corruption, prejudice and oppression. I would make you stand like a marble wall, and defy the assaults and encroachments of those wretches who dare to set a foot upon the sacred boundary and landmark of liberty. But, at the same time I would fill your souls with a deflation of every thing like violence, rancour, and cruelty. O that I could make you feel the true determination of generous valour, and that you might be as wise and benevolent as you were determined and resolute!

How is it to be done? How shall I steel your breasts, and soften your hearts at the same moment? If I knew how to do this I should then indeed be fit to stand in this Tribune, and be listened to by my fellow citizens; because I should then be able to point out to you the certain means of redress, and insure you success in your struggles for the happiness of future ages, without aggravating, even for an hour, the misery of the present generation.

I am sure, however, that this effect is not to be produced by intimidation or by ignorance. I have seen, since I last had the honour of meeting the countenances of my enlightened fellow citizens in this place; I have seen some of the lamentable consequences of the miserable ignorance, in which the governors of this country contrive to keep the people. I have been rambling, according to my wonted practice, in the true democratic way, on foot, from village to village, from pleasant hill to barren heath, recreating my mind with the beauties, and with the deformities of nature. I have traced over many a barren track in that county (Surrey) which is called the

Gentleman's county; because, forsooth the beggarly *sans culottes* are routed
out from it; their vulgar cottages, so offensive to the proud eye of luxury,
are exterminated, and nothing but the stately domes of useless grandeur
present themselves to our eyes. I have been travelling over those spots; I
have enjoyed the fine prospects from Leith hill; and have turned round,
with a sigh, to behold how many a little uncultivated valley there lies
waste; how many a beautiful spot lies desolate, which a thousandth part of
that revenue which has been so madly wasted in the present detestable
war, might have converted into smiling gardens and luxuriant fields, yielding food and raiment to many a poor family, while their little smiling
cottages might have imparted delight, where now nothing but gloomy sterility is to be seen.

In the course of these rambles I have dropped, occasionally, into the
little hedge ale-houses to refresh myself. I have sat down among the rough
clowns, whose tattered garments were soiled with their rustic labours; for I
have not forgot that all mankind are equally my brethren; and I love to see
the labourer in his ragged coat—that is I love the labourer: I am sorry his
coat is obliged to be so ragged. I love the labourer then, in his ragged coat,
as well as I love the Peer in his ermine; perhaps better; for indeed I should
not be sorry if the ermine of the Peer were employed in keeping the children of the poor ragged-coated peasant warm of a winter's night. I have
mixed, therefore, with these people; and I have grieved to hear their sentiments. Commotion and violence they can readily commend. They can
applaud the frantic proceedings of those, who have seized upon the shambles, the mills, and the bakers' shops; and thus have endeavoured, by their
arbitrary proceedings, to reduce the price of provisions. Thus far they think
the interference of the people right: But as to political enquiry, to this they
are too many of them dead. The generality of them still cherish the prejudices that have caused their misery. They hate a Frenchman, for being a
Jacobin, as much as they formerly hated him for wearing *wooden shoes*, tho'
they know no more of the meaning of the word *Jacobin*, than they did
before of the guilt that was attached to shoes of wood. Nay too many of
them idolize the name of a contemptible wretch whose father's reputation[11]
was the sole cause of his popularity, and whom a few grains of enquiry
would lead them to execrate as the author of that very scarcity of which
they complain. I have argued with these men upon the impropriety of
tumult and violence: for I abhor commotion more than I abhor any thing,
except despotism and corruption; and I never meet with the advocate of
violence, but I endeavour to show him its wickedness and absurdity. But,

alas, the uninformed mass love this violence. They uphold the propriety of it, because they are ignorant of the real sources of their calamities; because they do not know that the miller, the baker, and the butcher, against whom their violence is directed,[12] are as much oppressed as themselves; and that they must look higher if they would find the real instruments of their oppression; that they must think more deeply, if they would learn the means by which that oppression is to be removed.

The fact is, as I shall shew you in the course of this enquiry, that though the causes are multifarious indeed, that have produced this oppression, the greater portion of them is to be traced to the errors, to the vices, to the selfish usurpations of those ministers, and their predecessors, who think that no man has rights who was not wrapped in a swaddling band of ermine, and that no man can be entitled to reason, unless he has, either in possession or expectation, a bit of blue ribbon, or a few gold and silver spangles embroidered on his night-gown.

There can be no doubt that the advocates of administration must be anxious enough to prevent enquiry; because enquiry must point out who are the causes of the wrong; and what is the mode by which redress is to be obtained. There is no doubt that tumult and violence are pleasant things to them; because they give them pretences for giving additional force to the arm of authority; and for drawing tighter those reins of government, which, though the poor may bleed at the mouth while the gag presses hard upon them, it is pleasant enough for those who only drive, and whip, and spur them, to be holding with a hard hand. They, therefore, have little objection to the butcher, the baker, or the miller being sacrificed to the ignorant indignation of the people, provided thereby they avert the dreaded calamity of calm enquiry, and shun the light of political truth, which brings conviction to the minds of the people, and threatens, by the unanimous sentiment of virtue and justice which it might inspire, to drive them and their crimes from the seat of power. This they must abhor; because whenever that unanimous sentiment of common sense and justice shall prevail among mankind, down drops the curtain upon the mighty puppets of the day; the wires they have been moved by, will no longer make them perform their evolutions, and Punchinello[13] and his family strut in their embroidered robes no more.

Citizens, the field of enquiry that opens before me is immense. The present subject involves almost every question connected with finance; it involves the consideration of that delusion which has been so long upheld, paper credit; it involves the system of taxation; it involves the present mode of partitioning land into farms and tenements; it involves the scandalous neglect which has occasioned one third of the land in this island, (taking England, Scotland and Wales, together) to remain in an uncultivated state.

On the succeeding evening I shall give you the facts stated by the committee of the board of agriculture, and prove to you that one third of the lands of this country absolutely lie waste. What a scandal to the government of this country! What a shame that pensions, places, and emoluments so immense, should be wasted upon a few worthless individuals, while so large a portion of the country lies useless, which, with a tythe of that money, might be converted into regions of plenty and population!

The despotism of China would blush at such absurdity. Go there; behold the population thick almost as the bearded grain that grows upon the cultivated ground. Behold every street swarming with human beings. What is the reason, that even in the midst of despotism the human species can thus be multiplied? They have no pernicious system of paper credit; they have no monopolized system of external commerce; they have no monopoly of lands into the hands of a few holders; they are not year after year, and month after month, turning the little tenant out of his farm, to throw a huge province almost into one concern, and on the speculative mercantile trafficker in land bestow that which might produce the comfortable support of numerous families, and tend thereby to the happiness and prosperity of the country.

It is not my intention to enter into the whole of this wide field on the present evening. I shall confine my observations during the remainder of this Lecture to a few particular points, which are immediately connected with the abuses of government, and with those circumstances that press particularly upon the present moment.

There are undoubtedly circumstances which have occasioned a gradual increase in the price of articles of the first necessity, in this country; there are other circumstances which have tended to produce an absolute scarcity, not only in England, but in Europe.

Amongst those which have tended to increase the price of provisions we may reckon the enormous growth of corruption among the higher orders of society; by which the expences of government have been greatly increased. We are to consider, also, among the causes of permanent evil, the restrictions upon the exportation and the importation of corn;[14] and we are to consider, also, a burden rendered venerable by its antiquity, but whose grey hairs can no longer preserve it from contempt, I mean the oppressive bur-

den of tithes,[15] and a variety of other causes, which shall be enumerated in
their turn. The part, however, which I shall particularly dwell upon this
evening, is that which relates to the present war, and which, as all other
wars in some degree, but the present more than any former, has occasioned
a considerable increase of the price of provisions, independent of taxation,
independent of the additional burdens which encumber traffic—as the increase of freightage and insurance, and the like.

The former of these is paid upon all articles of consumption, which are
removed from one part of the coast to another; and therefore corn, coals,
and other articles which are of home consumption, as well as sugar and
articles of foreign produce, partake of the consequent increase in price.

Now, Citizens, I shall state a few facts relative to an individual article,
which will shew you, by analogous reasoning, how considerable an increase
in the price of the necessaries of life must have been produced by the
present war, by the operation of these two species of burthen alone. The
freightage of sugars was only four shillings per hundred weight before the
war, now it is ten shillings; the insurance upon the same article, which
used to be six pounds per cent. is now increased to sixteen.

You will please to remember, that the increase of freightage arises from
so many individuals who used to be employed in commercial navigation,
being pressed on board our men of war, to be cut to pieces and destroyed
for the glory and honour of William Pitt and Co. Such is the price which
one half of the community pays for having the other half cut and blown to
pieces in ridiculous wars!

With respect to the increase of the insurance, that is to be attributed to
the activity of the enemy. For as they sometimes take the liberty of sweet-
ening their tea with the sugar we have paid for, the under-writers of course
must take a greater premium before they can insure the respective cargoes.
And by the way it should be observed, that these gentlemen under-writers
do not fail to take advantage of these circumstances. War is a sort of harvest to these legal gamblers; so much so, that I remember, at the close of
the American war, hearing one of them lament that hostilities were over
so soon—for, that if they had continued a year or two longer, he should
have feathered his nest completely.

Citizens, I do not mean to contend, that the freightage and insurance of
all articles have increased in the same proportion; but this will show you
how to account for one part of the increase of the price of the necessaries
of life resulting from the present war. In short, there is a thousand ways in
which it affects them, besides the wholesale accumulation of taxation, and

the obvious inconveniences of decaying manufactures and stagnated commerce.

See, then, the advantages of going to war, to those whose destiny it is to
survive at home; as to those poor beings who had their heads knocked off
abroad, according to Mr. *Burke*, they are gone to receive their reward; and
therefore he might tell you the faster our brothers and friends have their
heads knocked off the better, because they are going so much the faster to
heaven. And as he had the honour of being educated among the Jesuits at
St. *Omer's*,[16] I am sure I shall not contend points of religion with him. But
admitting this to be the case, there can be no doubt that heaven has been
very well peopled by the triumphs of the present war; the last campaign
particularly, the exploits of which it is unnecessary to enumerate: and,
indeed, it would put one out of breath, as it did the French, to follow them
from field of glory to field of glory—from the frontiers of France to the
marshes of Flanders, and from the marshes of Flanders to the dykes of
Holland, and from the dykes of Holland to heaven knows where.—It
would be impossible to enumerate the achievements which will immortalize the name of the British Frederic, and cause posterity to go down upon
their knees and bless the wise heads of *Pitt*, of *Jenkinson* and *Loughborough*,
and all the sapient projectors of this most glorious, salutary, and triumphant war. Paying a little more for the sugar to sweeten our tea, or drinking it without, or having a plumb-pudding or pye or two the less every
week, are trifles in comparison with the permanent advantages reaped from
undertakings so wise, and exploits so glorious.

There is another thing has produced an increase in the price of all necessaries to be shipped from one part of the country to another, namely, the
embargo laid upon our merchandize, in order to enable Mr. *Pitt* to get more
sailors to fight *his* battles for him.

But there are, in the present war, circumstances of peculiar aggravation,
which it seems our state politicians could not calculate.

It was boasted by that great teacher of the Rule of Three, the Chancellor
of the Exchequer,[17] that we should have for our allies all the powers of
Europe. It was well answered by his powerful opponent in the House of
Commons[18] (much more powerful he would be still, if he would shake off
the trammels of party!)—It was well answered by him, that the greater our
alliances, the greater our calamities; because the consequence was, that all
Europe being engaged in war, no port would be left open, no place would
be neutral, and therefore the greater would be the stagnation both in our
external and internal commerce.[19]

But he might have gone further; he might have said, not only our commerce is stagnated, but the very sources of subsistence are dried up, in
consequence of this grand alliance. All Europe is at war. Your own produce, scarcely ever sufficient for your own support, is now to be sent in
large quantities to the continent, to supply all the armies of all the despots
of Europe. Stripped, as you will be, of every necessary article of life, where
is the neutral nation that is to supply you? None.—You have plunged all
Europe into war; all Europe, of course, must neglect the cultivation and
tillage of its land; all Europe must lose the opportunity of supplying you
with the necessary articles which your profligacy will destroy.—Where
then are you to seek, in the midst of those blessed victories which you
anticipate (how well they have been fulfilled we have since seen)—where
are you to seek for food to sustain the soldiery who are to fight your battles
abroad, and to feed the poor manufacturers who will be languishing in
disease and want at home?—Will you expect it from America!—from
America, who, if she has one grain of justice or common sense, must love
the cause of your enemy, and abhor your's?—America, who must regard
every success you may happen to obtain, as a signal of alarm to her independence?—America, who must regard your violation of treaties, on the
banks of the *Miami*,[20] as a bone of contention purposely preserved, to furnish you with a sorry pretence, if ever you should think yourselves strong
enough, once more to attack her, and attempt her subjugation?—According to this calculation has been the event. Hence neither wheat nor any
other grain has been imported since the last harvest, except oats, and very
small quantities even of these; most of them from Ireland; very few, indeed, from Hamburgh.

This accounts for the rise of 75 *per cent.* in the price of that article,
which has been mentioned before. The very great supplies of oats, which
used to be sent through the ports of Holland from various parts of the
continent, have entirely ceased.

The states, also, on both sides of the Rhine, the Austrians, and the
united Netherlands, have either neglected their tillage, or what little they
have produced has fallen, not into the hands of Britain, but into the hands
of Britain's enemy.—Your allies have left half their lands unsown; and
what has been the fate of that which they have cultivated? The triumphant
republican, with his sword in one hand, and his sickle in the other, has
reaped the harvest, and carried it into his granaries.

Let us observe, also, the conduct of our good and gracious ally the King
of Prussia, that illustrious sample of the faith of monarchies, that demon-

strative reasoner in favour of treating only with *regular and established governments*. Even when he pretended to be our friend: that is to say, while he
showed an inclination to receive our money;[21] for he never showed any
inclination to do any thing else for us, but to lighten us a little of that of
which he saw we had so much as to make us proud!—Seeing that taking a
great deal of it away would bring the people to their senses, he very kindly
helped the Minister off with it. But even during the time that he was
receiving this money, he absolutely prohibited the exportation of corn to
any nation whatever.

Now, whether in reality he was afraid that this corn should fall into the
hands of the French, or whether he was afraid there would be a scarcity in
his own country, it matters not with respect to my argument. Suffice it to
say, that it being known to our wise Minister that he forbid the exportation of corn, yet our wise Minister thought proper to pay for a quantity of
that article; hoping, I suppose, to be able, by weighty arguments, to persuade the King of Prussia, after he had paid for it, to let him have it. And
now we may find, perhaps, that the eloquence of the French Convention is
more powerful in Prussia, than the eloquence of Britain:—that Court having been a long time studying the French language, tho' I have not yet
heard, that any English grammarian has been sent for to instruct them in
ours. One part of the English language, however, the King of Prussia understands very perfectly: that which I mean is generally written in characters of the brightest yellow, and which is considered in our senate, as com-
posing the most solid, weighty, and persuasive part of eloquence. The
ornamental part of rhetoric, however, he imports from another country;
and to these (as there are some reasons to doubt the soundness of his royal
capacity) he may chance to be most attached.

But there is a still more important circumstance to be taken into consideration; namely the exportation to the armies. This is not easily calculated;
because I am credibly informed, that, in many instances, what with the
shifting of ground, retreating from place to place—for, you know, we have
been gravely told in the ministerial papers, that "notwithstanding their
successes, the French have never been able to take possession of any
ground, till the British troops had first of all removed from it," thereby
demonstrating a well known physical proposition, that two bodies cannot
occupy the same space at the same time.—Well then, what with the
bodies of the English armies moving first from one spot and then from
another, and the bodies of the French moving on to them; what with
sometimes burning the corn and sometimes drowning it, that it might not

fall into the hands of the enemy; what with its sometimes actually falling into those hands, it has been known that the orders of the Commissaries have sometimes been three times executed, before the stores have actually arrived at the army for which they were intended. So that even the powerful genius of *Brook Watson*[22] has sunk beneath the weighty duties, and still more weighty profits of his office; and he is said to have exclaimed in despair, that it was impossible to supply a flying army.

Here then is waste for you. Here is a source of aggravated scarcity. The waste and consumption of a camp is always double the quantity that would provide for the same number of individuals in their own peaceful habitations: and the support of a flying army is always three times as much as an army that is successful would require.

But this is not all the wicked and mischievous policy of the present system: It adds wantonness to misfortune, and aggravates with wilful devastation the calamities of the human race. It is reported that even so large a quantity of haystacks as would cover a whole mile and a half of ground in the neighbourhood of Rotterdam, was set on fire by the retreating English and Hanoverians, because it should not fall into the hands of the enemy.

A precious legacy this to bequeath a people whom we had forced into a war they did not wish for; and whom we were incapable of defending!

Magazines of hay having been so destroyed, do you suppose that magazines of corn and beef have not been destroyed in the same way?

O feeble sense of reason and of virtue!—O neglected spirit of justice and humanity! That any being who has capacity enough to count his fingers, or who can put down as many units upon a paper as will make ten, should ever think of plunging continents into war for the gratification of their ambition, when the consequences must be destroying, thus, by wholesale, the means of the existence of so many thousands of their fellow beings, who have the same right to the accommodations of life with themselves; but who, together with their families, are to be reduced to misery and the lingering death of famine, while mad revenge, the avarice of office, and the intoxicating love of power, stalk with inflated insolence over the globe, affect the nod of deity, and snuff the incense of human sacrifices!

Citizens, the evening is far advanced. But late as it is, there is one subject I cannot pass over without some animadversion. I mean the conduct of the Minister of this country with respect to Poland; that country whose struggles for dawning liberty warmed the heart of every generous Briton;[23] that country to which every man who had one spark of veneration for any thing that looked like liberty in the constitution of this country, must have sincerely wished success; that country has been beaten down; its spirit has been annihilated; its population thinned by massacres perpetrated by the *regular Government* of Russia; every spark of liberty has been trampled out; the Hyaena of the North,[24] and the vultures of Germany, have torn its mangled limbs; have feasted upon its gore; and have been supplied by British gold, with the means of this destruction and inhuman partition.

This conduct will shew you, that it is not Jacobinism only, that is hateful to the present minister;—that it is not republicanism only that he detests; that he is a worshipper of unqualified despotism; that he wishes to establish it throughout the world; and that even the most temperate and moderate reformation; even the merest half-way attempt towards liberty and the amelioration of the condition of the human species, is sufficient to set his gall afloat, and provoke him to glut his appetite for blood.

Look at the history of the attempted revolution in Poland. Were there any appearances of Jacobinism there? Did they set up for that liberty and equality which has been so misrepresented? No: if they had they would have triumphed; and *Pitt*, and the despots of Europe would have been disappointed. But they were too moderate in their views to warm the souls of the great body of the people; too little careful of the rights of the mass of mankind, to awake the glowing enthusiasm which liberty and equality inspires. They could not unite in one effort the congregated energies of the nation: but the congregated despots and cabinets of Europe were united against them. For their destruction hard British gold was sent over to the Despot of Prussia, in subsidies.

What use did he openly make of it? Did he assist the alliance against France? No. Did he not, in the most bare-faced manner, apply that money to the destruction of Poland? and did not *Pitt* still continue to send the money of this country to that Despot, even after he saw the use that he made of it? And was he not thereby enabled to hold out against the vigorous exertion of the Poles, till the Hyaena of the north was ready to pour her Barbarians upon them, and to repeat the *massacres of Ismael*[25] *in the streets of Warsaw.*

Yes, this tiger in human shape, this royal savage, is one of the allies with whom our virtuous administration thinks a free people ought to coalesce, for the destruction of republicanism in France, and for the restoration of the despotism of the Capets, and the contemptible superstition of his holiness the pope.

But it may be said, "he was deceived. He was so busy with his calculations, with his arithmetical plans and schemes, that he could not attend to what was doing upon such a spot of the continent as Poland; that he knew nothing of the exertions made by those brave people; and but little of the attempts made by the tyrants of Europe against them." But no—he has abjured all such excuses: with that matchless effrontery which nothing but a *William Pitt*, backed by *Henry Dundas*, could possibly assume, he steps forward and tells you that, "even if he could have foreseen the manner in which the subsidy paid to the King of Prussia would have been applied, he certainly would have paid it."[26]

Here then is a direct avowal of his guilt.—I wish not for punishments; I wish for redress; but if other persons, not as philosophical in their feelings as I wish to be, should ever take it in their heads to redress the wrongs of Europe by coercion, let him take care. When the principal goes to rack, I fear he will find but little security from his plausible harangues. Nor will it be easy, perhaps, for men of honest and ardent hearts, that wish to keep the cause of liberty unstained by wanton vengeance, to preserve such a culprit from the gripe of a severe retaliation.

Citizens, I shall dwell no longer upon this subject this evening. I have already extended this lecture to an unusual length. I shall therefore adjourn till Friday evening; leaving you for the present with this invocation. Think I conjure you—deeply think of all the facts that can be collected relative to this subject. It is a subject in which your own happiness is involved; in which is, also, involved the happiness of your posterity: the children yet unborn may bless your patriotic activity, or reprobate your selfish sluggishness, in proportion as you exert yourselves to redress the grievances under which the nation groans. And when I invoke you to redress those grievances, I do not invoke you to deeds of cruelty and violence. I invoke you to the energies of the mind. I invoke you to trace, to the very source, the causes of your calamities. I am convinced you will find almost all those calamities to result from the total want of a representation of the people in parliament. I am convinced that you will find that the corruption, the rottenness, the profligacy which have crept into your administrations, in consequence of the want of this representation, is the genuine source of your calamities; and that *there is no redress for a nation situated as we are* (to repeat those treasonable words which were to have brought the axe of the executioner upon this neck) *there is no redress for a nation situated as we are, but from a fair, full, and free representation of the people in the Commons House of Parliament!*

THE TRIBUNE. No. XVII.
THE SECOND LECTURE *on the Causes of the present* DEARNESS *and* SCARCITY *of* PROVISIONS, *delivered* Friday, May 1st, 1795.[27]

(Many of the occasional reflections in this Lecture will not be understood, if the reader is not reminded that a known agent of the Treasury planted himself in a very conspicuous situation this evening, and made several attempts to interrupt the Lecturer.)

CITIZENS,

IN my Lecture of Wednesday evening, I began with observing the vast and evident disproportion between the increase of the price of provisions and the price of labour. I proved to you from *Hume*, or rather a writer quoted by *Hume* as an authority, that about 230 years ago, when the common price of labour throughout the country was eight-pence per day, many of the articles of consumption were cheaper in a degree of twenty-two to one, than they are at this period. I afterwards proceeded to shew you, that, in all probability, a considerable degree of difference had taken place between the proportionate price of the luxuries of life and the mere necessaries, and that, therefore, perhaps some deduction ought to be made from this calculation. But I believe I gave you data sufficient to authorize me in the conclusion, that after all allowances of this kind, it was but a very moderate calculation indeed to suppose that, in order to have kept any pace between the increase of the price of labour and the increase of the necessary articles of consumption, (that is to say, to make the condition of the laborious part of the community precisely the same as it was 230 years ago), the wages paid for labour ought to be, considering what the prices of provisions now are, between five and six shillings per day. I endeavoured to show you, that it was not my intention absolutely to point out that such ought to be the wages at this time, but to show you this fact—that either very great injustice has been done to the common people, with respect to the prices paid for their labour, or else a very extravagant augmentation has taken place upon the necessary articles of life, inconsistent with the quantum of specie in circulation.

I might have pushed this subject a little further; and when I was enquiring what ought to have been the prices of labour in order to make the comforts and conveniences of the lower orders of society the same as they

were 230 years ago, I might, perhaps, with very great propriety, have enquired whether the condition of the lower orders of society ought not, at
this period, to be considerably better than it was at that time. For if it is
admitted, society has been in a rapid state of progress, if it is true that
knowledge has extended to a very considerable degree, that the mechanical
arts have been brought to much greater perfection, that all the different
employments to which men are devoted, are now performed comparatively
with much greater facility (that is to say, a greater quantum of production
may be effected with the same labour and in the same time)—if all these
circumstances are true, it would be, perhaps, a fair object of enquiry,
whether that class of society, to whose industry and exertions we are to
attribute this improvement, ought not, at least, to have had some share in
the advantages resulting from it; and instead of living in a worse situation
than at that time, whether they ought not to be enabled to live in a situation more comfortable than they then did; for I cannot see what sort of
justice there is in the great body of the people labouring eternally, if the
whole advantage is to be monopolized by a few idle drones, placemen and
pensioners, some of whom, if I were so inclined, I could point out in this
assembly. I cannot perceive the justice or propriety of the great body of the
people labouring and exerting themselves to increase the accommodations
of society, if the whole benefit is to be seized by a few aristocratic oppressors, who are sending their spies and emissaries into every corner to
catch up every word that may drop from a friend of Liberty.—Let me
observe, however, that I am glad they do send such persons here, because
they may chance to hear some truths that will incline them to be active
and useful converts, especially if the audience treat such persons with the
candour they are entitled to: for men ought not to be censured on account
of the situations in which they are placed. They have frequently been the
choice of unexperienced youth, frequently the choice of their parents, and
frequently have been adopted from accidents in life over which they could
have no command. I do not, therefore, make this observation to stimulate
ungentle feelings in your hearts; those persons who frequently attend these
Lectures will bear witness, that I have always been anxious to prevent any
intemperance even towards the emissaries of those who have absolutely
entered into conspiracies, first to knock out my brains by hired bludgeon-
men, afterwards to kidnap, and send me, perhaps, as Lady Grange was
sent, into the distant solitary islands of Scotland,[28] and lastly, to carve me
into four quarters, and stick my head upon a pole.

Pursuing, Citizens, the chain of reasoning from which I have been led into this digression by the illiberal interruptions of this man, I say, perhaps, I might have been entitled to argue, that while the nobleman rides in a carriage twice as superb, while he lives in an apartment twice as splendid and convenient, the poor peasant has a right to expect, that he should live in a cottage twice as commodious, and wear twice as comfortable a cloathing for himself and family. (TREASURY RUNNER, interrupting— "And so he has.")

I shall show the honourable Gentleman who has made that reply whether it is so or not, by and by. I will state, not assertions, but facts. If Gentlemen will make such observations it must spring from their ignorance— however, ignorance is no improper qualification for a tool of Government. I will state the facts, I will tell Gentleman, that[29] from the facts contained in the records of times past, and known state of the industrious orders of society, it can be proved that their situation is three times as miserable, instead of being twice as comfortable as it was.

I shall not, however, occupy your time by replying to the significant nods and monosyllables of one individual. It is my business to investigate this subject; and I shall investigate it upon general principles, in defiance of all the idle vermin in office, which our pockets are so incessantly picked to maintain.

I was going to add, that I might have argued, that if the liveries of a Prince are to be increased from fifty to one hundred guineas per suit, that the poor ought to have the opportunity of putting upon the legs and feet of their children twice as good stockings and shoes as they did before. Citizens, I next examined the rise of provisions and the increase of the prices of labour, within the last twenty or twenty-five years; and as these are facts, of which a larger proportion of those who heard me could judge, I think it a little curious, that an individual, who has apparently lived thirty or forty years in the world, should attempt to contradict the conclusions from them.—For as every article of provision has considerably more than doubled in its price, and as the wages of labouring men have not increased one fourth part, I should like very much to know, from some of the scholars into whom Mr. Pitt has flogged his arithmetic, how, with so small an increase in wages, at the time when so great an increase has taken place in the price of the necessaries of life, a man can get twice the comfort and accommodation now for fourteen or fifteen pence, that he used to get for a shilling before.

But, Citizens, when I am speaking of the increase, such as it is, of the prices of labour, I ought to animadvert upon the special care which the laws of this country, from a laudable desire to preserve the peace and harmony of society, have taken to place the lower orders entirely in a state of dependance upon those who employ them; the consequence of which is, that when any general national hardship takes place, by means of which the prices of the articles of life are always increased, but by the means of which, at the same time, a quantity of labour becomes less, the master takes a convenient and snug opportunity to scotch, as they call it, the wages of the journeymen.

Many of you, I dare say, have read, and I hope such of you as have not will take an opportunity of reading, the excellent pamphlet of Citizen *Frend*,[30] for which that admirable advocate for the cause of Liberty was so scandalously expelled from the university of which he was so illustrious a member. You will remember that, in that pamphlet, he takes notice of a very affecting circumstance of his kind: Just after the war had been declared, Citizen *Frend* (for I believe he will be better pleased to be called Citizen than Reverend and Mr.) happened to follow some poor women, who had been to a market-town to take home their work; and who, as they walked along, rung in the ears of each other the doleful and angry complaint, "We are scotched 4d. in a shilling, on account of this war."—I repeat not the words, but the substance.—"O!" says *Frend*, "that the voice of truth and humanity might penetrate the walls of cabinets; and that I might resound in the ears of Ministers and Princes—The labouring poor are scotched 4d. in a shilling, to maintain your ambitious projects and destructive wars, without common sense, common virtue, or principle of justice?"[31]

Citizens, I have had some opportunities, also, of observing the dependent situation of these lower orders of society. Some years ago, before my mind had taken that strong bias in favour of political pursuits, to which it is now attached, going into the native country of my parents, I took the opportunity—being generally desirous to see as much as I could, and, not like those poor wretches condemned to the ignorant confines of the office of a Secretary of State, to know no difference between truth and falsehood, right and wrong, but what was taught me by the lying documents of spies and their employers, which it is the duty of those poor ignorant beings to copy—my employment not being of that description, I took the opportunity of seeing, as far as I could, the condition of those orders of society, about whose happiness in the country I had heard so many romantic stories, while I was an inhabitant of the town, and took my ideas of rural felicity from novels and pastorals. I beheld there poor women, doubled with age, toiling, from morning to night, over their wheels, spinning their flax and hemp; and I found that their condition was so miserable, that many of them were positively obliged to take their work once or twice a day home to the persons who employed them, in order to get the scanty pittance that was to purchase the meal by which they were to sustain their emaciated frames. (*Vide* PERIPATETIC, vol. I. p. 143.)[32]

I was astonished, I own, at this picture of misery. I had read a good deal in poems and romances about rural felicity. I did not know that rural felicity consisted in sitting over a wheel until one is double, and getting neither comforts nor conveniencies—no, nor the necessaries of life, to sustain and prop one's declining years, by this eternal drudgery.

This made, I own, a deep impression on my mind; which, though it did not operate immediately, stimulated me to a train of enquiry, which could not fail of its ultimate effect.—I had hitherto been a high government man, a supporter of prerogatives, and an advocate for venerating the powers that be.—O! that some way could but be invented to keep mankind (all but the chosen few) in utter ignorance! Then might placemen, pensioners, and the usurping proprietors of rotten boroughs, enjoy, indeed, a golden age, and the *swinish multitude* (driven as their *swineherds* list, and slaughtered at their will) should grunt forth sedition no more!—But it will not be. Enquiry will some how or other be awakened; and, when it is awakened, the mists of delusion melt before the rising sun of truth, and the midnight hags of despotism bind us in their spells no more.

I soon found myself compelled to acknowledge that, where such was the condition of so large a portion of society, all could not be right—that "there was something rotten in the state of Denmark";[33] and every fact which, in the progress of investigation, came under my observation, tended to confirm the opinion.

Among other abuses, I soon found that one of the causes of this calamitous situation was the unfeeling manner in which these poor beings were left to the arbitrary discretion of their employers, who took the liberty, when these poor creatures took home their work, to scotch them as they thought fit; so that, under various pretences, for every pound that was spun by the poor individual, she never got paid for above three quarters, when it came to be estimated by the masters and employers. So much was to be considered as waste, so many deductions were to be made; and the poor individuals, where they are not numerous enough to associate, have no appeal—none at least that they have any hopes from; for you know but little of Justices of the Peace, if you believe a country magistrate will listen to the complaints of a poor friendless being, against the tradesman who has arrived at opulence by his oppression.

Thus then we find, if we regard the facts which history furnishes, that the inevitable consequence must be, from the increased price of the articles consumed, and the want of a proportionate increase in the wages paid to the industrious poor, that within twenty-five years the condition of the latter has been so reduced, that they cannot obtain half the necessities of life they formerly used to obtain; while their opulent oppressors, the place-men, pensioners, and contractors of the day, enjoy more than twice the luxuries and extravagance with which they formerly debased their nature.

I have stated to you, also, that oats and barley, which, in many parts of the country, be it remembered, are used as substitutes for wheat, have still more extravagantly increased; and that oats, in particular, have increased 75 *per cent.* since the year 1790.

Perhaps the *honourable Clerks of the Treasury* will not be inclined to contradict this. They will have had some opportunity of knowing the truth of it.—But, Citizens, since I met you before, I have had an opportunity of getting possession of some other facts, relative to this very important part of the question. I find, from a person who has been many years in a very considerable way of dealing in those articles, that twenty-seven or twenty-eight years ago, the common price of oats, in the retail market, was from 9s. to 10s. 6d. per quarter; that, till within these twelve years, 12s. was the common price, and that they were never higher than 14s.—But now, what is the price of them? Thirty-five shillings! an increase nearly four-fold, in so small a distance of time, as that which I have stated to you.

Now, remember, what a very important article of consumption these are for the labouring poor in certain parts of the country. Remember, that throughout the whole of the country parts of Scotland, wheat is a luxury which the poor man never tastes; that oats, that barley, field peas, and other pulse of this description, constitute the whole sustenance of large proportions of the people there: and I could instance a poor being, of the name of Crawford, who emigrated to America on account of this miserable situation, and who has now, merely from the profits of his own manual labour, been able to take a little farm of his own, and to become a master Farmer, in his turn; but whose sole sustenance, for himself and family, while he resided in Scotland, was one meal a day of meagre potatoes; and that, in the horrors and excesses of their hunger, they gnawed the peelings and fragments for their supper, having no other sort of sustenance whatever to keep themselves from absolute starvation.

Now, Citizens, in parts of the country where this was the case, consider what must be the monstrous accumulation of their grievances, and the miserable situation of the poor, when such an accumulation has taken place upon the price of that article in particular (oats) which constitutes the most strong, the most wholesome, and the most important part of their subsistence.

So much for the increased comfort, the double accommodation, the twice as good apartments, and the twice as good raiment and food, which the common people of Scotland maintain at this time.

Such being a small, very small part, indeed, of those monstrous facts which show the blessings of a system of rotten boroughs, and the corruptions of faction, I think myself called upon, as a good Citizen (that distinction, beyond all others, which men ought to be most emulous to deserve) to stand forward and investigate, as far as I am able, the causes of the mischief under which the people groan. Yes, groan, I say: for many a poor, meagre, emaciated, depressed, and heart-broken wretch, in this country pays, with groans and slavery, for the pampered luxury of those, who, because they wallow in the wealth of which they have plundered the nation, think they have a right to stop the mouths of the poor, and the advocates of the poor with the gag of persecution; and, if they cannot effect that, think it right to employ their pimps and perjurers, "Old-Bailey solicitors and the sweepings of the stews", to disturb their investigations, misrepresent their sentiments, and deprive them of their lives.

Citizens, there is another reason why I am desirous of investigating this subject, and it is this:—That the investigation of such subjects has a tendency to prevent tumult, insurrection and confusion. How desirous some men, who call themselves friends of Government and the Constitution, are to excite such tumults, we may learn from this fact—that whenever they believe a number of persons are assembled, to enter into peaceable enquiry, they send some one or other of their agents to prevent that enquiry, and disturb the peace. Thus, the very night that I had the honor to be arrested, in this place, upon the ridiculous trump'd-up charge of High Treason, Mr. *Walsh*, the Treasury spy,[34] absolutely told me, that he took, to the meeting of the King's Arms tavern, the great over-grown athletic Irishman, that created the riot and confusion there, and gave the Lord-Mayor a pretence for preventing in future the meetings of that peaceable assembly.

Citizens! Citizens! we know, and our enemies know—and their conduct shews that they know it—that if men will enquire, with impartiality and temper, into the causes of these calamities, they will have no occasion for turbulence; they will find that the individuals, against whom they are inclined to direct their fury, are generally as innocent and oppressed as themselves; and that it is not the *miller*, against whose machine they direct their fury—it is not the *butcher*, whose commodity they seize, it is not the *baker*, whose shop they break open and rifle,—that these are not the men who are the causes of the calamities under which they groan; that the real causes are of much too weighty a nature to be removed by turbulence. They are so serious, so fortified, so deeply rooted, that they can only be removed by the unanimous spirit of enquiry diffusing itself through the country, and awakening to unanimous effort, by a spirited, firm, and determined (but at the same time peaceable) disposition, to represent their grievances to each other, in the first instance, and then with one congregated voice to that government, which, however it may pretend to make it high treason to overawe any branch of it, will never fail to respect and reverence, as it ought, the sentiments and opinions of the people, whenever, in a firm and unanimous manner, they are thundered in their ears. It was from this conviction that I undertook the present enquiry, and you will remember that on the last evening I traced some of the causes of the evil. I endeavoured to shew you that the evil resulted from impolitic regulations and excessive exactions. I endeavoured to shew you, in part, what I conceived to be the bearing of this question upon the subject of the present war; and I traced, among other circumstances, the great increase of burthens which lays upon many commodities; the increased expence of those transactions, in which they must necessarily be engaged, before they can bring their commodities to market, and I shewed you, that these were, in many cases, increased threefold, from the drawing off of so large a number of sailors and useful labourers for the war, from the superior vigour and ability of the marine of the French republic, which while it has left to England the empty honour of gaining victories in general engagements, and boasting of the barren sovereignty of the ocean, has never failed to sweep our commerce into republican ports, which it was the duty of the administration of this country (if they had understood their duty) to have protected.

I noticed, also, as another cause, the embargo which has been laid upon all, and still continues upon a large portion, of our most essential merchandise; it is true from one or two articles it has been taken off, but the evil was done, and the effects continue to be felt. I stated that the tillage of both sides of the Rhine, from which we used to be supplied with various sorts of grain, &c. had been neglected and destroyed;—that this evil had been aggravated by the prohibition of exportation from the country of our good ally of Prussia; and also the very considerable mischief which had resulted to this country, from the large exportations that have been made of all the necessary articles of consumption to the armies on the continent, which on account of the calamitous and disgraceful circumstances, in common with other machinations of our blessed and immaculate minister, have been sent three times before they reached the army for which they were intended; having fallen into the hands of the enemy, or been destroyed, sunk in the waters, or consumed in flames, to prevent their falling into the hands of the enemy; and I noticed a particular circumstance, of a whole mile and a half of hay stacks, in the neighbourhood of Rotterdam, being set on fire, in order to prevent them falling into the hands of the enemy.

Now, Citizens, those persons who have been used to hear the arithmetic of Pitt will not, I suppose, readily agree with the conclusion I shall draw from these facts: namely, that *it would have been better for this country*, that this hay and these provisions should have fallen into the hands of the enemy, than that they should have been thus destroyed.

I mean in general, Citizens, to draw my arguments in this Tribune, not from partial interest and *political expediences*, but from broad and universal principles; to consider universal justice and humanity the deep root and solid trunk from which my arguments are to sprout and my conclusions grow; and to teach you that these, and these alone, are the proper objects of your veneration. But when I speak of the measure and maxims of ministers it is impossible to talk of general principles, of philanthropy, and humanity. They have abjured all principle both by word and deed. It is a sort of watch-word of alarm, which they never use but to couple it with the indefinable stigma of Jacobinism, when they want to hunt the persecuted patriot to *Botany Bay* or *the Scaffold*. I must meet them therefore on the ground of expediency; and it is the fate of these muddy-headed oppressors, that chuse what ground they will, they must be beaten.

You will please then to remember, that every considerable destruction of the necessaries of life has a tendency to produce not only a scarcity in the individual country in which the devastation is committed, but mediately in the general stock of the universe—that is to say, in the aggregate stock of the whole of the productive countries from whence these resources spring. All the world suffers, in some degree, in point of real wealth (the wealth that consists in the quantum of real necessaries and comforts) and, to a very considerable degree, when the devastation is so monstrous as that

which has been committed by this foolish, revengeful, malicious disposition—the system of mad havock and extermination upon which the present war is conducted.

Now let us attend a little while to a consideration of what is the fair and
honest system of commerce: not such a system of commerce as placemen
and pensioners are desirous of promoting. Remember that the fair system of
commerce is this—that whatever one country produces more than necessary for the consumption of that country, it sends to another country that
is in want of that article, in order that it may bring back some other article
of necessity, or luxury, of which it stands in need.

This is the fair, the just, and rational system of commerce. And, with
respect to *articles of the first necessity*, this is the system upon which commerce must inevitably be conducted. Suppose, then, as is the fact, that the
whole produce of those parts of the world that have any commercial intercourse together, taking all the different articles, is pretty nearly in proportion to the whole of the necessities and consumption of all those countries.
This I say is nearly the fact; and must be so: for I take it for granted, that
man does not toil for the mere pleasure of toiling. He toils to produce as
much as he can find a good market for; and is never disposed to produce
more than he can consume himself, and turn to his advantage, by disposing of it to others. It will therefore follow that the quantity requisite to
supply the demands of the civilized world, will bear a pretty general proportion to the quantity actually produced, when the whole of that produce
comes (as by means of commerce it cannot fail, in effect, to come) to a
general market. Now the system of commerce being, thus, a general mart
for the universe, it follows of course that, with respect to my argument, it
matters not whether these productive countries, having intercourse together, be three or three thousand. I will take therefore the smallest number, for the sake of simplicity and convenience. I will suppose that two
countries are at war together, and that there is a third country which is in
possession of abundance of necessary articles, grain for example, which it is
the nature of war to render scarce, and of which, in consequence, the
other two hostile countries will be in a considerable degree of want. Now
what will this third country do? You may make as many treaties as you
choose, to bind the merchants and government of the pacific nation; for
treaties are not even packthread—they are nothing but rotten paper, or
parchment at best; more feeble than Falstaff's men in buckram;[35] they stand
for nothing at all when the parties have the power of breaking them.—If
you wish for a comment upon this text I refer you to the works of the

present King of Prussia. Well, Citizens, the country that has corn to spare
will send it to the best market, and if there are two markets in want of the
commodity, will find its interest, and will follow its interest, in sending
part of its surplus to one and part to the other.

Suppose England then, that England were, at this time, the only country
that felt this scarcity, the whole superfluity of other countries would, of
course, find its best market here; or if the scarcity be greater here than in
France, the consequence must be that those who have, would bring it to
the English market, because there it would fetch the best price. But suppose you have produced a scarcity and famine in both countries, reflect,
only for one moment, what must be the consequence? Will the country
that has abundance of corn bring the whole of it into the English market,
by which means the price would be smaller than if they had sent only half
of that commodity to England, and the remainder to the market of France?

Now, I ask you, Citizens, if this is not a clear and plain demonstration
that the common scarcity, produced by the profligate and abandoned system of burning, drowning, and destroying the articles of human sustenance, is an aggravation, instead of a mitigation of your misfortunes? and
that you are in reality by these means in a worse situation than if the
provisions destroyed had fallen into the hands of the enemy? Mr. Pitt and
his coadjutors would have sophistry enough I make no doubt to answer all
this, in their own way, and to carry the question against me *in the House of
Commons*: but I put it to you as plain men, understanding a plain question—Men whose calculations are not merely confined to multiplication
and subtraction;—understanding also that there is such a thing as political,
as well as numerical, arithmetic—calculations of the desires, wants and
propensities of men, as well as treaties, compacts, plans, and cabinet pro-
jections—taking these things into consideration, (of which *Pitt*, I believe,
is as ignorant as the hobby horse that he rode upon when a boy at
school)—I ask you whether, in defiance of all the treaties you can make, if
you produce a general scarcity, you do not produce a much worse effect
upon your own population and country, than if you have produced that
scarcity in your own country only, and suffer that produce (which you so
ridiculously destroy) to fall into the hands of the enemy?

Thus you see that the generous, humane, and benevolent system of policy, is the best policy, at last, for the country that adopts it, as well as for
others to whom it may be extended?

Citizens, there is another circumstance of a very curious nature, and
almost as disgraceful as it is curious, which it is necessary for me to dwell

upon. But disgraceful circumstances will never put the present administration to the blush; and so I need not have any tenderness for them on the occasion. I mean the conduct of the cabinet of this country with respect to neutral vessels.

There was a time when Britons had an open, manly and courageous spirit. There was a time when Britons had a sense of honor, and a feeling of benevolence; when they would have disdained to set the example of violating all the admitted laws of neutrality between nation and nation.[36] There was a time, when the people of this country knew that neutral vessels were sacred, whatever war might exist between the two contending countries. But this, Citizens, was a time when Britons disdained all weapons but those of open and manly exertion. This was a time when the detestable policy was not understood, nor could ever have been suggested, of attempting to starve twenty-four millions of brave and virtuous men, because they were struggling for their emancipation from unheard of despotism.

Yes, Citizens, there was a time when this country, upon the very eve of a war with France, freely permitted to go to that country large quantities and supplies of corn, because it was known that the rival country was in want of such assistance. I believe it is well authenticated that *George the second*, for George the *second* was a gentleman!—and I say it is well authenticated, there was a time when George the second, actually engaged in a war with France, yet suffered a supply of wheat to be sent into that country, to prevent the people from perishing with famine.[37]

This was glorious and magnificent conduct, worthy of a Briton! and if I had any nationality about me, it would prompt me to regret that the man who did this act was not born in the country which gave me birth.

There was also a time when the laws of nations were respected;—there was also a time when the brave and hardy Briton met his enemy face to face in the field—I mean not to stand up here as a panegyrist of slaughter, I hate massacre and murder however disguised: yet, comparing the two periods, and the two lines of conduct, I cannot but admire the man who prefers to stand openly forward in the field of combat, to the man who wishes by artificial famine to rid the world of enemies he dare not meet, because he knows his degeneracy of mind has sunk him below the gigantic powers of those who are struggling for freedom and justice. There is a chance that the man who meets his enemy openly in the fields supposes he is right, detestable as the acts of murder must always be by which such enmity must be supported. But the wretch who attempts to starve, to poison, or assassinate, who hires perjured spies and tumultuous assassins to breed confusion in a neighbouring country, that he may charge that confusion upon those whom he has basely and insolently injured; such a man, by his detestable arts, and sneaking tricks, proves that he knows himself to be a juggler, and that his cause is as rotten as his heart is hollow.

Well, Citizens, while the generous spirit of freedom still remained, Britain respected the laws of nations: and neutral vessels went free. What has been the conduct during the present war? I shall not recapitulate the circumstances which I stated the other evening, relative to dragooning one nation and another into this mad war with the French Republic: I shall confine myself to the capture of the vessels of those nations which in defiance of the juggling and bullying cabinet of this country, have continued their neutrality. And here even the Treasury runners will not have the face to contradict me. They know the facts. They are a little more in their way. There can be no doubt, when a man begs pardon, whether he has committed the offence. And *Pitt* it is notorious has done so more than once.

He seized every neutral vessel; and brought them into the ports of this country—What has been the consequence? Whether by mismanagement or what not, even the corn seized in the first instance proved good for little upon the hands of the seizers. But the neutral countries began to see this juggling; and they began to juggle in return. They put all their rotten corn on board proper vessels, and threw them in the way of the ships of England, that they might be seized; knowing very well what sort of shallow-pated bullies they had to deal with, and that, sooner or later, they should have full indemnity for them.

Well, the ships were captured in due time; and what did they do with them? Why they sent this blessed harvest, which they had thus reaped by their system of piracy, into the granaries and storehouses in this place, and that place, and the other place; and you may now some of it by the smell, if you go along bank side in the Borough at this time. But do not mistake it for dunghills, or night carts, I pray you. It is the corn your governors intended you should eat. For they sent all the good corn out of the country, as fast as they could, to supply their good allies; and behold when they came to open their magazines, (having been obliged already to pay down a good price for the commodity, and make sneaking apologies, as bullies usually do, to the neutral nations they had insulted) they found precious stocks of stuff, the greatest part of which was obliged to be sold to the real swinish multitude: not to the two legged swine, but the real swinish multitude, who run on all fours: many of whom even had the seditious and treasonable presumption to toss up their snouts and refuse the ministerial banquet that was offered to them.

Citizens, the evil consequences of this war, and the system upon which it has been conducted, have not stopped here. We must take into consideration the injury which has been done to our own agriculture, at home; the loss of those hands by which the agriculture ought to have been promoted, by distress and misery, by emigration to America, by manning our armies, and by the laudable and excellent science of kidnapping. The individual whose plough should have furrowed the earth, and produced the smile of plenty, has been sent with his sword to gore the breasts of the friends of the human race, and spread devastation and misery throughout Europe.

If this has not produced an absolute decline of the cultivation of our farms, it has at least operated to prevent the improvement and continued increase of production, which the improved state of society would otherwise have insured. We are to recollect, that when war sounds his soul-chilling trumpet, when the shrill blast of revenge and carnage is sounding from one end of a country to another, all other concerns stagnate; commerce droops, the arts expire, science languishes, and agricultural improvement is no more: and they must be miserably ignorant indeed of the condition and state of this country, who do not know that there is room enough for improvement with respect to agriculture among us. I shall give you upon this head the best sort of authority to argue from upon such an occasion: aristocratic authority. I find by the "Report of the Committee appointed by the Board of Agriculture, to take into consideration the state of waste lands and common fields in this kingdom", that the whole soil of Britain is supposed to consist of about 49,436,160 acres.[38] Now let us consider what is the quantity of this that is cultivated, and what the quantity is that is waste. We are informed that the waste lands in this kingdom amount to 6,259,472 acres; we are informed that the waste lands in Wales amount to 1,629,307 acres; and we find that the waste lands in Scotland amount to 14,218,222 acres; the whole together amounting to 22,107,001 acres, uncultivated; while the whole cultivated land is only 27,329,159 acres. So that there is almost half of this happy, this glorious, this wisely governed and flourishing country lies waste and uncultivated, under the influence and auspices of so blessed a constitution and so blessed an administration as we have the happiness to boast. Almost one half of one of the finest countries in the world lying positively uncultivated, and producing no one advantage hardly to man or beast! These are facts I state not from the visionary conceptions of my own brain; not from the ravings of democrats; not from the insidious inventions of Jacobins, but from the agents of government themselves, from committees appointed by their own Board of Agriculture.

Let us consider then, in the language of their own report, "what a difference would it make in the state and prosperity of this island, were only one half of these extensive wastes to wave with luxuriant crops of grain—be covered with innumerable herds and flocks, or cloathed with stately timber!"[39]

It has been objected that a large portion of this waste land could not be cultivated. This objection also the Committee of the Board of Agriculture has been kind enough to remove. For it states that the lands incapable of all improvement are only one million of acres; that the lands fit to be planted are three millions of acres; that the lands fit for arable and pasture are fourteen millions; lands fit for tillage three millions; and lands capable of being converted into meadow, or water meadow, one million. So that we have eighteen millions of acres in this country, now uncultivated, which are capable of being applied to the most important uses: those uses directly connected with the subsistence and comfort of the inhabitants.— We have three millions fit for timber, and which therefore would be useful, in a secondary degree, to the maintenance of the life and comfort of man; and only one million absolutely sterile; and even this one million might, perhaps, be covered with flocks of goats, which, though they yield no fleece, to increase the commerce of the country, yet afford a wholesome food, by their milk, and their flesh, while young, which would be better than for so many inhabitants of the country to be in want of all wholesome and necessary comfort, as they are at this time. Now, Citizens, we are told from this same author, that those lands might annually produce as much provisions as would be worth 19,500,000 pounds per year; and that they would produce wood for building, firing, &c. and other uses, as much as would be worth several millions more.

Consider then, for a minute, what blessings a wise and peaceful administration of this country might have secured; by applying our resources to improvement and cultivation; and reflect what curses they have procured by the mad havock and confusion into which they have plunged us, and the rest of Europe.

Let us consider, Citizens, how many deserts might have been made to smile in fertility, by a proper application of our resources; for though it has been said, and I am much inclined to agree with it, that the inclosures which have taken place in this country, have been a great calamity; yet I am sure of this, that inclosure, upon a fair and honest principle, might be productive of the greatest advantages.[40] For you are to remember that, in consequence of inclosure, you may have a greater height of cultivation, you may have a greater quantity of cattle, and other necessaries of life, produced; that your wool is less injured and of a superior quality, and therefore more advantageous to the producer, and better for the consumer. But inclosures ought not to be conducted upon the principle that has been usual among us. The rich man ought not to have an act of parliament to rob the poor freeholder of his estate. I say the poor freeholder: for I challenge the greatest casuist of the law to produce me a better title, by which the first nobleman in the land holds his estate, than I will produce in favour of the estate which the poor man has in that right of commonage, which may have been bequethed, or made over to him, by the nobles and great landed proprietors of former generations.

Citizens, our nobles had once some nobility. I wish not to recall to your admiration the ages of feudal barbarism; but I wish not to have the chains of feudal barbarism without any of the advantages of feudal munificence. I remember, from the pages I have turned over, accounts of the manner in which our great nobility enjoyed their revenues in former times: the hundreds and thousands of individuals supported by their bounty; their open halls of hospitality; the recreations, sports and pastimes with which they enlivened the people, at particular periods; the bounty which they displayed towards them. But in these times they had not learned to consider it as their best grandeur to loll themselves into apoplectick diseases, in a stupid gilded coach; they thought, on the contrary, that the splendour and greatness of their nobility and fortune was best displayed by having their tenants around them, enjoying the comforts and relaxations of life, about them, at their expence. However, in other circumstances, they might be inclined to oppress those individuals, they had some degree of liberality, at least, in their conduct towards them, in these respects.

Among the most conspicuous of them, in point of this endowment, was *John of Gaunt, Duke of Lancaster;*[41] for Dukes, even royal Dukes, were not always made of such stuff as they are made of in the present day! Among the foremost of those Dukes, whose liberality kept some pace with their possessions, was *John of Gaunt, Duke of Lancaster*, who bequeathed a great quantity of land to the poor inhabitants, in particular situations, to be held by them, and all future inhabitants of such districts, for ever.

Now I should like to know of those gentlemen who cry out about *Repub-*

licans and levellers of property, and all this stuff and nonsense, which originated in their own distempered brains: I would ask which of them holds
their estates upon a better tenure? But the greatest plunderer and oppressor
always cries stop thief first; because he is desirous of creating that confusion
which will prevent his own villainous practices from being detected.

What then is the system upon which inclosures are now carried on? and
what ought it to be?

With respect to agriculture, two objects ought always to be kept in view:
namely to produce the largest quantity of the necessaries of life that the
country can produce; and to promote the most equal distribution of those
articles of comfort which can peaceably and justly be effected. This is my
system of equality and justice. This is my idea of the first and genuine
principles of just government, with respect to agriculture—to produce the
largest quantity of the necessaries of life, and to promote the most equal
distribution of those articles. A little observation will shew us that the last
of these, the most important, has never been attended to at all; and that
the first has been attended to in a very imperfect manner: witness the
waste lands I have just stated to you.

Citizens, the fact is, that there is a third object which, though it ought
to be no object at all, is the only object with governments in general;
namely REVENUE! because without revenue, that is to say without taxation, the expences and extravagances of ministers and their favourites cannot be supported; pimps and parasites cannot swell to power and grandeur;
numerous trains of spies, informers, and assassins, cannot be supported;
and, in short, the whole system of that grandeur, luxury, extravagance and
folly, which constitute what ministers call the grandeur and prosperity of
the nation, must tumble into ruin if this revenue were not to be kept in the
most flourishing and prosperous condition. In order to support this revenue, it has been necessary to oppress, in a great degree, the agriculture of
the country: for as *Soame Jenyns*[42] (who though an aristocrat, could sometimes find out the truth) observed, the commerce of this country may be
considered as a hog—You see he thought the rich merchants the swinish
multitude!—The commerce of this country may be considered as a hog—:
if you touch but one bristle upon its back, it immediately begins to make
such a grunting, that it throws the whole sty into confusion; and the country is distracted with its clamour; while agriculture, like a poor sheep, is led
up silently every year, to yield its fleeces to the shearer, without uttering
an individual murmur.

Now, Citizens, such being the pacific disposition of agriculture, or the
individuals who are employed in agriculture; and such being the turbulent

disposition of our rich aristocratic merchants, it is easy to see that ministers will have as large a portion as they can, out of the labour and sweat of the industrious poor.

But let us now consider how inclosures are at present carried on. A bill is brought into Parliament, that virtuous and immaculate assembly, concerning which I always want words to speak with becoming reverence!—A bill is brought into parliament, by a rich proprietor, who has got a large estate, by the side of a common; and thinks that common would be a very good addition to this estate, and is, therefore, desirous that this common should be inclosed for his benefit and advantage. Well what is the mode of proceeding? A time is appointed, and sometimes no time at all, for you will remember, that, some years ago, a Mr. William Tooke,[43] had an estate in the neighbourhood of a brother of the Lord Chief Justice De Grey,[44] which Chief Justice was a very useful friend to Lord North. And this relation of the Chief Justice had a mind to inclose Mr. Wm. Tooke's estate, for his benefit and advantage. A bill was brought into Parliament. It was introduced, read, and re-read on the same day, and committed to be read the third day, and passed the day following. How was this prevented? Why John Horne, who has since taken the name of Tooke, and who has done many gloriously audacious things in the cause of liberty; and who, notwithstanding the assassin-like attack that has been made upon his aged life, by the Reevites and Pittites of the day, during the last summer, by keeping him shut up in a close unwholesome room,[45] I hope he will live to do many more gloriously audacious things in the same cause—This John Horne Tooke wrote a libel upon the Speaker of the House of Commons: and I have heard him say, that it was certainly the most outrageous libel that was ever penned.[46] He got it immediately inserted in the newspaper. This libel kicked up, as he expected, a monstrous riot in St. Stephen's chapel:—not the present House of Commons to be sure:—I speak only of former Houses of Commons, about which there is no treason to speak one's mind freely. These, however, have been formerly the most riotous and sometimes the most blackguard assemblies in the nation. The present parliament is undoubtedly very much reformed: but I hope the next will be reformed still more. The Speaker, in a very great fury, took the chair; and immediately declared, he would not sit there and have the dignity of the House attacked through his sides, in this way. A warm debate was produced, and the attention of the public was called towards the subject.

They attempted, but were not wise enough to know how to do it, to punish the author of the libel: but they never dared to bring in the bill a third time; and the relation of the great, and upright, and immaculate Lord

Chief Justice, who was the great and powerful friend of the great and powerful Lord North, never had his bill brought in again; and was glad to make his peace, in a fair and honourable manner, with the said Mr. Wm. Tooke, whose estate he had attempted to inclose as his own.

In the usual course, however, a bill is brought in, and petitions may be presented, and which, when they are supported, some little compensation, to be sure, is generally made to the lower orders of society. But suppose it happens, as it does frequently happen, and must frequently happen, that those poor individuals have no friend even to put it into their minds that they have the power of doing such a thing: and the great are not very anxious that the poor about them, should be very well informed as to their political rights! No: they are to be fleeced as bare as can be, and their very bones are to be picked, after they are fleeced, by the rich man, who having committed a highway robbery upon their little properties, talks of the security of property, and enters into associations, with Reeves and his cabalistical informers, to prevent *Republicans and Levellers* from enquiring into the right by which these robberies have been committed.

But, Citizens, it is very evident that a tenth part of that expence, which has been devoted in this mad and ridiculous war, and in supporting the places, pensions, and emoluments of the corrupt set who have produced the war—a tenth part of this revenue would have cultivated, or made considerable advances towards *cultivating, all the waste lands throughout the country, for the benefit and advantage of the common people;*—not a bare common, with here a blade of grass and there a blade of grass, and here a dangling briar and there a copse to destroy their little flocks. No, they may turn them into a plentiful, luxuriant, smiling country, from which they might reap a part of their subsistence; and not be compelled to toil from their bed to their table, and from their table to their beds, and thus from day to day, in one constant succession of labour, as if the great mass of mankind were only born to breed slaves for the higher orders of society; and to toil and sweat, and die, without comfort and accommodation.

Go even into the neighbourhood of this metropolis; where manure is abundant; where the means of cultivation are easy; go which way you will; turn to the east, the west, the north or south;—see what tracks of land lay bare and desolate, which, with a little of the care of government, if they had time to bestow it upon such *insignificant subjects*, might procure a comfortable subsistence for innumerable families, whose little cottages, rising here and there, with a little assistance, might turn this waste into a blooming Eden, and make this country, as one of our poets has called it, "the exhaustless granary of the world!"[47] But all our resources are swallowed up by this mad and ruinous war. Nothing can be thought of but the annihilation of freedom. Nothing can be thought of but spreading the name of a *Pitt*, over the continent; and the empty boast, of a shuffling individual and his coadjutor, *Dundas*, having given a constitution to a country, who would neither accept of that constitution, nor suffer either the one or the other of them to be door keeper to the Convention for which they would form the laws.

For this, agriculture is to be neglected, the arts are to be destroyed, Wisdom is to be forbidden to open her lips, infant Genius is no more to plume its unfledged wings in popular assemblies, least it should soar to the realm of light and truth. Every thing is to be neglected; every thing is to be overthrown; the poor are to be starved in myriads, and only have the melancholy alternative to turn their throats like sheep to the butchering hand—I was going to say of *their* enemy—No, not of their enemy, but of the enemy of *Pitt* and his *Pittites*, and *Dundas* and the asses which follow him!—for this, I say, every right, every happiness, every social duty, are to be swallowed up! carnage is to reign, year after year, campaign after campaign! mad project after mad project!—Disappointment, instead of producing wisdom, is only to produce desperation!—and the wretched inhabitants of *La Vendee* are again to be seduced, we are told, from their allegiance; that war may again rage through that devoted country, and the minister of this devoted country may have occasion to plunge it still deeper, into misery and desolation. From calamities so aggravated I was going to call for guardian angels—I was going to call for preserving Deities to rescue us. But no: I call upon the good sense—I call upon the virtue—I call upon the spirit, and integrity of the people, to snatch the people from the precipice upon which they stand, and preserve us from the desolation which else must inevitably swallow us.

THE TRIBUNE. No. XVIII.

Consequences of depriving the MASS *of the* PEOPLE *of their share in the* REPRESENTATION. *The* THIRD LECTURE *"on the Causes of the present* DEARNESS & SCARCITY *of* PROVISIONS," *delivered* Wednesday, May 6th, 1795.[48]

CITIZENS,

THIS is the third time I have met you upon the subject of this night's Lecture: if I were to meet you again and again till I have gone through the whole of my subject, I know not when this course of lectures could possibly close. The further our researches extend, the more we find to investigate. This, so true in sciences, is perhaps more conspicuously true with respect to the sources of those great national calamities under which we are sinking.

I anticipated to you on the first night the very wide field of enquiry into which this topic would lead me. I was not aware, however, of its full extent. In short, it would be totally impossible to do justice to the subject in a course of lectures that professes to be miscellaneous; and I feel myself called upon, from the pressure of temporary matter, to bring it to a conclusion this evening.

In my mode of investigating it I have divided it into two general heads: that is to say, the immediate causes of aggravated scarcity and dearness; and the general regulations which have unfortunately been adopted, in this country, by which the gradual increase has been occasioned. For the sake of methodical arrangement, it would have been proper, perhaps, to have begun with the latter. Circumstances, however, led me to a different arrangement: particularly my having announced as a part of the subject a topic which necessarily connected itself with that branch of the enquiry, at a time when I was not aware that I should deliver any more than one lecture upon the subject before me.

The greatest part of what I then had to say upon the causes of the temporary scarcity, I have brought to a conclusion in the former lecture. I am now going to the immediate investigation of what may be considered as the permanent, though growing, causes of the dearness of provisions in this country. And, among these, I shall consider paper credit; the corn laws; the monopoly of farms; the encouragement of the breed of horses; tythes; the neglect of our fisheries; and contracts and monopolies between fishermen and fishmongers; from whence I shall digress once more to the affairs of Poland, and then lead you back to that which in fact is the fountain of all the other causes, the monstrous growth of barefaced corruption in this country.

With respect to paper credit, it may not, at first view, appear to be immediately connected with the subject. But this opinion will vanish, if you remember that it is an admitted principle, making exceptions for accidents which may produce temporary scarcity, and also for the contracts and monopolies between the holders of particular articles, that the price of commodities must necessarily be regulated by the quantity of circulating medium;—or in other words, that gold and silver and all other arbitrary signs of property, decrease and fluctuate in their value, in proportion as they become more abundant, but that the real articles of necessity always remain precisely the same. The calculations and customary language of the world lead us indeed to a contrary conclusion. But the fact is, that it is gold that is purchased with commodity, and not commodity with gold: the gold being in reality nothing but the counters or the figures, if I may so express myself, by which the quantum of wealth is calculated. Whenever, therefore, the numeral or nominal wealth is more abundant than the production, you must put down a greater quantity of these counters, or the signs of these counters, to tell how many sheep, how many oxen, or how much corn you are worth, or able to buy.

You are to consider that paper credit, though it does not increase the specie, but on the contrary may be proved to occasion its diminution, yet increases the circulating medium: that is to say, that paper is taken to market, particularly the wholesale market, instead of specie, and, passing in common with the circulating specie, increases the quantity of nominal wealth in circulation, and of course occasions any given quantity of money to be worth so much the less. Thus then you will find that the circulation of paper begets an increase in the price of all the articles of consumption which the great mass of the people have occasion for. It is so important that this part of the subject should be understood, that I would rather be guilty of tautology than be obscure. I will state it therefore in another way: As the price of the article which can be brought into the market, must be proportionate to the quantity of circulating medium which can be carried into the market, it follows of course that if I, having 5000l. in specie, can circulate my paper to the amount of 5000l. more, and thus carry in effect 10,000l. into the market, instead of 5000l. I produce an inevitable increase in the price of the articles to be consumed. This, with respect to the dealers in this paper coin, is matter of no inconvenience. It is a struggle of credit. It enables them to carry on their commerce with greater facility; and he whose word passes most current has the best of it. But the common people, the working man and the little shopkeeper, have no part of the credit resulting from this circulating paper. They must take it indeed, sometimes, in payment; and they must abide by the loss of the exchange, and the delay. But their notes will not be accepted; their accommodations between individual and individual will not pass current; they are not permitted to swindle the public, though the rich are; but they must bear their part of the increased price of the necessaries of life, in consequence of this swindling in which they have no share.

And yet, Citizens, no sort of property is protected with so much jealousy as this fabricated, circulating medium. The laws of this country, severe and sanguinary enough in many respects that relate to the treatment of the lower orders of society, have thought it necessary to be still more rigid than usual with respect to this paper credit: and consequently we find that forgery is among those crimes and offences which never escape the last sentence and punishment of the law.

Why is this? There must be some reason for it. Surely we cannot admit that forgery is a crime peculiarly marked with the blackest stains of turpitude.—I stand not up as an *advocate* for crimes that violate property; but I wish that a scale should be observed between the punishment and the turpitude of actions. Surely, then, I say we cannot suppose that there is more moral turpitude in the act of forgery than in many actions that are passed by with a much slighter degree of punishment. The common feelings of mankind revolt at such a supposition: and nothing but that commercial influence which, of late years, has contaminated our councils and our laws, could have countenanced the unremitting severity with which this crime has been pursued. We find accordingly that where individuals have not been misled either by commercial connections, or by particular attachments, to the modes and practices of the times, that a great disposition arises among mankind to condemn or blame this extreme severity: nor could all the arguments of commercial expediency and the inviolable barrier of mercantile credit, stifle the voice of public sympathy in the recent cases of Peru and Dodd.[49]

A very ludicrous anecdote, applicable to this subject, was once related to me by an officer whose duty is to attend one of the circuits. A man had been indicted for forgery at the assizes; and a jury of farmers and graziers was impannelled to try the offence. The facts were proved beyond the possibility of contradiction; but the honest farmers did not understand how it should happen, that a man who committed a robbery without any sort of violence, or injury to the peace of society, should be punished in a manner so much more severe than many whose crimes were marked with deeper turpitude. They therefore consulted among themselves, and presently agreed, that tho' the thing to be sure were proven, yet as for matter of that, it was impossible to hang a man for a bit of paper. If he had stole a sheep, it would have been another thing; but to hang a man for a bit of paper, no they could never agree with that matter: as they had just been trying a man, who had killed another by an unlucky blow, and which the

Judge instructed them to find only manslaughter, they agreed to bring this in manslaughter also; and manslaughter it was.

But however much at a loss, reasoning like speculative moralists, we might be to account why a superior degree of severity should be adopted, for the preservation of this particular species of property, practice will soon give us a clue. Nothing is so friendly to individual accumulation and monopoly.

This the legislators of the ancient world very well knew. They knew that in proportion as you can compress property into a small compass, a few will have an opportunity of ingrossing to themselves a larger proportion of the riches of the country, and of keeping the other portions of society in misery and depression. Lycurgus[50] therefore invented a species of coin, which has been rendered famous through succeeding ages, by the name of iron money. So that if a man in Sparta was worth twenty or thirty pounds, he was obliged to hire a waggon, to remove it from place to place: an expedient which could not fail of producing the desired effect, of preserving a considerable degree of equality among the citizens.

A contrary object has been kept in view by modern legislators, and of course, a contrary practice has been appealed to. It was found beneficial to the revenue, it was found beneficial to corruption, to luxury, and to usurpation, that property should come into the hands of as few individuals as possible; and therefore methods have been devised to favour this monopoly.

The history of the progress of wealth, or rather of the medium of wealth, would be a very curious one if I had time to enter into it at large. In the first instance undoubtedly all wealth must have consisted in what is now called *kind*:—Persons who have collected or who have paid tythe in kind will understand what I mean. But this unwieldy sort of wealth would be very inconvenient upon the present system. It would undoubtedly clog very much the wheels of what ministers call Government—that is to say, corruption. This, however, you would not perhaps consider as a very grievous calamity; and you might even be tempted to exclaim with Pope

"O that such bulky bribes as all might see
Still, as of old, encumber'd villainy!
A Statesman's slumbers how this speech would spoil!
Sir, Spain has sent a thousand jars of oil;
Huge bales of British cloth blockade the door:
A hundred oxen at your levy roar."

Essay on the Use of Riches.[51]

Specie, then, was soon introduced; but was found not sufficiently convenient: for James I having ordered a large sum to be given to one of his favourites; but happening, by strange accident, to have a minister who had a little honesty, he took him into the room where the money was all spread out. James was astonished at the formidable appearence of so many guineas; and declared it was too much for any individual. He ordered therefore that his favourite should be content with half.

Nor is this the only kind of inconvenience which politicians have experienced from transactions in specie. It has been found that guineas, like roaring oxen can tell tales. Of this I will satisfy myself with one example. A great politician, in the time of William III. had been desirous of a private audience with Majesty, and had accordingly crept up the back stairs: for whether you have a *Whig King* or a *Tory King*, there must always be a back stair-case to the royal closet. What the important intelligence was which he had to communicate was never known, for the affair was conducted with becoming privacy. Nor would it ever have been known what was the occasion of the subsequent alteration in his sentiments and conduct, but for an unlucky accident. But just as he was stealing down again, the bag, in which his bribe was contained, which was to pay him for his future votes in Parliament, happened to burst, and the whole secret was revealed.

> "Once 'tis confest, beneath the patriot's cloak,
> From the crack'd bag the dropping guinea spoke,
> And, gingling down the back stairs, told the crew
> Old Cato is as great a rogue as you."[52]

But, Citizens, paper credit has at once given wings and secrecy to corruption. There is now no necessity for cumberous waggons to take away your heavy iron wealth; no occasion for canvas bags to hold your millions; or cloaks to hide them from the public eye. A little bit of paper that may be "passed thro' the hollow circle of a ring", may answer every demand of Government or corruption—may purchase a whole House of Commons, or transport a band of Patriots to Botany Bay.

> "Blest paper credit! last and best supply,
> That lends Corruption lighter wings to fly:
> Gold, wing'd by thee, can compass hardest things,
> Can purchase states, or fetch, or carry kings.

A single leaf can waft whole navies o'er,
Or ship off armies to a distant shore;
A leaf, like Sybil's, waft us to and fro,—
Our fates, our fortunes as the winds do blow!"[53]

The next article to which I shall call your attention you will imme-diately perceive to be most intimately connected with the subject. I mean the corn laws.

It is not necessary for me to enter into an investigation of all those commercial regulations which have so strong a tendency to favour the wealthy few, and keep the rest of society in a state of depression and pov-erty. I shall only notice such of those regulations as relate immediately to the subject in question: though undoubtedly every one of them in some degree eventually affects the price of all commodities and necessaries of life.

Commerce, in fact, ought to be no part of the subject now before us: for the object of agriculture ought not to be *commerce*, but the comfort and accommodation of the people. But our regulations have not always had this beneficial object in view. We find but too many of them which have a particular tendency towards favoring the opulent land-holder, and bolster-ing up, thro' his means, the System of Rotten Boroughs and Corruption. We find many precautions taken to increase the weight and influence of those gentlemen: and for a very good reason: they are not only proprietors of land; that might be of no more estimation in the eyes of a minister than any other species of commodity, but they are proprietors also of those rot-ten boroughs, which Lord *Mornington*[54] and Mr. *Pitt* are pleased to suppose constitute so sublime a part of the excellence of our constitution, that, if we were to tear them away, there would be but little left in the glorious fabric to demand our veneration, or promote our felicity.

Citizens, it is very clear that the higher corn and cattle sell, the higher the landlord can raise his rent. For he will always take care (especially now that long leases are out of fashion) not to lose his share of the advantage, whatever it may be, which the industry or the ingenuity of the farmer may produce. The higher, therefore, the market, the higher will be his rent, and the greater his opportunities of indulging in those gratifications to which, undoubtedly, the higher orders are entitled, though it would be something like blasphemy to attempt to extend them to the lower classes of the community.

Hence we find that, among other *wise* regulations, there is a bounty upon the exportation of corn, whenever it shall be below a given price: and as the persons who have an interest in fixing this standard as high as it can be fixed, are the very persons who, by the present Constitution of Borough Jobbing and Aristocratic Influence, have the power of altering it whenever they please, we have—or rather, THEY *have*, by means of this politic regulation an infallible means of keeping up the price to the improvement of their own fortunes, it is true—but to the beggary and starvation of the multitude. And yet, while our wealthy land holders are thus associated and represented for the advancement of their rent-rolls, and our unrepresented labourers and mechanics are punished like felons for associating for an increase of wages, Aristocrats have the audacity to talk of the liberties of Britons—of equal laws, and equal justice.

But the injustice does not terminate here. I have repeatedly proved, on a variety of occasions, that, as all taxes must be paid out of the profits of productive labour, the whole burthen of taxation must, in truth, eventually fall upon the shoulders of the laborious part of the community. Who is it then that pays the bounty?—The laborious poor!—Who is it that receives the benefit of that bounty?—The landholder!—the indolent rich!—Is there any doubt of the accuracy of this statement?—Reflect awhile.—Are not the taxes paid by the people? Is not the bounty paid out of the taxes? Does it not follow therefore, of course, that the more Government pays in bounties the more taxes must be levied upon the people?—And all for what? Why truly for the noble privilege of paying a greater price for every bit of bread they put in their mouths.

How monstrous to plunder the poor peasant and artisan, in this manner, of the very means of purchasing the necessaries of life, and then to tell them that they must pay so much the more for having been so plundered!!!

Nor is this all. Having taken precautions to prevent the price of the necessaries of life falling below the minimum which our land-holders and borough-mongers will condescend to accept, they have also taken other precautions to mount it up to the *maximum* which their *consciences* would suffer them to exact. For this barriers are to be erected to prevent the free progress of mercantile intercourse;—the first great maxim in the communion of nations ("Let the abundances of each be exchanged, that the scarcities of each may be removed!") is to be violated;—and commerce, the boasted glory of our isle!—Commerce, who from her very essence should be free as air, is to groan in manacles!

Unless the average price in our markets should be upwards of 50s. per quarter, no corn can be imported from foreign countries.

Now, Citizens, be pleased to remember that though 50s. is or was a very high price, yet good wheat may be considerably more than 50s. Nay, and must be so before the ports can be opened; because all the wheat sold at market is not good; and as it is the *average*, and not the *maximum*, that opens or closes the ports, the average price may be 50s. while all the good wheat may be sold at a price very considerably higher. I will instance this by a calculation. The average is fixed by the inspection of officers who attend the markets for the purpose of taking an account of the quantities sold in different districts. Suppose that 50 quarters are sold at 53s. that will give you 132l. 10s.; suppose 200 quarters at 52s. the amount will be 750l.; then suppose 400 more at 49s. which is 980l. for the whole. The result is, that 650 quarters of wheat selling for 1632l. 10s. the average price becomes 50s.; but the good corn has been sold at 52 and 53s. Thus then you see, that till good corn has amounted to 53s. or upwards, the ports must be shut, and no foreign corn must be admitted to come to competition with the corn produced in this country; because such a competition would do what? Injure the great mass of the people?—No; do them good—make bread so much the cheaper. And who can dispute that it would be good for the great mass of the people, that all the necessaries of life should be sold as cheap as possible?—No; the injury would be to the rich landholder, who would not be able to charge so great a price for his land: a thing so monstrous, that the happiness of millions ought not, in the eyes of wise and beneficent legislators, to be held in competition with it for a moment. But even this average, extravagant as it would once have been thought, is not fixed. It is fixed, indeed, with respect to you and me; it is fixed that it shall never be altered for *our* advantage; but it is not fixed that it shall never be altered for the advantage of our borough-mongers and legislators. The fact is, that it is altered whenever it suits their conscience that it should be. At no great difference of time, the average was 48s. instead of 50s.—But mark the consequence of your having no voice, no interest in the choice of your *representatives*; of having your legislature with those individuals who are to make your laws and regulations—the rich landed proprietors—the owners of rotten boroughs—the sapient individuals who happen to possess, upon their estates, the fragments and relicks of Druids temples at Old Sarum; or to see from the wave-invaded shore the ruins of a church; still struggling with the surrounding sea, whose shattered spire continues to be represented, though the spot that encircled it is no longer the habitation of man.

It is natural enough that those persons, being the only individuals represented, being the only individuals who have any power of controul over the representatives, their interest should be particularly attended to; and that, therefore, in proportion as the price of corn increases, the average price fixed in the act of parliament should also be altered: nor should I be at all surprized, if, in a few years, we were to run from 50 to 60, to 70, to 100. Why not? The individuals who make the laws having an interest in making this average as high as it possibly can be borne, what should restrain them but a dread of the enlightened spirit of the people? And who shall dare attempt to inspire that dread? To put the borough-mongers in fear, you are told, is to overawe Parliament; and to overawe Parliament, you are told, is High Treason: and as no one, it may be supposed, is very desirous of being hanged, drawn and quartered—

"Must not things mend in their common course,
From bad to worse, from worse to that is worst?" SPENCER.[55]

Yet, notwithstanding all this, a sapient magistrate in the northern extremity of the country—(a place for the magistrates of which I dare say we all have a becoming esteem)—I mean to say the Lord Justice Clark, on the trial of Morton and others for sedition, chose to observe that "the poor of this country, particularly those infatuated people stiling themselves The Friends of the People, pay no taxes at all. It is the landed-property men alone that pay all the taxes; for look you, my Lords, we pay the poor for their labour; and so, as we gi the poor the filler to pay the taxes wi, it is we, in truth, that pay aw the taxes. And if they be not content with our good laws and wise government, they may e'en tack their alls upon their backs, and pack off wi themselves. And let them gang, we'll be better quat o' them. But we can't take our land upon our backs: Na; we mun stay."[56]— So that, notwithstanding the increased price of rent—notwithstanding the encreased price of the commodities of life, upon which, by the way, all taxes ultimately fall—notwithstanding every burthen and imposition which the laborious poor are subject to, we are told that they pay no part of the taxes: and, as a notable proof of this, we are told that they have nothing left, but that which they can put upon their backs, and go off whenever they choose: and as an equal proof that the rich people, the landed property men pay all the taxes, they tell you they have the misfortune to be encumbered with such valuable estates, that it is impossible for them to go, let things be as bad as they will. They cannnot put their land upon their backs, and consequently they mun stay.

Citizens, I might here animadvert upon the unchangeable nature of court politics. *Justice Clerk* tells the common people they may get themselves gone, as soon as they will. They may put their alls upon their backs, and away they may trudge; for that it will be a good thing to be rid of them.—What does the cabinet of this country say at this time? Why, it issues a mandate (legally, I grant you, but mark how consistently) saying, that though you are upon the brink of starvation—though your children are crying to you for bread—though distress and misery of every description encircle you round, you shall not attempt to depart from this country, if you have not the permission of *Mr. Secretary Dundas*. It shall be esteemed as a crime of a very high magnitude. You shall be dragged from the ships, and the ships shall be detained, and not permitted to proceed upon their voyage. You shall have but one alternative—either to starve in your cottages, or be both starved and butchered too, in the ranks of those armies who are fighting for a cause from which undoubtedly you will receive very great advantages; though I very much doubt whether any of you are wise enough to discover in what that advantage will consist. But why animadvert upon inconsistencies? If men can sit upon the bench, and talk such rank nonsense as this, what matters whether they contradict to-day what they said yesterday, or to-morrow what they say to-day?—The labouring part of the community may take their alls upon their back, and quit the country!!! Suppose they did, what would *Lord Justice Clerk's* landed estates be worth, after they were gone? what would it produce? I will tell him what it would produce—Such innumerable swarms of vermin as would threaten him with immediate destruction, and to deliver him from which he would pray for the restoring arms of those Sans Culottes whom oppressive cruelty had banished from the country. What can *Lord Justice Clerk*, and all the Lords and the Justices—and the Lord knows who to help them, produce from their estates? Let them sow them with the musty records of the courts of law; let them plant them with acts of parliament, and manure them with the sanguinary sentences of the Court of Justiciary; let them, if they choose, dig holes, and bury that gold which they so idolized. What will it produce? Briars, thorns, thistles enough undoubtedly. Every sort of annoyance it will produce. But bread, the food of man, the barley that should make him wholesome liquour, will it yield him these? Will it feed their sheep or oxen, or make them broad cloath? No.—No sort of commodity whatever, for sustenance or comfort, will their land, their law, or their acts of Parliament produce them. Nor will all the mandates of the Privy Council, nor the grave decisions of the Bench make a potatoe grow without cultivation, or turn acorns into melons and peaches. No: these they must receive from the labours of that common rabble, without whom the *Lord Justice Clerk* has the wisdom to say, they could do a great deal better than with them.

O what sort of system is it we live under, when Judges sit upon the Bench and preach doctrines so absurd and so pernicious: doctrines which nothing can equal but the intoxicated cruelty of the late aristocrats of France, who, while in their gilded carriages, they rolled carelessly over some poor tattered beggar, whom they disdained to turn out of the way to avoid, have been known to exclaim "It is no matter. It is only one of the common fellows; and we had always too many of these wretches!"

We have seen, Citizens, what has been the consequence of such doctrines in France, I hope we shall see no such consequences here. But if we do, whose is the fault? Does it rest with those who call out to the oppressor "forbear your inhumanity—Reform your ill policy"? or does it result from those who pollute the sacred vestments of authority by doctrines so diabolical as that which I have read?

Another cause of the growing scarcity to which I shall refer you, is the monopoly of farms. The time has been, as Goldsmith beautifully expresses it, the happy time, "when every rood of land maintained its man."[57] What is the case now? Where will you go for those little farms which supported in comfort, and supplied with all the simple necessaries and decencies of life, a family healthy from its industry, virtuous from surrounding necessities, and whose interests were inseparably united by the humble situation it was placed in with that of the great mass of the people? Those little farms are no longer to be found. Large proprietors have grasped whole provinces, almost, in one concern; and that useful order of men is annihilated, to make room for the spacious granaries, and unwieldy opulence of monopolists and speculators, who, by reason of their wealth and fewness, find combination and compact easy, and rule the market at their own will and pleasure.

A correspondent, residing in Shropshire, gives me the particulars of some circumstances which have taken place in his own neighbourhood. He tells me that, in two villages, in the neighbourhood of his own residence, he remembers, at no considerable distance of time, nine farms to have been contained in the one, and seven farms in the other: each of which supported, of course, the families of the occupiers in decency and comfort. What is the condition now? The *nine* farms are reduced to *three*; and the *seven* are reduced to *two*. Thus then you have two families living in luxury, where you used to have seven maintained in decent competency; and you have three exulting in their large possessions, where you used to have nine carrying their produce to a fair and early market, to the accommodation and benefit of society.

Whose is the advantage of this? There can be no doubt: the landed proprietor's. He collects his rent with less trouble. He finds it more easy to obtain it immediately at the time when it is due; or the proprietor, forsooth, is a man of capital and credit; and if he cannot get specie from him, he can get circulating paper. He finds, also, that he is enabled to demand a higher rent; because when only one family is to be supported, where three were to be supported before, the farmer can be content with a more moderate ratio of profit, and yet his family live in greater abundance than the three families could afford.

This is not all. The mischief does not stop here. This monopoly of farms destroys competition, and encourages speculation; and consequently creates an artificial, and increases the real, scarcity. The little farmer was obliged to take up his commodity into the market, when he wanted to make up his rent, or other payments; the great farmer can keep it in his barns till he meets with a chapman at such a price as he chooses to put upon it. The little farmer could not speculate upon the chances of scarcity, and thus create one where otherwise it would never have existed; the great farmer can: he finds no inconvenience in such speculation; because, being a man of considerable property, a man of *respectability*, (as we denominate those who have the power and the inclination to starve their fellow beings by wholesale) he knows that, if he is pressed for an immediate supply, he can have it, by means of the fictitious circulating medium. The fact is, that the very character of a farmer is almost annihilated.[58] In many parts of the country you see no such thing as an individual who tends to his own farm, and is thus brought to something like a level with the labourers whom he employs. Instead of this the land is divided between vast proprietors, who consider their farms as objects of commercial speculation, and who look down upon the poor dependent drudges who toil for them, as beings who have no sort of title to commiseration and fellow feeling.

Citizens, we must immediately perceive, if we use a moment's reflection, that in the present state of human intellect and human passions, absolute equality of property is totally impossible. It is a visionary speculation which none but the calumniators of the friends of freedom ever entertained.

Reeves[59] and his associates might deem it convenient to suppose persons to entertain such notions; but they existed only in the distempered brains of Alarmists. But though this is not attainable, there is another state of society perfectly practicable, and which is the best substitute for this poetical vision—this golden age of absolute equality: I mean the imperceptible gradations of rank, where step rises above step by slow degrees, and link mingles with link in intimate and cordial union, till the whole society connected together by inseparable interests indulges that fellow feeling between man and man, from which, and from which alone, the real fruits of humanity and justice can be expected.

Alas! "What can we argue but from what we know?" This argument, so often applied as the test of science, we may apply to feeling also. We must know what calamity is, before we can feel for it. The calamities of the order of society but just below us!—an order into which we see the possibility that we may ourselves descend, press home to our feelings. We enter into the particulars that constitute their poignancy—we understand their nature, and we feel them in their full force. We are disposed both to respect and relieve them. But he who has been nursed in pomp and luxury, looks down upon the poor drudge, by whom he is supported, as a beast of burden, created for his ease and advantage; and feels no more for his calamities, in three instances out of four, than for the pangs of the expiring brute who bleeds beneath the stroke of the butcher to supply his table.

But these imperceptible gradations are destroyed by the present monopolizing system. There are but three classes of men left among us—the monied speculators, among whom may be classed the great farmers I have been describing; the proud high towering drones, who hum, and buz, and make a noise in the hive; but who never brought a morsel of honey into the cells; and the poor hard-working drudges, who toil from day to night, and almost from night to day, and receive for their useful and important services the bitter inheritance of unpitied poverty. In great towns it is true gradations something more various may be traced; even in these we are hastening to the same dismal state of separation. Hence it is, from these wide gaps, these chasms in society, that there is no common interest, no general affection, no universal sympathy, binding man to man, and constituting one great united, harmonious mass, having but one object, and adhering steadily together for the preservation of each other and the attainment of that object.

Perhaps it is not proper for me, who certainly am not very far advanced in agricultural speculations, to lay down any particular regulations; but I doubt very much whether it would not be to the happiness of this country, if no farm was held by any individuals of more than two hundred acres.[60] But we now have thousands of acres held in one farm.—What wonder, then, that there are monopolies? What produces monopolies? When great competition exists monopoly cannot flourish. But when the power of competition is in the hands of a few individuals, they have nothing to do but to agree to do that which their mutual interest will prompt them to fulfill, and they have the whole public at their mercy; and the power of starving them into a compliance with their extravagant demands.

Citizens, I do not intend to indulge myself frequently in speculative projects. But one has been submitted to me which I think worthy of attention. I have formerly shewn you, that almost half the land of this island remains in an uncultivated state. "Now we will suppose", says my correspondent, "that four millions of acres of this was parcelled into small farms of 80 or 100 acres; this would become a receptacle for 50,000 families put into possession of a comfortable subsistence; and would give us in a few years, by the increased accommodation and comfort of these families, an addition to the rising generation of many thousand individuals. Take into consideration also the advantage that would result to agricultural production: and if we suppose only 30 acres of tillage in one farm, this, on low calculation, would produce us 12,500,000 measures of nett grain." I do not pledge myself to the accuracy of the calculations made in this proposal: But it is easy to see what advantages might result by employing our revenues in such improvements instead of lavishing them in projects of sanguinary ambition. These are the means by which our grandeur and power might be indeed increased, instead of depopulating the continent, and rushing into frantic crusades to extinguish the principles of Jacobinism, and restore Royalty and popish Idolatry.—Restore Royalty in France!—We restore Royalty in France!—What absurdity!—What injustice!—Whether the principles of Royalty be right or wrong—whether Republicanism be right or wrong— whether Jacobinism ought to triumph, or Jacobinism ought to fall, what was it to us in the present instance? It was the affair of France, and France ought to be left to settle it; nor had we any more right to go to war to compel that nation to adopt a government according to our taste than I have to break into your houses, and say you have no right to any sort of food upon your table but such as I choose for you. You like roast beef, perhaps; but you shall have nothing but boiled. You, perhaps, are a Jew and will not eat pork. I tell you you shall have nothing but pork; and if you do not forego your damned Judaical infidelity, and eat pork when I command you, I will pull every hair out of your chin, and turn you out as bare as ever your King Nebuchadnezzar was turned out, to graze upon the common, and eat cold sallads with the beasts of the field.[61]

Another circumstance connected very closely with the state of agriculture is the encouragement given to the breed of horses. No person can be at a loss to conceive how very large a proportion of those commodities which might administer to the comfortable support of man, is devoured by the numerous train of horses kept for a variety of purposes in this country. If we turn our eyes to the studs of Noblemen and Princes; if we consider that many, for mere pomp and vanity, have kept hundreds of horses in stables vying for splendour with the palaces of our nobility, erected at an expence that would build cottages for all the poor in the neighbourhood of London:—if we consider the monstrous quantity of steeds trained for the purposes of gaming, to increase the detestable art of lavishing property on vice and profligacy, instead of bestowing it upon benevolence and charity;—if we take all those circumstances into the calculation which will arise in your minds at the bare mention of the subject, we cannot but immediately reflect, what a large decrease must be thus occasioned of the produce which would otherwise contribute to the support of man. Consider how many cattle might graze, and how much wheat might grow upon the tracts of land allotted for these steeds; tell me if in this article of luxury and fashion you do not find one of the permanent, though growing causes of that scarcity of provisions of which we at this time complain.

This, also, is extended still further. The farmer must have steeds which occasionally he can convert into horses of pleasure. His very plough would be disgraced by having an ox in it; every part of labour, some of which might even be better performed by oxen, is performed by horses.

To this, also, we ought to add the waste, the profligacy, the dissipation, and destructive vices which result from the scandalous practice of keeping an enormous train of lounging fellows in liveries, the whole of whose labour is devoted, not to increasing the necessaries of life, not to add to the useful productions of society, but to increasing the vice, the licentiousness, the luxury, the pride of their employers, swelling them up with the monstrous idea that one set of men was formed to cringe at the footstools of another; and that there are, in reality, distinctions of society besides those of wisdom and virtue. It would be digressing too far to describe all the mischiefs that result to the morals both of the *Lord* thus waited on, and the *Slave* that waits. My present concern is only with the effects upon the production and consumption of the necessaries of life; and these are obvious to the most casual observation. I cannot, however, pass by an opportunity of observing, that the very practice of being waited on by a train of insolent slaves in Merry andrew's[62] coats, besides its other pernicious consequences to society, has a necessary tendency to encourage the idea that one set of men is formed of baser materials than another; that they were born to cringe, and to bow to a few terrestrial deities; or to be hewers of wood, and drawers of water, mere beasts of burden, for the convenience and pleasure of the erect and lordly few, who call themselves the higher ranks of life: When the fact is, that these characteristics, which we so properly despise, result not from the original nature of man, but from the vicious institutions of society, which make many administer to the luxuries of one; instead of cultivating that spirit of equality to which I hope, one day or other, to see the human race aspire.

It would be unpardonable, when talking of the inconveniences under which our agriculture lies, if I were to pass over the subject of tithes: an oppressive burden, which presses with particular hardship upon those articles to which a considerable degree of favour ought to be extended, in adjusting the burthens of the State. The necessary articles of consumption ought, surely, by the wisdom and care of every Government, to be put under such protection and regulations that they can be sold at the easiest possible rate. How is this to be done? By taxing the farmer, first of all, in common with the other inhabitants of the country, thro' every gradation of his profession, and in every form which the ingenuity of financiers can devise, and then in addition to all this, laying upon his shoulders the aggravated burden of priestly imposition to the amount of a tenth of the gross produce of the soil! A burthen, which, when we consider what has been expended in rent to the landlord, in cultivation of the land, in gathering in the harvest, and a thousand incidental expences, will be found to amount to at least one third part of the profit. This might, perhaps, have been endured with patience at a time when superstition reigned over every mind—when priests were considered as Gods, and had sometimes the audacity openly to call themselves such. But now that the eyes of mankind are opened—when they begin to perceive that every one has a right to save his soul in his own way, and that the pulpit is but too generally prostituted to purposes of political usurpation, the motive for chearful compliance with so heavy a contribution is no more, and the burthen falling without alleviation upon our shoulders, we cannot but reflect on the immediate effect which this must have on the price of the necessary articles of consumption.

But let us consider also, not only the immediate, but the secondary operation of this *sacred* tax. Has it not a tendency to depress the spirit of agricultural improvement? What encouragement have I to labour from the increase of the produce on my land? What temptations do you hold out to me to improve the soil upon which I live, and to invent new methods of tillage and agriculture, by which society would be benefited? Why this is the advantage: You tell me that a man to hear, whom, perhaps, I may piously go three times every Sunday; or to whom, perhaps, I may think it greater piety not to go at all; either because his doctrines are averse to the prejudices in which I have been educated; or because my mind has, some how or other, towered above, or sunk below (for it is not for me to decide) the objects to which he would direct my attention:—This man is to reap the profit of my toil. This man is to reap the harvest I have sown. And, in addition to the increased rent which I must pay to the landlord, in consequence of the benefit I have conferred upon his land, I am to have an increased burden upon my shoulders to the pious gentleman in the black gown, from whose assistance, I am told, I am not to reap any advantage in this world; but am to receive a copious harvest in the world to come. I have heard say *there are but two sorts of bad pay-masters: those who pay before-hand, and those who never pay at all.* But unfortunately every one of us is obliged to be a bad paymaster in this particular. We are obliged to give prompt attention here: but we must trust to the other world for remuneration: where, if we should be deceived, we shall have no opportunity of bringing the individual to the bar of the King's Bench, to receive compensation from the verdict of an honest jury.

It must, however, be admitted that these men have their *uses* in society. When the country is plunged into war, no matter how, there are generally, you know, fasts and prayers appointed, in order to influence the people to exert themselves courageously to procure a successful issue to that war. Now it must be admitted, that these *pious gentlemen* have considerable influence in persuading the people to yield their throats to the knife, for the grandeur and emolument of ministers, and, of course, you know, for our glorious constitution. But to speak a little seriously, whatever might be the objects in view in establishing such an institution as this, is the imposition I am speaking of a means to make that institution successful? Is it consistent with policy, even, that the teachers and hearers should be in a perpetual state of warfare? Yet what but a perpetual state of warfare results, or can result, from this system of tithes? Every person at all acquainted with the

history of any country village knows the disgraceful litigations, scandalous
to the character of man, with which the parishioners are harrassed by their
ministers, who preach forbearance, and practice intolerance; who tell them
they are not to throw their debtor in jail for the sake of a little property,
and yet put their debtor into worse than any jail whatever, the Spiritual
Court, for what common sense and justice cannot discover to be any debt
at all.

I believe the best thing for the happiness and morals of mankind is, that
every individual should choose his own religion, according to the conviction of his own heart. If he chooses with TOM PAINE to say THE
WORLD IS MY COUNTRY; and DOING GOOD MY RELIGION,[63] I
see no reason why he should be persecuted for that faith. If he chooses to
bow down to the Trinity; believing that one is three, and three is one, it is
scandalous to interrupt the freedom and tranquillity of his worship. It is
equally scandalous to interrupt that freedom and tranquillity if, on the one
hand he chooses to worship God in single Unity, or to bow down, on the
other, to all the wooden Saints or moulton calves "which God-smiths can
invent, or Priests devise." Let him hear all. Let him listen to all. Let him
judge of all with candour, and let him remember that *his* grandmother, and
his nurse (generally the first formers of our religion) are no better judges,
nor more infallible Doctors in these matters, than the Pope of Rome, or
any other old woman that might happen to model the infant faith of his
neighbours. Let him determine according to the dictates of his conscience.
(He can have no other guide than conscience or fear. Let those take the
scoundrel passion—the principle of fear, whose minds have not nerve
enough for bold enquiry. I am for the British manliness of internal conviction!) Let him hear whom he chooses; and let the instructor and the pupil
settle their own terms. It is no business of your's or mine where our neighbour goes, or what he believes, or what he pays. All our business is
whether he is a good member of society, whether he exerts his faculties,
mental or corporeal, to advance the interests of society.

If so general and benevolent a sentiment is adopted, the diabolical "rancour of theological hatred" must be exterminated from the mind of man;
and difference of opinion would no more beget that rancour and animosity
that have so long deformed the universe; and, under the mask of propagating the religion of peace, spread fire and sword and desolation through the
world: while not content with external ravages, the baneful rapacity with
which it has been accompanied has seized upon the vitals of national in-

dustry; has damaged the improvement of the most useful arts; checked the progress of agriculture, and aggravated the dearness and scarcity of those articles necessary for the subsistence of human life.

Such, Citizens, appear to me to be among the leading causes that affect the *agricultural productions* of the country. There is another branch, however, of this subject which must not be passed over in silence. Corn and cattle are among the most important articles of consumption; but they are not the only resources of life. This country is so happily situated that both these may fail to a considerable degree, and yet barring impolitic regulations, no famine reach us. We are surrounded by seas and watered by innumerable rivers: yet what is the situation of the fisheries of this country? Look to our northern coasts, in particular, (you might look at every coast) and see what neglect prevails. Consider how long the people of Holland, more industrious and more politic than ourselves, have caught our own fish upon our own shores; salted them, and preserved them; and afterwards sold them to us, at a price extravagantly increased, in diminished quantities. I have dwelt, in a former lecture, upon this subject; and upon the impolitic duties and regulations, with respect to salt. In my lecture upon the genuine means of averting national calamities, I entered considerably into the subject; and, as I have printed that lecture, in the first number of my Tribune,[64] I shall not go into it again. There are some facts, however, not noticed there, which ought not to be passed over in silence.

Some provisions, under pretence of checking the growth of this evil, have been made: but they are very inefficient; and perhaps, were even intended to be so. In Aberistwith, in Wales, in particular, it is common for the fishermen, during the season, to go out in the morning, and catch as many fine cod, and fish of that description, as they think they shall be able to sell in their own market. These they throw upon the beach; and the people, of all descriptions, come down and purchase what they want—the finest large fish at a penny a piece. An attempt was made, some years ago, to raise them to two-pence; and the common people were so indignant, that they threatened insurrection; and the fishermen were obliged to keep them at the old price. My correspondent, from whom I have the anecdote—a person who has sent some literary productions into the world, enquired why they did not catch a large quantity, as they seemed to procure them with so much ease; but he was answered—To what use shall we catch more than we can sell? We can get no cheap salt to keep them with. Upon enquiring what was meant by cheap salt, he found that a regulation had been made, some years ago, which required a given quantity of salt to be sold, without any duty, at the salterns or manufactories in that part of the country; in order that the salting of fish might be encouraged, for the benefit of the poor of that neighbourhood in particular, and of the interior of the island in general. But what was the consequence? Did the poor fishermen, the common class of the people, reap the benefit of this? No. They had more wealthy, and more powerful neighbours, whose turn (for they are represented in Parliament) was first to be served; and the swinish disfranchised herd, who have no voice by which their complaints can be made known, were to be deprived of the means of laying up, in the plentiful season, that which might support them in the time of scarcity. A few wealthy individuals, in order to prevent the trade from getting into the hands of these little retail haglers, which they thought would be injurious to their monopolizing plans, contract, regularly, for the whole of the salt that is thus permitted to be sold without duty; and the poor are not permitted to have a single grain of it for their own tables. Thus, instead of the common people salting the fish, and preserving it for themselves, or carrying it to market, the cheap salt is absolutely bought up, and, as it is said, not made use of at all; lest the produce of the fisheries, which monopolizing individuals have a particular interest in keeping at as high a price as possible, should get into the hands of the common people, and be sold at reduced prices.

That there are many practices of this kind it is impossible for us to avoid concluding, when we consider the present price of fish; and what it used to be in former times;—when we consider that the inhabitants on the banks of the Severn, where the finest salmon is caught, can rarely get a single fish; and that in almost every place, where these luxuries used to abound, the same complaint is to be heard. The reason is, that the fishermen are under contract with certain great factors, to sell them the whole of the fish that they catch; and are bound by engagements, to destroy what is not wanted for their limited markets. This statement, at first view, would appear like fiction; but I have the facts from persons who reside in the neighbourhood of the Severn, and who have had opportunities of ascertaining them. I know that, at first blush, it would appear that this is impolitic in the contracting parties; for that the more they sell, the larger would be the profit. But this is not the case. If the individual can obtain any thing like the sum for a tenth part of the commodity, which he would obtain for the whole—If he obtains even the half, he receives a very advanced emolument: because the agents to be employed in the sale, the care to be taken to prevent the whole from being spoiled, the expence of carriage, &c. &c.

are much less when he sells a small, than when he sells a very large quantity.

But how should any individual have the right of making such regulations? Why should the streams which flow from the liberal urn of nature; which are fed by the waters of heaven, and break their unbidden way through the veins of the earth—those streams which are cultivated by no man—which are stocked by no man—which receive no benefit from this man's capital, or that man's capital—why should they be the property of individuals? Are they not the bounties of nature? and has not every one of nature's children a right to share her bounties? Unless, forsooth, you choose to tell us the great are the only legitimate children of nature, and that the rest are bastardized by those statutes of aggrandizement which have lifted a few to rank, emoluments and distinctions, which the mass can never hope to attain!

Such then are a part, and but a part, of the causes of that increasing dearness of provisions, and consequent misery of the mass of the people, of which we complain. That the effects of these gradually operating causes have lately been very much aggravated by others of a temporary nature, has been already shewn; nor shall I attempt to recapitulate them at this late hour of the evening. Suffice it to say, that, like the present war, with which they are so intimately connected, they may all be traced to the same original spring of action—a systematic aversion in our cabinet to the principles of liberty.

There is one of these topics, however, upon which I slightly touched at the conclusion of the lecture of Wednesday last, that seems to demand more ample notice than I then had time to give it; not only as it is most intimately connected with the immediate subject of these lectures, but as it tends to illuminate, in a most eminent degree, the real character and views of our Ministers. It will be obvious that I allude to the affairs of Poland.

It cannot be unknown to you that Poland, in a very considerable degree, was considered as the granary of Europe. What must have been the consequence of the devastations of last Summer?[65] Consider that this granary of the world, instead of being cultivated by the peaceful plough-share, has been rent by the iron scythe of military tyranny;—that the industrious peasants, who used to cultivate the soil, have been prevented from that cultivation by the trumpet, which has called them to arms; by the gnawing thought, that what they produced another might reap; that the sons of Liberty might plow the earth, but that the demons of Despotism might come with their scythes and claim the rich harvest, and carry that which ought to have supported a race of men proud of hard-earned independence, into the granaries of northern savages, whose only refinement is slaughter, and whose only appetite, blood and cruelty.

Consider also the devastations of war which have raged through that fine country. Consider the extent to which this calamity has been diffused during that struggle, whose glorious energy, and whose prospects of success, so frequently cheered my heart, while confined within the mansions of the Tower, at a time when prospects of the happiness of other countries were the only consolations of the generous Briton;—for every thing at home laid tamely prostrate at the feet of a despotic faction.—Poor devoted Poland! you might have calculated largely upon the hardships and calamities you had to struggle with; but you had one enemy which, perhaps, never entered into your speculations. You did not expect that corruption would be employed by a British minister, to blast and palsy your glorious efforts, and to string with increased energy the tyrannic arm of the Prussian despot!

Citizens, this conduct of the minister of this country—this underhanded exertion to crush the liberties of Poland, discover to you a dismal secret. If you reflect, it will unfold to you the real objects which that minister has in view. Compare this conduct with the conduct of those ministers in the time of Charles II. who, it is now universally admitted, aimed at the establishment of despotism. What conduct did they pursue? Wherever the dawn of liberty was to be discovered, there the British cabinet found a foe. The republic of Holland felt the eternal hostility of the British court. Why? Because the flame of liberty, such as it was in Holland, was thought to be inimical to the project of Charles's ministers for extinguishing the remaining spark of liberty in Britain. Therefore it was that attempts were made to destroy republican Holland.[66] Therefore it was that Charles's ministers intrigued with the despot of France, for the destruction and overthrow of Holland. That destruction he did not effect; for, just at the time when the brave Batavians, despairing of being able to defend their country, were about to embark, and transport themselves to the East-Indies, the genius of British liberty burst forth, and compelled the court of Britain to alter its detestable measures.[67]

Compare these facts with the conduct of our ministers in the present struggle on the continent. Why should the minister of this country, who deals forth his hypocritical admiration of the constitution of this country, be hostile to the liberties of the Poles? They were not Jacobins. They did not proclaim *liberty* and *equality*. They did not erect guillotines. They did not pretend that *sans Culottism* was to be the basis of their constitution.

They did not venture (they were not enlightened enough—they were not wise enough—if they had, they would have triumphed!)—they did not venture to proclaim the equal rights of man. They did not attempt to set up a government, in which every individual should have an equal share in the appointment of the legislature. They were not Robespierrists:—they were not even republicans! Why then was there such animosity on the part of the British cabinet against the Polish revolution?—Citizens—Citizens! I fear we shall be compelled to conclude, that the real hatred of our ministers is not against republicanism, but against liberty; not against Jacobinism, but against the least shadow and appearance of independency, and the rights of human beings; a settled abhorrence for every thing like free, just, and humane laws.

O hypocrisy! how transparent is thy veil!—Pitt pretends to approve of limited monarchy: yet Poland attempted to establish a limited monarchy, and Pitt subsidized a German despot to counteract the attempt; and this very Pitt has since told you in the House of Commons (for the audacity of some men is equal to their profligacy!) that if he had been aware of the use to which the subsidies *he* granted would be applied, he would nevertheless have subsidized the King of Prussia.[68] We have therefore his own authority for pronouncing that he was at least friendly to the subjugation of the brave and virtuous Poles. But for this subsidy, it is clear Prussia could not have resisted the brave efforts of the gallant *Kosciusko*.[69] He did not resist them effectually at last. He felt (and trembled while he felt) the zeal, the ardour of that brave peasant.—Yes, *peasant* I will call him; for *Kosciusko*, like *Stanhope*, was an aristocrat only by birth: he could perceive that the peasantry are the life, the soul, the existence of society; and therefore he gloried in the character, and assumed the appearance: like a peasant he fought—like a peasant he conquered—and, at last, like a peasant fell, to *chains* indeed! to *anguish*! but not to *infamy*. No: he fell *from prosperity*; but he rose *to glory*. His name will be resounded; his memory will be beloved. Posterity will bow adoration to his bust, when *Pitt* and all his dependants, are swept down the tide of oblivion; or if their names are preserved, will only be preserved to infamy.

O Poland! Poland!—Yes there was a time when the friends of liberty might flatter themselves with a hope, that not the General of the Poles, but the *despot* of Prussia (for it is now no longer treason to speak of him as he deserves!) would have felt the galling of chain. But, alas! the gold of Britain enabled him to hold out till the Russian barbarians were ready to take the field.

The Russian!—How my blood curdles at the name! O Poland! O exhausted country! O depopulated Warsaw! whose brave exertions against
one despot had robbed thee of the energy that should have defended thee
against another!—what heart bleeds not for thy fate! Behold the fiend
Zuwarrow,[70] hot from scenes of massacre and cruelty, where Ismael's sons
groaned and bled, by thousands, at his command; nor even Circassia's
daughters, the beauties of the east, no, nor the smiling infants at the breast
escaped his butchering knife. Zuwarrow comes, and Warsaw's streets groan
beneath his blood-stained steps. And thou, Imperial Daemon! thou cursed
Hyaena of the north, thou pouredst thy savage fury in his soul, and gavest
the dagger edge.

Thus Poland fell. It sunk beneath the sanguinary grasp; and scenes of
bloodshed and horror marked its fall. Liberty expired; humanity groaned; the
hero and his bride; the infant and his parent fell together, in one promiscuous
carnage. Such are the triumphs—such the humanity of that regular government, by whose assistance Order and Justice are to be restored in France.

What then was the consequence of this subsidy to Poland? Desolation
and massacre. What was the consequence to Britain? The produce of that
country, which, if our Cabinet had yielded to the wishes of the people, for
the people's hearts were with the Poles (where the heart of the Minister
was—if, indeed, he has such a thing, which may be called into question).—The produce of that country, which might have been sent into our
ports—that abundance which might have relieved our distresses, is gone.
It is not only *robbed from us*: It is destroyed, annihilated. It is worse than
lost to us; worse than *fallen into the hands of our enemies*. It has fallen into
the wide womb of non-entity: it has perished, and we can never recover it.
Is this then—this Machiavelian policy of our rulers, not connected with
the causes of our calamities?

We were told, at a former period, when our blessed Sovereign had the
misfortune to labour under certain derangements of his transcendent intellects[71]—we were told by the right reverend fathers in God, the Bishops in
conclave assembled—and what right reverend Bishops tell us who shall
venture to call into question?—we were told, that the crimes of the people
had caused the calamities of the Sovereign.[72] Whether this be true or not,
I shall not dispute. I do not pretend to be as well versed in the occult
sciences, as the reverend bench of Bishops. But this I know, that whether
the crimes of the people produced the calamities of the Sovereign or not,
the crimes of his Majesty's Ministers frequently produce the calamities both
of prince and people.

Thus in the time of Charles I. when the *apostate Wentworth*[73] once a bawling advocate for liberty, became minister of the crown, and Earl of Strafford, we find that his bad policy brought the nation into a civil war, and the Sovereign to the block. We find, also, that when *Louis* XVI. yielded the reins of government to that profligate wretch, *Calonne*, that *Calonne*, by his arts and intrigues, plunged the country into bankruptcy and misery; and afterwards, his intrigues plunged Louis XVI. into perjury, and eventually the country into anarchy: an anarchy which Pitt and his coadjutors would persuade you was occasioned by the friends of liberty; but which, in reality, was occasioned by the intrigues of the friends of despotism: by the cabals of that wretch Calonne, the crimes of him, of Condé, and Artois,[74] and the profligacy of the court of France.

Citizens, I am no advocate for the doctrine of constructive treason. But if it could be admitted, must we not determine that those ministers are guilty of high treason, who seeing the effects of this misconduct, pursue precisely the same line of conduct, which *Calonne* and the apostate *Wentworth* had pursued before.

The fact is, Citizens, that the worst calamities of every nation result from the profligacy of ministers. Ever careless of the welfare of the people, and ever grasping to increase revenue and the wages of corruption, they continue the ravages of oppression, till the energies and resources of the country are exhausted, and desolation appears in every corner. And mark how that corruption has swelled of late among us. See the torrent which it has spread over the country. Once it was a little rippling stream, it played and murmured round the purlieus of the court; in time it became a spreading river; now a mighty torrent, it has burst its banks, and swelling like another Nile, has drowned the nation in one general inundation: and behold the half-formed monsters of vice, of misery, and luxurious deformity, which rise from its polluted slime!

Yes, Citizens, there was a time when corruption had its bounds; when one place was sufficient for one man. But now, so intrepid becomes the honesty of our courtiers, so zealous and enthusiastic are they in preserving the rights of the people, so much additional energy have they acquired, that to sap their independence requires not one place only, but a dozen, before they will consent to support the measures of the court, and become hostile to the welfare of the people. I shall not attempt to illustrate this by enumerating all the places possessed by *Pitt* and his family in England, by *Dundas* and his family in Scotland, or by *Beresford*[75] and his family in Ireland. In short, such is the power and patronage grasped by these three worthless beings, that England, Scotland, and Ireland seem to contain but three men; each of whom, if you touch but the hair of his head, or threaten to remove him from his places, even though you leave him his salaries and emoluments, can threaten you with a civil war, and, perhaps, the wreck and ruin of the whole government.

From this monopoly of places arises another misfortune. For you know *ministers must be supported*; and if they monopolize all the old places to themselves, they must create so many more new places for their dependants. . Thus we find, that instead of two Secretaries of State, we have three: all *principal Secretaries of State*, though one of them,[76] forsooth, is hardly permitted to sign his name to a warrant of any description, unless it be to arrest a Jacobinical fellow for high treason, without permission from his high and mighty master and coadjutor, Dundas.

As to the creation of these lesser places, it were in vain to enumerate these—Boards of Controul, Offices of *Police*, and Boards of Agriculture, with salaries for apostate secretaries;[77] and I know not what. I will refer you, however, for an instance to the Tower, where if you should have the good fortune to experience the same opportunities of information that I have had, you may learn, that in consequence of the oeconomical arrangements of that great reformer, the Duke of Richmond, wherever there are three labourers doing any sort of work, there are always six clerks to see that they do it.—I beg pardon, Citizens, I have been guilty of a slight inaccuracy in this statement: the language of the Tower is, that wherever there are three labourers doing *nothing*, there must always be six clerks to see that it is done. Then we must take into consideration, also, the increase of pensions and secret service money; and the compromises which the ministry coming in always makes with the ministry going out. Once it was thought sufficient, when one set of rogues—I beg your pardon—I meant to say ministers went out, for the other set who came in to promise them indemnity; and that they would not impeach them, and bring them to the block. But now, indemnity! they will say with a sneer—indemnity! holding their hands behind them as they retire—I must have something besides indemnity, or I will become so flaming a Patriot, I will not only oppose your measures, but blow up the whole system—let the people into the secrets of office, and make your places not worth your holding. Your contracts, your monopolies, your discounts upon subsidies, your pensions from foreign Courts, all shall be exposed.—Indemnity, indeed! I say indemnity! Give me a good pension, and I will oppose you only in a parliamentary way. But if you don't, take care of me, I shall grow desperate, and

> "Let in the light to Pluto's drear abodes,
> Abhorr'd by men, and hateful e'en to Gods."[78]

If you want authority for all this, I refer you to Fitzwilliam's letters; and if he does not say the same thing in other words, I have no wit in decyphering the courtly character.[79]

That this inordinate growth of corruption is the spring and fountain head of all our calamities cannot be doubted: for it is clear and evident that this corruption, as it leads to waste, extravagance, and dissipation, as it leads to the decrease of productive labour, and an increase of those inordinate burthens and taxes that consume the profits of productive labour, must tend to increase the price of the necessaries of life.

For evils like these, where shall we seek for redress? From tumult and violence? From destroying market houses, and breaking open the shops of butchers and bakers? fie, fie, fie! Can imagination be so dull as to suppose that outrage and tumult can redress calamities so enormous. A little partial evil may, perhaps, sometimes get redress from these enormous exertions; but calamities so great require the peaceful but determined energies of the national mind!—A loud, a fervid, and resolute remonstrance with our rulers. And a union and association among ourselves that may command the respect of those, who have the boldness to despise our individual efforts. We must lay the axe deep to the root of the evil, and not suffer our attention to be diverted by tearing the lesser branches. The plain and simple fact is, that the happiness of the lower and middling orders of society, (for let us not be so deluded as to suppose, that the lower orders can be oppressed and the middle orders not feel the oppression!) the great body of the people are neglected, because the great body of the people are not represented in the legislature; and those who make the laws are not at all dependent upon their favour or approbation.

If you will have redress, seek it quietly, but seek it firmly. Redress the evils of corruption, by reforming the source of corruption.

There is no redress for a country situated as we are, but by restoring to the people their right of universal suffrage and annual parliaments: rights which nature dictates, and which no law can take away: rights which the constitution of this country has stamped with approbation; and which, if we wish for happiness and prosperity, we must seek to restore: for the plain and simple fact cannot be more concisely expressed, than in those words in which I have so often repeated it, that "there is no redress for a country situated as we are, but from a fair, full, and equal representation of the people in the Commons House of Parliament."

THE TRIBUNE. No. XXV.

Report on the STATE OF POPULAR OPINION, *and the Causes of the* rapid Diffusion *of* DEMOCRATIC PRINCIPLES. *Part the Second. Including Definitions of* Democracy, Aristocracy, *and* Monarchy. *Original Meaning of the word* KING—*Consequences of* MINISTERIAL AMBITION, *&c. Delivered at the Lecture Room, Beaufort Buildings, September 9th, 1795.*[80]

CITIZENS,

THE last lecture that I delivered in this place was the commencement, or rather indeed the continuation of a report of the state of popular opinion. I endeavoured to state, as far as my means would enable me, (and candidly to shew you what my means have been), the progress of popular opinion, since I had the honor of meeting this company; and I concluded with observing, and giving you, such reasons as appeared to me necessary to shew that there was a considerable increase of the democratic principle in this country. I proposed then, on a future evening, to enter into the causes of this increase, and to endeavour to point out the particular conduct of goverment to which we are indebted for this increase.

But, before I enter into the particular causes, it is necessary that I should give some explanation of my terms; because words of almost every description, are considerably abused in disputes between contending parties; those, to which I allude, in particular. It frequently happens, that appellations, of the highest virtue and excellence, are used by the enemies of liberty, as terms of the most contemptuous reproach.

When we consider the use of the word Democracy, we find that there are two interpretations to be given to it.—The Aristocrats are very fond of fixing an interpretation to it, which the word never did,—nor ever can, bear in this or any other language.

There are, however, two distinct senses, in which an Englishman may naturally be expected to use this word. If we look back to the real meaning of the term, we shall find it to be a government by the great body of the people. Now, a government by the great body of the people, taken in its strict and original sense, does certainly describe a *pure republic*. Nay, more, it describes a republic without any *intermediate* order, such as we now call a representative assembly. But this is a system whose advocates, in the present day, if any, are extremely few; for the improvement of political science has enabled us to discover very considerable defects in all the ancient forms of government: and it has been found that a democracy, purely and simply considered, can never exist, save, only, in a small country, consisting, perhaps, of a single city and a few miles of territory around it: Nor even in such a state, can this species of government exist long, without occasional tumult and disorder. Modern legislators, therefore, have invented what is called a representative democracy; which is, in reality, if you adhere to the strict definition of terms, no democracy at all; because, if the representatives are vested with the complete and full powers of the state, I think I shall be able to state to you, that this is the only thing which really, justly and properly, can be called an *aristocracy*.

Aristocracy, in fact, originally meant a government of the *wisest*: and who can have so great a right to be deemed the wisest, as those who, for their wisdom and supposed integrity, have been selected, by the great mass of mankind, to be their rulers and governors. This representative democracy is the real essence of what was formerly, theoretically, called aristocracy;—the realization of the visions of sublime philosophers, who, in their attempt to discover how an aristocratic government ought to be constituted, were never able to hit upon this project. They foresaw, indeed, as every one would, that a country ought to be governed by the wisest; and were, therefore, anxious to establish a government of the wisest; *Plato* in particular, considered an aristocracy—as the best government in the world.[81]

But how was this wisdom to be discovered? Why, forsooth, a few philosophers, among the musty cobwebs that hung about their cells, were to dictate, by a sort of divine right, to the rest of the world, and, like the priests of the deluded multitude, were to triumph by a sort of superstition, of which they, themselves, were the authors, and from which they, alone, could be expected to receive any advantage.

Having given these two definitions of democracy, I think I shall be enabled to prove that every Englishman ought, in reality, to be, in a certain sense of the word, *a democrat*. I think I shall prove to you, that, what I shall call *constitutional democracy*, ought to animate every breast; ought to glow in every bosom; ought to dictate to every intellect; and that it is only by cherishing this glorious constitutional democracy—this emanation arising from the *principles*, not from the *corrupt practice*, of our constitution—that we can ever expect to relieve ourselves from the burden of immoderate taxation, and to attain the peaceful and quiet enjoyment of the fruits of our talents and industry.

Let me then, Citizens, put to your consideration this question:
WHAT IS THE CONSTITUTION OF BRITAIN?
If we consider the external forms of our government, we shall find that it consists of a Chief Magistrate and a Senate of two chambers—the one elective, and the other hereditary. If we consider the description of this government which the spirit of our constitution has dictated, we shall find it to consist of *King, Lords,* and *Commons in Parliament assembled.*

Now, Citizens, to substantiate the assertion I have made, that *every true lover of the British Constitution ought to be at heart a Democrat,* it is only necessary to consider the meaning of the plain, simple word—*Commons.*

I should suppose, Citizens, notwithstanding the variety of abusive epithets that have been invented to obscure the real meaning of this phrase, (such as *wretches, rabble, swinish multitude,* and the like)—that it is still impossible for any individual to be so dull, as not to know what the word *Commons* means. There is no man, not even *Mr. Burke,* himself, in the very paroxysm of his frenzy, who can mistake a human being for a *swine.* No man can be so ignorant of the English language, as to suppose that the word *wretch* is a description of a class, or order of beings. There are *wretches* enough, indeed, in this country; and woe to the wickedness of that aristocracy, which has made them so wretched! There are miserable beings, indeed; but it ill becomes those, who have plunged us into this misery—this swinish ignorance, to reproach us with *their* crimes, and to think that their present usurpations are a justification for usurpations still more abominable and atrocious. The fact is, that the word, *Commons,* carries its own meaning with it. Every body, when you talk of the *king,* as one of the constituent parts of our government, knows very well, that you mean the chief magistrate of the country, invested with certain powers and authorities, by the constitution, for the benefit of the people.—Yes, for the benefit of the people. This is the express condition of his power: and the chief justice *Eyre,* himself (who did not seem very anxious to make acknowledgements to the friends of liberty) was obliged to declare in the outset of his speech, that it was only for the protection, advantage, and happiness of the people, that the laws of the country had raised particular fences around the person of the king, and attempted to make him inviolable from the attacks of common incendiaries, or individual violence, which revenge might dictate, or ambition lead to.[82] The *king*, then, is the chief magistrate,—the executive power; and he, our constitution tells us, is one, and *only one*, branch of the constituted authority. By the *Lords* we very well know what is meant; though it would be difficult to find what is the meaning of some persons being made lords, who have got that title. It is, however, very well known, that by Lords we mean a certain number of individuals walking, like other men, upon two legs; but, unlike other men, decorated with stars and garters, and such other ornaments, as you might have seen represented in gingerbread, a few days ago, at Bartholomew Fair. They are called *Peers*, that is, the *companions, equals*, and *counsellors of the King*; for such I believe is the original meaning of the word, and the constitutional sense in which it is to be taken; because every peer of the realm has a right to demand, whenever he chuses, an audience of the king, and has a right to give him his counsel and advice:—leaving it to his *wisdom* whether that advice shall be followed or not.

Thus, then, having found out that king means the only person we call king in the country, and *Lords* the whole of the persons called Lords in the country, I shall conclude, that *Commons* means all those persons who do not presume to be considered as either kings or lords, or any thing else than mere common people.

It is true, there are some amphibious animals who are in one sense *Commons*, but who are called *Lords* by courtesy; and Mr. *Windham* and Mr. *Burke*, by their metaphysics, might prove, perhaps, that there are *uncommon* men who may be called *commons by courtesy*, also. But if they possess the capacity, the shape, and other attributes common to mankind, I conclude that they are entitled, at least, to be considered as *common men*; and, consequently, that by "Commons in parliament assembled" we mean the democracy of the country, who by their representatives are (ought to be I mean) represented in the commons house of parliament.

Thus, then, Citizens, the constitution of Great Britain may be properly defined a *democracy, admitting* some mixture of aristocracy in its legislature, and adopting an hereditary Chief Magistrate, to be responsible for the execution of the laws, and who is called the *King*.

Citizens, Modern Theorists—for modern theorists we have had in abundance, who have been very anxious, by general denunciations against modern theories, to abuse themselves; Mr. *Burke*, Mr. *Windham*, Mr. *Wilde*,[83]

and some other champions of the fallen cause of chivalry, are a little confounded at the old constitutional language which lawyers of two or three
hundred years ago were accustomed to use. They do not like to hear of the
British Commonwealth: for commonwealth and republic are they know
synonymous; and, therefore, they have hunted for new theories and new
coined phrases, and have chosen to use a very curious phrase, *mixed monarchy*.

Now, if these gentlemen, instead of studying metaphysics, had chosen to
study their dictionaries a little, they would not have made use of so nonsensical a phrase. Monarchy means a government in which the supreme
power and authority are vested in *one person*. How that can be, and yet,
Lords and Commons have a right to share that power and authority with
him, is a paradox that will require all the subtlety of these metaphysicians
to explain.

The fact then is, that, instead of talking of a *mixed monarchy*, we ought
to call our government a *limited* or *restrained democracy*; the theory and the
maxims of our government teaching us, that it is for the sake of the democracy (that is the great body of the people) that all our laws and institutions
are made; and that all constituted functionaries are, in reality, as they
always must be in practice, whenever practice is called for, subordinate to
the grand object, the welfare of that great *body from whom all power is
derived, and for whom all power ought to be exercised.*

How, then, came this government to be called a *mixed monarchy?*—or
how can a monarchy be *mixed?* Lately, indeed, they seem disposed to get
rid of the *mixture*, and the chief justice Eyre, in plain and direct terms,
calls the government of this country a *monarchy*. "To pull down and subvert that glorious fabric the British Monarchy", are his plain and unqualified words.[84] Let me ask this learned lawyer, *Who made it a monarchy?* Not
the ancestors he talks of. They made it not a monarchy; a *despotic government of one*. They vested, indeed, in the hands of one man the executive
power; but the real sovereignty, the right of making and altering the laws,
they vested—or, if their language be supposed an image of their hearts,
they meant to vest, in the great body of the people, by their representatives by them chosen: imagining, that their councils would be rendered the
more wise, by having a house, filled with men well educated and of superior knowledge, which they called a *House of Peers*. But little did they
foresee, that in some future period, not at the close of the 18th Century; it
will undoubtedly be the 19th before it takes place.—Little did they foresee
that, in some future period, boxing and brutality were to be the qualifica-

tions of the ermine robe: and that pimps and parasites were to be decorated with those ornaments, which, if they are to be worn at all, ought to be the badges of honor, virtue and actual service.

But these learned men, happening to understand more of *languages* than *principles*, and being able by the use of these languages, to confound to-gether the words *King*, *Rex* and *Monarch*, therefore, endeavoured to make you believe that a *kingdom*, a *government by a Rex*, and a *monarchy* are one and the same thing.

But let us enquire the meaning of the word *King*; and we shall find it to be of a very different signification from the words *rex* and *monarch*; as a learned etymologist informs me—for I profess myself to be but a plain man, and neither etymologist nor scholar. I want to discover the truth; and a truth of six minutes old is as much revered by me, as a truth that has the stamp of 6000 years. Words and derivations, therefore, have little to do in deciding my principles. I will use, however, when I can, the knowledge of others to any good purpose. King, then, is an old Saxon word, or rather a contraction of an old Saxon word. It is derived from the word *konning*, which was sometimes pronounced kenning, and sometimes cunning—and from cunning or kenning—*ken* and *King*.

Thus, then, in reality, *King* means the *cunning man*.

You will please to remember, however, Citizens, that I do not mean to "call the KING a SOLOMON" again. I have been once tried for High Treason for calling the King a Solomon already. Mr. *Groves*,[85] you know, alias Mr. *Powell*, after saying that I spoke in the most contemptuous and reproachful terms of his most sacred Majesty, when he was asked by the judge what he meant by contemptuous and reproachful terms, said he had "heard me call the *King a Solomon*"![86] You have heard the old proverb, that the burnt child dreads the fire. I am determined, therefore, never to call the King a Solomon again; being very well convinced that it is as high treason to call the King a Solomon, as it would be a high absurdity to call any of his ministers by that name.

However, Citizens, to be a little more grave, the plain and simple fact is, that Kings, according to our *ancient Saxon constitution*, and according to the original meaning of the word, were persons of eminence, *chosen* to fill the office of first magistrate, on account of their superior wisdom—real or supposed. I say chosen: for notwithstanding the boasts made by the sup-porters of divine right of lineal descent from the God *Woden*, or the devil knows what other gods or godlings, I will venture to affirm that, legally speaking, *the crown of this country never was hereditary, till the revolution in*

1688; and that at this very time it is only hereditary, under certain restrictions: that is to say, upon condition of a strict compliance, on the part of the *House of Brunswick*, with the compact and terms under which the crown was granted.

Citizens, It is very true that our Saxon ancestors had a notion (so ancient, and consequently, so venerable is prejudice!) that wisdom is confined to particular families; and, therefore, they always chose their *King* or their *cunning man* from one particular family; but that they did chuse him, is evident to every one who has read the history of his country. They did not always take the elder son, in preference to the younger. An infant or idiot was never suffered to reign upon the throne; and, if they had the misfortune to be mistaken in their first choice, they repaired the evil by setting him aside, and putting up another.

This was the practice of our Saxon ancestors; and I defy any historian to contradict the assertion, and bring facts of history to support his contradiction.

What was the practice also, after the invasion by that band of plunderers called Norman conquerors? How did they succeed?

Did the bastard of a woman-servant at an inn succeed to the throne of Great Britain by the divine right of lineal descent? Certainly not: he seized the throne by power; and conscious, even in that barbarous age, that power was not principle, and that possession is but an unquiet state without some semblance, at least, of right he assembled the states of the country, and procured himself to be formally elected: upon certain conditions it is true, with which he did not afterwards conceive that the *faith of regular government* obliged him to comply.

After his death, did his crown descend to his eldest son? No, with the consent of the states of the kingdom he bequeathed his crown to his second son.[87] That second son was succeeded by his third, in violation of what is now foolishly called the *right* of primogeniture. And in fact, if you trace the whole line of kings, from the time of the Norman invasion to the period of the revolution, in 1688, you will find *that there never were more than three persons of the same family, who, from father to son, took the crown in regular descent, and held it during the period of their natural lives.* Some circumstance or other (sometimes real election, sometimes pretended election, and sometimes usurpation and violence, under colour of election) deposed one and set another on the throne. Nay, to take no notice of Henry VII. who could claim no sort of descent from any family whatever; being a bastard—and of course, according to the *perfection of wisdom,* as revealed in the orthodox code of our law, being no sort of relation either to his father or his mother.—Setting him aside, we find Henry VIII. (convinced of this truth which I am now enforcing) occasionally consulting HIS parliament (HE also had a tolerably obsequious parliament!) to get them to settle the descent of the crown on the head of one or other of his children just as his caprice happened to dictate or his passions prompt.

Thus I think my position is proved; and I could enter into a longer detail if it were necessary, which it is not, as every individual can satisfy himself by referring to history, that *till the revolution of 1688, there was no such thing as a legally established hereditary succession to the crown of this country.*

For what then was the revolution of 1688 made?—Every man who pretends to be an admirer of the constitution of this country, as then established, must acknowledge that it was made, not for the purpose of enslaving, but of further emancipating the people. Well, then, what is the reasoning that results from this? Our revolutionary ancestors had found that certain inconveniencies, and very great ones too, resulted from this species of elective succession. They perceived, and rightly, that a crown, such as it has always been held, is much too great a temptation for ambition, much too important an object to be made subject to what is called election; but what, under circumstances of such strong temptation, must conduct to, or found itself upon, civil war, rebellion, or intestine commotion. But citizens, though they established an hereditary throne, under certain restrictions, which it is not now necessary for me to dwell upon, they certainly did not mean to abandon the *Democracy*. This part of the constitution they proposed to leave entire.

I believe, if they had thought a little more deeply, they would have found that the only way to keep it entire was to introduce an immediate reformation into it: to destroy the subterfuges of corruption, by means of which that representation may be so debilitated as to be rendered a mere nullity—a phantom—or, to speak more properly, a fiend-like instrument of oppression, veiled in the angelic semblance of Liberty. To prevent this, they would, I believe, if their attention had been sufficiently directed to this object, have restored the people to their natural and unalienable right (confirmed by the spirit of their constitution,) the right of *annual parliaments and universal suffrage.*

Well then, citizens, if it be true, that originally the democracy was the basis and foundation of the British constitution; if it be true that the revolution in 1688, was not made for the purpose of weakening liberty, but for the purpose of strengthening it, I have a right to conclude, that democracy is of right, the basis of our government; and that *we ought to consider the government of this country, as a representative democracy, admitting at the same time, the check and controul of an hereditary aristocracy, called a House of Lords, and vesting the executive government in a person whom we call, not a* MONARCH, *but a* KING.

This then is a sense in which the word democracy is not only justifiable, but proper; and to vindicate the democracy is equally legal, equally constitutional, as it is consistent with the fundamental principles of justice and of reason.

In this sense, and in this only, I beg the audience will understand me, when I recommend the purification and support of the democracy of this country, and a zealous attachment to the principles of that democracy.

But, Citizens, it has been observed by Hume, and he brings a great number of facts to support this part of his observation, that the government of this country, which for a long while before had been running strongly towards *a sort of democracy*, had, when he wrote, that is to say, fifty years ago, for a considerable time been setting very strongly in towards *absolute monarchy*: and this man, who calls himself a Briton, has the degeneracy of mind to declare, that absolute monarchy is not only the natural tendency of the government of Britain, but the desirable end to which the constitution ought to arrive.[88]

But while theorists of one description are talking of promoting the power of the crown, and increasing the monarchic authority; and while theorists of another description are talking of supporting the dignity of the democracy, by vesting larger powers in the House of Commons, the plain and simple fact is, that *the government of this country, practically speaking, is no longer either a democracy, or a monarchy, nor a mixture of monarchy and democracy; but a usurped oligarchy, constituted by a set of borough-mongers, who have stolen at once the liberties of the people, and abused the prerogatives of the crown.*

To these men every species of reformation, every species of discussion, seems equally abhorrent and frightful. To them, the democracy which I described in the first instance, and the constitutional democracy which I described in the second, were equally dreadful. Every thing that should have a tendency to give any sway or influence to reason, or to throw any authority into the hands of the people, appeared so formidable, that they looked with equal malevolence and hatred upon the most moderate reformer and the most violent revolutionist.

This was evident from the commencement of the revolution in

France:—a revolution which, I will be bold to say, till it was disturbed by the intrigues of foreign despots—till it was counteracted by the machinations of *Pitt* and his coadjutors, was conducted upon principles so philosophical, with a humanity so astonishing, and with a benevolence so enlivening, that it has almost lifted one's ideas of the human species beyond the ordinary level upon which we have been used to contemplate them, and painted to us that regenerated country as a nation of philosophers indeed!—or rather of a guardian genii dropped from the skies, to restore peace, wisdom, and happiness, to every quarter of the globe. Oligarchic usurpers dreaded, however, the appearances of such a revolution: they dreaded it more than they would have dreaded even the sanguinary proceedings which, by their artifices, have since taken place, and upon which they have openly boasted their hopes of a renovation of that system, which would be friendly to the continuation of the orderly regular governments of tyranny and corruption, among the nations of the continent, and to the system of rotten boroughs, by which the people of this country have been so long oppressed, taxed, and insulted.

Men who dread the truth, and who have a cause to support, whose most characteristic attribute is a rottenness at the very core, always attempt to calumniate those who enter into discussion. And I remember a couple of little anecdotes of this kind, which perhaps will form some degree of parallel to the ravings of Mr. *Burke* and his followers. The former of these is from an "Essay on Demonaic Possesions", printed in a recent volume of the "Transactions of the Manchester Society", in which there is a quotation from an old book, written by a pious divine of the church of England, one of those inspired gentlemen, whose holiness may be discovered by their lawn sleeves, and who are vulgarly called Bishops. This venerable and right reverend book was written to prove the existence of *witches*, *ghosts*, and *hobgoblins*; and the holy man who wrote it ventures to say, that, if you begin once to doubt the existence of witches, ghosts and hobgoblins, farewell to all hopes of the salvation of your wicked soul: for "as it is a well-known maxim, that they who are for no Bishops are for no King; so it is equally well known, that they who are not believers in ghosts and witches, cannot be believers in God."[89]—The other anecdote has come to me only in a traditionary way: you must not therefore expect chapter and verse. But I am told that one Mr. Toplady,[90] in one of his sublime and terrible orations, laid down a maxim equally clear and demonstrative of the damning dangers of investigation, and the consequent necessity of making a wide gulp, and swallowing down the whole of the established creed at once, without any chewing. According to him, once you begin to waver and enquire, you are lost; and the steps to perdition are these: from *Calvinism* you go to *Arminianism*, from *Arminianism* to *Arianism*, from *Arianism* to *Socinianism*, from *Socinianism* to *Deism*, from *Deism* to *Atheism*, and from *Atheism* to the *Devil*.[91]

In the same way argues that mirror of *political orthodoxy* Mr. *Burke*—for intolerance, religious or political, is the same in principle; and must consequently appeal to the same mode of reasoning. If these enquiries, says he, in essence, at least, if not in words—if these enquiries are permitted to go on in the world—if political reformations are tolerated by the regular governments of Europe, from overthrowing the despotism of France, they will begin to reform the corruptions of *rotten boroughs* in *Britain*:—from reforming the corruptions of *rotten boroughs*, they will attack *places* and *pensions*; and from attacking *places* and *pensions*, they will proceed to *grumble* at *enormous taxes*;—from grumbling at enormous taxes, they will attack the *enchanted castle* of the *British Constitution* itself, overthrow the venerable remains of feudal necromancy, break down the magic tripos of *ancestral inspiration*; and hurl the *great magician* from his chair; throw all things into anarchy, and hence fall headlong into political perdition.

In the pious hope therefore of saving us from this calamitous fall, he wrote the most raving and fantastical, sublime and scurrilous, paltry and magnificent, and every way most astonishing book ever sent into the world. A book, I will venture to say, which has made more democrats, among the thinking part of mankind, than all the works ever written in answer to it; or all the labours of those, who according to the cant phrases, and nonsensical jargon of our minister and his agents, *organise* anarchy and *establish* confusion, in every corner of the world.

Yes, I will venture to say, that it is impossible for any thinking man, really meditating upon the consequences of the facts and principles which every now and then escape from the pen of this Burke, even in this very publication, and marking the shallow pretences upon which his favorite doctrines are built—it is impossible for any man, be his prejudice ever so strong, to read that book without being convinced, that Mr. Burke is entirely in the wrong; and that the truth lies on the side which he is so eager to calumniate.—I confess for my part, that this was the impression the book made upon me. I had like many others, been educated in the high veneration of certain high-sounding words, and could not think that any thing could possibly be wrong in so *glorious and happy a constitution* as that enjoyed by *this most favoured corner of the world*, where felicity blossoms like the primrose under every hedge, and happiness towers like the lofty oak in every forest. But when I came to read Mr. Burke's book (and I had a professional reason for reading it with very serious attention) I was astonished to hear the man talk of the revolution of 1688, as of an act by which the privileges and liberties of the people were taken away! as an act by which our ancestors relinquished for ever a natural and imprescriptible right, to which formerly he seems to admit we might have laid some claim.

When I found him laying down theories so contradictory to sense and history; and when I found him in order to throw unmeritted calumny on the friends of liberty, representing a woman[92] whose monstrous vices would have rendered her an object of disgust, but for the particular situation in which the accident of birth had placed her, as a star descending from heaven upon the earth, to warm, illuminate, and cheer mankind—when I found him laying down principles which destroy his own conclusions, and asserting facts which destroy his own principles—when I found him, in the same breath denying the rights of a people whom he calls free, to judge of the conduct of their rulers, and rejecting with disdain the supposition that such rulers ought to consult the feelings and stand in awe of the opinions of the people, and yet contending that it was impossible for the members of the constituent assembly of France, to effect their purpose of giving freedom to France, because "To secure any degree of sobriety in the propositions made by the leaders in any public assembly, *they ought to respect in some degree, perhaps to fear, those whom they conduct*:—To be led any otherwise than blindly, the followers must be qualified, if not for actors, at least for judges";[93] that is to say, the people must either be driven like wild beasts, or else they must be enabled to judge for themselves; and how are they to be enabled to judge, but by that very diffusion of information, the very mention of extending which to the *Swinish Multitude*, throws Mr. Burke into such paroxysms of frenzy—"To be led otherwise than blindly", says he, "the followers must be qualified, if not for actors, at least for judges; they must be judges also of *natural weight and authority*";—not the factious authority of tyranny and wealth—but "NATURAL WEIGHT AND AUTHORITY"!—When I found in this farago, every part of which, that is not founded in gross falsehood and misrepresentation, militates in principle against his own conclusions, nothing (to speak in Johnsonian phraseology) but the *frenzies of sublimity, the contradictions of reason, and the tortuosities of sophistication*, could I avoid suspecting, that there was "something rotten in the state of Denmark",[94] which this State Juggler wanted to conceal from view; and that there was in reality something so excellent in the principles espoused by the *French Revolutionists*, that it was impossible for a man even to write against them without promoting them? The fact is, that nothing can be fatal to truth but silence (or commotion). Do but write or speak, no matter how absurd the principles you set out upon, and it must triumph. Nay, perhaps the best way to promote it, in an enquiring age, is to write away against it as fast as you possibly can.

The writing of this book was certainly one of the first active causes of the growth of democracy in this country. Discussion was no doubt considerably promoted by the immortal writings of *Thomas Paine, Joel Barlow, Thomas Cooper* of Manchester, *James Mackintosh,*[95] and many other enlightened men, who took up the pen to vindicate the revolution in France: little imagining that because *they* had thus vindicated the French revolution, persons in this country, some of whom had never read their books, were to be tried for high treason for that which they had written.

But however these books assisted, and undoubtedly they did very considerably assist the progress of the cause of Democracy, it is to be observed, that they owed their existence to the publication of *Burke*; and therefore we are to look upon him as the great father and first propagator of the principles of democracy in this country.

But mark the step that followed!—It was thought that the reading of these answers would be a very pernicious thing indeed. It was never attempted to prevent persons from reading the book itself: for you know that there is no harm in reading or inquiring upon one side of the question— but to attempt to examine both—O 'tis most horrible! and on the opposition side, all *regular government* will agree that the press ought to be shackled, as much as possible. Shackled, therefore, it was resolved it should be; and the *Diabolus Regis* (as in ancient times the king's Attorney General was called)—the *Diabolus Regis*, that is the *King's Devil*, was instructed to launch forth the subterranean thunders of his legal Pandemonium. Proclamations were immediately issued to forbid the people to read or think[96] but the devil was in the people (nor the *King's Devil*, but *Tom Paine's Devil*, or a devil of some other description) and the more they were forbidden to read or think, they did but think and read the more. These proclamations instead of preventing their career of enquiry, made them enquire with more avidity, and judge with greater profundity: and I understand it was very common, on market days, in little country towns, for the country people who had never heard of *Paine's* name before, to go to the little book-shops, and, not knowing any other way to ask for it, to make themselves understood by saying, "Why Maister, we want that there book we maunt read." Thus were proclamations against Democrats, a second effective cause of promoting the principles of democracy.

Proclamations not succeeding, the next thing was to proceed to prosecutions: accordingly we find, that men have been prosecuted by wholesale, some for *writing* books,[97] others for having published them, and others for having read them. For my part, my case was a little singular; for I was prosecuted, and that to the jeopardy of my life, *for not having read them*. Joel *Barlow's* book, in particular, which was one of the things from which large extracts were read upon my Trial, I had never seen till after my acquittal. Since, indeed, I have read and admired it very much: for I thought it necessary, as I had been in danger of being hanged for it, that I should know what it contained.

That excellent and worthy citizen, *Frend*, was also to be persecuted in the university of which he was so ornamental a member, for having written a book professedly with a view of reconciling the contending parties, and preventing the excesses which he and every man foresaw that the mad extravagances of the minister were plunging us into.[98] *Winterbottom* for preaching sermons in which nobody can discover what were the passages that were called seditious, was thrown into Newgate, where he is to lie four years;[99] and *Holt*, the printer of the Newark Herald, while the *Duke of Richmond* and Mr. *Pitt* are the principal members of the cabinet of this country, is actually prosecuted, condemned, and imprisoned,[100] for re-publishing the letter, which the Duke of *Richmond*, Mr. *Pitt's* patriotic coadjutor, so industriously disseminated throughout the country,[101] as containing the best and only means of restoring our constitution to its ancient vigor and purity.

But it was not enough to prosecute men for books. Perjured spies, men known to be inflamed with the utmost rancour and hatred against the parties, were permitted to swear in courts of justice, from their loose recollections of conversation still more loose and unpremeditated; and, upon such evidence, men were condemned for indiscrete and idle words: words which, not being deliberately spoken, ought to be considered, as all hasty and unpremeditated words must be in the view of candour and reason, as perfectly innocent.

Breillat was condemned for expressions of this kind, alledged by his prosecutors to have been uttered almost a year before the time of his prosecution.[102] In the hour of inebriation, in a coffee-house, the master of which gave the information, poor *Hodgson* was taken into custody, crammed in a vile dungeon; and now forsooth lies in jail, for laughing over a bargain, which no good man will approve,—made between the *Prince of Hesse Cassel* and the *Elector of Hanover*, respecting the sale of their subjects at £30 per man; and having therefore called his most sacred and august majesty "A Hog-butcher"![103] What is majesty if it can be wounded by a nickname?—And who ever heard of any prosecution commenced against that most infamous slanderer *Edmund Burke*, for calumniating the still more sacred and august majesty of the people by calling them a *Swinish Multitude?* Yet for this foolish piece of levity and buffoonery, (while the bespectacled buffoon of St. Stephen's is yet at large) is poor *Hodgson*, forsooth, also confined in Newgate, with a fine upon his back, in violation of the constitution of the country, Magna Charta and the Bill of Rights, which expressly says that no judge shall, at his peril lay unconscionable fines upon any man, which must weigh him down for ever. There he lies loaded with an enormous fine, evidently for the express purpose of keeping him a prisoner for life: because those who imposed the fine, know that neither he nor his connections are worth the sum of money fixed upon his head.

The case of poor *Frost*[104] was still more wicked. He had been drinking with his friends at a coffee-house, when a man stopped him as he was going through the coffee room: "I think you are *Citizen* Frost"—"Yes, I am"—"You have been in France lately?"—"Yes, I have." "How do you find things going on in France?"—"Oh very gloriously, every thing goes on just as it ought."—"Oh you are a liberty man; you are for liberty and equality I think." "Yes, I am for liberty and equality."—"What for liberty and equality and no king?"—"Yes Sir, for liberty and equality and no king"—"What are you for liberty and equality and no king in England?" Vexed and indignant as every one must feel, under such circumstances, he replied, "Yes, Sir, I am for liberty and equality and no king in England."[105]

I was present in the court when this cause was tried: and I heard this *Diabolus Regis*, fulminate such a volume of horrible denunciations, and opprobrium against the culprit, that one would have imagined, if one had only heard his speech, and not known the particular crime for which the man was tried, that he had absolutely endeavoured to murder the king, put his sons to the torture, and violate the purity of his daughters.

Indignation and not fear was stirred by these proceedings; and men became more and more democratic, when they saw the violence and injustice with which those who were the enemies of democracy proceeded.

The next step, however, instead of being a milder was of a more severe description. Men for speaking their sentiments in a convention—sentiments, many of which may be traced to the glorious Alfred himself, the founder of our liberty[106]—sentiments which, at the period of the revolution, would have been thought to be the boast and the glory of Englishmen. Britons—Men for speaking these sentiments, under that constitution which pretends to be the same as was established at the Revolution in 1688, were transported, like felons, to Botany Bay.[107]

However what is the consequence? How ignorant must those men be who think opinions will be beaten down by persecution?—Are they ignorant of the history of their country? Are they ignorant of the history of that christianity, which they profess, but which they disgrace by their conduct? Do they not know that, when opinions are persecuted, if they have but the least portion of comparative truth, they will grow ten times stronger in consequence of that persecution?

Men who never troubled themselves with the investigation before, felt their blood boil within them at this treatment; and stepped forward to shew that they were not ashamed of being the advocates of men thus cruelly treated: and from being advocates of the men, they became advocates of the cause. Though they would not have been so but for the injustice with which those opinions were persecuted.

Well, finding every thing they had done to prevent the progress of liberty had only increased its progress—what was the next object? *Blood! Blood! Blood!* Ferocity could no longer be restrained. Those beings whose glaring eyes, rolling like fiends, and convulsive lips, quivering like beasts of prey, with savage expectation, exulted over those beings whom they thought they had in their power, and thus made a place, which ought to be the seat of wisdom and of sanctity, a sort of bear-garden by their ferocity— and who treated the persons who were brought before them like reptiles unfit to be looked at—these wretches—pardon me if I am too warm in my expressions. Humanity cannot always bear with patience, the recollection of such insulting brutality, as I have encountered!—These beings attempted to take away the lives of men for persevering in doctrines they themselves had set afloat; and upon the stream and current of which they had sailed into the port of power.

In the midst of their ferocity, however, they were cowards. They did not dare to act a wicked part like men: and in order to fortify themselves against the consequences of so illegal an act, they seduced persons, who, till that time were supposed to have some little character, to join them, and make a most unnatural coalition, and Whig and Tory joined together in a faction[108] so heterogeneous, as was never before thought of: that thus by their united power they might venture to destroy a few plain, simple, fortuneless, unconnected men, who had dared to tell their fellow citizens that they ought to be free, and that the principles which were true when these men were out of power, continued to be so now they are in. Hence came forward, from the same cowardly spirit, the assassin-like attempts of toad-eating scribblers and hired journalists. A pamphlet was published by Mr. *Reeves's* Bookseller, the very title of which treated us as if we were already convicted; speaking of *the treason committed by the persons now in custody upon a charge!*[109]

What affirm that a treason was actually committed, and send these affirmations in heaps to every corner of the country, while the men remained yet untried; and the minister and all the lawyers around him had not found out what specific crime to charge upon the warrant? What, was the prejudication to be permitted in this *land of liberty?* Yes, and more flagitious prejudications still.

Sir *John Rose,*[110] the Recorder of London, and one of the commissioners, by whom we were afterwards to be tried, if the papers justly recorded his speech on that occasion, stood up in his judicial capacity upon the swearing in of the new Sheriffs, and accused us, as though we had been men already convicted, of having conspired against the life of the King. "Gentlemen, you will have in the discharge of your functions, duties of peculiar importance to fulfill. You will have to take charge and custody over men who have had the profligate audacity to lift the arm of treason, against the sacred life of the King".[111]

These are our *Judges!!!* O Britons! Britons!—What is our situation if upon such Judges, and such witnesses as those who sent us before such judges thought fit to provide, the pure administration of justice is to depend.

But Citizens, these continual calumnies and prejudications would not do; these are attempts which the passions of men cannot endure. These are attempts which even the perverted judgments of Aristocrats will not approve. They had stretched the cord till it broke: and the men whose lives they sought, found glorious champions among the foremost leaders at the bar; they wanted not the assistance of honest men in another branch of the profession; and they found a glorious asylum in that port and harbour of British liberty—AN INDEPENDENT JURY! which all the arts (and arts enough were appealed to) of courtiers and ministers could not corrupt.

This attempt broke the charm of popular infatuation. The furious Aristocrats hid their heads in confusion; and I am happy to say, the Democrats had the virtue and the wisdom not to abuse their triumph. Instead of becoming more furious, they became more moderate; and shewed the genuine excellence of their principles, by not falling into that intemperance which the enthusiasm of weak minds is too apt to produce, but which must be always injurious to the cause of truth and virtue!

But citizens, there is another way in which these persecutions served the cause of liberty. It was pretty universally believed, that one of the terms of agreement made with certain parties when they came into the Grand Cabinet Coalition, was, that the minister should absolutely prove us to have been guilty of High Treason, and convict us accordingly.

Having found with what security and confidence he could *promise and vow in the name of a House of Commons*, without the trouble of a previous consultation, the minister was ready to offer himself as a godfather also for a British Jury: but a British Jury is not a British House of Commons; and that which he promised in their names, they did not think, *when they came to meet, that themselves were bound to perform.*

The country perceiving two such strong and mighty factions, become so weak and so impotent, that they were obliged to combine together in this extraordinary manner, and to adopt such extraordinary measures, against a few simple unconnected men, began to enquire what the reason of this could be; and they immediately found that the real reason was *corruption*— that these virtuous Whigs finding they had no longer any chance of having all the loaves and fishes to their own share, very prudently consented to take half the loaves and fishes, rather than have none at all!

This then destroyed all confidence in party: and confidence in party has always been the greatest enemy to the principles of liberty, and the genuine rights of mankind. It is in principles only that you can confide; and no man can be entitled to countenance or affection, but as he is subservient to those glorious principles upon which the rights and happiness of mankind are built, and upon which alone those rights and that happiness can be supported.

The enormous taxation with which the people are burdened is another of the operating causes: and when they found themselves, by the multiplication of places and pensions, burdened with additional loads, this led them to consider a little more deeply the principles of that democratic branch of the constitution, without which the constitution of this country would be worth nothing at all. When they found that not only *aristocrats* but *opposition men* had places and pensions; when they found that not only the Tory *Pitt* and the Tories that adhered to him, but the Whig *Stormont*, now *Mansfield*,[112] and other Whigs held places of some thousands a year,

paid by the toil and industry of the people—when they found that illustrious ornament, in point of intellect, to the country in which he lives—
that man of powerful mind whose exertions have contributed alone to
furnish any respectability to the Whig Party during the last half century—
that even *Fox*, though in truth he *holds* no sinecure place, has *spent the
money for which he sold one*:[113] and that therefore he found himself bound to
contend that patent places are property so sacred that you must not venture to attack them; not even in the shape of taxation; when they found all
this was it possible for them not to see through the juggle of the present
system, and to wish for an assembly in which the democracy should be
purely and truly represented?

In this then it is palpable, that both parties are agreed. Administration
and Opposition are in harmonious concert: when Mr. *Harrison*[114] brought
forward a motion for laying a tax upon the places of persons receiving
favours from the Crown[115] Mr. *Pitt* thought it impossible any *honourable
gentleman* could suppose the *honourable gentleman* to be in earnest. No, no,
he could not suppose the honourable gentleman could mean any thing but
a joke. Astonishing assurance! as though he should have said in direct
language, "What does the honourable gentleman suppose, after we have
been grasping at power so long and so successfully—after we have devised
so many expedients to turn that power to our own advantage—after we
have laid such burdens upon the shoulders of the people, in order that we
may fill our own coffers—after we have taken such pains to secure to ourselves the plunder of the country, does the honourable gentleman suppose
us to be so weak and inconsistent, as, that we will now suffer by our own
free will and consent, any part of that plunder to be taken away from us!"

Thus, then, whatever disagreement there may be between Whigs and
Tories, as to who ought to have the largest share of those places and pensions, and the like, it is evident that they are perfectly agreed, that no part
of this sacred property shall be touched for the purpose of lightening the
burden of the people. Nor is *John Bull* so blind as not to perceive the
juggle: and hence an additional reason for wishing the restoration of that
true Democratic House of Commons by which alone this juggling can be
put an end to.

Citizens, I am afraid I shall not be able to go through all the subjects I
proposed this evening. I believe I shall not be able to enter at large into
the blunders, the ridiculous professions, the bravadoes and boastings with
which the present war has been attended. Suffice it to say, the people have
opened their eyes, and, having discovered the real objects of the war, are

dissatisfied with its continuance. They have begun to enquire how this war came to have been undertaken; and they perceive it to have been undertaken, in consequence of their having no organ to represent their interests in the national Council—and they begin to think also that the man who earns every thing, whose labour creates all the wealth of the country, has almost as much right to have some voice in naming the representatives by which the country is to be governed, as those who produce nothing but consume the whole.

Something too towards opening the eyes of the people, has been done by the imbecility with which this war has been conducted—which began with bullying, was carried on with absurdity, and is likely to terminate with disgrace. This war and this conduct of the war has tended to a considerable degree to open their eyes: and blunders and disgraces, tho' they have not made the Minister a whit wiser, have had some effect upon the people; and, if I am not much mistaken, *he will find* that *they* are somewhat wiser than they were.

I hope they will be wise enough; that whatever they attempt they will attempt by peace, reason and justice: not by tumult and violence. Commotion and coercion are the game of the Minister; enquiry and reason are the game for us: because we have truth on our side, and if we once persuade the great multitude of the people (and soldiers are people as well as we are)—if we can once convince the great body of the people that they have rights; and persuade them peaceably and firmly to demand their rights, I should like to see the four or five hundred men, or the four or five thousand, who would have the impudence (not to say the courage) to stand against the congregated voice of the nation. It is the very nature of men, who are wrong, who feel they are convicted of wrong, and are confronted by millions having truth on their sides, to blush and retire; and violence is only rendered necessary by the intemperance of those who have not patience enough to wait for the peaceful operations of human reason.

Citizens, there is one very important thing however which the present war has taught us, it has taught us the absurdity of the idea that *one Englishman can beat half a dozen Frenchmen*. It has taught us that if Englishmen, formerly, had any advantage over Frenchmen, it was only because the English were more free than the French: for that liberty and enthusiasm are every thing, and climate, feature, and complexion nothing at all.

The infatuation of Ministers however still continues. They have rummaged all the universe almost to find out persons, who would accept of pensions, commonly called subsidies, in order to support the alliance; and having ranged almost the whole of this terraqueous globe, I suppose the next step will be to subsidize the Prince of the infernal regions himself, and get him to become their ally; as being a fit—perhaps the fittest agent for their purpose.

Nay, there are strong symptoms of some negociation of this sort already: for they have lately acquired an Ally who may be supposed, by some, to have dealings with that great personage—and to be in no small degree in his confidence: and I should not be at all surprized if Mrs. *Williams*,[116] of *Store Street*, who so timely stepped forward to boast her loyalty to the King, and acquaintance with the Queen of this country, and dedicated her work to her,[117] foretelling that *Louis* XVIII. would be restored to the Crown of France; that the Stadtholder would be restored in Holland, and that the arms of Britain (in defiance of the false prophecies of Brothers)[118] would be triumphant, and the house of Brunswick preside upon the British throne for ever—I should not be at all surprized if this august personage should by and by produce her formal credentials, and take upon herself the character of Minister Plenipotentiary from his Sooty Highness:[119] and then both the Pope and the Devil may have their Ambassadors at Court; and the atheistical practice of burning them in effigy on the 5th of November, disgrace the country no more!

But there is one reason why, perhaps, an alliance of this kind might not so very much contribute towards increasing the spirit of democracy among us as some other alliances have: for we are informed that spirits neither eat nor drink; and that the Devil has wealth enough in Pandemonium already. He will not, therefore, want either subsidy or loan; and it will not be necessary to send our bread and beef to the lower regions to feed these new allies. This, however, we are obliged to do for our other allies, and the common people finding themselves reduced to misery and starvation, as in the most fertile parts of this country you may, if you chuse, see that they are reduced!—I say, the common people finding themselves so reduced, for the sake of supporting the principles of aristocratic domination and usurpation, is it not natural that they should be repelled with disgust from principles the maintaining of which cost them so dear; and be led to enquire whether the cheaper dominion of pure justice and free equal representation is not to be preferred to the expence of aristocratic corruption?

Citizens, I cannot part from you without saying a few words relative to the condition of the lower orders of society. You who listen to me are most of you persons who are raised, in some degree, above the misery which I have been condemned to view: but do not suppose, because you are a few steps higher on the ladder of society, that the lower steps can be broken away without securing your destruction.

Citizens, in the Isle of Wight, where Nature seems to have poured her beauties, her sublimity and her fertility with the most lavish hand, where the common average of production upon every acre of land is a third part more than the average of the other parts of Britain—in the midst of this fertility, in the midst of this abundance, in the midst of all the sublime beauties and romantic scenes which that enchanting country presents, how often has my heart ached to behold the beggared misery of the great body of the people.—*Great body!* No, there is no great body of people there. Population is wasting away. Turn wherever you will, you see cottages falling into ruin; you see mansions of luxury rising, the fine feelings of whose masters cannot endure the sight of wretchedness: and who, therefore, permit not a cottage to rise within their vicinity. There you may see the little farm-house turned into the summer house of some gentleman or lady of quality; the grounds upon which the farmer lived turned into *Fermes Ornés*,[120] where the produce is grasped by the luxurious individual who has laid out the country for his pleasure and amusement. It is true that it is better that they produce corn there than that they should lay it out entirely in articles of pleasure and luxury. But what is the consequence? The wealthy individual hoards up the grain. He has no calls for rent; he has no particular necessities to compel him to do justice to society, and bring his corn to a fair market; and therefore he speculates, and waits for an opportunity to take advantage of the artificial distresses of mankind: and to such a height are these speculations carried, that corn in the *Isle of Wight* has been sold this summer at 20l. and 24l. a load, standing on the ground: though in the memory of the oldest man alive in that island it was never 12l. before.

Citizens I have not concluded the picture. It happens that this island produces in one year, as is admitted by all the historians, as much grain and cattle as would maintain the inhabitants ten. It produces, also, the greatest abundance of shell fish, particularly crabs and lobsters, which are sent to the London market. The markets, also, of Portsmouth, Gosport and Southampton are supplied with vegetables from this spot—and boats, and even large vessels, are built in the ports and creeks. Yet with all this, except in a few particular spots, the country is almost a Desert in point of population; and sometimes they are reduced to the greatest distress to get in their harvest.

You will suppose, then, that the peasantry being so few, live in happiness and comfort; that they have decent apparel, decent education, eat a little meat twice or three times a week at least. But, alas! No such thing. Their wages are not sufficient for bread. Their children run in barefoot beggary in groups, at the chariot wheels of their oppressors; and they will run for miles to get a halfpenny by opening a gate to let you pass through; save your servant the trouble of dismounting, as if the curse of Canaan[121] had fallen upon them that servants unto servants they should be. And thus is the universal condition of the peasantry of that country. I have been grieved at my heart to see human beings thus brought up in ignorance. I have been grieved to my soul to see beings whom nature made my equals thus subjected by usurping man to cringing beggary: and doomed to play tricks and anticks to extort that from the levity of their beholders which compassion will not impart. I have grieved to see the finest forms in the world (for the rustic females of the island have peculiar advantages in point of person) climbing over rocks to collect lampets—miserable shell fish that stick to the shelves and shingles, to sustain an existence destitute of comfort, destitute of intelligence, destitute of every enjoyment—nay of every decent necessary of life.

Oh citizens, reflect, I conjure you, that the common class of mankind and you are one! that you are one in nature! that you are one in interest! and that those who seek to *oppress the lower*, seek to *annihilate the intermediate orders*. It is their interest to have but two classes, the very high and the very low, that those they oppress may be kept at too great a distance—and in too much ignorance to be enabled to seek redress; and that those who partake of their favors may take as little as possible from them of the wages of corruption and iniquity.

I have generally been most anxious about the condition of the most distressed orders of society, because they have seldom an anxious advocate: we are apt to feel disgust at abject misery and wretchedness, and the sickly imagination turns away from such objects of contemplation. It is therefore that I dwell particularly upon their case. But it is not to one class of people I wish to confine myself; I wish not to limit justice to a particular sphere.— I would have it extend throughout the universe, and be participated to every being, whatever be his condition, his colour, nation or his circumstances. It is universal, and not partial justice that I contend for: the rights and happiness of the universe, not the amelioration and benefit of a particular class.

Let me however conjure the middling orders of society to remember that they are particularly interested: that if we have not peace and reform in time, those who are now the middling, must soon be the lower orders; for oppression, though it begins with the poor and helpless mounts upwards from class to class till it devours the whole: and let it be remembered, even by the wealthy and unfeeling merchant, who is now but too often the ready instrument of ministerial tyranny, that the only favor reserved for him is like the favor of *Polyphemus* to *Ulysses*: "You have endeavoured to gladden my heart", said the one-eyed monster, "by the beverage you have imparted; and therefore when I have devoured your companions; when I have torn their limbs to pieces, and banquetted upon their flesh, you shall be the *last sacrifice that shall be made to my rapacious maw*."[122]

THE TRIBUNE. No. XXVIII.

Report on the STATE OF POPULAR OPINION, *and Causes of the Increase of* DEMOCRATIC PRINCIPLES. *Part the Fifth. Including Sketches of the affairs of* SCOTLAND *and* IRELAND, *with a History of the Progress of* DEFENDERISM, *and Reflections on the Fate and Deportment of* O'CONNOR. *Delivered at the Lecture Room, Beaufort Buildings, Strand, September 18th, 1795.*[123]

CITIZENS,

IF the state of opinion in England is not very flattering to the champions of aristocracy, let us consider whether, by turning their eyes towards *Scotland* and *Ireland*, they will find much more reason for consolation and satisfaction. Let us consider what is the state of the public mind there: and let us keep it constantly in remembrance, that we ought to to be equally anxious about every part of the opinions of every part of the nation, and that we ought to be equally desirous of promoting the peace, happiness, and prosperity of all the *three divisions*, as they have been hitherto considered, but as I would say the *three integral parts*, of a state, which I should wish to see to the end of time one and indivisible, in sentiment, wishes, and in exertions.

With respect to *Scotland*, we cannot but be aware that there is a disposition to dissatisfaction, and that a very strong bias, indeed, towards immediate and thorough reform has been manifested, even before it displayed itself with equal strength in this part of the nation. We cannot but be aware that the principles of liberty are there very widely diffused; and that a considerable degree of indignation and anger still boils in the breasts of Scotchmen, on account of the abject situation in which they are held by corruption, and the slavery imposed upon them by *royal Burghs* and other rotten corporations,[124] by which their rights are extinguished and their suffrages monopolized.

It is very true, Citizens, that from the unfortunate circumstance of *Scotland* being a country where there are no laws, an inquisition has been established, in that part of the country more successfully than Mr. *Reeves*, and his honourable associates, have been enabled to establish here.—I say from *Scotland* being a country where there are no laws: for when Judges from the Bench shall declare, as the Judges of the *Court of Justiciary* have declared, that an opinion delivered by the Privy Council is binding upon the consciences of Judges, because undoubtedly some of the Judges of the country were members of that Privy Council—I say when opinions like these are delivered, which, in other words, is asserting that the Judges have a right to make whatever laws it is convenient for them to execute, then the state of the people, as to any hope of legal redress, as to any hope of public virtue and justice, is absolutely that of having no laws at all. Nay, I speak too favourably: they are in a condition much worse than if they had no laws at all: for to have laws *to punish*, but *none to redress*, to have laws to *crush*, but none to *protect*, to have laws that can trample us into the dust; that can subjugate us to a tyrannous aristocracy, and no laws to obtain a redress against the usurpations of that aristocracy, is a state infinitely worse than that of savages who run wild in the woods, and seek for protection only from their own strong arm.

In consequence then of the modes of proceeding in the Courts of Justiciary, in consequence of the *public prosecutor* being able to appoint, in the most open and palpable manner, the jury, by the majority of whose voices being able to appoint, in the most open and palpable manner, the jury, by the *majority of whose voices* the person brought before them is to be tried, they have been enabled to produce a degree of terror never equalled, except under the tyranny of that *Gallic* dictator, *Robespierre*, so frequently abused, and so frequently imitated by those who abuse him most. On this side of the *Tweed* there is more difficulty in executing the arbitrary will of a few inquisitors. Exertions after exertions have been made to crush opinion: and yet freedom of opinion still lifts its head on high, and braves the thunders of ministerial and inquisitorial vengeance. Magistrates have tried all means to suppress discussion, and all would not do. They have tried cabals and intrigues of every description—nay they have winked and connived at violence; and even sent into rooms, where persons were assembled for the purpose of free discussion, their police officers to create riots. Yet still the treasury papers call aloud for the magistrates to repeat those fruitless exertions to crush every individual who dares to speak the truth, and to find *honest juries* to acquit him for having so spoken.

Yes, Citizens, the oracular diurnal pamphleteer of a certain great treasury scribbler, has been calling very loud upon the magistrates to suppress assemblies, in which it is wickedly maintained that *cruelties and murders have been committed by crimps and press gangs.*

Citizens, I should like to know what sort of exertion it is that magistrates are to appeal to, in order to suppress *the Jacobinical crime of reason. Police officers* have already kicked up riots and have neglected to take themselves up for such rioting—*Police officers* have brought huge deluded coal-heavers, to bellow forth outrageous songs within these walls—but who, as soon as they heard the voice of reason, well convinced of the truth of the principles they were sent to decry, departed from the room with denunciations against those who had attempted to delude them, and to inflame their minds against those who, instead of enemies, they found to be their best friends. *Reeves*—the grand arch inquisitor! *Reeves,* the chief magistrate of this district, has given orders to every constable and officer of the Dutchy[125] to crimp me—for I can call it nothing else, to take a man up without warrant, authority or criminal accusation, with what view no one has ever been able to discover or divine—but probably to conduct him on board a ship to fight his Majesty's battles, and maintain the honour of the British flag, in defiance of the blasphemous thunder of republican cannon. A pert little gentleman perhaps, also, who though at present no magistrate, may perhaps be one some day or other—a little prating Jack a Dandy, of the name of *Jenkinson,*[126] employed on a certain occasion fifty bludgeon men, to knock Lecturer and auditors o' the head, and all has failed—nuisance has failed, sedition has failed, and high treason itself has failed. I should like to know what are the fresh exertions magistrates are called upon to make, that they may rival the triumphant glories of the *Court of Justiciary,* and crush the monster discussion, in this part, also, of Great Britain.

To return, however, to *Scotland.* If we are to judge from mere external circumstances, the sentiments of liberty there lie prostrate at the feet of those to whom liberty is always offensive, and reason always a crime. But let us not conclude too hastily, appearances are frequently delusive; and

the rage and indignation that is smothered and pent up within the bosoms
of individuals who dare not speak, frequently engenders fury more destructive, and dispositions more inimical to the preservation of peace and happiness, than all the flaming sedition, as it is called, ever breathed from the
lips of those who, boldly speaking their minds, and investigating their principles, are liable to be contradicted at all times; and if they speak falsely to
be convicted of that falsehood, and overwhelmed with the shame and disgrace due to the wretch "who dare think one thing and another tell."

Citizens, we cannot be ignorant of the character of the Scotch nation;
we must be narrow minded, infatuated beings, if we do not admit that our
brethren on the other side of the *Tweed* are a brave, a gallant, an intrepid,
and a reflecting people. We must be lost to all knowledge of the human
character, if we suppose that such men relinquish their principles merely
because they are not permitted, for the present, to speak them. We must
be blind indeed to all conviction that results from an observation of the
conduct and character of mankind, if we are not convinced that, by attempting to smother and suffocate the discussion of opinions, and forcibly
to suppress the expression of popular sentiment, we alienate the affections
of these men whom we thus treat like vanquished slaves, and create in
their bosoms a determined enmity against that government which thus
compels them to be *enemies* when they wish only to be *reformers*.

What can you suppose, at this time, must pass in the breast of the
Scotchman, who feels himself no longer enabled, on account of this system
of persecution and inquisition, to unbosom himself to the friend of his
heart, or speak his sentiments over the chearful glass? What must be his
feelings, I say, when he finds sentiments thus immured in his bosom? Must
they not be eminently hostile to the aggrandizement of those who have
thus chosen to be dreaded masters, when they might have reigned in the
affections of men who, owning no master, look only with veneration and
esteem to their benefactors—and, above all, to the public benefactor,
whose eminent situation enables him to dispense felicity to thousands.

Citizens, the plain and simple fact is, that there is but one source of
national peace and popular attachment; and that is the unforced affections
of the heart. You may *compel* men to *hate* you; but their *affections* you must
win by kind and gentle means—they can never be forced; and not less
ridiculous is any attempt to coerce mankind, and compel them to applaud
your measures, or be attached to your government, than was the attempt of
the oriental Tyrant in the fable, who attempt to compel, by arbitrary laws,
every person throughout his Court to wear the smile of gladness upon his

face. All the gloomy, all the malignant passions you may extort; but if you wish for dispositions friendly to happiness and virtue, you must win them by gentle means—and if you will not, by wise, virtuous, and just regulations, secure the affections of the people; if you will not, by equal laws fairly and justly administered, secure to the magistracy of the country that veneration which virtue and wisdom can alone obtain, farewell to all hopes of enjoying any peace and tranquillity in the elevated situations to which fortune may have exalted you, or to which you may have aspired by intrigue and artifice.

But let us turn from Scotland to a picture still more gloomy and unfortunate. Let us behold the condition of our sister country *Ireland*. Here, I believe, we shall find still less to exult in, still less to be satisfied with. Here we shall find discontent disseminating itself through all ranks and conditions of the people; and we shall find (melancholy to relate!) that coercive measures have driven many an excellent and upright individual into the mistaken notion of looking for protection from a foreign army, and wishing rather for the assistance of those who hitherto had been considered as their natural enemies, than the protection of those who ought to be their natural and their zealous friends.

Perhaps, Citizens, it may not be improper, in this part of the investigation, to take a brief view of the former history of the country I am speaking of. We are to remember that *Ireland* was in the first instance a conquered province;[127] and we ought therefore, perhaps, to be the more anxious to treat the people with kindness; since it is only from this kindness that we can possibly expect to fix their attachment, and unite them to us in the firm bonds of amity.

The barbarous maxims of ancient conquerors always reduced the natives of a subjugated country to a situation little better than that of slaves; and, accordingly, the descendants from the ancient *Irish*, to this day (for we have not yet entirely conquered those prejudices which early tyranny taught mankind) are to be found principally among the most neglected orders of the commuity; while the generality of the gentry trace their descent from English families. Hence we have not yet that thorough incorporation of the different classes which must be the zealous wish of every good friend to the peace and happiness of mankind: since without this the gentle intercourses and sympathies of life, the reciprocations, produced by intermediate and gradual steps of accession and declension, have never been known in *Ireland* as once they *were* in *England*.

Citizens, the abject condition of the lower orders in *Ireland* is such as no individual of feeling and humanity can contemplate, without regret and anguish. Ignorance—savage ignorance reigns triumphant: and what has been the blessed consequence? There have been ministers, in modern times, who were very anxious to suppress all enquiry, and who considered it as an enormous crime to impart information to mankind. If you wish to rule people in peace and keep them in proper order, say they, you must keep the swinish multitude in ignorance. Thus, and thus only, are you to make them quietly submit to their lordly drivers. Yet look at *Ireland*. Is the maxim supported by the experience of that country? a greater degree of ignorance, I should suppose, than prevails among the *wild Irish*, as they are called, even the Ministers of this country would not wish to prevail. And yet the history of *Ireland* is little else than a continued narrative of ferocious depredations commited by these ignorant people, linked in tumultuary combinations, to extort by violence what they have not improved intellect to demand by the voice of manly and intrepid reason.

Citizens, I speak not from national feelings, I wish to triumph over all nationality: and with me, indeed, there is no such national distinction between *Irishmen, Scotchmen and Englishmen*. I care not which name is articulated first. It is only contending which brother of the same equal family shall first be named: and as *I abhor the rights of primogeniture*,[128] I am satisfied with which soever you begin; so that you will but admit that they have all the same common rights of happiness and fraternity.

But at the same time I must observe, that in almost all cases, the brothers and sisters of the same family have a different character. From the little intercourse I have had with *Irish gentlemen*, I have found it pretty uniformly agreed, that even among the higher classes of society, information, generally speaking, is but too much neglected. Hence it is that there is a greater disposition to neglect the rights and interests of the lower orders. I know there are brilliant exceptions. We have had repeated proofs of the strong genius and energetic understanding of the *Irish nation*—proofs that make one still more lament that a mistaken sort of hospitality, too nearly allied to drunkenness and debauchery, should have obscured the faculties which might have contributed so much to the happiness of the universe. Let me observe, however, that nothing can be more unfriendly to the happiness, and consequently to the contentment of the laborious orders of society than that men of the higher (that is to say the *more useless*) ranks should be lost in extravagant debauchery, and insult the starving wretchedness of the poor by the wasteful profusion of privileged licentiousness.

Another circumstance, contributing to this discontent, is the common practice of many of the gentry in *Ireland*, farming out their estates, as they generally do, in large portions, to intermediate proprietors, whose trade being extortion, trample still more upon those from whose industry the happiness, the grandeur, and the strength of the country is alone to be supported. This being the state of society in *Ireland*, we shall not be much surprized to find that, for centuries, the history of that country has been uniformly marked by the excesses committed by combinations of the common people.

The first instance I shall particularly mention is the *Rapparees*, a set of persons whose history you will find amply detailed in "Sir *John Dalrymple's Memoirs*":[129] and perhaps you will be a little amused by tracing the very great resemblance between those depredators and the "virtuous peasants of *Poictou*", as the assassins and midnight plunderers in *Brittany* have been affectedly called; and whose sole virtue is being the tools of an insolent swarm of Priests and aristocratic oppressors, and lurking in woods, at the corners of roads, to cut the throats of every individual whom they think differs from them in opinion. That such is the real history of the *Chouans*, if I were disposed to enter further into the digression, might be easily proved. And but too nearly such is the picture drawn by Sir *John Dalrymple*, of the *Rapparees* or Tories; and who were the individuals who had the merited honour of conferring a title upon the high flown aristocrats in this country.

After these *Rapparees* arose another sect, rather of a different description, but still who unfortunately marked the history of the country by associations highly inimical to public peace and welfare.

But let us mark, if you please, how they arose, as it may be a useful lesson to those who, in this country, are so very fond of the inclosing system.—Not that I find fault with the mere circumstance of inclosure, but with *that system of enclosure by which the rich monopolize to themselves the estates, rights, and possessions of the poor.*

The men of whom I am now going to speak are the *White Boys*; and who, in the first instance, were called *levellers*.

It may not be unimportant to tell you how they obtained that name: for even they were not levellers of *Reeves's* description. The sublime idea of levelling all intellect and plundering all property, was left for discovery to the keen and penetrating genius of that great lawyer—*the founder of inquisitions, and the organizer of the system of spies and perjured treachery.*

The *Levellers of Ireland* took their name from the following circumstance.

There were, in that division of Ireland where they first arose, very considerable commons, which had been long assistant to the comfortable support of poor families. But certain persons of considerable power and distinction, took it into their heads that they could make a better use of these commons, than the poor people did; and therefore, without any act of Parliament or legal authority whatever, they seized those commons and inclosed them with what are called *dry walls*—that is to say, walls of stones piled one upon another, without any cement. The common people, not very well liking this system of encroachment, levelled those dry walls constantly by night which the aristocrats constantly built up in the day. Hence they were called *levellers*. The usurpers of the people's rights were thus compelled to build wet walls, that the joints of the *aristocratic stones* being combined by the democratic lime, might resist the encroachments of these *levellers*. Such is the early history of these associators, but as they afterwards adopted a strange fashion of "wearing their shirts over their coats", from that circumstance they came to be called *White Boys*.

Under this denomination they continued their depredations; and, at last, in an unaccountable disposition to do some degree of justice to these common people, who shewed that they would never be quiet till they got it, those commons were restored, by an act of Parliament—to the right owners. But, (as generally happens, when rulers struggle against their rights of the people) the repentance came too late. *The seeds of sedition were sown, as they are always sown, by the tyranny and ill management of the rulers. And concessions were made, as usual, when those concessions could no longer heal the wounds which tyranny and usurpation had inflicted.*—May the concessions of modern Aristocrats be made in better season; before the discontents, which their present system of oppression cannot fail to disseminate, have taken such deep root as to be fatal to the tranquillity of the community! that we may thus avoid the consequences which must inevitably result from a determination to uphold *the rights of borough mongers*, in opposition *to the rights of man!* and *the privileges of a few*, in opposition to *the just immunities of all!*

Citizens, I shall proceed to observe that there are other circumstances, which result from the maxims of policy equally unjust and ridiculous, which have a tendency, at this time, to excite in Ireland even the wildest dispositions of democracy.

I mean, in particular, the universal dissatisfaction which at this time prevails, in consequence of the refusal of an act of justice to the consciences of a great majority of the people, which was so peaceably demanded, and which there was at one time reason to hope would have been so honourably conceded. We cannot, Citizens, avoid observing that, even since the revolution, there has been a disposition, almost in whatever party happened to be uppermost, to cherish a division of sentiments upon speculative opinions. This is one of the engines constantly employed to divide the people: it being the maxim with those whose principles are weak, and whose ambition is strong to divide first that they may conquer afterwards. Thus, for a whole century almost, have the minds of the *Irish Catholics* been agitated against those of the *established religion*, and the minds of the *Protestants* agitated against the *Catholics*. Hence, also, in this country, have *the ridiculous test and corporation acts*[130] been supported with a view, as one would imagine, to no other end but to keep alive the unnatural ferment and dissatisfaction, which has so long subsisted between *Protestants of the Church of England and Protestant Dissenters.*[131]

This maxim, however, of division upon religious sentiment has been strained too far: as has always been the case with respect to dishonorable expedients. If you go upon the plain, simple principle of justice, you can never strain too far: because the farther you go in the right road, the nearer you get to the great standard of truth. But if, on the contrary, you adopt principles of ambition, and *paltry expedients* for the gratification of that ambition; those very expedients, carried to an excess, recoil upon those who have attempted to support themselves by such means, and destroy the power they were intended to aggrandize.

Such has been, in a considerable degree, the case with respect to disputations and jealousies upon religious subjects. Mankind have been taught, by artifices so frequently discovered, to consider these as intrigues of state tricksters and jugglers; and have therefore come pretty unanimously to the adoption of this plain and self-evident axiom—that *if you wish for the full and ample enjoyment of the rights of religious opinion, you must first acquire the full and actual enjoyment of political liberty.*

When you have annihilated usurpation, tyranny and monopoly—when you have made the voice and sentiments of the people a fair and just rule for the principles of legislation, you have done away with the power of one faction to tyrannize over another; and having established liberty upon so broad a basis, you are enabled to found a temple so capacious, as to afford every honest heart an opportunity to indulge every sentiment, and exercise every inclination, not hostile to the peace, happiness, and welfare of mankind.

We have talked, Citizens, of toleration. We have made an empty boast of *granting a part of their rights* to particular classes of people, till mankind have discovered that *the very word toleration is but an insult*: that *no person has a right to tolerate the opinions of another: because no person has a right to call the opinions of another in question*. The right to form our own judgment upon every abstract question is a right which can never be taken from man, though its exercise may be tyrannically suspended. (*Interruption.*)

Toleration means putting up with the opinions of others. But I should like to know what right any person can have for supposing it a matter that depends upon his inclination whether another man shall have an opinion, will, or inclination of his own. Nay, opinion is not only an inviolable right; but a right that mocks the folly of persecution; because it can never be taken away. You may make men hypocrites, indeed, (and perhaps governors, not being very much attached to sincerity, may not have any particular objection to hypocrites!) but you cannot compel them to change their opinions. To talk, therefore, of toleration is rank absurdity. It is the *right*, not the *indulgence* of the free exercise of the convictions of judgment, upon questions which society has no right to interfere with, that is claimed by every enlightened advocate for the happiness of mankind.

But let us consider what has been the conduct of the Minister in this respect. We cannot, Citizens, be blind to the truth, that the whole people of *Ireland* have, of late, expressed a strong inclination that the *Catholics* should be emancipated from the restrictions under which they lay.[132] It has not only been the wish of *Catholics* themselves; it has been the wish of Protestants. This unanimous wish inspired a rational expectation in the minds of the people, that compliance and not coercion would follow. This expectation we know to have been considerably increased by the appointment of *Earl Fitzwilliam* to the Viceroyalty.[133] I shall not dwell upon events which are fresh in your remembrance. Suffice it to say, that *Ireland* expected emancipation; but that *Ireland* was disappointed; and was taught to remember that she was dependent upon the Cabinet of *London*: or, in other words, upon King *William* the fourth—alias KING PITT; whose sovereign will and pleasure was, that the Catholics should not be emancipated; and that the wishes of the people of *Ireland* should not be indulged.

The fact is that a sort of congenial sympathy affected his mind. He was exceedingly unwilling that the *Ponsonbys*,[134] who monopolized all the power, patronage, and wealth of *Ireland*, should lose any part of that power, while he himself, monopolizing all the power, patronage, and property of *England*, had the power of preventing so disagreeable a circumstance. But what were the pretences for refusing the emancipation? Why

forsooth we are told, all of a sudden, that the Catholics, hitherto proscribed as the most violent advocates for despotic power, by a sort of magi-
cal *hocus pocus*, are turned to violent democrats, and that they would overturn royalty, and aristocracy, and all the peaceful and regular institutions
of orderly government. This it is true may appear strange! Such an alteration, in so short a time! But the wonder vanishes when we observe how
rapid a progress certain principles are making; and that even the *Pope*[135]
himself has turned Jacobin, and forced his bull to bellow forth VOX PO-
PULI VOX DEI: "*the voice of the people is the voice of God*! and therefore
you, my good son *Louis*, must submit to the will of God, expressed in so
clear and audible a manner!"[136] If, therefore, Sir *Infallibility* himself has
proclaimed this great truth, it is certainly not impossible that the devotees
of his *infallible holiness* should entertain the same faith. Be this, however, as
it will, the catholic emancipation was rejected; and, instead of the abolition of ridiculous distinctions between one religion and another, a system
of military coercion is established in *Ireland*, and the reign of a new Viceroy
was proclaimed by the arrival of thousands of *English Fencibles*, into a country where *English* and *Irish* ought to be no further distinctions than right
hand and left of the same body; one of which could not be employed
against the other, without involving an act of suicide.

But what must be the tendency of such a measure? Depression and terror
for the present, a civil war for the future. Disunion and destruction, and
scenes of slaughter, in which brother, perhaps, must shed once more (as on
the plains of *America*) the blood of brother, and the *Irish relative* glut the
keen poinard in the breast of his *English friend*.

Measures of this description mark a desperation which can only be ascribed to phrenzy. That the Minister of a great country should hope to
enforce these measures, which he cannot carry by trusting fairly to the
hearts and wishes of the people, by rendering one part of the country an
instrument to coerce the other, is a wickedness so wild and extravagant,
that one would be astonished any human being could adopt it without
some preconcerted scheme to separate the two parts of the Empire.

But it is impossible this system should succeed. The light of reason has
gone abroad, humanity has warmed the breast of man; and we have found
(strange indeed that we should have been so long in making the discovery!) that even the sooty *African* is our brother: that even the poor "whip-
galled slave", in the *West Indies*, deserves our commiseration: and, this
being the case, do you suppose we can be blind to this still more evident
truth, that *English, Scotch and Irish*, are one and the same—that they are

united and bound together in the chains of inseparable interest—and that to attempt to employ one of them, as an instrument of coercion against the other, is an attempt to make men the assassins of each other, who, upon the first moment's reflection, instead of poignards, instead of coercion and malice, will extend the hand of fraternity to each other, and rush forward, not to each other's destruction, but with open arms to the embrace of concord, peace, liberty and affection, exclaiming with ardour—*think not to make us brutes and savages, to tear each other's breasts, we are all men,* WE ARE ALL BRETHREN, *and will not shed the blood of those whose manly hearts are warmed with affection for us, and whose generous virtues call for our admiration and esteem!*

But, Citizens, notwithstanding all this progress, generally speaking, towards this union of sentiment, it cannot but be acknowledged, that the measures adopted by Ministers have, in particular bosoms, stirred up a spirit of disunion: and I am much deceived if there are not in *Ireland*, at this time, strong dispositions to an absolute separation from this country.

I speak not wishes but fears. My sentiments are certainly congenial to the indivisibility of the three countries. I think we are not too large, considering the great and powerful nations in our neighbourhood: and though I have hopes that the system of hostility is dying away—though I have great expectations that the present hostilities are the last agonizing and convulsive throws of that system of perpetual war and devastation, which has so long depopulated *Europe*; yet, at the same time, I cannot but think that some degree of proportion between the strength, power, and population of neighbouring countries, may have some tendency towards protecting them from the renewal of that system. Therefore I do not, in this case, "speak by tropes", nor, "by my fears express my hopes."[137] To whatever degree this disposition may have spread, certainly the measures at present adopted, must have a considerable tendency to increase it: For can we be extravagant enough to suppose, that, by mere military force, we can retain *Ireland* as a dependant colony? No—She has a right to be considered as an equal part; possessing all the immunities that we ought to possess; and, therefore, in subjection she never will be held.

Observe what dissatisfactions make their appearance. When prosecutions for high treason are going abroad, there is generally a conviction, in the minds of those who institute them, that their measures are such as justify attempts of that description. When we perceive the manner in which they have behaved lately towards the *defenders*;[138] and when we consider how these *defenders* are apparently increased in number, I think we shall perceive that we are not strengthening the bonds of union and affection. And though these *defenders*, in many respects, bear great similarity to the *White Boys* or *levellers* of former times, yet I think the late trial[139] will lead me to suspect, that there is a powerful and formidable conspiracy to effect a separation between *Ireland* and *England*. I should wish, from the bottom of my soul, that no such conspiracy existed; but if it do, can the late event promise much for the frustration of such a design? quite the contrary. What has been the conduct of the man who, upon the oath of a single witness, swearing himself to be foresworn, has been condemned to execution? Think of his manly, his intrepid, his magnificent conduct! Hear, in every word and sentiment that he speaks, the feelings and convictions of an honest enthusiasm—misled and deluded, it is true, or rather driven, by the persecutions and oppressions of the times, into notions and projects offensive to the laws, and opposite, I believe to the real interests of his country—yet an enthusiasm so powerful—so fascinating—so encouraging—as cannot fail to produce an effect the very reverse of panic, depression, and dispersion. Let us be just to those whose actions we do not applaud. Let us confess then that this man could not have so deported himself—could not have so expressed himself—could not have waked this glow of involuntary admiration in our hearts, if he had not been prompted and animated by an internal feeling of the justice and propriety of his conduct. And who knows how widely this delusive feeling may have spread? or how much warmth, enthusiasm, and revenge, may have been generated in the breasts of his followers, by his heroic intrepidity? Do we, who disapprove the *cause*, feel this veneration for the *man*?—What then may be the emotions of those who participate in his political feelings? Let us remember, also, that these Defenders in general, if there were not a great mixture of justice and truth in their pretensions, could never have become so formidable to government. *Wat Tyler*, that great and glorious character, so infamously assassinated, and so wickedly blasphemed by courtly historians, would never have been the leader of a powerful body of the populace, if the pretences for which he had armed had not been founded in justice and natural equity; nor would these Defenders ever have been formidable if there had not been oppressions, and acts of injustice, which stimulated the feelings of many an honest but impatient being, rather than endure the miseries of his country, to appeal to means unjustifiable, but which, from the ignorance they are retained in, are the only means they know how to devise.

In short, I am convinced that this act of coercion, and the magnanimity with which the man has perished, will rather promote the cause of *defend-erism* than beat it down; and that, if we would in reality check the progress of this evil, we must not appeal to coercion, but must ameliorate the condition of society; and reform those abuses which have reduced the lower orders to their present melancholy situation.

THE TRIBUNE, No. XXX.
On the Causes of the CALAMITIES and DISTURBANCES that afflict the Nation. *Part the Second—Including a Vindication of the moral CHARACTER of the LABORIOUS POOR, against the insulting Calumnies of their OPPRESSORS; with Sketches of the starving Misery of the BRITISH PEASANTRY.* Delivered at the LECTURE ROOM, *Sept. 25, 1795.* [140]

CITIZENS,

I concluded the Lecture on Wednesday evening with some animadversions on the calumnies which are so frequently thrown on the character of the lower orders of society. But it appears to me that it is not right to pass over that part of my subject, in so slight a manner; because those who wish to prevent a further diffusion of the rights and liberties of mankind, and of the knowledge necessary to such diffusion, have generally sheltered themselves under this subterfuge—that the vices and depravity of the common people render it totally impossible for them to be benefited by more liberal institutions; and would refer to this want of morality among these classes, all those disturbances which occasionally break out in this and every other country.

Let us then examine this subject, and see how far these calumnies are well founded: because, if it be really true, that the industrious part of the community are persons unworthy of the same advantages with others, a great part of my arguments will fall to the ground; and I shall not be able to prove that the late disturbances have entirely originated in the calamities of the country; and that the calamities have originated in the corruptions which have crept into the state and sapped the foundation of all that is dear and glorious in the constitution of Britain.

Let us compare a little the moral character of this despised, oppressed, and injured part of our fellow beings, with the other classes of society: and if we find that they are by no means that set of beings which their oppressors are anxious to represent them; but that vices and virtues are common to all the different orders of society, we shall be bound to pronounce this judgment—that if they are even worse than those who abuse them, it must arise simply from the circumstance of their depression; and that if they are not worse, they have a right to some indulgence, for if we can bear the vices of the great, we ought also to bear with the vices of the little, especially when we consider that they are made so little by the vices and oppressions of the former.

Admitting, I say, for the present, that the moral character of the laborious orders of society is in reality worse than that of the other ranks, what conclusion could possibly be drawn from this, unless another conclusion could be linked with it, that it was inherent in the nature of their being, and did not spring from their situation; and that therefore we ought to consider it as the dispensation of Providence, that those who bore this original sin about them should be hewers of wood and drawers of water, while those who look no more like men than themselves, but who have a certain aristocracy of intellect and moral feeling, infused into them by the divine spirit of transmitted property, or the magic influence of hereditary institutions, are thus lifted to a rank to which the more unfortunate plebeian can have no claim.

But can we believe that the laborious part of mankind are more depraved than their indolent *superiors*? or can we believe that the old woman's cant with which our nurseries and our pulpits are continually resounding, that the world is growing worse and worse? and that depravity is growing upon us, day after day, till every thing but the show of man is lost?

If we were really to admit this original difference of classes, if we really saw that marrying with a plebeian brought forth only a brood of mules, who could never afterwards perpetuate their race, aristocracy indeed might arrogate something from the argument. But if this cannot be supported, then what force is there in the objection about the depravity of the laborious poor, but what must support my side of the question, instead of that in which it is advanced. This would indeed shew us the most odious picture of the system of starvation, for it would prove, that this depression is equally fatal to the morals and the condition of man.

They must be kept in subjection, we are told; we must not pamper their appetites, for fear they should grow insolent and unruly, believe no longer what the priest asserts, nor do any longer what their lordly masters command. But, if it is true that the peasantry of the present day are not to be compared for moral virtue and good demeanour, with those of the glorious days of the good queen Bess, as she is called, how does all this hold together?—It has been proved from this Tribune, that, at the beginning of her reign, the common price of one day's labour was equal to the price of two fat pigs, whereas now no fat pig is ever permitted to smoak in the nostrils of the profane multitude. And yet aristocrats tell us, that turbulence, dissatisfaction, and immorality, are much more common now, than in those days of insolent prosperity and abundance.—If it is also true that soldiers, in the time of *Edward* the Third,[141] were less disposed to mutiny than at present, here is another most blessed proof of the benign influence of the system of Starvation; for the soldiers have been also proved, by historical quotations, to have received at that time equal to what five shillings per day would have been fifty years ago, (which was the time when *Hume* wrote,) and equal therefore to considerably more at this time. If therefore they be, as is asserted, more unruly and turbulent at present than formerly, where are the blessed consequences of the present system of depressing them lower and lower?—If, in short, the lower class be less worthy of esteem and veneration than they were in former ages, this is an incontrovertible argument why you should devise measures to restore them once more to that comfort they formerly enjoyed, and which ought not to be still more amply dispensed, under the improved, glorious, flourishing, and happy constitution, under which, since the Revolution in 1688, we have so boastfully lived.

But, Citizens, the whole of this calumny is totally unfounded. It is not true, that, in the language of Spencer,

> "This world is winding, in a common course,
> From good to bad, from bad to that is worse."[142]

It is not true, that the common class of mankind have all this aggravated vice to answer for. The fact is, that the moral characters of men are stamped, not by the quantity of reward they receive for their labour, but by the degree of information which is prevalent among them.

Brutality and violence will be the prevailing feature of every people, in what country, soil, or climate soever, where man is nursed in ignorance.

There turbulent passions will be his only guide; and acting only from that stimulus, he will be raised but little above the level of the brute, who, stung by hunger, roves from place to place, seeking what he may devour. This is the characteristic of Ignorance and Barbarism: and, if you look at the early history of this and every country, you will find the most incontrovertible evidence of the truth of the picture. But, when the sun of Reason begins to dawn—when the light of Truth diffuses itself over the land—that Truth, whose hand maid is Virtue, and whose offspring is Liberty—the moral character of nations, generally speaking, is considerably improved.

I am very well aware, that there are certain circumstances that counterbalance this tendency to moral improvement, with respect to particular classes and individuals: I am well aware, that it is not uniformly the case, that the man who is most enlightened will have the best moral character. Not instruction itself can always counteract the ill effects of baneful institutions, which dispose men to a listlessness of disposition, unnerve the soul, and plunge the apparently favoured being into a sink of vice, degeneracy and corruption, more odious than all the barbarous ignorance of the most uncultivated ages.

I do not, therefore, mean to apply the argument I am now making use of, to individuals universally, nor to the higher orders of society. With them, the improvement of intellect has long been at a stand, and morality has been long declining; because they are cursed with the debilitating conviction that they can command outward respect at least, knee-worship, and tongue-service, without either those virtues, or that wisdom, which is necessary to lift the plebeian from the dust, and procure him that esteem which is the wish of every honest and generous mind.

Citizens, it will be my attempt to prove, during this course of lectures, that the present institutions of society are equally baneful to the virtue and to the happiness of the higher, as of the lower, orders of society: those institutions, which trample the poor labourer into the dust of insult, slavery, and cruel injustice, contaminate the heart, debauch the understanding, and undermine the principles of those proud oppressors, who swell to unwieldy opulence by their depression and wretchedness.

Yet, in defiance of the maxims which arise from these causes, the maxim I have laid down will hold good. The nation that is most enlightened will possess the greatest quantity of virtue. It may also possess the greatest quantity of vice, among those few who are privileged beyond the necessities of mental exertion and moral rectitude: as was the case in France.

There, one of the most conspicious consequences of intelligence, and refinement, was, for a long time, that a large body of proud luxurious beings,
decorated with titles (as if the only intention was to shew how insignificant
titles are, and to what beings they can sometimes belong) were privileged
to trample every sacred principle of morality and justice under foot, and to
grind the people to powder under the mill-stones of their oppression. Such,
indeed, were the *nobles* of enlightened France—O! most ignoble beings
indeed! for 70,000 of them, we are told, ran away at once, terrified by the
grim and formidable countenances of the enraged *Sans Culottes*, and came
crying to England, begging and praying that the Aristocrats of this country
would plunge them into a mad and ridiculous crusade, which may send
them, perhaps, ere long, to Russia or Arabia on the same errand.—You
will remember, Citizens, that I am prophecying, and not praying: it is the
inspiration of the prophetic spirit that I yield to, not the fervour of devout
petition for the fulfillment of the prediction. That such an intelligent,
virtuous, enlightened, useful order of men, as the nobility of this country,
should be sent packing, it is impossible that I should ever wish. No, Citizens, let us but get rid of our placemen, our pensioners, our sycophants, our
commissaries and contractors, and the old ladies who wrap themselves up
in scarlet cloaks may sleep in undisturbed security.

There are many circumstances, which, at the same time that they increase the opportunities of mental improvement, increase also the opportunities of luxurious gratification. A nation has but little opportunity for
either, till it has obtained a considerable degree of perfection in the necessary and laborious arts of life. Then only it is, that people have leisure and
inclination to cultivate the improvements introduced into society by literature and scientific information: and I think there can be no difficulty in
proving that the progress of information has commonly produced a progressive advancement in the general standard of human character. If you
look back to barbarous ages, and compare the state of intellect with the
state of morals, in this country, in those times, when great and mighty
potentates, reverend bishops, and illustrious peers, were permitted by express act of parliament to claim the benefit of clergy although they should
not be capable to write, you will see that the moral character has kept pace
with the intellectual; and that the mass of the people in Britain are now
much more worthy of esteem and liberty, than the highest ranks of men
among those barbarous ancestors to whom ignorance sometimes looks up
with such blind admiration. I am sorry however to add, that all the advantages of this improved state of society seem to be exclusively engrossed by

those classes of beings who have contributed little to the common improvement; and whose morals appear to have received the smallest portion of this amelioration.

But citizens, we need not be surprized at the calumny which those who have all the power in their hands, and therefore cannot be punished for the abuse of it, lavish on those who have no power at all, and who therefore may be punished for telling them the truth. These privileged classes, though not themselves very famous for works of genius, have, in a considerable degree held not only the sword but the pen. For money will make the pen to go as well as the mare: nay, power and patronage will command it without the assistance of money: and therefore it is, that more than one half of the romances which are sent into the world under the denomination of histories, political surveys, views of society and *morals*, topographical descriptions, and the like, are stuffed with nothing but servile adulations and time-serving misrepresentations, to gloss over the conduct and characters of the higher, and calumnious abuse and false descriptions of the lower orders—calculated to steel the hearts of the readers against them. And thus it is that they render their productions pleasing to those great men who can recompence them with sinecure places and pensions.

Topographers, in particular, whom we generally consult, to learn the real condition of the people, will be found guilty of this offence in the most abject degree. Every fact is misrepresented, and the grossest falsehoods are foisted upon us to make their court, forsooth, to the great men who have proud mansions in those neighbourhoods they describe. For they know very well that there is nothing to be got by pleading the cause of the swinish multitude.

Thus it is, that the *laborious* ranks of the community have had so many calumniators, and the *indolent* so many apologists. Were we *Lions* painters, says the *Lion* in the *fable*, how many pictures could be exhibit to you of men who were torn to pieces by lions, for this one of an opposite nature of which you are so proud. Chaucer speaks to the same purpose in his Wife of Bath's prologue:

> "Perdie, If women had written stories,
> As men have, in their oratories,
> They would have told of men more wickedness,
> Than all the works of Adam would redress."[143]

In modern English thus:

By heaven if women had written histories as men have, they would have told more bad actions than all the sons of Adam could retaliate on their heads.

Thus then the powerful orders have the opportunity of painting the common people in whatever light it suits them; and to the disgrace of literature it has hardly ever happened that any man of considerable talents has had the disinterestedness and independence of mind to enlist himself in the service of the latter. But I believe, if characters were fairly delineated, there would have been few lords or great ministers of state, who might not blush at the comparison between the two pictures of luxurious affluence and laborious indigence.

Citizens, there is another reason, why the comparison has been drawn so unfavourable to the laborious part of the community: it must be admitted, that though the industrious poor are not in reality more vicious than the higher orders, yet there is some degree of difference in the kind of vices into which they respectively fall: and we are always inclined to think those vices the greatest which we have no opportunity of committing, or no particular inclination to commit. Butler says, in his Hudibras—

"We compound for sins we are inclin'd to,
By damning those we have no mind to."[144]

But after all, the difference is rather in the manners than the thing, in the extent of luxury with which those views are gratified, than in the nature of the vices themselves.

It is very true, that the poor peasant may now and then be found out in some *faux pas* with the farmer's maid in the barn, and will be exposed accordingly to the severity of *impartial* justice, whilst his wealthy landlord, who knows how to hide such irregularities from the eyes of the world, satisfies his inclinations by debauching beneath the canopy of splendour, the wife or daughter of his bosom friend: the mechanick, it is true, will sometimes be found reeling from the alehouse intoxicated with the vulgar fumes of a liquor, which it would shock the ears of this polite auditory to name; while the great lord reels nightly from the tavern with half a dozen of claret or champaigne in his head, and escapes from censure, or at least from chastisement.

These are the pleasures of a gentleman; they are not of that low, base, vulgar kind in which the plebeian, now and then, and but rarely, indulges himself because he can afford no better. The poor countryman also indulges himself sometimes perhaps, in drinking his pot of fivepenny ale, instead of paying a trifling score he has run at the chandler's shop; but the illustrious potentate drinks his *Tokay* at *five guineas* a bottle at the very time when he is calling on his tenants and neighbours, in addition to the exhorbitant rent they afford him, to subscribe thousands upon thousands, to enable him to enter into a composition with his creditors and secure the payment of their demands in twelve or fourteen years.

It must be admitted also, Citizens, that the labouring poor are sometimes guilty of pilfering a stick, or so, from the hedges and fences of their landlords, or perhaps of breaking down a pale or digging up a post for fuel, to warm their shivering limbs. But the Statesman and imperious Lord never steal sticks from hedges, nor pales from fences. No: they commit no felonies—they satisfy themselves—they do things in stile; and the worst that they can be accused of, in this way, is only desolating whole nations, and plundering their country by millions at a time:—Actions which, as there is no law powerful enough to correct, cannot be set down in the catalogue of crimes.

There is also another cause for the very unjust character which is given by the opulent ranks to the laborious part of the community. They draw their information from polluted sources, and a contracted survey of human society. It is true that people of rank, as they are called, are not shut up, like sultans, in the seraglios of the east; but they are kept in almost as much ignorance:—If they travel, it is inclosed in a vehicle of modern luxury, called a coach or a post-chaise, and the only persons they converse with, except the pageants of their own cast, are the innkeepers and postillions on the road. At home, they remain in equal ignorance of the real character of the peasant and artificer: the former stands trembling in his presence, and with the latter he scarcely ever encounters: so that his ideas of the character of the poor is derived from the lacquies, panders, and low retainers, who hover about the scenes of their debaucheries, and whom their own luxurious vices have corrupted. In short, the class of the poor they know any thing about, is that small and really despicable set of vagabonds, who are no where to be found but in the purlieus of brothels and gaming-houses, and other seminaries of vice, which spring from the luxuries and dissipation of great cities.

These are the unfortunate beings, I would fain have the candour to believe, whom they falsely consider as the representatives of the whole of the common people, when they call them a pack of profligates and wretches. And wretched enough indeed they are. But who made them so wretched? Who made them so profligate? Could such beings as I am now describing—men that sleep on bulks, and loiter in loathsome recesses, without visible occupation or permanent residence—could such poor calamitous outcasts as these exist to infest society, if it were not for the luxurious vices of the higher classes, which first brought them into so degraded a situation?

But if from this scanty number—this refuse of debauchery—a class of beings, who never yet were found in any well ordered, well organized society, we draw our ideas of the laborious poor, nothing but our ignorance can be pleaded in our excuse. Visit the garret of the artificer, go into the workshops of the manufacturers, go into the cottages of peasants, the proper scenes to teach you the real character of the poor, and I will be bold to say, you will meet with persons of a very different kind of description.

Citizens, a very able writer, (who is certainly no Jacobin, no metaphysical reformer,) has lately stepped forth to vindicate the poor from such infamous calumnies. The person I mean is a Citizen *Davies*,[145] whose book now lies before me.—I say *Citizen Davies*—for though he has some aristocratic prejudices lurking about him, as appears, among other things, from the price of his book, yet I call him Citizen, because I see, in *his* book, virtuous and generous feelings which are of the true *Civic* cast; and by *Citizen* I mean only a member of civilized society whose heart is softened, and whose affections are warmed by a genial love and sympathy for mankind.

This writer will shew you, by facts well substantiated, that the calumnious charges of indolent profligacy, levelled against the industrious poor, are unjust. Nay you need not take his word. You need not depend on his authority. If you will use your own eyes, if you will use your own understandings, you will perceive that though the common people have their foibles, and their vices, it can never be admitted that indolence is one of the number; all that I have heard of negro slaves, and poor wretches condemned to the gallies, does not in point of laborious exertion exceed what I have seen and know of the incessant toils of one industrious part of the community of this country. Do they not labour for twelve, fourteen, sometimes sixteen hours a day, in all sorts of weather, and in all sorts of drudgery, and this for six successive days in every week: and yet there are who can calumniate these men as a set of beings whose profligacy and inattention subject them to the wants and miseries they experience.—Shame on the wretch who can see the most valuable parts of his fellow citizens thus depressed, and hear them thus calumniated, and not stand boldly forth to plead their cause, and risk every thing that man can stake, in the hope of vindicating their rights, and obtaining an amelioration of their condition; but let us turn to the passage I was about to quote to you. You will remember that the writer is a Minister of Religion, Record of *Barkham*, in *Berkshire*. You will not therefore suspect him of making misrepresentations, from Jacobinical motives. The clergy do not frequently lean to that side of the question.

"In visiting the labouring families of my parish, as my duty led me, I could not but observe with concern their mean and distressed condition. I found them in general but indifferently fed; badly clothed; some children without shoes and stockings; very few put to school; and most families in debt to little shopkeepers. In short, there was scarcely any appearance of comfort about their dwellings, except that the children looked tolerably healthy. Yet I could not impute the wretchedness I saw either to sloth or wastefulness. For I knew that the farmers were careful that the men should not want employment; and had they been given to drinking, I am sure I should have heard enough of it. And I commonly found the women, when not working in the fields, well occupied at home; seldom indeed earning money; but baking their bread, washing and mending their garments, and rocking the cradle."[146]

Such is the picture this writer draws of the manners and morals of the industrious poor. I shall presently shew you, from facts in this book, that even if they had the disposition, they have not the means of intoxication and criminal indulgence; and that therefore the charges which we lay upon the whole of the industrious parts of mankind, on account of a dissolute few, are only disgraceful to ourselves.

Citizens, I shall now be obliged to draw your attention to a part of the subject which must necessarily be rather dry. I am going to state to you a few instances of weekly expences and weekly earnings of poor families, collected from diligent enquiry and actual observation, by this Citizen Davies, in 1787. I shall afterwards have occasion to shew to you how considerably these calamities have increased since that time.

In the eighth page are the following statements:

Accounts of the Expences and Earnings of Six Labouring Families in the Parish of Barkham in the County of Berks., taken at Easter 1787.

No. I.   *Weekly* Expences of a Family, consisting of a Man and his Wife, and five Children, the eldest eight years of age, the youngest an infant.

	s.	d.
FLOUR 7 gallons and an half, at 10d. *per* gallon	6	3
Yeast, to make it into bread, two-pence halfpenny; and salt one penny halfpenny	0	4
Bacon, 1lb. boiled at two or three times with greens; the pot-liquor with bread and potatoes, makes a *mess* for the children	0	8
Tea 1 ox. two-pence;—3 quarters of a lb. of sugar, six-pence;—half a lb. of butter or lard, four-pence	1	0
Soap, 1 quarter of a lb. at nine-pence *per* lb.	0	2¼
Candles, 1 third of a lb. one week with another at a medium, at nine-pence	0	3
Thread, thrum, and worsted, for mending apparel, &c.	0	3
Total	8	11¼

Weekly Earnings of the Man and his Wife, viz.

	s.	d.
The man receives the common weekly wages eight months in the year	7	0
By task-work the remaining four months he earns something more: his *extra* earnings, if equally divided among the fifty-two weeks in the year, would increase the weekly wages about	1	0
The wife's common work is to bake bread for the family, to wash and mend ragged clothes, and to look after the children; but at bean-setting, haymaking, and harvest, she earns as much as comes one week with another to about	0	6
Total	8	6
Weekly expences of this family	8	11¼
		6
Weekly earnings	8	
Deficiency of earnings	0	5¼

I have thought it the more proper to state these circumstances in my lectures, because unfortunately aristocratic prejudice has caused this book to be
published at the price of half a guinea, which ought to have been sent into
the world at so easy a rate; every person in the middling and even humbler
spheres of life should have been able to procure it, if we wish that reformation
should come peaceably and quietly, it is necessary above all things that the
people at large should know what the condition of the respective classes is. It
is only by this that a unanimous desire of justice can be produced. It is only by
this that we can know what justice in real life requires. It is only by this that
corruption can be peaceably removed, and tumult and confusion be prevented: for one part of society being ignorant of the distresses of the other,
oppressions are too grievous to be borne, heats and animosities, are the fruits
of reciprocal ignorance, and men at last become determined to procure their
rights even at a price which they would not wish to pay: for they argue, and
perhaps they argue rightly, that it is better to have redress, even at any price,
than to go on for ever from misery to misery, from one calamity to another,
till the world becomes one desert waste, where horror, tyranny, and desolation, like a bloody triumvirate, exult in the sacrifices made to their ambition.

Thus, in the weekly expences only, you have a deficiency of five pence
farthing. But to these is to be added the weekly proportion of the expences,
which are proved, by this accurate observer, to amount to three shillings
and a farthing more. There is, therefore, a weekly deficiency of three shillings and five pence halfpenny.

No. II

Weekly Expences of a Family, consisting of a Woman, whose Husband is run away, and six Children, the eldest 16 years of age, the youngest 5: four of the Children too young to earn any thing.

	s.	d.
Flour for bread, 6 gallons, at 10d. per gallon	5	0
Ditto, half a gallon for puddings, and thickening the children's messes	0	5
Yeast for the bread, 2d.; salt three halfpence	0	3½
Bacon, 2 lb. at 8d. (with sometimes a sheep's head)	1	4
Tea, one ounce and a half, 4d.; sugar half a pound 4d. butter, half a pound, 4d.	1	0
Soap, something more than a quarter of a pound, at 9d. per lb.	0	2½
Candles, one-third of a pound, one week with another, at 9d. per pound	0	3
Thread, worsted, &c.	0	3
Total	8	9

Weekly Earnings of this Family, with the Parish Allowance

	s.	d.
This family receives from the parish, weekly,	5	0
The eldest boy earns per week	2	6
The next, aged 13 years, but not constantly	1	6
The mother, (whilst an old woman looks after the younger children), earns, one week with another, about	1	6
The amount, supposing none of them to lose any time, is	10	6

But some deduction must be made from this sum, because they are an unhealthy family, one or other of them being often laid up with the ague or rheumatism; disorders to which poor people, from low living and working in the wet, are very subject. The woman assures me that their earnings with the parish allowance do not exceed 9s. per week on the average; therefore deduct

	s.	d.		
	1	6		
Total of earnings, with the parish allowance	9	0		
Surplus of earnings	0	3		
Weekly proportion of annual out-goings	3	2¼		
	0	3		
Deficient	2	11¼		

No. III

Weekly Expences of a Family, consisting of a Man and his Wife, with four small Children, the eldest under 6 years of age, the youngest an Infant,

	s.	d.
Flour, 6 gallons, at 10d. per gallon	5	0
Yeast, 2d.—salt 1½d.	0	3½
Bacon, 1 lb.	0	8
Tea, 1 ounce, 2d.—sugar, ¾lb. 6d.—butter ½lb 4d.	1	0
Soap, ¼lb 2¼d.—candles, ⅓lb. 3d.—thread, &c. 3d.	0	8¼
Total	7	7¼

Weekly Earnings of the Man and his Wife, viz.

	s.	d.
The husband, if he has constant health and constant employment, earns on average	8	0
The wife, like No. 1, does not earn above	0	6
Total	8	6

Weekly earnings of this family	8	6
Weekly expences	7	7¾
Surplus of earnings	0	10¼
Weekly proportion of annual outgoings	2	10¼
	0	10¼
Deficient	2	0

No. IV.

Weekly Expences of a Man and his Wife, with three Children, the eldest under 5 years of age, the youngest an Infant.

Flour, 3 gallons per week, at 10d	2	6
Yeast, 1d.—salt 1½d	0	2½
Bacon: the farmer of whom they rent their dwelling, lets them have a fatted hog, weight about 14 score, (on condition of their not keeping any pigs or poultry) at 1s. per score under the market price: this at 6s. 6d. per score (1787) comes to 4l. 11s. and as it lasts the family the whole year, it is per week exactly	1	9
Cheese, about 28lb. at 4½d. per lb; 10s. 6d. per ann.—per week	0	2½
Tea, ¼lb. per month, at 3s. per lb. per week 2¼ lb; sugar, 8d.; butter 4d.	1	2
The wife having an infant at the breast, and fancying *very* small beer better than mere water, brews a peck of malt once a month, which costs 1s. 4d.—hops, ¼lb. 4d.— this is per week	0	5
Soap, 3lbs. at 9d. per lb. lasts 2 months, this is per week	0	3
Candles, ⅓lbs. at 9d. per lb. lasts 2 months, this is per week	0	3
Total	6	11¼

Weekly Earnings of this Family, viz.

The man's business is to follow a farmer's team, for which he has 8s. a week throughout the year	8	0
He has, besides, either his diet in his employer's house 6 weeks in the harvest, or instead of it 18s.; which divided into 52 parts, is per week	0	4
The wife earns at a medium, about 8d. per week	0	8
Total	9	0

Weekly earnings of this family	9	0		
Weekly expences	6	11¼		
Surplus of earnings	2	0¼		
Weekly proportion of annual outgoings			2	8¼
			2	0¼
Deficient			0	7½

No. V.

Weekly Expences of another Family, consisting of a Man and his Wife with Three Children, the oldest six Years of Age, the youngest an Infant.

	s.	d.
Flour ½ a sack per month, or nearly 5 gallons per week, say		
4½ at 10d	3	9
Yeast and salt	0	3
Meat, bought a pig and fatted it; price of the pig 10s. 6d. cost 6d. a week for 42 weeks before fatting, 11. 1s.; was fatted with one sack of beans, 15s. one sack of pease 16s. and 5 bushels of ground barley 25s.; total 41. 7s. 6d.—When killed it was estimated to weigh about 14 score pounds; it cost therefore 6s. 4d. *per* score; this, with a few sheeps' heads and shins of beef, will last all year, and is *per* week	1	8
Beer; they seldom brew but against a christening	0	0
Tea, sugar and butter	1	0
Soap, starch, candles, worsted, on an average	1	0
Total	7	8

Weekly Earnings of this Family, viz.

	s.	d.
The man has, summer and winter, the common pay, 7s.; and he has also a mess of milk for breakfast, and small beer worth at least 1s. more	8	0
The woman earns, as she believes, by washing and needle-work, by breeding poultry, and at harvest work, when she has no child to nurse, about 1s. *per* week	1	0

	s.	d.
Weekly earnings of this family	9	0
Weekly expences	7	8
Surplus of earnings	1	4
Weekly proportion of annual outgoings	2	8¼
Subtract	1	4
Deficiency	1	4¼

No. VI.

Weekly Expences of a Family consisting of a Man and his Wife, with two young Children, the eldest seven Years of Age, the youngest four.

	s.	d.
Flour 5 gallons, at 10d.	4	2
Yeast and salt	0	3
Bacon 1½ pound, at 8d.	1	0
Tea, one ounce, 2d.; sugar ½lb. 4d.; butter ½lb. 4d.	0	10
Soap ¼lb. 2¼; candles 3d; worsted 3d.	0	8¼
Total	6	11¼

Weekly Earnings of this Family, viz.

	s.	d.
The man earns, one week with another, if constantly employed	8	0
The woman on an average, not more than	0	6
Total	8	6

Weekly earnings of this family	8	6
Weekly expences	6	11¼
Surplus of earnings	1	9¼

Weekly proportion of annual		
outgoings	2	6¼
Subtract	1	6¾
Deficiency	0	11½

N.B. The weekly expences and earnings of another family, consisting of the same number of persons, are so nearly the same with the above, that it is not worth while to set them down separately.

This was the case at the price provisions bore in 1787. I shall now just mention a few facts, which prove the oppression to be much more grievous at this time.—Since the year 1787, there has been a most rapid increase in the price of provisions. Flour is here stated at ten-pence per gallon. While I was in the Isle of Wight, it was sold at two shillings and three-pence per gallon; so that seven gallons and a half, at two shillings and three-pence per gallon, amount to sixteen shillings and ten-pence halfpenny; while the whole earnings of the man and his wife are but eight shillings and six-pence.—Here you have a deficiency of eight shillings and four-pence half-penny, even if flour alone were the only article the poor man had to buy. (*A laugh.*)

Citizens, there may be some who are disposed to laugh at this. The circumstance may appear trifling to them, that millions of our fellow-beings, more useful to society than themselves, are pining in absolute want. But such facts ought surely to inspire some sympathy with however little ability such facts may be stated—with however ungraceful a delivery they may be accompanied: and I confess they come from the lips of a man not much used to the statement of mere numerical calculation, who has been more desirous to study the heart—the intellects—the feelings of the human race—than the *tare* and *tret*[147] by which human life is now to be estimated; and who laments that he is obliged, from the unfeeling neglect of rulers and oppressors, to descend to minute particulars of arithmetic in such a case, that he may drive the nail of conviction into the hard block of a heart which dwells, but too frequently, in the bosom of the proud being we call man.

I know Citizens, that by courting your prejudices, by flattering your individual importance, I can command more of your plaudits; but if I bring conviction to one deluded Aristocrat, if the flame of truth arise in one human bosom from my efforts, take my reputation—tear it into shatters—and let neither my name nor my person be thought of more. I stand up here the advocate of my suffering and miserable fellow-beings, and not to count the applauses which any set of men can possibly confer upon me.

Citizens, since this period the calamity has been monstrously aggravated. We had had, generally speaking, of a glorious and abundant harvest. Yet what is the condition of the poor now? What is the price of bread at this time? What is the comparison between the condition of the common people now, and in the year 1787, at which period even the calamities of mankind were calling aloud for relief? At this time our flour is one shilling and ten-pence per gallon. Remember, Citizens, that the gallon loaf is the same as your half-peck. What then is the present condition of the labourer? Our gallon of flour is one shilling and ten-pence—seven gallons and an half amounts to thirteen shillings and nine-pence—the earnings are eight shillings and six-pence—and you have still for bread alone a deficiency of five shillings and three-pence. Such is the portion of every poor unfortunate being whom nature has cursed with servility. He is doomed to feel the anguish of not knowing how to satisfy the hunger of those little infants who cling to his heart, and at every call of want tear the fibres of his existence, and make him curse the hour which proved propitious to his love; but, worst of all, execrate the fatal moment that made his passion fruitful, and gave him children, once the best blessing, now the worst torment of the marriage bed.

But, citizens, to shew you how rapidly, of late, our burthens have increased, and our comforts declined, let us see the alteration which has taken place during the last eight years. We are told in this book that in the year 1787, the earnings of a laborious man and his wife were just hardly sufficient to support the existence of themselves and two small children. But what is their condition now? Will their present earnings support them? Will they find them even in bread alone? Alas! when I state the fact, I know the feeling heart will deeply mourn; though perhaps an individual may indulge his levity, where his sympathy ought to be exerted. Every article consumed by every individual is already considerably increased in price. But let us confine ourselves to bread, for bread and water are the labourers fare at present. Flour instead of 10d. is 1s. 11d. *per* gallon. Five gallons of flour, we are told by this book are requisite for the weekly supply of a man, his wife, and two children. Five gallons at 1s. 11d. amount to 9s. 7d.: add to this article (upon the supposition, which is not true, that nothing else had increased in its price) the other expences, leaving out the scanty morsel of bacon they used to have, and you will find the amount to be 13s. 10d½. Now will any man tell me in what county the labouring peasant gets 13s. 10d½. a week for his labour? I do not mean to say in the harvest month, but taking all the year into the account for the whole 52 weeks. In very few places indeed is it more than 8s. in none more than 9s.—Taking it here at the average of 8s. 6d. you have a deficiency of 5s. 4d½.; or admitting the propriety of such a luxury as a bit of bacon once a week, of 6s. 4d½ per week, in the means of support for a man and his wife, and even two small children. And where is the well-wisher to his country, who would not wish that every labouring man, should have more than two children? else what is to become of our population—of our strength—of our power—of our very means of existence as a nation? How is the consumption of great cities, of luxury, of war to be supplied? Suffer me to repeat once more—

"Princes or lords may flourish or may fade,
A breath may make *them* as a breath has made;
But a bold peasantry, their country's pride,
When once 'tis lost can never be supply'd."[148]

Yet, citizens, will humanity believe it, while I was in the Isle of Wight, a circumstance I have mentioned before, the farmers were disposed to raise the price of labour, and came to a resolution for that purpose, when a certain aristocrat, one of the great proprietors of the island, I will not mention his name—I wish to allay personal indignation not excite it—and to promote general inquiry, not to strike at individuals, who, after all, are the creatures of circumstances, and who if they are base and ungenerous, are made so by circumstances resulting from impolitic institutions. This nameless aristocrat, called a meeting the Sunday following, after service, in the vestry of the church, to shew how much the doctrines he had heard had softened his heart, and used threats and complaints to influence the farmers to alter their resolution; telling them that they would make the common people insolent, and would never be able to reduce their wages again.

Why should they be reduced? when wars, taxes, and the profligate schemes of despotic and corrupt ministers have increased the price of those commodities necessary to the support of life? Does the return of peace ever restore the prices of those commodities to their ancient standard? No! the landed proprietor takes advantage of the rise of the product, to raise the price of his lands, and thus perpetuates the mischief which would otherwise be only temporary.

But there is another circumstance that increases the calamities of those classes of society, I mean the degeneracy of aristocracy with respect to their conduct to their tenants, and the surrounding cottagers: I hope it is no high treason, though it is a certain truth, to say, that our aristocrats are degenerated.

Citizens, I do not mean to stand up as an advocate for the ancient feudal system. The barbarous Barons of elder times, and the system of vassalage charm not me: but let us remember, that if there were vices of very considerable magnitude in the ancient aristocratic body, there were also virtues which made some degree of compensation for them. Brutal ferocity, and rapacity marked their conduct; and they held the surrounding country in miserable dependence upon their greatness: but they considered the whole of their vassals as their family, and thought they shewed their power and grandeur best by their liberality to the industrious, the poor, and the unfortunate. For them the hall of the great man was open, and they could taste at least on particular days the charming beverage of his cellar. Where is this hospitality now? The house of grandeur it is true, invites you by its beautiful appearance; but when you knock at the gate, insulting, suspicious avarice turns you away with bitter disappointment; and thus seems to say— it is reward enough for your toil that your eyes partake of the grandeur which your hands produce.

I need only refer you in support of this, to a few facts from Hume's history.—Oh blind and foolish ministers! when you were determined to adopt a system of prosecution and persecution, for the suppression of popular enquiry, why did you not make it high treason to propose to publish histories in cheap editions, like these. Such books, though written by *high-flown* Aristocrats themselves, are strong advocates for reformation.—Such books are pregnant with facts that, if properly known and digested, would hurl Corruption from its high-built seat, and restore the reign of Liberty and Justice.

In what did the power and grandeur of our ancient nobility consist? not in fine coaches and splendid equipages; not in pompous buildings, or lofty colonades, raised at an immense expence to obscure the mansion they were meant to adorn: no, but in hospitality—in gladdening the heart of the poor, and filling the hungry. "The earl of Warwick, commonly known from the subsequent events, by the appellation of *King-maker*, particularly distinguished himself by his gallantry in the field, by the hospitality of his table, by the magnificence, and still more by the generosity of his expence and by the spirited and bold manner which attended him in all his actions. The undesigned frankness and openness of his character rendered his conquest over men's affections the more certain and infallible. His presents were regarded as sure testimonies of esteem and friendship; and his professions as the overflowings of his genuine sentiments. No less than 30,000 persons are said to have lived at his board in different manors and castles which he possessed in England."[149]

This was nobility, this was solid grandeur; unlike the selfish, and tinsel fopperies of modern times. But these were the days of chivalry, and "the days of chivalry", you have been told, "are gone";[150] and the days of corruption, of placemen, and borough-mongers are come in their stead.

There is, however, one redress, we shall be told, still left,—though the nobility and rich proprietors open their doors no more with ancient hospitality to their surrounding tenants—though a man is now unable to earn so much bread alone as will supply his wants, yet *the parish offers its generous assistance*, and large contributions are made to supply the poor with rice and potatoes. But is this a proper way to provide for those whose industry ought to secure the independent enjoyment of the necessaries of life? Besides, as to parish relief, it is the interest of overseers, who must bear a proportion of the rate, to provide for them as miserably as they can. But what is worse, this charity, as it is called, breaks the spirits of those who ought to derive support from their generous efforts to render fertile that earth, which, without their aid, would be waste and sterile. This drives them, also, frequently to desert their families, and thus increases both the distress and the burthen. Add to this the unjust and unnecessary load accumulated on the shoulders of the middling orders by this system of supplying, by mock charity, what in justice ought to be dispensed as the merited return for labour. A considerable part of what is levied for these purposes never go to the relief of those for whom it was contributed. There are parish feasts, parish jobbs, and parish patronage, as well as feasts, jobbs, and patronage, among statesmen and courtiers. One must have a grand workhouse to build, another must have a new portico to the church, and a third must be employed to paint a cupola, or boil some pitch in a belfry, and thereby if he happens to set the house of God in flames, and burn it to the ground, it is only another job to build it up again. Aristocracy and ornament must be attended to whatever the common and middling orders feel. And then the tax falls not where it ought to fall on the higher, but on the middling orders of mankind. I suspect I have already trespassed on the time which ought to be alloted to this lecture; in the further investigation of which I shall enter pretty largely into the history of the national debt and taxes; and the application of that debt and taxes not to the aggrandizement of the people, but to that of a few Placemen and Pensioners.

[Selections from Volume 3]

THE TRIBUNE, No. XXXIV.[1]
The Connection between the CALAMITIES of the PRESENT REIGN, and the System of BOROUGH-MONGERING CORRUPTION—LECTURE THE SECOND—*including* Sketches *of the* Connection *between the* Growth *of* Taxation *and* Corruption, *and the increasing Miseries of the* Industrious Poor; *and Reflections on the Metaphysical Sophistries of* WINDHAM, *and the pious Ravings of* BURKE. Delivered *Friday October 9, 1795.*

CITIZENS,

A Portion of that indulgence shewn me on the last evening it is necessary you should again extend; for though my health is considerably improved, I am very far from being in a condition to make the wished-for exertions.

I come before you to resume a subject of considerable importance, and to enter particularly into that branch of the enquiry whose importance is, perhaps, greater than any other.

All however that I shall be able to do this evening will be to enter into a statement of facts and principles, and the conclusions that result from them in as methodical a manner as I am capable, and with as little exertion as possible; because it will be eminently imprudent for me to enter into digressions which would rouse my passions and feelings, and occasion me to speak with particular warmth and animation.

Citizens, you will remember that I have dwelt very largely upon the burdens which have accumulated upon the shoulders of the people. You will remember also, that I then laid it down as an axiom, that this increase of burden may be traced to the increase of corruption in the legislative branches of the government; and that there is not only a necessary connection in theoretical reasoning between the two, but that there is also a practical connection, demonstrable from facts that may be brought before you. Some little progress on the two preceding nights I have made with respect to the proofs of this strong assertion. I shall go on this evening with shewing some other facts which will prove the connection still further. I shall begin with shewing you that this connection is no forged invention of Jacobinical innovators; for that the aristocratical writers of the present century have themselves perceived this truth, and have stated it pretty strongly in some of their most celebrated writings. I shall particularly instance *Hume*; for I am particularly desirous of bringing before you, as often as possible, quotations from writers who take the opposite side of the question to that which I endeavour to maintain: because I wish to impress it upon you, that whatever degree of conviction you possess in your own hearts, with whatever confidence you may express that conviction, yet, if you have not examined both sides of the question, and read the aristocratic productions of the avowed champions of corruption and despotism, as well as those on the side of reform and liberty, the impression upon your minds can be nothing more than a *prejudice*, which perhaps the first violent declamation on the other side may brush away. Nothing deserves the name of *opinion* but what results from a determination to be in possession of all the facts you can accumulate, and to examine with equal candour the arguments against you and those in your support.

It was therefore, I confess, that I spent almost the whole of the last summer which indisposition and the little recreation of the country permitted me to devote to study, in reading aristocratic writers alone, and in marking, with my pen, innumerable passages which are stronger and more forcible weapons to enforce democratic principles than any thing that ever came from any of the writers who are professed and acknowledged champions for the Rights of Man.

Citizens, I shall bring you a passage I think of that description. It is well known that *Hume*, besides the very partial and pleader-like history he wrote, has also produced several political works; and particularly a collection of Essays. In one of these he has examined, in a very *ingenious*, but, at the same time, in a very *sophistical* manner, the important question, "Whether the constitution of Britain is more likely to terminate in a republic or an absolute monarchy?"[2] *Hume*, from the manner in which he states the question not only argues the probability, but even affirms the desirability of absolute monarchy, in preference to a republic. I also shall discuss this question in the course of these lectures: and in the first place, denying that either one or the other is necessary, I shall maintain it would be better for us to have a republic than an absolute monarchy. Nay, I think I shall compel you to conclude, that, if we cannot have a reform without republicanism, it is better to have a republic than to endure all the consequences of that borough-mongering corruption which is growing so fast upon us.

This, I say, will be a question for future examination: and it will also be a fair question for examination, whether the arguments are well founded which have been asserted by *Hume*, formerly, and by *Peacock*[3] and others of later times, with some plausibility and ingenuity, that one or other of these must be the case. At present I shall satisfy myself with a single passage from *Hume* relative to the influence and corruption which result from increasing the burdens of the people; or in other words, from augmenting the favourite system of revenue.

Having spoken of the British spirit of liberty, which is supposed, by certain persons, to prevail very strongly in our minds, "It may be said", says he, "that this spirit, however great, will never be able to support itself against that immense patronage which is now lodged in the hands of the King. Upon a moderate computation", says he, "there are now, (in 1742) near three millions, at the disposal of the Crown. The civil list amounts to near a million: the collection of all the taxes to another million; and the employments in the army and navy, along with ecclesiastical preferments, to above a third million." He then goes on to add, after making a comparison between these three millions, and the whole revenue of the country—"when we add to this immense property, the increasing luxury of the nation, our proneness to corruption, along with the great power and prerogative of the Crown, and the command of such numerous military forces, *there is no one but must despair of being able,* WITHOUT EXTRAORDINARY EFFORTS, *to support our free government much longer.*"[4]

Now, Citizens, in the first place, let us enquire where does the danger lie? The decrees of the Cabinet are not yet laws; It is true we have had decrees relative to increasing the accommodation of soldiers, that have had no sanction from Parliament, and yet have been carried into execution; and we have had proclamations stuck upon every sign post, and every watch box, public house door and church door throughout the country, to scare ignorant rustics with rumours of soldiers and conspiracies; but nobody yet presumes to say that the proclamations of the Cabinet are laws. The making and altering of laws is vested in the Parliament. Well, then, how does *Hume* suppose that this patronage of three millions in the Crown, can affect the liberties of the people? How does he suppose that this great military force can affect the liberties of a people whose *representatives* annually vote their continuance or dismissal? It is then by buying up the Parliament, by means of this patronage, that the liberties of the people can alone be threatened: and therefore the direct and immediate conclusion is, that the growth of taxation is the growth of corruption: because the revenue, with which people are to be corrupted, is the result of taxation—ergo, *the greater your taxes the greater your corruption!!!*

Then, Citizens, let us consider that it is full 50 years since this paragraph was written: let us consider that during those 50 years, the burdens of the nation, and the consequent patronage of the Crown, have been growing to a most immense extent.

It is not my intention to enter very amply into minute particulars: if I can shew you gross amounts, upon good authorities, I shew sufficient for my conclusions.

I will, however, give you a few instances of the growth of this patronage and corruption, in one or two particular instances. For example, respecting ministers to foreign courts—here are a few curious *items*. In *William* the Third's time we find the amount of these embassies was not more than 45,000l. per year. In the last years of *George* the Second, which was somewhat after the time when *Hume* wrote this Essay, they had only increased 5000l. that is to say 50,000l. a year was the amount of the burdens laid upon the people for this article: but in 1778, they had swelled to 98,000 per year; and it is notorious, that at this time, this article of expenditure is immensely and extravagantly more. It is even asserted, with some degree of confidence, that the embassy of Lord *Macartney* to the Emperor of *China*, to exchange baubles, and bring back a copy of an *Imperial poem*, cost this country half a million of money.[5]

Citizens, I have not been able to be so active during the last week as has been my general habit, and to hunt from place to place till I can get the facts I desire; and therefore I have not been able to get the present amount of the *secret service money*; but, Citizens, I can tell you that, in *George* the Second's time, this was no more than 44,000l. per year, that in 1777, it was no more than 86,000l. a year, but if we consider the present posture of affairs; and remember, that we carry on the present war, upon the system of *secret services*—if you remember the tricks and cabals continually playing in the interior of *France*—our communications with the rebels and outcasts of society in Britanny—if we consider the great stress that is laid upon this *secret dagger work* (if I may be permitted so to express myself)—we must suppose that the growth of expence is inordinate beyond all description.

Citizens, there is another article which I cannot trace down to the present time: The pensions avowedly upon the civil list: But you will see that *this part of the revenue* is in the same progressive state of *improvement* with the rest. In the last reign they amounted to 68,300l. In 1777 they had grown to 127,000l. and they have been growing ever since.

But let us turn to the wholesale articles insisted upon by *Hume*. He estimates the civil list at less than one million. It is notorious that, since the present King came to the throne, there have been considerable augmentations to this list; and that it is now, taking all circumstances into consideration, about 1,200,000l.

I know, Citizens, that this great revenue having been complained of in certain *seditious* publications, it has been replied in the House of Commons, that this revenue is not all consumed by the King. Certainly, Citizens: we know very well that being a King neither so much enlarges the stomach of a man, nor so much extends the capaciousness of his back, that he should be able to eat, drink, and wear 1,200,000l. worth of commodities in a year. Tho' it has been said that there are Stadtholders who can eat whole legs of mutton for their dinners, yet we know that, generally speaking, Princes are only ordinary men; and that they eat and drink in the same manner and proportion with other men. But remember, that it is a much worse thing for the nation that this is not all consumed by that royal Personage, to whom it is impossible that we should grudge any thing which can contribute to his real enjoyment, than if it were. For if it is not consumed by the Sovereign, it must be consumed by other persons thereby rendered dependant upon him;—or, more properly speaking, upon his ministers. It is, therefore, more to my point to shew you that it is not consumed by him, than if I could prove it is—for the consequence is, that there is so much influence created by patronage, destructive of all independence, in the House of Commons. This patronage and the influence it creates, extending to the members of that house, and their relatives, they will be sure to vote for whatever measure is brought forward by the Court, though that measure should be to load the people with thirty millions of taxes more than they are loaded with already.

But let us consider what the increase of patronage has been with respect to the other two articles.

You will remember that *Hume* estimates the patronage, from the collection of taxes, at one million: that is to say, an emolument of one million to those officers by whom the taxes were collected. Well then, the more taxes you have to collect, the greater the expence of collecting them; the greater number of hands employed, the greater degree of patronage—or, in other words, of corruption. Mark then: in 1742, the time when *Hume* wrote this Essay, the taxes amounted to but about six millions. In 1795, at which time we still, notwithstanding our burdens, have power to breathe, our annual taxes amount to upwards of twenty millions.—Now then, to exercise you a few minutes in arithmetic—call to mind, that if the levying of six millions of taxes produce one million of patronage to the Crown, the levying of twenty millions of taxes must produce to the Crown a patronage of three millions and a half:—that is to say, the collection of six millions of taxes bringing a profit of one million to the persons by whom these taxes were collected, the collection of twenty millions of taxes must bring a profit of three million and a half, at least, to those who do collect those twenty millions of taxes. Nay, this is reckoning much too low—for as you increase taxation, you increase the difficulty of the levy. You cannot levy three or four times the taxes with three or four times the trouble with which they were before levied; because every individual having more temptation, and more necessity to attempt to evade those taxes, a greater proportion of tax-gatherers is necessary to prevent that evasion. Hence the increasing swarms of Collectors, Excisemen, Supervisors, Supervisor's Clerks, Auditors, Auditor's Clerks, and persons of all classes and descriptions in the department of Customs and Excise are increased to such a degree as would stagger credulity, if it were not that so many of us have such good reason to be very well acquainted with the fact.

Now every appointment has, and must have, its *political* price. Every vacant place is marked, like bales of stockings in a hozier's shop, with the *minimum* of *parliamentary*, or which is the same, of *electioneering* influence it must bring. And such are the obligations of corruption in which every minister is bound, that if he sell his commodities under price he must shut up shop; he must become bankrupt, and his political opponents, like unfeeling assignees, seize upon his effects, and carry on the trade for their own advantage; while the great body of his creditors (I mean the public) suck their fingers for a dividend, and continue to be cheated as before.

Let us now turn to the patronage resulting from the increased expences in the army and navy. Is this to be considered as much less than the former? I believe we shall find it quite the contrary. When we find that the supplies voted for the army this year are 11,241,000l.—when we recollect that those for the navy are 6,315,000, we must remember that this *army* must have officers, must have contractors, must have attendants and dependants of various descriptions; that this *navy*, also, must have its officers, contractors, &c. &c. and that these officers and these contractors are so many dependants upon the administration in possession of the reins of power. If, then, upwards of one million was fifty years ago charged by *Hume*, who was always favourable enough to the Court party, to the account of influence arising from the distribution of offices, &c. in the navy and army, we shall be obliged to acknowledge an immense weight of this patronage in the present instance. I will give you one instance, to shew you what this increase must be. In 1755, which was a little after *Hume* wrote, we find that the extraordinaries of the army were only 504,977l. in 1778 the extraordinaries of the army were 3,026,137l. and that, in 1795, the extraordinaries of the army were 3,600,000l. Such has been the increase in this individual article. If the increase of expence in other articles has borne any proportion with this, patronage must have increased at the rate of at least seven to one. However, that we may not be over extravagant in our estimate, let us conclude that if the patronage in 1742 was three millions, we must now admit, considering the monstrous growth of taxation, considering the extent to which our military establishment, in particular, and our naval also, are extended; we must now suppose, that there is, at least, a patronage of between nine and ten million, per year, vested in the Crown.

With respect to the *Church*, I believe that stands pretty much as it did. It does not, therefore, require any particular animadversions.

Citizens, a question immediately results from this statement. How is this patronage connected with the system of borough-mongering corruption? I have stated to you, already, that the great evil is to be attributed to this circumstance—that, by the great patronage of the Crown, Ministers, who hold the reins of patronage in their hands, are enabled to buy up the votes of those who *ought to be* the representatives of the people. It may therefore be perhaps suggested, if it is by the representatives being bought up that you are reduced to the calamities under which you at present groan, how are you to be assured that parliamentary reform and the annihilation of borough-mongering interest would relieve you from these excessive burdens? For it may be said, it is as easy to buy up a man who is sent into parliament by one set of people as by another; and that he who has been returned to parliament by 10,000 or 20,000 votes may be purchased at the same price as that man who is sent by one or two voters, or perhaps by no voters at all.[6]

If this statement contained no fallacy, I grant it would be vain to reason about reform: it would be more wise to look about for ourselves what comforts might yet be enjoyed, and to trouble ourselves no farther about the miseries of our fellow-beings. But I flatter myself that I shall prove, that nothing but the system of borough-mongering corruption could enable any set of men to buy up the representatives in parliament, be their patronage what it would: yea, though the revenues of the country were increased a hundred fold; for mark—If every man who has a seat in parliament were annually chosen by the unbiassed suffrages—by the uninfluenced ballot, for I know no other way by which votes can be given, without influence—of the great mass of the people—If he were to return every year, with his responsibility upon his head, to the bar of that public who, if they are displeased with his conduct, would reject him from that seat he formerly held; then mark the consequence—every year the minister would have to buy his majority afresh, or else what had been done one year towards the establishment of despotism, would be undone the next by the purity of a renovated representation.

Now what revenue could possibly enable any administration annually to repeat this corruption? The mines of *Mexico* and *Peru*, even if they could be worked without expence, would not be sufficient. Men who stand forward in any degree of respectability are not to be bought for trifles. However base and degenerate the individual who may have been unworthily honoured by the confidence of the people, he will remember that public estimation is of some value, and it is not a paultry bauble, that will induce him to renounce his fair fame. Our business then is not to trouble our heads whether men are, nor are not pure, but to consider how we are so to frame our system that even the vices of mankind shall have no longer the power to hurt us.

This, I think, Citizens, is only to be done by annual parliaments, and universal suffrage. I might, if this were the proper time, quote a long string of arguments from the most unsuspected authorities, in support of this opinion; from *Whig* writers, and *Tory* writers; supporters of the House of *Stuart*, and supporters of the House of *Brunswick*. In short I know no writer of strong mind, not even *Burke*, but has advanced facts and arguments upon which this opinion might be supported: but suffice it at present slightly to observe, what the influence would be relative to the system of corruption and consequent taxation.

I have shewn you insuperable difficulties attendant upon corrupting the *real* representatives of a people. I shall now show you how very easy, under the present system this corruption must be. Remember, Citizens, they have not now to buy men every year—no—nor even to purchase them once in every seven years. It has indeed been regarded by some as a sort of seven years purchase; and therefore they have supposed that the simple circumstance of shortening the duration of parliaments would remedy the grievance, by rendering the purchase too frequent to be supported. But, Citizens, be not deluded by half-way measures; he who recommends a mid-way path, between right and wrong, means to make you the instruments of his own ambitious views. Think what your rights are, and determinately persevere, with tranquil and benevolent firmness to the attainment of full and complete justice, for you will find half-way expedients always defective. Even annual parliaments, so long as the borough-mongering system continues would be no relief. For how is it that corruption plays its game at this time? by purchasing individual votes? No, they are put up by wholesale in large lots, and knocked down to the best bidders. The very succession is bought; and the *votes*, though not the *seats*, are rendered in effect hereditary: I say hereditary; for whatever faction so possesses the purse of the nation, as to be enabled to purchase the boroughs by which the seats in the House of Commons are filled, they are as completely and effectively hereditary, as to the principle, as the seats in the House of Lords. Nay, they are worse than hereditary, for they are transferable property which every one can buy and sell, which is not the case with peerages and titles.

But borough-mongering corruption is a mere system of disgraceful barter; and he who is ashamed to hold this *property*, as it is called, any longer, would not be ashamed to sell it to one who has more effrontery than himself. There are two ways then by which this corruption is effected, either by buying up the proprietors of rotten boroughs, and thus securing, so long as the party so bought, or his successors, continue in possession of these boroughs, two, four, six or eight representatives in parliament, and their heirs and successors in the representation for ever! Another way is, to let some clerk of the treasury, some pander of political profligacy, collect so much property as enables him to buy half-a-dozen boroughs; and then you have the members who *represent* them, entirely at your devotion. Both these modes of corruption are practised, which is notorious to every one who hears me.

If you doubt, whether borough-mongers are bought, look to the list of new-created peerages. If you doubt that clerks of the treasury, and other dependants upon government, are enabled to scrape together so much of the public plunder, as to buy rotten-boroughs by wholesale, study the political life of Mr. *Rose;*[7] you will find that by prostituting peerages, bestowing places and pensions upon particular individuals, promoting their families (no matter how worthless or insignificant) and the like; what is called a government interest in certain boroughs is secured—or in other words, a right in the administration to return whatever men they choose to represent, *not the people*, but the *administration* in parliament, and to vote as they shall nod and direct.

Now, Citizens, permit me to take a short review of the consequences of all this, and with that short review I shall close that dry part of this course of Lectures, which consists in the statement of calculations. I am not sure that I shall not now and then have occasion to intersperse my Lectures with such statements, but they will not, for the future, furnish the body. I began with stating facts: I shall now go on to demonstrate principles: and, having done that, I shall endeavour to point out in what manner the grievances may be removed, and those principles may be peaceably carried into execution.

Let me then beg your serious attention, because I know these facts, however feebly I may state them to you, will furnish matter for important deliberation. Let us consider, in the first place, what is the effect of all this to the great body of the people. In the first place, the wages of this corruption must be paid from the revenue; and what is the revenue? Is it not the produce of the taxes? And how are these taxes paid? They have been divided, fancifully enough, as *Paine* observes, into two classes—direct and indirect.[8] But I think a very little time will enable me to show you, that of these taxes (direct and indirect) every sixpence is paid by the lower and middling orders of society: that is to say, every thing is paid by the productive labourer: I shall admit, at the same time, that people of small independent property, who have no means of increasing their property, are also most grievous and heavy sufferers by the growth of taxation. But I think I shall be able to prove, that though the great proprietor and wealthy merchant talk of taxes, they in reality pay none; the whole is paid by the productive labourers; who are the great strength and pillar of every community. For what is the taxation? Every tax is, it is true, so much money taken out of the pockets of the respective people on whom it is assessed. But what is that money? It is only the sign and representative of that which really constitutes the wealth of the nation. What then constitutes the real wealth of the nation? The fruits of the national industry: its agricultural productions! its manufacturing productions! These are the real wealth, the real riches, the real grandeur and power of the state.

By whom are these produced? Are they produced by the great lord, in his ermine robes? Are they produced by the wealthy merchant? or by those respectable and truly valuable (though despised and neglected classes) the labourers in husbandry and manufactures?

But this is not the only way to prove that all the taxes are paid by the common people. I think I can shew you, that every class of people, except those I am now speaking of, have the power of shifting the taxes from their own shoulders; but that no such power is possessed by the productive labourers: and therefore upon them, in the last resort, must the burden of taxation fall.

As taxes increase, and the necessaries and luxuries of life advance, the landed proprietor increases his rent; he breaks up his little farms and makes them into large ones, to collect a larger revenue; and by a thousand ways takes care that his income shall keep pace, at least, with the growing burdens of the state. Nay, he does more; as public burdens increase, the luxury and extravagancy of the higher orders of society are increasing also.

The farmer, in his turn, increases the price of his commodity. In proportion as his rents are raised, he raises the price of the corn he takes to the market:—and he has a right to do so: I do not blame him—I do not blame individuals—I blame the vices and diseases of the system. I wish to eradicate these: I do not wish to stir up ungentle feelings in your minds against any man or class of men.

Does not the merchant, in the same way, increase the price of his articles? Does not the manufacturer increase the price of his commodities? and are there not combinations of these great dealers to raise the price of their commodities whenever it is necessary, and to keep down the price of labour, in such a manner that *commerce may not be hurt*—while the laws punish the laborious classes who associate in the same way as criminals, and confine them as felons?

I grant, there are particular trades which do not come under this description; whose labourers are numerous and pressed together; and who, by a sort of insurrection, extort that justice which they cannot otherwise obtain. But is this a thing to be desired? Will you uphold a system by which the common people can have no relief but from violence? If you will, you are the *organizers of anarchy*, and make *confusion and insurrection the order of the day*. But, can the great mass of the labouring people combine together? Can the labourers in agriculture—these main pillars of social life! nay, those very germs of our existence!—have they the powers of associating, and compelling those who employ them to proportion their wages to the burthen? On the contrary, I have known even the wishes of the Farmers themselves, to do them justice, frustrated by a few purse-proud individuals, who have stepped forward, with cruel and insulting menaces, to prevent the raising of their wages, in conformity with the exigencies of the times.

Thus the higher orders shift the whole of the burden from themselves;

and the middling orders shift off the greater part of it, in their turn. The middling orders, however, when the burden becomes very inordinate, have their share of it: the little shop-keeper must be ruined: the man who used to maintain his family in credit must be reduced to bankruptcy; he cannot always increase his prices proportionately; his commodities, from general distress, decrease in their consumption; and thus, from the decay of trade, bankruptcy, misery, and bare-foot wretchedness, succeed to decency, plenty, and expected competency.

This is the situation of many who once vainly hoped, in their old age, to lay their heads in the lap of Indulgence, and smile to see a family flourishing in happiness and opulence.—But the great oppression certainly lies upon the labouring poor; which in some of my statements I have shewn. I find, however, that some suppose I have misrepresented the fact; not recollecting that the facts I stated related to the pay of labourers in husbandry, which is much smaller than that of workmen in large cities. I shall beg you, therefore, to remember that I am speaking only of the country labourers; but that the facts, with respect to *proportionate calculation*, though not with respect to the particular prices, would equally apply in the case of artificers and manufacturers.—If it is true that workmen in great cities receive greater wages now than the labourers in husbandry, it is true that it always was the case, and therefore the proportionate diminution is the same; and it is the proportionate diminution to which I principally wish to call your attention.

Now then for a few facts, to shew the connexion between *taxation, corruption*, and the growing miseries of the industrious orders of society.

In *Davis's* excellent book, which, without his seeming to know it, contains in every page the most strong and decided facts to prove the necessity of a complete reform in our system of representation—in this book, "The Case of the Labourers in Husbandry", we have a comparative statement of the prices of labour and of the necessaries of life, at five different periods, to which I shall add a sixth, to bring the question home.[9]

Now, take this great fact with you, that the nominal price of labour is nothing. It matters not whether a man receives five farthings or five shillings a day. The quantity of the necessaries of life which he can get by his labour, is the real price of his industry: and if I can prove that a man could get four times as much for his two-pence a day formerly, as he can for his fourteen-pence per day now, I prove that the condition of the lower orders is four times worse than it formerly was.

Now, Citizens, in the middle of the 14th century (when we had no taxes, and no corruption) the ordinary price of a day's labour in husbandry was 2d; the price of a quarter of wheat from 3s. 4d. to 4s.: the medium was 3s. 8d.—Now follow some calculations drawn from facts, for which this author refers you particularly to Bishop Fleetwood's "Chronicon", Burns's "History of the Poor Laws", and Dr. Price "on Reversionary Payments."[10] In the middle of the 14th century, it seems, 22 days labour would purchase a fat hog two years old; 20 days labour, clothing for a year for a common servant in husbandry; six days labour would purchase a quarter of beans or peas; five days, a quarter of barley; two days labour would purchase a pair of shoes; and one day's labour, of common husbandry, would buy two gallons of ale.

About the middle of the 15th century (a period also when we had neither taxes nor corruption) the pay of a labourer per day was 3d; the price of a quarter of wheat 5s. and 5s. 6d.—You will find then, Citizens, that here the increase in the price of provisions, and the increase in the price of labour, had pretty nearly kept pace. You see the condition of the labouring people was even in some degree ameliorated. It cost at that time from 20 to 22 days labour to purchase a quarter of wheat; 16 days labour to purchase a quarter of malt; eight days labour to purchase a quarter of oats; seven days labour to purchase a stitch of bacon; four days labour to purchase a yard of cloth, for a shepherd; and one day's labour to purchase two or three gallons of ale.

Now, Citizens, for the third period.—At the former part of the 16th century, the price of a day's labour was 3d. halfpenny, and the price of a quarter of wheat about 7s. 6d.—(It is worth observing how nearly the price of labour here was regulated, for nearly three centuries, by the price of the principal articles of necessity!)—26 days labour would purchase a quarter of wheat; 13 or 14 days a quarter of malt; seven days, a quarter of oats; one day, eight or nine pounds of beef, pork or veal: and one day's labour would purchase 7lb. of cheese, or 4lb. of butter.

Now let us go to the fourth period (the middle of the 17th century) when taxation and corruption had begun, and see what an immediate change took place in the condition of the industrious orders of society. In *Essex*, the day's labour had then risen to 1s. 1d. One would suppose, from this great and sudden rise of wages, that in that period, of about 120 years, the labouring poor had got into a paradise of plenty! and yet mark the facts, and see how grossly we abuse ourselves, when we say, because wages increase, that the price of labour has kept pace with the price of the necessary articles of consumption. The price of wheat, at that time, was from 40 to 42s. per quarter, so that, instead of 22, they were obliged to employ 37 days labour to purchase a quarter of wheat; 22 days labour for a quarter of malt; seven days for a quarter of oats; and four days and a half's labour to purchase two shirts ready made.

Now, Citizens, I will come, if you please, to the latter part of the eighteenth century; that is, in reality, to the years from 1790 to 1792. I shall state a few facts of this aera, and then you will see what advance has been made in the price of the necessaries of life, and what advance on the price of labour. You will see when Corruption, like an overflowing flood, began to sweep away every valuable principle from the heart of man, and when the lust of power banished each generous and gentle feeling from the soul, what became of the just balance and proportion between the prices of labour and the prices of the necessaries of life. You will see who are the people that bear the burdens while great Ministers and politic Lords are swelling to immense wealth and luxury.—In the latter part of the eighteenth century, the price of a day's labour is 1s. 2d. It is so now throughout that part of the country I have visited. I enquired scrupulously myself, of the masters who employed, and of the men who were employed. Wherever I went, I put my head into the farmhouse to collect what facts I could, and into the little public-house, and the cottage of the poor, where I have seen the husbandman, time after time, making his meal off a bit of bread and a little skimmed milk; and, where they had not the opportunity of keeping a cow, bread and water—bread and water, fellow-citizens! was all that rewarded the toil of those individuals, but for whom bread itself would not be enjoyed by the luxurious and the proud! Fourteen-pence per day then, two or three years back, as now, was the price of a day's labour; and the consequence was, that (wheat being 48s. and malt 42s. 6d.) 41 days labour was necessary to buy a quarter of the former, and 36 days to buy a quarter of the latter. In short, instead of 22 days labour, 41 were necessary to purchase a quarter of wheat; instead of 16 days, 36 and a half to purchase a quarter of malt; and instead of 20, 96 days labour to buy a good fat hog: instead of six days labour, 27 or 28 were requisite to buy a quarter of beans or peas; instead of five days labour, 20 or 21 days, to purchase a quarter of barley; instead of seven days, 41 days labour to buy a stitch of bacon; instead of four days, nine days labour to purchase a yard of cloth for servants; instead of two days, six days labour to purchase a pair of shoes; and whereas one day's labour would purchase two or three gallons of ale, in the middle of the 14th century, one day's labour was then the price of a single gallon; one day's labour also would procure then but three pounds of ordinary cheese, or a pound and a half of butter, instead of seven pounds of cheese, or four pounds of butter; and instead of labouring 20 days, 40 days labour were necessary to purchase raiment for a year, for a common serving man.

But, Citizens, great and enormous as this increase appears, it shrinks into insignificance, when compared with the increase that has taken place since the commencement of this desolating war—a war, in which, seeking to ruin France, we have ruined ourselves: raving for the destruction and annihilation of Gallic liberty, we have destroyed the sources of our own felicity, till ruin and misery have lifted up their fiend-like arms, and brandishing the scourge of famine over our heads, have rendered misery, unspeakable misery, the lot of that branch of the community who deserve the warmest affections of our hearts, and our most zealous efforts for the amelioration of their condition.

I have extracted from The Morning Chronicle an account of the returns of the Corn-Market; and I mention the fact more particularly, to shew you what infamous and barefaced falsehoods are palmed upon you by the ministerial papers—for the purpose, one would suppose, of stirring up confusion in the country, that thereby they may give the Minister an opportunity of establishing a military despotism over us. Yes, Citizens, the wretch who wishes to point out the Miller, the Baker, or the Butcher, as the oppressor, can have no other view but to excite commotion; and produce the destruction of these innocent men. Innocent, I say; for though I do not mean to say there is no such thing as monopoly—yet I am sure that monopoly could not exist, but for that system of borough-mongering corruption, a part of the spawn of which it is. But, generally speaking, I am conscious that the dealers in the necessary articles of life are themselves as much injured and oppressed as the consumers: and he who endeavours to make you believe the contrary, can have no other view but to divert your attention from the real source of the calamity, and fix your indignation upon men who, being within your reach, may fall, perhaps, victims to mistaken vengeance, and thus furnish a pretence for that despotism, for the establishment of which nothing but *a pretence* is wanted.

When day after day I read in "the True Briton",[11] as it is called—O that *Britons* should bear that name to be thus libelled, and scandalized by the dirtiest dependent of the dirtiest scribe of a corrupt administration!—I lose all patience—I forget disease and infirmity, and can restrain myself no longer, when I find this once brave and generous nation so basely insulted and degraded.—When day after day I have read in this paper, and in the "Times", accounts that the prices of those articles were falling in the markets—that the commodities are coming in in great plenty, and that therefore monopolies among the bakers and butchers, and the connivance of the *Lord Mayor*, for such things they dare to insinuate, are the real causes of the misfortune; I have burned with indignation to observe circumstances thus stated, which whose who state them must know to be false; and which there is reason to believe are nonetheless sanctioned by high authority: for I have been told, by one of the proprietors of the "Times", that scarcely a paragraph is inserted but what is formally transmitted in the French language; the production of some of those emigrant rascals who enjoy the confidence of *gentlemen high in office*, and who, having brought calamity and ruin upon their own country, come here to bring the same ruin and calamity on us. But, Citizens, I have here accounts of a different kind, in a less questionable shape, which I am going to state, and the accuracy of which I have ascertained by proper inquiries and authorities that cannot be doubted, and which enable me to say, at the very time when the ministerial papers had the audacity to say, that the prices of these articles were lowering in the market, they were actually rising every day.

Having shewn the foundations I have to depend upon for the statement before me, I proceed to observe—that new English wheat was last market day from 82 to 86s. per quarter; the average 84s.; which was from one to two shillings more than it had been sold at the preceding market day, though the "Times" of that day asserted, that it had considerably fallen. Foreign wheat was from 70 to 76s.; medium 73s.; English barley, new, 35s.; malt 4s.; old field oats 26s.; new oats 25s., and flour 70s. per sack.

Now then, Citizens, what is the result? That a man who could once get a quarter of wheat for 22 days labour, must now work 74 days for the same quantity. Remember I am speaking of the labourer in husbandry; the proportionate decline, as I told you before, is the same in town; the exact quantum of injury is the same, though the nominal sums are different. He must now labour 46 days to purchase a quarter of malt. To this let me add, that instead of *six* days he must labour from 48 to 65 days to buy a quarter of beans or peas. Such then, Citizens, with respect to the articles of the greatest necessity, are the monstrous inconveniencies to which the labouring part of the community are at present subjected.

If you put together the whole of the facts I have thus stated, this conclusion immediately results; that as corruption and taxation have kept pace, so has the misery, the ruin, and depression of the great body of the people, gone hand in hand with these burdens. They will oblige you to draw this conclusion also, that with respect to the great mass, whatever may be the case with the intermediate orders, it would be better that even the age of feudal tyranny were restored, than that the tyranny of rotten borough-mongers should be established over us: a tyranny the most expensive, and, as it is supported by the labour, the groans and anguish of the great body of the people, ought to be considered as the greatest scourge that ever afflicted the universe.

What signifies then the fine, metaphysical, high-spun arguments of *Windham*? I speak not from irritation—I wish not to stir up any ungentle feelings. I am not hurt at being called "an acquitted felon." If it be felony to speak truth, and to unmask corruption, I glory in being a felon; and will endeavour to be the greatest felon in Britain: and if I do not attain it, it shall be for want of power, not of endeavour. I am prouder of that title, gained in such a cause, than Mr. *Windham* or any of his family can be of the titles and dignities they carry about them. I would rather bear this title with a halter round my neck, as the badge of my order, than wear the *blue ribband* apostacy round my knee, or be decorated with any of those baubles which please the minds of men in their second childhood when they become once more pleased with a rattle, and tickled with a straw.

But to a hungry people what signify the metaphysics of *Wyndham*, splitting the hair of nothingness in twain, and then arguing which portion of *non-entity* is most *substantial*? What signifies listening to such hyperboles and scientific nonsense, as make up the *airy nothing* of this gentleman's speeches, when he attempts to demonstrate our *negative successes* and mystical felicities? Let us appeal to facts: and if the condition of the people is growing worse and worse, and if we can trace these calamities to the corruption of borough-mongering usurpations, let us join heart in hand to redress these corruptions—Let us, with the voice of reason, with the energies of intellect, seek for the remedy where alone it can be found. Let us call aloud, again and again, till redress is given to our wrongs, and till the people are restored to their ancient inherent right to annual parliaments and universal suffrage.

What signify the *lullabies* of *Burke*—the narcotics and soporifics with which he would charm us to sleep? or the visions and frenzies with which he would disturb our slumbers? What signify his pious ravings and meditations of the rewards to be conferred upon us in another world? Why should not this world, also, be rendered tolerable to us?

Citizens, it is true, as a well-known Citizen observed, when he first heard this reflection, it is very well to have a good inn in prospect, where one may put up at night; but why should we be starved to death upon the road? Let us think also where we are to breakfast and to dine. As for the rest, stay till the time comes when you are to put on your night-cap; and doubt not, if the day be well spent that the slumber will be sweet. Do not suffer yourselves to be deluded with the idea that the Deity (if a Deity there be) can be such a Being, that the only way to obtain his favour hereafter is to be miserable while we are here: as though he had not the power, or the inclination, to impart felicity both in this world and the other!

THE TRIBUNE. No. XXXV.
The Connection between the CALAMITIES of the PRESENT REIGN, and the SYSTEM of BOROUGH-MONGERING CORRUPTION—LECTURE THE THIRD.—*The Connection between Parliamentary Corruption and Commercial Monopoly: with Strictures on the* WEST-INDIA SUBSCRIPTION, &c. Delivered *Wednesday Oct. 14, 1795.* [12]

CITIZENS,

I have this night particularly to request of the numerous friends of liberty and order, that they will be cool, and collected, and not suffer the illib-erality of a few beings of another description to throw them into confusion. I have also, to admonish those few individuals who came for the purpose of disturbance, that it will be for their credit not to be over hasty; because if they begin to hiss before they have heard any thing, people will know they came with a determination to disturb and not to hear; and therefore it will be impossible for their conspiracy to have any effect. When men calling themselves *gentlemen*, and in the *garb* of gentlemen, begin to hiss at the bottom of the stairs, and ill-treat the door-keepers, we know what sort of beings they are; they proclaim themselves at once to be part of those rep-tiles spawned and cherished in the pool of corruption, who are fearful lest the rays of truth should dry up this stagnant pool, and deprive them of the sources of their noxious existence.

Let them not however flatter themselves, that a few such reptiles, spit-ting their frothy venom in my way, can check my course. I should ill discharge the duties of my situation, were I, from such poor terrors, to forbear the free investigation of every species of abuse which the corruption of the times engenders. I knew from the first, that this investigation must inevitably create innumerable swarms of enemies among all classes of men: for where is the class in which corruption is not to be found?

But these circumstances, although they may put us upon our guard, cannot, if we are seriously attached to the cause of liberty, turn us from the course of enquiry. He who feels his mind actuated by the love of the human race, regardless of such enmity, and despising such hostility, will proceed with fortitude—sometimes annoyed and wounded, and sometimes victorious, but always calm! seeking for consolation in the consciousness only of his own rectitude, and for reward in the affection and esteem of the worthy part of that species whose rights he vindicates, and whose happiness he endeavours to promote.

The particular part of the subject which it is my duty to investigate this evening, is the aristocracy of the Royal Exchange; an aristocracy which, though sanctioned by no legal authority, and decorated with no trappings of distinction, is I believe in reality as important a pillar in the temple of corruption, as any of those that are to be found in the avowed plan of the state architects of this temple. Let me not, however, be misunderstood, when I speak in terms of strong reprobation of the aristocracy of commerce.—If I find myself compelled to mark with decided censure the present corrupt and monopolizing system, at the shrine of which not only the happiness and the liberties, but even the very lives of the great mass of mankind are inhumanly sacrificed, let it not be supposed that I mean to condemn the system of commerce altogether.

Commerce, uncorrupted by monopolizing speculation, is one of the greatest advantages that result from social union. It is by this that the comforts and accommodations of each quarter of the globe are transplanted to every other, and that every individual spot of the universe might be benefited by the knowledge of all the rest. A fair and liberal spirit of commerce has a considerable tendency to inform the understanding of mankind, to increase the progress of intelligence, and above all, to do away the ridiculous and destructive prejudices of nationality.—The intercourse of man with man, and nation with nation, of the trader of one country with the trader of another, if conducted on liberal and equal principles, must certainly remove the delusive idea that humanity and virtue are the attributes of a particular soil, and convince us that we ought to extend the narrow sphere of our affections, and in all our schemes of justice and policy, to regard alike the happinesss and welfare of the whole universe; because all the inhabitants of the universe are but one family, linked together by correspondent sympathies, and endued with the same faculties of sense and reason—the same passions and necessities—the same powers of virtue and frailties of vice—in fine, the same faculties to impart and to enjoy the reciprocations and improvements which constitute the happiness and security of the whole.

But it is one thing to admire the genuine principle of commerce, it is another to countenance its abuses. It does not follow, because commerce, simply considered, is good, that the present system is good also: a system in which speculation has banished the fair and equitable process of exchange, and in which monopoly has destroyed the free energies of the human character, and counteracted all the benevolent tendencies which I have before described!

A Citizen, whose name is Wadstrom,[13] has very lately obliged the world with a publication of very considerable merit, in which he even doubts whether the system of "Speculation-Commerce", ought to be tolerated in the world at all.[14] He is disposed to consider that the only kind of commerce really advantageous to mankind, is that which he calls "Commission Commerce",—by which particular individuals undertake to supply the wants under which other individuals actually labour; instead of seeking to produce or accumulate commodities in hopes thereby of exciting artificial wants, provoking the demand and increasing the consumption.

It is not my intention to enter this evening into a question so complicated and abstruse. You will perceive at once that it involves the important dilemma of simplicity or luxury; and many other considerations that would shake several of the most settled habits of what is called refined and polished society; and I shall freely acknowledge, that to do any thing like justice to it, would demand a much larger portion of commercial knowledge than I pretend to possess. But I will say, that undoubtedly there is great force of conviction in parts, at least, of the system he has laid down; and that we shall certainly find, if we examine and probe the subject to the bottom, that the spirit of speculation has destroyed the fair, honest, and manly character of traffic; and that at present (though the open barter only appears in the infamous African slave-trade) almost all the inhabitants of the universe are rendered, as it were, the saleable commodities of a few engrossers and monopolists, who still assume the name of merchants, but are no longer worthy of the character once attached to that name.

Notwithstanding all this, there are many who still maintain that the mercantile system, even as it now stands, is friendly to Liberty: and a fanciful writer, who has lately stepped forward to support the corruptions of the Commons' House of Parliament, has carried this opinion to a most wild extent. This author's name is *Peacock*. He is, it is true, a member of one of those privileged orders, who are very unwilling that any existing corruption should be touched, even with the little finger of Reform, and has accordingly endeavoured to support that excellent position laid down by Mr. *Pitt* and Lord *Mornington*, that *the corruptions of the House of Commons constitute the principal excellence of the British Constitution*, and that, if you remove these corruptions, every thing that is admirable and excellent in that constitution will fade and crumble away. This *Peacock*, in the midst of his wild vagaries, has taken it into his head to maintain, that the commercial interest in this country is a republican interest; and that, in fact, the republican interest is in danger of getting too much ascendancy in the constitution, in consequence of the share of representation already possessed by the mercantile interest.

This opinion is not peculiar to this man; and therefore I shall examine it a little. I know that many specious arguments might be advanced, from history, that would tend to substantiate this opinion. We might be told, for example, that *Athens*, one of the greatest commercial cities of antiquity, was a republic. But remember, *Athens* did not owe its republicanism to its commerce; neither did *Athens* owe its commerce to its republicanism. The republicanism of *Athens* sprung from an example of such generous and magnanimous virtue as, I am afraid, we shall not see imitated by many Kings of the modern world. *Theseus*[15] ascended the throne of *Athens* as hereditary sovereign of that country; but, some how or other, *Theseus* got the mad jacobinical idea into his head, that it was not for the welfare and happiness of the human race, that even such a territory as *Athens* should be under the controul of one man. With a disinterested patriotism, that must endear his name to all true lovers of Liberty, *Theseus* therefore, resigning his power, laid the foundation of that republic, whose energies of mind astonished the admiring universe, and have left the modern kingdoms and empires of the world, "with base despair, to wonder at its greatness, and mourn their fall degenerate"!—This republic was afterwards consolidated by the wise and excellent laws of *Solon*;[16] and, so long as his institutions remained pure, and unadulterated with the baneful mixture of aristocratic corruption, the genius, the grandeur and power of that republic rose triumphant: and so far was this freedom from owing its origin to commerce, that, when commerce had swelled to an inordinate degree, and had poured into that city its tide of riches, luxury, and corruption, down fell the splendid edifice of Athe-

nian Liberty, and Aristocracy, and consequent Anarchy, spread devastation, not only through that particular state, but through the whole Grecian
confederacy.

But, Citizens, it may be supposed that this tendency of commerce to
republicanism may be better supported by the example of the Italian republics; and *Genoa, Venice,* and *Florence,* may be brought forward to substantiate the strange assertion that *Peacock* has made. Remember, however,
that the commerce which prevailed at the time when these republics were
founded, was a very different system from that which now prevails, and to
which, alone, Mr. *Peacock,* if he means any thing, must mean to allude.
Remember, also, that all is not gold that glitters; and that it is not the
mere name of republicanism that produces liberty. In fact, republicanism,
both in the ancient and modern world, has been but too frequently made a
cloak to conceal the usurpations of the most tyrannical aristocracy. Surely
the advocates of Commerce cannot boast much of the liberty enjoyed by
those Italian republics, when we reveal their internal structure, their system of spies and informers, so excellently imitated of late by those supporters of the present administration, who, with a sort of Harlequin's dagger of
lath, have converted Mr. *Reeves* into a lion's mouth, to receive and act
upon all the anonimous calumny which political prostitution or revenge
may dictate. *Carthage,* at a time when a few monied aristocrats exercised
the most despotic tyranny over it, was still called a republic. *Holland,* before the late revolution, still maintained the name of a republic; yea, and
had its House of Representatives, with this difference, indeed, from ours—
that *their Representatives* were *openly* and *avowedly* named by the aristocracy
and adherents of the chief magistrate of that country. *France* also was
called a republic in the days of *Robespierre:* whose sanguinary measures the
Dictator of another country seemed so well disposed to imitate, though he
had neither courage nor genius to carry his intentions into execution. Nay,
the present Convention, at the very instant when they are trampling upon
the glorious principles of Liberty and Equality, for which the nation has
been so long contending, and endeavouring to force a tyrannic degree
down the throats of the people (in imitation of an honourable assembly in
another nation) by a garbled report, patched and fabricated in a Secret
Committee—at this very instant the Convention talk of consolidating the
Republic.—It is high time that men should be awakened from their trance,
and see that not names, but principles, should be the object of their attachment; that it is the liberty of the human race, and not the nick-name
that may be given to a constitution, that is worth contending for. It is not

pulling down one tyranny, and setting up another, that is worth contention. It matters not what shape a government may assume, if its real operation is to sacrifice the happiness of the many to the interests of a few: nor is
it matter of much consequence whether the Aristocrats that domineer over
us, were nursed in the lap of Nobility, brought up in the counting-houses
of monopolizing merchants, or produced in the ferment of civil commotion, from what are insultingly called the dregs and refuse of the people.
The tyranny of the Dagger, and the tyranny of Monopolists, equally destroy the freedom of the human character—nay, equally destroy the comforts and *lives* of the human race, though the assassinations of the latter are
more silent and secret than those of the former.

The fact is, Citizens, that there can be no liberty where there is not a
simplicity of manners, a fortitude of character, and a pure and generous
system of morality. This simplicity, this fortitude, and this morality constitute the true essence of liberty so necessary to the welfare and happiness of
mankind: but which never can be maintained where the true equality of
man is not recognized in this plain maxim, that *laws made for the government of all ought to receive the sanction and approbation of all, either personally,
or by representation.* Every individual defrauded of the right of giving his
sanction to these laws is, in reality, a slave: and freedom is to him but an
empty sound that vibrates upon his ear, but conveys no privilege to his
heart.

This liberty, though never yet enjoyed in absolute perfection, has, I
shall shew you, existed in a much more considerable degree in countries
that were not commercial than in countries that are. For example, will any
man pretend to say that *Switzerland* owes its liberty to commerce? Does the
little republic of *San Marino* owe its liberty to the commercial aggrandizement of a few individuals? No, a just system of mild and equal laws has
contributed to secure the happiness of that little republic; and shewn us
(such a bubble is the pretended balance of power) that the weakest and
smallest state, adopting the principles of justice, moderation, peace and
liberty, may maintain its independence, in the midst of powerful and rival
nations. It is true, indeed, that in the ancient republic of *Acaia* commerce
was carried on to a very considerable extent: and yet, in the midst of this
commerce, *Acaia* of old (like San Marino of modern times) a small diminu-
tive city, maintained its independence, its freedom, and its virtue, without
the assistance of *Jannissaries* to protect it, or combinations of military despots to fight its battles. But the commerce of *Acaia* was conducted upon
principles which at this time are not understood. Commerce was not then

carried on for the exclusive advantage and emolument of a few. No, by the excellent institutions of the state it was made to produce equal advantage to every citizen of the community. Every man participated not only in the labour, but in the profit: unlike those countries where all the burden is thrown upon one class of the people, and the whole of the advantage is engrossed by another.

Let me be understood. I do not wish, by this example, to enforce any ideas of pecuniary equality. These notions, wickedly broached by Reeves and his coadjutators, I leave to those who had the profligacy to attempt to set them afloat.[17] I would not recommend that those institutions should be shaken which enable men individually to reap the profit of their individual exertions. No, I am convinced that it is by this individual independence that the general happiness and welfare might, in the present state of society, be best promoted. But at the same time, do not fall into the opposite extreme by countenancing laws that throw all power and emolument into the hands of those who, from their superior wealth, possess already too much authority. I would not have you, by countenancing systems by which this monopoly is supported, sacrifice the interests of the great body of the people, to an ideal notion of wealth and grandeur; which means neither more nor less, when properly translated, than the depression, beggary, and starving misery of the great body of the people. This may sound like paradox, but it is nevertheless true: for what do you mean to describe when you talk of the grandeur, wealth, and prosperity of a country? Do you mean that all the people are grandees? that all are wealthy?—all are flourishing?—Certainly not.—You mean neither more nor less than this—that a few particular individuals are enabled to display a pomp, luxury and splendour that dazzle the beholder, and inflate his imagination with ideas of superfluous affluence—that your great merchants, courtiers, and favourites of ministers are capable of making expensive feasts, in which the revenues of a province are wasted at a meal, while the people at large—But who thinks of the people? They are nothing. It is the splendid opulence of the heads of the nation that constitutes the power and grandeur of the nation. As for the people: they are only the feet—or, in reality, the dust upon which the feet of greatness ought to trample.

But, Citizens, there is a certain sense in which commerce, even as it is generally conducted, may be favourable to liberty: that is to say, it favors the cause of liberty to a certain extent. It has a tendency to dispel the midnight of ignorance, and to introduce some feeble rays of light and knowledge among mankind. It has a tendency, also, by the respectability that attaches to mercantile opulence, to weaken that veneration for names and hereditary distinctions, which, however excellent in their way, ought not to monopolize all the admiration of mankind. In this point of view commerce has been useful in this country. At the first revival of knowledge, after the darkness and ignorance of the middle centuries, the spirit of trade did much towards the emancipation of mankind; and by setting up a formidable barrier against the feudal despotism of the Barons, broke, undoubtedly, that yoke of intolerable slavery which those military barbarians had imposed upon the great mass of the people. But if commerce formerly broke the chains of *feudal tyranny*, it is now riveting the equally intolerable chains of corruption and influence.

To illustrate this observation I will refer you to the bargains and agreements made between a few great commercial houses, and the leaders of the administration of this country: and you will, then, I believe, admit that the present system of corruption could not be supported, if it were not for a certain combination between the monopolists of the Royal Exchange and the Borough-mongers of St. Stephen's Chapel.[18] This combination has been for a considerable time in existence. Its extent and power, however, are growing day after day: and its fatal effects have never been so considerable as at present.

Unfortunately for the happiness and repose of mankind, at the altar of this combination every principle of justice and humanity has too frequently been sacrificed. War and destruction, not peace and political amelioration, are the means by which it is supported; and however strange it may appear—however contradictory to our general speculations, the harvest of our commercial prosperity, as it is called, is to the great body of the people, continual havock and desolation.

It is very true that, generally speaking, Peace is the nurse of Commerce; and therefore it may be supposed that I advance an hypothesis that cannot be supported, when I say that the emoluments of these commercial monopolists are as considerable from the system of war and desolation as the profits of ministers are admitted to be.—I say *admitted*, because every man knows that war is a great promoter of patronage; and patronage is the harvest of a corrupt administration.

But remark a distinction here. It is true that the *national* advantages of commerce can only be secured by peace. But the general advantage is one thing, the particular is another: and it is to the particular advantage that I wish to draw your attention. For this purpose it is necessary to digress a little into a history of the commercial system.

Commerce, in the first instance, undoubtedly consisted in the mere exchange of commodities: one country bringing its superabundant production to another where it was likely to find a superabundance of some other commodity of which it stood in need. So long as this system continued commerce must, undoubtedly, have promoted the general welfare of mankind. Nay, when the more improved state of society introduces a medium to supersede this cumbrous barter, still the benefit to society continues, so long as the commodities necessary for the sustenance and comfort of man are the real objects of commerce. But when the comforts of the many come to be exchanged for the luxuries of the few—when the hatchet of the husbandman is enhanced in its price to load the side-board of the noble, or the merchant, with the guilty produce of Mexican or Peruvian mines—and above all, when the necessaries of life (particularly grain) become articles, not of *open* traffic, but of commercial speculation;—when tricks of every description are played to aggravate their price, and government itself presumes to dabble in these speculations, then commerce which should be advantageous to the universe, becomes destructive to the happiness, and even to the existence of man.

In the progress, however, of commercial degeneracy there is another step that ought to be noticed. Commodities, when commerce is fairly considered, are the *objects* of exchange: but money, from having been agreed upon as a token, and common medium to facilitate exchange, has become itself the object of traffic. *Money* (not commodities) is the article in which your great commercial monopolist wishes to become a dealer: and it is easy to prove that war is peculiarly favourable to *this* trade; though most unfavourable to a fair and honest traffic.

I am well aware, Citizens, that this part of the subject will require some degree of pains on my part, and on your's more attention than is usually paid in places of this kind. We have so long been used to consider commerce in the aggregate, that few of us are disposed to make these necessary distinctions. My distinctions, however, are simply these—Fair commerce deals in commodities necesary for the comfort and advantage of mankind. Monopoly deals, not in these articles, or, at least, not exclusively in these articles; but builds its profits upon a traffic in money itself: a traffic which frequently raises a few individuals to enormous opulence—but produces no benefit whatever to the people at large. It is, in short, a sort of political whirl-pool, which having once acquired a given force, sucks every thing into its vortex, and in proportion as it encreases in power and magnitude, extends its destructive influence through a wider circle. This traffic is principally carried on between the speculative monopolist and the government: as for instance, in the article of loans. A minister bargains with a merchant, or given number of merchants, to furnish him, or rather *cause him to be furnished*, with such a quantity of money; for which he secures him such and such an avowed interest; such and such a premium to augment that interest; and such and such bonuses and douceurs, as they are called. Thus the minister is enabled, on the one hand, to keep the wheels of corruption going, and the merchant, on the other, reaps an emolument by the sale of his money—or as it may frequently happen, by the mere *pawn of his credit*, which no other species of commerce could bring into his coffers.

Now the necessity of loans is produced by immoderate expenditure: immoderate expenditure is encreased by war; this traffic of money, therefore, so destructive to the people, at whose expence it is carried on, but so profitable to the opulent speculatist, is carried on to a more considerable extent in time of war than of peace; and thus have your monied men, so long as national credit will hold, an interest in promoting that system of war, which mankind at large, have so much reason to execrate. If this had been thoroughly understood there would have been no difficulty in accounting for the avidity with which the meeting in Merchant Taylors' Hall plunged the country into a ruinous and profligate war.[19]

From this mutual interest proceeds a sort of compact between certain individuals at one end of the town and certain individuals at the other; which fairly translated into the vulgar tongue means this—Do you protect us in our monopoly of boroughs, and we will protect you in monopolizing particular branches of traffic. To this combination it is that both parties so frequently sacrifice every principle and feeling of humanity. To support this secret convention it was that the minister, who upon all other occasions can command a majority, suffered his power to be paralized when the interests of humanity were at stake; and, while he indulged his *feelings* by vehemently exclaiming against the most atrocious system of murder and depradation that ever was dignified by the name of commerce (I mean the detestable Slave Trade) rather than offend his city connections, gave a sly wink to his condescending majority, to vote in opposition to his arguments: and thus, Citizens, what with this fine management, and the finesse of that great politician *Henry Dundas*, the English nation, after having expressed its almost unanimous wish for the abolition, was compelled to continue this abominable traffic.[20] But France abolished it,[21] though we would not; for abolished in effect, it is:—more than abolished:—premature emancipation is rushing upon the kidnapped sons of Africa. What the scenes may be, through which these unfortunate islands have yet to pass—what the calamities of this struggle of emancipation, I cannot pretend to divine: and fain would I draw a veil over the melancholy prospect. But with respect to West-India slavery, it is abolished: its final doom is fixed. It may, perhaps, keep up a struggling, feeble existence, for a little time; but the period cannot be distant, when the West-India islands will be cultivated by slaves no more—when the West-India islands will be no more dependent upon any European power: and for my own part, Citizens, I own that I cannot very much lament the prospect of this separation. I am convinced, that the doctrines of Justice are always the doctrines of Expediency: and that, when you suffer Principle, god-like Principle! above all things, to dictate your conduct, you do in reality the most politic thing that can possibly be done. Every country having a right to independency—every country having a right to chuse its own government, I should be led, in the first instance, to suppose it for the happiness and welfare of the whole, that these rights should be exercised and enjoyed. But it is not only by argument *a priori* that I am induced to form this conclusion. What examination I have been enabled to give the subject, convinces me that it would be a happy thing for the universe in general, and for Britain in particular, if there were no such a thing as a colony or dependency in the political system of the universe. I am convinced the people would be more happy; that a more extensive, but a more fair and equal commerce would be spread all over the world; and that population and happiness would be essentially promoted. I grant at the same time, however, that this would not be equally advantageous to those commercial monopolists of whom I am speaking; for if this independence should ever take place, Trade must be open! Traffic must be free! and every individual, and every country, must have a fair and equal opportunity of struggling for a share of this general commerce. The consequence would be, that, from the spirit of general rivalry, every article would be sold at the lowest price by which a living profit could be obtained: and do you not immediately perceive, that it would be for the happiness of the people that every article should be so disposed of?

But your monopolists would be injured; and therefore a fresh armament is to be equipped for the *West-Indies*, with the vain and hopeless expectation of preventing a catastrophe which is inevitable: which may be delayed, perhaps, for a few years, but which never can be permanently prevented. The principle is broad awake; and no drug, in all the shops of all the political quack doctors, who have so long been dosing us with their

potions and their pills, can send it to sleep again. But still we are to struggle with Despair: like men who, in their sleep, dream they are running,
and though their feet are clogged with the bed-cloaths, endeavour to kick
and sprawl about; so in our dream of conquering the *West-India* islands, we
send our fleets, with the best blood of the country, stored with necessaries
for which our poor at home are starving, to flounder and sprawl, and buffet
the adverse elements, till, faint and exhausted, we wake from the delirious
slumber, and find that we have toiled in vain.

Thus do we plunge the country in still deeper anguish, to prolong the
feverish existence of that system of monopoly with which the Minister has
much reason to be pleased, but which the people have equal reason to
curse, from their very hearts.—It is not enough that magazines of provisions are to be established upon our coasts, that the *Chouans* and *Vendeans*
may have bread, while Britons starve. Stores are also to be sent to the
West-Indies, and, in the chance of war, perhaps, are to be committed to
the waves or the devouring flames; while the starving people fix their im-
ploring eyes upon their betrayers, expecting in vain for their iron hearts to
melt in compassion for their miseries and their sufferings.

Citizens, there is another part of this curious system upon which I must
say a few words: I mean the subscriptions which you have seen advertised
in the public papers.—Citizens, I am aware how ungracious a task it is to
represent, in unfavourable colours, a transaction of this kind. But let the
facts be stated, and let Reason judge, whether this indeed be charity, or
only a state-trick to bolster up the popularity of a measure which so many
circumstances conspire to render odious. I wish not to assign a selfish motive where a generous one can be found; unless the weight of argument is
such that justice, eternal justice! to which all considerations must bow
down, calls me to incline my judgment to the unfavourable side: but let us
consider a little the nature of this subscription. It is called an act of charity:
but Charity has lost its meaning, if it signifies the giving of alms to promote desolation, cruelty, and war. What charity can make amends to the
widow who shall lose her husband in his mad crusade? to the child who
shall lose his parent? or the aged father who shall lose his child? I shall take
no particular notice, at this time, of the strong reasons there are to suspect
that collections of this kind are frequently abused and perverted in their
application, and rendered subservient to the purposes of political prostitution, instead of being applied to the noble purposes of benevolence; but I
shall take the liberty of shewing you who the movers of this subscription
are, and then leave you to judge whether it is, in reality, an exertion of

manly liberality, or an artifice to give popularity to a measure to which the people are found to have sense enough to be generally averse.

Permit me to remind you of the circumstances under which this subscription has been brought before you. Let me ask you, in the first place, What is the purpose of the expedition to which this subscription applies? Is it not clear and evident, that the hope of recovering the *West-India* islands is, in reality the foundation for continuing, during another year, this war of unparalleled desolation?—In what manner is that war to be carried on? An immense loan is to be raised, *in a great measure from these very subscribers* to the predicted widows and orphans of those who are going to inevitable destruction in the West-India expedition!—Here is disinterestedness! This mad crusade is thus to be carried on another year, to the destruction of thousands and tens of thousands more of our fellow beings!—Here is humanity!—This is *commercial and political charity*! Thousands more are to be massacred, and a subscription is opened by the West-India Merchants and Money-jobbers to make the massacre popular. Millions are to be borrowed, to carry on this massacre; and the people are to bear the burthen! Aye; but the *West-India* Merchants are to have the loan. But remember that lending is in this instance, the most profitable use to which they can apply their money. Nor is this all: the loan itself is made—the war is continued—to defend their monopoly.

Will the mass of the people in this country ever receive 20 millions of advantage from the possession of the whole East India Islands, if it were possible to possess them? If not, who are the persons to be advantaged? The combinations of West India Merchants; who, having got the planters in their power, reap the profits, and command the price of the article which they dispose of. These are the men who are to reap the advantage! For them this war is to be carried on another year! for them 20 millions more of British treasure are to be expended, and the miseries of aggravated famine are to seize upon the vitals of the people. Desolation is to rage on, in *England, France, Germany,* and the *West-Indies,* that a few individuals may be enabled to carry on one system of monopoly at the East end of the town, and to support another system of monopoly at the West end of the town, which has robbed the people of their rights, their independence, and their suffrages!

A brief statement of facts relative to these loans will shew you how well it is worth the while of these monied men to bolster up a war by an occasional subscription. You are told, it is true, that the money is borrowed at 3 per cent. Yes, but perhaps you borrow at the rate of 58l. for 100l. *ergo,* you pay 100l. for every 58l. which makes it 5¼ per cent at once. But this is not all. There are the profits of a lottery, by which the morals of the people are to be debauched for the benefit of the higher orders; and there are, also, your bonuses, your douceurs, and a heap of complicated &cs. too mysterious for us plain men to understand. Add to this, the subscriber to these loans is to receive interest from the day the bargain is made, without advancing a single shilling of the capital for six weeks or three months; and a part of it for nine months after subscription. Thus you see, at once, that the stagnation of commerce is compensated to the monied man, by the quick return, and immense interest of his money; and by the power and patronage so advantageous in a thousand shapes and forms, which he thus procures.—Well then who are the men that have brought forward this subscription? Read over the whole list, and scarcely a man will you find amongst them who is not a dealer in government loans—a government contractor—a government agent—or a West India monopolist. These are the men, then, for whom the people of Britain are to groan, and sweat, and bleed through another campaign; and who, to encourage us in this unnatural contest, make an ostentatious display of their benevolence in subscribing for a month's bread and water for the widows and orphans of those who expose themselves to pestilence and slaughter in their quarrel.

If men want to shew their charity, let them not confine it to sects and descriptions. Let them relieve distress, by whatever cause it may be produced; and not thus hold out their pretended liberality as a lure to tempt mankind to shed their blood in a struggle in which that class of society from which the soldiers and seamen are selected, can have no possible interest.

I now proceed to the remaining branch of my subject, the East India Company; another great pillar of that system of monopolizing corruption which is the source of our calamities. Here we have at once a single mercantile firm who are said to have entered into a *conspiracy to buy the House of Commons.*[22] Guy Vaux[23] entered into a conspiracy to blow up the parliament—Charles the Second entered into a conspiracy to do without one; and certain terrible fellows, since known by the name of *acquitted felons*, were accused of a conspiracy to reform it. But ask Mr. *Pitt*, and he will tell you that the most terrible conspiracy of all was that of the East India Company to *buy the parliament*. But after calling up their accounts, and finding they could only buy up one third, they resolved to save their money, and leave that honourable house to its native purity. But though they did not execute their plan, their Nabobs are very well represented in the Commons' House of Parliament: and so long as their charter depends upon parliamentary influence, it is but in little danger. I shall not, at this time, enter at large into the validity of the arguments by which the perpetuity of this charter is supported; nor enlarge upon the parliamentary influence which this company possesses. The late election in the city of London has sufficiently convinced me of this;[24] and the night is too far spent to suffer me to enter upon a detail so full of the enormities of corruption; neither shall I, at this time, enter into a speculative examination of the foundation upon which charters stand; because it would lead me into a wider field of enquiry than time will permit. I recommend, however, this subject to your serious enquiry; confident that you must agree with me, that all monopoly is injustice, and political abomination: confident, also, that when you have enquired, you will find that the systems of monopoly and borough-mongering corruption are so intimately entwined together, that it is impossible to remedy the mischiefs of the one without reforming the abuses of the other. Twin plants from one common root of political depravity, they must flourish or must fall together. And if flourish much longer they unfortunately should—farewell to all the blossoms and herbage of human comfort, for like the Upas of Java, the blighting dews shed from their noxious branches spread desolation and sterility throughout the land.

Having thus shewn the interest which ministers and opulent money-dealers have in promoting the system of war, I shall proceed, in the next Lecture, to shew the horrors of the system itself, and the miseries it brings upon the great body of the people.

THE TRIBUNE. No. XLIII.

The Second Lecture on the UNFORTUNATE RESTORATION *of the* HOUSE *of* STUART, *with Strictures on the Differences between the* ENGLISH REVOLUTION 1649, *and that of* FRANCE, *in 1792, and the Impossibility of restoring Royalty in the latter Country: including a Delineation of the* CHARACTER OF CROMWELL. *Delivered Wednesday June 3, 1795.*[25]

CITIZENS,

THE subject upon the investigation which I enter for the second time this evening undoubtedly demands a very considerable degree of attention, and requires that the man who attempts to investigate it with that freedom and boldness without which no advantage can arise from investigation, should have all his watchful faculties about him, that he may avoid unguarded and rash expressions, with which people of warm imaginations sometime outstep their better judgements. The person indeed who stands periodically in a situation like this, ought to have a patent of infallibility to preserve him from those accidents to which the persons and tempers of mankind are liable. For an audience is seldom disposed to make much allowance for the accidents with which a man may be visited. They judge his oration or his book according to the execution, and never enquire into the particular embarrassments under which he laboured at the time of production. It is my misfortune, however, not to be sufficiently acquainted with his Holiness the Pope, to attain this patent of infallibility; and therefore I have been frequently obliged to come before you under circumstances of considerable embarrassment. At this very time you may perhaps perceive, that I labour under an inconvenience of health, peculiarly unfavourable to the exertions of oratory: and though it is long since I was in the habit of being frightened at my own shadow, it may happen in the course of this Lecture that I may be so much frightened at the sound of my own voice, that it may embarrass me very much.

Those who attended on the former evening will remember I entered as largely as time would permit into a consideration of the mischiefs brought upon us by the unfortunate restoration of the House of *Stuart*; and particularly from the very disgraceful manner in which that restoration was effected, by the intrigues of *Clarendon* and *Monk*[26] by which the better part of the nation were prevented from laying *Charles* under those restrictions which otherwise perhaps would have saved this country from a considerable part of the calamities brought upon it. I ventured, however, to consider the very circumstance of restoring a family so disgraced by every tyranny and usurpation as a national calamity.

Whether any persons differ from me in this respect or not, at any rate, when we consider the mischiefs resulting from the unqualified restoration, there is no dread of being convicted of high treason for saying, that this event, so frequently celebrated, by the preaching of sermons, the ringing of bells, the firing of guns, and the mounting of standards, is in reality one of those disgraceful events which stigmatize the wisdom of this nation.

Citizens, I took a considerable survey of the tyranny, the injustice, the artful falsehoods of that reign, together with the plots and conspiracies of *Charles* and his courtiers (*for kings and courtiers can be conspirators*! and indeed it is generally within the verge of courts that real conspiracies originate!) The innumerable calamities that were brought upon the country, the profligate expenditure of public money, the corruption introduced into every branch of the government, and all the mischiefs of this reign, it is not necessary for me now particularly to dwell upon. Suffice it to say, they were such as to compel the country in a few years after this restoration, to appeal to another revolution; to drive the brother of *Charles* the Second from the throne; to bastardize his son by a ridiculous act of parliament, and afterwards to cut him off the entail, and introduce another family to the throne.

Now, if we admit that revolutions are calamities, we must lament, also, those still greater and heavier calamities which necessitate a country to appeal to revolutions: and if we mean to say that the revolution in 1688, was justifiable, proper and necessary, we pronounce the *restoration of the House of Stuart* a calamity: for whatever advantages resulted from the *Revolution in* 1688, (though whig historians boast that it cost no blood) it has deluged not only great portions of the British empire, but the whole of Europe with blood for near a century. To this circumstance we are to attribute a great part of the wars in which *Britain* since that period has been engaged, since the pretensions of French despotism (now so fortunately and happily overthrown) for interfering with this country to restore the House of *Stuart*, are certainly to be considered among the causes of those wars, which have produced so considerable a depopulation and so enormous a debt.

We are to consider, also, that though in *England* no bloody battles were fought for the maintenance of that revolution, yet that in *Ireland* there was a long train of battles, cruelties and horrors which imagination sickens to contemplate, and that *Scotland* was disgraced by the massacre of *Glencoe*[27] —a massacre which, in my opinion, fixes an indeliable stain upon the memory of *William*,[28] and is a dreadful drawback from that general applause so frequently poured upon him.

But, Citizens, this is not all. The *Revolution* in 1688, (glorious and happy as it was) did not entirely remove the calamities and mischiefs brought into this country by the restoration of the *Stuarts*. I shall take no notice now of the pretences made use of for perpetrating the innovation of a standing army. I shall take no notice of the perpetuation, and continual growth of that monstrous system of taxation called excise. Independent of these circumstances, the calamities produced by the profligate expenditure of public money by *Charles* the Second, did not die with him, with the debts that he contracted, or with the immediate mischiefs produced by his own personal extravagance.

At this time we continue to pay heavy and grievous taxes, in consequence of his licentious pleasures: among the vices of *Charles* the Second, good care is taken that we shall not forget his attachment to the Turkish fashion of keeping a grand seraglio.

Citizens, some Christian princes are Turks, some are Heathens, and some are Centaurs. Some Christian princes choose to keep grand seraglios, and some Christian princes choose to keep great studs, and heigho for Newmarket! and 300l. a day more than their revenue is expended; and some Christian princes choose to lock up million after million in their strong chest, to show their devotion to the god Plutus.[29] I shall, however, take the liberty of observing that neither grand seraglios, nor gambling at Newmarket, nor strong boxes are of any benefit to the people of this country; and that princes are then valuable and then only, when blending benevolence and liberality, and making prudence keep pace with generosity, that the nation may not be burdened with unnecessary taxes, they extend that revenue which is liberally granted them by the people, in rewarding independence, virtue and ingenuity; and, in short, to sum up all perfection in one short sentence, princes are only valuable when, like the present sovereign upon the throne, they dispense universal peace, happiness, and felicity through the country over which they reign.[30]

To return from this digression—having considered the calamities which resulted from the unfortunate restoration of the house of *Stuart*, let us now proceed to investigate the causes of that restoration.

People who have read in a superficial way—and sometimes even great ministers are very superficial fellows!—Persons who have read history superficially, observing the catastrophe of the *English Revolution* in 1649, are inclined to suppose that a similar catastrophe will take place in *France*; and that either the present Dauphin[31] will be restored to the throne, like the son of *Charles* the first; or else that some other *dynasty* will be set up by the great men of that country, and royalty be again triumphant in that nation. But Citizens before we jump into conclusions, let us look at our premises; let us see that there is no ditch on either side into which we may be in danger of falling, and breaking the neck of our logical reputation. Were the revolution of 1649 in *England* and of 1789 in *France* produced by similar causes? Are the circumstances of society in *France* now such as the circumstances of society in *England* were at that time? and have the same steps been taken or the same phenomena appeared in *France* during the present struggle as appeared in England during the struggle to which I am appealing? If we can answer these three questions in the affirmative, there is a strong presumption (be it remembered however it is nothing but a presumption) that a similar catastrophe will take place in France.[32]

Let us compare then the genius of the two revolutions.—The English revolution in 1649 was produced not so much by the luxury, the extravagance, and the profligacy of the court, together with a state of bankruptcy in the nation, as it was by certain causes, powerful indeed in their operation, but confined in their immediate action to a narrower sphere. The plain and simple truth is, that since the overthrow of our Saxon institutions, the sun of Liberty had never shone, with unclouded beams, upon this unhappy country. A band of *Norman robbers* had laid prostrate at their feet every thing that looked like law and justice. They had trampled down both liberty and property, and seizing every thing into their own arbitrary hands, had dispensed again to the original proprietors part of those lands, tenements and effects, in vassalage; and thereby held the country in progressive links of slavery, from the greatest baron to the poorest peasant who was sold, like the cattle, with the estate upon which he laboured, and treated with more indignity than the very tools he worked with. In process of time, the rising spirit, first of the nobility, afterwards of the country gentlemen, and after that of the trading interest of the country, made considerable encroachments upon the tyranny which the Normans had established. It was fortunate, also, for the country, that some of the memorials of ancient liberty were still in existence: some of the maxims of common law (which certainly afford the only foundation there is for boasting of the particular excellency of our system of jurisprudence) still survived the general wreck; and from these fragments men began to comprehend what the structure was when entire, and were eager to build again that Gothic shrine of Liberty, beneath which their ancestors had once lived in happiness and security.[33] Time after time, the contentions between the kings and the great barons gave the people opportunities of recovering part of their rights. It happened, however, that the progress of information was more rapid than the progress of political improvement.

When literature began to dawn over the western hemisphere, knowledge (though we were rather late in hailing the sacred beam) was not entirely neglected in England. In the reign of Elizabeth, who certainly was not less tyrannical than most of her predecessors, yet, as letters became considerably cultivated among particular classes of society, mankind began to awake from their lethargy; and though, under her vigorous administration, they were not strong enough boldly to demand their rights, yet the growth and progress of literature enabled them, under the succeeding reigns, to claim, with a firmer tone, a restoration of the ancient rights of *Englishmen*. They succeeded in a considerable degree, time after time, in the work of political amelioration. Unfortunately at that time, however, the light of science was diffused only through a narrow circle: it had broken down, indeed, the walls of cloisters and monastaries: it had travelled beyond the studies of bishops and great peers; and the gentry of the country began to think that it was no disgrace to be able to read and write. But unfortunately the great mass of the people were not enlightened; and therefore we find that, in the reign of *Charles* the First, the people were only led forward by a few intelligent minds—men of great capacity and great personal courage, who led on the people, not so much by disseminating information, as by that dependence in which, on account of their large property, they continued to hold such a large proportion of the country.

There was, however, a very *active spirit* of another kind among the people. They had light indeed (inward light) which, though it came not through the optics of reason, produced a considerable ferment in their blood, and made them cry out for that liberty, the very meaning of which they did not comprehend. In fact, the mass of the people were quickened, not by the generous spirit of liberty, but by the active spirit of fanaticism. Such, then was the state of society at the time of the Revolution, that terminated in the first stage in 1649, and in the second stage with the restoration of *Charles* the Second. Among the leaders who stood forward, and signalized themselves in that cause, there were certainly men whose virtues, courage, and transcendent talents, will demand admiration, so long as the *English* language shall exist. It is to be lamented, however, that all the characters in that revolution were not men of equal virtue. I need only name *Oliver Cromwell*;[34] who, though he set out perhaps, with as large a portion of the love of liberty as was possible for a hypocritical fanatic, yet undoubtedly in the end proved himself to be, not a reforming patriot, but an ambitious usurper. Unfortunately, however, the state of the public mind was such, that the hypocritical pretender to divine inspiration could lead a larger portion of the people with him, than those men whose pure and enlightened spirit was dictated to by the philosophic principles of liberty and universal justice. Indeed, it will generally happen that men who are capable of flattering the prejudices of those whom they wish to make instruments of their ambition, will be more successful than those upright individuals, who, disdaining to feed the expiring lamp of error, endeavour, with the strong breath of reason, to extinguish every sentiment injurious to human happiness.

We must, however, take things as they are. When a nation has the misfortune to be plunged into such a situation, it must seize all the advantages it can. It can have no other rudder than its own energy, and ought to have no other.—But it is necessary to dwell a little longer upon the character of *Oliver Cromwell*, he having been a principal actor in some of the most important scenes at that period exhibited on the theatre of Europe and possessing, even at this day, many enthusiastic admirers, who do not scruple to uphold him as the greatest champion that Liberty ever had in this country. I cannot see him in that point of view. I cannot read the historians of that day, without feeling a conviction that, at the latter period of his life at least, ambition became his predominating motive, to which he sacrificed every principle of justice and public welfare. Be this as it will, *Oliver Cromwell* was a very considerable actor in the revolutions of that period, and therefore his character and capacities form a considerable part of the argument to be brought forward on the present evening. What, then, was *Oliver Cromwell*? What was the size and capacity of his mind? and what were the projects in which he was engaged, and the nature of the system which he attempted to establish?—The acuteness of Cromwell's talents cannot possibly be denied. Every person who peruses the history of the period, will perceive that, through every stage of his political conduct, he always seized, and turned to his own advantage, every political event, whether in the first instance apparently prosperous or disastrous, that occurred. He had therefore a mind not only bold and enterprising, but capacious, versatile, and penetrating. It could seize occasions when they presented themselves: it could create them, when they did not. It could controul the genius of his enemies, and turn their projects, nay, even their very successes, to his own advantage. He was therefore never at a loss for expedients necessary for the propping of his own authority; and for supporting, so long as he himself existed to direct it, the system which he wished to support; a system by which he became the first man in this country, and the terror of all Europe. But *Cromwell* was always obliged to depend upon the expedients of the moment. The whole *system* of *his* government—I should say the whole *history* of his government—for I mean to shew you that there was nothing like system in it!—the whole history of his government is nothing but a history of expedients, to which he appealed under the particular circumstances in which he was placed. He was now building up one sort of legislature, and then pulling it down: now setting up another, and then pulling that down again: then erecting a house of mock Lords, and then pulling them down again; just as the exigencies of the moment prompted. Thus the *Protectorate*, or, as it is called, the Republic, continued as long as he lived, because the superior *activity* of his mind, the terror of his name, and that sort of fanatic eloquence which he possessed, kept all other persons in awe; and, so long as the architect remained, the pillars of the revolution appeared to be secure, whatever change might take place in particular parts of the building. But *Cromwell* had not a mind capable of calculating upon the passions of mankind in the mass, nor of viewing in distant prospect the events and causes likely to influence the politics of future years: he was therefore incapable of forming a system that could be rendered permanent, and contribute to the advantage either of his own particular family, or of the nation in general. Accordingly, we find that this government of expedients crumbled into dust as soon as he expired: the plain and simple fact being, that every thing rested, not upon digested principles, which are permanent and durable; but merely upon his shoulders; therefore, of course, no sooner did he fall, than anarchy and debility were exhibited in every part of the state; and the nation, destitute of able and popular leaders, and wearied with incessant fluctuations, was driven to seek repose again in its ancient despotism.

Thus, then, the revolution in 1649 was not the revolution of the great body of an enlightened nation, but a revolution produced in the first instance by a few intelligent minds, who stimulated the people to act upon principles which they did not comprehend, and was afterwards supported upon the shoulders of an individual, whose talents, though equal to the task of supporting the weight he had taken upon them, were not sufficient to frame a system by which that weight could be supported, when he was taken away.

There is another circumstance also of considerable importance, relative to the revolution of 1649; and by means of which *Cromwell* was enabled to usurp the dominion of the country.

Citizens, there are two species of popularity upon which power may be built, independent of that power which is vested by ancient opinion and hereditary succession: namely, the popularity obtained in the senate, and the popularity obtained in the field of battle. The former of these is obtained by the intrepidity with which the senator steps forward, upon all occasions, to strip the mask from pretended patriotism, to lay the axe to the root of corruption, and point out to the people the means by which that corruption can be remedied. The other kind of popularity is also ex-

ceedingly important in times of tumult and confusion: I mean the popularity of the soldier, who shows himself ready to shed his blood in the field
of battle, in defence of his principles; and, feeling a conviction of the
propriety of the cause in which he is embarked, proves, by his actions, that
no danger can impede him, no prospects of death intimidate him.—Now,
Citizens, these two kinds of popularity, for the benefit and advantage of
the people, in times of revolution in particular, ought to be kept separate;
for, when they are united, they throw so great a weight of influence into
the hands of the individual so uniting them, that he always eventually
possesses the power, and generally makes use of it, of overthrowing the
liberty for which he appeared to contend, and usurping to himself that
tyranny which in the first instance he professed to overthrow.

Cromwell possessed this united popularity. He had spoken for the people,
and braved all the dangers of being their champion, in the senate; he had
exposed his breast, with manly resolution, to the daggers of courtiers, the
intrigues of crown lawyers, and the insolent usurpations of those who, because they possess all power, think they have a right to dispense with all
law. In defiance of these, he had dared to step forward, to vindicate the
insulted rights of Britain; and had been successful, in his senatorian exertions, in rousing the people to a manly and virtuous resistance. Cromwell
also was a leader of armies: he fought for the cause for which he spoke: he
conquered in that cause, and thus attached to himself the united popularity
of the citizen and of the soldier; and thereby obtained an ascendancy
which must inevitably endanger the liberties of a nation, and put the individual in possession of the means of grasping the tyranny.

Such, then, were part of the causes of the weakness of the revolutionary
principle in *Britain*. Such were, in part, the causes of the power which
Cromwell possessed, of usurping dominion in the country, instead of establishing liberty and justice.

Seeing, thus, what was the genius and nature of the revolution in 1649;
and perceiving that it was propt in the first instance only by a few, and in
the latter period only by an individual man, we cannot be surprized (the
leaders of that revolution being cut off, and the great prop and support of it
having fallen beneath the stroke of fate) that the revolutionary spirit became extinct; and that the house of *Stuart* was restored, with all those
disgraceful appendages of unlimited power; which that house of *Stuart*, to
its own destruction, exercised upon this harrassed and insulted nation.

Now let us consider the genius and spirit of the *French revolution*.—
Having been so particular in describing the genius and spirit of the revolu-

tion in 1649, it perhaps may not be necessary for me to enter into the same detail with respect to the revolution of *France*. You will immediately perceive that the same causes which produced the revolution in 1649, did not produce the revolution in *France*; that the causes which enabled *Oliver Cromwell* to usurp a tyranny over this country, and make himself Protector, do not exist, nor ever have existed, at any period of the French revolution; and, finally, you will perceive this still more material difference, that the revolution in France is built upon the broad basis of public and almost universal opinion, and is therefore materially different from the revolution in 1649 in this country. We have therefore no foundation whatever to expect a similar catastrophe to that which took place in this country. Where causes are dissimilar, the effects cannot be the same; for effect and cause would be nonsense, if we did not admit that the one is the inevitable consequence of the other: that is to say, that every cause must be proportioned to its effect, and every effect proportioned to its cause; and that therefore, where the causes are different, the effects cannot be the same, and where the causes are the same the effects cannot be dissimilar.

But I shall not satisfy myself with this abstract statement of the question. Let us review the nature and genius of the revolution in France; let us survey the nature of the causes which produced that revolution in the first instance.

The extensive despotism of France had its peculiar characters, originating from the circumstances under which it was placed. It was a despotism, in some degree, of a liberal nature. It was, it is true, very tyrannical as to its political operation; but it was, at the same time, in this respect liberal— that it encouraged the diffusion of knowledge, the cultivation of science, the improvement of literature; and accordingly, philosophical truths, and abstract speculations on government, were spread through a much wider circle in France, previous to the commencement of the revolution, than there were through this particular country at the commencement of the revolution of 1649.

I do not pretend to say, for I do not believe, that, at the time the revolution broke out in France, political information was as widely and as generally diffused as in this country at this time. If there had been, I believe, the calamities and mischiefs that have taken place in France would have been in a considerable degree avoided. But whether this is the case, or not, certain it is, that the despotism of *France* was not built upon as general an ignorance as the usurpations of the house of Stuart were in this country. Accordingly, when the Revolution broke out there, the light of political science flew with greater rapidity, and through a wider circle, than during the revolution in this country: for, when the middle orders of the people, or a considerable proportion of the middle orders, are informed, they quickly disseminate information throughout the mass. The whole mass being quickened, the whole mass acted—not for a faction, but for themselves. They did not blindly follow a few particular leaders, to whom they were attached: they were themselves the revolutionary principle; and they created the leaders who afterwards conducted them to the objects they had in view.

But this is not all. The *immediate causes of the revolution in France* were very different from those in England. A general bankruptcy had been produced, by unnecessary wars and profligate expenditure. No longer able to procure the revenue by which their system of tyranny was to be carried on, the government was obliged to appeal to the great body of the people, and set questions afloat, which, under no other circumstances, could have been so widely agitated. Another cause was, the universal detestation drawn upon the *French* royal family, by their extravagance, dissipation, and total contempt of the interests, welfare, and good opinion of the nation. This, also, was another cause which provoked general investigation. Profligacy and bare-faced vice, extravagance and unqualified dissipation, are circumstances which strike immediately upon every mind: they provoke enquiry, from the chateau of the noble to the cottage of the peasant. The very labourers in the field, the ploughmen at their homely toil, and the mechanics labouring in their shops, seize the opportunity of investigating the questions that result from this extravagance, and consequent dissipation of the public money.

There were, it is true, a variety of other causes. It is not necessary, however, for me to run through them. Suffice it to say, the aristocrats of *France* themselves, who fled to this country on account of the downfall of despotism—even that raving and frantic aristocrat *Montgaillard*[35] himself, acknowledges that the revolution in *France* does not depend upon the popularity of particular leaders: that it is the *Sans Culotism* (that is to say, the great mass of the people quickened to a sense and indignation of the wrongs and injuries they have suffered) which is the vital principle of that revolution, and that their most conspicuous leaders, and even *Robespierre*, might go to the guillotine, but the revolution remain unmoved. In other words, it is not the revolution of *Marat* or *Robespierre*—it is not the revolution of *Brissot* and the *Girondists*—it is not the revolution of the Abbe *Seyes*,[36] or of *Tallien*,[37] and *Bourdon of Oise*[38]—but the revolution of the people. Their souls were altered, their habits were altered, their modes of thinking were altered, their capacities of acting were altered,—there was an universal moral revolution throughout the country; and, whenever an universal moral revolution takes place, no power on earth—no power of human combination, though leagued with the fiends below, (if fiends there are) can prevent political revolutions also, or overturn a revolution standing upon such a basis. The whole substrata of political institution is in such case affected, and therefore every atom of political existence must be annihilated before that revolution can be destroyed, or the principle of despotism can be restored, in a country where such events have taken place.

You see, Citizens, the aristocrats themselves are compelled to furnish us with these arguments. In short, if you wish to be a thorough democrat, read every aristocratic book that is published: Begin with *Burke's* Reflections, for I declare to you, that it was not *Tom Paine* but *Edmund Burke* that made me so zealous a reformer, and convinced me of the necessity of annual Parliaments and universal suffrage. Read the aristocratic works of *Arthur Young*: take for their comment, if you please, the democratic works he published[39] before he got a *place*, that they may explain each other. Read the works of the French Emigrants, and learn every word of *Montgallaird*[40] by heart; and if you are not convinced by what he has written, to persuade this country to continue the war, that it is vain and fruitless, take my lungs for a pair of bellows to blow an alchymist's fire withal.

They may keep up, by their infernal system of bribery, the ferment and discontent in *Paris*, but if they had levelled *Paris* with the dust, that work will convince you their business would be yet to begin. It is impossible to tread out or exterminate the spirit of liberty, sometimes enlightened, and sometimes mistaken, but always warm and ardent, which glows in that country.

But, Citizens, there are other circumstances which tend to prevent, in the first place, the usurpation of a protector in *France*; and, in the second place, the restoration of royalty; namely, that in the whole progress of the *French Revolution*, the senatorial popularity has never been united with the military. No one man has been, at the same time, a great leader in the convention, and a great leader in the field of battle; and I have no doubt in the world but that the French people will take care that no one man ever shall concentrate in his person so dangerous an accumulation of political and physical power.[41] This being the case, the popularity is divided, the attachments and influence are divided, and the consequence is, that there is no blind and implicit bigotry in the people, no unbounded authority in any leaders. Fortunately for the French nation they have got a little way past superstitious bigotry to particular names: their devotion is fixed upon principles. In those principles they may be sometimes mistaken: but their errors more frequently proceed from the passions and vices engendered by the old despotism, and which impel them to an opposition to their own principles. But it is principle they are in pursuit of, and not individual men; and therefore standing upon the faith of no individual, no individual can betray them; and all that the powers in alliance can do is to hire so many men for the guillotine—bribe them to sacrifice their own lives, and endeavour to bring a stain upon the revolution of France, which ultimately must be brought home to the person in whom that criminality originated: and woe to the man who shall be obliged to stand at the bar of his country and answer to the dread account.

But, Citizens, there is another circumstance that tends to convince me that royalty will not be restored in *France*: and much as I esteem and venerate royalty in *England*, I shall venture to declare that I hope and trust, for the welfare of mankind, that monarchy never will be restored in *France*. I will tell you why. I am going to broach a bold opinion: for it stands in opposition to the generally received maxim which people who call themselves philosophers, and gain credit as such by retailing stale maxims, without examining them. In spite of all the grave faces of these gentry, I shall venture to assert, that a country so large and extensive as *France*, never can be vigorously and virtuously governed but by a republican constitution.

Having thrown down this gauntlet, I shall now bring forth the weapon with which I mean to maintain my challenge. It has generally been upheld, that a republican form of government is only suited for a small territory.[42] This maxim is, I believe, 2000 years old; but I could mention some palpable absurdities that are 5 or 6000 years old. I could mention some that, if you will believe the writers in support of them are 40 or 50,000 years old. But antiquity is no test of truth: add to which, words change their meaning in the process of time, and the maxim originally being true, might become false in the new signification of the terms. What did the ancients mean by a democratical republic? Why they meant a country in which every individual citizen throughout the state assembled when public business was to be transacted, and voted and debated in his own person. If that is the only meaning of a democratic republic it is granted at once that the country must be very small in which it can prevail. But that is not the meaning of the word republic in modern acceptation: by republic we now mean a government so constituted and organised that the whole body of the people may convey their will to the heart and centre of government, and by means of representatives and properly appointed officers, conduct the business of the country according to the general voice of the people.

Now let us examine what are the impediments to the establishment of such a government over a large territory. Let us next examine the nature of limited monarchy: and then proceed to this great question, whether limited monarchy can exist in a territory so large as *France*.

Citizens, perhaps I shall be obliged to be a little dry and prolix in making my meaning clear: for when we have new ground to tread, we must be more cautious than when we are pursuing the beaten path. But let us consider what is the nature and operation of government. Every territory consists of centre and circumference. If the circumference is small, a small power can be extended all round it: if the circumference be large and the government merely central, as is the case with all regal governments, a very great power must exist in the centre, or the extremities must be in positive anarchy. Well then, what do we mean by despotism? and what do we mean by limited monarchy? By despotism we mean a government so energetic that it can strike even to death at any extent of the country, and produce obedience by terror. By a limited monarchy, we mean a country in which the governing or central power is restrained—that is to say, it is not so strong but what the other parts of the constitution, and particularly the great body of the people, can put *a peaceable, but yet efficacious restraint* upon it. For the *monarchy is not limited with respect to its operations upon the people, unless the people have a power of checking and restraining it to a certain degree.* To talk of a limited power that cannot be controuled, would be the most absurd nonsense imaginable. Well then, let us consider in the next place what a republic is. I have already defined it to be a government in which the power is diffused and extended through the whole body of the people. Every part of the state has of course its due share of governing power and principle essential to its own particular preservation: in other words, though for the perfection of its organization and unity of its operations with respect to foreign powers, it has a visible and acknowledged centre, the republican government is in fact omnipresent throughout the whole extent of the empire.

Having thus defined the *mode of operation* in the three forms of government, a little consideration would lead us to expect, and a little experience will convince us that the expectation is well founded, that under every species of monarchic government, the extremities or distant provinces of the empire must always be under a more rigid controul than the centre. Thus accordingly we find that a justice of the peace in a distant territory has more power to crush any individual or set of individuals, or to check the progress of investigation, than the whole Privy Council with all its powers and authorities at its back ever can exercise in the capital: accordingly you find that bolder enquiry and a more liberal communication of the heart exists always in the capital than it does in the provinces of every nation. This is the case however small the territory may be. This is the case even in the *British* empire, and accordingly we find that the judges of *Scotland* could dare to pronounce, and the aristocracy of *Scotland* to give countenance and occasion to the pronouncing sentences so monstrously illegal that the very hearts even of aristocrats in *England* revolted at them.[43]

Why is this? Because public opinion rallies round the centre of government, and wherever public opinion rallies round, there will be a certain degree of check and controul upon the operations of government: for after all, it is impossible to prevent enlightened intellect from having its effect, whatever may be the disposition of particular persons to destroy that intellect, or prevent its dictates from being known.

Another circumstance is that a monarchic government, whether limited or absolute, acts in its proper person only in the centre. It may have, and it has its deputed authorities and delegated functionaries; but its *proper force* is exerted only in the capital and its environs. In proportion as government approaches to individuality, its native influence or authority must become confined to the sphere and compass of individual observance and exertion.

Well, then, it must delegate its powers to others, to act in the extremities of the country. It must have certain appendages, certain subordinate governors, who in the distant provinces of a large empire, must cause the law (or will of the sovereign, where that happens to be law—and precious law it generally is) to be carried into execution.—Now either the functionaries in the provinces, must have a great degree of power, to execute the mandates of government, or they must have a small degree of power, and depend for the execution of them upon other means. Now if the delegated functionary has a small degree of power, it is evident that the distant parts of the country will be falling into anarchy, because in the distant provinces he cannot have that assistance from the immediate interference of the regular government which may be necessary in particular extremities to enforce order or adjust the fit expedients to the times. If on the other hand, his power is unlimited, which provincial governors generally seem to think they are, then there are two dangers. Either he may make use of that power in such a manner as to oppress and destroy the province over which he domineers, and then you have a limited government in the centre only and a despotism in the extremities, or he may make use of it in so lenient and popular a way as to attach the province to himself; and then who shall answer for his loyalty.

That great power must therefore be checked and controuled by one of these two means—(I speak of an individual, but remember it is equally applicable where the power is delegated to a body of individuals, and branched into a variety of hands) either the check must exist in the central government, or in the people. If in the people farewell to your limited monarchy, for you have established separate republics, and every province must become in effect a separate and independent state. If, on the contrary, it exists in your central government, then what must be the monstrous tyranny of that government? What must be the system of spies, assassins, and informers which must be employed in every part of that province to enable the central government to crush and destroy its agent? and how unjustly must this tyranny be occasionally exercised?

The result I think of all these considerations is, that if you have a regal government, in proportion as that territory is large, the monarchy must become absolute. For the extremities must be strong, and to have the extremities stronger than the centre is preternatural and must lead to dissolution. The government must, therefore, be strengthened beyond the possibility of controul, where the territory is very large: for it must be either dismembered, or become an absolute and perfect despotism. But a republican government, when fairly constituted, does not exist only in the centre. It exists in every part and portion of the empire: every province has its power of operating with respect to those circumstances which depend upon the immediate existing circumstances in its own boundary. Every province has the power of communicating its will to the centre. The government of a well regulated republic is in fact an organization of the whole mass: it is not an oppressive weight laid, according to the anecdote of Alexander the Great, and the Indian philosopher,[44] upon one part only, and which must therefore be laid just in the centre, to extend an equal influence to all the extreme parts: the weight and the elasticity are equal in all its parts. It is that sort of combination among the people, that sort of intelligence, communication, and organised harmony among them, by which the whole will of the nation can be immediately collected and communicated; and therefore there wants neither the tyranny in the distant provinces which must depress, nor the check and controul that would expose them to the probability of dividing.

Thus, then, is a republic the proper form of government for a large

territory like *France*. And when in such a territory, a republican government is once formed upon right principles, it bids fair for immortality,
especially now that by means of the liberty of the press, the whole must
quickly become informed: for ignorance is the parent of a servile disposition; and wherever intelligence is disseminated, the intrepid spirit, can
never be trampled down; and though a *Robespierre*, or any other tyrant,
may domineer for a time, in the stormy aera of revolution, his usurpation
must end in his own destruction.

Thus I conclude that the larger the territory the greater the necessity for
a republican system, on the principles of liberty and equality. The walls of
the ocean shutting us out from that extensive territory which *France* seems
destined to possess, if we have virtue, and a steady determination, while
we revere the monarchy, and put up with the aristocracy, not to forfeit our
democratic rights—we may preserve a limited monarchy. But in such a
country as *France* there are but two things to choose, either absolute despotism, or absolute republicanism. Therefore, abhorring despotism from my
soul, I cannot but hope, that *France* will, by becoming a free and independent republic, break the fetters of prejudice in which the understandings of
mankind have so long been bound by the erroneous maxims of a too much
reverenced antiquity.

THE TRIBUNE. No. XLVII.
A WARNING VOICE TO THE VIOLENT OF ALL
PARTIES; *with Reflections on the Events of the* FIRST DAY
of the present SESSION *of* PARLIAMENT; *and an Enquiry*
whether CONCILIATORY *or* COERCIVE MEASURES *are*
best calculated to allay POPULAR FERMENTS. *Delivered*
Friday, Nov. 6, 1795. [45]

CITIZENS,

THE war-hoop of faction once more resounds through this distracted
country; and persecution is about to rage, perhaps, with more ferocity than
ever. No sort of toleration it seems is to be allowed by persons of one class
to those of another. Those, in particular, who are in power, and possess
the offices of magistracy, seem to be infected with a baleful anxiety who
shall be foremost in singling out the stigmatized reformer for destruction;

and in exercising the new authority which they seem to think may be created by those *edicts of the cabinet, called royal proclamations*. With so little moderation is this power exercised—with so little discretion, that even the man who lifts his voice in behalf of moderation, and wishes to allay the furious passions of the times is singled out as an object of indignation; and even to talk of warning "the violent of all parties", of the danger of their furious prejudices is regarded as a crime not to be endured.[46] The poor bill sticker who stuck the bills of this day, has been seized by the merciless hand of power, and thrown into prison.[47]

Still, however, unmoved by resentments, uninfluenced by any sentiment but that love of mankind which inspires in the enlightened breast an ardent enthusiasm for liberty, once more I step forward to warn you with the voice of reason and candour to allay the furious tempests of passion which seem to threaten the total dissolution of all social virtue: and chiefly on you, my fellow Citizens, embarked in the great cause of liberty—on you I call with confidence: by you at least I expect, that the voice of warning will not be heard in vain. Let reason, I pray you, be your sole guide in that pursuit of parliamentary reform which I trust you will never abandon but with your lives. Believe me, Citizens, in all the situations in which man can be placed, in all circumstances of society, moderation, well understood, is the first of virtues. The exercise of this virtue dignifies the character of man, and lifts him from that brutal state to which ignorance and aristocratic fury would degrade him.

But, Citizens, however useful this moderation in all the circumstances of society, it is particularly necessary at a time when persecuting fury endeavours to deprive us at once of our rights and faculties, and to provoke us by every species of irritation and insult into excesses and tumults which might furnish pretences for the usurpations of a corrupt and vicious administration.

When I speak of moderation, however, understand, I pray you, the sense in which I use the word. Properly understood it describes one of the greatest virtues that adorn humanity: but it has frequently been abused to the most corrupt and vicious purposes. The hypocrite, or the coward, who dares not look any principle in the face, and pursue it through all its moral consequences, or a part of whose system of politics it is, to confound for party purposes, all distinctions between right and wrong, talks of moderation and abandons truth. This is not the sort of moderation I wish you to adopt: this is a moderation I abhor: I would rather be at once the prostituted pander of corruption, than the sneaking half-way *moderé* who bawls for liberty and yet shrinks from the manly investigation of rights and principles.

Principle, glorious principle, eternal, immutable principle, should be the standard around which the friends of liberty should always rally. Round this standard then let us rally in the present hour. Like the *Spartan* at his landmark, to whom I have frequently alluded, let each man stand inflexible at his post; and though the fury of persecution should heap all the rubbish of perverted law upon him, till mountains of oppression lifted upon mountains bury him for ever,—a monument of persevering virtue.

Yes, Citizens, let us come to a determination rather to die than to abandon the glorious privilege of liberty; but let us die like the *Spartan* I have alluded to, not like ruffians and banditti; let us shew what we are ready to endure in a good cause; not what we are anxious to inflict. It was said yesterday at the meeting in commemoration of Hardy's acquittal, by that veteran in the cause of liberty, *Horne Tooke*, that "we should resist oppression (and while we have life oppression shall be resisted) but it must be the resistance of the anvil to the hammer."[48] It was as well replied by another Citizen, that perhaps the time might be near when something more than the resistance of the anvil to the hammer would be necessary. Citizens, that time is already arrived; and I will tell you what this further resistance is: it is not the resistance of violence and fury; but the resistance of an honest enthusiasm, that, peaceably and boldly advances through every danger, and determines to reiterate, instead of relaxing its virtuous efforts for the emancipation of the human race. Let us not be merely stationary. Let us boldly advance to the heights of principle. Let us go forward in knowledge, truth, and justice; and I defy the utmost pride and insolence of persecuting power to prevent the ultimate attainment of our object.

But let us not think we are getting forward, if we plunge into headlong violence. Mark, I pray you, the state of the public mind: do we seem as near the attainment of our object now as we were before these unhappy excesses took place, which will form in a great part the investigation of this evening? In principle, then, not in violence I would have you get forward. In active exertion of mind, not in tumult, I would have you advance. Now is the time to cherish a glowing energy that may rouse into action every nerve and faculty of the mind, and fly from breast to breast like that electric principle which is perhaps the true soul of the physical universe, till the whole mass is quickened, illuminated and informed.

Think not, Citizens, that I address this invocation to one sect or party of men alone: I would have the same zeal glow in every breast, so it be attem-

pered with the same moderation. Remember it is candour, it is the philosophical conviction at once of the dignity and of the fallibility of human
intellect that should stimulate us to enquiry.

Our moderation ought not to be the consequence of a fear that dares not
look principle in the face: it ought not to be a consideration of danger to
ourselves: it ought to be the fruit of candid research: it ought to spring from
a deep-felt conviction that judgment is fallible; but, at the same time that
there is no guide more infallible. The same moderation you expect from
your opponents, therefore, that moderation you are expected to exercise
towards them. Nay, I will go farther—moderation and candour ought to
proceed from us especially. We are the party who pretend to be making
discoveries in the regions of truth and political justice. We profess to have
surmounted prejudices: shall we then, by our intemperance, shew that we
are still prejudiced? We complain of the intolerance and persecuting spirit
of the old system: shall we then shew that we are ourselves intolerant? We
complain of wars, of bloodshed and of violence: shall we shew by our conduct that we are also violent and sanguinary? Do we wish to make proselytes to the principles we have adopted? Let us shew by the calmness and
reasonableness of our deportment the confidence we have in the truth and
justice of our cause. Mankind are prone to believe, and I suspect they are
right, that where there is violence there is no heart felt conviction of
truth. Could we really shew this principle in all its naked loveliness, its
irresistible charms must gain the affections of all. We have nothing, therefore, to do but patiently to strip off the cumbrous sophisms with which it
has been disguised, and our work is done. But if we endeavour to tear them
away with impassioned hands, we maim and disfigure our principle, and
create disgust, instead of fixing attention, and conviction can never be
expected. Of those who are now the antagonists of political truth; how
many are only so because they have had no opportunity of candid examination? Let us allure them by our candour—Let us convince them by the
unruffled mildness of our conduct, that our principles are not of that terrible nature which they have been represented. Let us convince them, by
the striking contrast of our behaviour, who are the foes and who are the
friends of order and humanity.

Citizens, it is easy to demonstrate that there needs no stronger argument
that a man has not a perfect conviction of the truth and justice of his
principles, than his being anxious to appeal to violence: for if we believe
that our principles are true, and those of our opponents' false, what can we
desire better than the peaceful opportunity of bringing principle against

principle fairly into the field? Under such circumstances truth must bear away the palm of victory.—Have we any doubts upon this subject? Let us appeal to our own breasts. Who that hears me has not felt at different times different sentiments upon the same subject? Where is the man who calls himself a champion for the rights and liberties of man who cannot recollect a time when he did not see the question in the same forcible points of view? We must be children in intellect as well as limb before we can be men. It is only by exercising intellect in the one case, as our limbs in the other, that we can attain the upright dignity of manhood. I freely acknowledge that I recollect the time when my mind, swaddled in religious and aristocratic prejudices, struggled under the imbecillity of passion against those who differed from me upon dogmas which I had never before examined; and indeed because I never had examined them. Shall I now then show the same blind fury against all who disagree with me? If I do, then instead of rising from error to truth and knowledge, I have only changed from ignorance to ignorance; and end the same blind bigot I began. Let me appeal to the judgement of others, if the history of their minds exhibit not similar changes.

Among the most enlightened friends of liberty I believe I could point out material changes of opinion. How was this change produced? By persecuting fury? Perhaps it was. Perhaps they were dragooned into the opinions they now hold: but it was by the persecuting fury of those with whom they formerly corresponded in sentiment, but who repelled them by their unjust and irrational conduct. Persecution does indeed make converts; but it is *from*, not *to*, the cause it endeavours to uphold.

If, then, you have changed your opinions, it is because the arguments in behalf of your former prejudices were feeble and yielded to the superior force of the arguments of liberty. It is therefore that you have abandoned old prejudices, and have become the advocates of what is called a new system: that is to say, the glorious system which says, one human being, not disqualified by crime, is as worthy in the eye of justice as another, and ought to be so in law; and that although property ought to be secured to him who by his industry and talents has obtained it, yet there is no reason why his property should give him the liberty of tyrannizing over and oppressing those who have been less fortunate.

Well, then, Citizens, let this warning voice ring in every ear; that *violence can but lead to destruction!* Let aristocrat and democrat be alike convinced that if he has truth on his side he need only bring forward that truth in plain and unsophisticated language, and he will be sure to make converts: but that, if he is supporting the cause of falsehood, force and coercion will be in vain. They may awhile keep off the day of reform, but truth, virtue, and justice must ultimately be acknowledged. Let it be remembered, also, that if the demands of the reformers are just, to keep off the day of payment instead of mending the matter only makes it worse. It is adding all the consequences of litigation to the first demand; and woe to those who may thereby be thrown at last into the power of the irritated and defrauded creditor.

As for us, if we are not convinced that we have truth on our side let us abandon our pursuit; but if we are convinced, as I trust we are, let us make use of reason as long as they will suffer us to reason. When they will not suffer us to reason it will be impossible for us to argue with our fellow citizens, and shew them the necessity of forbearing from violence; let what will ensue, therefore, the crime is with them who padlock the mind with unjust restrictions: but so long as we can use our reason, let us make the best use of it, by imprinting on every mind the necessity of investigation: and believe me, Citizens, if you have an anxious desire of knowledge you will find opportunities of improvement. The very coals burning in your grates will be eloquent in the exposition of oppressive corruption: every thing you eat, drink, or wear, will plead reform, and pronounce philippics against the burdens of taxation; and convince you how impossible it is for the great mass of mankind, under the present system, to obtain even common necessaries to support that strength and that toil, by which, and by which alone, the necessaries and enjoyments of life are created.

Read, Citizens, and think. If you read with attention, you will find matter enough for thought: and if you will not think, it is to no purpose that any man should exhaust his health and strength in inculcating the principles of truth and justice. I do not profess to make judgments for you—I do not pretend to create understandings—I do not pretend to implant even principles upon your minds—all that I can hope is to rouse and stimulate you to enquiry. And if you will but think, though the voice of all discussion were sealed up—though every book were destroyed, you will soon be convinced of the necessity of reform.

The glorious seeds of liberty are sown, and let oppression do its worst they will spring up in due season. *Charles I* shut up the coffee-houses, lest sedition, as it is called, should be talked: that is to say, lest the frequenters of those houses should dare to say that he was surrounded by sycophants, hypocrites, plunderers, and oppressors, who pretended to make him a great prince, but used their authority to destroy the people. But did this, or the persecution that ensued under the reign of *James II.* destroy the fruit of liberty? No. The elastic spring of British energy was not destroyed. The more it was compressed, the greater its reaction. The strong determination of awakened intellect drove the house of *Stuart* from the throne: and I hope every house that shall dare to tyrannise as the house of Stuart did will experience the same fate.

But who are the real authors of your oppressions? The ministers, and not the prince, are in reality guilty. Nay Pitt has told you that under *existing circumstances* he is virtual sovereign of Great Britain.[49] I say, Citizens, that this has been declared almost in express words. Mark his speech. He talks in a royal stile from beginning to end; and assumes to himself the whole dignity and importance of regal power. Here is a ministerial paper professing to quote his own words, marked with inverted commas, to shew that it has been taken verbatim. "If *I find*" (says Mr. PITT) "that all these facts, supported by the authority of the most intelligent Frenchmen, have contributed to *our* general welfare, and to the consequent improvement of our *affairs*, I cannot help expressing *my* astonishment, that any man should be bold enough to accuse *me* of insulting *my country*, when on that account *I declare* MY *satisfaction!*" ORACLE, *October 30.*[50]

Now this is said in the debate on the speech from the throne. This is said in reply to the animadversions made by Mr. Fox on the passage in that speech which professes so much satisfaction at the *improved state of our affairs upon the continent.* This satisfaction, therefore, and this speech Mr. Pitt takes home, at once, in the first person. "It is *I* who speak", says he, "it is *I* who declare MY satisfaction. Majesty is but my representative organ—my mouth-piece. I am King *Stork*; and I cannot help expressing my astonishment that any frog among you should be bold enough to croak out his disapprobation of my royal word!"

If this is not the stile of usurpation, what is it? Do I go too far, when I accuse him of having assumed to himself the stile of royalty?

Citizens, I have professed to treat this evening particularly upon the events of the first day of the present session of parliament. There are two parts of these proceedings which might be dwelt upon, to illustrate the necessity of that candour I have endeavoured to inculcate. I have already said something upon what passed in the inside of the House of Commons. I shall dwell more particularly on what passed without those walls. Upon this subject, as upon all others, there are two statements, made by the opposite parties. The aristocrat affirms, that the tumults of Thursday[51] originated in these lectures, and in the popular societies; and particularly the meeting at Copenhagen House.[52] The democrat, or reformer, affirms, on the contrary, that the tumults of Thursday arose from the bad conduct of the administration: from the present corrupt and profligate war, and that system of measures equally unconstitutional and unwise, which have plunged this country from misery to misery, into the abyss of ruin, till, at last, to close the great climax of human affliction, famine begins to stare us in the face; and our only way to remedy the scarcity of bread is to do without it. The aristocrat says, if you permit political discussion, treasonable lectures (as they are called) and seditious societies, where people enquire into their rights, and wrongs, the consequence will be tumult and disorder. The friend of liberty says:—if you oppress the people they will be tumultuous; if you ruin trade, you will turn numbers of families out of employment, and overwhelm the people with distress; and, in consequence, poor beings who know nothing but their distresses—no principle but the stimulus of want, will commit depredations upon society.

Now let us fairly investigate these two statements. Remember, Citizens, that the aristocrats have yet brought forward no argument whatever, to shew the connexion between political investigation and these disturbances. Perhaps they think assertion and authority better than argument, especially when they come from a man who wears a great wig in Westminster Hall or Lincoln's Inn. We have heard of a great number of persons being apprehended; and the magistrates, I conclude, would have been anxious enough to find it out, if it had been the case, and yet it does not appear that any of them were members of the popular associations. What is the conclusion? Why that political associations have prevented the outrage, since those only have been outrageous who were no members of them; and that, therefore, if every man had been in the habits of political enquiry no outrage would have happened. Political enquiry and association shew a better way of redress. Tumult only gives fresh handle to the minister for adopting measures of worse oppression. It is true that a proclamation insinuates, and that a great and learned authority of the law absolutely asserts that there was a connection between the meeting at Copenhagen-house and the tumult which took place four days afterwards. The learned Lord, indeed, to whom I allude,[53] makes a little mistake in order to support his statement; and says that the meeting was called the day before the meeting of Parliament: whereas the meeting took place on Monday, and it was not till Thursday that the tumult happened. Now, Citizens, what idea must we form of the inflammatory proceedings of a meeting that could keep the public mind without sleeping three whole days and nights till the opportunity should come to throw mud and stones against the gilt coach of majesty, and thus insult the sacred person and institution of royalty. Citizens, a part of these proceedings was a speech of an hour long on the necessity of using nothing but reason in the pursuit of reform, and a demonstration that every act of violence would only give the minister an opportunity to increase the chains and fetters of the people.[54]

But what are the arguments by which the democrat and reformer support this side of the question. The arguments are of two kinds, the deductions of abstract reason, and the experience of all ages, from the first period of history to the present hour. These will shew, that the persons fondest of violence are those who are most ignorant. Violence always begins either with those oppressors who wish to destroy all knowledge but their own, or among those who, though they can feel the oppression, can neither write nor read—among poor, harrassed, and degraded beings who have neither opportunities nor inclination for enquiry.

When WAT TYLER,[55] whose name has been so infamously slandered, and who, though an ignorant man (one of the swinish multitude!) had an honourable mind that disdained every subterfuge of art, and in the midst of triumph could trust his life in the hands of Kings, Lord Mayors, and Courtiers—who, to their honour be it remembered, assassinated him, because he did not chuse, when he had it in his power, to sacrifice them to an injured people! When *Wat Tyler*, and his insurgents, oppressed by the hardships brought upon them by mad and frantic crusades for the subjugation of France,[56] spread terror to the very recesses of the court; were these insurgents men of enquiry? Were they men who had been in the habit of political association? Were they members of *Corresponding Societies*, or did they attend *Lectures in Beaufort Buildings?* No, neither lectures in Beaufort Buildings, nor London Corresponding Societies then existed. Political associations were unknown; and the men who committed the violence had never heard of meetings for the discussion of political principles. Stung with the wretchedness and misery of themselves and families, and not having the knowledge or ability to seek redress by argument, they appealed to the only logic which the politics and institutions of the times permitted to the mass, the logic of clubs and long-bows of which (for they had hands) they could not be deprived.

Let the whole history of the universe be searched—what does it shew?— that the more savage and ignorant people have been, the more they were disposed to tumult and violence. Who are the men at this time most inclined to tumult and violence? How are quarrels settled by the various descriptions of men? Men of enquiry sometimes get warm in controversy, it is true; but their heat evaporates in a few expressions of intemperate passion: while persons not used to enquiry vent their fury by knocking down their antagonists, and rushing into battle and destruction. As for reformers, the men accused of being the instigators of the recent tumult, it has been proved to have been their constant maxim—"Let us venerate the laws, and an honest jury will defend us, even tho' law should be perverted, and lawyers leagued in phalanx for our destruction." I say, Citizens, it has always been our maxim—although the laws should be ever so bad (and where is the country that has not bad laws?—and why should we be so bigoted as to hazard those that are good, rather than reform the bad ones)—venerate the peaceable execution of these laws; but do all you can to reform them. I say the same of constituted authorities. Venerate them as long as they act consistently with the authority vested in their hands. Attack not the magistracy, even if you should not like that magistracy; for what right have you to attack that authority of which the uplifted voice of the people has not demanded the alteration? If you by violence assault the magistrate in the execution of his office, assassination, and not reform, must be the order of the day; and tumult and desolation must prevent that happiness of mankind which is the anxious wish of every true lover of the principle of equality and justice. The constituted authorities, while discharging the duties of their respective offices, must be regarded as the representatives of the law, and their persons of course are sacred, although, in their individual capacity, they are no more than other men. The wild Indians, in this respect, set us an example worthy of imitation. Having chosen their chief to lead them into battle, they yield him implicit obedience in the camp: but when they return to their cabins and their families, they want no such magistrate, and he is treated only as a comrade. It is not the man who is sacred, it is, in reality the office. I do not mean that you have a right to assault the magistrate at any time; but I mean to say that the veneration you owe to the magistrate is attached to him only while he is discharging the duties of his office: at all other times you ought only to regard him as a man and an equal.

I believe these opinions will be implanted on every enquiring mind. I believe every man that argues will abhor violence; and particularly that violence committed against the constituted authorities. I believe reason and enquiry will discover better means of redress.

The tumult arose, not in consequence of reason and enquiry, but from the misery in which the people are plunged. How great and aggravated this misery has been is proved from documents collected not for any purposes of party; by documents collected even by persons of aristocratic principles. Remember I have proved to you that a man now gets but a fourth part of those necessaries of life, by a day's labour, which he got 3 or 400 years ago by less labour. Remember I have proved to you that a man bought as much corn, as much beer, as much meat, as much cloathing for one day's labour, when he got but 2d for that day's labour, as now, when he gets 14d. Nay, the disproportion is still greater; for this was calculated from the state of facts in the year 1787: the necessaries of life are since increased two-fold; and, in many instances, a man must now labour 6 or 8 days to procure the necessaries that formerly he could procure for one day's labour. The result is, that the great body of the people are slaves; that they toil for arbitrary masters from morn to night; and almost from night to morn again; and get not even the common necessaries of life; but are obliged to go, with suppliant voice, to beg for that to which they are entitled as the reward of useful labour. Thus men having no longer the means of getting even a scanty subsistence, fly into tumult. But are these members of political societies? Where should they find even the small pittance that should keep up those societies, or pay for admission to these lectures? Oh! that I could extend my voice to those poor individuals whose necessities preclude them from attendance. I have no doubt that, if I could have an opportunity of collecting these lower and despised orders of society around me, from all the nations of the earth, that I should be able to persuade them to lay all dispositions to violence aside.

I am convinced that the arguments I could bring forward would be irresistible to minds uncorrupted by the arrogance and selfishness, which debilitates and exhausts the understanding of the higher orders. I am convinced that I could bring the conviction of truth to their minds; and that the tyrants of the earth would no longer be able to get military slaves to commit fresh murders to promote their ambition.

Regarding even this slight, hasty and imperfect sketch of the arguments on our side, it is obvious that it is not in consequence of political association—not in consequence of the investigation of the principles of truth and justice—not from pursuing parliamentary reform, that tumults and violence have taken place: but that they are to be attributed to that misery which renders enquiry impossible, because it takes from man the means of purchasing the knowledge which could illuminate his understanding. This misery, while it checks information, diffuses irritation: and the minister, to allay this irritation, aggravates the cause. A wise physician would, perhaps, apply palliatives—not provocatives. But palliatives are not in favour with our state quacks. In their whole political pharmacopoeia there is not a nostrum of this description.

The ministerial papers tell you that they foresaw the late disturbances;—that they saw inflammatory hand-bills about town, exciting to these excesses. If they did, why did not they send forth answers? Why did they not exhort the people to come peaceably and quietly, or to send their delegates peaceably and quietly to represent their grievances? that if they had wrongs justice might be done? But no—mark the only use they made of the foreknowledge; and then see which is most precious in the eyes of certain *supposed loyal persons*—the life of the monarch, or of the minister! A brave, honest and virtuous minister, aware that the indignation of the people were roused, would have asked his own heart, who roused that indignation? His own conscience must have convinced him that he was the man. If, therefore, there was any danger, and if he had any loyalty, he would have been the first to brave the tempest, that its fury having been spent his *royal* master might have passed in safety. But did he do so? Did the minister, whom the "*True Briton*" and *all* the ministerial papers tell you, knew of the tumult that was to happen—did he go first and expose himself as a brave man would have done, and have said, "Citizens—deluded Citizens—or, if he liked it better, deluded swinish multitude—why are you tumultuous? If any crime of government has caused your miseries, the guilt lies on me, not on that royal master whom I serve, and whom it is my duty to protect."

This candour, generosity, honour, and fortitude would have dictated; and that very honour, generosity and fortitude, would have disarmed resentment. But instead of this, he sends his royal master to the House, and stays behind himself, till he knows that the tumult is over; and then he sneaks to the House of Commons in a *hackney coach*! Is this the conduct of a man conscious of his own integrity? or is his zeal for royalty like his attachment to the constitution, which while he extols in verbose panegyrics, he is stabbing to the vitals—or his care for the protection of liberty and property, for the security of which he encourages *loyal associations* in every parish, while he himself is destroying the one to gratify his ambition, and plundering the other to carry on a mad and ruinous war?

Citizens, I shall dwell no longer upon this subject at present: but before I dismiss you, I shall say a few words on the crisis to which we are arrived. I feel the solemnity of the situation in which I stand. I feel the solemnity of the situation of my country. My heart grows too big for the breast that contains it. I feel it impossible even to restrain my voice or my feelings within that compass necessary for the preservation of my health—perhaps of my life. For the prolongation of my exertions, I wish I could command a moderation of feeling, as well as that candour and humanity I am endeavouring to inculcate. Fain would I discover the secret, by which, without losing one atom of the energy, I might restrain and moderate the strong emotions of my heart, that I might imprint the same truths upon your understandings, without doing any injury to my own frame. But if the two things cannot be united together—if this zeal and this energy cannot be exercised without this wreck of health and constitution, take what remains of this poor life; for I will not relax my exertions till uncontroulable force prevents their continuance.

The crisis approaches—the hour of trial comes, persecution and calumny usher it in; and however the storm may end, I must brave its fury. Rage and resentment I know are launched against me by the violent of both parties. While ministerial hirelings post me about the streets as a *miscreant*, and that scandalous and profligate paper called the "*Times*", accuses me with hiring the mob that committed the tumults of Thursday,[57] I am informed that the poor, infatuated, deluded people, at the east end of the town, who in the present hour of distress throng about the shops to buy for themselves the garbage and offal formerly consigned to dogs, and pay 4d a pound for bullock's liver, will turn sometimes indignantly away, and after first cursing the wicked administration that brought them into such miseries, will accuse me of preventing them, by my pacific doctrines, from redressing their grievances.

I know the danger of the situation in which I stand. I know that those whose designs are not honest, and those whose knowledge is not accurate upon the causes of our grievances, and the means of redress, will be indignant against the man who endeavours to arrest the up-lifted arm of violence, or calls on kindling vengeance to forbear.

For my part, however, my object is the peace, happiness, and welfare of society: I wish for the emancipation of the human race. I wish for equal rights, equal laws, and universal peace and fraternity, the branches and members of genuine liberty. In proportion, therefore, as the fury of the storm increases, as far as I am able, I will increase my efforts; and as I find in different parts of the town, the arm of authority is stretched forth to prevent political discussion, I will increase the frequency of discussion in this place as long as I have strength, and no absolute and determinate law forbids.

I shall, therefore, henceforward, continue my Lectures on Mondays, Wednesdays, and Fridays, and may the spirit of enthusiasm that glows in my breast spread through every audience, and by them be diffused through wider circles, till liberty, equality, and justice become the wish of every heart, and the theme of every tongue.

SOBER REFLECTIONS [1]

ON THE

SEDITIOUS AND INFLAMMATORY

LETTER

OF

THE RIGHT HON. EDMUND BURKE,

TO

A NOBLE LORD.

ADDRESSED TO THE SERIOUS CONSIDERATION OF HIS

FELLOW CITIZENS,

―――――

BY JOHN THELWALL.

―――――

" Next Anger rush'd—his eyes on fire,
" In lightnings own his secret stings." 2

―――――

LONDON:
PRINTED FOR H. D. SYMONDS, NO. 20, PATERNOSTER-ROW.

1796.

AS the following pages are intended, in some sort, as a reply to the inflammatory misrepresentations and incongruous principles of a recent pamphlet, from the elegant and abusive pen of Mr. BURKE, it might have
been expected, perhaps, that I should have followed the example of my
antagonist, by throwing my observations into the form of a letter, and
addressing it either to some great personage, or to that antagonist himself.
But it has long been a principle with me, that, as far as is practicable, at
least, in the state of society in which we live, our open profession and our
real object should always be the same; and I have been frequently disposed
to suspect that all colourable pretences, all habits of subterfuge, even in
circumstances of the most apparent indifference, have a tendency to
weaken the moral feelings, and produce a bias of mind eminently unfavourable to rectitude of judgment, and that enthusiastic attachment to the
cause of truth, which is, in reality, the noblest attribute of a cultivated
understanding. There is a manly and an independent energy of mind, encouraged by a scrupulous adherence, not only to the *essence*, but even to
the *shews* and *forms* of sincerity, which a friend of liberty ought to be
particularly zealous to preserve. I therefore address these animadversions on
one of the most extraordinary pamphlets that ever were published, openly
and avowedly to my fellow citizens, for whose advantage they are principally intended; and from whom, alone, I have the vanity to expect any
considerable portion of attention: for I have not the fortune (good or
bad—as "the zealots of the *old* sect in philosophy and politics",[a] may
choose to consider it) to be either the pensioned *dependant*, friend, or correspondent with any noble lord, with whose honours I might emblazon on
my title-page; and, as for Mr. *Burke* himself, the distemper of his mind is so
evident in every thing which of late years he has either said or written,
that it is impossible to expect from him the smallest degree of candid attention to the arguments of one whom, upon no better evidence than the
suggestions of his own furious prejudices, he stigmatises as "a wicked pander
to avarice and ambition".[b] The hydrophobia of alarm rages too fiercely in
his mind, to suffer him to wet his lips with the sober stream of reason, or
turn to the salutary food of impartial investigation. All is rage, and foam,
and headlong precipitancy; and the individual must be as mad as himself
who expects any thing but to be torn by his invenomed tooth, from an
attempt to stop him in his career, or turn him to the right, or to the left,
to examine the grounds over which he is so furiously running.

[a]Letter, &c. p. 1.
[b]Ibid. p. 47.

Let me, however, be understood: I apply this metaphor not in the bitterness of malevolence, but in the kindness of pity. I would not willingly—
even if my feeble lance were capable of piercing the seven-fold shield of
literary and aristocratic pride by which my opponent is defended,—I would
not wantonly tear with fresh wounds, a breast already bleeding with the
keenest anguish of paternal affection.[3]

Mr. *Burke* does not, perhaps, expect so much candour and moderation
from one whose principles are diametrically opposite to his own; and who
does not even shrink from the imputation of being a *Democrat*, a *Jacobin*, or
a *Sans Culotte*: (for it is too much the habit with the violent of all parties,
to suppose that there can be nothing virtuous or liberal in the character of
any man who is of an opposite principle to themselves): yet when I peruse
the pathetic passage in this beautiful, but mischievous letter, *I feel*, though
prejudice may not *believe*, that I can sympathise with the afflictions of an
enemy, even when, from that perversion, from which the finest understandings are not exempt, he happens, according to my judgement, to be
the enemy, also, of the human race. In one respect, also, I have ever been
ambitious of emulating the *chivalrous spirit* of our ancient heroes. I can
venerate the talents and enthusiasm employed against my own cause; and
(in the more liberal acceptation of the phrase) as *Shakespere* expresses it—

> "*Envy* their great deservings and high merits,
> Because they are not of our determination,
> But stand against us as an enemy."[4]

I should not, therefore, exult if Mr. *Burke's* "*feelings*" were, in reality,
what he calls them, "nearly extinguished";[a] I do not exult to find them, on
the contrary, the most irritable that ever burned (like a hot-ash) under the
frost of age: far less do I exult in those incongruities of mind, which exhibit
reason in its dotage, while the imagination is still rioting in all the vigour
and luxuriancy of youth. I bow with veneration to the gigantic powers of
his unwearied intellect; I gaze with rapture upon the splendid effusions of
his inexhaustible fancy; and I have not the savage ignorance to suppose
that if I had the will, or the power, to destroy his reputation, I could
transfer his genius to myself, or plant his honours upon my own brow. Nor,
indeed, when the subject is weighed in to important scale of effects and
consequences, have the friends of liberty any serious cause to lament his
exertions. The provocation of political discussion is the grand desideratum

[a]Letter, &c. p. 2.

for political improvement: and, so far is the gall of personal animosity from my pen, that, in the fervent sincerity of soul, I can exclaim—"Far, far may that period be removed, when fate or caprice shall inflict upon him either the silence of death, or the death of silence!"

I could wish, indeed, that a mind so rich, so cultivated, so powerful, were upon the side of truth: but if he will but write, take whatever side he will, I am sure that truth will be derived from his labours: for I defy Mr. *Burke*, or any other individual of penetrating and energetic mind, under what unfortunate delusion soever he may labour, to publish a pamphlet of eighty pages, without bringing forward some important observations, which, on account of their firm foundation in justice, will remain, while those which are false will be exposed and rejected by the discussion which such publications cannot fail of producing. Nay, the very absurdities and sophisms of a vigorous mind are subservient to just conclusion: for, from the energy with which they are expressed, they take fast hold upon the imagination, and compell the reflecting reader to give them that repeated revision which, unless the mind is very considerably warped by the strong bias of interested prejudice, cannot fail of conducting the enquirer to principles of liberty and justice.

In this point of view, the cause of liberty has essential obligations to the pen of Mr. *Burke*. He has written books which have converted such of his *disinterested* readers, as were in the habit of thinking for themselves, *from* the cause he endeavoured to uphold, *to* that which it was his object to overthrow; he has provoked answers, which, extending the boundaries of science beyond the narrow pale of opulence, have carried the invaluable discussion of political principles and civil rights to the shopboard of the artificer, and the cottage of the laborious husbandman; and his ungovernable phrenzy has hurried him into *expressions* and *epithets* so repugnant to every principle of justice and humanity,[a] and so revoltingly disgusting to the common sympathies of nature, as could not fail of producing a very general conviction, I will not say, as some have said, of the rottenness of his heart (for who shall judge of the *motives* of man, or set bounds to the omnipotency of self-delusion!) but of the weakness and injustice of that cause which could reduce such talents to the necessity of appealing to weapons so gross and so unmanly.

In this last species of warfare the fury of my present antagonist has been at least sufficiently seconded by the *metaphysical* phrenzy of his friend Mr.

[a]*Reflections*, &c.[5]

Windham. Indeed, if this *gentleman* had been *hired by the Jacobins of Paris to disgust all ranks of people* (placemen, pensions, and dependants alone excepted) *with the laws, government, and constitution of this country*, he could not have proceeded to more wanton insults upon their feelings. To say nothing of his quotation, and direct application of that line from *Shakespere*,

"If *Richard's* fit to live, let *Richmond* fall:"[6]

Which, if it meant any thing, was referring the question to this bloody arbitrement—*either these reformers ought to die by the hands of government, or the governing party by the hands of the reformers*;—what shall we say to "acquitted felons", "killed off", and a variety of other sentences, of whose "*vitality*" this subtile, Machiavellian secretary (terrified by the lingering echo of his own frenzy) has so pathetically complained? It is difficult to conceive how human nature could become callous enough to give utterance to these, and other expressions, still more inhuman, of which I shall have occasion to take notice: But Mr. *Burke*, in the very pamphlet I am answering, furnishes us, according to his conception, at least, with a sufficient explanation. "Nothing can be conceived", says he, "more hard than the heart of a thorough-bred metaphysician. It comes nearer to the cold malignancy of a wicked spirit, than to the frailty and passion of a man. It is like that of the principle of evil himself, incorporeal, pure, unmixed, dephlegmated, defecated evil."[a]

In what particular country Mr. *Burke* has met with those philosophers and metaphysicians, from whose example he has drawn this definition, I shall enquire more particularly hereafter; and on the validity of his arguments, in this respect, I may perhaps be admitted to decide with the greater impartiality, from having the misfortune (for such I believe it is, to be deficient in any branch of knowledge) of being liable to no part of that rancorous animosity, with which he is *sometimes* disposed to regard both the science and the professors of metaphysics. In the mean time, that I may not appear to prejudge the question, permit me to declare, that, if it can be shewn that these subtile disquisitions and abstract enquiries are necessarily hostile to the principles and practice of humanity, I shall hold myself in readiness to reject with equal abhorrence "the philosophy that would eradicate the best feelings of the heart", and that system of private attachment and obligation, which, preferring a part to the whole, would sacrifice to *individual gratitude* the interests and happiness of mankind![7]

[a]Letter, &c. p. 61.

But the most powerful of those champions, for whose efforts in behalf of liberty we are indebted to the ungovernable fury of Mr. *Burke's* attacks, have not been found either among the metaphysicians, or the ferocious violators of the principles of humanity. The strong, rude, sometimes incoherent, but always gigantic mind of *Thomas Paine*, had been neither fashioned nor debauched by the subtilties nor the sophistries of metaphysics; and he has approved, at the peril of his life, the settled aversion of his soul, not only to the massacres, tumultuary or legal, which have disgraced the *French Revolution*, but even to that "penal retrospect" which rendered the faithless and perjured Louis a victim to the treacherous duplicity with which he conspired for the destruction of his people. And as for those other distinguished antagonists of Mr. *Burke*, whom this country may more exclusively challenge as her own; they are men whose social virtues have either never yet been questioned, or being questioned, have been put to the ordeal, and passed, like pure gold, through the fire, undiminished either in weight or lustre.

The energy of some of the most celebrated of these has, it is true, been relaxed awhile, by the enervating influence of party attachment; while others, infected by the temporary mania of alarm, have *appeared*, at least, to desert the sacred cause: but let the tools and advocates of corruption beware; for if tyranny should advance with too audacious a stride—if those who have already provoked so much discussion, encouraged by a temporary supineness, should insult too outrageously the feelings and understandings of the nation, these champions may be provoked to resume their neglected arms, or others, still more irresistible, may step forward to supply their place. The manly spirit of Britain is not dead but sleepeth. Sampson in the lap of Dalila[8] (*the Dalila of dependance and corruption!*) slumbers it is true, amidst his bonds: but he is not yet shorn of his strength; nor is the mystic secret yet discovered: and should he chance but to awaken from his lethargy, the *new cords* may be burst asunder, and the *Philistines* be compelled to fly!

Behold then the unwearied services of *Edmund Burke*, whom corruption has pensioned for its own destruction! who defends the privileged orders by overwhelming their privileges with contemptuous ridicule! and protects the inviolability of places and pensions, by tearing asunder the venerable veil of prescription, and undermining the foundations of hereditary property!

But what reason soever the noble personages attacked in this letter may have to hurl back the charge upon their assailant, and accuse the *ministerial faction* of being "executors in their own wrong",[a] the friends of popu-

---

[a]Letter, &c. p. 2.

lar enquiry "have nothing to complain of"—"It is well! it is perfectly well!
We have to do homage[a] to" his zeal in the cause of political investigation.

The discussion provoked by his inconsiderate "Reflections" was nearly
exhausted; the *nine days wonder* of the State Trials had subsided; political
persecution had become familiar, and, like the daily bread of a land in
plenty, was taken as a matter of course, and digested without comment or
observation; and whatever spirit or energy hitherto remained among the
people, seemed to have evaporated in the struggle provoked by Mr. *Pitt's*
and Lord *Grenville's* bills,[9] and to have left them, in this respect, like the
fallen angels, after the toils of unsuccessful fight, reposing in the oblivious
pool, equally forgetful of the disgrace they had experienced, and of the
energies by which it might be retrieved. Mr. *Burke*, however, knew that
this was not the state in which it was their duty, or their interest to remain; and he determined, accordingly, to awaken them from their lethargy. He seized, therefore, again the trump of political controversy—

> "With a withering look,
> The war-denouncing trumpet took,
> And blew a blast so loud and dread,
> *Were ne'er prophetic sounds so full of woe!*
> And ever and anon he beat
> *The doubling drum* with furious heat." (Collins.)[10]

Such a peal, at such a time was certainly of all things most desirable. No
other circumstance could, perhaps so soon, and so effectually, have revived
the energies of popular exertion, or have dissipated so effectually the lazy
mists of torpor and despondency which hung on the sickening ear of British virtue, and threatened it with eternal blight: so true is it that those
advantages which the ardour of friendship labours to produce in vain, are
frequently conferred by the over-active zeal of our bitterest enemies.

But it will be said, if such is my exultation at the appearance of this
letter, why have I called it a "mischievous pamphlet"? To this I answer,
that the advantages to be expected from this letter are consequential—
certainly not intended; but that the mischief is in the thing itself. Mischief
and good are merely relative terms; for nothing is exclusively productive
either of the one or the other: and with respect to intellectual, or literary
exertions, the balance is always eventually, I believe, favourable to the
happiness of mankind. In short, it seems to be past the time, in this part of

[a]Ibid.

Europe at least, when it is in the power of any book to be productive of ultimate mischief. Mankind now read too many books to be permanently injured by any. Whatever mischief is to be apprehended, must be rather from the *stagnation* than the *nature* of their enquiries: and, perhaps, the best advice that can be given them, is to read every thing that comes their way, from a Grub-street ballad to a Royal proclamation. There are, however, some publications which, abstractedly considered, and independent of those answers likely to be produced in a busy, literary, disputatious age, like the present, must be considered as most pernicious in their tendency: and such, above all that ever fell under my cognizance, is "A *Letter from the Right Honourable Edmund Burke to a Noble Lord.*"

So rash—so intemperate—so imprudent—I cannot help adding, so *unprincipled* an attack upon the peaceful security of all property, never has been made, I believe, before, since England had a language in which that attack could be conveyed. Sir *Thomas Moore*, it is true, has visited the closets of speculative men with the fascinating picture of a society in which incessant toil is not the portion of any man, and every thing is enjoyed in common:[11] But there is nothing in the "*Eutopia*" that is irritating or inflammatory; nothing that is calculated to hurry the uncultivated mind into rash conclusions, or shake the foundations of society with sudden convulsion. *Thomas Paine*, also, in the second part of his "Rights of Man", projected,[12] what *Servius Tullius* partly executed in ancient Rome,[13] a scheme of progressive taxation, by which the towering pride of wealth might be humbled and restrained, and the burthens of government be lifted from the poor man's shoulders: And *Licinius*,[14] and the much celebrated, and much slandered, *Gracchi* laboured hard for the establishment of those *Agrarian* laws which constituted an important article in the original compact of the Roman government, and must be regarded as among the *constitutional rights* of that nation.[15] But for Mr. *Burke*, alone, of all the demagogues I ever read or heard of, was reserved the *honourable* distinction of assailing, with *popular fury*, the very existence of all property; stirring up the passions of a distressed and irritated people, by representing the "overgrown" fortunes of the nobility as "oppressing the industry of humble men",[a] "trampling on the mediocrity of humble and laborious individuals"[b] and the like.

In short, Mr. *Burke* is the first complete *leveller* I have met with: the only man who has had the audacity, in direct and popular language, ad-

[a]Letter, p. 33.
[b]Ibid. 39.

dressed at once to the perceptions and passions of mankind at large, to represent all wealth—all territorial possession, as plunder and usurpation— as the fruit of blood, of treachery, of proscription!—as being obtained by "the murder of innocent persons"[a]—"from the aggregate and consolidated funds of judgments *iniquitously legal!*" and from "possessions *voluntarily surrendered* by the lawful proprietors *with the gibbet at their door*";[b] nay, to complete the climax, as having been augmented (*as some fortunes are at this very day augmenting!*) by "bringing poverty, wretchedness, and depopulation on the country", and swelled by confiscations produced "by instigating a tyrant to injustice, to provoke a people to rebellion."[c]

I do not stand forward as the champion of prescriptive rights, nor wield the sword of reason for the perpetuity of ancient prejudices, or the vindication of hereditary honours. I am more solicitous about the living than the dead: more anxious for the happiness of posterity than the reputation of long buried ancestors. I leave therefore to the avowed advocates of the illustrious and the great, the easy task of repelling a considerable part, at least, of that outrageous obloquy which, though directed against a particular family, does in reality, more or less, bespatter the whole body of the nobility and great proprietors of the land. But if such *were* the real foundations of property—if such were indeed the stuff of which all estate, and wealth, and grandeur were composed, what good and considerate man— what friend to the peace and order of society—to the sweet sleep of security, and the humane emotions of the heart, would have laid bare those foundations with *so rude* a stroke?

There are even some truths of the utmost importance to the improvement and happiness of society, which the true philosopher, though he will not suppress, will unfold with a tender and a trembling hand. He will proceed with a caution almost bordering on reserve; and will accompany every advance towards the requisite developement with the most solicitous exposition of every appendage and consequence of the respective parts of his doctrine; left by pouring acceptable truths too suddenly on the popular eye, instead of salutary light he should produce blindness and frenzy! and from premises the most just, plunge into conclusions of the most destructive nature. Such in particular are many of the speculations which relate to the subject of property. These are indeed of so delicate a nature—the

[a]Ibid. p. 42.
[b]Ibid. p. 42.
[c]Ibid. p. 44. and p. 48.

abuses relating to them are so closely interwoven with the very texture of society—and the principles upon which they stand are so liable to misapprehension and abuse, that it is almost doubtful whether mankind is yet sufficiently enlightened and humanized for the investigation, and whether the subject had not been as well omitted even in the *abstract and speculative quartos of William Godwin.*[16] For my own part, at least, conscious of the difficulty of keeping clear from all dangerous misapprehensions, I have never ventured to enter much into the subject: not but that I can see with as much clearness, and feel with as keen a sympathy, as Mr. *Burke* (when it suits the purposes of his political frenzy and personal resentments) can himself pretend, the vices, the miseries, the unsocial pride and abject wretchedness too frequently produced in society by those huge masses and immeasurable disproportions of property, which unjust laws and impolitic institutions, more than the rapacity of individuals, have tended to accumulate.

Perhaps there is no humane and reflecting man who does not, occasionally at least, wish that respectability were more attached to other things, and less to wealth; that the great body of the people were redeemed from that necessity of unremitting drudgery, penurious food, and consequent ignorance and depression of intellect, to which they are so invariably doomed; and that the huge and unwieldy masses of wealth and territory (too vast for enjoyment—too dazzling for just and prudent distribution) were in the way of being gradually and peacefully melted down, by the salutary operation of wise and equitable laws. There is perhaps, for example, no one who does not occasionally question the justice of the law of primogeniture—the great root of all the evil; and the propriety of marrying together contiguous and overgrown estates, without regard to the inclinations, dispositions, tastes, aversions, and consequent morals of the parties, who are to be the instruments, or perhaps the victims, of these schemes of family aggrandizement. In short, there are undoubtedly a thousand evils resulting from the present state of things, in this respect; and there are perhaps a thousand palliative remedies that might be applied without lacerating the social frame, or dissolving the sacred ties of reciprocal security and protection. Whatever can be done, in this or any other respect, for the emancipation of mankind, and the advancement of general happiness, it is right that we should enquire into the means of doing; and the wider the real knowledge of those means can be disseminated, the better for the peace and happiness of the world. Every thing that relates to this subject

ought, however, I repeat it, to be treated with extreme delicacy and caution; for there are conclusions so false, and consequences so terrible, laying
within a hair's breadth, as it were, of the truths we aim at, that he who
rushes forward with too boisterous a precipitancy, is in danger of provoking
all the horrors of tumult and assassination; instead of ameliorating the condition of the human race. No tricks and arts of eloquence, no gusts of
passion, no inflammatory declamation, nor the least incitement to personal
animosity or resentment, ought to be admitted in the examination of such
a question. It is a new and untried navigation. Almost all that we know
about it is, that the shoals are dangerous, and the quicksands innumerable.
And under such circumstances, above all, it must certainly be the duty of a
cautious mariner to "heave the lead every inch of the way he makes".[a] But
Mr. *Burke*, who, when a few places and pensions were all the freight he
had on board, thought these precautions necessary tears from its moorings
the vessel of hereditary property, and, notwithstanding "the aweful state of
the time",[b] giving the rudder to his resentment, exposes it, at random, to
all the fury of the tempest which himself has raised.

Is it possible that Mr. *Burke's* new patrons can countenance all this? Has
the zeal of his *pensioned gratitude* transported him too far? Or is it a part of
the long-digested conspiracy of political panders and rotten borough-mongers? Is no property to be sacred, but the *property of seats and votes* in the
House of Commons? And are the foundations of all other inheritance to be
shaken, that these usurpations may be rendered the more secure, and the
authority of the *Steeles*[17] and the *Roses*, who measure their estates by the
square inch on the planks of St. Stephen's chapel, be relieved from the
checks and counterpoises that may hitherto have controuled the exercise of
their spurious sovereignty?

Let us hope, at least, that we are not to look for the solution of this
mystery to some blacker cause. Let us hope, at least, that this insidious
new-created *oligarchy* have not, on the prospect of failure in their ordinary
resources, turned to the *bird's-eye prospect* of new "confiscations of the ancient nobility of the land",[c] to support their all-devouring system of corruption. Let us hope, at least, that this inflammatory farago of denunciation
and proscription—this portentous retrospect of two hundred and fifty years

[a]Letter, p. 23.
[b]Letter, p. 36.
[c]Ibid. p. 41.

is not sent out, as the *avant courier* of a sanguinary faction to prepare the way for the meditated catastrophe of other "innocent persons of illustrious rank",[a] whose fate, according to Mr. *Burke's* superstitious mode of calculation, might atone for "the butchery of the Duke of Buckingham",[b18] and the "pillage" committed upon that "body of unoffending men",[c] the *monks* of Tavistock and Wooburn Abbey.[d]

Inflammatory pamphlets, and ferocious scurrilities in the daily prints, have however paved the way, of late, for attempts equally daring and unexpected: and the axe, which has passed over the humble weeds without inflicting a wound, may be destined to try its edge upon the stateliest oaks of the forest.

Some, perhaps, may put together the circumstances of Mr. *Burke's* education, the pathetic lamentations which he has poured forth in a former publication[e] upon the impious invasion of the sacred slumbers of the cloister,[19] and the frequent allusions in this pamphlet to the wrongs of monks and abbots, priests and Cordeliers, Capuchins, Carmelites, Franciscans, and Dominicans;[f] and hence they may suppose, at least, that they have discovered another reason for the intemperate zeal of *the pupil of St. Omer's*. They may trace, perhaps, in this bitter and inflexible malevolence against *the inheritor of the crimes of former centuries*, the seeds of that *metaphysical piety*, so consistent with the mystical refinements of a Jesuit's college, which ascribes all the sublime attributes of the Deity to whatever is connected with the priesthood, and of course, considers the wrongs of that sacred order, according to their own language, as neither past nor future— as existing always in the present tense—accumulated and concentrated in the ONE ETERNAL NOW!!!

If, however, we appeal to internal evidence, we shall find that motives of a more personal nature have not been entirely without influence in the production of this pamphlet. That unsocial vanity—that irritable self-love—that proud impatience of all question or controul, which regards all opposition as insult, and "all insult as a wound";[20]—in short, that proud and revengeful egotism, which has formed so distinguishing a trait in the character of all inveterate aristocrats, from *Appius Claudius*[21] to *Edmund*

[a]Letter, p. 42.
[b]Ibid. p. 68.
[c]Letter, p. 42.
[d]Ibid. p. 68.
[e]Reflections, &c.
[f]Letter, p. 41, 42, 43, 67, 68.

Burke, must be admitted to have had something to do, at least, with the colouring of the piece, to whatever instigation we may attribute the sketch, or the original design. What but this could have hurried such a man into such extravagant inconsistencies! What but this, even pensioned as he is, could have rendered him so blind an instrument to the usurpations of a faction which he cannot but despise, and have driven him with such headlong violence to the destruction of every principle which he had hitherto pretended to revere?

There are, it is true, persons who have at all times regarded Mr. *Burke* as a splendid instance of the depravity of genius—as a man of base and time-serving disposition, whose patriotism was the mere purchased property of a party, which held him in dependance by the loans granted to him by the Marquis of *Rockingham*;[22] and it was, therefore, thought consistent enough, when his patron, by a last act of liberality, had cancelled all legal obligation, that he should set himself to sale to the opposite party, and become the furious opponent of every principle he had been hired to defend. I have endeavoured, however, to judge him with greater charity. I have sought for, and thought I had discovered, a principle that would account for his conduct in a less dishonourable way. My solution, it is true, would still have left him among the number of those deluded men whose judgments have been perverted by a mistaken sense of private obligation; but it would not have reduced him to the level of sordid corruption.

In short, I conceived Mr. *Burke* to have been throughout a Republican of the old Roman school! or, in other words, a high-toned aristocrat. And I readily accounted for this twist in his understanding from the patronage which it had been his misfortune to experience. For it is but too natural with us to regard those institutions as every thing, without which we should ourselves, apparently, have been nothing. It was, therefore, not extraordinary that Mr. *Burke*, finding himself redeemed, by the powerful and generous patronage of the leader of an aristocratic party, from the necessity of being a *public lecturer* in a provincial university, and transplanted to the more genial soil of political influence, should think himself bound in *gratitude* to exalt that aristocracy to which alone he owed his exaltation.

Upon this solution, his conduct, apparently so opposite, with respect to the *American* and *French* revolutions, is perfectly reconcileable. For with pure, genuine, whole-length aristocrats, princes and people are alike indifferent: alike obnoxious, when they aspire to any share of power; and alike acceptable, as the tools and instruments of their ambition. But as, in all mixed governments, their power is of a very doubtful and amphibious na-

ture, but little recognized by the avowed maxims and spirit of the constitution, and depending rather upon the influence of their property, and their
talent for intrigue, than either the weight of their functions, or real attachment of the people, as circumstances vary they are obliged to vary the
fashion of their sentiments and conduct. Their principle and their object
is, however, always the same; and always has been so, whether they instigated the people to destroy a *Tarquin*, or created a *Tarquin* to destroy the
people.[a] Law and liberty are alternately in their mouths; but their liberty is
the unrestrained license of monopolizing oppression, and their law the arbitrary exercise of their own discretion. The dignity of the sovereign, and
the sovereignty of the people, are alternate stalking horses for their usurpations. As Mr. *Burke* expresses it—"Popularity and power they regard alike.
These are with them only different means to obtain their object; and have
no preference over each other in their minds, but as one or the other may
afford a surer or less certain prospect of arriving at their end."[b]

Such are the characteristics of inveterate aristocracy—of the high-toned
optimates of mixed and limited governments: a set of men widely different
from the ancient Tories of this country:—more dangerous, I believe, to the
peace and happiness of society; certainly more destitute of all support from
rational and consistent principle. Such is the party to which the first talents, the most capacious understandings, perhaps the best hearts in the
nation, have been too long enslaved! Such is the party to which I imagined Mr. *Burke* to be inseparably wedded.

This supposition is countenanced by his whole political history. This
supposition is confirmed by his own account of what he calls his public
services; that is to say, his services to this party. And, upon this supposition, his conduct with respect to the French revolution, is perfectly reconcileable to his conduct respecting America.

The principle of the two revolutions was, perhaps, the same: though this
may be contested, at least, upon very plausible grounds. Their operation in
this country was, however, widely different. Party disputes ran high, it is
true, on both occasions; and the nation was unhappily divided into the
most inveterate factions. But in the former instance, it was the gentry, the
optimacy, the aristocratic interest, that moved—that agitated, and conducted every thing; in the latter, the great body of the people—the *com-*

---

[a]The reader is particularly recommended to peruse with attention the account given by Dionysius of
Halicarnassus (B. IV.) of the murder of Servius Tullius, and of the expulsion of the Tarquins.[23]
[b]Letter, p. 15.

mon mass, had the audacity to judge for themselves, and inquire into the nature of their rights.

Could an inveterate aristocrat be expected to tolerate this? Was it not to be expected, that persons of this description, (like the aristocracy of Spain, upon a similar occasion) should cling to the throne for protection, against what they regarded as the *invasions of Liberty*, and permit themselves to be degraded and enslaved, rather than suffer the people to be free?

Thus did the candid and liberal part of mankind account for the apparent inconsistencies of Mr. *Burke*; and, by referring his whole conduct to the influence of aristocratic prejudices, exonerate him from the charge of venal apostacy. But what shall we say now? What opinion shall we form of the present work? To what principle shall we refer the incongruous sentiments it contains? Certainly not to that abhorrence of uncontrouled prerogative which inspired him with the enthusiasm of opposition during the American war, and made rebellion for liberty lovely in his eyes; these sentiments were relinquished, for the reasons stated above, at the very dawn of the French revolution. Certainly, not to those feelings which, during the discussion of the *regency bill*,[24] occasioned that exulting, indecent, and unfeeling exclamation—"The Almighty has hurled himself from his throne"![25]—Mr. *Burke* has learned a very different "style to a gracious benefactor"![a] His Majesty is now "a benevolent prince", who "shews an eminent example, in promoting the commerce, manufactures, and agriculture of his kingdom"; and "who even in his amusements is a patriot, and in his hours of leisure an improver of his native soil":[b] a position, the truth of which no one will call in question. But is it more true at this time than before the above-mentioned period? I, for my part, can perceive no alteration. The benevolence and patriotism of the present reign has been steady, uniform, and consistent. At least, the only important difference is, that Mr. *Burke* has now a *pension* from his "mild and benevolent sovereign"; and that then he expected a *place* from his successor! Still less can we refer this extraordinary pamphlet to those aristocratical principles which offered the only solution of his former conduct.

"The government of France", says that great oracle, Sir John Mitford,[c27] "was totally overthrown in consequence of the total failure of the good opinion of the people"; and hence that profound and subtile logician thought

[a]Letter, &c. p. 10.
[b]Ibid. p. 44.
[c]Trial of T. Hardy.[26]

himself entitled to infer, that it must necessarily be high treason to shake the foundations of popular opinion: but if this conclusion were just, never was so capital a treason committed against the aristocratic branch of the constitution, as by the publication of Mr. *Burke's* pamphlet.

Is the composition of aristocracy such as Mr. *Burke* represents it?—Then is the very institution of aristocracy radically vicious!—Is it "the offal thrown to jackals in waiting", after "the lion has sucked the blood"?[a] and are "innocent persons",[b] and "bodies of unoffending men"[c] the "prey" upon which both are pampered?—I am afraid these premises would carry us further than Mr. *Burke* and his new friends are yet prepared to go. I am afraid it would be something like high treason, at least, under Lord *Grenville's* new act, to draw the conclusions that inevitably result from such data!!! And yet if such pamphlets are put in circulation by the *advocates* and *pensioners* of government, what act of parliament can prevent the consequences?

Mr. *Burke*, an advocate of government! Mr. *Burke*, the champion of aristocracy! Mr. *Burke*, the political Atlas who supports which such "great zeal", and such "success",—"those old prejudices which buoy up the ponderous mass of nobility, wealth, and titles"![d] Judge for yourselves, my fellow citizens: but before you pronounced, too positively, read with attention his eighty pages of virulent abuse against "overgrown dukes, who *oppress the industry of humble men*"![e] "who hold large portions of wealth" ("the prodigies of profuse donation")[f] "without any apparent merit of their own"![g] and by their "vast *landed pensions*"[h] (obtained by the blackest crimes of treachery and oppression)[i] "so enormous as not only to outrage oeconomy, but even to stagger credibility",[j]—"trample on the mediocrity of laborious individuals"![k]

But it is not only with the battle-axe of moral indignation that Mr. *Burke* assails the aristocracy of his country. With equal expertness, and

[a]Letter, &c. p. 41.
[b]Ibid. p. 42.
[c]Ibid. p. 42.
[d]Ibid. &c. p. 34.
[e]Letter, &c. p. 33.
[f]Ibid. p. 39.
[g]Ibid. p. 39.
[h]Ibid. p. 38.
[i]Ibid. p. 41, 42, 43, 44, and 46.
[j]Ibid. p. 37.
[k]Ibid. p. 39.

equal ardour, he wings the light, keen shafts of satire and ridicule: nay, so
blunt is his sympathy, and so exquisite his animosity, that he even tears it
occasionally with the rude hand-saw of pointless scurrility.[a] The rage of
Juvenil,[28] and the playful levity of Horace[29] are not sufficient; and Billingsgate and the shambles are forced into alliance with the muses, the classics,
and the sciences, to supply him with terms and metaphors sufficiently forcible to express the mighty hatred with which he labours.

Youthful intemperance may furnish some apology for hasty and indecorous language; but if grey hairs expect our reverence, they must purchase
it by discretion, wisdom, and moderation. Mr. *Burke*, however, retains, at
three-score, his juvenile contempt for these cold qualities—"this well selected rigour"!—this "preventive police of morality"![b] The hungry lioness
rushes not with so blind a fury upon her prey, as he upon the victims of his
resentment. I am told that a noble attendant of the bedchamber (I mean
Lord *Winchelsea*)[30] who turned several of his tenants out of their farms, &c.
for being guilty of distant relationship to me, and of having read my publications, among other things, complained very bitterly of some passages in
my "Peripatetic", which he considered as calculated to inflame the minds
of the common people against the opulent and the great. I will not venture
to affirm that there are no expressions or sentiments, in that hasty publication, which, upon mature consideration, might demand some softening or
apology. But to say nothing of the much more popular and "questionable
shape" in which Mr. *Burke's pamphlet* comes before the public, I defy all
the lords of the bedchamber together, to find in the work before-men-
tioned, or in any other of my publications, passages of any thing like the
inflammatory nature of those in which the "Letter to a Noble Lord"
abounds. I have pleaded, it is true, and while I have a tongue or a pen to
exercise in so just a cause, I will continue to plead, the cause of the oppressed and injured labourer. I have reproved the unfeeling and fastidious
pride of greatness; and offered something in extenuation for the pilfering
vices of laborious wretchedness. I have even presumed to hurl back the
charge of dishonesty upon "mighty lords, and descendants from the loose
amours of kings", who "rob us, by letters patent, and suffer not a coal to
blaze in our grates, nor an action to be brought for the recovery of a just
debt, till they have levied contribution upon us": But Mr. *Burke* flies at

[a]Ibid. p. 37, 68, 69.
[b]Letter, &c. p. 34.

higher quarry. He pounces at once at hereditary property; calls the birds of prey around him, and excites them to the promised banquet.

In short, if the daemon of anarchy wished to reduce the social frame to chaos, what charms more proper could he select for his incantations than the ingredients of this troubled cauldron? Should some prophet of pillage and massacre in reality arise, what more could he wish for than such a Koran? what further instructions could he give to his apostles and missionaries than to comment upon the text of *Edmund Burke*, and push his principles to their most obvious conclusions?

I trust, however—and, in this one respect, my opportunities of forming a just conclusion have been much superior to my antagonist's—I trust, that what are called the common people of this country are in no danger of being stimulated to such excesses as this letter sometimes pretends to deprecate, but more frequently appears calculated to provoke. I too have laboured "with very great zeal, and I believe with some degree of success"[a] (rather more, if I am not mistaken, than Mr. *Burke* can boast of in his attempt to "support old prejudices")[b] not indeed "to discountenance enquiry"[c] but to give it a just direction;—to point out to the poorer sort in particular of my fellow citizens, smarting and writhing under the lash of oppression and contumely, the peaceful means of redress; to shew them the distinction between tumult and reform—between the amelioration and the dissolution of society—the removal of oppression—and the sanguinary pursuits of pillage and revenge. I trust that the salutary lesson has not been enforced in vain—that *whatever calamities may result to society, from the present enormous inequality in the distribution of property, all tumultuary attacks upon individual possession, all attempts, or pretences of levelling and equalization, must be attended with massacres and assassinations, equally destructive to the security of every order of mankind; and, after a long struggle of afflictions and horrors, must terminate at last, not in equalization, but in a most iniquitous transfer, by which cut-throats and assassins would be enabled to found a new order of nobility, more insufferable, because more ignorant and ferocious, than those whom their daggers had supplanted.*

The friends of liberty know that, sooner or later, the progress of reason must produce (perhaps, at no distant period) an essential reformation in the government and institutions of this country: but (unless the frantic and

[a]Letter, &c. p. 34.
[b]Ibid. p. 34.
[c]Ibid. p. 34.

desperate councils of such men as Mr. *Burke* and Mr. *Windham*, should unhinge all society, *under pretence of preserving order*) no part of the excesses which have rent and convulsed the devoted land of *France* need be dreaded in *England*: for the causes of those excesses do not exist among us. Reform, like a long-woo'd virgin, shall come at last, in the unsullied robes of Peace, and, in the Temple of Concord, shall give her hand to Reason. But such hymeneals suit not the tastes and dispositions of Mr. *Burke*; for placemen and pensioners will not be invited to the banquet. The marriage of Tyranny and Corruption, in a robe of blood, would be more in harmony with his disordered and irritated imagination; with a legion of foreign mercenaries to protect the pomp, and a procession of Inquisitors, and an *Auto da Fé*, to close the accustomed revels!

Such, at least, are the only orgies, for which the vows and the offerings of Mr. *Burke* are calculated to prepare. Such alone are the systems to which his maxims and sentiments are reconcileable: For if, on the one hand, all democratic innovation—all reform is to be pertinaciously resisted, and on the other, all respect for rank, fortune, and hereditary station are to be torn away, by the impassioned hand of personal rancour and factious malevolence—if the people, deprived of all legal weight and influence in the legislature of the country, and therefore of all attachment from rational and well-placed affection, are to be stimulated to personal hatred and animosity against the noble, the wealthy, and the great, whom they are to be taught by *ministerial hirelings* (oh! that such a mind could ever be included in such a description!) to regard as the plunderers of their ancestors, and the oppressors of themselves, what but tyranny the most unqualified—what but blood—what but foreign mercenaries, and the united horrors of inquisitorial and military despotism, can long sustain that rule which ministers pretend to be so anxious to preserve unaltered?

What *but* this?—Nay: *not this, nor more!!!*—Britons may be led: but driven they will not be. They have spirit—they have intelligence—they have a manly firmness—they have some knowledge of their rights, and a keen desire to possess them. In short, they are men who live towards the close of the eighteenth century, and have seen two Revolutions: and if Bishops continue to preach, that "they have nothing to do with the laws but obey them"; and Lord Chancellors to declare, that "the laws they are to obey ought to be couched in such terms that they cannot comprehend them"!—If wasteful wars are to create famines, and illustrious peers are to console the half-starved people with the reflection, that "their scanty mess would have been still more scanty, if so many of their friends and relatives had not been slaughtered"; or, as Mr. *Windham* would call it, *killed off*, "in foreign expeditions"!—If every door is to be closed against peaceful remonstrance and complaint, and Secretaries at War are to thrust obnoxious statutes down our throats with the sabres of armed associators!—and if, finally, every gallant patriot, noble or simple, who has the generosity to stem the torrent of corruption, is to be beset by treasury blood hounds, and hunted with threats of confiscation and proscription: by the great terror that swells my heart, as imagination conjures up the picture, I do not believe that heaven or hell have power to sustain the system; but that which *France* has been, *Britain* too soon must be!

If such events should take place, whom has the country to thank but the *Grenvillites*, the *Westmorelands*[31]—the *Pitts*, and *Windhams?*—If property should be shaken, and nobility go to wreck, who sounds the Indian yell of pillage and desolation, but the Right Honourable *Edmund Burke*, with his "Letter to a noble Lord"?

In vain shall the advocates of this political maniac accuse me of misrepresenting his arguments, by generalizing observations which he has confined to a particular instance. I do no more than every reader of his pamphlet must inevitably do. It is the Duke of *Bedford*,[32] indeed, that is ostensibly attacked; but the whole body of nobility and landed proprietors, are wounded through his side. Let not the partizans of the minister weakly and wickedly suppose, "the rival honours of the house of *Russell* are blighted by this pamphlet, and public odium excited against their wide possessions; but we have yet—

> "Golden opinions from all ranks of men,
> Which may be worn still in their newest gloss." Shakespeare.[33]

Let them not, I say, "lay this flattering unction to their souls."[34] There is not one argument of moral reprehension—one stroke of satire, or ridicule—one intemperate expression of degradation or abuse, that does not equally apply to them all. Old nobility and new, all are included—all are alike the victims of Mr. *Burke's* irritated pride and immeasurable resentments. Their patents, their deeds of gift, their titles, and their rent-rolls, all—all are consumed together in this conflagration of his inflamed and allinflaming mind!

If the estates of the Duke of *Bedford* deserve the odious appellation of "landed pensions",[a] are not the estates of the Dukes of *Portland*, of *Rutland*,[35]

---

[a]Letter, &c. p. 38.

of *Richmond*,[36] of the Earls of *Westmoreland*, *Winchelsea*, *Lonsdale*,[37] and the long train of *et ceteras*, "landed pensions" also? Is the Duke of *Bedford* a "Leviathan among the creatures of the crown, who plays and frolics in the ocean of royal bounty", (by which, I suppose, we are to understand that the king, whenever his virtuous and disinterested ministers shall so advise, may withdraw his *bounty*,[a] and transfer these "landed pensions", to more *grateful* servants!) is not the Earl of *Fitzwilliam* a "Leviathan" also? and, would not all the disgusting details of this figure, in which Mr. *Burke* indulges his imagination, equally apply in one instance as in the other? Does he not, also, "lay floating many a rood"?[b] And if the "overgrown" bulk of the one "oppresses the industry of humble men",[c] are not the unwieldy proportions of the other equally oppressive? Was Mr. *Russel*, in the time of *Henry* the eighth, a "*Jackall* in waiting"?[d] What are the *Hawkesburies*,[38] the *Loughboroughs*, the *Macdonalds*,[39] and the long list of new-created peers, whose wholesale elevation has tended, not a little, to shake the prescriptive reverence, or in Mr. *Burke's* own words, "those old prejudices",[e] which can alone support a house of *hereditary legislators*? If it is a disgrace to the Earl of *Bedford* to have been "swaddled and rocked, and dandled into a legislator",[f] have not the whole body of nobility, by descent, become legislators in the same ridiculous manner?—If I were not afraid of being suspected of courting the favour of party, (than which nothing, I believe, is more destructive to the energies of genuine patriotism) or bowing to that splendour of wealth and patronage (than which nothing is more degrading to the free-born mind!) it would be only a tribute of justice, to the value and ability of late exertions to say, that it would be well for the country, and for the honour of that house, of which the Duke of *Bedford* has *rendered himself* a *distinguished ornament*—if this legislative *swaddling*, and *rocking*, and *dandling*, had been uniformly as efficient to the end proposed. On the contrary, how many of our illustrious nobles (aye, and of those whom Mr. *Burke* must now rank among the number of his friends!) are no better, to this day, than "mewling in a nurse's arms";[40] or, what is worse, with a criminal supineness, equally dishonourable to their rank and to their nature, are abandoning every thing to the spoil and usurpations of a set of jobbers, loan contractors, Change-alley calculators and adventurers, who

[a]If this is not the meaning of his language, what does it mean?
[b]Letter, &c. p. 37.
[c]Ibid. p. 33.
[d]Ibid. p. 41.
[e]Ibid. p. 34.
[f]Ibid. p. 28.

have no other claim to the implicit confidence they enjoy, than what is derived from the disgrace and misery, the ruin, desolation and famine, which their mad projects, and desperate speculations have brought upon the country—and, indeed, upon the whole of Europe?

But this is not the only instance in which the flail of Mr. *Burke* strikes harder behind than it does before. I do not trouble myself to enquire whether this first leaf of *"Burke's new Peerage"*, afford a specimen of accuracy and impartiality, or of misrepresentation and malevolence. The question with me (and the only question of real importance to society) is, not how property was acquired three hundred years ago? but—how is it now employed? If the Duke of *Bedford* is disposed, as I hope and trust he is, to employ his great property and influence to the protection of the liberties and happiness of his country, the people will have an interest in the protection of that property. If there be others who are disposed to abuse their advantages, to the slavery and destruction of mankind, let them beware, lest they urge the people to do that in *self-defence*, which, from principle, they would abhor: for it is not very strange that grinding oppression should sometimes force the harrassed multitude to reflect, that the rights and happiness of millions are of more importance than the security and possessions of a few. The alternative, it is true, is dreadful: but the crime is with those who compel a nation to choose between such hideous extremes.

Regarding property in this point of view, I enquire not how "the first Duke of *Bedford*" acquired the vast estates which he has transmitted to his posterity;[41] nor by what title *John a Gaunt* held those immense *commons*, which he bequethed *in perpetuum* to the poor of the respective districts. I would not even be very curious to enquire into the means by which the wretched peasantry have been deprived of these freeholds, and their estates transferred to a few wealthy proprietors; unless it were with a view of preventing future encroachments. But, surely, Mr. *Burke* does not suppose us ignorant enough to believe, that Mr. *Russel* was the only founder of a family, whose merits it would be painful to probe. Does he call us to look back to the reign of *Henry* the eighth?—who, by the way, tyrant and monster as he was, (and even Mr. *Burke*, it seems, is aware that kings can sometimes be such) by exterminating from the country those lazy and pestiferous drones, the monks and religionists "of his time and country"[a] made some atonement to society for all his crimes!—Does Mr. *Burke*, I say, call upon us to look back to the reign of this eighth *Harry*? Let this

[a]Letter, &c. p. 43.

"*defender* of the high and eminent"[a] reflect, that we can look further! or we need not look so far! Let him ask the house of *Bentinck*,[42] whether there were no "prodigies of profuse donation" in the time of *William* the third? Whether the "lions" of the house of *Nassau*[43] had not their "jackalls", as well as those of the house of *Tudor*?[44] Let him ask the proudest he that ever traced his genealogy to the times of the Norman robber, whether there were no instances, even in *those good old days*, of "immoderate grants taken from the recent confiscation of the ancient nobility of the land"?[b] Had none of the landed pensions of that day their "fund in the murder of inno-cent persons, or in the pillage of bodies of men",[c] more truly "unoffending" than those cloistered drones and juggling visionaries, whose dispersion Mr. *Burke* so pathetically bewails?

Could the monks of *Wooburn* and *Tavistock*, and the murdered franklins and freeholders of those days of old, rise at once from their graves, (like the furies who pursued *Orestes*)[45] to harass the present possessors of their re-spective seats, whose wrongs would sound most terrible in the affrighted ears of nobility?—whose appeal would be most forcible to retributive justice?

Mr. *Burke* has done an irreparable injury to the cause of aristocracy by provoking this discussion; and, if an antidote is not applied, which I trust it will, by fair and manly exposition of the subject, has set a poison in circu-lation most dangerous to the health and existence of the social frame.

The attachment, however, of this polemic to aristocracy, appears at least to be as sincere as his religion. He pretends to foster and protect the for-mer, and he tears it up by the roots from that only soil in which any institution can flourish—the opinions of the people over whom it spreads. He pretends to be a zealot in behalf of the latter, and he acts on the direct converse of the position upon which the morality of that system is pro-fessedly built. The decalogue only denounces vengeance upon the posterity of offenders to the *third and fourth generations*; but promises mercy to thou-sands of the righteous and good. Mr. *Burke*, on the contrary, visits the sins of the forefathers upon generations without end, and passes by their vir-tues, as of no account at all.

I repeat it—for I am no simulator; nor have the popular schools in which I have been fashioned, (whatever contempt Mr. *Burke* may *now* think fit to entertain for them) have made me so keen a disputant, as to be

---

[a]Ibid. p. 42.
[b]Letter, &c. p. 41.
[c]Ibid. 42.

willing, for the sake of victory, to appear the thing I am not. I repeat it, therefore, I do not stand up as the advocate of hereditary distinctions, or hereditary honours. All honour, and all shame, are, in my calculation, merely personal. Goods and chattels may be heritable property; and in such a society as we are members of, I am convinced that it is necessary they should be so. But moral and intellectual distinctions, (the fountains of all real honour) are neither heritable nor transferable; nor is it in the power of human laws to make them such. They begin and they end with the immediate possessor. I admit, at the same time, that ancestral reputation sometimes operates very powerfully in the way of example. Strong instances of this are to be found in the history of the ancient and the modern world: and if the Duke of *Bedford* has been roused to his late exertions by a proud admiration of the conduct of that ancestor who, in the infamous reign of Charles the second, sealed his attachment to the principles of liberty with his blood,[46] I rejoice that he had such an example to set before his eyes; nor is it justice to society to suffer that example to be forgotten. If his Grace, in defiance of Mr. *Burke's* admonition,[a] should ever condescend to attend my lecture, (where I have sometimes been honoured with the plaudits of as fine scholars, as distinguished patriots, and almost as exalted geniuses as my calumniating antagonist) I would endeavour, it is true, to convince him that there is a surer and better motive of virtuous action: that the love of mankind is better than the pride of ancestry: that it is more noble to enquire how nations and generations can be most effectually served, than what our forefathers did, or what they would have done: and that to be what we ought, is to be something more than the most virtuous ancestor has ever been! But if mankind are still to be estimated, not by individuals, but by families—if the whole race is to be regarded as a body corporate, and the living representative to be accountable for the actions of the whole, still let us pay some little regard to justice—let us balance fairly the debtor and the creditor, and set down the good as well as the bad.

If this is the way in which we are to proceed, the house of *Russel* has nothing to dread in the settlement of the long account. Let Mr. *Burke* paint the first Earl of *Bedford* in the blackest colours his imagination can supply—let all that he has asserted pass unquestioned, and more, if more can be found, be added to the account; the virtuous resolution of Lord *William Russel*, who, in the full possession of all that youth, and rank, and wealth, paternal pride, and conjugal affection could bestow, disdained to

[a]Letter, &c. p. 35.

preserve his life by shrinking from his principles, is an ample atonement for all.

But is it not strange that Mr. *Burke* should be blind, not only to justice, but to the interests also of the order he professes to defend; for what so blind as the headlong fury of selfish and irritable pride? What so precipitate as the passions and resentments of a mind evidently and avowedly uncontrouled by any curb of principle?—which, regardless of the unity and immutability of truth, professes to submit its calculations and conclusions to the fluctuating decisions of interest, favour, or aversion—and on questions that relate to "the theory [and practice] of moral proportions",[a] to use "one style to a gracious benefactor; another to a proud and insulting foe"?[b]

That such were the motives and causes that produced this pamphlet, the pamphlet itself has put beyond all question and dispute. "Why will his Grace", it is said, "by *attacking me*,[47] force me reluctantly to compare my little merit with that which obtained from the crown those prodigies of profuse donation."[c] &c. "Let him remit his rigor on the disproportion between merit and reward in others, and they will make no enquiry into the origin of his fortune"![d]

Was ever rectitude of mind more publicly disavowed than in this sentence? Was ever self-love and resentment so openly proclaimed paramount to all principle? Either the enquiry is right, and ought to require no inducement from personal motives; or it is wrong, and no personal motive ought to provoke it. But this, I suppose, is the *gratitude* about which Mr. *Burke* makes so much parade:—"You do injustice to mankind, that I may reap the benefit of it; and I will do the like injustice, that the benefit may be reaped by you"!

Such is the *common traffic of gratitude and private obligation*! Such, according to "the *old sect* in politics and morals", is the square rule of virtue! This sentiment is still more nakedly expressed in another place. "*Had he permitted me to remain in quiet*, I should have said 'tis his estate, that's enough. It is his by law; what have I to do with its history? He would naturally have said on his side, 'tis this man's fortune.—He is as good now, as my ancestor was two hundred and fifty years ago. I am *a young man with very old pensions; he is an old man with very young pensions,—that's all*"![e]

---

[a]Letter, &c. p. 9.
[b]Letter, &c. p. 10.
[c]Ibid. p. 39.
[d]Ibid. p. 47.
[e]Letter, &c. p. 39.

What is this but saying, in other words, that men of estate and property, and the nobles of the land in particular—the *hereditary guardians of the rights and properties of the people*, are bound in good policy to countenance all the growing peculations of corruption; and, if they refuse to do so, that the *new peculators* will turn round upon the *old proprietors* will all the fury of a dangerous and desperate revenge, shake the foundations of their property, and endeavour to excite against them all the popular odium that may lead to pillage and tumult! But if these passages reveal the *selfish irritability* and *lax morality* of the writer, what shall we say to the sentiment exposed in the ensuing?—"Since the total body of my services have obtained the acceptance of my sovereign, it would be absurd in me to range myself on the side of the Duke of *Bedford* and the *London Corresponding Society*"?[a]

What, then—are we to understand that if *the whole body of his services* had not been accepted, that is to say, rewarded by the *animating soul of a good pension*, he would have ranged himself on the side of the Duke of *Bedford* and the London Corresponding Society?—In other words, are we to understand that his hostility to liberty, and the negociation for his pension, began at the same time?

For the honour of human genius, I would fain hope, in defiance of so many concurring circumstances, and of Mr. *Burke's* own testimony, that this is not entirely a correct statement of the case, and that it is yet possible to find some way of accounting for his conduct, without referring every thing to conscious and voluntary corruption. Be this, however, as it may—I trust that the public are not at any loss to decide which of the important services, so ostentatiously displayed in this splendid farrago of abuse and egotism, it was that occasioned that "*able, vigorous, and well-informed statesman*,"[b] Lord *Grenville*, to have the "goodness and condescension" both "to say" and do such "*handsome things* in his behalf."[c] I will not enter into the personal merits or demerits of Mr. *Burke*, nor into the general question of the propriety or impropriety of his pension. I leave this enquiry in the hands of older and better judges. Mr. *Burke* would, of course, object to my "being on the inquest of his *quantum meruit*"[d]—(may his fate never be in the hand of a less than candid juror!) He, of course, "cannot recognize in my few" (he cannot, however, add my "*idle*") years, the competence to judge "of his long and laborious life";[e] and I am certainly as well attached,

---

[a]Letter, &c. p. 59.
[b]Ibid. p. 3.
[c]Ibid. p. 2.
[d]Letter, &c. p. 9.
[e]Letter, &c. p. 9.

as he, at this time, finds it convenient to be, "not only to the letter, but to
the spirit of the old English law of trial by peers";[a] and should be sorry
either to prejudge him by a *garbelled and inflammatory report*, fabricated in
the guilty-concealing cave of *secrecy*, to present him with a packed jury, or
to traverse his challenges. But Mr. *Burke* will not himself deny that from
"the total body of his services", it is easy to single forth the limb or feature
whose grace and attraction won the rich prize of royal—or rather of ministerial favour. Mr. *Burke* himself will not pretend to doubt that, great and
important as those services might be, which he has so well enumerated, his
"unexampled toil in the service of his country",[b] his "oeconomical reforms",[c] his "studies of political oeconomy", which he had pursued "from
his very early youth", and by which "the house" [of commons] "has profit-
ted" so much, "for above eight and twenty years",[d] together with all that
"preparation and discipline to political warfare", by which he "had earned
his pension before he set his foot in Saint Stephen's chapel",[e] all, all
would have been neglected and forgotten, but for his conduct with respect
to the French Revolution. All that he "did, and all that he prevented from
being done",[f] even at that time (1780), when "wild and savage insurrection
quitted the woods, and prowled about the streets in the name of *reform*",[g]
and "a sort of national convention" (of which his new friend Mr. *Pitt* now,
perhaps, *recollects* that he was a member) "nosing parliament in the very
seat of its authority",[h] threatened England "with the honour of leading up
the death-dance of democractic revolution"![i] all, all would have lain in
thankless oblivion—even the *eternal impeachment*, "on which (of all his
services) he values himself the most",[j] would have failed to influence "ministers to consider his situation",[k] if it had not been for the zeal and ardour
with which he sounded the trumpet of alarm against the *ideal danger* of
"rude inroads of *Gallic tumult*",[l] called up, with his hideous yells, the hell-
born fiend of political persecution, and, turning the house of commons

[a]Ibid. p. 8.
[b]Ibid. p. 6.
[c]Ibid. p. 6.
[d]Letter, &c. p. 28.
[e]Ibid. p. 27.
[f]Ibid. p. 23.
[g]Ibid. p. 13.
[h]Ibid. p. 14.
[i]Ibid. p. 13.
[j]Ibid. p. 27.
[k]Ibid. p. 6.
[l]Letter, &c. p. 54.

into a mountebank's stage, dagger-struck every imagination, and plunged his country—plunged all Europe, into the most frantic, the most terrible, the most desolating war, that ever scourged the universe!

This was the crown of all his labours—"the Corinthian capital", that gave the finishing grace to the temple of public utility his life had been spent in rearing. But for this "the four and a half per cents had been kept full in his eye"[a] in vain. He might have enjoyed, it is true, in vista, the prospect of this trophy of "the oeconomy of selection and proportion",[b] but never would he have beheld the minister entering the porch to consecrate the spoils and offerings at his shrine.

If I were not impatient to enter into more important matter, and unwilling to extend too far the limits of this pamphlet, I would fain make some few animadversions upon these four and a half per cents. I would fain enquire into the grounds of that exultation with which Mr. *Burke* compares the funds and sources of his pension, with those that administered to the exaltation of the house of Russel. I would fain enquire whether it be more vicious to enrich oneself with the plunder of *dormitories*, and by the extermination of slothful, juggling, monks (who, like devouring *locusts*, prey on the green leaf of useful industry, and blight its hopeful fruitage in the bud) or *even* with the confiscations of attainted nobles, the descendants, according to Mr. *Burke*, of former "jackalls in waiting"—for the argument holds equally true *ad infinitum*; or to draw the means of luxury and profusion from taxes extorted from the hard-earned pittance of the labourer, and thereby to make the spare meal of poverty still more scanty and comfortless. Mr. *Burke* has quibbles and sophistries, and his friend, Mr. *Windham*, has metaphysical subtilities, I make no doubt, to repel this charge; but if I had time to push the question home, I could prove, by calculations as incontrovertible as any in the minister's arithmetic, that every pension that rewards the baseness of political apostacy, strips the wretched family of the peasant and the manufacturer of a portion of their scanty bread.

Mr. *Burke* may therefore congratulate himself, as much as he pleases, upon the "spontaneous bounty" of "the Royal Donor", and "the goodness and condescension" of "his ministers";[c] but his pension is, in reality, a beggar's cap, thrown by the way side, to receive the farthing of the poorest passenger; while, to aggravate the disgrace, taxation, like the crippled sol-

[a]Ibid. p. 25.
[b]Ibid. 33.
[c]Letter, &c. p. 6 and 2.

dier in *Gil Blas*,[48] rests its blunderbuss upon the stile, and converts the
pretended "charity"[a] into an act of plunder.

But my pamphlet is swelling beyond its intended proportion; and I must
hasten to more important matter. I leave, therefore, all consideration of
the general merits of the pensioner, all comparison of the proportion between the services and the reward; and all enquiry into the operation of
the pension, that I may examine the particular conduct without which all
his other services would have been of no avail; and canvas the principles
upon which that conduct was professedly built.

"If I am unworthy", says the pamphlet, "the ministers are worse than
prodigal":[b] and if with respect to *French affairs* his conduct has been inconsistent with justice, policy, and the security and happiness of mankind, the
greater his former services, the more criminal those ministers must appear:
for the system indeed must be rotten to the core, when a life of honourable
service can only obtain its reward by an old age of depredation and mischief.

Mr. *Burke*, it is true, modestly declines "the high distinction", and "the
glory" of being considered as the exclusive "author of the war";[c] and as I am
not at all desirous of removing *responsibility* from the shoulders where the
constitution has placed it, I am ready to exonerate him from the charge. I
believe that the ministers of this country had resolved, from the first dawn
of the *Revolution in France*, to seize the earliest opportunity of attacking
that nation. I believe, that but for the ministers of this country, the profligate and fatal treaty of *Pilnitz*[49] never would have been signed; *France* and
the Empire would not have been embroiled in war; the excesses which
have disgraced the greatest and most glorious event in the annals of mankind, would never have been perpetrated; and that *Louis* XVI might, perhaps, to this day have continued "King of the French". I believe, also, that
if no such man as Mr. *Burke* had been in existence, Mr. *Pitt*—or more
properly speaking, Lord *Hawkesbury*, would nevertheless have plunged us
into this unhappy contest. Mr. *Burke* and his *dagger*[50] were therefore the
only instruments (powerful instruments, however,) in exciting that terror
and alarm, which gave, among certain classes at least, a degree of popularity to the measure, without which the minister would have found it
difficult to fulfil *his continental engagements!*

[a]Letter, &c. p. 33.
[b]Ibid. p. 7.
[c]Letter, &c. p. 79.

It was Mr. *Burke* who assisted him, in this embarrassment, by sounding the *tocsin* of alarm, and creating a real danger by proclaiming one that was imaginary. It was Mr. *Burke* who made himself cryer to the new inquisition, and prepared the way for the *Reeveses*, the *Devayneses*, and the *Idesons*,[51] whose *departmental star Chambers*, and *Revolutionary Committees*[a] have polluted the stream of administrative justice, and debased the character of the nation. He it was that, like a political dog-star, shook "from his horrid hair"[52] distemper and delirium; till the brain-fever of property maddened the whole land; and great bankers and wealthy merchants, surrounded by their clerks and dependants, (the myrmidons of the ware-room and counting-house) turned Merchant Taylor's Hall into a bear garden; put Billingsgate and Bedlam to the blush by their disgraceful, and outrageous conduct; and thus presented us with a modern illustration of that profound and indubitable remark of *Machiavel*, that "tumults and disturbances are more frequently created by the wealthy and powerful, than by the poorer classes of society."[b] In short, it was Mr. *Burke* who condescended to be the

---

[a]This phrase may sound rather harshly in the ears of *loyal associators*! but it should be remembered, that there are revolutions against liberty, as well as revolutions for it: revolutions made by governors against the people, as well as revolutions made by the people against the government. The latter of these have always, I believe, proceeded from necessity; have been actuated, in the first instance, by right principles; and have been productive of ultimate good. The former have as uniformly resulted from the ambition, rapacity, and tyranny of wicked counsellors, and have been productive of oppression and misery, and generally of *ultimate revolt*! These revolutions are, in reality, the causes, and the justifications of the other.—But of this more in the text.

[b]See that invaluable work "Discourses on the first decade of Titus Livius."[53] Versions of this neglected book, both in *French* and in *English*, are to be met with upon almost every stall: and my readers cannot do better than transplant it, and, indeed, the whole of this author's works, into their libraries. The doctrine above quoted, will be found at some length in book i. c. 5.

Some, perhaps, may think that I have treated this "respectable body of men"! rather too harshly in this passage: but the turbulent yells, the grinning distortions of impassioned countenance, the jostlings, and personal violence, with which every individual was assailed who attempted to oppose their resolutions, cannot but live in the memory of all who were present at that meeting. The outrageous and assassin-like attack made by a part of this *respectable body* upon Mr. *Favel*,[54] as he was departing from the hall, fixes a stain of a deeper dye, and would furnish some colour, at least, to the arguments of those who might wish to persuade us, that the boasted police of this country, is not so much intended to preserve the peace, and protect the persons of the people, as to enforce a blind and abject submission to the will of the governing party! The conduct of these same *respectable gentlemen* at Grocer's Hall[55] was, I understand, still more outrageous. Let any person compare these facts with the tranquil, firm, and orderly proceedings of the immense multitudes of *common people* assembled at *Chalk Farm, Copenhagen House*, and *Mary-le-bone Fields*,—the regularity with which they transacted their business, and the peaceable manner in which they dispersed, as soon as it was over; let them add to this, an attentive examination of the behaviour of the plebeians and of the patrician order, in what are called the *seditions* of ancient Rome, and then let them draw what arguments they can in favour of the maxims and system of the present administration.

"jackal", not of a *lion*, but of an *ape*, who, having run through all the tricks and metamorphoses of apostacy, determined, at last, to become a beast of prey, though he had neither the courage, nor the sagacity, to start his own game.

His new ally, however, caught up the scent with all imaginable keenness. No sooner did the troubles in France make their appearance, than he began to beat the war-provoking hide of "old *John Zisca*",[a] and call out for carnage and blood.—Like *Collins's* personification of Anger, forth

> "—he rushed: his eyes on fire
> In lightnings own his secret stings!"[56]

and, this too, at a time when every thing in that country was going on so humanely, so philosophically, so benevolently, that every generous heart in Europe sympathised with the triumphs of Gallic liberty; and mankind began to lose their nationality, and nobles their prejudices, in the unbounded admiration of an event that promised a speedy extinction of those systems of devastation and ambition, which have hitherto been the greatest scourges of the universe.

It is in vain that Mr. *Burke* now raves about massacres, and sanguinary executions. It is in vain, that he disgusts our imaginations with tedious rhapsodies about "foul and ravenous birds of prey—obscene revolutionary harpies, sprung from night and hell, or from that chaotic anarchy which generates equivocally all monstrous, all prodigal things"![b] At the time when his first wild and frantic publication on this subject ministered to the insidious designs of his present patrons, no excesses had taken place which could justify his abuse, or afford the least colour for regarding the French revolutionists as maniacs who thought "*The whole duty of man* consisted in destruction."[c] The revolution was then in the hands of "philosophers", and "literary men"![d] It had not yet fallen (as afterwards, from the unprincipled interference of foreign despots, and the still more fatal influence of *foreign gold*, scattered among emissaries "in the night cellars of *Paris*", to hire intrigue, and provoke insurrection, it did most undoubtedly fall) under the management of "bravoes and banditti"—of "robbers and assassins". If his

[a]Letter, &c. p. 3.
[b]Letter, &c. p. 21.
[c]Ibid. p. 57.
[d]Ibid. p. 57.

declamations against the changes that have taken place in that country, had never been heard of till the system "of pillage, oppression, *arbitrary imprisonment*, confiscation, exile, revolutionary judgment, and *legalized premeditated murder*",[a] had been adopted; and those declamations had been abandoned when the cruelty and wickedness of this system were relinquished, he might have claimed some credit, perhaps, for his humanity; and have laid less open to the suspicion of a grounded abhorrence to every principle of liberty. Even then, however, we must have pitied the confusion of intellect that could not separate principles from unprincipled actions; and continued to revere the sentiments of truth and justice, however they might be violated by their professors: or rather by individuals of the country in which they were professed.

But it is the profession and occupation of this singular writer, to confound all distinctions by affected *antithesis*; to destroy all unities of time, place, and action, for the purposes of misrepresentation; to bewilder the misunderstandings of his readers by incongruous mixtures of fact and fiction, and to build his conclusions upon artful transpositions, that unite things together which have no connection, and make causes the consequences of their own effects. His mode of analysis is to break down the whole series of events into one chaotic mass; and then, selecting such parts as are best suited to his purpose, and arranging them according to his own arbitrary fancy, to draw conclusions that contradict all the facts of history, and all the dictates of unsophisticated reason. Thus, for example, the French Revolution having at different periods, and under different circumstances, brought into action, upon the political theatre, some of the most enlightened philosophers that ever adorned, and some of the fiercest cannibals that ever disgraced, the modern world, Mr. *Burke*, that every thing French, and every thing revolutionary, may be brought into abhorrence at once, confounds the two classes together under the denomination, "of the Cannibal Philosophers of France";[b] and exclaims, with affected astonishment, "In the French Revolution every thing is new; and from want of preparation to meet so unlooked for an evil, every thing is dangerous. Never, before this time, was a set of literary men converted into a gang of robbers and assassins. Never before, did a den of bravoes and banditti, assume the garb and tone of an academy of philosophers."[c]

[a]Letter, &c. p. 64.
[b]Letter, &c. p. 56, 59.
[c]Letter, &c. p. 57.

Never before! No, nor now. The author of the "Reflections on the French Revolution", and the author of the "Rights of Man", are not more distinct—the sentiments of *Edmund Burke* on the American war, and the sentiments of *Edmund Burke* on the present crusade, are not more opposite than the men and the motives he has thus confounded together. They were men, not only distinct, but in positive opposition. As well might the till late unheard-of maxims of despotism, said to have been delivered by the Bishop of *Rochester* and Lord *Loughborough*,[57] be attributed by future historians to the Earl of *Lauderdale*, by whom they were so spiritedly and so properly exposed![a]—as well might *Thomas Paine* be reproached with the virulent and unprincipled malignancy of stigmatising the oppressed, laborious, and most valuable classes of society as a "swinish multitude", because he lived and wrote in the same age with the being who outraged humanity with such scurrility, as the crimes of *Robespierre*, of *Couthon*,[59] and of *Marat*; of the ATTORNEY GENERAL *Fouquiere*,[60] and the hangman *Le Bone*,[61] be charged to the account of the *Condorcets*,[62] the *Isnards*,[63] the *Rochefoucaults*,[64] and the *Rolands*,[65] who were the *victims*, not the *authors*, of the crimes which we deplore.

That the philosophers of France were too cold, too speculative, too slow and cautious, to have saved their country, in the desperate condition into which they were plunged by the coalition of German despots, and the intrigues and corruption of courts *pretending neutrality*—that they had too little of the energy of men of business for the stormy times they had to steer through, and that the profligate and detestable proclamation of the Duke of *Brunswick*, (the true *proximate cause* of all the massacres and horrors in *France*), required other antidotes than fine-spun theories and speculations, however just and excellent, I am ready to admit: nor shall I be backward in stigmatising with just epithets of abhorrence, the ferocious barbarity, the enormous, the almost unparalled cruelty (I say *almost*—for I have not forgotten *Ismael* and *Warsaw*!) with which the more energetic party abused their power! But if it was the misfortune of *France*, that her philosophers were deficient in the powerful energies of manhood,[b] and her energetic

---

[a]Debates on Lord *Grenville's* new treason bill.[58]

[b]"France", says Madam Roland, "was in a manner destitute of *men*. Their scarcity has been truely surprising in this revolution, in which scarcely any thing but *pigmies* have appeared. I do not mean, however, that there was any want of wit, of knowledge, of learning, of accomplishments, or of philosophy. These ingredients, on the contrary, were never so common:—but as to that *firmness of mind*, which J.J. Rousseau[66] has so well defined, by calling it *the first attribute of a hero*, supported by that *soundness of judgment*, which knows how to set a true value upon things, and by those *extensive views* which penetrate into futurity, altogether constituting *the character of a great man*, they were sought for

characters destitute of the humanising temperament of philosophy, surely it is not therefore just, to attribute to the former the savage ferocity that deformed the latter; or, by confounding them together, to involve the whole in one indiscriminating censure, and endeavour to bring all science and philosophy into disgrace, and represent "*knowledge*" itself as "rendered *worse than ignorance*, by the enormous evils of this dreadful innovation."[a] Still less will it be admissable, to attribute the mischiefs that sprung from these unfortunate combinations of circumstances to the principles of the revolution, if it can be proved (and the proof I think, would not be difficult), that *the imbecility of the philosophic, and the ferocity of the energetic party, had their remote causes alike in the vices and cruelties of the old despotism.*

Is Mr. *Burke* really so ignorant, or does he presume so far upon the ignorance of his fellow citizens—upon the "stupefaction of the dull English understanding",[b] as to pretend that the *philosophers* and the *Septembrizers* of France were the same persons;—that the promulgators of the humane, the incontrovertible, the glorious principles that breathed through the speeches and declarations of the National Assembly, and enlarged, at once, the boundaries of science and philanthropy, were also the perpetrators of those horrid massacres, and still more horrible executions, by which all principles, all humanity, all justice, were so outrageously violated? Reason, at once, revolts at such a conclusion. But, fortunately, this argument, so important to the human race, does not rest upon the conclusions of speculative reason. Fact—strong, stubborn, incontrovertible fact (so hateful to the juggling philosophers of *the old sect*) stares us in the face so openly, that one knows not how sufficiently to admire the confidence of the man who could so grossly misrepresent *events and affairs of yesterday*, or the supineness and voluntary ignorance of those whom such misrepresentations could deceive!

Who are the philosophers and metaphysicians of France, whose subtile theories of humanity, and refinements of universal philanthropy, have been so mixed and confounded with cold barbarity, or savage ferocity, as to

---

everywhere, and were scarcely any where to be found."[67] These observations display at once great penetration and great prejudice in this extraordinary woman. The latter prevented her from looking for *real greatness of mind* beyond the boundaries of her own party; but the former compelled her to acknowledge, that within this pale it was not to be found. The qualities, however, of which the Girondists were so obviously deficient, were most eminently possessed by several of the Mountain party, and by *Danton*, in particular, perhaps in as high a degree as by any individual whose "name is destined to live in the pantheon of history."

[a]Letter, &c. p. 21.
[b]Letter, &c. p. 63.

justify this favourite Claudian figure of rhetoric[68]—"cannibal philosophy", with which we are so frequently indulged? Which of the *metaphysicians of France* has been "ready to declare", either by word or action, "that he did not think a prorogation of humanity for two thousand years, too long a period for the good he pursued?—or that his imagination was not fatigued with the contemplation of human suffering, through the wild waste of centuries, added to centuries of misery and desolation"?[a]

I could point out, with infinite facility, certain *English metaphysicians*, who go much beyond all this; whose "humanity", (and whose liberty also) may be truely considered as "at their horizon; and like the horizon, always to fly before them":[b] who would put *Liberty to sleep*, that she might be able (when they thought it convenient) to open her eyes—preserve the freedom of the Constitution, by establishing despotism upon its ruins; shew their hatred of violence, by incessant appeals to military coercion; their love of justice, by sanguinary persecutions *iniquitously legal*; and their humanity, by a conspiracy to starve twenty-four millions of people: and who, so far from being "fatigued with the contemplation of human suffering, through the wide waste of centuries, added to centuries of misery and desolation", wish for *eternal* war—*eternal* massacre, pillage, and desolation;—pronounce, that peace with regicides *never* must be made;[c] and seem to wish, that when their *tongues* can no longer call for blood and carnage, "their *skins* may be made into *drums*, to animate Europe to eternal battle."[d]

It is easy also to point out metaphysicians in this country, who answer too well some other of Mr. *Burke's* descriptions—who "wish[e] their sophistical *Rights*" (not "*of man*", it is true, but) of *rotten-boroughmongers*, "to falsify the account, and the *sword*[f] *as a make weight* to throw into the scale", profess to have armed one part of their fellow citizens for the subjugation of another; and protect the freedom of senatorian debate, by threatening to answer the arguments of their opponents with the sabres of a *praetorian cavalry*.

How gracefully appeals to humanity and virtue come from such lips as these! How fit and appropriate to such men, the moral indignation which bursts forth in reproaches of *Barbarism* and *Cannibal Philosophy*!

[a]Letter, &c. p. 62.
[b]Letter, &c. p. 62.
[c]Letter, &c. p. 80.
[d]Ibid. p. 3.
[e]Ibid. p. 54.
[f]See debates on Colonel M'Leod's motion on the subject of the Fencible Cavalry.[69]

I wish not to degenerate from argument to abuse. I trust I have conducted myself throughout these strictures with a temper and moderation which will shew, at least, that *Sans Culottism*, in its true signification,[a] is not inconsistent with the urbanity and mildness of polished life; and I should be sorry, towards the close of my labours, to forfeit a character so essential to public utility: but if hard words must be used—if our adversaries, in defect of argument, will appeal to abuse, can it be helped if the ill directed ball rebounds? and may it not be admissable, so far, to retort upon them, their *uncitizen-like* (or, in their own language, *ungentlemanlike*) epithets, as to ask them, whether these are not the real literary assassins—the real philosophical banditti, and metaphysical bravoes, from whose example they have derived those extravagant and incongruous definitions which, by a strange jumble of characters and events, they endeavour, in their virulent rhapsodies, to apply to the *philosophers* and *literary men* of France?—But the jaundiced eye of prejudice sees every thing discoloured, and knows not that the distemper exists in itself.

I mean not to deny that crimes and excesses have been perpetrated in *France*. Deeds have been done "at which the face of heaven glows with horror"![71] But let not Mr. *Burke* hide the deformity of his own cause in this black cloud of indiscriminate abuse. Let him bring forth his lists of philosophical banditti and assassins; and let us see this pretended connection between the *metaphysics "of the new sect"*, and the crimes that have torn that sometime distracted country, or his attack upon *French principles* must fall to the ground. If the *excesses* cannot be proved, either logically or experimentally, to have been connected with the *principles*, coincidence of time is nothing to the purpose, and the one cannot be said to have produced the other. Now if the principles did not produce the excesses, the excesses must have been produced by something else: and nothing can be more illogical than to condemn any set of principles on account of consequences that never resulted from them.

It matters not, I repeat it, that the principles were propounded, and the excesses committed nearly about the same time. If a philosopher and an assassin happen to take shelter at the same inn, is the philosopher therefore a cut-throat, and the assassin a metaphysician? But Mr. *Burke's* way of arguing is still more inconsistent and unjust.—A banditti of ruffians, or

---

[a]I beg leave to quote from the earliest of my political works, my own definition of a *Sans Culotte*.— "An advocate for the rights and happiness of those who are languishing in want and nakedness." *Pol. Lect.* p. 26.[70]

"cannibals", if he pleases (for I can find no epithet too strong for their crimes) having broken in upon a company of philosophers, who were teaching the principles of justice and philanthropy to a throng of newly emancipated slaves, they killed and devoured the greater part of them, and then began to fall upon the pupils: and for this reason, and for no other, (unless it be that the philosophers had assisted the throng in escaping from the tyranny of their masters) this acute logician confounds together, the devourers and the devoured; and because one party were philosophers and the other cannibals, calls them a set of cannibal philosophers.

Is not this, I demand, a fair statement of the case? Consider, I conjure you, my fellow citizens, for the question is well worthy of serious examination; and it is time we laid aside our animosities and our heats, and examined it with temper and moderation. The misrepresentations that have too long inflamed our minds "are not wholly without an object"![a] While we are waging war with Gallic Liberty, we are losing our own. Corruption has been long assailing us on every side; and though her shafts may have been steeped in anodynes to prevent the present smart, the wounds are, for that very reason, the more dangerous. Despotism is now approaching with gigantic strides; and, distracted and alarmed by a thousand incoherent terrors, we are sinking, for shelter, into the vale of abject submission. But let us dissipate, in good time, these visionary delusions,—these vapours of the drowsy brain; lest, when awakened at last upon the extreme verge of destruction, we should be obliged to return by that uphill path whose rugged activities have occasioned so many strains and bruises to our unhappy neighbour.

"Awake! arise! or be for ever fallen!!!"[72]

Be not deluded by idle rhapsodies and arbitrary combinations. Excesses and cruelties are not forms of government. Actions are not principles—either *old* or *new*. Philosophy is not a cannibal; nor can a cannibal be a philosopher! The *new principles of France*, as they are called, are good in themselves:—the principles of equal rights, and equal laws. They are, in fact, the *oldest principles in the world*: the principles upon which the wisest and happiest governments of antiquity were founded: expanded and improved, it is true, but not fundamentally altered, by the wisdom derived from the improved state of human society—the wider diffusion of intellectual acquirement—and the more general intercourse of mankind.

These principles, I repeat it, in themselves are good. If our antagonists

[a]Letter, &c. p. 4.

are seriously of a different opinion, why do they not examine them, without misrepresentation or abuse, on the simple foundation of their own merits or defects? Why confound them with other things? Why pretend to discuss principles, and talk of nothing, in reality, but the actions of unprincipled men? Is time unsteady, because my watch goes wrong? Is it not noon when the sun is in the meridian, because the parish dial is out of repair? Can *principles*, which are the sun of the intellectual universe, be changed in their nature or their course by the vile actions of a few ruffians? Prove to me, by dispassionate argument, that the *principles* of the French Revolution are false and pernicious, and I will relinquish them at once, and thank you for delivering me from my errors. But while my reason tells me that they are consonant *in themselves* with truth and justice, it is not calling them *French* principles—it is not calling them *new lights*—it is not *the hoary prejudice of six thousand years*—it is not calling me *Jacobin*, nor calling others *cannibal philosophers*—it is not talking of the "ignorant flippancy"[a] of a man whom the learned solidity of colleges and consistories have never been able to answer—it is not all the declamatory bitterness of *Burke*, the metaphysical frenzy of *Windham*, the sanguinary rage of *Pitt*, nor the long-winded sophistry of *Scott* and *Mitford*, shall compel me to relinquish these important truths:—no; not though it could be proved that the crimes of *Marat* and *Robespierre* surpassed the savage wickedness of the fiend *Zawarrow*, and the ferocity of Croats and Hulans.

Marat and *Robespierre* were no more to be regarded as integral parts of the *new principles of France*, than *Pitt* and *Dundas* as parts of *the old principles of England*; or than the *fire of London* as having been part of the river Thames, because its waves were blackened by the rubbish of falling houses, and the blazing rafters floated along the stream. The rafters and the rubbish were swept into the sea, and the Thames regained its wonted clearness: *Marat* and *Robespierre* are swallowed up in the ocean of eternity, and the new principles of France remain; and if *Pitt* and *Dundas* were to die of a surfeit, after a *Wimbledon* dinner, I do not believe, for my own part, that our liberties would be less secure.

As men are not principles, so neither are particular actions. Mr. *Burke* might as well contend, that barracks and subsidized mercenaries, and the short memory of a minister on a trial of life and death, are the British constitution, as that the tyranny of *Robespierre* was the new French system of philosophy and politics. To come still closer to the point, it were as

---

[a]Letter, &c. p. 77.

rational to affirm, that the massacres of Glencoe were the principles of *our* Glorious Revolution, as that the massacres of September were the principles of the Revolution of France!

That the revolution had had its "harpies",[a] as detestable as either *Virgil*[73] or Mr. *Burke* has described, who feasted on the general wreck, and were for leaving "nothing unrent, unrifled, unravaged, or unpolluted",[b] there can be no doubt: nor is it necessary, to account for the generation of "these foul and ravenous birds of prey",[c] to descend with the poet to the regions which superstition has peopled with more than mortal wickedness; or to mount with the political declaimer to the regions of philosophy and metaphysics.

What sort of figure *Fouquier Tinville* would have made by the side of the metaphysical Sir *John Scott*, I do not pretend to say; but who ever suspected either *Marat*, *Robespierre*, *Le Bon*, or any of that sanguinary party, of visionary subtilties and metaphysical abstraction? Which of those fine-spun metaphysical theories, whose abstract perfection is so abhorrent to Mr. *Burke's* "instincts"—which of those breviaries of fundamental principles which commanded the assent, and excited the admiration of the philosophical world, is attributed to either of these men? *Robespierre*, it is true, was a member of the Constituent Assembly; and we find him, at an early period, in possession of considerable popularity; but his popularity was not of a description to class him with those *speculative literati* against whom the politicians of the *old sect* have conceived such an inveterate abhorrence.

However this country may be disposed to indulge its vanity in comparisons, they are not always to our advantage. The *French* Robespierre was no *apostate*. There was a certain steadiness and consistency in his conduct and character, which, (together with some grand traits of simplicity and disinterestedness) even in the midst of abhorrence, compel us to respect him. Again, I repeat it, comparisons are not always in our favour: in the character of the *French* Robespierre there was nothing to excite our contempt. He had vices—demons of desolation! bear witness, he had vices: but they were not the vices of corruption. He neither maintained himself in riotous luxury, nor enriched lethargic brothers, and imbecile relations with the plunder of his country, disguised under the specious names of places and pen-

[a]Letter, &c. p. 21.
[b]Letter, &c. p. 21.
[c]Letter, &c. p. 21.

sions. He had cruelty too, the thought of which makes one's flesh creep: but though he issued a decree to give no quarter to *Britons* or *Hanoverians*, found in arms, he never entered into a conspiracy to *starve* twenty-four millions of men, women, and children![74]—He had virtues too—grand magnificent virtues! for "pure unmixed, dephlegmated, defoecated evil", exists no where but in the inflamed imagination of Mr. *Burke*. He was superior to all the sordid temptations that debauch the little mind—the allurements of luxury, ostentation, and rapacity. Surrounded by all the temptations of unlimited power, he lived like a private citizen, and he died a pauper.

Robespierre was, however, from the first a man of blood. He was for giving every thing to the people, it is true; but he was for giving it them not by the cultivation and expansion of intellect, but by commotion, and violence, and sanguinary revenge: and therefore it was that the revolutionary movements of *Robespierre*, perhaps, in despite of himself, hurried him into the most insufferable of all tyrannies, instead of conducting the people to freedom. There can be no freedom in the world but that which has its foundations in the encreased knowledge and liberality of mankind. Tyranny comes by violence, or by corruption: but Liberty is the gift of Reason.

Of this important truth the Revolutionary Tyrant seems to have been entirely ignorant; and from this defect, and the want of personal courage, proceeded, I believe, all the errors and all the horrors of his administration. Nay, so far was he from that metaphysical abstraction, which places its confidence in fine spun theories and bird's-eye speculations, that his conduct has given birth to a report, that he cherished almost as inveterate an abhorrence against philosophers and literati, as Mr. *Burke* and his new friends—So far was he from upholding the dangerous heresy of illimitable inquiry, that he would have roasted an atheist at the stake with as much satisfaction as the most pious bishop of the church.

During the reign of his desolating tyranny, philosophy was silenced, science was proscribed, and daring speculation soared no more. France was threatened with midnight ignorance; and in the *Club of the Cordeliers*,[75] at that time one of the instruments of his tyranny, a motion was even made to consume the public libraries.

Away, then, with these shallow pretences for degrading the noblest exercise of human intellect; Away with this idle jargon of cannibal philosophers and literary banditti! So unnatural an alliance never yet was formed; nor ever will. The assassins and ruffians of every clime, whether in the pay of *regular* or *revolutionary* tyrannies, have a sort of universal instinct whispering to them, that knowledge and oppression cannot thrive together.

"If we do not silence the press", says *Woolsey*, "the press will silence us":[76] and *Robespierre* (a little wiser in this respect than *Edmund Burke*) prohibited, in the Jacobin Club, the publication of his own speeches; lest his intemperance should provoke discussions which his tyranny could not afterwards controul.

But though the pretences of Mr. *Burke* for confounding together the *philosophy* and the *crimes of France* are thus completely refuted, I do not expect that the ground will be abandoned. It is too important a part of the permanent conspiracy against the liberties of mankind to be readily given up. Remove but this delusion from the eyes of the people, and the reign of Corruption could not last—"no, not for a twelvemonth." The principles of liberty are so consonant to the general good—the cause of the rotten borough-mongers is so destitute of all rational support, and the miseries produced by that system are so numerous, that nothing but the groundless terrors so artfully excited—nothing but the prejudices inspired against all speculation and enquiry, by confounding together things that have no connection, could possibly prevent the people of Britain shouting from every village, town, and street, with one unanimous and omnipotent voice—

"REFORM! REFORM! REFORM!!!"

Of this the faction in power are sufficiently aware; and there it is, that their hatred and persecution are principally directed, not against the furious and the violent, but against the enlightened and humane. Therefore it is, that they endeavour to confound together, by chains of connection slighter than the spider's web, every sanguinary expression, every intemperate action of the obscurest individual whose mind has become distempered by the calamities of the times, not with the oppressions and miseries that provoke them, but with the honest and virtuous labours of those *true sons of moderation and good order* who wish to render their fellow citizens firm and manly, that they may have no occasion to be tumultuous and savage; to spread the solar light of reason, that they may extinguish the grosser fires of vengeance; and to produce a timely and temperate reform, as the only means of averting an ultimate revolution. These are the men against whom the bitterest malice of persecution is directed. These are the men against whom every engine of abuse and misrepresentation is employed; to calumniate whom their "Briton" and their "Times"[77] and their dirty Grub-street pamphleteers, are pensioned out of the public plunder—and against whom grave senators from their benches, and *pensioned Cicero's* from their literary retreats, are not ashamed to pour forth their meretricious eloquence, in torrents of defamation, and to exhaust all the fury of inventive (or *deluded*) malice. These are the men for whose blood they thirst; and whom they endeavour to destroy by new doctrines, not only of accumulative and constructive treason, but of *treason by second sight*: making them accountable for actions they were never consulted upon, books they never read, and sentiments they never heard. These, in short, are the men for whose destruction laws are perverted, spies are employed, and perjurors are pensioned: and when all these artifices prove inadequate to the end, these are the men to stop whose mouths bills have been proposed, in parliament, subversive of every principle of the constitution, lest the nation at large should be in time convinced that they are not what they have been represented: but that *the friends of Liberty and Reform, are the true friends of Humanity and Order!*

This would be, indeed, a terrible discovery for those who are supported by corruption: and in this point of view one cannot blame them for the selection they have made of the objects of their persecuting hatred. To let their vengeance fall at once upon the really violent, would be an act of impolicy, that would shew them "to be foolish, even above the weight of privilege allowed to wealth"[a] and power. Were these suppressed (arguing upon their own supposition, that persecution can suppress) what would become of those pretences by which, alone, they have rendered the advocates of reform obnoxious to the fears, and consequently to the hatred, of the alarmists? But if they could destroy the real reformers, the men of reason, of humanity, of intellect, they would destroy the magnets (if I may so express myself) around which, whenever their influence shall become sufficiently diffused through the intelligent atmosphere, the good sense, the spirit, the virtue of the country, must be attracted; and when it is so attracted, and when the parts shall firmly and peacefully cohere, and, thus brought under the influence of the true laws of nature, shall press together, with the united force of attraction and gravitation, to one common centre of truth, the seven days work of creation is complete—the system is restored to order; and the unruly tempest of tyranny and corruption shall endeavour in vain to prolong "the reign of chaos and old night":[78] the planet shall roll on, regardless of the storm—grace, beauty, fertility, happiness, shall flourish in full luxuriance, and the meteors of delusion shall burst and expire. But were this principle destroyed—were those powers of intellect and virtue by which, alone, this grand harmony can be produced, suppressed by the timely interference of superior power, and every thing left to the misguidance of those *ignes fatui* of intemperance and revenge, which, in the night of ignorance, a foul corrupted atmosphere never fails

---

[a]Letter, &c. p. 55.

to ingender, in the low, rank, marshy fens of vulgar intellect, the friends of liberty would be no longer formidable; but while they floundered about in a thousand wild directions, destitute of any common principle, and unconscious whither they were going, must presently be swallowed up in the bogs, and swamps, and quagmires of their own delusion.

In simpler language, though commotion and violence are the watchwords of alarm, it is the progress of reason—the power of presiding intellect, of which, in reality, the borough-mongering oligarchy stand in dread. This, they are justly apprehensive, may in time disseminate what they call its *infectious influence*, so far as to palsy the very hands of corruption, and cause the sceptre of their surreptitious authority to fall, by the mere operation of its own weight, from their enfeebled grasp. But as for actual violence—this they can despise:—this, some parts of their conduct, and many of their sentiments, would almost lead one to suspect them of being desirous to provoke. Their military, they may suppose, would quickly suppress any insurrection; the tumult would afford a convenient opportunity of ridding the country of obnoxious individuals[a] and, while the victorious sword was yet out of the scabbard, who could blame them, if they took the opportunity of organizing a *military despotism?* But the friends of liberty are aware of this; and their conduct has proved how little they deserve the calumnies of Mr. *Burke*, and the ministerial faction. Intemperate language may sometimes have been used, and even received with intemperate applause; but the voice of reason has always been the commanding voice; nor could the grossest insults, nor the most methodised attempts of treasury hirelings, police ruffians,[b] and ministerial fanatics, (for there are fanatics, it should be remembered, of all sects) ever throw them into confusion, or provoke them to violence.

But Mr. *Burke* would be ill qualified for a champion in behalf of that

---

[a]I understand that a certain officer, of some rank in the army, has avowed that instructions of this kind have been given: "If any tumult should arise", he is reported to have said, "we know our game. We should not spend our fury on the *rabble*", (such is the language they use towards those useful members of society, whose industry supports and feeds them!) "we should look out for those prating rascals ······, and make sure of them, wherever they were to be found." I shall not insert the names that were placed at the head of this black list of proscription, for more reasons than one. Suffice it to say, they were such as fully to justify the above chain of reasoning. They were not men of blood—not men of violence—not men who yelp for tumult or revenge; who call out for rebellion, or breathe forth slaughter. No—no:— such characters are safe (for the present). They are the nest eggs: the hen pheasants, whom the keen sportsman must spare, that they may breed fresh game. Let us hope, however, that this was only gasconade: a *military bounce*: and that human nature is not yet so depraved, that such instructions could be either given or accepted.

[b]For a striking illustration of the propriety of this expression, see "Narrative of Facts", prefixed to "Political Lectures," vol. 1. part 1, p. xii. and xiii.[79]

cause he has *now* undertaken to support, if he could not confound together the clear and obvious distinctions between intellectual firmness and tumultuous violence—the energies of the mind, and the energies of the dagger! Ill would he be calculated to support the tottering cause of oligarchy and corruption, he if could not divert popular attention from the abuses and violence of his own party, by exciting unmerited odium against all intellect and enquiry, and throwing upon the philosopher and the philanthropist the imputation of those crimes which the enemies and persecutors of those characters in reality perpetrate, whether in France or Britain.

The sophistries, however, and misrepresentations of my antagonist end not here. Not only has he confounded together characters and events that were in reality distinct—not only has he charged the crimes of a few ferocious usurpers upon a whole people, and made the philosophers of France the authors and promoters of that very system of cruelty, in resisting which so many of them lost their lives; but he has assigned the excesses and crimes of the revolution *altogether* to a wrong cause; and charged upon *republicanism* the guilt of ingendering those hideous propensities—those enormous depravities of gigantic wickedness, which nothing but *despotism* ever did, or ever can produce. His talent seems, indeed, to lay quite in this way. In his "Reflections", in defiance of the well-known fact, that the famine, or *great scarcity of bread*, was one of the principal causes of the revolution, he charged the revolution with having caused that famine.[80] I am not, therefore, surprised to find him still obstinately persisting in charging all those cannibal dispositions upon the Republic, and the *Rights of Man*, which could not have existed at all, if the old despotism had not generated them; and which, at any rate, the revolution would only give their proprietors an opportunity of displaying in deeds of open violence and commotion, instead of employing them to perpetrate the secret cruelties and assassinations of the court—in devastations sanctioned by *regular authorities* and oppressions *"iniquitously legal"*!

That popular commotions call all the vices, as well as the virtues of the community into action, cannot but be admitted. That when "the cauldron of civil contention" is boiling over, the foulest ingredients will sometimes be at the top; and that, in the general fermentation, combinations the most deleterious will sometimes be formed, no reflecting man has ever yet denied. It is an additional argument why the rulers of the earth should take care not to render such commotions necessary and inevitable.

Happy, thrice happy shall it be for those princes and governments, who derive a useful lesson from the events that have passed before us! Happy, thrice happy shall it be for those wise and moderate rulers, who, in this busy, changeful, and enquiring age, put not their trusts in *janissaries* or *Swiss Guards*; but, adopting the salutary advice of the great Lord *Verulam*, shall illustrate by their conduct that profound and salutary maxim, that "the surest way to prevent sedition is not by suppressing complaints with too much severity, but to take away the matter of them."[a] In other words, the best way to manage the distemper, is not to amputate the limb but to remove the cause.

But whatever vices and dispositions the heat of popular commotion may call into action, must have been generated by former circumstances. Extraordinary exigencies place men in strong lights, and shew them such as they are: but they do not create characters of a sudden; nor manufacture mankind anew. Revolutions are touchstones for the real dispositions; but they do not, like the whisp of a harlequin's sword, change the dove into a tyger, or the tyger into a dove. If, therefore, we were to admit that all the revolutionists—the whole body of the French people, were indiscriminately involved in the guilt of those excesses so exultingly quoted, and so wickedly exaggerated by the foes of liberty—what would be the conclusion? Where would the blame in reality fall, but upon that old system of despotism, for the restoration of which Mr. *Burke* "would animate Europe to eternal battle."

The revolution in France, or more properly speaking, the philosophers and patriots who first set the *new order of things* in motion, did not create their agents. They did not sow the earth (like *Cadmus*) with dragon's teeth, and reap a harvest of men to carry on their projects.[82] They were obliged to make use of the instruments already made to their hands; and when the game was on foot, the bad as well as the good would have their share of the play. If, to resume the allusion, a race of contentious homicides did burst from the ground, and alternately destroy each other, the seed was sown by the *old despotism*, not by the *new philosophy*.

Mr. *Burke*, indeed, himself seems conscious, that the wild and ferocious characters he declaims against, could not have been formed by the revolution—he knew that *the men whom he stigmatizes for projecting and forming the Republic, could not have been formed and educated by the Republic*. Unwilling, therefore, to assign, in plain terms, the generation of the monsters he describes to the right cause, he calls in the aid of poetry, and tells us, that

---

[a]Essays, Civil and Moral, p. 77. and 80. *edition* 1725.[81] Title—Of Seditions and Troubles. Query, Why has Mr. *Burke* overlooked this essay!

these "revolutionary harpies, sprung from night and hell, and from chaotic anarchy, which generates unequivocally all monstrous, all prodigious things."—True, Mr. *Burke*, I thank you for the allusion. The revolution *harpies* did spring, most assuredly, from what with classical precision of metaphor you have called *hell*, and *night*, and *chaotic anarchy*. They sprung, indeed, from that hell of despotism, into the very abyss of which *France* had for whole centuries been plunged—They sprung, indeed, from that night of ignorance in which the best faculties of the human mind had been so long enveloped and extinguished—They sprung, indeed, from that chaotic anarchy of vice, licentiousness, profligate luxury, and unprincipled debauchery, into which the morals of the country had been thrown by the influence and example of the court, and which, it is rightly said, *generates equivocally all monstrous, all prodigious things!* These were, indeed, the infernal sources of all the evil: and but for that "night, that hell, that chaotic anarchy", of the old despotic system, such "obscene harpies", such "foul and ravenous birds of prey", never could have been in existence, to "hover over the heads, and souse[83] down upon the tables", of the revolutionists, and "rend, and rifle, and ravage, and pollute, with the slime of their filthy offal", the wholesome banquet, which the philosophers of the revolution had occasioned to be spread for the social enjoyment and sustenance of mankind.

Such *were* the monsters generated in the infernal region of the old tyranny; and in such regions such monsters always *must be* generated, till effects shall cease to be commensurate to their causes, and nature's self shall change. Was it not time then, think you, that this "great deep" were broken up—that the chaotic mass of tyranny and corruption might be thrown into new motion, by the addition of some fresh principle, or stimulus by means of which (through whatever noise and uproar) a more wholesome arrangement might be produced—

"And from confusion bring forth beauteous order?"[84]

It is vain to tell me, that these harpies were no harpies to mankind till they shewed themselves as such. Despotism had always its harpies, and they were always well banqueted. They banqueted in silence, indeed, under the *old system*: they were not garrulous, as under the *new order*: nor did the press trumpet forth their atrocities. But they rent, and ravaged, and rifled, and polluted, and devoured, and acted all their horrors and abominations, with avidity and diligence enough, for centuries before the revolutionary system was set in motion. Of this Mr. *Burke*, and every man who is travelled, either in climes or books, is well informed. They had their public theatres, in which they tore the quivering limbs of their prey, for the amusement of courtly spectators; and they had their cages—their cells—their Bastiles, or, as Mr. *Burke*, more delicately calls them, "king's castles",[a] where they might banquet in silence, and riot undisturbed in all the horrid luxuries of cruelty. The revolution gave them nothing but a voice: and this attribute was ultimately beneficial: for their hideous shrieks and yells, and the audacious publicity of their cruel ravages, concentrated, at last, the general hatred of the country they infested. They were hunted to their caverns; and the race has become extinct.

I do not, however, mean to affirm that the harpies of the new system were the same individuals as would have been the harpies of the old: though, in many instances, it was probably the case. Cruelty is cruelty, under whatever system it acts; and an inquisitor, a Fermier General, and the president of the revolutionary tribunal, in the *reel* of political mutation, might join hands, turn round, and change positions *ad infinitum*, without ever appearing out of place.

But this is not all. Inhuman oppression generates inhuman revenge. All strong impressions produce strong effects. That which we passionately detest, we are sometimes in as much danger of imitating, as that which we passionately admire. How often does the hatred of cruelty degenerate into the very thing we abhor? How often does the hatred of tyranny render men most tyrannical?—for the hatred of tyranny is one thing—the love of liberty is another. The former is a common instinct; the latter is the noblest attainment of reason. Add to which, that *lex talionis* is, with the generality of mankind, the law of moral action: "Eye for eye, and tooth for tooth", is inculcated as the mandate of Deity. But the nobility and clergy of France, had not eyes and teeth enough to answer this account. Can we wonder at what ensued?

It would have been well for France, if the influence of the old tyranny upon the moral character of the people, had terminated with the evils here enumerated. If the cruelty of long-established oppression had only made the irritable ferocious, and the ignorant revengeful, these destructive passions might have been controuled by the energy of more cultivated minds, till they had been softened and humanized by the influence of more favourable circumstances. But tyranny had not left to the revolution the possibility of the crime with which Mr. *Burke* has charged it in a former pamphlet. It had "slain the mind[b] of the country" long before that revolution

[a]*Reflections, &c.*[85]
[b]*Reflections, &c.*[86]

took place. Literature, it is true, had been highly cultivated. Science had been liberally patronized, in the upper circles; and even that republican talent, *eloquence*, had been cherished with a diligence most important, in its ultimate consequences, to mankind. But the jealous nature of the government—the terrors of the Bastile,—the shackles of an imprimatur—the homage exacted by birth and fortune, and, above all, the frivolity and effeminacy of character imposed on the nation by a profligate, thoughtless, and luxurious court, which, having nothing manly in itself, could not be expected to tolerate manhood in its dependants, "dwarfed the growth" of that mental energy which the tastes and studies could not otherwise have failed of producing. Hence originated the circumstance of which the female citizen *Roland* complains, that the revolution produced no *men*. The course of study had been perverted by the influence of the government. The closet of the philosopher was infected by the contagion of the court. Solidity was sacrificed to ornament—the virtues to the graces. In acuteness, subtility, penetration, and even profundity, their literati were not deficient: but they wanted that boldness—that active energy—that collected, unembarrassed, firmness and presence of mind, which nothing but the actual enjoyment of liberty, and an unrestrained intercourse with a bold, resolute, bustling and disputatious race of men can possibly confer. This energy of mind, without which it is impossible, in any useful and important sense of the word, to be a man of business, must be sought among "thronged and promiscuous audiences", "in theatres and halls of assembly"; for there only it is to be found. The philosophers of France, however, from the necessities under which they were placed by the government and institutions of the country, either mingled with the gay circles of the dissolute and great, and became infected with servile effeminacy, or indulged their speculations in a sort of sullen retirement, where the masculine boldness of the true philosophic character was chilled by solitary abstraction.

Thus did the genius of the old despotism destroy, alike, the humanity of the bold, and the energy of the humane and enlightened. And thus it was that, the philosophers being feeble, and the men of intrepidity being ferocious, the republic was torn and distracted by the crimes which the despotism had prepared.

If it were necessary to strengthen this argument with historical evidence—if it were necessary to prove by particular records, that the disposition to these inhuman crimes did not originate in the nature and influences of *republican government*, we might appeal to the *massacres of St.*

Bartholomew; to the barbarous oppressions and wanton cruelties described by *Arthur Young*, in the first edition of his travels,[87] as spreading misery and desolation through the lordships and seigniories of what Mr. *Burke* calls "the *virtuous* nobility of France";[a] and, above all, to the inhuman punish-ments—the savage protraction of lingering, but exquisite tortures, with which inventive cruelty, in some notorious instances, gratified the appetite of royal vengeance.[88] Nay, whatever might be the conduct of particular leaders, rendered cruel at first by their intolerant zeal, and afterwards, still more so by their dread of retribution, it would not be difficult to prove, that *the character of the people* was *humanized*, and *improved*, instead of being rendered more ferocious by the influence of the revolution. I appeal, in particular, even to the very circumstance of the decree, that no quarter should be given to the *British* or *Hanoverians*. What was the consequence of that decree? The brave soldiers of the republic refused to execute it, even in an individual instance; and the dictator was obliged to recal a mandate which he found himself unable to enforce. Would the soldiers of the old despotism, who perpetrated the horrors of the night of St. Bartholomew, have so refused? Did the military slaves of our good ally, the Empress, display the same obstinate repugnance to a still more inhuman order? Let the ghosts of murdered babes and sucking mothers, that still hover unap-peased over the captive towers of *Ismael* and *Warsaw*, answer the solemn question!

Having thus replied to the arguments, or rather to the abuse, of Mr. *Burke*, against the revolutionary philosophers of France; and having shewn, in the first place, that the cannibals and the philosophers were not only distinct, but opposite, sets of men; and, in the next, that the cannibalism proceeded not from the revolution but from the old despotism; it is not necessary to examine, very elaborately, the truth of his assertion, that "every thing in this revolution is new." If my arguments are just (and they are advanced in the very sincerity of my heart) it is matter of little conse-quence whether every thing is new, or every thing derived from ancient precedent. All that I shall do, therefore, is to quote from *Machiavel*, his brief abstract of the causes and progress of revolutions, that the reader may see how far the observations of that fine historian and acute politician will countenance this bold assertion.

"At the beginning of the world", says this author, "the inhabitants being few, they lived dispersed after the manner of beasts. Afterwards, as they

[a]Letter, &c. p. 49.

multiplied, they began to unite, and, for their better security, to look out for such as were more strong, robust, and valiant, that they might *choose one out of them to make him their head, and pay him obedience.*"[a]—He then briefly sketches the progress of society to another stage, when the people having emerged in some degree from barbarism, "being to make an *election of their prince,* they did not so much respect the ability of his body, as the qualification of his mind, *choosing* him that was most prudent and most just. But by degrees their government coming to be hereditary, and not by election, according to their former way, *those who inherited degenerated from their ancestors, and, neglecting all virtuous actions, began to believe that princes were exalted for no other end but to discriminate themselves from their subjects by their pomp, luxury, and other effeminate qualities; by which means they fell into the hatred of the people, and, by consequence, became afraid of them;* and that fear encreasing, they began to meditate revenge, oppressing some and disobliging others, *till insensibly the goverment altered, and fell into tyranny.* And these were the first grounds of ruin, *the first occasion of conjuration and conspiracy against princes;* not so much in the pusillanimous and poor, as in those whose generosity, spirit, and riches would not suffer them to submit to such dishonourable administrations. The multitude following the example of the nobility, took up arms against their prince; and having conquered and extirpated that government, they subjected themselves to the nobility which had freed them. These detesting the name of a single person, took the government upon themselves; and, at first (reflecting upon the late tyranny) governed according to new laws, devised by themselves, postponing particular profit to public advantage; so that both the one and the other were preserved and managed with great diligence and exactness. But *their authority afterwards descending upon their sons, who, being ignorant* of the variations of fortune, as not having experienced her inconstancy, *and not contenting themselves with a civil equality, but falling into rapine, oppression, ambition, and adulteries,* they change the government again, and brought it from an Optimacy to be *governed by a few, without any respect or consideration to justice or civility: so that in a short time it happened to them as to the tyrant: for the multitude being weary of their government, were ready to assist any body that would attempt to remove it.* By these means, in a short time, it was extinguished, and forasmuch *as the tyranny of their prince and the insolence of their nobles were fresh in their memory, they resolved to restore neither one nor the other,* but concluded upon a popular state."[90]

[a]Discourses on first decade of Livy, Book I, chap. 2.[89]

Such then is the brief abstract, drawn from the masterly pen of *Machiavel*, of the origin, progress, and revolutions of political society: and though some particular instances may be marked with partial varieties in one feature, and some in another, such is the general picture which the histories of the revolutions of the most celebrated nations of the ancient and modern world exhibit. The lesson it teaches is most important. Well would it be for the rulers of the earth, if they would lay the instruction to their hearts; and instead of producing by one sort of revolution the necessity of another, would pay that *respect* to the liberties of their respective countries, which they are so anxious to exact towards their own persons and authority. It is true, that in the style and language of history, in general, there is but one species of revolution, specifically marked as such— the revolutions by which governments are overthrown: but if we seriously attend either to this abstract, or to the histories of the nations, of which it is so just a summary, we shall find that these have uniformly been preceded by revolutions of another kind—the revolutions by which governments become tyrannical.

In one respect, then, at least, and the most important of all—in respect to its causes, there was nothing like novelty in the French Revolution: nothing that could surprise or astonish us. The *pomp, luxury, and effeminacy of the court* had been long notorious. The extravagant and profligate dissipation of the princes, their *neglect of all virtuous actions*, and their indulgence in every vice, was a common theme of reproach against them, through all the nations of Europe. The *sanguinary and vindictive spirit of the laws*, the *rapine, oppression, and jealous tyranny of the government*, and the consequent misery and destruction of the people, (in this country at least) were become proverbial; and *slavery and wooden shoes* was the logic by which we justified our hatred of the French nation.[a] Surely these were causes enough to justify a revolution—causes enough to produce one. The only astonishment must be, that it did not come before.

The only novelty in this event, as far as relates to causation, consists in the circumstance of the nobility and the monarchy being overthrown together. But this very circumstance shews the profundity of *Machiavel*, and the accuracy of his reasoning; and exposes the "flippancy" of Mr. *Burke*. It is novelty of combination in the history of facts; but not novelty of combination in the history of cause and effect. It is an additional argument in favour of the assertion, that popular revolutions are consequences of the

[a]And yet, now we are to hate them for throwing their slavery and their wooden shoes away!!!

revolutions of tyrannny and oppression. In *France*, two revolutions took place at the same time; because two kinds of tyranny[a] domineered together, and therefore two revolutions were necessary. The nobility, by "their natural ignorance, their indolence, and contempt of all civil government";[b] and still more by their unbounded rapacity, their wanton insolence, their barbarous exactions, and all-desolating pride—or, in the language of my quotation, by *the rapine, oppression, ambition, and adulteries*, which they indulged *without respect or consideration of justice or civility*, had brought themselves into general abhorrence and detestation, even before any *conjurations and conspiracies against the prince* had arisen. They had made themselves partners in the guilt, and were therefore partners in the punishment of the tyranny. Instead of being a bulwark between the prince and the people, to preserve the latter from the oppression of the former, they were indeed the chief battery from which the destructive engines of Gallic tyranny spread ruin and desolation through the land.

And are these persons whom Mr. *Burke* pretends "are so like the nobility of this country, that nothing but the latter, probably not speaking quite such good French, could enable us to find out any difference"?[c] I would not for the whole pension of this "defender of the order", that this comparison should be true: for if it were—if the titled great of Britain were what those of France had been, then should I exclaim, in the bitterness of my soul, that their crimes and their oppressions ought no longer to be endured—no longer protected by the laws and institutions of the land; but that they, also, in their turn, ought to be driven into ignominious banishment.

Never—never (let us hope) will our nobility and great proprietors realize the simile Mr. *Burke* has so imprudently made! Never—never (let us hope) will the vices, the profligacy, the insolent oppression, and immeasurable rapacity of the French aristocracy, ravage and depopulate this country: for if they should, not all the rhapsodies of pensioned eloquence—not all the treason and sedition bills of *Pitt* and *Grenville*, can avert the terrible catastrophe.

But the danger to this country comes from another quarter. It is not

---

[a]I might say three. But I omit the ecclesiastical tyranny, because it does not fall immediately in the way of my argument; and because the same reasoning will evidently apply in this instance as in the others.

[b]Montesq. Spir. Laws, b. ii. c. 4.[91]

[c]Letter, &c. p. 59. Mr. B. it is true, applies the comparison only to the Duke of *Bedford*; but it applies either to all or none.

from the aristocracy, properly so called, that we have most to dread. It is not even from the prerogatives of the executive power. It is from the oligarchy of the rotten borough-mongers. It is from the corruption of that which ought to be the representative branch of the legislature. This it is that is undermining (I must not say has undermined) the constitution and liberties of Britain. This it is that is realizing, with fatal rapidity, the prophesy of *Montesquieu*—"As all human things have an end, the state we are speaking of will lose its liberty. It will perish. Have not *Rome, Sparta,* and *Carthage* perished? It will perish, when the legislative power shall be more corrupted than the executive!"[a]

Such, at least, are the apprehensions that have crowded upon my mind. Such are the dangers which, during the last five years, I have endeavoured, with the most laborious diligence, to avert, by the only means through which they can be averted—by provoking popular enquiry; by rousing, as far as I had power to rouse, the energies of peaceful but determined intellect; and by endeavouring, with all the little persuasion I could muster, to wean my fellow citizens from the prejudices and delusions of party—from all the idolatrous attachment to names and individuals, and to fix their hearts and affections upon principle alone—the great principle of philanthropy—the principle of universal good—the source and fountain of all just government—of *equal rights, equal laws, reciprocal respect, and reciprocal protection.*

These are the principles I have endeavoured to inculcate, in political societies, at public meetings, in my pamphlets, in my conversations, and in that lecture-room (that school of vice, as Mr. *Burke* is pleased to call it) at which he is so anxious to dissuade the "*grown* gentlemen and noblemen of our time from thinking of finishing whatever may have been left incomplete at the old universities of this country."[b]

If to have inculcated these principles with a diligence and perseverence which no difficulties could check, no threats nor persecutions could controul—if to have been equally anxious to preserve the spirit of the people, and the tranquillity of society—to disseminate the information that might conduct to reform, and to check the intemperance that might lead to tumult—if these are crimes dangerous to the existence of the state, the minister did right to place me at the bar of the Old Bailey: and, if perseverance in these principles is perseverance in crime, it may be necessary

[a]Sp. Laws, book xi, c. 6.[92]
[b]Letter, &c. p. 35.

once more to place me in the same situation of disgrace and peril. If to assemble my fellow citizens for the purpose of political discussion—if to strip off the mask from state hypocrisy and usurpation—if to expose apostacy, confute the sophisms of court jugglers and ministerial hirelings, and drag forth to public notice the facts that demonstrate the enormity and rapid progress of that corruption under which we groan, and by means of which *the rich are tottering on the verge of bankruptcy, and the poor are sinking into the abyss of famine*—if this is to keep a public *school of vice and licentiousness*,[a] then was it right in ministers to *endeavour* to seal up the doors of that school with an act of parliament; then was it right that I should be held up to public odium and public terror, by the inflammatory declamations of the *Powises*[93] and *Windhams*, the tedious sophistries of the *Scotts* and *Mitfords*, the virulent pamphlets of the *Burkes* and *Reeveses*, and *the conjectural defamations* of Godwin.[b] But upon what sort of pretence, even the inflamed and prejudiced mind of Mr. *Burke*, can regard me as "a wicked pander to avarice and ambition",[c] I am totally at a loss to conjecture. I have attached myself to no party. I have entered into none of the little paltry squabbles of placemen and oppositionists, by which, alone, profit or promotion can be expected. My heart and soul, it is true, and I believe the heart and soul of every man who entertains one grain of respect for the rights and liberties of mankind, was with the *Whigs* in their conduct and sentiments relative to the two bills, to which, as they are now passed into laws, I shall give no *epithet*. I trust they have an epithet, sufficiently descriptive, engraved upon the heart of every *Briton*. I thought, and I still think, that the man must be extravagant, indeed, in his expectations, who was not satisfied with their behaviour in this respect; and particularly with the firm and manly opposition of *Fox, Erskine*, and *Lauderdale*:[95] from the first of whom, I confess, I did not expect a conduct so bold and *unequivocal*. If any thing can preserve the party from that perdition into which, by

[a]Letter, &c. p. 36.

[b]It is painful to see such a name, in such a list. But if men of great powers, however sincerely attached to liberty, voluntarily, by cold abstraction and retirement, cherish a *feebleness of spirit*, which shrinks from the creations of its own fancy, and a solitary vanity, which regards every thing as vice, and mischief, and inflammation, but what accords with its own singular speculations; and if, under these impressions, and regardless of the consequences to an isolated individual, assailed already by all the malice and persecutions of powerful corruption, they will send such bitter declamations into the world, as are contained in the first 22 pages of "Considerations on Lord *Grenville's* and Mr. *Pitt's* Bills", they must expect to be classed with other calumniators.[94] The bitterest of my enemies has never used me so ill as this *friend* has done. But nothing on earth renders a man so uncandid as the extreme *affectation* of candour.

[c]Letter, &c. p. 47.

its *cold, half measures*, it has so long been falling, it is persevering in the temper, spirit, and sentiments of *that* opposition. So long as they do persevere in that temper and spirit, I hope, and trust, that the hearts and souls of Britons will continue to be with them. So long as they do so persevere, my heart and soul, for one, will be with them, most undoubtedly:—not as a *partizan*, for that I abhor—but as one who, coinciding with them in a particular principle, is anxious to neglect no opportunity by which that principle can be promoted. But if ever, which, I trust, will not be the case, they should be again weighed down by the pondrous millstone of that sort of aristocracy already described,[a] which so long hung round their necks, and prevented them from soaring to the heights of consistent principle, INS and OUTS, WHIGS and TORIES, will become once more objects alike of indifference—of contempt!

Thus, then, I have coincided, upon a particular point, with men from whom, upon other subjects, I have widely dissented; and I have even persuaded myself, that if these men persevere in the sentiments and conduct displayed on that occasion, the introduction of Mr. *Pitt's* and Lord *Grenville's* bills will ultimately prove to have been proud days for *Britain*. But amidst these feelings, I have forfeited no consistency. I have shrunk from no principle. I have become no "pander to avarice and ambition": nor have I courted the patronage of wealth or greatness, by relinquishing any particle of that independance, which does, indeed, render me "prouder by far" than all that frippery "of the Herald's College", which Mr. *Burke*, so scientifically, details;[b] in as much as the pride of manly principle is superior to the infantile vanity of the age of toys and baubles.

Neither have I sacrificed to interest nor gratified avarice, by my particular pursuits: whatever the narrow-minded and the envious may suppose. What I have received from the public, as the voluntary price of my labours, has been spent in the public cause:—in redeeming myself from the incumbrances produced by incessant persecutions; in alleviating (where I could) the sufferings of other victims; and in the expences with which my exertions have been attended. I may say of my politics as *Goldsmith* of his muse,

"They found me poor, and still have kept me so."[97]

But though I murmur not at this, neither should I hold myself a "pander to avarice and ambition", if I had really been enriched by my lectures. Whatever emolument I might have reaped, surely I also might have said, "I

[a] P. 24 to 27.[96]
[b] Letter, &c. p. 39.

have not received more than I deserve":[a] for assuredly every man deserves all that he can get by the honest exercise of his faculties, whether of mind or body. To increase the burthens of an almost starving people, by receiving pensions from the product of public taxes, may be base. To extort money, under pretence of propagating doctrines which those who *must pay* are neither desirous to promote nor willing to hear, may be a species of public robbery: but to derive support, *however liberal*, from a course of public instruction, to which *the only persons who pay are the voluntary pupils*, Mr. *Burke*, if he had succeeded to that professor's chair, of which, it is said, he was once ambitious, would certainly have been ready to prove, not only blameless, but honourable.

If avarice and ambition had been my ruling passions, it is surely admissable for me, "thus attacked", to say, that with my talent for public speaking, I should not have abandoned, from scruples of principle, the profession of the law; which lays open so fair a field for the gratification both of the one and the other. If selfish principles actuated my conduct, I needed not the insinuating message of a man (whose eminence in a learned profession ought to have lifted him above the shameful office of a *go-between to male prostitution*) that, "if I chose, I might do something better for myself than delivering public lectures." Even without adopting these words in a sense which, coming from such a quarter, I suppose them to convey—even without becoming what my calumniator has called me—"a pander to avarice and ambition"; I have some confidence in my own resources; and I persuade myself, that with my habits of industry, and with my little stock of reputation, I *could* derive a better subsistence from some of the profitable branches of literature, than my politics ever brought me, or ever will bring.

If I have any motives of personal interest, I deceive myself, and am a fool. If I were to regard myself alone, I believe no act of parliament could affect my interests: and certainly no interest—no reward can compensate me for the ravages upon my constitution, and the sacrifices of social enjoyment (which, as a husband and a father, constitute the dearest gratifications of my soul), occasioned by those exertions in which I have been so incessantly and laboriously employed. But how sweet and alluring soever the blossoms of domestic felicity, we must not, in the selfish enjoyment of our own gay *partierre*, neglect to root out the thorns from the road of the way-faring traveller, who is too heavily laden to stoop and remove them for himself.

[a]Letter, &c. p. 10.

I have, therefore, renewed my exertions; and, although an act of parliament has prohibited lectures "on the laws, constitution, government, and
policy of *these realms*",[98] have opened my school again, and shall continue
to open it, at such intervals as health will permit, to give lectures on the
laws, constitutions, government, and policy of *other* realms, which it is not
yet prohibited to discuss;[99] to investigate the elements of *political science*,
and trace the *causes and consequences of the various revolutions which the
tyranny and oppressions of various governments have in different ages produced*:
and though I possess no infallibility—no patent of exemption from occasional flights, or rather *flounderings*, of verbose nonsense, I think I may
venture to promise that "no *grown* gentleman or nobleman", who shall be
desirous "of 'finishing", at *Beaufort-buildings*, "any thing that may have been
left incomplete at the *old* universities",[a] will lose his time in listening to
such jargon as the following passage, with the exposition of which I shall
close this pamphlet.

"I conceived nothing arbitrarily, nor proposed any thing to be done by
the will and pleasure of others, or my own; but by *reason*, and by *reason*
only. I have ever abhorred, since the first dawn of my understanding, to
this obscure twilight, all the *operations of opinion*, fancy, inclination, and
will, in the affairs of government, where only a *sovereign reason*, paramount
to all forms of legislation and administration, should dictate. Government
is made for the very purpose of opposing that reason to will, and to caprice,
in the reformers, or in the reformed; in the governors, or the governed; in
kings, in senates, or in people"![b]

In the name of common sense how many gods has Mr. *Burke* in his
mythology?—Who is this *Sovereign Reason*? In which of the seven heavens
does she reside? For he has told us that in this blind world she is no where
to be found! At first, indeed, I suspected my antagonist (for whom no
incongruity, no contradiction is too glaring) of having slipped unawares,
into rank democracy; and of describing, by this *new Gallicism—Sovereign
Reason*, the collective reason of the SOVEREIGN PEOPLE; or, in other
words, the concentrated opinion of mankind: but upon looking a little
further, I find that this cannot be his meaning, for he expressly says, that
"government is made for the very purpose of opposing this [Sovereign] Reason (whatever it is) to will, and to caprice, in the reformers or in the
reformed, in the governors or in the governed, in kings, in senates, or in

[a]Letter, &c. p. 35.
[b]Ibid. p. 24.

people": that is to say in all human beings. Now that which is to oppose the will and caprice of all human beings (or even to decide, in opposition to all human beings, what is *reasonable*, and what is *wilful* and *capricious*) must be either positive, existing *institution*, or it must be some *being* who is more than human. That it cannot be positive, existing institution, which is to be regarded as the standard, is evident; because Mr. Burke talks of "reformers and reformed"; and, *if positive existing institution is the standard of Sovereign Reason, there can be no reform at all*; for every attempt to reform is, upon this hypothesis, an opposition of the will and caprice of the reformers (whether kings, senates, or people) to this Sovereign Reason. What was this reason, then, which was not the operation of the opinions either of others or his own, but without consulting which he neither conceived any of *his* reforms, nor proposed any thing to be done?—Why does he thus bewilder our judgment, without amusing our imagination? Why leave us benighted in those cold fogs of mysticism? If he is inclined to impose upon us a belief in something more than mere vulgar human faculty, by which his reforms, and the all-perfect wisdom of government, are to controul the will and caprice of the human race, why not strike us at once with some grand flight of inventive fancy, that we may at least have something pleasurable and amusive in exchange for the common sense we are to surrender. Could not *Numa Pumpillius* have lent him his *Egeria*? or *Socrates* his *Daemon*? or St. *Dunstan* his red hot tongs, to lead the devil about the country, for the amusement of gaping rustics?[100]

Of all the fictions, romances, and impositions that bewilder mankind, the most insipid, as well as the most absurd, are these dull, canting, metaphysical rhapsodies!

The reader will judge between us; but for my own part, I have ever considered reason as nothing more than the operations of the mind, employed in the research, comparison, and digestion, of knowledge by which efficient understanding can alone be produced. For the sanity or perfection of this faculty, I believe that there is no positive test or standard; and that the most confident deduction of the most cultivated reason is but "an opinion" still; except in as much as relates to that *one science*, which is known to admit of demonstration. Considering, therefore, that all questions of government, must ultimately be decided either by the aggregated *reason* (or as Mr. *Burke* may call it, the aggregate *will* or *caprice*) of society, or, as is more commonly the case, by the reason, will, or caprice of the governors; and, considering, also, that the multitude can have no interest in reasoning wrong; I have thought it of the highest importance to awaken my fellow citizens, in this time of peril and affliction, to the exercise of their faculties on questions of the greatest importance to us all; and to inculcate, not as matter of dogmatical opinion, but of useful enquiry, such sentiments and doctrines as to me appeared conducive to public happiness. This, notwithstanding the calumny and persecution with which I may be assailed, I shall still continue to do, not rashly, I hope—I am sure not fearfully; varying my means, according to the circumstances under which new impediments and new restrictions may place me. Among other things, I have thought it my duty to make some reply to this seditious and inflammatory libel of Mr. *Burke* (for so to me it appears in the most eminent and alarming degree); making it, at the same time, a vehicle for the inculcation of principles favourable at once, I believe, to the *Rights of Man* and the *interests of humanity*—for they are indeed body and soul, and can only exist together.

I would fain hope that this pamphlet, and the answers it has provoked,[101] and will provoke, may rouse, once more, that general spirit of enquiry, so essential at this time; and that notwithstanding the temporary panic produced by the new treason and sedition acts, we shall return once more to the manly and vigorous exercise of those innumerable means, which still lay open for enforcing the bold enquiries of reason, and the sacred love of humanity and justice; that thus, if the wild and desperate projects of the minister should unhinge the system he professes to support, and produce that dissolution of all social bonds, which he professes such anxiety to avert, the *principle of order* may still remain, indestructible, in the hearts, feelings, and passions of my fellow citizens; and (as Dr. *Darwin* so beautifully says of *Nature*, from the rude mass, in which he supposes Death, and Night, and Chaos, will sometime or other mingle the whole planetary system)

> "High o'er the wreck, emerging from the storm,
> Immortal *Freedom* lift her changeful form;
> Mount from the funeral pyre on wings of fame,
> and soar and shine, another and the same!"[102]

RIGHTS OF NATURE,

AGAINST THE

USURPATIONS OF ESTABLISHMENTS.

A SERIES OF

LETTERS TO THE PEOPLE,

IN REPLY TO THE

FALSE PRINCIPLES OF BURKE.

PART THE SECOND.

CONTAINING

*First Principles: or Elements of Natural and
Social Rights.*

The Origin, and Distribution of Property.

And—The Feudal System.

BY JOHN THELWALL.

LONDON:

PUBLISHED BY H. D. SYMONDS, NO. 20, PATERNOSTER-ROW;
AND J. MARCH, NORWICH.

1796.

Letter the First

There is a class of Readers to whom it may, perhaps, appear necessary to apologize for somewhat of a different temper exhibited towards Mr. B. in the present pamphlet, from that which has been admitted, on all hands, to have distinguished my Answer to his former Letter.[1] But the apology must be sought in the publications of my antagonist himself. If I have become more warm, it is because the sentiments of Mr. B. have become more atrocious. His former attack was upon individuals: this is an outrage upon human nature: and he who can seek excuses to palliate the enormous pro-ligacy of a wretch, who would extirpate opinions by the sword, and devote eighty thousand of his fellow-citizens to judicial, or military massacre, must be deficient in that ardent benevolence, which, while it pants for the hap-piness of man, cannot but detest the sanguinary ferocity that yelps for wholesale carnage. Some, however, may think, that I am not without a sense of personal interest, to stir me, on this occasion. Perhaps it may be so: But I am not, at the same time, without my consolations. If the govern-ment should act upon the advice of Mr. B. my eyes will not be cursed with the horrors that must inevitably ensue: Mine will be the glory, and the comparative felicity, of being one of the first victims.

Beaufort Buildings, 5 Nov. 1796.

POSTSCRIPT TO THE THIRD EDITION.

Some blemishes, arising from hasty composition, principally in the first sixteen or eighteen pages, and some inaccuracies of the press, in the latter sheets, which escaped observation while the two former Editions were at the press, are corrected in this. A note, or two, has also been added, or enlarged; but in all essential points this Edition corresponds with the former; and it is hoped the earlier purchasers will not consider themselves injured by these critical amendments in the latter impressions.

The Second Part, now at the press, and treating matters of much higher import to the welfare and happiness of man, has been composed with greater deliberation and care; and, it is presumed, will require no such after-thought, as the stile of some passages, in this part, seemed to demand.

November 26, 1796.

LETTER I.
INTRODUCTORY REMARKS; ON THE SPIRIT AND TEMPER OF BURKE'S LETTERS ON THE PROSPECT OF A REGICIDE PEACE.

The *tocsin* of aristocracy sounds once more—the *generale* is beaten on the tortured hide of "old John Zisca",[2] and the yell of persecution rings through the harassed country. But the din of ravening oppression is no warning to a sluggish and insensate people. A drowsy stupor, creeping over the frozen nerve of misery, at once soothes, and threatens with the sleep of death.

The blood of friends and relatives is "poured out like water" in a profligate crusade of the powerful and wealthy, against the poor and weak—of governments, and government contractors, against the human race: Thousands and tens of thousands of our British youth are annually sacrificed by the yellow pestilence (that high priestess to the Moloc of West Indian avarice) for the perpetuity of the African slave trade:—Woes are aggravated by insults, and complaints are answered by persecutions which outrage humanity, and make law a mockery: the burthens under which we groan, have produced an organized system of monopoly, which, worse than a blighting mildew, hangs on the full ear of our vain prosperity, and, in spite of an abundant harvest, denies to the craving family of the artificer and the peasant, even the *negative blessing* of a plenteous meal: yet all these calamities, accumulated in one horrid mass, cannot urge us to the manly energies of reason, and the decided tone of *authoritative* complaint. But if neither invocations nor sufferings can warm you to sympathy, or rouse you to reflection, yet, listen, my fellow-citizens, to the prophetic fury of the arch-enemy of freedom: peruse the portentous leaves he has thus wildly scattered, and think upon the fetters that are still forging for you. Attend, I say, to the threats so liberally distributed, stamped as it were, with the currency of authority, from the very mint of court confidence, and issued by the pensioned hand of an apostate,[3] paid by the produce of *your labour* to encrease your burthens, and destroy your rights: and, when you have heard these denunciations, sink down again, if ye can, in wonted supine-ness, till the "salutary, but critical terrors of the cautery and the knife"— the relumined fires of Smithfield,[4] and the axe upon Tower Hill, awaken, and warn you that your hour is come.

To what an abject condition is the spirit of the country beaten down, when riotous paupers (to support whose wasteful luxury the labourer must sweat, so much the more at his hard drudgery, and return at night to so much the worse hammock and the worse meal) can dare to give public utterance to these sentiments of unqualified tyranny. The former publica-tions of Mr. B. were sufficiently explicit. But this is a declaration of open, inveterate, irreconcileable war, on the part of the governing few, not only against the lives, properties, and liberties, but against the sentiments and feelings of the subject multitude.[a] It is a direct vindication of the doctrine of exterminating opinions, and enforcing creeds and ceremonies by the sword—and denounces, at once, a computed number of eighty thousand people, (according to the author's own account, the stem and flower of British intellect) to the prompt and destroying fury of "a vigour beyond the law."[5]

The state is diseased when such men *dare* to utter such sentiments. I say *dare*—for though I wish not to stop discussion, either by legal persecution, or the fury of a mob, yet most certainly I do wish to uphold the salutary

[a]It has been the fashion, in certain assemblies, to rail against the practice of separating the government from the nation, as a new-fangled Jacobinical artifice; and Mr. B. is most outrageous against the French Directory on this account: Yet he himself out-jacobinizes Jacobinism in this way. There is, however, nothing new in it. The ancient historians teach us by their sentiments, as well as their facts, that when governments set up an interest opposite to that of the people—the people must seek an interest in opposition to their governments.

awe of popular opinion; and, notwithstanding some doctrines of supposed treasons, propagated in the late never to be forgotten parliament, and retailed again (if retail it could be called) in the nine hour harangues of Adair,[6] Scott,[7] and Mitford,[8] I shall venture to affirm, that in whatever country this salutary awe does not operate, not only upon the tools and dependants of government, but upon the government itself, *even to its highest head*, there tyranny, in its essence, is already established, and liberty is but a name.

And, how is this salutary awe to be enforced? By the manly energies of the people—by their active vigilance, in watching the conduct of their governors, and comparing it with the sentiments of their advocates and known retainers—by that intellectual courage, which dares to give utterance to whatever the heart feels; and, above all, by that sturdy, restless, jealous exertion of the inalienable prerogative of reason, which contends, inch by inch, for the great charters of birth-right and nature, and instead of shrinking, with panic terror, at every triumph of *legal* innovation, is roused to fresh exertions, and exercises, with greater ardour, the privileges and rights that remain. These are the means by which a brave and enlightened people *overawe* their governors, and compel them to exercise a wary and modest caution, salutary to the nation at large, and ultimately beneficial to themselves. These are the true and genuine checks of a free government. Without these, I repeat it, no government can be free. Different shapes and modes of political institution, may give to these checks a different mode of operation—a better or a worse—a more permanent, or a more precarious organization; but the principle is in the heart of the people; and where this principle is active, monarchy[a] itself may be attempered with a degree of liberty; without it, republics are but despotisms in masquerade.

How stands it in this country with respect to this salutary check, grounded (as in the ensuing letters I shall prove it to be) in the essential rights of nature, and the very principles of political association? Does the government—does the legislature—do the ministers, or even the hireling

---

[a]By monarchy, the reader is to remember, that I mean something very different from kingly power. The former means a government *by one man*, who holds his power by some supposed or assumed *individual* right: the latter is a delegated trust, conferred by, and held for the acknowledged *benefit of the people*. Where monarchy begins, kingship ends; and the people who bargained for a king, are not bound to submit to a monarch. If authorities were necessary for this distinction, I might refer to Polibius (Gen Hist. B. VI. Ext. I.)[9] The English reader may consult either *Hampton's* translation, vol. III, where (p. 5, 6, 7, 9, and 14) the distinction is repeatedly and clearly marked; or that of *Ed. Spelman*, affixed, together with the Greek text, to the first vol. of his edition of Dyonisius of Halicarnassus, p. 393, 395, 399, 403, and 405.[10]

scribblers of those ministers, feel and acknowledge this controlling awe? No. The legislature (the *late* legislature) has ventured to call this over-awing influence of popular opinion, high treason; the ministers have de-clared, in express terms, that they lay taxes on our shoulders for the sup-port of an immense troop of cavalry, to out-awe this awe, to destroy this check, to suppress this opinion, to ram it down our throats with the broad sword, or drown it with the murderous roar of musquetry; while grey-headed apostates bewail the pretended "relaxation of all authority", and call aloud for laws of more sanguinary promptitude, because "the crown", forsooth, cannot destroy, at will, whomsoever it chooses to arraign, but "retires from *its courts*, defeated and disgraced" by the groundless prosecu-tions with which its ministers insult the justice and the feelings of the nation. Could these things be—could we be thus dragooned and trampled upon—half gagged, and half bullied into silence, if we were the men we have been?—if we inherited the spirit of those ancestors, over whose hon-ourable graves we stalk, an abject and degraded progeny? No, the evil is here. A greedy and unsocial selfishness absorbs our faculties. A base tim-idity bows our soliciting necks to the yoke: and a want of all kindness, all good faith and common justice, to those who embark fairly in the common cause, palsies every effort of patriotism; and leaves the isolated wretch, whose desperate honesty still prompts him to contend with powerful usurpation, a prey at once to persecuting violence and malignant envy. These dispositions have had more to do in prostrating the hopes and liber-ties of the people, at the footstool of borough-mongering usurpation, than all the proclamations and persecutions of the last five years, backed and supported with the new-fangled laws of treason and sedition, the *formidable* legions of military associators, and all the troops of fencible and yeoman cavalry which inflate with such audacious confidence *the MARAT of the British cabinet.*

While these dispositions remain, the cause of liberty will be retrograde, the beggary and wretchedness of the multitude will continually encrease, and the growing insolence of authorised plunder will exult in apparent omnipotence. In short, while each man continues to care for no one but himself, all will be trampled upon and oppressed; and while the friends of liberty,[a] instead of considering themselves as one common family, cherish

---

[a]It is really lamentable to recollect how large a portion of those who have been persecuted for their attachment to the public cause, have either been driven to America for bread, or are pining for want of it at home. Aristocrats will not employ the men whom they have injured, and democrats neglect the veterans who have served them. Every instance of such neglect plucks a feather from the wing of freedom.

their private jealousies, and forget their common interests, so long will fresh projects of usurpation be formed and executed with impunity, and mankind be treated like a herd of cattle. But when the people, recovered from their panic, and roused from their insensibility, shall feel the importance of a persevering fortitude, and (yielding to that generous enthusiasm, which annihilates, or at least suspends, the petty factions of jealousy and envy) with a generous confidence and unanimity, shall resolve to demand their rights; then shall the fantoms of corruption fade away, and the dark mists of hovering despotism flee before the rising sun of British freedom. Then shall the hireling Burke, with the whole clan of pensioned scribblers, instead of yelping thus audaciously for the blood of their fellow-citizens, bow, with becoming awe, to the tribunal of popular opinion, and learn to respect the rights and the feelings, not only of "four hundred thousand political citizens", but of seven millions of enlightened Britons, all conscious of their natural and civil equality; all asserting their equal share in the common inheritance of *rights*, and producing "(in their persons) their title deeds."[a]

In the meantime, let us hope that this new outrage upon the rights, and feelings, and security of mankind, will not be without its influence in producing the desired effect: for, if ever wholesale denunciations could inspire a sense of common danger—and a sense of common danger could knit men together in the bonds of common interest, these pamphlets contain sufficient warning, that we must be no longer supine, selfish, and divided—unless, indeed, we mean to be reduced to the dreadful alternative of either abandoning, for ever, all opposition to the measures of government, however corrupt or tyrannical, or resigning to proscription, legalized massacre, and hired assassination, an acknowledged fifth—perhaps a third—perhaps more than half of the informed, reflecting, reasoning part of the community. This, I say, is the plain alternative, laid down by Mr. Burke. But I shall not, according to his fashion, satisfy myself with assertion. I shall proceed to proof.

Mr. B. I should premise, is a very desultory, and excentric writer. His combustible imagination fumes, and boils, and bursts away, like the lava from a volcano (as bright, and as destructive) in a thousand different directions; apparently without art or design. Order and arrangement appear to be entirely despised; proportion of parts is expressly laid down, in his only elementary work,[b] to be no ingredient of the beautiful; and his political

---

[a]*Paine's First Principles of Government*. Intrinsically the most valuable of all his productions.[11]
[b]Treatise on the Sublime and Beautiful, part III. sect. 2, 3, 4, and 5.[12]

publications may be regarded as illustrations of this curious doctrine. Tropes, sentiments, and propositions, are every now and then starting up, one knows not why, or whence, or wherefore.

> "The things, 'tis true, are costly, rich and rare:
> But wonder how the devil they got there!"[13]

Every metaphor becomes an allegory; every embellishment a digression; and every digression a voluminous episode. But the reader, who, on this account, should calculate upon the artlessness of Mr. Burke's mind, would do no credit to his own penetration. "If this be madness, there is method in't."[14] In this excursive frenzy of composition, there is much deep design and insidious policy. He not only writes with a two-fold object—but his objects are in diametrical opposition to each other. It is his intention at once to instruct and to confuse. Even in that small proportion of the people of Britain, whom he calls "the British public", there is a still smaller subdivision (men of complete leisure, and of trained political education) whom he regards as the initiated few, and who, of course, may be expected to catch up, and put together, many of the loose disjointed hints, scattered here and there, with such studied carelessness as to escape the observation of those who "read as they run". Hence, if we want to know the whole meaning; and real object of this master of political controversy, instead of following him through the regular succession of pages and paragraphs, we must seek for the leading traits and positions of his work, and then, putting together the disjoined parts of the syllogism so artfully divided, we must extract the enveloped conclusion for ourselves.

Having furnished the reader with this clue, let him turn to the *"Letters"*, p. 66 to 71, or the *"Thoughts"*,[15] p. 16 to 21, then to the *"Thoughts"*, p. 63 to 68, and to the *"Letters"*, p. 19 to 23, and he will find the dilemma I have stated to be very fully unfolded: that is to say, he will find the pensioner of an administration in the constant practice of preparing the minds of a certain class, by means of the pamphlets and paragraphs of its hirelings, for the promulgation of every pre-concerted scheme of tyranny and usurpation—he will find this grey-headed procurator of proscription and blood, seriously recommending, by the "severe" and "unshrinking operation" of some new means of persecution and *"force"*, the utter extermination of every sentiment of reform—or, as he very accurately, though insidiously, calls it, change.[a]

[a]See p. 42 of this Letter.

In the first of these passages above referred to, Mr. B. after observing that, "it cannot be concealed, we are a divided people", proceeds "to compute, and to class those, who, *in any political view,* are to be *called* the people."—"In England and Scotland", says he, "I compute that those of adult age, not declining in life, of *tolerable leisure* for such discussions, and of *some means of information,* more or less, and who are *above menial dependence,* (or what is virtually such) may amount to about *four hundred thousand*": (*Letters,* p. 66)[a] to which, in his original *Thoughts,* he had added— "In this number I *include the women* who take a concern in these transactions, who cannot exceed twenty thousand." And thus did this *preux chevalier,*[16] though so furious an antagonist of the *Rights of Man,* in an unguarded, perhaps a *tender* hour, confess himself a proselyte to the *rights of woman.* And this, says he—this petty fraction of the population of England and Scotland—these four hundred thousand males and females, who alone, out of three or four millions of adults, by whom this island is peopled, have leisure for discussion, or the means of any degree of information—"*This is the British public!*"—this is the *natural* "representative of the people!"

This the British public!—and what are all the rest? Political non-entities!—A dash of the pen has blotted them out of the book of life. But, by what right, by what omnipotent power, what uncreating, and re-creating authority, does this renegade doom to political annihilation nine-tenths of the inhabitants of the world? Where are the fate-commanding locks of this painted Jupiter, that thus he thinks to *nod* away the existence of millions?—Where are his thunder-bolts and his lightnings?—But I forget myself: the lightnings and the thunderbolts are all prepared. Windham (the armed progeny of his prolific brain) keeps the key of the arsenal; and if he but turns the massy lock, the thunders roar, the conflagration spreads, the heavy clouds bear desolation on their wings, and the million trembles and obeys. But waving these thundering arguments (and I trust that the time is not distant when the conductors of reason will disarm them of their terrors, and the tempests of ministerial fury rage innoxious!) upon what foundation do these calculators take a tenth for the whole, and call four hundred thousand (men and *women*) "the public of Britain"? Why, truly—the reason is even more profligate than the assertion itself!—because of our whole population not more than a tenth-part have either "the *leisure,* or the means for any degree of information, more or less!" And is this your boasted state of civilization and refinement?—Is this the wealth, grandeur,

[a]Rivington's edit.

prosperity, and flourishing condition of the country?—Is this good order?—Is this *government* (or is it grinding and murderous oppression) which dooms the mass of mankind to incessant toil, and comfortless assiduity, and assigns the leisure, and the means of any degree of information or discussion, to a tenth-part only of the inhabitants? And, even of this tenth, how large a portion are to be ranked, not among the *promoters*, but the *destroyers* of the prosperity so much vaunted:—not among the productive labourers, but among the caterpillars and locusts, the blights and mildews of social industry![17]

Are these the institutions which Mr. B. wishes to support? Are these the perfect models of social jurisprudence which it is blasphemy to approach with the unhallowed finger of innovation or reform? Are these (in their effects) the regular and orderly fabrics of the ancient legitimate "government of states", whose plans and materials were "drawn from the old Germanic or Gothic customary", and of which those famous architects, "the civilians, the jurists, and the publicists", have given us such flattering draughts, ground plots and elevations? If they are, away with your idle jargon of *venerable* antiquity:—that awful, but endearing epithet, belongs not, Mr. *Burke*, to grey hairs alone!—away with your pompous boasts of grace, beauty, and sublimity, of swelling proportions, and polished symmetry. If such are the effects of these fabrics, they are hateful and accursed; and, though crowned with "Corinthian capitals", though hung with antique trophies of renown, and adorned with offerings of ancient and modern piety, they must perish; they ought to perish; and they will. They are Augean stables that must be cleansed.[18] They are Bastilles of intellect, which must be destroyed. They are insulting mausoleums of buried rights, and are ready to totter from their base; for the day of the resurrection is near at hand; and "the vail of the temple shall be rent in twain".[19]

But, no: Mr. B. slanders the institutions he is so zealous to support. Things are not yet so bad as he represents them; though if they proceed in their present career, there is no knowing how soon we may sink even to a lower state of degradation. The number of those, who, some how or other, find, or *make*, the means and opportunities of obtaining *some degree* of information, is not yet reduced to one in ten. I, indeed, affirm (and I shall argue the right hereafter) that *every* man, and every *woman*, and every *child*, ought to obtain something more, in the general distribution of the fruits of labour, than food, and rags, and a wretched hammock, with a poor rug to cover it: and that without working twelve or fourteen hours a day, six days out of seven, from six to sixty. They have a claim, a sacred and inviolable claim, growing out of the fundamental maxim, upon which alone all property can be supported, to some comforts and enjoyments, in addition to the necessaries of life; and to some "tolerable leisure for such discussion, and some means of such information", as may lead to an understanding of their *rights*; without which they can never understand their *duties*. It is true, in the present circumstances of society, the mass of the people are far from the enjoyment of this right: let Mr. B. determine whether this is to be attributed to the nature, or the corruption of our institutions. But still, notwithstanding the scandalously inadequate price of labour—wages being, in many instances, rather a mockery than a support;—notwithstanding the unreasonable number of hours through which the labour of the day is protracted, and the impediments thrown in the way of a cheap, and, therefore general, circulation of knowledge, by the duties on paper, stamps on newspapers, advertisements, and the like; yet, judging of the whole country, from the parts which I have seen, and making all possible allowances for local and accidental advantages, Mr. B. will not be able to contract his *new aristocracy of thinkers and discoursers* into any thing like the narrow circle of four hundred thousand.

This champion for the few, to the exclusion of the many—this advocate for the noble and gentle, at the expence of the useful and the honest, may exult in the luxuriancy of his imagination, his various stores of science, his hours of literary leisure, and his familiar intercourse with the wits and literati of half a century, but there are hundreds, nay thousands, in those classes excluded from his calculation, who though they could neither endite,[20] nor comprehend his learned metaphors and dashing periods, would yet blush at such flimsy sophisms as he sometimes covers with a cloud of splendour; and with the weapons of plain, solid, Socratic argument, would beat half a dozen such combatants out of the arena. I could point him to whole companies, whose neighbourhoods,[a] nay, almost whole professions

---

[a]I might refer particularly to Sheffield. My stay in that place was very short; but it was long enough to see that there is a great body of virtue, and well grounded principle among what may be called the *Sansculotterie*: but it is a body without a head. They have unfortunately no leaders. There are, indeed, several people of considerable property and influence who *think* with them; but who have not the courage, or the energy, to take that open and decided part which might promote the real peace (for *oppression is not peace*) of the neighbourhood: and as for that *Chicken-witted thing* that calls itself a Whig leader in those parts, *it* is the being most despised for aristocratic domination of any creature in the county: and I am sure I mean no disparagement to '*Squire, Justice, Colonel* ALTHORPE!!![21] If any three or four persons of weight and pecuniary consequence in that place, would take these honest, intelligent manufacturers and their cause, fairly and publicly, by the hand (as persons of that description, to their immortal honour, have done in Norwich) in the now trampled Sheffield, as in virtuous Norwich, the petty tyranny of provincial prosecution would presently be at an end; the instruments of power would feel, and practically confess that salutary awe of which I have spoken above; and no jack in office would dare to exercise, or to threaten, the exertion of a vigour beyond the law.

of labouring manufacturers, who understand the principles of government much better than himself, and who want nothing but practical fluency to render them most formidable antagonists to the whole college of aristocratical declaimers.

The fact is, that the hideous accumulation of capital in a few hands, like all diseases not absolutely mortal, carries, in its own enormity, the seeds of cure. Man is, by his very nature, social and communicative—proud to display the little knowledge he possesses, and eager, as opportunity presents, to encrease his store. Whatever presses men together, therefore, though it may generate some vices, is favourable to the diffusion of knowledge, and ultimately promotive of human liberty. Hence every large workshop and manufactory is a sort of political society, which no act of parliament can silence, and no magistrate disperse. Socrates, therefore, (the first democratical lecturer, mentioned in history, and the founder of the unsophisticated, and unrestricted system of *Sans-culotte* philosophy) when he wished to expose "the corruption and venality of the times",[a] and those "false tenets and opinions which were contrary to the happiness of the human race",[b] acted consistently with his high character for wisdom and penetration, in visiting, among other places of resort, the shops where workmen assembled to pursue their vocations.[c] "He began", says the biographer, "to oppose *sophistry* and superstition with success, and to teach his fellow *citizens* wisdom and virtue. In the open streets, in the public walks and baths, in private houses, in the *workshops of artists*, or wherever he found men whom he could make better, he entered into conversation with them, explained what was right and wrong, good and evil, holy and unholy, &c." The nature and tendency of these conversations we learn from a variety of passages. We are particularly informed that such was his intrepid zeal for the promotion of truth, and the assertion of human liberty, that "As soon as any opinion or superstition occasioned an *open violence*, the invasion of the NATURAL RIGHTS OF MAN, or the corruption of their morals, no threats or persecution could deter him from declaring against it."[d] And, again, we learn that when a senate of tyrants (a vile and detestable Oligarchy)[e] assisted by an armed force, and a sovereign alliance, trampled on the rights and liberties of the Athenian people, and exercised

[a] Cullen's life of Socrates, prefixed to his translation of Phaedon, p. 23.[22]
[b] Ibid. p. 15.
[c] Ibid. p. 12.
[d] Life Socr. p. 32.
[e] Ibid. p. 35.[23]

an authority beyond the law—"robbing the most upright men of the republic of their property and their lives, *under the pretext of punishing rebellion and treasonable offences*,[a] banishing others, and driving many more to seek for peace and safety in voluntary emigration; in the midst of these persecutions and proscriptions, Socrates was found, as usual, in the places of public resort—in the workshops of the artists, and among the labourers in the manufactories, uttering seditious allegories, and condemning the desolating tyranny of the Oligarchy. "It is wonderful indeed", he is reported to have said, "if shepherds make the herd which is entrusted to their care grow smaller, and more meagre, and yet shall not be accounted bad shepherds; but it is still more wonderful, if the guardians of a state make its subjects grow fewer and worse, that they should not be accounted bad guardians."[b]

Now, though every workshop cannot have a Socrates within the pale of its own society, nor even every manufacturing town a man of such wisdom, virtue, and *opportunities* to instruct them, yet a sort of Socratic spirit will necessarily grow up, wherever large bodies of men assemble. Each brings, as it were, into the common bank his mite of information, and putting it to a sort of circulating usance, each contributor has the advantage of a large interest, without any diminution of capital.

But such men, I shall be told, are out of the question: let their capacities, their acquirements, their understandings be what they may, they form no part of "the British public"; they are in a state of "menial *dependance* (or what is virtually such.)"—Dependance and independance! Fine distinctions! But in what do they consist? Are they to be sought in the station, or in the mind? Do wealth and rank give independance? Does industrious

[a]Ibid. p. 35. N.B. The book from which I quote, was dedicated to the Right Honourable Henry Dundas, in 1789.

[b]Cullen's Life of Socr. p. 36. The reader will not, after these specimens, be surprised that an act of parliament was made by the tyrannical Oligarchy to stop the mouth of Socrates; and that Critias and Characles, two of their sophists, or state lawyers (see p. 36) were employed to entrap, impeach, and destroy him; while their buffoons were set to work, to ridicule and defame him to the people, and "the priests", and other venal wretches, "who felt Socrates a thorn in their side", made use of their pious cant and holy mummeries "to turn the minds of the Athenians against him." (p. 24, 25). Such was the origin of the conspiracy against Socrates. A victim to that conspiracy he fell[24]—the wisest, the greatest, the most virtuous of mankind. Yet a pedantic fellow, one Dr. Bisset,[25] in a certain ridiculous farrago of ignorance and misrepresentation, which he calls a "Sketch of Democracy", represents him as the victim of democratic envy and injustice; and, by a curious perversion of facts, makes Critias and Characles (the two sophists, or lawyers, employed by the tyrants to destroy him) "two lecturers, who earned their bread by gratifying the prejudices of the people, and incensing them against *dignified* characters."[26] Socrates was so far from being a dignified character in Dr. B's sense of the word, that his mother was a poor midwife; his father a stonemason; and he himself worked several years in his father's yard. His dignity was of a nobler kind than that which kings confer and Dr. B. would defend.

poverty of necessity degrade the man? An anecdote shall settle these questions.

During the late election at Nottingham, one of the principal manufacturers of that place, who had always deprecated, with great severity, the present war, and the whole system of ministerial measures, was observed, of a sudden, to become reserved and wavering. The ministerial candidate had concerns with a banking house, which, by means of acceptances, discounts, and the like, was exceedingly useful to him, in his large dealings. Dr *Crompton*[27] was the candidate for the people: but he had no connection with any bank, but that of virtue and patriotism; and their notes, you know, are not current in commercial transactions. The wealthy manufacturer deliberated—he doubted—he calculated—he resolved—to vote for the ministerial champion. He determined to canvass for him. "William", said he, to one of his journeymen, "I hope you mean to vote for Mr. *Smith?*"[28]—"No, Sir", replied the *menial dependant*, "indeed I do not. I am surprised that *you* should ask me such a question. However, if *you* are not independent, I AM!" This, however, I am aware, will be no argument, *ad hominem*, as they call it, to Mr. B. It will rather enflame than moderate his prejudices. He will regard it as a flagrant act of *Jacobinism* and insubordination; an overt-act of treason against the sovereignty of wealth; a "revolt of enterprising talent against property."[a]

I grant, also, that this argument will not universally apply. Though some men have energy of mind enough to act in this independent way, upon such occasions, many, under such circumstances, feel themselves compelled to bow. During the same Nottingham election, an instance of this sort occurred, which, to minds of a particular stamp, at least, cannot fail to be interesting.

A poor manufacturer, who was past his best days, and to whom, therefore, it was of serious consequence to be dismissed from an established shop—especially as he had a large family to support—was pressed by his employer, in very authoritative terms, to vote for this same Mr. Smith. He hesitated: but the very sustenance of his family was at stake; and he yielded. Going up to the hustings, and having given in his name, he was asked by the poll-clerk, for whom he voted? "Why, I have two votes; have I not?"[29]—"You have."—"Well, then, I give one of them to Mr. Smith— but that's not mine: it's my master's! The other's my own, and I'll give that to Dr. Crompton—for he's the man for the people!"—"Thank you, my

---

[a]What homage does talent owe to property? But of this in another Letter.

good friend", (exclaims the *courtly* candidate)—"thank you, for me. Let me
have the pleasure of shaking hands with you."—"No, I'm d—d if I do",
replied the voter; "I was obliged to vote for you, but I an't obliged to shake
hands with you, neither. But I'll shake hands with you, Dr Crompton; for I
gave it *you* from my heart!" Mr. B. may despise the sans-culottism displayed in this anecdote—and I am, certainly, no enemy to soothing manners and decorum;—but yet such energy of mind, however rudely fashioned, is of ten thousand times more real worth than all the polished
periods of pensioned apostacy, and all "the dressed up smiles that ever
flickered on the curled lips" of obsequious courtiers! And whatever sentiments a master of the ceremonies might entertain upon the subject, he is
but a shallow politician who excludes such men from the account, in his
calculations of the weight and force of opinion. Such men have not, it is
true, all the advantages of free agency:—so much the worse for Britain.[a]
The generality of them have no votes at all; and many who have, are
under coercion in the exercise of their privilege—so much the greater
scandal to justice and humanity.[b] But though they have not votes, they
have opinions. They are a part of "the British public", even of Mr. Burke's
informed, discussing, garrulous public, upon which "more than the legal constituent, the artificial representative", is supposed (falsely supposed) to depend. An oppressive combination of employers, the cold grasp of penury,
or the brutal violence of a mad-headed, drunken, profligate magistrate
(armed, for the sake of the constitutional system of checks, with the united

[a]I do not mean the mysterious, allegorical thing, which *statesmen* call Britain. I mean the aggregate of
British population. That is my idea of a country, or a state.

[b]I ought not, while speaking of humble patriotism, to forget the *independent, poor* voters of Norwich;
among which there are six or seven hundred, whom (even in these seasons of distress) no threats, no
interest, no bribery can shake: but who will vote for the permanent liberties of themselves and families,
at the hazard of their temporary bread. Upon any *strong exigency*, this number (I mean, among the
labouring freemen of that city) would be nearly doubled: that is to say, it would embrace almost the whole
class. If *Bartlet Gurney*,[30] the late candidate, had stood forward manfully (or rather, if his family had not
held him back)—if he had even done those things, which, under *existing circumstances*, any candidate
may fairly and honourably do—I mean, brought up the London and other out-voters, who were in his
interest, (which would not have been the tythe, or twentieth part of what his opponent[31] is *known* to
have done)—nay, had he even shewn himself on the hustings, and convinced the people, that he was in
earnest, (instead of *running into the north* to avoid them) he would have driven the War Secretary from
the market-place, with a majority so decisive, as would have sunk that *blustering puppet of a day* into
political annihilation. Even as it as, Bartlet Gurney had a majority of 143 *resident votes*. Never was there
a finer enthusiasm, on such an occasion, than the common people, and some of the higher, displayed.
The Quakers (that body of men, whom, of all religionists, I most revere and love) must pardon me, if I
say, that the timid bashfulness of sectarian pride lost Freedom a triumph, of which no other
circumstance could have deprived her.

powers of the police, and of the sword) may suppress, for awhile, the due influence of this opinion; but, ultimately, it will have its weight: and its weight will be greatest when its exertion is of most importance. In the mean time, it has a degree of influence even now; though not in its natural and rightful place—that assembly which *calls itself* the Commons House of Parliament;—the honourable and right honourable members of which (as we are expressly told) are in such a state of "menial dependance, (or what is *virtually* such)" that the *votes* of the majority are directly opposite to their *dispositions*.[a] But it has its influence—a powerful influence, upon the resources of the country; upon the expence and the facility of filling the ranks of the army, and upon the spirit of enthusiasm in the day of battle. It has its influence, also, on the pillow of the minister; where it requires no second-sight to perceive, that it haunts his imagination, and disturbs his slumbers. There, in prophetic visions, it foretells the sad catastrophe of his ambition, and points out, in the *continuance* of this war, the means of British renovation; the approaching failure of the funding system; the demurs of money-lenders, and the prudent desertion of those "life and fortune men", who, repenting the madness of Merchant Taylors Hall, and finding the bankrupt state no longer competent to support, at once, the burthen of public credit, and the enormous prodigality of the present system, will be obliged to *abandon the borough-mongers to preserve their property*.

To appease this opinion, to lay this wandering ghost[b] of popular discontent, the simulator, Pitt, has drawn once more around him the magic circle of delusion, with charms and spells of pretended negociation, and backward mutters of arrogance and recantation. But lift up your voices, ye artificers, ye mechanics, ye manufacturers of the land! ye genuine props and pillars of the nation! Be not amused with pretended treaties: for what is peace, but war, to you, while ye drudge in servile misery for inadequate rewards, and your families pine in want and ignorance? Wear not your lungs with sighs and sullen murmurs—let not only the nocturnal phantom, but the living body of your complaints appear before your oppressors. Exert once more the manly energies of reason; and tell them, with a clear and decided tone, that "peace is not peace, without reform"; that "your discontents can never be allayed, without the restoration of equal rights, and

[a]Letters, p. 63; and Thoughts, p. 14, where it is put still more strongly.

[b]The body is reported to have been buried, at the beginning of December last, in St. Stephen's Chapel, with this inscription—"Pitt and Grenville's Acts"; and underneath, "in a state of *internal tranquillity*". Thus much by authority. To which is added, by an unknown hand, "but in hopes of a joyful resurrection."

equal laws, and the adoption of a pure and independant organ, through which the opinions, not of a *tenth-part*, but of the whole nation, can be freely delivered, and distinctly heard."

But no: we are told, the nation wants no such organ. The opinions of the *menial, dependant mass* must be taken for granted from those of their *betters*. In those more reputable orders, in that privileged four hundred thousand, who, by virtue of their situation, have an exclusive license to enquire and to discuss, the people have, already, "a *natural* representative". Natural representative!—Of what excellent use, in the science of confusing mankind, is this prerogative of coining new phrases! Natural representative of the people! The people itself, as the word is here used, is an artificial, or corporate body—for it means the aggregate population of a particular state, or body politic: and how there can be a *natural representative* of an *artificial corporation*, I am yet to learn. I can understand, indeed, that the parent is the natural representative of his infant children, armed with the right, and bound by the duty of judging and acting for them. I can, also, understand, that children are the natural representatives of a departed parent; and, as such, are entitled to those portions of the produce of his labour, which have neither been consumed by him, nor legally set apart to support the profligate luxury of placemen and pensioners. But how it should happen, that four hundred thousand people (*men and women*) from the mere *accident* of living in more comfort, and with less toil, should be the natural representatives of three or four millions of other full-grown—full-aged beings, of the same structure and faculty with themselves, but to whom they have neither relationship nor affinity, and, as such, should be entitled to act for them, speak for them, think for them, and almost eat for them (for even this privilege is scarcely left to the personal exercise of the million) is a problem which the "jurists and publicists" must solve. I give it up entirely.

But Mr. B's *Nature* and mine are widely different. With him every thing is natural that has the hoar of ancient prejudice upon it; and novelty is the test of crime. In my humble estimate, nothing is natural, but what is fit and true, and can endure the test of reason. With him the feudal system, and all its barbarous, tyrannical, and superstitious appendages, is natural. With him, all the gaudy, cumbrous fustian of "the old Germanic, or Gothic custumary" is natural; and all the idolatrous foppery and degrading superstition of the church of Rome are natural, also. Nay, with him, that detestable traffic in blood and murder—that barter of groans, and tortures, and long lingering deaths, the *Slave Trade*, is also natural!!! Nor do I doubt, that, with equal facility, and upon the very same principles, as he maintains the masters and employers of this country to be the natural representatives of the workmen they employ, he could prove, also, those very humane, and very, very respectable beings, who, as they walk upon two legs, I shall continue to call men, by *courtesy*, (I mean the West India planters, and their Negro drivers) to be the natural representatives of those poor, harassed, half-starved, whip-galled, miserable slaves, whom they, also, *employ* in their farms and factories.

In short, this champion of the privileged orders adopts, most unequivocally, the principles of this similitude. Having assigned the exclusive privilege of opinion to the favoured four hundred thousand—a mixed herd of nobles and gentles, placemen, pensioners and court-expectants, of bankers and merchants, manufacturers, lawyers, parsons and physicians, warehousemen and shop-keepers, pimps and king's messengers, fiddlers and auctioneers, with the included "twenty thousand" petticoat allies—ladies of the court, and ladies of the town!—having secured this motley group (the favoured progeny of Means and Leisure) in the exclusive, and unquestioned enjoyment of the rights of information and discussion, he proceeds to observe, that "the rest, when feeble, are the *objects* of protection!"—Objects of protection!—so are my lady's lap-dog and the Negro slave. It is easy to determine, which, of the two, *polished sensibility* will shelter with the most anxious care!—Ye murky walls, and foul, straw-littered floors of the plantation hospital! Ye full-crammed, noxious workhouses of Britain—vile dens of tyrannic penury and putrescence![a] speak—Ye roofs and floors of wretchedness! speak ye (for that part of nature which should be loud and eloquent, is spell-bound in panic apathy)—What is the *protection* which the feeble labourer, or the sick Negro finds? and then refer, for comparison, to the down pillow of yon pampered, snarling cur; or the commodious chambers of the canine palace at *Godwood*.[b]—But to return to the description.—"The rest, when feeble, are the objects of protection—when *strong*,

[a]There are some few, and but few exceptions, to this general description. At any rate, however, a workhouse is but a gaol; and, therefore, a fit receptacle only for those paupers, whose infirmities make confinement necessary to their preservation.

[b]A splendid edifice, erected by the D. of Richmond for his dogs, with commodious kitchens, parlours, dining-rooms, bed-rooms, lying-in-rooms, pleasure-ground for the morning sun, pleasure-ground for the evening sun, baths, &c, &c. — N.B. It is a strict rule at Godwood, that no servant be permitted to give a morsel of broken victuals either to mendicant travellers, or neighbouring peasant. Poor women, who presume to pick up withered sticks from under the trees in the park, are taught, by a "severe and awful" administration of "justice", to respect the sacred rights of property.

they are the MEANS of force".[a] So is the dray-horse; and the poor ass that drudges day and night in the sand-cart! So are the bludgeon, and the pistol, with which, under *existing circumstances*, every man (at least, every obnoxious man) will do well to be provided, as preservatives against assassination.[b] But foul befal the government, that considers the great mass of the people as brute machines; mere instruments of physical force; deprived of all *power*, and destitute of all *right* of information; and doomed, like the dray-horse, or the musquet, to perform, mechanically, whatever task of drudgery, or murder, a few "counsellors and deliberators" may command! And yet, Mr. B. tells us, that "they who *affect* to consider that part of us" (to wit, nine-tenths of the adult population of the country) "in any other point of view, *insult us while they cajole us!*"

Such, my fellow-citizens, is the language of pensioned indolence. Nine out of ten of the human race (it will, anon, be nineteen out of twenty) are born to be beasts of burthen to the remaining tythe: to be hewers of wood, and drawers of water—to be exposed to heat and cold, winds and waters, rocks and tempests, for these privileged masters; and, finally, to be "listed as soldiers for battle", to defend, or to aggrandise a country, in which they have neither voice nor right. And he who dares to assert their claim to "any tolerable leisure for discussion, or means of information":—he who dares to maintain their pretensions to opinion, or title to be regarded "in any political view", as part of "the people", is an hypocritical jacobin incendiary, revolts against the sovereignty of wealth, and "insults us while he cajoles us"! Such is the soothing and *grateful* language, for the pleasure of being amused with which we are taxed in a yearly pension of four thousand pounds![33]

But beware, Mr. Burke, and you, his hypocritical employers, how *ye* cajole and insult *us* too far. Abuses, when discovered, inspire the sober wish of peaceful and rational reform: but when wrong is added to wrong, and coercion to coercion; when remonstrance is answered by the goad and the yoke, and insult is heaped upon oppression, reason may be overpowered, and madness may succeed; and the philanthropic few, who admonish in vain, may deplore the destiny from which they cannot preserve you. In

[a]Letters, p. 67.

[b]See "An Appeal to Popular Opinion Against Kidnapping and Murder: Including a Narrative of the Atrocious Outrages at Yarmouth, Lynn, and Wisbech"; and the motion made by Mr. Erskine, in the Court of King's Bench, on Saturday the 19th instant, on the subject of these flagitious aristocratic violations of all law and order.[32]

vain do you shudder at the cannibals[a] of Paris—in vain do ye colour, with exaggerated horrors, the "tribunals of Maroon and Negro slaves, covered with the blood of their masters"; if, obstinately vicious, instead of being warned, ye are irritated by the example.

I deplore, as ye do, the "robberies and murders", committed by these poor wretches—the blind instruments of instinctive vengeance. But, I cannot, like you, forget by whom those lessons of murderous rapacity were taught. I cannot forget, that slavery itself is robbery and murder; and, that the master who falls by the bondsman's hand, is the victim of his own barbarity.

I am no apologist for the horrible massacres of revenge; whether perpetrated by negroes, by monarchs, or by mobs. I abhor revenge. Vengeance, Mr. Burke, with me is crime. All retrospective principle is crime; and to its criminality adds folly. In your own sort of language I should say—we were *made* with our eyes in our foreheads, that we might look onward to the future, not linger upon that which is gone by, and cannot be recalled. Give me *security for the future*, I will dispense with what is called *justice for the past*. But we are not to expect whole nations (whether of Maroon negroes, or of feudal vassals) to become of a sudden so entirely speculative. Revenge, it cannot be concealed, is a rude instinct, common to all animated being, which nothing but deep reflection, and well digested principles can eradicate. It is an instinct, also, when it dares to shew itself, strongest in the most feeble, fiercest in the most submissive, and most fruitful in the steril soil of ignorance. The bleak frost of severity nourishes it to wild luxuriance. It perishes beneath the warm manure of kindness. It is a wild growth of nature, it is true: but it is fatally cherished by authoritative example: and if tyrants will teach bloody lessons, it is unreasonable in them to complain of the aptitude of their scholars. Add to which, Mr. B., this *detestable vice* is one of the *virtues* of the *ancient and venerable* part of that religion you so anxiously uphold. The maxim of forgiveness to enemies, is, comparatively, a *modern innovation*: which accounts for its being so seldom practised by governments or priests. "Eye for eye, and tooth for

---

[a]The reader will, of course, give me credit, for using this word in a figurative sense. Mr. B. in the very dotage of credulity, applies it literally. "By cannibalism, I mean their devouring, as a nutriment of their ferocity, some part of the bodies of those they have murdered; their drinking the blood of their victims, and forcing the victims themselves to drink the blood of their kindred, slaughtered before their faces." *Let.* p. 105. Can Bedlam surpass the madness that could write, can idiotcy match the credulity that should *believe*, this trash? There is another passage, in the same page, still more hideous. Mr. B. is a *romance writer* of the German school: If he can but excite horror, no matter how incredible the tale. But surely there are scenes too terrible to amuse a benevolent mind, even in *fictions and poetic legends*!

tooth",[34] will not satisfy them. Theirs are the dread instructions, "which, being taught, return to plague the inventors".[35] Theirs, indeed, too generally, are the crimes unprovoked: the crimes of revolutionists are only the crimes of revenge. Had the Maroons and negroes never been most wickedly enslaved, their masters had never been murdered. Had the chains of France been less galling, they had never fallen so heavy on the heads of French oppressors. To avoid their fate, let governors avoid their crimes. To render sanguinary *revolutions* impossible, let them yield to temperate *reforms*. To avert a dreaded vengeance, let the provocations of injustice be instantly removed; and the padlock from the mouth of an injured people, be transferred to the lips of pensioned indolence!

But the politician of Beaconsfield,[36] "the doctor of the constitution"[37]— or rather the doctor's doctor, has found a shorter way.—"The cautery and the knife" are more sovereign than the emollient and the balm. Extermination (even of eighty thousand men of talent and capacity) is more easy than reform. Desolation itself is not to ministerial ears "a word of such ill sound"[38] as "change"; and Jacobins and reformers are therefore to be submitted to the "severe and awful operation", in a manner that will expose "the crown" to no sort of danger of again "retiring disgraced and defeated from its courts." "Of these four hundred thousand *political citizens*", says he, "I look upon one-fifth, or about eighty thousand, to be *pure Jacobins*; *utterly incapable of amendment*; objects of eternal vigilance", &c. "On these, no reason, no argument, no *example*, no *venerable authority*, can have the slightest influence. They desire"—What? "A *change*; and they will have it if they can." True: And they ought to have it; and they must, or the nation is undone for ever. If all are Jacobins who wish for a change, Mr. B. most miserably under-rates the Jacobins of this country. Some wish for a greater change, and others for a less. There are, I fear, almost as many different opinions, among reformers, as to the extent of that change, as there were among the allies about the objects of that ever to be renowned and glorious confederacy of kings, by being chief trumpeter to which—or, more properly speaking, drum-major (for we must not forget old Zisca) Mr. Burke has accumulated so considerable a portion of spoil, at so small an expence of danger. But, barring the idle terrors which state jugglers keep so artfully alive, by repeating, at due intervals, and with due solemnity, the cabalistic words, *French massacres! republicans and levellers! horrid atheists! dreadful anarchy! bloody regicides! cannibal philosophy!* and the like, I believe there is scarcely a single reflecting man, unconnected, by interest or expectation, with existing corruptions, who does not, in some degree, wish a change. But says Mr. B. "England has been happy; and change is a word of ill sound to happy ears."[a]—England *has been* happy!!! Perhaps so. England was not always infested with such a pestiferous swarm of placemen and pensioners, borough-mongers and contractors, as, at this time, devour the harvests, and blast the verdure of the year. Will Mr. B. pretend to say, that England *is* happy now? Will he pretend to say, that even that small portion, that tythe, which he calls "the British public", are happy at this time? And if they were, what right has a tenth part to be happy at the expence of the misery of all the rest? But, can even these be called happy? Are those middle classes (which we middling people are apt, so selfishly, and so wickedly, to consider as the whole!)—are even they happy? Alas! how dismal the reverse!

Ye tradesmen, ye manufacturers, ye noiseless proficients in the arts, the sciences, and the gainful branches of learning (the bulk and mass of all those callings and professions *nick-named* RESPECTABLE)[b] tell me—tell *the world*, can ye look in the innocent faces of your children, and, contemplating the prospect before them, say, that ye are happy? Can ye look upon your own condition, your blighted prospects, and your stinted comforts, and, even barring future prospects, say ye are happy? Alas! how many of you are, at this very time, descending, and how rapidly, down the ladder of degradation! A few (I grant it) prosper. A few swell to uncontroulable pride, and incalculable affluence. The more is your disaster. To be, like Tantalus, in a lake of misery, with the prospect of abundance constantly before our eyes, and never to taste it, is to be doubly miserable. But what is the condition of the mass?—*Your little* mass, I mean. As for *the great mass*—it is trampled in the dust, and forgotten. How many of you have been obliged to relinquish your little country house, or country lodging?— sweet recreations of health and pleasure! which at once prolonged existence, and decked it with a ruddier smile! From the tables of how many has the tax-gatherer snatched the cheering wine? How many, many a family, that once basked in the inner, has been pushed to the outer circles of this temperate zone? How many from these outer circles have been thrust into the chill regions of penurious labour? And, how many thousands, upon

[a]Thoughts, p. 1.—In Rivington's edition this is omitted. A qualm of modesty seems, unaccountably, to have seized the author, and this insult to our feelings was struck out. But, thanks to Mr. Owen![39] (honourable mention of him in the journals of political literature!) we have the first thoughts, as well as the after thoughts. Of the writings of Mr. Burke we can never have too much.

[b]Respect is not the attribute of property, calling, or condition. It belongs, in reality, to nothing but virtue; and to that which is a branch of virtue—well applied talents.

whose moderate toil the sun once cast his oblique, but cheering gleams, now shiver at the dark bleak poles of comfortless distress?

If, then, our happiness be reduced to a mere "has been", this terrible *change*, is the burthen of *a dirge*, rather than a *word of omen*; and must impress us rather with plaintive than terrific sensations. We might, therefore, with strict propriety dismiss the subject, in Mr. B's own style, by declaring that the objection "will not apply"; and accordingly, "put it out of court: and so far as that goes, let the counsel for existing abuses take nothing by his motion."

But the counsel in this cause is a deep politician. He can practice popular arts against the people. His motion was not made with any view to the decision of that high court of reason, to which he appealed, but for the sake of the general impression expected from the mere motion itself. Change is a word of ambiguous meaning; and, under certain circumstances, the worst construction is sure to be put upon every ambiguity. It should be remembered, therefore, that *change, revolution*, and *reform*, are but modifications of the same idea: though the last, by established courtesy, is the most unequivocally admitted in a favourable sense. *Reform is a change*, or *revolution, from bad to good*. Every usurpation, and every concession, is a change. Every alteration of the law, the repeal of an old act, or the passing of a new one, is a change. The whole history of government is nothing but a record of changes, or revolutions, gradual or sudden; and the worst revolutions are those that are never called so. In short, abstractedly considered, there is nothing terrible in change or revolution. Violence and cruelty are to be abhorred. Humanity is to be loved and cherished. First and greatest of all virtues! parent of all blessings! fountain of all social joys! it is to be wooed, and fostered, and reverenced with the fondest care! to be clasped to the breast, and entwined with the very texture of the heart—only to be torn away with the last, dearest fibre. But when violence and cruelty are established—when they are surrounded by privileges, and fortified by power, revolution itself becomes humanity and justice.

The question, then, is, what sort of change do we desire? Does Mr. B. mean to say, that one-fifth of the people of that class which he regards as "the British public", *desires a change* of tumult, ferocious anarchy and slaughter?—O woeful Britain! if this were indeed the case: for there would scarcely be a paper partition between thee and the flames of the most hideous desolation. But if, by change, he means, as I do, redress of grievances, and reform of long-growing corruptions, I repeat it, not a fifth, but four-fifths of the thinking part of the community, do, in their hours of sanity, when the tertian of alarm subsides, wish for such a change: and when I look round on the condition of my country, and the scandalous abuses of government, proud am I to be considered, among the distinguished *incorrigible* eighty thousand, not the least obnoxious to Mr. B. and his *new employers*.

After having thus indulged his indolence, in a little faint and dubious colouring, the artist presently returns to his *old dashing style*. "If they cannot have this change, which they desire, by English cabal", says he, "they will make no sort of scruple of having it by the cabal of France, into which they are already *virtually incorporated*."[40] Thus, *all reformers* are Jacobins; and all Jacobins are of the French faction, virtually incorporated with that nation, and willing to secure the change they wish by foreign interference.

As for *virtual incorporation*, or *virtual presence*, whether in a *wafer*, or a *confederacy*, they are mysteries which, I profess, I do not understand. Mr. B. perhaps could explain the one, and some of our good allies might write commentaries on the other.[41] But I am not curious about occult sciences; and I shall only observe, that if the French republic derives no greater benefit from our *virtual incorporation* than the grand confederacy from the virtual co-operation of the Empress of Russia's manifestoes, it would be most gratuitous prodigality in government to be at any further expence for special commissions, and trials for high treason: or even for Mr. B's darling expedient, *the ancient wholesome practice of Bill of attainder*! For my own part, at least, I have no objection to avow all the incorporation I am conscious of with French Jacobinism.

I do confess, that so long as I imagined it even possible for the republic to be overthrown, no prospect was accompanied with equal anguish: For, notwithstanding the many adventitious horrors which have clouded the revolution, I regarded it as a great and glorious effort for the emancipation and moral improvement of the human race. But the thought has long ceased to agitate my mind. The Republic stands upon a rock; and Aeolus Burke[42] may blow till he cracks his cheeks, but all the blasts of his eloquence will never shake it. We must have miracles; or all is safe. "The sluices of heaven must be opened, and the waters of the great deep be broken up";[43] for nothing less than a general deluge can destroy it.

As for English reform by foreign cabal, I shall only observe, that I hold, with respect to England, the same doctrine that I held with respect to France. I deny Mr. B's law of vicinage altogether; and shall reply to this sophism in my following letter. In the mean time, I would have the reformers of all nations keep for ever in their minds the monitory remembrance, that hatred may be forced, but love cannot; that chains may be *imposed*, but freedom must be *acquired*.—In other words, that no country can have freedom, which cannot obtain it for itself; and that *foreign interference can only, at best, produce a change of masters.*[a]

But, this is by the way. All I have to do, at present, with Mr. B's charge, is, to shew the point of view in which he regards, or pretends to regard, the opinions of eighty thousand of those people of Britain, who, by virtue of their pecuniary situations, *are licensed to think on politics.* This, together with what he says of the talents and capacities of these men, will form the first branch of what I shall venture to call *Burke's new syllogism of massacre.*

"I have a good opinion", says he, "of the general abilities of the Jacobins."—In his very last publication, they were a herd of "fools aspiring to be knaves";[b] and the reader cannot have forgotten his vehement declamations at the beginning of the French Revolution, against "the vilest, the most despicable, the most ignorant of mankind; who, unlike the English Revolutionists of the last century—for they were men of genius and intelligence—that was a struggle of talents for their natural ascendancy—a transfer of power, from the aristocracy of birth, to the aristocracy of mind; but these men, on the contrary, had overthrown *all* distinctions, and transferred dominion, not to the wisdom and the intellect, but to the folly and ignorance of the nation!"[c] But now, "I have a good opinion of the general abilities of Jacobins." Who knows, but that bye-and-by, he may take another turn, and entertain a good opinion of their principles? Change is with him no inconsistency. Mr. B. and the weather-cock, are only out of character when they are fixed. "Strong passions", says he, "awaken the faculties. *They* suffer not a particle of the man to be lost. The spirit of enterprise gives to this description the full use of all their native energies."[d] And again, in his second Letter[e]—"It is a dreadful truth, but it is a truth

---

[a]This maxim, however, applies only to those nations in which foreign mercenaries are not employed by the government. It is no impeachment of the conduct of the Dutch. They were, already, under a foreign yoke. Their government coerced them by British and Prussian mercenaries; and they had no choice but that of accepting the aid of French fraternity.

[b]Letter to a Noble Lord.[44]

[c]I have not the speech before me: but this, I know, was the strain and sentiment of that furious philippic.[45]

[d]Letters, p. 70. Thoughts, p. 20.

[e]Letters, p. 144. Thoughts, p. 87. Compare this with his picture (Let. p. 145. Thoughts, p. 89) of "the tribe of vulgar politicians" that throng the court of princes!!! and who can doubt the issue of the struggle?

that cannot be concealed; in ability, in dexterity, in the *distinctness of their views, the Jacobins are our superiors.* They saw the thing "right from the beginning!!!" &c.—Such is the picture drawn by this sublime politician of that "great and formidable minority" (not, gentle reader, the whig minority of the House of Commons!) of whom he wishes to put the men of family and property in terror, that he may put them into *blood.* To complete the picture, in the true style and colouring of alarm, he adds, "I do not know whether, if I aimed at the total over-throw of a kingdom, I should wish to be encumbered with a larger body of partizans. They are more easily disciplined and directed, than if the number were greater."[a] Nay, and so disciplined, and so directed does he conceive us to be, that he ascribes to us a sort of omnipotence, and supernatural power of metamorphosis— "passing from place to place, with incredible velocity, and diversifying our character and description, so as to be capable of mimicking the general voice!"[b]

And what has all this to do (you will naturally enquire) with the argument against a Regicide Peace? Will the government, by exhausting the resources of the nation, be better enabled to struggle against such a faction (admitting its existence)? Will the increase of burthens, the beggary, misery, and consequent discontents, growing out of the prolongation of war, make such a faction less formidable? (Though not anxious myself for peace, I argue the question openly and fairly. In cases so momentous, there ought to be no disguise.) Would the unthinking, the desperate, the fickle and the wavering, be the less likely to fall into the hands, and be rendered instrumental to the views of such men, from the accumulating miseries, which, from such prolongation, must inevitably result? Mr. B. is not such an ideot as to believe it. His hyperbolical statement might, indeed, supernaturally account for a general *exclamation,* without admitting a general *desire,* for peace: supposing, indeed, that such *general* exclamation had been raised. But this I deny. The moderates (the patchworkmen—place-hunters, and dupes of place-hunters) wish for peace, I believe; and such of the monied men as have no advantage from loans and contracts, or as dread the consequences of a fresh loan: but as for the Jacobins—indeed, Mr. Burke, (maugre[46] all your profound penetration) they are very indifferent about the matter: they know (as you do) that peace, under *existing circumstances,*

[a]Letters, p. 68. Thoughts, p. 18.
[b]Ibid.

could only be a hollow truce[a] that the over-burthened labourer would still continue to be taxed for enormous sums to be squandered in foreign intrigue, to disturb the tranquillity, and irritate the government of France; and that "what now *stands for* a government" in England, (I mean Pitt and Hawkesbury's discordant cabal) has injured the French Republic too outrageously ever to forgive it. In short, they know that there is no peace for Europe, so long as the unnatural alliance between the funding system and the borough-mongering system lasts; and that, therefore, any thing (in how "questionable a shape" soever it may come) would be, ultimately, a blessing, that should bring this unnatural alliance to the crisis of a divorce. Sooner or later, this crisis, I believe, must come: and when it does come, "Perish, the Borough-mongers", I say, for one, "and let the public creditor be secured!"—In other words, let Corruption be destroyed—let plunderers and ruffians be dismissed from power, let pensions be abolished, sinecures be totally abrogated, and the salaries of all officers reduced to a level with the mere necessary expenses of the table and the library, of a man of science and public business: Let simplicity and virtue be substituted for ostentatious debauchery; and thus let the peasant and the manufacturer be redeemed from misery; and, at the same time, the thousands, and tens of thousands of virtuous families, whose *well-earned competence* is now vested in government securities, be preserved from hideous ruin. Thus it is, and only thus, that the joint object can be attained, and the jarring interests of the stock-holder, and the productive labourer, be united.

But if Mr. B's extravagant picture of British Jacobinism has nothing to do with the argument on Regicide Peace, it has something to do with that which is of infinitely more importance: it has something to do with our palladium, Trial by Jury: it has something to do with all the yet-remaining fences of our little, little liberty—with all that stands between the head of the patriot and the axe of ministerial vengeance.

But take it not upon credit. Trust not to my assertion. Read the book yourselves—or rather the books: for the parts in which they differ, and the parts in which they agree, are equally important to the just display of the

---

[a]Since this was written, I have seen a spirited and well-written pamphlet, "*Utrum Horum*:—The Government, or the Country", in which this idea is further pursued; and the distinction between a *real* peace, and a peace concluded by our present government, is ably marked.[47] D. O'Brien—I observe, with pleasure, that he has not daubed his title-page either with *Mr.* or *Esq.*—D. O'Bryen, and myself, differ upon some points—our habits, and, perhaps, our objects, are somewhat dissimilar: but different mediums do not prevent us from seeing the same great glaring truths.

temper and views with which they were composed. Consider the whole. Compare together the retrospective parts; and if ever you execrate again the names of Robespierre and Marat, without glowing with superior detestation for Edmund Burke, it is only, because it is in the nature of man, that reason should be the fool of imagination, and that guilt should lose its guiltiness in our eyes, when impotence prevents the perpetration of its malice.

Hear, for example, his affected lamentations over "the total relaxation of all authority",[a] the "inefficiency of tribunals", the backwardness of whose "most essential members" (the juries, I suppose, he means) to execute the bloody mandates of a minister, is described, with insidious obscurity, as a "disowning of the goverment". See, also, his furious attack upon the House of Lords, because that "highest tribunal of all", would not indulge his rhetorical spleen with condemnation of Warren Hastings.[48] There was no evidence, it is true: no case can be made out. But what of that? Mr. Burke can have no idea of "the reason, and equity, and justice", of that "severe and aweful—living law", to which he so pompously appeals, unless trial and accusation, sentence and execution follow each other with as mechanical a certitude as the conclusions of a mathematical problem result from its premises—Without this, it is "dread and putrid; insufficient to save the state, but potent to infect and to kill."

But "the very storm and tempest of his rage",[49] are reserved for the *treasonable* acquittals—for treason, it seems, it was, that we should be acquitted. That Lords and Commons should have joined together in votes of prejudication—that Ministers and Crown Lawyers should have projected and planned such elaborate prosecutions; and twisted and twined, and distorted all law and common sense, till the very statutes of the realm, and the English language itself, were turned inside out, and logic and jurisprudence walked topsy-turvy, like the captive king of the Antipodeans, in Chrononhotonthologos[50]—that his own most sublime and *inventive* genius should have been employed in arranging, drawing out, garbelling and embellishing "Reports of Secret Committees"[b]—that Courts of Special Commission should have been adorned with such pomp and circumstance— Bedlam, Bridewell, and the stews, ransacked for collateral evidence, and nature's loose analogies have been explored for moonshine links of uncon-

[a]Letters, p. 19, and 20. This is one of the additions, for the purpose of working up which to due sublimity, the work has been kept six months in the press.

[b]This, is believed to be one of the *important services* for which Mr. B. received that pension of £4000 a year, which he so modestly assures us, "is no more than he deserved!!"—*Letter to a Noble Lord.*

nected facts: that Judges, Counsel, and Witnesses, should have been so well chosen, and so well paid[a] and Juries so carefully selected, with such due proportions on each pannel, of contractors, police magistrates, and tradesmen to the royal family;[b] and yet, after all, that we should come off with our heads upon our shoulders, and "the CROWN retire disgraced and defeated from ITS courts", with only the solitary, *ambiguous* consolation of executing one of its own spies[52]—this

> "Is grief too fierce for nerves like his to bear,
> And claims the horrors of a last despair!"

He raves till he is lost in the maze of his own frenzy. Like a wounded elephant, his enemies having escaped, he turns his fury upon his friends— upon himself—upon those very pavillions and edifices of state he was armed and caparisoned to defend; and four dread pages of splendid ruins, are covered over with froth and blood.

"The highest tribunal of all is deprived of all dignity and efficiency."— "Public prosecutions are become little better than schools for treason; of no use but to improve the dexterity of *criminals*" (i.e. *reformers*) "in the mystery of *evasion*", (i.e. of *avoiding the society of perjured spies!*) "to shew with what complete impunity men may conspire against *the common* WEALTH", (that is to say, in plain English, against *the corruptions of a gang of borough-mongers—the* PLUNDER *of a hord of placemen and pensioners!*) "to shew with what safety *assassins* may attempt its awful head!"

There is a gradation, it seems, in *honourable obloquy*: but surely we are now at the ladder's top. Mr. Windham made us *white-washed felons*; Lord Grenville *stained us with moral guilt*; and Mr. B. has dubbed us ASSASSINS. It would be curious to know what epithet this *Gentleman!!!* would

---

[a]All the witnesses were not paid alike; or with equal good will. The honest fellows from Sheffield were dismissed with the price of an outside passage on the coach, and about 7s. for expences on a journey of 200 miles. My very valuable and lamented friend, the late John Stuart Taylor, of Norwich,[51] when he applied to a certain gentleman in office, or Jack in office, which ever you please to call him, for those fixed and regular expences, which the subpoenaing party always pays, to every professional man, during the time he is withheld from his business, was answered with surly insolence—"Expences, Sir, for such a witness as you! Do you think it was for this you were brought up to London? You were expected to give evidence on the part of the crown, not on the part of the prisoner!!!"—When the Lynams, the Taylors, the Groveses, the Timses went for their *expences*, was there any demur??? No, they had said all that was expected—and almost every word of it had been proved to be false.

[b]To the immortal honour of those men—to the honour of our national character, this was not a sufficient inducement to English jurors to bring in a verdict for the crown against the evidence.

give to those ruffians (*mostly in the pay of the Government*) who were concerned in the meditated, *attempted* massacres of Lynn and Yarmouth!—In
the mean time, I wonder how *juries* relish these things. But it matters not.
They are not to be used any more, I suppose, *on such occasions*.

Having exhausted his stock of Newgate wit, the metaphorical Proteus
now turns his hand to medicine and surgery, and cures low fevers with
amputation and the caustic. It must be confessed, however, that his *language* is sufficiently scientific. "Whilst the distempers of a *relaxed fibre prog-
nosticate* and *prepare* all the *morbid force* of *convulsion* in the body of the
state, the steadiness of the *physician* is overpowered", &c. "The *doctor* of
the constitution shrinks from his own *operation*. He doubts and questions
the salutary but critical terrors of the *cautery* and the *knife*." The doctor
thus disgraced, anon he becomes a soldier, learns the Brunswick march,
and "takes a poor credit even from defeat." Then again he is a eulogist; a
politician; a lawyer; a resurrection-man, dealing in rotten carcasses; a "ju-
rist"; a letter-founder, and a printer's devil; an engrosser of parchment
rolls, and an engraver of brazen tablets: and all in one single page.

And now he is a dancing master, whimsically employed in "*bowing* to
the enemy abroad", which, it is sagaciously remarked, is not the way "to
subdue the *conspirator*"[a] who is breaking the fiddle "at home". Having displayed these harlequin tricks in his own person, he proceeds to try his
dagger of lath upon other objects. In ten little lines "anarchy" is a rat-
tlesnake; a "*focus*", endowed with magnetic powers; a "venomous and
blighting insect", that "blasts and shrivels, and burns up the promise of the
year", occasions "salutary and beautiful *institutions* to yield *dust and sweat*",
and turns "the harvest of the law to stubble." At last, to crown the whole,
tired of agriculture and natural history, and having panted round the whole
circle of metaphor, he returns, like a hare to the squat he started from,
takes up his old profession of physic once again, and gives us an emetic of
pustles and blotches, and "eruptive diseases", which "sink in and re-appear
by fits". The malady, however, which is now under his care, whatever it
may be, has, somehow or other, *a conversable faculty*—a sort of *intellecual*
"*fuel*", which holds treasonable correspondence "with the source of regicide", and cunningly "waits for the favourable moment of a freer communication to exert and to encrease its force." This is really the most intelligent, artful, intriguing, philosophising disease I ever heard of. What a loss

---

[a]*Conspirator!* singular number!—"A man may conspire with himself!!!"—*Chief Justice* EYRE.—
State Trials, King v. J. Thelwall, *fifth day*.[53]

to the readers of "Medical Transactions", that the doctor has not favoured us with its name, its diagnosis, and the peculiar characteristics of its exterior symptoms.

Wonderful man! most incongruous, and most brilliant phenomenon of genius! how hast thou the power to make even nonsense fascinating, and give charms to sheer malevolence! Thou art, indeed, a compound at once strange and terrible: but, it must be confessed, thou art an entertaining mongrel. Full of beauty, and of ferocity, as "the *royal* beast of *Pegu*";[54] and driven onward by the same blind impulse of rage and raving—thy hideous roar is ever prophetic of blood: But "the tyger is frequently lost in the ape"; and indignation is disarmed by splendid absurdity:- while the tricks and antics of a wild, extravagant, frantic imagination have a sort of witching charm, that defies the sober severity of judgment, and occasions even the absurdity itself, to be accepted as a sort of atonement for the depravity we should else abhor!

But let us not forget—for if we should, there are others who will remember, that these tropes, and metaphors, and allegories, however wild and incoherent in themselves, all point to one determinate object—all lead to one conclusion: namely, that the eighty thousand jacobins (more or less) who are so firmly grounded in the truth and purity of their sentiments, that no sophistical "reasoning", no hackney "argument" of prejudice or corruption, "no example" of government spies caught in their own vile nooze, "no venerable authority! can have the slightest influence on them"; and whose conduct is so strictly consonant with benevolence and justice, that when the crown (that is to say the minister) brings them before a jury, howsoever selected, and of whomsoever composed, it retires from its courts defeated and disgraced—That these detestable jacobins—these eighty thousand criminals, against whom no crimes can be proved—these conspirators, who never yet conspired—these assassins, whose only dagger is reason, and whose only sword is truth—the meridian sun itself being their dark lanthorn, and publicity their only cloak—these are to be submitted to the prompt execution of the cautery and the knife; to be cut and burnt away, like warts, from the eruptive body. All, who dare to complain, though oppression were heaped upon oppression, "till it o'ertopped Olympus"—all, all who dare to wish for change, (though tyranny grew black as the thickest night, and corruption stank in our very pottage,) all are to be swept away. Jurors (unless juries can be regulated by some new fashion) must no more be trusted with such conspirators: for jurors are conspirators themselves—"the acquittal of the conspirators is a proof of the extent to which the conspiracy had spread."[a] Juries will not do: our present tribunals are not efficient. They were instituted for the purpose of chastising criminal ACTS—they cannot reach OPINIONS with sufficient certainty; *but the SWORD can*. "Out the word came; and it never went back":[b] nor ever can get back. Mr. B. indeed soon repented that he had let it out; and endeavoured to recall it: but in vain. It had escaped into the hands of Mr. Owen; and by means of a fortunate quarrel, between the apostate politician and the apostate bookseller, behold—we have it. It is before the world. It is in print. "The type is black and legible"; and both "the *letter*", and the spirit are "*clear*".

"I have formerly heard", says he[c] *with more surprise than* "*satisfaction*", that "opinions are things out of human jurisdiction",—that "you can never extirpate opinion, without extirpating a whole nation." He then proceeds to argue both the practicability, and the propriety of this forcible extirpation; maintaining the justice of "war against opinion",[d] and even affirming, in round terms, "when I am told it is a war of opinions, I am told it is the most important of all wars."[e] He does not, however, neglect the opportunity of exposing the inconsistency of his antagonists. I am glad he does not. I would not have the intemperance, or the injustice, of either party spared. All persecution, from whatever quarter it come, (and I call all war upon opinion, all prosecution for opinion, persecution) is equally detestable: nay, if the thing, in itself, is capable of aggravation, that aggravation it receives, when it is appealed to by the friends of liberty. Let priests and tyrants take shelter in their inquisitions, their star-chambers, and their courts of law, where their *blind* deity, with the two-edged sword, uplifts her scales, in pageant mockery, but strikes as power directs. We have a goddess of more perfect organ—far-seeing Reason, with steadier balance, and an unweaponed hand; but, yet, of force that can never fail of victory, if we have but faith, and trust in her omnipotence.

Why should any advocate for freedom have lost his temper, or his consistency, on account of any nonsense which Mr. Reeves might choose, or be hired, to write, about the trunk, or the branches of a rotten tree? In the name of wonder, what can we wish for more, than that *such talents* should

---

[a]Such was the audacious language of William Pitt.[55] His mind seems pretty well disposed for the adoption of *the cautery and the knife. His steadiness would not be much overpowered by the operation.*

[b]Letters, p. 171.

[c]Thoughts, p. 63.

[d]Ibid. 64.

[e]Thoughts, p. 66.

be employed in *such a cause*. I, at least, have never suspected Mr. Reeves of being one, who, if the Thames were a fire, would know where to run for water to put out the flames. But if ever it should please the gods to enable him to write any thing worth answering, let us hope that pen, ink, and paper will not be wanting. Write away, then, Justice Reeves, and support your cause. Scalp headless wights[56] with Grub-street "Tomahawks"; and indite new "Thoughts"[a] for men who never think. I, meanwhile, proceed to examine the arguments of your more potent coadjutor.

"As to the *mere matter of extirpation*", says he, "of all kinds of opinions, *whether right or wrong*, without the extirpation of a people"[b]—O certainly: it is not necessary to extirpate the *whole* people: Cut but the throats of *that portion* of a people who hold the obnoxious opinion—*Saint Bartholomise* them—nay, that *informed, discussing* portion of them—that *awakened*, able, energetic band, such as the proscribed eighty thousand of this country, over whom "NO *example*" (however terrible) "*no venerable authority* can have the slightest influence"—*Do but Bartholomise them*, and the business *appears* to be done. And this, says the Oracle of aristocratic abhorrence of massacre and cruelty—"this is a thing so very common, that would be clouded and obscured, rather than illustrated by examples."

Mr. B. was very much in the right to save himself from the confusion, in which particular statements would have involved him, by this round and general assertion; for certainly, if he had come to close quarter with facts, none of the particular statements would have answered his purpose: certainly the massacre of the protestants, by the *humane* and *politic* old despotism of France, would not: though for this our *serious* Machiavel[58] (for the Italian did but jest) could, perhaps, assign a reason. The thing was not thoroughly done. It is true, that the *Grand Monarque* having determined to "exert a vigour beyond the law", and having given orders accordingly,[c] "there were killed in the city of Paris, that day and the next, above ten thousand, whereof above five hundred were barons, knights, and gentlemen, who were purposely met together, from all parts, to honour the King of Navar's marriage."—It is true, "Gasper de Coligny,[60] the famous admiral" (one of the leaders of the Hugonots) "was pulled out of the stable, and cruelly abused by the fury of the common people", (this was a royalist

[a]Thoughts on the English Government.[57]
[b]Thoughts on the Regicide Peace, p. 64.
[c]See English translation of *Davila*, p. 374, 375, and 376, edit. 1647. See also for the horrible particulars, "History of the Bloody Massacres, &c. in 1572 (extracted from Thuanus's Hist. of his own times", and translated.) Lond. 1674.[59]

mob—a mob hired, instigated, marshalled by the *regular*, constituted government) "who detesting his very name, *tore* his head from his shoulders, cut off his hands, and dragging him through the streets to the place of execution, left him hanging by one of his feet upon the gallows; and a few days after" (these were royal cannibals!) "they set fire to it upon the same gallows, half burning it, with barbarous rejoicings; their cruelty finding no end, till two servants of the Marechal de Momorancy[61] stole away the relics of his miserable carcase, and buried them, secretly, at Chantilly." It is true, also, that "the day before this terrible execution, the king dispatched posts into divers parts of the kingdom, commanding the governors of cities and provinces to do the like."—It is true, that "on the same night at Meaux, and the days ensuing at Orleans, Rouen, Bourges, Angiers, Thoulouse, and many other places, but above all, at *Lyons*, there was a most bloody slaughter of the Hugonots, *without any respect of age or sex*, or quality of persons." But it is true, also, that through the great extent, and out of the whole population of France, there were *only* forty thousand men, women, and children put to the sword. There ought to have been eighty thousand, reasoning, discoursing, enquiring adults, even if the population of France had only equalled that of Britain. Hence, perhaps, it was, that *Hugonot Jacobinism* and *Hugonot infidelity* (or *Hugonot heresy*)—for with *established priests* they are *essentially* the same!) instead of being "extirpated" from "the vicinage of Europe", have been gaining ground ever since, both in number of proselytes, and extent of principle.

Neither will "the wars of Charles V. and his successors", against this same *Hugonotism*,[62] better support his cause; as indeed he confesses: though at the same time he cautiously observes, that whether those wars "might or might not" be justified, "is a matter of historical criticism!" Nor yet will he be able to quote, among his "cloud of examples", the early persecutions of the Christian system of innovation and reform: a system which, whatever Mr. B.'s *mode of faith* may suggest, went much greater lengths, with respect to a very tender subject, than the wildest *Atheism* either of the French or English Jacobins. The primitive Christians (as every scholar knows) both upheld and practised, not only *equality of rights*, but *community of goods*: (a wild and absurd scheme, I confess; and not practicable upon any *large scale*: but I speak to the doctrinal and historical fact:) nor can the man who has seriously considered the essential doctrines of that religion, view, without contempt, the ostentatious mockery of a modern congregation, who call it Christianity to keep "the poor, the halt, and the blind",[63] standing, at due distance, in the aisles, while the well-dressed classes are closeted up in pews, lined, elevated, and embellished, according to the rank and station of the occupants, listening to a drawler in an awkward habit, and cooped up in a mahogany box, to soothe the pride of greatness with obsequious exhortations, and terrify the abject and oppressed into trembling subordination, and reverence for their *betters*. Edifices, thus *set out*, are Pagan theatres; not Christian churches. What degree of persecution this system met with in Pagan countries, is a subject of so much controversy among the learned, that I shall not venture to decide. However, that it was persecuted in "that centre and focus of attention", Judea, where it first broke out, is evident; and that with tolerable severity. It was persecuted. Christ became popular. His doctrines became popular.—How could doctrines fail of popularity, which contained so many elementary political truths, and vindicated, so directly, in many respects at least, the Rights of Man? He did not spare corruptions, either in Church or State. He exposed the doctrines and the practices of the priests and the aristocrats, the Pharisees and the Sadducees,[64] the powerful, the wealthy, and the great. He collected the people together, in great numbers, and lectured them against existing abuses; in the streets, in the wilderness, in the fields, and on the neighbouring hills. The government was alarmed. They "sought to destroy him"; and when they could not "lay hold of his words", they set gangs of ruffians upon him, to knock him on the head, with bludgeons and stones. But "he escaped out of their hands, and got away." In the midst of these persecutions, the number of his proselytes continually encreased; and some of the *great men* among the Jews (like the *great man* I had mentioned in the "Narrative of my arrest and treatment"[a]) thought, "that men who had a heap of people running after them, were best in a place of security." He was secured. A certain apostate (his name was neither *Edmund Burke*, *William Pitt*, nor *William Windham*—it was *Judas Iscariot*) took it into his head to persecute the doctrines he had formerly supported; betrayed the cause; and accepted a pension for "his public services." In short, Jesus Christ was crucified, as *Joseph Gerrald* has been transported, for exposing the corruption and degeneracy of the times, and preaching a great reform. But it was all in vain. Hang, transport, and crucify, as long as you please: the spirit of a great reformer, martyr'd for a glorious principle, will rise again. The phoenix mind springs triumphant from the pyre; and the winds, that scatter the ashes of the martyr, propagate the principles for which he fell.

Thus fared it with Christianity. The persecutions it suffered, by drawing

[a]Tribune, vol. 1, p. 89.[65]

attention to its doctrines (many of which, particularly in the state of society then prevailing, were excellently calculated to impress the general mind) contributed, more than all the tales of prophecies and miracles, with which it *became* incorporated, to spread through the system, not only through Judea, but through "all the surrounding vicinage." *It did continue to spread so long as persecution continued; and never was overthrown till* POLITIC EMPERORS (*finding it a useful instrument of ambition*) ESTABLISHED THE NAME, AND DESTROYED THE PRINCIPLE.

But, says Mr. B. opinions may not only be forced; you may even force men into the forcible persecution of their own opinions:—"Instances enough may be furnished of people who have enthusiastically, and with force, propagated those opinions, which, some time before, they resisted with their blood."[a] True: but it is a truth which makes terribly against *one* part of his argument, and nothing for the other—for it tends to shew (if brought to the test of facts) the great advantages which new opinions have over the old, when driven to the issue of coercion. The proselytizing army is always encreasing; the army of establishments always falling away. Many thousands, in every long-continued struggle, begin with "resisting opinions with their blood", on account of their *novelty*, which they conclude with "propagating (even enthusiastically, and with force,") from a conviction of their *truth*. An Arnold,[66] or a Dumourier, may be dragged from the retreats of infamy, to prove that the Champions of Liberty may be bought by its foes. But the examples are worth but little, in the scale of argument; and, I speak it with glowing satisfaction, they are but few. As for the voluntary, and unbought recantations, they are all on the other side. In short, "in the event of a struggle", settled governments may rest almost assured, that they must conquer immediately, or not at all. It is, therefore, a serious thing, to bring matters to such an issue.

I rather suppose, however, that Mr. B. had his eye upon examples of another kind; for specimens of which, not to burthen the reader with quotations, especially, as I have cited the passage in a former publication;[b] I refer to "Burnet's Summary of Affairs before the Restoration."[c] There he will find *Lutherans, Catholics,* and *Calvinists*—that is to say, Lutheran, Catholic, and Calvinist *Princes*—Electors, Dukes, and Palatines, in abundance, changing, and re-changing their religion, as policy of state directed;

---

[a]Thoughts, p. 64.
[b]Pol. Lect. p. 55. *On Pros. for Pol. Opinion.*
[c]*Own Times,* vol. 1, p. 14 fol. edit.[67]

and propagating, with *force*, at one time, "those opinions which, before, they resisted with *their* blood": that is to say, with the blood which they regarded as *their property*—the blood of their subjects: the fact being, that, like princes and statesmen in general, they had no settled opinion of any kind; except, that whatever tended to gratify their usurping ambition, was to be pursued; and that every thing was to be "judged by moral prudence" (of which they were the sole umpires) "and not by any abstract principle of right".[a]

But, continues the advocate of extirpation—"Rarely *have ever* great changes in opinion taken place, without the application of force, more or less."[b] True, Mr. B.—and for this plain reason—governments have rarely wanted such counsellors as yourself, to persuade them to drive the question to that issue. Establishments (however pure in the outset) have never failed, in process of time, to be infected with innumerable corruptions. These the governors have an interest in perpetrating; and, indeed, for the sake of that interest, the corruptions have been generally introduced. To them, "the beauty of all Constitutions consists in those very corruptions of which others complain";[c] for it is by the latter, not the former, that their ambition is flattered, their rapacity indulged, their patronage extended, and places and pensions heaped upon themselves, their families, and dependants. These corruptions are therefore artfully confounded, and incorporated, with the original institutions; and the institutions themselves, under one pretence or other, are artfully abrogated by their pretended supporters; till, at last, the whole is infected; and nothing but corruption remains. The enormity of the evil produces complaint. Remonstrance, rejected and despised, provokes to keener discussion, and more bold enquiry. New theories and new systems are started, more consonant with the nature of man, and principles of justice; and the old, corrupted, disjointed patchworks of obsolete institution, and new-fangled usurpation, are attacked with all the strength of argument, and the ardour of principled conviction. But corruption cannot stand the test of enquiry. It shrinks from the galling probe of truth. Its strength consists in "the morbid force of convulsion", not in the conscious energies of temperate health. It therefore flies from argument, and appeals to force: leaving, to the proscribed reformers, only the sad alternative of perishing in thousands, according to the example of

[a]Thoughts, p. 64.
[b]Ibid. p. 63.
[c]Speeches of the Right Hon. W. Pitt, and Lord Mornington, on the Motion for a Committee to take into consideration the Petition of the Friends of the People.[68]

the Hugonots, and the advice of Burke and Windham, by "a vigour beyond the law", or of repelling force by force, with death or victory on their banners, and on their hearts.

Such has been the case in many a nation—in Greece—in Switzerland—in Holland *twice*—in America; and such was the case in France. Opinion had grown till it had burst its chains; circumstances concurred that gave opinion weight; and court seemed to yield; but coercion was prepared. Monopolies (gigantic in wickedness) were planned and executed, to put the subsistence of the people in the power of their oppressors; and fresh massacres were decreed, and organised; but the project transpired: force was repelled by force: *Lambesque*[69] was discomfited; the people flew to arms; the Bastille was taken; *Broglio* fled; and Paris escaped a second feast of Saint Bartholomew. But still there were *silver-headed* traitors to the cause of man, pensioned profligates, at the ear of royalty, advising coercion—from within, or from without— it mattered not. A foreign combination produced a foreign war; and Louis XVI, who had sworn to defend the *constitution of new opinions*, kept up (as *Mallet du Pan*, his confidential agent confesses, in his *Correspondance Politique pour Servir à l'Histoire*)[70] a secret intercourse with the despots who had leagued for his destruction. But surely the "great changes in opinion", resulting from "the application of force", in these instances, are not much calculated to encourage established governments to a repetition of the experiment.

I do not meant to assert, that coercion has no influence over opinion. I have not forgotten that the despotisms of China, and Japan, (despotisms in which that prompt conductor and disseminator of intellect, the press, is yet unknown)[a] did, by nipping Christianity in the very bud (long before it was eighty thousand—perhaps before it was eight hundred strong) exterminate that religion: or, more properly, prevent it from taking root. Neither do I forget the prophet of Mecca and his armed apostles; who carried conviction on the sabre's edge, propounding circumcision or death. But Mahomet, and his Arabs, also, war against Mr. B: for here the *new opinion prevailed*. And why did the new opinion prevail? The answer is a dreadful warning to old establishments not to be eager for contests of blood. The new opinion prevailed, because there is an incalculable distance between the energy and enthusiasm of a new conviction, and the science and mechanism of ancient habits: because it is the former, alone, that rouses the full force of

---

[a]The Chinese have an art of printing. But it consists in the use of logographic characters, instead of an alphabet: it is, accordingly, a labour of many years to learn to read their language.

intellect and valour, and "suffers not a particle of the man to be lost": because the old opinion depends upon rotine; the new upon intrepidity and merit: because in one, the mass feel that they are nothing; in the other, they may be every thing they dare: because the establishment takes its leaders, and must take them, by a *sort of lottery*, from the court cabal; the innovation *selects* them "from the ranks". In one case commands are conferred, that laurels may be reaped: in the other, laurels are reaped that commands may be obtained. Such, "in the event of a struggle", are the advantages in favour of the innovating army: and Mr. B. sees, and acknowledges them in all their strength.

Yet, still, this champion of old systems maintains, that new opinions may be, and ought to be extirpated by force. They ought to be extirpated for three reasons. I. Because "*Opinion is the rudder of human action.*"[a] Granted. Granted, also, that "*as the opinion is wise or foolish, vicious or moral, the cause of action is noxious or salutary.*" But who is to judge of this wisdom or this folly—of this vice or this morality? *Government!* says Mr. B. I say no: for that thing called government, if there be corruption in the state, is, of necessity, the focus of that corruption: That thing called government, is composed of a privileged few, who always may have, and, the history of the world assures us, frequently have had, an interest diametrically opposite to that of the state. Was the court of Tarquin,[71] or of Nero,[72] of Caligula,[73] of Domitian,[74] or Heliogabalus,[75] fit to be consulted for standards of moral and intellectual taste? Did they not mow down all virtue and all wisdom, and propagate the most detestable vices, and the most atrocious barbarism? Are the governments of Japan, of Morocco, of Algiers, fit to be consulted as oracles upon these subjects? If they are not, none are: and for this reason, if the government were ten times blacker than all that I have instanced, it would say that it was pure; and the fouler it was, the more dangerous to deny the assertion.

How then is it to be decided? *By precedent!* you say—No; for precedent is infinitely diversified. All things may be supported by precedent; and all condemned. It would, therefore, revert to governments to decide what precedents were good, and what were bad; and all my former objections recur.—*By antiquity and established usage!* No; that would be to proscribe all improvement—for all improvement is change of established usage. That would be to make the weakness and simplicity of childhood a standard for the vigour and intelligence of maturity; and to prohibit all the advantages

[a]Thoughts, p. 65.

of experience. As Lord Bacon observes, in this respect, *we, who live now, are, in reality, the ancients; they are the younger generations that have passed before.*[76]

Every thing useful to man has resulted from this great principle. Every improvement, every invention, is an innovation, resting upon the substantial data—that, by having all the experience of our ancestors, with the addition of our own, we are wiser than they; and have a right, not only to imitate, like apes, but to improve—to alter—to choose, and to change, as men.

And is political science, alone, upon whose improvement depend the happiness, and the lives of millions, and the creation, as it were, of new worlds of population, whose embryons are now perishing in the dark and comfortless chaos of devouring despotism—Is political science alone to be an exception to the rule, and never to be breeched in manhood, because it has formerly been encumbered with swathing-bands and long coats? Certainly; and, for this obvious reason—The nurses, who hold the leading strings, have a profit in its weakness; and must lose their places, and their perquisites, by such a change. The case of governments, and of arts and sciences, in this respect, are said to be essentially different; but the difference consists in this alone: that if we had a government of tanners, and a priesthood of lawyers, I have no doubt that it would be high treason to dress a hide after a new fashion, and blasphemy to invent machines for splitting timber.

2. "*It has ever been the great, primary object of speculative and doctrinal philosophy, to regulate opinion.*" Certainly, and this object has always been, and of necessity must be, most effectually answered when opinion is most free; and indeed the very terms, "speculative and doctrinal philosophy", when used in any sense of approbation, take for granted. Every body knows that *philosophy* means the *love of wisdom*; and that to *speculate* is to *conjecture, and pry, and enquire, with a view to the discovery of truths as yet unknown.* So that speculative philosophy evidently means the *love of that wisdom which consists in making enquiries and conjectures, with a view to the discovery of new truths;* while *doctrinal* philosophy, or the philosophy of *teaching,* must of necessity mean *that love of wisdom which displays itself in imparting to mankind the truths which, in the process of our conjectures and enquiries, we may have discovered.* Now how can we speculate without the liberty of speculation? How can truths, hitherto unknown, be discovered, if we are not free to conjecture and enquire?—And how can new truths be taught, if the philosopher is not permitted to communicate what his con-

jectures and enquiries have led him to regard as true? In short, how can there be any such thing as "speculative and doctrinal philosophy", if opinion is not left unshackled? It is not by coercion, but discussion, that opinions are to be regulated, and the consequent effects of morality and social order obtained. But,

3. "*It is the great object of political philosophy to promote that [opinion] which is sound.*" Certainly, it is the duty of every political philosopher, and of every philosopher, by every motive of reason, and every opportunity of discussion, to promote whatever appears to him to be sound. But the disposition to decide between soundness and unsoundness by the faggot and the axe, comes not from the schools of philosophy, but from those of theological contention. What follows, therefore, "*and to* EXTIRPATE *what is mischievous, and which directly tends to render men bad* CITIZENS *in the community, and mischievous neighbours out of it*", is a sophism both in terms and substance. It is a sophism in substance, in as much as the statement being general, vague, and hypothetical, furnishes no just foundation for the particular conclusion meant to be inferred. It is a sophism in terms, in as much as the phrase, "extirpating what is mischievous", being spoken in reference to the antecedent "political philosophy", demands assent only to the propriety of extirpating the supposed mischievous opinion by philosophical means—that is, to say, by means of reason, or setting one opinion against another; while the whole tenor of the argument would apply this assent, not to extirpation by philosophy, but by the sword.—In this sense of the word, therefore, I deny the proposition: a proposition, indeed, which absolutely begs the question; and affirms the very point it pretends to argue. I, on the other hand, affirm, that political philosophy has no right (according to Mr. B.'s jargon) to extirpate, by force, any opinion whatever:—no, not even "the opinion, that it is a man's duty to take from me my goods, and to kill me if I resist him." The sophist who should propound such a doctrine, would be easily confused. (To say, that he could not, is to admit that he is right; or to affirm, that falsehood is more convincing than truth: a dictum that destroys all morals.) He who should *act* upon the doctrine, would, undoubtedly, be hanged. But so long as indolence, or fear, restrains him from action, *the opinion*, however absurd, is perfectly harmless; and society ought to be satisfied. It is sufficient for the *law*, that we fear the *gallows*: Our friends and companions, it is true, the guardians of our interests, and the instructors of our children, we would seek among men who act upon more generous principles.

As for pulling down governments—in addition to the preceding arguments, I shall only add, that *no man* can pull down a government, But when, not a Man, but a *People*, wills a grand renovation, to feel the *will* is also to be conscious of the power: and, when the will and the power cooperate, sophists may string syllogisms, like beads upon a rosary; but while they are reasoning, the thing is done.

Fortunately for mankind, this will is not lightly inspired. It is not to be produced by declamations or logic. The speculative few will have their preferences, their theories, and their projected improvements. Sir Thomas Moore had his Eutopia;[77] and Hume, himself, sketched a sort of ground-plot for the French Republic:[78] but to the mass, even of those who have some "tolerable leisure for discussion, and some means of information", (so long as their grievances are not very galling) that which *is* will generally appear to be best; merely because it *is*; and because that spirit of nationality, which belongs to the whole species, occasions us to imbibe, with our very nutriment, a prejudice in favour of our national institutions. Nay, even the speculative few, themselves, from their very love of speculation, till roused by some extraordinarily provocative, prefer the very establishments they disapprove, to the dangers, and the trouble of a change.— Hume's Commonwealth slept for sixty years, and the Eutopia for whole centuries, on the shelves of the learned; and even the popular language of Thomas Paine would not have provoked any very alarming discussion, if the general *condition* of mankind had not pre-disposed them to exclaim— *We are wretched!—Let us enquire the cause!*

In short, in all the pages of history I have perused, there is not a single instance (and most assuredly I have not forgotten France) of a great, popular revolution taking place, till grinding, and long-continued oppression, had rendered it absolutely necessary:—till groaning Nature called for the dire relief.

It is not, therefore, by the extermination of eighty thousand malcontents and theoretical reformers, but by the alleviation of burthens, and the restoration of equal justice, that such revolutions are to be avoided. It is not by the persecution of *new opinions*, but by the reform of *old abuses*, that contentment can be restored, and tranquillity preserved to a state; and governors secured from the terrors of retributive justice.

But, says Mr. B. I do not mean to persecute all *new doctrines*. "Theological opinions", for example, "whether sound or erroneous, do not go directly to the well-being of social, of civil, or of politic society." (If I were disposed to give a clue to one sort of persecution, while I reprobate another, I could mention some theological opinions which appear, to me, at least, to go more directly to the destruction of all social, moral, and political virtue, than any thing of which Atheism itself was ever accused. "If I were the Deity", says Plutarch, who, by the way, was himself a priest—but he was, also, a philosopher—a moral philosopher!—"If I were the Deity, I would rather that men should deny my existence, than say, that I was cruel, jealous, lascivious, or revengeful.")[a] The theological dogmatists, he continues, "did not preach vice or crimes." (How, Mr. B.—did they not preach the crusade? Did they not preach murder, assassination, poisoning, *despotism of Kings*, the axe, the halter, and the faggot? And did they not practise what they preached?—But I forget myself—With the single exception of *deposing kings*, all that I have objected, instead of vices and crimes, are virtues, in Mr. B.'s *politico-moral* code. Nay, even such deposition itself, provided the power be transferred only to the privileged bodies, and feudal proprietaries of the "old Germanic or Gothic custumary", may be perfectly innocent, and even praise-worthy: for "indeed, the force and form of the institution, called States, continued, in *greater perfection*, in those republican communities [in which the classes, orders, and distinctions, such as before subsisted, or nearly such, were still left] than under monarchies.")[b] "The parties", says he (the religionists) "disputed on the best means of promoting virtue, religion, and morals." And what do the Atheist and the Christian dispute about?—Why, whether religion is, or is not, the best instrument for promoting morals and virtue.[c] Men may differ upon this point, as well as upon the question, of which sort of religion (from the Egyptian faith, in calves and onions, to the orthodox metaphysician's, in an incomprehensible, immaterial, triune Deity) and yet both parties may be good members of society. Do you try our lives by our opinions, or our opinions by our lives? Neither would be just: for man is an incongruous animal. But surely, the latter were more candid: and, upon this foundation, I would be bound to bring Atheists into court, before whom the pious, impetuous, hireling apostate of Beaconsfield must hide his head in confusion.

Opinions certainly have their tendencies with respect to moral character. But opinions are multitudinous. They proceed not from any one common stock. They spring up from many a wildly scattered seed. They blossom on innumerable stems. Detested, therefore, be the bigotry that

---

[a]I quote from memory: but I know, that in sentiment, I am correct.[79]
[b]Letters, p. 111.
[c]They dispute, also, whether religion be true or false. But with this abstraction, the politician has nothing to do.

condemns the soil, on account of one rank weed: that, from a particular doctrine, however erroneous, would argue the immorality of a general character!

But "is there no distinction between an innocent and moral liberty", and opinions that are "the direct highway to every crime and every vice?"—Must government "either throw the bridle on the neck of headlong nature, or tie it up for ever to the post?"[a] The sophism is stated with most plausible subtilety; and the simile is truely fascinating: and when mankind shall acknowledge themselves to be horses—or that their governments are created for the express purpose of riding them, then will it strictly apply: then will it be right, that opinion should be lashed round the station-post, till it is broken-in to the taste of the rider. But so long as men and their governors are animals of the same order—so long as the great body of a people have a *common weal*, and that little corporation called Government, a *particular* one—so long as rulers have an interest, and betray an inclination, to consider every thing as "an innocent and moral liberty", which tends to pamper their ambition and rapacity, or encrease their power; and to represent all opinion inconsistent with their views, and hostile to their corrupt and despotic pride, as "the down-hill way to every crime and every vice"—so long (that is to say, as long as political society exists) will it be much more dangerous to the peace and welfare of the universe, to give the reins to that dread War-Horse, Constituted Power—*whose neck is clothed with thunder, the glory of whose nostrils is terrible, and who swalloweth the ground with fierceness and rage,* than to throw them loose on the neck of the headlong colt Opinion, who, though he may snort, and curvet, and frolic through a thousand extravagancies, will never, unless cruelly lashed and goaded, commit any serious depradations, or do irreparable mischief, either to himself or others.

This metaphor is, however, an important part of Mr. Burke's statement; inasmuch, as it proves, that his observations on the forcible extirpation of opinion, are intended to apply, not only to the foreign war, but, also, to the *Domestic Enemy.* Here, then, the argument, as far as relates to the development of the mind and objects of the writer, is complete—And thus it stands:

There are, in this country, "eighty thousand Jacobins, so utterly incapable of amendment, over whom no argument, no example, no venerable authority, can have the slightest influence."

[a]Thoughts, p. 66.

These Jacobins have been tried, in the persons of their supposed leaders; but "the tribunals have been found inefficient"; the Juries, (by finding them "Not Guilty") have "disowned the government"; and "public prosecutions have been mere schools of treason."

But opinions, if they cannot otherwise be checked, ought to be "extirpated by force": the practicability of which may be proved "by a cloud of examples".

Ergo—Eighty thousand Jacobins are to be *forcibly* gotten rid of, at any rate; "by the caustic and the knife"; by fire and sword—by mock trial, without Juries to "disown the government",[a]—or by the murderous tumults of Lynn and Yarmouth bludgeon-men.

Such, my fellow-citizens! are the propositions and denunciations of the confidential hireling of a court, which yet fills the world with senseless howlings against cannibal philosophy, and affected exaggerations of revolutionary massacres!!! And to shew you that the insinuations of Mr. B. are not rashly, or unadvisedly made—to shew you the object of his insinuations—and that these hints do actually, and *bona fide*, come from the governing powers, for the purpose of preparing the public mind for some fresh member of "that *previously digested plan, or series of measures*", hinted at in the memorable debates of the last session;[81] essential parts of the language of these pamphlets—important branches of this *syllogism of massacre*, are incessantly propounded by all the members and dependants of the government; no opportunity is neglected of insulting and reprobating the Juries who were guilty of the *deplored* acquittal; the circumstance is openly connected with every motion and proposition for encreasing the military force; and Mr. Pitt (even since these sheets have been at the press) in a debate (Oct. 31) upon that very subject, affirms, that notwithstanding the issue of the trials, nine-tenths of the nation are convinced of our guilt.[82] The inference is plain. It is a commentary (a tremendous commentary, coming from such a quarter) on the intricate, yet not obscure text of the arch-apostate to Aristocratic moderation! The ordinary physic of the state cannot cure the disease; even extraordinary potions have been administered without

---

[a]That is to say by Bill of Attainder. That this is one of the "efficient operations" to which Mr. B. alludes in that intricate and purposely obscure passage (p. 19) will no longer be doubted, when we recollect and compare his sentiments upon former occasions—"If", said he, on the prosecution of Warren Hastings, "we cannot have justice by the *slow, formal mode of Impeachment*, we must resort to the ancient, *wholesome practice of Bill of Attainder!*" Let the reader but look back into the History of his Country for the cases and precedents of this *ancient* practice, and he will presently determine how *wholesome* they were; and *who* they were wholesome for![80]

effect; and as soon as the body politic (that is to say, the body of "political citizens",—the privileged "four hundred thousand"), can be properly prepared for the operation, recourse must be had to "the cautery and the knife."

If this is not sufficient to open your eyes, the last trumpet alone can awaken you. If this is not sufficient to rouse you to fresh vigilance, fresh exertion, closer intercourse, and intrepid unanimity, ye are dead—ye are lost, not only "in the oblivious pool",[83] but

> "In bottomless perdition; there to dwell
> In adamantine chains."[84]

Think, I conjure you: What is the prospect held out to you?—For yourselves—unqualified submission, or the prompt and destroying vengeance of some new mode of legalized massacre, or military execution:—for your children—the tombstones of progenitors, who, though born to a degree of freedom, which they were bound to improve, and had no right to alienate, yet relinquished the patrimony, with criminal supineness, and left to them, for their inheritance, beggary, and accumulating chains!

Rouse, then, once more, to the investigation of your rights: for, if ye will be ignorant, ye must be slaves. Trust not your hopes to a blind fatality. Repose not in the indolent expectation, that the corruption of the system will work its own cure. That corruption will, I believe, inevitably destroy itself: But the destruction of the tyranny is not, of necessity, the emancipation of the slave. Almost all are tyrants when they have the power: and the being, or the nation, that knows not how to maintain its freedom, when one yoke is broken, will find that another is prepared. Even if a continuation of the war, or the *winding-up* of a peace, should bring affairs to a crisis—If, as is not unlikely, ere the close of this century of ambition, usurpation, and carnage, prodigal expenditure should come to open bankruptcy, and the obstinate infatuation of courtly pride, should bring, at once, to their catastrophe, a system of horrors and a ministry of crimes; how shall ye be assured of benefitting by the event?—How shall ye secure yourselves from new modes of corruption, and new systems of oppression? How, but by vigilant discussion, and well-grounded principles?

Awake, then, once more, to the important enquiry. Compare what ye are with what ye have a right to be. Compare your powers and your faculties with your condition: the bounty of nature with your scanty enjoyments, and unsatisfied wants: the wealth resulting from your productive labour, and the abject wretchedness of your general state. Compare these things, and consider well the causes. Trace them to their sources, in the nature of some, and the corruptions of other, of those very institutions of the old Germanic, or Gothic custumary, at the prospect of whose approaching overthrow, the volcanic imagination of Burke pours out such deluges of flame and smoke. Contrast the gloomy intricacy of these oppressive systems—these antique temples of fraud and violence, with the simple plans of reason, and of nature; and learn what to avoid, and what to pursue.

In the furtherance of this great enquiry, despise not the warnings, nor reject the assistance of a friend, whose sincerity, at least, has been, more than once, tried in the balance, and has not been wanting; and who still, unsubdued by persecutions, unawed by the daggers of assassins, unchilled by the cold neglect of an unsocial world, and forgetful of his own misfortunes, and his own personal cares, incorporates himself with the public, and with the warm enthusiasm of conviction, proceeds to advocate the cause of man against the usurpations of establishments.

Among the vindicators of these abuses, the most formidable, assuredly, is Edmund Burke:—nay, he is the only one who, in any literary point of view, can be regarded as formidable at all: for the talents of this country are, generally speaking, pure: they have not been debauched by court favour, nor rendered dependant by the liberal patronage of an administration of Mecaenases[85] and Medici.[86] In brilliancy of imagination, extent of general knowledge, and richness and versatility of talents, Mr. B. is, however, by himself a host: though, at the same time, such a host as no champion of reason, of an inductive mind, and an enthusiastic impression of truth, need be afraid to attack. Armed with the firm confidence inspired by the latter of these advantages, and hoping to be found not quite destitute of the former, I appear once more in the lists; and, not conscious of any disgrace in a former skirmish, proceed to closer and more decided conflict. He has stated what he calls his principles: mine shall be stated still more explicitly. I shall demonstrate the misery produced by his feudal institutions; and shall endeavour to display the social and moral advantages, the improved felicity and extended intellect, which would result from more simple and equitable systems dictated by the laws, and by the rights of nature.

In the pamphlet, or rather pamphlets, I am replying to, there are three important objects of discussion. 1. The spirit of Jacobinism, in this country; and the manner in which it ought to be disposed of, or extirpated. 2. The excellency of the old established systems of government, as now administered, and the folly, wickedness, and profligacy of attempting to shake them, either by sudden or progressive change. 3. The justice and propriety of the present war; the capability of this country to pursue it, till what are affectedly styled regicide and atheism, by establishment, shall be utterly destroyed; and the virtue, the wisdom, and even the necessity of staking our national existence upon that issue.

Of these, the first only (which, though artfully incorporated with the rest, forms, in reality, a distinct subject) is particularly examined, in this letter; to which I have given entirely a controversial form; as the nature of Mr. B.'s attack, in reality, necessitated me to do. The other two belong to the comparison of the respective systems. I shall, therefore, in the following letters, proceed to a sort of systematical developement of the rights of nature, and genuine objects of social institution; and shall, of course, controvert the axioms and declamations of the arch-champion of feudal barbarism (which he calls polished society) as they fall in with the following heads: and shall thus endeavour to present, in living colours, the contrasted pictures of the usurping establishments, which court sycophants would have you worship, and those natural and inalienable rights, against which they entertain such inveterate abhorrence.

END OF LETTER I.

NOVEMBER 27, 1796.

The Second Part of this Pamphlet is now at the press, and will be published in a few days—containing as follows:

LETTER THE SECOND.　First Principles: or Elements of Natural and Social Rights.—I. *False Principles of Burke examined and exploded—Rejection of the Gothic Custumary—Fallacy of the Argument of Vicinage.*　II. *Man considered as an Individual—his Rights and Faculties—Original Equality of Man.*　III. *Foundations of Civil Society—its genuine Object, not decided by Precedent but Reason—Institutions subservient and responsible to general good.*

LETTER THE THIRD.　Origins and Distribution of Property.—I. *Use and Abuse of History in Political Discussion.*　II. *Progress of Society—1. Man in the savage State—2. In the Pastoral—Property in the Pastoral State.—3. The Agricultural State—Influence on Condition and Institutions of Society.* III. *Basis of Landed Property—Original Distribution—Accumulation of Land—from natural Causes—from artificial—Duty of Governments to discountenance Accumulation—Digression on Laws of Primogeniture.* IV. *Distinction of Proprietor and Labourer—Abuses of that Distinction—Rights of Labourers—from Nature—from implied Compact—from the Principles of Civil Association—Condition of the Mass—compared with the Savage—with the Negro Slave—Tyranny of Property*[a]—*Amelioration of Condition of Labourers—in America—in France.*

LETTER THE FOURTH.   The Feudal System.   I. *Progress of Arts and Knowledge—of Accumulation—Supposed Advantages of an idle Class—disputed—Knowledge is Tyranny unless diffused.* II. *Monopoly of Knowledge— of Arms—Consequent Usurpations.* III. *Feudal Establishments—Vassalage and Servitude—Origin of Nobility—of Gentry—Norman Conquest—Tyranny of Force.*

———◆———

Should the countenance given to the Second Part encourage the Author to proceed, a *Third Part* is intended to be published in a few weeks, embracing the following subjects.

LET. V.   The Mercantile and Manufacturing Systems.

LET. VI.   The Funding System.

LET. VII.   The Causes of Popular Revolutions; and Means of Preventing them, or lessening their horrors.

LET. VIII.   Idea of an improved State of Society. Its Practicability, Means, and Objects.

———◆———

[a]Not that all property is tyranny (rightly understood it is, and ought to be, sacred) but that there is a species of tyranny, and that a very grievous one, frequently growing out of large accumulation. This distinction the reader who has curiosity to peruse the work, will find distinctly marked: but, in times like these, I deemed it necessary to avoid even a momentary misunderstanding upon so tender a subject.

[Second Part]

"The greatest part of the governments on earth must be concluded tyrannies, impostures, violations of the natural rights of mankind, and worse than the most disorderly anarchies."

EDMUND BURKE.[87]

Letter II.
First Principles: or, Elements of Natural and Social Rights.

I. *False Principles of Burke examined and confuted—Gothic Custumary rejected—Reply to the Argument of Vicinage.—* II. *Man considered as an individual—his Rights and Faculties—Natural equality.—* III. *Origin of Civil Society—its genuine Object—Subserviency and Responsibility to the general Good.*

I. "The operation of dangerous and delusive first principles", says Mr. B. "obliges us to have recourse to the true ones."[a] Let us see, then, how far his own principles are dangerous and delusive, and refer to the great code of Reason and Nature, to discover what are the true.

It is not, indeed, very easy to extract Mr. B.'s principles. His mode of writing is at once declamatory and dogmatical in the highest degree. Assertion and metaphor mingle in such splendid confusion; and facts without proofs, and conclusions without arguments, are so accumulated and involved, that it is almost impossible to decide what is to be regarded as premises, and what is illustration. The following, however, appear to be the principles upon which he rests his arguments.

---

[a]For the quotations at the beginning of this letter, see Rivington's edition of Burke's "Letters to a Member", &c. p. 108 to 116; or Owen's edit. p. 47 to p. 55.

1. That "Men are neither tied to one another by treaties and compacts", nor by "interests"; but "are led to associate by resemblances, by conformities, by sympathies."

2. That "War is the sole means of justice among nations": and that "nothing can banish it from the world."

3. That "the cause of why many nations in Europe have been less separated, in later times, in the course of long and bloody wars, than communities, apparently at peace in other periods, must be sought in the similitude throughout Europe of religion, laws, and manners."

4. That the sources of this similitude are "the feudal institutions emanating from the old Germanic or Gothic custumary, improved and digested into system and discipline by the Roman law."

5. That "the several orders (which are called States) arising from this system, may, if they choose, *cast off* Monarchy"; because the force and form of the "institutions called states, have continued in greater perfection in Republican communities, than under Monarchies." But,

6. That for any nation to form "a new scheme of manners, in support of a new scheme of politics", is an outrage against "the *aggregate* commonwealth of Europe." (Hence he concludes—that—"those miscreants", the French Republicans, have "made a schism with the whole universe.")

7. That "the analogies which form the law of nations, are to be drawn from the principles which prevail in the civil community."

8. That "the *Law of Neighbourhood* does not leave a man perfect master of his own ground":—as in the case of *nuisances*; which the neighbours "have a right *to represent to the* JUDGE, *who*, on his part, has a right to order the work to be staid; or if established, to be removed."

9. That "this right of denunciation does not hold when things continue, *however inconveniently* to the neighbourhood, according to the *ancient mode.*"

10. That "where *there is no constituted Judge*, as between independent states there is not, the vicinity itself is the natural judge."

11. That "what in civil society is a ground of action, in politic society is a ground of war."

From these premises, Mr. B. deduces, *generally*, "a right and duty", in the grand vicinage of Europe, to "prevent any capital innovation which may amount (in the judgment of that vicinage) "to the erection of a dangerous nuisance"; and, *particularly*, to persevere, by process of fire and sword, by pillage, murder, and desolation, to the abatement of that grand innovation, the French Revolution, and the restoration of the *ancient* (and therefore unimpeachable) nuisance of which, heretofore, we so unreasonably complained.—And this, I am told, is considered as the strong part of Mr. B.'s pamphlet. It may be so: but, to me, at least, its strength, like that of Sampson,[88] is wrapped in mystery. It must lie in the hair, or some other ornamental part; for, in the limbs and portions of the argument, I see it not.

In the first place, the premises are too many, and too unconnected to serve as a basis of just reasoning. First principles are, in their very nature, few and simple; and though the result of them, when demonstrated, may in their turns, be used as premises, yet they must grow out of some common data, like branches from the parent stock, in all the simplicity of induction. It is the trick of sophists to overburthen the memory with a crowd of intricate propositions, which dazzle where they should elucidate, and confound where they should convince.

1.2. With respect to the propositions themselves, the first and second, instead of simple *data*, or self-evident, elementary truths, are complex dogmas, which, at least, require much argument to establish them; and which, if established, would not answer the purpose for which they are advanced. Thus, although it should be admitted (as, "where there is no constituted tribunal" to enforce the compact, we must admit) that "papers and seals" cannot, and perhaps ought not to "tie men to one another", that, "the interests frequently tear to pieces the engagements, and the passions trample on both", yet the other branch of this proposition is by no means a concomitant truth. "Resemblances, conformities, and sympathies", have, it is granted, much to do with *individual associations*; but (torn and trampled upon by our unruly passions, as, in common with many nobler parts of our nature, they too frequently are) "the interests" have still more: and, even independant of all these, there are a thousand accidents or necessities, imperious in their nature, by which passions, interests, and sympathies are all, in innumerable instances, alike controuled. This, so true with respect to individuals, is still more so of *national intercourse*. "Distance of place", though it "does not extinguish the duties or the rights of men", not only alters their reciprocal claims and obligations, but weakens their sympathies, restrains their passions, and resigns them more completely to the influence of those interests, those necessities, and that habitual routine, the powerful operation of which, even in the closest intimacies of social life, cannot be rationally disputed.

I deny, then, in the main, the argument of sympathies and resemblances, as chief causes of confederacy, or intercourse among nations: trusting—or, at least (to speak with more modesty) *hoping*, that there is not much resemblance, not much conformity, no very strong and intimate sympathy (however close may be the alliance) between the Governors of this country and those German and Russian despots, whose sanguinary ambition tore, with *cannibal* ferocity, the bowels of dismembered Poland, and strewed the streets of Warsaw with unexampled massacre.[89] But I concede to Mr. B. that among nations, as among individuals, the wild and irritable passions of insolent prejudice, and fanatic pride, too frequently tear and trample upon the engagements of friendship and reciprocal interest. The senate of Britain, and the nations of Europe, bear recent testimony to this disgraceful truth: and the tears that, in the former, added dignity to its brightest ornament,[a] were prophetic of the torrents of blood by which the other has since been desolated. But that war ever was, or ever can be "a means of justice", is a proposition so contradictory to all reason and experience, that whatever may be Mr. B.'s faith in the *trial by combat, by wager, and by ordeal*,[90] and the whole catalogue of superstitious "feudal institutions, drawn from the Gothic Custumary", I for one must beg leave to demur; convinced that the justice of a cause is no more to be demonstrated by such appeals, than the existence of witchcraft (another practice "emanating from the said Custumary") by throwing old women into horseponds, burning them if they swim, and drowning them if they sink.

"When the sword is drawn", says Tacitus, "and the power of the strongest is to decide, you talk in vain of equity and moderation: *those virtues always belong to the conqueror.—*Victory transfers every virtue, and oppression takes the name of wisdom."[b] Similar was *once* the opinion of Edmund Burke, when in one of those sublime transports of Republican enthusiasm, in which he indulged himself, in the discussions during the American war, he indignantly exclaimed—"Rebellion!—what is rebellion?—*It is written on the backs of those who run away*!!!"[92]

War is, indeed, a mean of any thing rather than of justice. It is a mean of revenge—of desolation—of conquest—(It is a mean, also, of defence against hostile aggression; and as such, alone, to be defended; "The blood of man should never be shed but to *redeem* the blood of man. The rest is vanity; the rest is crime.") It is a mean of ambition; and a mean of plunder.

[a] I speak of Mr. Fox as an *individual*: and, considering him in that point of view, who will refuse the tribute of admiration, either to his heart or to his head? My opinion of *Party* is well known: the influence it has had in rendering his talents and virtues comparatively useless to the public, no one can more sincerely lament.

[b] Manners of Germans. Murphy's Transl. vol. iv. p. 36.[91]

It is a mean of multiplying places and pensions; of encreasing the emoluments and patronage of office; of murdering, oppressing, starving the useful mass to pamper the profligate and useless few: and so long as all power and government remain exclusively in the hands of these few, I fear, indeed, with Mr. B. that "nothing can banish it from the world." But the permanency of an evil can never justify its particular operation.

3. The dictum that follows is a perfect Burkism: cause is misstated for effect, and effect for cause. That a general harmony of *manners* endears the reciprocations, and prolongs the intercourses of social life, is readily admitted; and that, in the present state of human knowledge, and of human arts, these intercourses and reciprocations, extend beyond the narrow bounds of a family—a neighbourhood—a nation, is a truth which the philanthropist admits with triumph. But the general intercourse of Europe produced the similitude, not the similitude the intercourse: and the manners (upon which I lay the principal stress—for in this respect, laws and religion have only a secondary influence) instead of emanating from the boasted feudalism, have, in a considerable degree, abrogated its institutions, or controuled their force.

As for the reciprocations existing between nations "in the course of long and bloody wars",—it is of little consequence, I imagine, to the poor wretches who bleed, and *starve*, in these detestable struggles, whether the *enlightened* few, for whose advantage they perish, are sincere in their animosities, or "do but murder in jest!"—whether, as in more barbarous times, governments immolate their hecatombs at the altar of revengeful ferocity, or, with the refinement of commercial oeconomy, lead them to a common slaughter-house, to be butchered for a common benefit; and civilly shake hands over the bloody bargain. This, at least, we know—that in proportion as the boasted intercourse and urbanity improve, wars become more frequent, more lasting, and more destructive. In the lamented times, when nations were "more perfectly separated", war was only a sort of sabbatical pastime for our rulers: but now, it is pursued, with true work-a-day assiduity, (in preparation or in act) six days out of seven, as for daily bread.

It may appear paradoxical, but it would not be difficult to prove, that the frequency and obstinacy of wars, in later times, is to be attributed to the very circumstance which prevents the perfect separation of the hostile nations. This circumstance is not "similitude of laws"; for they are made to hang poor rogues who *suffer by the warfare*, not to regulate the conduct of governors, who *decree* it:—not "similitude of religion"; for the efficient rulers of the earth—the *trained politicians*, upon whose wise management the intercourse is supposed to depend, have seldom (in reality) been of any religion at all. With them, from the very nature of their education, opinions are mere engines of state; and the faith they gird on others, as a robe of sanctity, is to themselves a harlequin's jacket, that changes its fashion with the exigencies of the moment, or is thrown off, as an incumbrance, when some daring leap is to be taken. Thus CICERO,[93] *the oracle of the public forum*, upholds, with pious gravity, the very opinions which CICERO, *the philosophical correspondent of Atticus*, treats with contemptuous ridicule!—Thus, "the Monarchs of France, *by a series of wars and negociations*, obtained the establishment of the protestants of Germany, while they were destroying the protestants at home"![a]—and thus heretics draw the sword to protect the apostolic throne of St. Peter; as most Christian Kings once joined in holy league with the Imperial successors of the Arabian prophet.

The real cause of the phenomenon is to be sought in the commercial system; which, while it furnishes the pretences and means of war, still keeps up a circuitous and clandestine, if not a direct and open intercourse between the contending nations. This, also, it is which, not only more than treaties and compacts, but more than resemblances, conformities, sympathies—more than *vicinity* itself, binds together the aggregate of nations into what Mr. B. calls the community of Europe.

4.5.6.   From what remains, it appears—that, according to the *true first principles* of Aristocratic logic, all palatable and wholesome knowledge must be derived from the maxims and institutions of those polite and erudite constitution-mongers, the Goths and Vandals of the fifth century; hashed up (or, as Mr. B. has it, "improved and digested") "with the decrees of despots and praefects of the Eastern and Western Empire, into a sort of politico-salmagundy of superstition, barbarism, incongruous tyranny, and mock morality; sauced, seasoned, and garnished to the true taste of royal and aristocratical epicureanism, by those scientific cooks, the jurists and publicists of the Roman and Germanic schools. In other words, "the old Germanic or Gothic custumary, disciplined and systematised by the Roman law", is the great repository of all elementary truths, whether of politics, of morals, or of manners!—the source of all wisdom and all *civilization!*—the quarry from which are to be hewn the pillars of our freedom, and "the Corinthian capitals of polished society"!

By the said Custumary is also to be decided what revolutions may, and

---

[a]Letters, p. 183. Thoughts p. 126.

what may not be made; and under what particular circumstances, and for what particular purposes, monarchs may be *killed off:*—"Cast off", I believe, he calls it:—but it is much the same—"the states, or privileged classes, orders, and distinctions" (of ancient, or of modern times) in whose behalf this revolutionary right is admitted, seldom demurring much between *casting* and *killing* off, either monarchs or people, as best suited their ambitious purposes. In this country, in particular, they have generally preferred the latter: though instances of each abound. The *History of England*, from the Conquest, is little else than a chronicle of usurpations, and revolutions, and regicides. With the solitary exception of imperial Rome, there is not such a "Nation of Regicide" in the ancient or modern world:—But (barring one ambiguous instance) it was all for the "privileged classes, orders, and distinctions"; and therefore &c.—&c.—&c.—*See* BURKE'S RULES FOR KING-KILLING. *Rivington's edit.* p. 110!!!

(Aristocracy!—Aristocracy!—every thing is to be for Aristocracy!—Kingship may be annihilated, if Aristocracy does but monopolize the advantage; and the Revolution in 1688 was only right because "the Prince of Orange was called in by the flower of the English *Aristocracy; aristocratic* leaders, who commanded the troops, went over to him, with their several corps, in bodies; and *aristocratic* leaders brought up the corps of citizens who newly enlisted in this cause"![a]—As for what have been called the principles of that Revolution, it seems they are mere trash! visions and afterthoughts of Lock[95] and his disciples!—stalking horses to amuse 'the four hundred thousand thinkers': The real excellency of the event consisted in this, that the Aristocracy led the way, like herdsmen, and the people followed like sheep!)

To the whole of this dogmatism I shall certainly object; and of course to the jargon about "breach of community—outrage against the aggregate of nations", &c. and shall maintain the *political right* of France to make, within her own territory, whatever revolutions, when, and howsoever she should think fit: And by France, I certainly mean the *French people*—not the mere states or privileged orders; who were no more France, than the laced lacquies of Earl Fitzwilliam are *the ancient and noble* family of Wentworth. They were the *servants* of France; and, finding them to be unprofitable and unfaithful servants, she called them to account for their innumerable frauds and impositions, stripped them of their liveries, and turned them off.

---

[a]Sp. on Army Estimates, 1790. See Works of Ed. B. 4to edit. vol. iii p. 14.[94]

I repeat it, France, thus considered—the aggregate body of France, always had (and always must have) a *political* right to make, within her own territory, whatever revolutions she thought fit. I say nothing, in this place, of the *moral* right: that must depend upon the provocations, causes, objects: and one country has nothing to do with another, further than respects external political relations. Morality or immorality is an abstract question, to be decided by the conscience of the country, not by the *Military Tribunal* of the vicinage.

To proceed—In the first place, I deny that the Germanic or Gothic custumary is, or that any custumary or establishment can be, in point of right, the authoritative repository of first principles: and for this reason—Either that custumary or establishment must have been eternal, or it must have had an origin. This claim of eternity no European establishment has the modesty to prefer. They must have *originated*, therefore, in *chance*, in *usurpation*, or in *right*. If in chance, they can be no authorities; and we must look in them, not for elements, but for incongruities; not for first principles, but a chaotic mass:—If in usurpation, they are only precedents of wrong; and precedents of wrong cannot be authoritative sources of the principles of right. Right principles may, it is true, become incorporated with them—good fruit engrafted upon a bad stock: but you are not, therefore, authorised to pronounce, by mere reference to the trunk, that whatever it produces is good. If they originated in right, then had they a *right to originate*; and the very existence is a precedent sanctifying that principle of innovation they are so frequently quoted to bar.

Deny me this; and you deny to man, in one age and period of the world, that free, or moral agency, which, in another, you are obliged to admit: In other words—You unhinge the great system of the universe, and substitute in its place, a chaos of your own creation; in which man is no longer man—no longer an organised being of a distinct and regular species, propagating, from race to race, his particular kind; but an anomalous deformity, owing his existence to a sort of equivocal generation; neither deriving nor imparting a specific nature, nor holding a fixed station in the ranks of being.

Have I jumped too suddenly into this conclusion?—Mark the steps that lead to it. If these establishments had not a right to originate (I repeat it) they could not originate in right. The right of these establishments to originate could only arise from the nature and circumstances of man, *for* whom, and *by* whom, they originated. If it was right that they should originate by man, man had a right to judge of the propriety of their originating; and, consequently, of the propriety of the establishments themselves: and, if that propriety arose out of the nature and circumstances of man, his right to judge of their propriety necessarily included a right to judge of his own nature and circumstances, and to modify the establishments accordingly. The conclusion is—that either the nature of man is changed (for his rights grow out of his nature, and without change of nature there can be no change of rights) or else he is still at liberty to judge of his own nature and circumstances, and to originate such establishments as that nature, and those circumstances require. In other words—*Establishments cannot decide upon First Principles; but First Principles must decide upon Establishments.*

I say again—The very existence of establishments supports these principles: for (historically speaking) how came they to exist?—By *innovation*: by the overthrow of prior establishments, on the ruins of which they have been established. I speak not of particular cases. I speak *of all*—all establishments, civil or religious, of which history has preserved the traces.

Was not the present *Church of England* an innovation? Is it not founded upon the ruins of that papal establishment, which, in spite of the proud pleas of prescriptive reverence, and the sanction of adoring ages, was obliged to give way, with its whole train of adulterous corruptions, and their cowled and mitred hosts of *pensioned* advocates, to doctrines more congenial to the sentiments of the nation, and the establishment of more simple rites? And, where did the reformers of those days look for their authorities?—To the Customary of Rome—its legends of saints, and institutions of holy feudalism? No: these they rejected, as codes of obsolete prejudice and records of imposture, and appealed to the first principles (or what they regarded as first principles) of the religion they endeavoured to purify.

Was not *Christianity* itself established (if that which Constantine[96] established can be regarded as Christianity) upon the ruins of Paganism?—and did the first Christians appeal, for the principles and elements of their faith, to the codes and digests of the Pagan institution? or, did they refer to data which they accounted of a higher authority, more conformable to their reason, and more adapted to their nature and circumstances?

Passing from religion to politics—from Constantine the Great to George the Third—Is not our present establishment, with all the fruitful blessings of the *Brunswick succession*, an innovation on the prior establishment of the House of Stuart? And did not Sir Robert Filmer, like Edmund Burke, fulminate his anathemas, with pious rage, and dogmatise *his first principles of prejudice and absurdity*, drawn from the Pandects and Institutes of expiring despotism?[97] But the reformers and innovators of the age, with Somers, Locke, and Sydney[98] at their head, appealed to the code of Nature for more genuine principles; and the clouds of sophistry were scattered by the rays of truth.

Nay, was not *Hereditary Royalty*, itself, introduced by innovation into Britain? Our Saxon ancestors knew it not.[a] Their Chief Magistrate, it is true, held his office for life: but he was *elected* by the states; and the crown, at his demise, returned to those who gave it.

True it is, that from attachment, and from superstition (for the Saxon princes had also their pretensions of divine right—their fabulous descent from Woden,[104] and their expedients of papal consecration!) the choice was generally confined to a particular family; but infancy, crimes, or imbecility, were sufficient bars to the succession; and the title of the office still indicates the qualification once thought necessary for the important trust. But if the throne, under the Saxon, was the property of the people, the nation, under the Norman, became the property of the king. He bequeathed it, as we bequeath our chattels, by his will; and, if no fortunate adventurer happened to anticipate the nominee, in the seizure of the royal treasures, he succeeded, without a murmur, by the divine right of royal testament, and "held his crown in contempt of the people." At length the anarchy of regal robbery and testamentary succession, yielded to the settled order of hereditary descent; and, subject to the controul, and the wisdom of parliament, hereditary it has been ever since.

Finally—Does not even the old Germanic, or Gothic custumary, with all its emanating feudal institutions, derive its origin from a great and general innovation?—an innovation of the most dreadful kind; which was, indeed, every thing that Mr. B. would represent the French Revolution to be!—an innovation of ignorant barbarism; whose sole object was plunder; and whose sole means were fire and sword, rape, massacre, and desolation!—an innovation whose smallest crime (if among its crimes, all things considered, that circumstance can at all be reckoned) was to have broken

---

[a]See Lord Somers—(Judg. of Nations ¶ 6.)[99] and the authorities he quotes. "I never desire", says Mr. B. (Ref. on Fr. Rev. Works, vol. iii, p. 43)[100] "to be thought a better Whig than Lord Somers": And this observation he makes while combating Dr. Price's maxim of the right of electing Kings.[101] It is a little remarkable, however, that Lord S. in the book just quoted, maintains not only the ancient, but the *inalienable* right of Britain, and all other nations, "to elect their governors, and cashier them for misconduct".[102] It is still more remarkable, that this treatise of Lord S. should be one of those books which Mr. B. alludes to, as having been so charitably circulated by the Soc. for Const. Inform. but which he doubts whether any body was ever so charitable as to read. Refl. &c. p. 24.[103]

to pieces an institution the proud growth of twelve successive centuries, and subverted an Imperial establishment of five hundred years. And yet with the Alerics[105] (male or female)[a] who, to satiate their brutal "appetite for plunder and revenge", would "deliver to the licentious fury of the tribes of Germany and Scythia", the noblest city of the world; abandon to *military execution all who should dare to defend themselves*, or even neglect to *assist the invader, with all their might, and by every means in their power*; and, in the midst of rapes and general conflagration, "fill the streets with dead bodies", and "extend the promiscuous massacre to the feeble, the innocent, and the helpless"—With the Attilas,[108] who may boast, with ferocious pride, "that the grass never grows on the spot where their horses tread"[b]—With the Gundobalds,[110] who piously declare, that "war is the means of justice", successful slaughter the fiat of Providence, and conflagration the award of God[c]—With these we are to contend, to extermination, for the perpetuity of their system: if "in the progress of society, arts and sciences diffuse *new lights*", and new systems should, "by consequence", arise;[d] "mingling the

---

[a]The passages, in this description, marked with inverted commas, are quoted from Gibbon's account of the sack of Rome by the Goths, in the year 410. (Decl. and Fall of Rom. Emp. vol. v. p. 310, 311, and 344. 8vo. edit.)[106] Those in *italic*, from the *D. of Brunswick's famous Manifesto* (Art. 7 and 8.) and the *Additional Declaration*[107] with which it was shortly followed. For a practical comment, trace over the blood-track of the fiend *Zuwarrow*—consult the Russian massacres of Ismael and Warsaw; at the latter of which places, a vanquished, unresisting multitude of six-and-twenty thousand people, men, women, and children, were murdered by royal authority. I bring these circumstances together, that the reader may see at once what these *Goths* have been, what they would be, and what they are. I do injustice, however, to the dead, when I compare the ancient with the modern Alerics, or compute what Paris was threatened with, by what Rome suffered. The proclamation of the *barbarian of the 5th century*, "when he forced his entrance into Rome, exhorted the soldiers to spare the lives of the unresisting citizens." p. 311. The *barbarism* of the present day exclaims, with brute ferocity, "murder all who do not assist you"!!
[b]Ibid. vol. vi, p. 126.[109]
[c]"Is it not true", said the King of Burgundy, to the Bishop, "that the event of national wars, and private combats, is directed by the judgment of God; and that his providence awards the victory to the just cause?" Ibid. p. 352.—Where is the essential difference between the Barbarian of the fifth, and the Courtier of the eighteenth century?
[d]"Is it true", says a dedicatory echo of Burke's politics, "that in the progress of society, arts and sciences have diffused *new lights*, and the civil union, being *by consequence*, better understood", &c. MURPHY'S TACITUS, Notes, vol. iv. p. 187.[111] Thus is it directly acknowledged, that in proportion as new lights are diffused by the progress of knowledge, the principles of political association are better understood. Yet this faint copyist, like his eccentric master, is an advocate for the perpetuity of the old Gothic Custumary; and, with all the admitted improvements of social science, would fetter us to the institutions which, twelve or fifteen hundred years ago, were fabricated, by ignorant savages, in "the woods of Germany". I cannot resist the temptation of referring the reader to this curious *Commentary*; where, especially in the "notes on the life of Agricola", (if he has patience to wade through the heavy mass of common-place criticism and trite illustration, which, with true book-making assiduity the translator has heaped upon his invaluable author) he will find as curious a hash of inconsistency and

martial shouts of Barbarians with the sound of religious psalmody",[a] we are to wage eternal war, "not with their *conduct*, but with their existence":[b] and if we cannot succeed in securing immortality to Gothism, at least, we are to be "buried under its ruins";[c] and the evening is to close, as the morning broke, upon scenes of devastation and carnage.

7. As for "the analogies which form the law of nations",—I deny, in the first place, that any such thing as a law of Nations, does, in fact, exist. While that republic of princes, the Germanic constitution, was any thing more than an expensive mockery, there was, indeed, a sort of public law in Germany—or, more correctly, perhaps, a pact of conspiracy against the rest of Europe; as, in the ancient world, during the existence of the Amphictyonic league,[114] there was also, a public law of Greece: but as for a law of nations, in any accurate, or extensive sense, this is one of the sublime speculations of modern Jacobinism—a germ of *universal peace and fraternity*—a mere philosophical embrion, crude, as yet, and uncounted in the world of being; though so impregnated, I believe, with the quickening seeds of truth, that it cannot fail of an eventual birth. At least, I am one of those *incorrigibles* who expect to behold something more than the cradle of its infancy; and who expiate in the alluring hope of bequeathing to posterity the tranquil security and ever-growing blessings which the maturity of such an institution might dispense. At present, however, no such terrestrial Providence exists. The moral agency of governments is reduced to no fixed principle; and while individuals, in their particular communities, are condemned to the cells, and fetters, and strait waist-coats of oppressive and superfluous laws, the great community of nations remains in a state of anarchy; and madmen and ruffians pillage, murder, and destroy at pleasure.

Grotius and Puffendorf[115] may be quoted to eternity, and their learned dust thrown, upon *every occasion*, in the eyes of an ignorant multitude: but

---

contradiction as ever was produced by the despicable attempt to maintain a system in the teeth of all the facts of history. Tacitus,[112] with a mind imbued with all the principles of the old Republicanism, and a heart warm with all those humane and generous feelings, which it is the very nature of despotism to trample under foot, is, it must be confessed, an unfortunate text-book for an advocate of oppression; and the picture he has drawn of the jealous tyranny of Domitian, with his spies and informers, and mock trials for treasonable and seditious writings, is, one would imagine, a strange subject for illustrating the propriety of making "the common hangman" chief corrector of the press, and suppressing "innovations, clubs, and schismatics", by a system of persecution. Ibid. p. 346 to 349, in particular. Mr. M. however, gets through with it, as well as he can, and Tacitus is, for the first time, enlisted on the side of tyranny.

[a]Gib. vol. v. p. 313.[113] See also, our prayers and sermons for fast days.

[b]Letters, p. 141.

[c]"Under the ruins of *the civilized world*" is Mr. B.'s expression (p. 20): but he has before explained, that nothing in the world is civilized, but the Gothic Custumary.

the governments, who quote them, laugh at their own juggle. These equiv-ocal appeals are used by statesmen for no better purpose than to blind the people when they would lead them into war: as horses are muffled that they may be tied to the mill; or as the Spaniard, at his bull-fight, shakes his robe at the boisterous victim, and dazzles him while he strikes the blow.

8. The analogy, then, is deficient in an essential member. The *vicinage* can appeal to no common law,[a] declaring what is *nuisance* and what is not. It can plead no compact, no delegation or convention, real or *virtual*, in any period of the world, assenting to the establishment of such law: no impartial arbitrator—no constituted organ by which the decisions of such law could be pronounced. Mr. B.'s *vicinage* is a jury in its own cause. It is, indeed, upon a large and tremendous scale, a *self-constituted Revolutionary Tribunal* fulminating the barbarous decisions dictated by its own blind pas-sions and perverted interests, and alternately carrying them into execution, by military violence, or yielding its own neck to the triumphant victims it had wantonly and impotently condemned.

9. 10. 11. The very admission, in the tenth proposition, that "betweeen the independent states there is no constituted judge", before whom "the denunciation" can be brought, would, therefore, be sufficient to bar the analogy. But the objection rests upon still stronger grounds. The *reason* of the law of civil vicinity, does not apply to the vicinage of nations: and Mr. B. is too scientific a lawyer to deny in *theory*, though he may be too profes-sional a lawyer, having taken so good a fee, to admit in *practice*, that the *reason of the law* is its noblest and most essential part.

Neighbours in a civil community, have their *common*, as well as their *individual rights*; the former derived from nature, and secured (or meant to be secured) by the specific compact under which the community exists; the latter, generally speaking, created by the compact; and growing out of its specific provisions; and, therefore, fit objects of superintendance and re-striction to the authority under which they exist. (Nations have, also, their common as well as individual rights: but neither the one nor the other originate in compacts of vicinage—for between the community of

[a]Nothing in the regions of political dogmatism can be more ridiculous than Mr. B.'s idea of a law of nations. In the addendum to his last edition (p. 160)[116] he talks of "the treaty of Utrecht" as "one of the fundamental treaties that compose the public law of Europe." That is to say (to try him by his own test of analogy) two or three neighbours fall together by the ears, proceed to box, kick, cuff, break heads, and fracture limbs, till they are tired; and at last set themselves down over a bottle, reconcile old differences, and enter into some mad or profligate agreement of supposed mutual advantage; after which they take upon themselves to say—this shall be a part of the fundamental law of the vicinage. If our neighbours do not conform to it, let us set their houses on fire, and satisfy public justice by conflagration and plunder.

nations no such compact exists. *They* are bottomed, all, in nature; and by the principles of nature they must be tried.) It is the duty then of every civil community to take care, that the *subordinate rights of compact* do not encroach too far upon the *common rights of nature*, as, "if a man were left perfect master of his own ground", might be the case. Hence the right of denunciation in the respective neighbourhoods; and tribunals for the abatement of nuisance. But this nuisance, I repeat it, must consist in the particular invasion of some common right: The law, in this respect, being a sort of assertion of the original equality of man; who, though he has yielded much to compact and individual appropriation, yet retains a sort of quit-rent, as an evidence of his title, and a vestige of his common right. Thus, for example, *Man has naturally an equal claim to the elements of nature*; and although earth has been appropriated, by expediency and compact (for the basis of which appropriation see the following Letter) light, air, and water (with some exceptions) still continue to be claimed in common.

The light which illumines my premises, belongs equally to my neighbour as to me: it is therefore a nuisance to block it out. The air I breathe must be breathed, also, by him; and the stream that flows through my garden waters his: If I stop the one with a dam, or poison the other by "a pestilential manufactory", I make my individual right of compact a mean of usurpation upon the common and superior rights of nature: in other words, I commit a nuisance; and it must be abated.

In these, and like instances, the innovation, and rightly, constitutes the nuisance; and you cannot abate what is "according to the ancient mode": for property is, upon both sides, concerned; and all property, except the actual produce of individual labour, comes by compact: you must take it, therefore, as the compact gives it. With respect to "brothels and night-cellars for thieves, murderers, and house-breakers", the case is different. The common rights of the immediate neighbourhood may be, in some degree, annoyed; but the principal nuisance is to the community at large, and consists in the danger to the morals and security of society; over which the laws, made, or pretended to be made, by and for the whole, have "a right, and a duty, to preside." The proprietors, therefore, of these seminaries, the other parts of the denunciation being clearly sustained, would not, I conceive, be at liberty to plead "that they were *old creations*." Neither, I presume, would the plea of "old creation" answer the purpose of a proprietor indicted for not taking down a tumbling house: and even Mr. Justice Reeves (whose duty it is, in this district, to preside over such presentations) would be obliged to acknowledge, that buildings may become nuisances by being too old, as well as by being too new.—But how does this reasoning apply to nations?

Mr. B. tells us (and he gives abundance of hard words for proofs) that the *new erection*, in France, is a pestilential nuisance. Some French declaimer may, perhaps, as dogmatically affirm, that the old erection, in England, is a tumbling nuisance: that, partly by the ravages of time, and still more by the sapping and mining arts of its pretended guardians, the beams are disjointed and the foundations gone. But what of all this?—If their *innovation* is so pestilential a nuisance, so much the worse for them: for they must live in the stench. If our *old edifice* is a tumbling nuisance, so much the worse for us: for our houses will be endangered by the fall. But the pillars of our constitution will not tumble upon their heads: nor will their pestilential manufactory poison our air. Let them build, and brew, and innovate, in what manner they please; but the light will still shine as bright as ever—the air still refresh us with its wonted purity—the dews of heaven fatten our land, as heretofore, and the sea flow on, regardless of their dykes and mill-dams. As for the contents of their *night-cellars*, they would scarcely have come so far as to rifle *our* travellers, and break *our* houses; or, if they had, we have police officers enough to bring them to justice—as soon as they would *fetch their weight*.

In short—Hostility there may be between nation and nation, and injustice there may be in a thousand shapes; but there can be no such thing as nuisance. All that Mr. B. declaims about—all the arguments of ministers, and all the proclamations, declarations, manifestoes, &c. of all the allies, amount to no more than this—that France has *set an example* which the old governments of Europe (and I do not wonder at them) are not disposed to approve. But in what part of "the praetorian law" does Mr. B. meet with *the nuisance of example?*

If my neighbour upholds doctrines I do not approve—if he is addicted to practices which I consider as immoral—if he keeps a swarm of concubines, or, what I regard as still more vicious, swears at his servants and whips his children—if he makes his drawing-room his kitchen, entertains his guests in a cellar, stirs his fire with a silver spoon, and sleeps in the cock-loft, or the gutter, I may pity him as a madman, or renounce his acquaintance; but do I indict him for a nuisance, with an ass's plea, that I am in danger of being seduced by his example?—It is a most impolitic concession made by the old governments, when they so vehemently proclaim, that if their swords do not overthrow the French Republic, the example of the French Republic will overthrow them!

11. Having swept away the rubbish of the Gothic custumary, and proved Mr. B.'s first principles to be no principles at all, I proceed to examine the question upon the broad grounds of reason and moral justice: for though I deny, altogether, the right of foreign interference, and consider no war as justifiable, but a war of simple and absolute self-defence, war or peace, under existing circumstances, is an inferior consideration; and the present contest must be regarded with diminished abhorrence, if the principles of reason and justice will not vindicate the Revolution against which it has been directed.

Jacobinism then (like all other systems) is to be tried by reference to the first principles of nature. If it is constituted of these elements, then is it limbed in adamant; and in vain shall the puny lance of sophistry assail "its colossal form." If these elements enter not into the composition, then is it, indeed, "a vast, tremendous, unformed spectre", and "the overpowered imagination" cannot be too soon relieved from the delusion. Let the light of reason be the test; and we are willing to abide the issue. If Jacobinism be a spectre, before that light it will most assuredly flee. If it abides the searching rays of enquiry, I, for one, will lean against it, with confidence, as the bulwark of my integrity, and the rock of my strength.[a]

Let us enquire, then, *what* JACOBINISM *really is?*—not what it is represented by Mr. B.—*What the* OLD GOVERNMENTS *of* EUROPE *really are?*—not what their advocates would wish us to believe them.

Properly to decide these questions, we must travel a great way back, out of our present habits and modes of thinking: We must consider, *What man is by nature?* and *What society has made him? What are his powers and his faculties, and* (if I may so express myself) *his capabilities?* and, *What is his actual condition?*

The whole argument of the enemy—the soul that animates the splendid eloquence of Burke, and the vapour that inflates the mediocrity of Pitt,

---

[a]In this discussion I adopt the term *Jacobinism* without hesitation.—1. Because it is fixed upon us, as a stigma, by our enemies: and they who shrink from epithets of unmeaning reproach, are deficient in the fortitude necessary for diffusing a grand principle.—2. Because, although I abhor the sanguinary ferocity of the late Jacobins in France, yet their principles, generally speaking, are the most consonant with my ideas of reason, and the nature of man, of any that I have met with: and it might be proved, from B.'s own confessions, that their profligate conduct arose not out of the *new principles*, but out of the corrupt and detestable character formed under the *old system*. But though I adopt the name, I shall not servilely copy their maxims. I shall dare to think for myself. Having rejected the Old Testament of Gothism, I shall not adopt, with implicity submission, the new Koran of the Robespierians. I use the term Jacobinism simply to indicate *a large and comprehensive system of reform, not professing to be built upon the authorities and principles of the Gothic custumary.*

emanate from the hypothesis that in the old systems every thing is right: at least as right as the nature of man admits. If this be true, and I can be shewn the truth, *Be they immortal!* shall be my dying words. We, on the contrary, affirm, that there is, in these systems, much that is corrupt and oppressive; much that is injurious to the comfort and morals of mankind, repugnant to his nature, and hostile to his very existence. Nay, some there are, who consider the whole frame of society as radically vicious; founded upon false principles, and supported by systematic oppression.

In differences so important, to what authority shall we appeal? To the tribunals of our opponents?—to the fields of slaughter? No: Nature—the great frame and deducible principles of the universe, must decide the question. When I talk, however, of nature, and *the natural condition of man*, I do not refer to any supposed era of perfect happiness, or poetical vision of a golden age: neither do I mean to argue upon any theological or philosophical hypothesis of origin or creation. The fact is, that the world is known to us only as a populous world; and man as a gregarious animal. How he originated, and what was his solitary condition (if solitary it ever was) are questions that may amuse our fancy, or exercise our faith; but with political enquiry they have nothing to do.[117]

Little more concern have we with narratives, or fables, of the origin of civil institution. This is a subject more profitable in speculation than as a matter of history. It is of little consequence what circumstances produced, or what motives influenced the first formation of political societies: for precedents of wrong cannot alter the nature of right. It is more important to discover what the objects of association ought to be, than to be informed what they actually have been. Fortunately, the most important is, also, the most practicable enquiry. History, obscure with respect to the early transactions of particular states, is, of necessity, silent as to the beginnings of constituted society. But politics has its romance, as well as natural philosophy; and the former, as the latter, can produce its Burnets[118] and its Buffons,[119] to fill up the vacuum of authentic record with Histories of Unknown Ages, and Chronicles of suppositious Facts. Even the sage Polybius, like the eccentric Burke,[a] has indulged his fancy with discoveries in this *terra incognita* of human history; shewing us how government was first instituted, and wherefore it first began. Such whimsies amuse, but they cannot instruct us. The fact is, we are not only unacquainted with solitary man, but with society uninfluenced by political compact. Even the savages in

---

[a]Polyb. *Gen. Hist.* B. vi. Ext. 1.[120] Burke's *Vind. of Nat. Soc. Works* 4to Edit. Vol. I.[121]

the recently discovered islands, have their forms of settled institution, and have made *some* progress in the arts of government: and a "Society founded in natural appetites and instincts, and not in any positive institution"[a] is to be sought only in the pages of sophists and visionaries.

The only apparent exceptions (and they are exceptions big with instruction) are in the instances of *founding new states*; either by emigration (as in the case of Rome, and some of the American provinces); or by the breaking up of old governments (as in France and Holland.) To neither of these instances, however, can we look for examples of simple origin. They are only *great changes* in political society: and though, in the former, men seek new territories, to try new experiments, yet "communities" (as B. rightly expresses it) "do not consist in geographical arrangement, or a denomination of a nomenclator"; and, although, in the latter, they should utterly destroy the very basis of former tyrannies, yet they necessarily retain the ideas, passions, habits and experience, derived from the state of political society, under which they have lived: they are, therefore, in both instances, innovators, rather than founders. As far, however, as these habits and passions would permit, men have always, under such circumstances, appealed to first principles. The vague and floating ideas of equal and common rights, which no state of society can entirely eradicate, embody themselves on such occasions, and extort reverence even from the profligate, and homage from the ambitious. Thus, by the advice of Romulus[122] their leader, as we are informed, by Dionysus of Halicarnassus, (B. I. and II.) the promiscuous throng of emigrants and refugees who founded the Roman state, not only elected their government, and chose their governors by UNIVERSAL SUFFRAGE—from the king and the senators to the pettyest annual officer, (without excepting even *the King's body guards*); but, taking possession of an uninhabited, and unappropriated spot, they divided the land also among them, in equal portions.[123] Thus also in France, though the settled claims of property prevented a division of lands (and, whatever Mr. B. may insinuate, certainly it has not even been attempted), very determined efforts were made to establish an *Equality of Rights*: and although (through the bloodthirsty ferocity of some of its advocates) the attempt, in its full latitude, has miscarried, yet much, very much has been effected, and the franchises of mankind are considerably enlarged.

But though neither history nor observation furnish any examples either of unassociated man, or of society without some sort of political institution,

[a]Burke's *Vind. Nat. Soc. Works, Vol. I*, p. 11.

yet is it not difficult to form a distinct idea of what may be called the natural condition of man: that is, to distinguish, in our minds, between what the individual has derived from nature, and what has been conferred, or abrogated, by civil society. When I talk, therefore, of *man in his natural state*, I mean to consider him *simply as an individual, stripped of all the relationships of Society, independent of its compacts, and uninfluenced by its reciprocations*. This abstraction is absolutely necessary for the impartial examination of the subject: for the rights of man must grow out of the nature of man; and the excellence of all social institution must consist in its conformity to that nature, and the security of those rights. But how shall we know what those rights and that nature are, till we have properly distinguished between the qualities of the individual and the sophistications of society.

The rights of man, thus considered, are simple in their elements. They are determined by his wants, and his faculties; and the means presented by the general system of nature (that is to say, by the frame and elements of the material universe) for the gratification of the former, and the improvement of the latter. I repeat it, the natural rights of man, considered as an individual, are determined by his wants, his faculties, and his means. They have no other bounds. I care not upon what hypothesis of man you proceed: whether of creation, or eternal succession, of chance, of necessity, of inherent laws of matter and motion, or what not: for a treatise on government, like government itself, should be of no sect—but accommodated to all. All lead to the same conclusion: for here is nature, or the universe; and here is man, chief tenant of that universe! child and creature of that nature! and heir to its circumstances, its blessings, and its woes! However man came, circumstances came with him. However man received his intelligence, that intelligence gives him a certain power, and a right commensurate with that power, over the unintelligent, or physical universe; and his faculties themselves are a title to their enjoyment. Was the universe created by a God?—that God created man also, a part of that universe, with all his wants and faculties; and by creating both the wants and the things wanted, HE dictated the rights by the means.[a] Did man and his faculties exist from eternity?—then a universe, conformable to those faculties, has, likewise, eternally existed. The natural wants and the natural

---

[a] I do not mean to say that, *in morals*, the means necessarily include the right of gratification. This would be a horrible sophism: for the means of wrong frequently proceed from the wrong itself. My argument applies simply to wants created by nature, and the means furnished by nature for their supply.

means are still coeval; and *Fitness is the Law of Right.* The other doctrines are embraced in these two extremes; and thus we have a basis upon which all sects may argue the great, the universal cause of Justice, of Liberty, and Man.

This basis may be laid in the following axiom—*Man, from the very circumstance of his existence, has an inheritance in the elements and powers of nature, and a right to exercise his faculties upon those powers and elements, so as to render them subservient to his wants, and conducive to his enjoyments.* In other words, Man is the sovereign; the material universe is the subject; his faculties are the powers by which he enforces his authority; and expediency is his rule of right. He is a despot, to the limit of his power, over the physical universe; and he has a right to be so. But this very right precludes him from despotising over his species: for the argument that applies to one, is of force for all, and to know the natural rights of others, it is only necessary to know our own.

When I think upon this sovereignty—when I think upon these powers—when I think upon the means afforded for their exercise—when, indulging any large and generous scope of thought, I reflect upon all the wonderous faculties with which man is endowed—the vast funds of moral, physical, and intellectual wealth which the elements of nature lay open to his exertions, and the centuries upon centuries during which he has been so laboriously employed; and when I see him still so poor, so lost, so abject, and so vile—so gross in appetite, so bankrupt in happiness, so unshaped in intellect, and so dead to generous and expansive morality, I cannot but conclude, that the existing institutions of government are not the best that the nature of man is capable of—that they are dead weights on his exertions, instead of springs to his elasticity.—But to return—

III. That in a society where no compact, or regular association existed (supposing such state of society practicable) these rights would equally belong to every individual, is evident. It is demonstrable by reason. It is palpable to sympathy. The only question is—*Whether this equality of rights is surrendered—or rather, whether, in reason and justice, it ought to be surrendered, by civil compact, or political association?*

To answer this question properly, we must consider several others.— 1. *What is the rational object of civil association? Is it not the general good?*— 2. *In what does the general good consist? Is it not in the security of the rights* (and, what necessarily depends upon those rights, the happiness) *of the whole?*—3. *By what means can civil association best secure those rights?* I answer—*first,* by generalizing and ascertaining them; and, *secondly,* by establishing a universal reciprocation; and thus involving the particular good in the good of the whole, and securing the good of the whole by particular interests.

Herein consists, then, the main *distinction between natural* (that is to say, *individual*) *and social* (or *political*) *right*. Natural, or original right, is (if I may so express myself) merely *physical*: that is to say, it consists in the mere powers and means of the individual; in the direction and exercise of which he is himself sole umpire. (Hence the impossibility of such a state of society; for judgments will differ, even where judgments are consulted; animal strength and cunning will differ; desires will clash; and the anarchic *Tyranny of Physical Force* must inevitably follow: at least, such will be the case while man continues either what he is, or what he has hitherto been.—I mean not to bar the flight of speculative philosophy. I admit—I uphold the eternal improvability of man.[124] What he may sometime be, if governments do not check his course,[125] it were presumption to determine. What he may not be, bigotry will alone pronounce.) Civil Society, by creating a common interest, establishing reciprocations, and binding the respective individuals by mutual pledges, adds to the physical a *moral right*. In other words, it creates Duties commensurate with the Rights; and makes the former the guarantee of the latter. It proceeds, or ought to proceed, upon the inculcation of the maxim—*What I have a* RIGHT *to demand for myself, it is my* DUTY *to secure to others*. Thus, then, the superadded, or artificial rights do not destroy the original. Nature is still paramount: but it is nature *en masse*, instead of individual nature. It is the aggregate of individuals securing its parts, and judging for the whole; instead of leaving those parts to contend, and destroy each other. Its business is not to abrogate rights, but secure them; not to restrict our faculties and enjoyments, but to improve both the one and the other.

There is, I know, a very generally received maxim among the "jurists and publicists" (the politico-apostolic authorities of Mr. B.) which stands in direct opposition to the doctrine here laid down:—I mean the fundamental maxim (for as such it has been regarded) that *Man, on entering into society, resigns a part of his rights, that he may secure the rest*.[126] But this maxim is absurd, inasmuch as every surrender of right is a surrender of power; and, therefore, every right surrendered weakens the security of what remains. Thus, when the people of Rome were deprived of their natural and constitutional birth-right, equal universal suffrage, by the new states, or customary "of classes, orders, and distinctions", under Servius Tullius, the disfranchised class (the nine out of ten, who had no "leisure for discussions, or means of information") were cajoled into acquiescence, by the promise of exemption from taxes and military service: (Poor, deluded people! to suppose that your privileges could be enlarged by the abridgment of your rights!) but, when the franchises were gone, the privileges followed:—the old as well as the new. The successor of Tullius not only compelled their personal service in *his* wars, and oppressed them with heavier burthens than ever, to support *his* revenue, but even reduced them to the most abject drudgery to gratify his ostentation; "forcing them, like slaves purchased with money, to labour in a most shameful manner; to cut stones, saw timber, carry burthens, and waste their strength in deep pits, and subterraneous caverns, without allowing them the least respite from their miseries." (*Dion Hal.* b. iv. c. 81)[127] In the same manner, not a part only, but the whole people of this country, have lately been deprived of the important franchise of popular discussion; and persons of a certain class have been cajoled into a sort of compliance with this invasion, by the pretence of better security for their property.[128] (Property!—Security of property!—The authors of these bills talk of securing property!—and against whom?—the dextrous pick-pocket, at the door of the theatre, *pushes away the crowd*, and whispers you to take care of your handkerchief, while he eases you of your purse—or your watch.) But then the time shall come, as come, I believe, it must, when resources can no more be *anticipated*, and dividends can no longer be paid[129]—then, when the interests of borough-mongers and stock-holders shall stand opposed (as opposed they must be, from the very nature of things) and the latter shall wish to deliberate on the means of saving themselves, and the country at large, from such scenes of misery and ruin as never yet were witnessed—then, where will be the security of property?—Then will repentant alarmists, the deluded and jilted proprietors of moonshine securities, be compelled (as well as the London Corresponding Society)

"to hide and feed, by fifties, in a cave",[130]

or be silenced and dispersed by a hireling police-magistrate, and the sabres of a troop of cavalry.

Thus, then, the just and rational object of civil institution is, not to retrench, but to equalize and secure the natural rights of man, by substituting moral arbitration for physical force: that is to say, by instituting tribunals for the regulation of individual conduct; that whenever supposed rights (that is to say, particular interests) clash, violence may be prevented, and personal differences be decided by aggregate reason. Of this aggregate reason, Law ought to be the epitome, and Magistracy the organ.

It is upon these principles only, that a multitude of individuals can be melted and organized into one harmonious mass. Thus only can they really become a community, or body politic: for where one part tramples, with rude and brutal insolence upon another, it is not a body politic, but a state of unequal war. When the arbitrary will of a few, wallowing in wealth and luxury, decides upon the fate, the feelings, the existence of a starving multitude, it is not a compact of civil association, but a wicked and lawless anarchy, where Violence and Conspiracy usurp the chair of Government, and the caprice of domineering pride is substituted for settled principle.

Under such systems, it is impossible that the general intellect should properly expand, the heart be meliorated, or the condition of the mass improved. Better for man were the rudest barbarism of nature, than such a state of political communion!—better were savage nakedness, and the dowerless[131] freedom of his woods and caves, than the wretched mockery of such a state of civilization and refinement. To such a state of society, however, though but too prevalent, no body of men, no individual, ever voluntarily submitted: and if they had, such submission, instead of being binding upon their posterity, would have been an act of insanity, equally inconsistent with their duties and their rights; and therefore not obligatory upon themselves.

To conclude—It appears to me, fellow-citizens, that the rational object of political society is the promotion of the welfare and happiness of the whole; that the welfare and happiness of the whole depend upon the secure enjoyment of their natural rights; and that, consequently, society ought to protect and preserve those rights entire. It ought to do something more. It ought not merely to *protect*, but to improve the physical, the moral, and intellectual enjoyments, not of a few only, but of the whole population of the state. It ought to expand the faculties, encrease the sympathies, harmonize the passions, and promote the general welfare of mankind. This were national prosperity indeed!—national grandeur, and national glory. All that has hitherto assumed those names, is mockery and cruel insult.

When these principles are invaded, it follows of course, that the injured have a right to demonstrate and seek redress: when they are obstinately and systematically violated, "obedience becomes a question of prudence, not of morality"; and the people (all gentler means having been found ineffectual) have a right—a firm, inalienable right, to renounce the broken compact, and dissolve the system.

END OF THE SECOND LETTER

Letter III.
Origin and Distribution of Property.

I. *Use and Abuse of History in Political Discussion.* II. *Progress of Society—* 1. *Man in the Savage State—*2. *in the* Pastoral—*Property in the Pastoral State—*3. *The Agricultural State—Influence on the Condition and Institutions of Society.* III. *Basis of Landed Property—Original Distribution.* IV. *Accumulation of Land—*1. *from Natural Causes—*2. *from Artificial—Duty of Governments to discountenance Accumulation—Digression on Laws of Primogeniture.* V. *Distinction of Proprietor and Labourer—Abuses of that Distinction—Tyranny of Property—Rights of Labourers—*1. *from Nature—*2. *from implied Compact—*3. *from the Principles of Civil Association. Condition of the Mass—compared with the Savage—with the Negro Slave. Amelioration—in America—in France.*

I. Having contrasted, in the preceding Letter, the principles of Mr. B. and the principles of jacobinism; or, in other words, the principles of the Gothic Custumary and those of Nature, let us trace them through their respective systems, and illustrate their respective operations upon the condition, the morals, and the happiness of man.

"The property of the nation is the nation",[a] says the feudalist; and the

---

[a]Letters, p. 118. Thoughts, 57. "Had Cade[132] and his followers", says Mr. B. pursuing the idea, in the next page, "got possession of London, they would not have been the Lord Mayor, Aldermen, and

principle results from his premises. *The population of the nation is the nation!*
replies the exulting jacobin; and assenting Nature ratifies the proposition.
But in order that we may properly understand the maxim of Mr. B. and all
the important consequences that would follow, it is necessary to enquire
What property, in reality, is? and how that which is called property originated and exists? for property, as it is generally understood, is certainly
neither coeval with man, nor an immediate or inevitable consequence of
political Society: though, under proper regulations, it is an advantage to
which the compacts of society alone could have given birth. In this research, unlike the essential subject of the former letter, history affords
much light. Man without society, or society without government, has
never yet been known; but man, without what is vulgarly termed property
(and Mr. B. uses the term in its most vulgar signification) is still to be
found in several parts of the globe: and the discoveries of navigators, from
Columbus[135] to Captain Cooke;[136] the observations of recent travellers
among the Hottentots and Caffrees;[137] and the labours of the most eminent
historians, from the pregnant brevity of a Tacitus, to the smooth eloquence
of a Robinson,[138] and the elaborate splendour of a Gibbon,[139] have collected, preserved, and arranged abundant materials for a political history of
the progress of society, the origin and gradations of property, and the institutions by which it has been, at once, sanctified and violated, invaded and
secured.

When such assistance is offered, the politician does well to accept the
boon: for History, though never to be admitted as the *mistresss*, is an important *handmaid* of political science. In other words, history is to be consulted, not for *precedents* that must be followed, but for *examples* that
should be weighed: not for dogmas to restrain, but for circumstances to
illustrate, our speculations: and, as far as they extend, for land-marks to
direct our course. In short, it is a mere repertory of facts, of all descriptions—the good, the bad, and the equivocal; and (to borrow an excellent
distinction from Bacon) we must not forget, that (*like other sciences*) it has

---

Common Council." No: certainly: but if the inhabitants of London had followed Jack Cade, or any other
Jack, and espoused his cause, then would that Jack and his followers have been *something more* than Lord
Mayor, &c. They would have been London itself; and (barring the allegiance which London, as a part,
owed to England, as a whole), would have had a right to make, or unmake, Mayor, Aldermen, Common
Councilmen, Mace-bearers, and all. I speak not with any reverence for Cade. The Cades, Orleanses,[133]
and the Catalines,[134] may all have their advocates; and, for ought I know, some of them may have been
more blackened than they deserve: but I am not one of those who make no distinction between tumult
and reform. With me, every conspirator is not a patriot; although, in the present day, every patriot is
called a conspirator. I merely reply to the sophism of Mr. B. and vindicate my own definition.

its DESIDERATA, *as well as its* DISCOVERIES;[140] and that, of course, Speculation and Experiment have yet enough to do. He who regards this parent of all useful knowledge in any other light, makes her the gaoler, not the monitress, of man; cradles the human mind in eternal tutillage, and rocks it into lethargy, with the antiquated lullaby of "What has been, must be; now, and for ever more!"

II. Having premised this much, on the uses of history in political discussion, I shall proceed with a brief and general review of the progress of society, with reference to the origin and distribution of property, and its influence on the general liberty and happiness of the human race.

1. The simplest condition of man we are acquainted with, and that, in all probability, out of which every other state has arisen, by a series of progressive *innovations*, is *the Savage State*. In this first stage of Society, an almost absolute equality prevails. The earth uncultivated, or nearly so, is of course regarded as the common mother, rather than the private property, of the tribe that wanders over its surface; and the wild animals it feeds, and the spontaneous produce it affords, are the unquestioned right of the individual whose fortune, or whose assiduity, secures the first possession. Distinctions of power, under such circumstances, could only rise from inequalities of strength or intellect; and these must, of necessity, be small. Man, left to the wild growth of nature, uncramped, and unassisted, by the diversified accidents of *polished* society, attains, like other animals, a sort of common standard; or, if particularly feeble in his original constitution, perishes in the bleak wild of barbarism. And though incalculable circumstances may sometimes confer an extraordinary force of muscle, or a superior degree of *cunning* (for, in such a state, intellect can mount no higher), authority is too imperfectly organised for the abuse of such advantages to extend beyond a few particular instances of violence and injustice. It is by property alone that whole nations can be oppressed: by the science of cabinets only that generations can be enslaved.

These rude tribes, have their assemblies, their orators, their legislators, to whom they look with reverence in cases of public exigency; and whose power encreases in proportion as common dangers call for united exertions. The authority of the chief may, in some instances, become almost absolute, in times of war: but it leads to no permanent distinctions of wealth or influence; and the ideas of property are scarcely extended beyond the right of the individual to the trophies he may gain in the field, and the *temporary affluence* resulting from the fortune of the chace.

2. Passing from the savage to *the Pastoral State*, we make a stride of some

importance in the progress of government, of civilization, and property. Man having tamed a useful animal, led it to pasture, protected it from beasts of prey, and contributed to the multiplication of its species and the rearing of its feeble young, acquires the same property in his flock, and upon the same principle, that the savage acquired in the game he had ensnared or killed. Still, however, the property extends only to the animal. The earth, and its vegetation, continue the common inheritance of all: and for this, for reasons which, growing out of the nature of things, operate upon the rude minds that could not explain them. He who tames and protects a stock or herd, of whatever description, claims, by appropriation, only the profit of his own industry; and, generally speaking, does but grasp the exclusive benefit of that which, but for his assiduity, would not have, *beneficially*, existed. But in the earth, which he has not laboured—in the vegetation he has not cultivated, he can have no exclusive property. The former is a common element, upon which every individual has a common right to employ his faculties;—the latter, the spontaneous gift of Nature to all her children, in which all have a common inheritance.

Even in flocks and herds, the property of the individual, *in such a state*, may extend to usurpation: for if it were possible for one man to *reclaim* (as it is called) and monopolize the whole race of useful animals running wild in a particular district, he could have no moral right to do so: because he would, thereby, preclude all others from their common right of exerting their faculties, for their own advantage, upon an important part of the common gifts of nature.—It cannot be too often repeated, that *Property is the fruit of useful industry; but the means of being usefully industrious are the common right of all.*

Property, in this state, it is obvious, though grounded in the same principle (possession, resulting from the exertion of individual faculty upon the common gifts of nature) differs, in some essential characters, from property in the state before described. Among savage tribes, there is, indeed, scarcely any thing which, in the general sense, can be regarded as property at all: in a nation of shepherds, it assumes a sort of permanency, and a capacity for accumulation. It becomes, accordingly, a temptation to violence, on the one hand; and an object of jealous protection, on the other. Hence the necessity of more intimate association, and firmer compact. The stock must be guarded by more jealous laws, than were necessary in a state where all property consisted in a bow and a hatchet, and a few familiar articles, which the warrior-huntsman slung across his shoulder, or tucked in his girdle, when he followed the war-hoop, or the chace: and thus, though *Liberty and Property* are so frequently joined together, in popular exclamations, the very basis of the latter, by a sad necessity, furnishes the foundation of an altar upon which the former is too frequently sacrificed.

In the state of society, however, of which I am at present speaking, the degree of personal independence is very great. It is not till man has taken another step, in the progress of appropriation, that liberty can be considerably invaded. While the elements of nature are not monopolized, the distinctions of property and power must be, comparatively, small: and, if war could be avoided, the pastoral state would be a life of almost perfect freedom. But in all conditions of society, war is a mean of two-fold usurpation; *and the country that takes up arms against another, is destined to subdue itself.* It is true, the full weight of this penalty is reserved for *civilized* nations. In the savage state it is but transiently felt; for the power of the chieftain expires with campaign: and all the habits of mere pastoral life are inimical to the usurpations of authority.

But whatever may be the advantages of these rude states of society, in point of liberty and independence, they are little calculated for permanent establishment. While the earth remains uncultivated, the subsistence of man, even in the most genial climates, is scanty and precarious; the social passions are languid and joyless; the faculties are sluggish; the intellect slumbers, as it were; and all the nobler and finer feelings of our nature, lie benumbed in the oblivious bog of indolence: the endearing intercourses of friendship are scarcely known; the reciprocations of relationship are but a sad chain of domestic tyranny and servitude; and even the dearest and sweetest of those connections which give an interest, and a zest, to civilized life, exhibits, in the hut of the savage or the barbarian, a disgusting picture, that paints, beyond the force of words, the melancholy conviction, that *liberty, without moral and intellectual improvement, is only a privilege of the strong to tyrannise over the feeble.* In the mean time, a scanty sprinkling of population, scattered over an immense surface, perhaps of the most luxuriant soil, cannot so properly be said to inhabit, as to prove its miserable want of inhabitants. Yet so imperfectly does even such a soil administer to their simple wants, that an enlargement of territory is fought for with as much sanguinary ferocity, for the poor privilege of hunting and fishing, as, by more civilized barbarians, for fame, and glory, and power, and encreased revenue.—In short, the savage and pastoral states, are states of almost incessant war; and, if it were not that our funding system has, for the last hundred years, rendered *civilized* Europe a still more hideous Golgotha than the woods and pastures of the barbarians ever knew, this circumstance, alone, might be thrown into the balance against the rude boasts of liberty and independence. As for what may be called the accommodations of life, I might quote the descriptions of savage wretchedness from Robertson's America;[141] Gibbon's picture of the pastoral habits of the Scythians, in his "Decline and Fall" (chap. 26);[142] White's account of the New Hollanders, in his "Voyage to New South Wales";[143] and the miserable shifts of wild Hottentots, from the narratives of recent travellers into the interior of Africa. But I shall content myself with a single extract from Tacitus, in which he describes the way of living in one of the rudest of the German nations. "Nothing", says he, "can equal the ferocity of the Fennians, nor is there any thing so disgusting as their filth and poverty. Without arms, without horses, and without a fixed place of abode, they lead a vagrant life; their food the common herbage; the skins of beasts their only cloathing; and the bare earth their resting-place. For their chief support they depend on their arrows, to which, for want of iron, they prefix a pointed bone. The women follow the chace in company with the man, and claim their share of the prey. To protect their infants from the fury of wild beasts, and the inclemency of the weather, they make a kind of cradle amidst the branches of trees interwoven together; and they know no other expedient. The youth of the country have the same habitation; and amidst the trees, old age is rocked to rest."[144]

3. Such, my fellow-citizens, are the miserable and degrading circumstances attendant upon these rude conditions of society. From these circumstances, nothing can redeem mankind but the steady cultivation of the earth. The earth is cultivated; and the face of society is changed, and nature itself subdued and altered. But is the condition of the mass improved? Are their real enjoyments encreased?—their actual sufferings diminished? Are there no circumstances attendant upon the partial prosperity which cultivation has ultimately produced, more bitter in their consequences, to the laborious multitude, than all the miseries of penurious equality? Certainly, at least, it is, that agriculture, from the very first, if it brought its blessings upon the world, brought, with them, its mischiefs, also.

In savage nations, where the chace still continues to be the proud employment of man, and a rude and miserable species of cultivation is regarded only as an auxiliary, it has reduced the woman to a condition of absolute slavery. Among the pastoral tribes of Germany, to which Mr. B. would have us look for patterns of social and political wisdom; where the land was not even regularly appropriated; where stock and herds constituted the chief wealth, and agriculture was only a secondary consideration, the labour of cultivation had given birth to the iniquitous distinction of master and slave. The condition of the slave was not, however, as deplorable as in states of higher cultivation. "To punish him with stripes", says Tacitus, "to load him with chains, or to condemn him to hard labour, was unusual. Each had his separate habitation, and his own establishment to manage. The master considered him as an agrarian dependant, who was obliged to furnish a certain quantity of grain, of cattle, or of wearing apparel. The slave obeyed; and the state of servitude extended no farther."[145] But if we turn our eyes to the wretched Helotes of Sparta, and the whip-galled Negroes of our own West India Islands, what myriads of lacerated victims rise up in judgment against the system of cultivation, and deplore the tyrannous inventions that snatched them from their caves, their hovels, and their woods.

Not to dwell upon partial evils, let us examine the general operation of the agricultural system: admitting, in the outset, that its advantages are positive and inherent, and the evils it has produced, generally speaking, adventitious only; and, therefore, capable of correction.

III. An immediate, or, at least, a necessary consequence of the agricultural state, is the appropriation of land: an appropriation which, duly understood, and under proper restrictions, rests upon the joint foundations of general expediency, and of individual right. The basis of property has already been defined, as *the right of the individual to the advantages resulting from his own industry and faculties, employed upon the common elements of nature.* By the same right, therefore, that the savage appropriates the game transfixed with his dart, and the shepherd challenges the stock he has reclaimed and pastured, the cultivator, also, claims, as his own, the produce of the land he has cultivated: for the earth is a common element, in which he had a common inheritance; and the fruit it produces, under his cultivation, is the creation of his industry. Still, however, the earth itself was the common element: and the property, in this state, consisted, not in the land, but in the produce. For the foundation of what is called Landed Property, we must appeal, not to physical or abstract right, but to moral and political expediency.

In some particular cases, indeed, if we may rely upon the authorities that record the fact, agriculture has been the joint concern of the whole state; and the common territory has been cultivated by common labour. In all instances, the perfect appropriation of the land must have been gradually effected: for it is difficult for man, in any state, to dispossess himself of the idea of a right of common inheritance in the earth which he inhabits. The Germans, in the days of Tacitus, had made, in their rude way, considerable progress in the arts of government. Society was separated into casts and classes; and four distinct orders accurately defined the degrees of honour and of servitude among those fierce barbarians: yet we learn, that "in cultivating the soil, they did not settle on one particular spot. The lands were taken possession of, in turns, by the whole community, according to the number of cultivators; and were divided among them, according to their respective ranks. The extent of their plains rendered this division easy. The arable lands were changed every year; and the pastures remained uncultivated: for they did not proportion their industry to the extent and fertility of the soil. They neither planted orchards, inclosed meadows, nor watered gardens. The cultivation of corn was all that *was enjoined*."[a]

---

[a]Tacit. Man. of Germ. sect. xxvi.[146] Correspondent with this is Caesar's account of "the Suabians, the most potent and *warlike* Nation among the Germans." Comment. War in Gaul, b. iv. "They have no enclosures", says he: "no man has an acre of land he can properly term his own; nor are they suffered to continue above one year in the same part of the country. Their chief diet is milk and flesh-meat; and their diversion hunting." *Bladen's Caesar*, p. 60.[147] See also b. vi. p. 118. "They mind not agriculture", &c.—nor has "any man fields of his own distinguished from the common by boundaries", &c. This is applied to the whole of the German nations; as is, also, the remainder of the passage, quoted in the text. There is a most beautiful allusion in the 24th Ode of the 3rd book of Horace, to a similar practice among the *Geteans*: —

> "Better the savage *Scythian* lives,
> Who in a wain his household drives;
> Better the *Gette*, whose fruitful grounds
> No fence divides, unmark'd by jealous bounds.
> One year he tills the mellow soil,
> And rests the next from all his toil.
> No step-dames treacherously prepare
> The baneful cup for hapless orphans there." DUNCOMB[148]

What follows is in an exquisite strain of satire and morality; but not immediately connected with my subject. I refer the Reader, therefore, to the Ode itself.

I shall just add, that there is some difficulty in the passage of Tacitus above quoted: a difficulty which appears still greater in Murphy's translation. The only distinction which, in such state of society, could occasion any inequality in the distribution of lands, must have been that of chieftains or heroic leaders; who, as their followers were feasted at their tables, would require, of course, a larger district for their support: that is to say, their families were larger, and therefore they required more land, to supply them with bread, and to feed the stocks and herds that constituted their wealth. How different these distinctions were from what is called "rank and dignity" in these days, appears from the following passage: "No distinction is made between the future chieftain and the infant son of a common slave. On the same ground, and mixed with the same cattle, they pass their days, till the age of manhood draws the line of separation, and early valour shews the person of ingenuous birth." (*Murph. Tacit.* vol. vi. p. 23.)[149] That is to say, the bravest man is deemed the noblest born! What would some of our modern barons (the Chieftains of the Drawing-room and Levee) say to such a test of distinction?—But in whatever this dignity consisted, it appears, from Caesar, that the privilege annexed consisted rather in the power of dispensation, than in any right of superior appropriation, a material object being the preservation of "an equality of riches." Between the times of Caesar and Tacitus, however, some changes might have taken place in this respect.

But the tribes of Germany were of a warlike character (probably from their neighbourhood to the military government of Rome—or it may be, from that ferocious pride and thirst of military glory, which actuate all barbarians); and their other habits were decided by this circumstance. "To cultivate the earth, and wait the regular produce of the seasons, was not the maxim of a German. You would more easily persuade him to attack the enemy, and provoke honourable wounds in the field of battle. In a word, it was, in the opinion of a German, a sluggish principle to earn, by the sweat of your brow, what you might gain by the price of your blood." That this contempt of agriculture was really produced and cherished by this war-like character, is put beyond a doubt by Caesar, in the sixth book of his Commentary on the Gallic War; though he assigns, at the same time, some better reasons for the mode of distribution. Contrasting the customs of the Germans with those of the Gauls, he observes, that "their magistrates and princes yearly distribute to every canton such a portion of land as they think sufficient, in some part of the country; where they send them to continue only for one year, and oblige them to remove the next: which custom they observe, *lest the love of the place they had long inhabited, having changed the people's genius from the study of war, to that of tillage*, they should endeavour to *extend their confines, and the weaker become oppressed by the more powerful*; lest they should become curious in their buildings, to defend them from the summer's heat and winter's cold; but, chiefly, to prevent covetousness, *the root of all factions and discord*, and preserve *that equality of riches in the common-wealth, which produces peace and content.*"[150] But wherever the agricultural system preponderated, and the product of cultivation became a principal object, it is scarcely possible that experience should not soon suggest the *general expediency* of permanent possession in the individual who was to cultivate: for man is a selfish animal; and earth, that it may be abundant in production, requires, not only the plough and the seed, that prepare the particular harvest, but the manuring toil that improves it from generation to generation.

But though *production*, of necessity, became a principal object, *distribution*, in the early stages of agricultural society, would not be neglected. The ideas of primitive equality were not obliterated; and the temptations to monopoly were few: and the probability is, that every wandering tribe first taking possession of a district, with a view to cultivation, would, like the original founders of the Roman state, canton out the territory in equal portions: and, thus, would the equality of distribution, reconcile general expediency with the particular interests of the individual, and the principle of common right.

Every thing, indeed, in the rude stages of society, had a tendency to support this equal distribution. Population was thin; and the abundant territory offered to every cultivator more than he could occupy: and even when population encreases (as in the agricultural state it naturally will) the case is not materially altered. The degree of knowledge (or rather of ignorance) is nearly uniform. The feebleness of political institution, and the laxity of civil compact, encourage habitual independence. Legislation has not yet become the property of the few: and above all, the inequalities of physical force are not, in these rude beginnings of society, rendered more disproportionate by the exclusive appropriation of arms, the establishment of magazines, for instruments of destruction, to enable the few to plunder and overawe the many; and the employment of selected bands of ruffians, hired first, like mercenaries, and afterwards compelled, like slaves, to perpetrate the robberies, and protect the usurpations of despotic rulers.

Under such circumstances, it is true, the acquisitions of the father would, in the natural course of things, descend to the children: but they would descend under such restrictions as would render permanent property least inconsistent with the common claims of mankind. While any portion of waste land remained, they would feel and act upon the just and natural principle, that territorial property consisted, accurately speaking, in the cultivation—not in the earth; and that, of course, *land uncultivated is still inheritance in common*, and cannot, till labour makes it so, be the peculiar property of any individual. If, therefore, the cultivator had more children than one, the eldest, when he arrived at man's estate, would take possession of a fresh farm; in which example he would be followed by other of his brethren, till it came to the youngest; who, in all probability, the father growing old and feeble, would remain with him, as an assistant, till his death; and would succeed, of course, to the paternal farm. Some relicks of this state of society, as Judge Blackstone observes, still remain in this country, in the sort of tenure, once prevalent among the Northern nations, and among us, called *Borough-English*; by which the landed property, or "burgage tenement", descends to the *youngest son*.[a]

When the whole district inhabited by any community, had become appropriated by cultivation, except what was still thought necessary to preserve in common, for the purposes of pasturage (a thing, of course, to be decided, by actual or implied compact, by the whole community); a differ-

---

[a]*Commentaries*, book ii c. 6. p. 83.[151] He calls it, indeed, a relick of the *pastoral state*. But it is demonstrable, alike, from history, and the nature of things, that, in the mere pastoral state, no such thing as landed property is acknowledged. Inasmuch as it relates to mere *tenement*, the observation may, however, apply; and he shews it to be still the practice among the pastoral nations of Tartary.

ent mode of descent arose, by necessity, out of the new circumstances; and domestic migration being no longer practicable, the whole family remained *in a sort of dependence* upon the father, and divided the estate at his demise. We have the authority of history for affirming, that this was once, almost uniformly, the case in this country; and the simple and equitable law, under the name of descent in *Gavel kind*, still continues in force, in some considerable districts, in the happy and flourishing county of Kent. Such also is the case in many of the smaller cantons of Switzerland; where the law, upon the death of a proprietor, divides the estate equally among all his children, male and female. In cases, indeed, where the conduct of children has been remarkably vicious, the law permits the citizen to will one-half his property to any one child, who may have distinguished himself by an opposite disposition; but it compels him to assign the reason in his will, and does not allow him to extend his discretionary power farther than this distinction. The remaining half must be absolutely divided, in equal portions, among the other children: and as conscience is generally perverted, or informed, by existing institution, as the state of society is exceedingly simple, and as ambition, splendour, and luxury (those first provocatives to almost every crime) are precluded by the salutary regulations of these happy states, even this exertion of parental discrimination, (which is regarded, and dreaded, as a brand of indelible infamy) is rarely exerted; and never but in those cases where the conduct of the repudiated children has been marked with peculiar profligacy.

IV. From the necessities arising out of these new circumstances, it is evident, that a great and important change must be progressively induced in the condition of the human race.—From this time, we must bid a sad farewell to that equality of landed possession, which, if philosophy did not forbid me to hope, and humanity prohibit me from propagating, philanthropy would impel me to wish. I say, my fellow-citizens! and I call upon you to engrave the maxim on your hearts! that Philosophy and Humanity forbid the propagation of this levelling doctrine. Philosophy forbids it, because the ideas, the habits, the necessities of the present state of social progress—nay, the very circumstances naturally growing out of the system of cultivation, when carried to any high and advantageous extent, render such equality totally impracticable:—Humanity forbids it, because the vain attempt to execute so wild a scheme, must plunge the world into yet unheard-of horrors; must send forth the pretended reformer, armed with the dagger in one hand, and the iron crow in the other, to pillage, murder and destroy; and, after all, to no better end, than to transfer all property from the proud and the polished, the debauched, effeminate and luxurious, to the brutal, the ignorant, and the ferocious; and to constitute, from the vulgar band of plunderers and assassins, a *new* "Gothic Custumary"—a new order of proprietors and nobility. But though we ought not—must not sweep down all property in a torrent of blood, let us not "shrink from the *critical but salutary* duty" of examining the foundations on which it stands, and discriminating clearly between property and plunder—between right and usurpation. Nor let the high and affluent—for there are *some* among them whose hearts are warm and benevolent, and whose *alarms* are honest—and to such I address myself—Let not them shrink from the well-meant enquiry, nor impoliticly deem the friend of man their foe. If they are just, they have nothing to dread from investigation; and property, like morals, will stand more firm upon the solid foundations of reason and expediency, than upon the *arbitrary*[152] and mysterious bases of authority and superstition.

1. However equal the distribution of land might be at the beginning of that aera of cultivation, when there was no longer any waste to be divided—and till then (in the *natural* progress) there could be no other differences than such as might arise from different degrees of individual industry—it is evident that as soon as division became necessary among the children of the respective cultivators, a considerable inequality must arise. He who had a large family, must necessarily divide his farm into small portions, or the family must live upon it in common. He who had only a single child, would leave an undivided inheritance: and the family of several brothers, who should chance to have but one heir among them, must necessarily bequeath to that one a fatal accumulation: unless, indeed, by some wise and human regulation, the lands of the proprietor dying without children should revert to the state, to be divided among those citizens whose farms had been split into inconvenient fractions.

2. By some such salutary provision, the balance of landed property might have been, in some degree, preserved. But, unfortunately for mankind, governments have, too generally, been employed in aggravating the evils it was their duty to counteract. Instead of protecting the weak against the strong (as they pretend to do) and thus levelling, by the influence of moral principle, the physical inequalities of strength, they aggravate those asperities by the *privileges* of wealth, and the appropriation of arms. Instead of soothing and harmonising the jealous and hostile passions of tribes and families, and uniting the whole in one fraternal bond, they have multiplied the divisions and enmities of the human race, by splitting them into casts

and factions—into "classes, orders, and distinctions", different in their views, and hostile in their particular interests. Instead of correcting the tendencies to unequal distribution, naturally arising in the more advanced stages of civilization, every opportunity has been embraced to assist the growing mischief; and laws upon laws have invaded the equal rights of man, and annulled the common claims of relative and private justice. Hence all the provisions which, not content with *securing* property, load it with unjustifiable *privileges*—Hence corporations, patents, and exclusive charters—Hence (for the iniquitous reasons and pretences of which see the following letter) the hideous—the barbarous—the unnatural *Law of Primogeniture*:—a law which, if contemplated with any reference to the principles and rights of nature, is a most iniquitous usurpation, and what a religious man ought to regard as an act of blasphemy;—and if examined upon any principle of relative and social justice, or any rational basis upon which the claims of descendable property can be supported, is an act of aggravated robbery, perpetrated by the elder brother, upon all the branches of his defenceless family.

From that state of society, then, and those circumstances of distribution, the contemplation of which led me into this digression, necessarily arose the distinction intended to be marked by the vulgar application of the word Property—that is to say, the distinction between the large proprietor and the small. And this, I conceive, to be the distinction Mr. B. intends to mark by the extravagant exclamation—"The property of the country is the country"! Indeed, it is impossible he should mean any thing else—for as all mankind (as will be presently shewn) have property—essential property, in the genuine sense of the word, the exclamation would, upon any other interpretation, be totally without meaning. And thus is the political existence or non-existence of man, to be decided by the cube rule that measures his paternal acres, or the arithmetic that strikes a balance in his ledger.

V. But these circumstances were also fraught, in their progress, with still more important consequences. From the inequalities inevitably produced, and the means soon discovered of encreasing them; and from the indolence, prodigality, and disasters of some, and the peculiar fortune of others, arose, in process of time, the *distinction of* PROPRIETOR *and* LABOURER. The cultivator, whose farm was too small for the support of himself and family, or who had been obliged to supply some temporary want by bartering away his penurious inheritance, was necessitated, for subsistence, to become the hireling labourer of him whose possessions had encreased beyond the limits of individual culture.

In this distinction (however natural, and therefore, justifiable in itself), are laid the first foundation of what may be called the *Tyranny of Property*: that is to say—*the power and disposition of the wealthy few, to oppress and plunder the indigent and unprotected many.*

At first, indeed, this unhappy distinction would not be productive of any serious oppression. The proprietors must be too many, and the labourers too few, to give the former any very extensive power of taking advantage of the dependent state of the latter. Their contract would, therefore, be comparatively fair, and grounded in mutual advantage: the workman deriving a full subsistence from his labour; and the employer (himself a labourer also) deriving but little more. Of such a state of reciprocation (growing out of the very nature of things) it would be scarcely reasonable to complain: but when we look upon the consequences which have arisen out of the distinction, and trace the progress of its abuses to their present enormous height, I cannot but repeat the enquiry—*Is the condition of the multitude improved?*

The whole condition of the universe has been materially altered by cultivation. That cultivation has been conducted by the labour and diligence of the mass of mankind. Is it right, then, that a few should monopolize all the advantages of this new state of man, and leave to the toiling multitude only a dark vicissitude of woes—only a sad transition from penurious indolence to laborious wretchedness? It is not right. There is no argument to be devised by all the pensioners in the universe, that can justify such oppression; and the territorial monopolist, who thus grinds and tramples upon the laborious cultivator, without whose toil his vaunted estate would be a barren wilderness, alters the very nature of his tenure, and turns his property into usurpation and plunder.

Let the proprietor reflect upon the nature of his possession—let him reflect upon the genuine basis of property. What is it, after all, but human labour? And who is the proprietor of that labour?—Who, but the individual who labours? As for landed property, I repeat it—it has not its foundations in natural or physical right; but in moral and political expediency. But moral and political expediency refer not to the individual, but to the whole society. That which is expedient for the whole, is politically expedient. The expediency of individual interest, is the expediency of the swindler, and the housebreaker. If monopoly is not encouraged—if the possession of the land is left to flow and descend in its own natural channels, the laws of the country rather restraining than encouraging accumulation; and above all, if labour has its adequate reward, I maintain that the permanent possession of land is morally and politically expedient; because it assists production, without preventing distribution; and, thereby, benefits the whole human race. But if all this social order is inverted—if accumulation is not only encouraged, but enforced, and if the labourer, the *real cultivator*, is insulted with such wages as are totally insufficient for the decent and comfortable subsistence of himself and family, then (I repeat it—and I will abide by the text in all the courts of law to which I can possibly be summoned) that which is miscalled landed property, is the worst of usurpation and plunder.

We have heard much of the Rights of Property, and the Rights of Nations. (Of the Rights of Man, also, we have heard some things, well worthy of serious consideration.) Much also we have heard of the Rights of the Peerage, the Rights of Parliaments, and the Rights of the Crown; let us, for once, enquire a little into the RIGHTS OF LABOURERS: for rights, as labourers, they most undoubtedly have, grounded on the triple basis of *nature*, of *implied compact*, and *the principles of civil association*.

1. As for his *natural rights*—it will be admitted, I suppose, in terms, however it may be denied in practice, that the labourer is a man. As man he is joint heir to the common bounties of nature; and, in all physical and moral justice, is the proprietor, also, of whatever his labour and faculties add to the common stock. Were he still the rude inhabitant of such a state, where the blessings, and the drudgery of cultivation were unknown—the indolent wanderer of the woods and mountains, he would have, as I have shewn, some rights, some inheritance, some means of solace and support; and the imperious land-holder, the great funded proprietor, the prodigal statesman, yea, the sceptered sovereign of the most refined and polished state, who now, from the profits of his toil, banquets in luxury, and lolls on down, would have wandered, in savage nakedness, like himself; would have slept on the same cold earth, and shared in all his penury, and all his hardships.

Whatever were the worth of these rude gifts and accommodations, the very frame and constitution of society has robbed him of them. He comes from the hand of Nature into a state of cultivation; and finds the world of nature destroyed by the world of art. His inheritance is alienated, and his common right appropriated, even before his birth. He appeals to Nature—and how does this common parent of us all reply? She answers (through that organ of reason that dwells in every breast) *Society is responsible, in the first place, for an equivalent for that which society has taken away. For the rest, you have still a right to employ your faculties for your own advantage; and, in the reciprocations of society, to receive as much from the toil and faculties of others, as your own toil and faculties threw into the common stock. You have a right to the gratification of the common appetites of Man; and to the enjoyment of your* *rational faculties. The intercourse of the sexes, and the endearment of relative* *connection, are your right inalienable. They are the bases of existence; and noth-* *ing in existence—no, not even your own direct assent, can, justly, take them* *away.*

2. Does the employer reject this decision of nature? Does he plead some recent compact between himself and the labourer? *I agreed with you for so* *much; and I pay you what I agreed!* I answer, that an unjust agreement, extorted by the power of an oppressor, is, morally, and politically, void. Yet such, in a variety of instances, are the compacts between the labourer and the employer. The territorial monopolist dictates the terms upon which he will condescend to employ the disfranchised labourer, from morn to night, in the cultivation of his fields, and the repair of his hedges and ditches. Does the latter demur about the price—*Fellow! there are many* *labourers and few employers. If you do not choose to drudge through the whole* *day for half a meal, go home to your family, and starve there altogether. If* YOU *will not work for half a loaf, there are others that will: and if you* CONSPIRE *together to get a whole one, we will send you to the house of correction*!!! Is this a compact, or a tyrannous usurpation?

But there is a compact—a sacred compact, implied in the very distinction of labourer and employer: And the terms of this compact are to be decided, not by the power of the one, and the wretchedness of the other, but by the reason of the thing, and the rules of moral justice. This reason, and these rules, call upon us to appreciate, with impartiality, the comparative value of capital and of labour; since the former, without the latter, could *never* be productive; and the latter, without the former, in the present state of society, cannot have the means of production. Such an estimate, fairly made, would place the labourer in a very different condition from that to which he has generally been condemned. Such an estimate would teach us, that the labourer has a right to a share of the produce, not merely equal to his support, but, proportionate to the profits of the employer.

3. This argument of implied compact is, also, supported by the very principles upon which all civil association rests. Mankind, when they abandon their woods and savage independence, abandon them for a common, not for a particular, advantage. They do not consent, that thenceforward the many shall be more wretched; that the few may be better accommodated. No: the object is, to promote the accommodation of the whole. When they give up their common interest in the spontaneous produce of

the earth, and yield it to appropriated culture; they mean to increase the comforts and abundance of all, not the luxury and wantonness of a faction. Go on to what extent you will, the argument still holds. The state of cultivation exists only by common labour. Abundance, decencies, accommodations, embellishments of life, have grown out of it—education, knowledge, intellectual refinement, and all the sweets of polished society. Has not the labourer, then, a right (as his share of the benefit) to maintain himself, *and a family*, in decency and plenty; and to give his children such an education, as, according to the state of society, may be requisite, to enable them, if they should have the virtue and the talent, to improve their condition, and mount to their intellectual level—though it should be from the lowest to the very highest station of society? Not accident of birth—but worthlessness, indolence, depravity, should doom the individual to an abject state. It is a vile, unnatural compound, this over-boiling cauldron of society, in which the dregs of vice and licentiousness for ever play, and froth and bubble at the top, while usefulness and honest industry are incessantly pressed down to the bottom.

To conclude—From the whole of this argument, and from all the principles laid down in this and the preceding letter, it results, that the landed proprietor is only a trustee for the community; and although he has a right to compensation for the due management of the deposit, if he monopolizes the advantages, in which all are concerned, and for which all labour, he is guilty of robberies—robbery committed by the rich and powerful upon the defenceless poor.

I have not time—I have not space, to illustrate every principle, as I could desire—else could I call a blush upon the cheek of those who boast the advantages of civilized society—else could I call to view the comparative condition of the naked savage of America, who "sees his humble lot, the lot of all", and that of the poor, wretched, o'er-toiled, half-starved, ill-clad, and worse-lodged labourer of Britain; who, in the midst of surrounding luxury, splendour, and refinement, rears his half-naked children in savage ignorance, and hears them cry for bread, when bread is not his to give them. The naked savage of America!!!—I declare in the very bitterness of sympathy, that to me, the condition of the naked savage appears, by far, more tolerable than that of a large portion, at least, of the laborious classes in this happy, flourishing, cultivated island: blessed as it is with all the salutary institutions, drawn from the old Germanic or Gothic custumary! It has been said in our House of Commons, by the advocates for the Slave Trade, that the condition of the negro, in our West India Islands, is prefer-

able to that of many of our own peasantry. It may be so. I protest it does
not appear to me impossible. The argument is therefore conclusive—That
we ought to *begin* with redressing grievances at home; and to despise the
canting hypocrisy of a ministerial tool, who can feel no sympathy with any
sufferings but those which are too distant for his redress.

What then, it will be said, would you lead us back to savage barbarism?[153]
Would you strip Nature of all the embellishments and refinements of civilization, and turn her, wild and naked, again into her woods?—No: I answer, no. I would extend civilization: I would encrease refinement. I would
improve the real dignity of Nature. I would clothe her, completely,—mag-
nificently clothe her: but I would not load her with absurd decorations, nor
disguise her genuine proportions. I would have her decent, and, if possible,
elegant, in every part. I would not have her an incongruous patchwork of
lace and rags—of gaudy pageantry and obscene filthiness. Mine should be
no "drab-coloured creation"; but I would prefer a uniform Attic simplicity,
in the stile of social distribution, to the Neapolitan frippery of scarlet and
gold, without shoes or stockings. It is Mr. B. and his college, who would
drive us back into the woods, to learn the arts of civilization and government from the half-naked barbarism of the Goths and Germans. It is Sir
W. Blackstone, and the fraternity of Lincoln's Inn, that would refer us, for
"the element and principles of laws, to the custom of the Britons and Germans in the times of Caesar and of Tacitus."—*Black. Com.* vol. i p. 36.[154]
The crime of the Jacobin is, that he looks forward to a state of society more
extensive in its refinements—more perfect, and more general in its improvements, than any which has yet been known.

The practicability of such a state, I shall argue in the sequel to this
work. In the mean time let me observe, that in some countries, some
things have already been done towards the melioration we look for. In
America (for example) the condition of the labourer is much improved.
There, from the state of wages, every hired cultivator is enabled, by tolerable diligence and sobriety, to become, in time, a master and proprietor
himself; and servitude is not, of moral necessity, the life-estate of any man.
In France, also, (though France has not done all that she ought, and has
done many things which it is infamous to have done) yet has the condition
of the labouring mass been much improved. Nothing could exceed their
wretchedness before the revolution. What has been their condition since I
will not illustrate by the poetic strains of panegyric, but by the language of
dissatisfaction itself—"Such", said one of the denunciators of the Convention, "is the excess to which forestalling and monopoly are carried, that a

poor sans-culotte (one of the laborious multitude) "can hardly get a fowl for his pot."[155]

France!—And dare I quote the example of France? I dare—I ought to quote it; as an example, and as a warning. Let us see what France has done that was right: and that, when it becomes necessary, let us imitate. Let us see what France has done that was wrong: and that let us always avoid. Let our rulers also (if they shudder, as all nature ought to shudder, at the excesses which have there been perpetrated) consider what were the causes of those excesses. Let them remember, that if the despotism of the Bourbons had never existed, the tyranny of Robespierre had never stained with crimson horror the pages of history: had the licentious cruelty and profligacy of the Court of Versailles never unhinged the morals, and destroyed the sympathy of the nation, the Septembrizers[156] of Paris had never strewed the streets with massacre.

END OF LETTER III.

Letter IV.
The Feudal System.

I. *Progress and Consequences of Accumulation—Altered Condition of Labourers—Arts and Knowledge.* II. *Supposed Advantages of Accumulation—1. Necessity for encreased production—Answered. 2. Utility of an Idle Class—Disputed.—Knowledge is Tyranny unless diffused.* III. *Monopoly of Arms—1. Use of Arms in Civil Communities—First Institutions of Rome. 2. Tyranny and Injustice of arming particular Classes—Consequent Usurpations.* IV. *Feudal Establishments—1. Origin of Nobility—2. Of Villanage—3. Of Gentry. Historical Illustrations.* V. *1. Saxon Establishments—2. Norman Conquest. Tyranny of Force.*

Having traced, in the preceding letter, the origin of unequal distribution, and the consequent distinction of proprietor and labourer, I proceed in the present, to mark the progress of those distinctions; and to probe, with unshrinking hand, the evils to which they have given birth. In a future stage of the enquiry, I shall point out the appropriate remedies.

I. The distinction between proprietor and labourer, as I have already shewn, in whatever respected the actual condition and accommodations of life, must, in the first instance, have been very small. The dependence would be mutual; the terms of the compact, of course, reciprocal and fair. The wants of the proprietor, like those of the labourer, would be few and simple. There would be none of that distance between them, which destroys all sympathy, and substitutes in its place, contempt on the one hand, and, on the other, envy. The proprietor, possessed of more land than he can cultivate, looks round for assistance. He has land; he has stock; he has implements of husbandry. These constitute the sole wealth of the little capitalist. He invites his less fortunate neighbour to assist him in his toils, and the produce is naturally divided, with some degree of attention to impartial justice.

Of this state of society, where the proprietor, or farmer, was joint and equal labourer with the persons he employed, some traces remained in this island, in the memory of many who are still alive. It exists, to this day, in all its primitive simplicity, in several of the happy Cantons of Switzerland. But as accumulation increased—that is to say, as the proprietors became fewer, and labourers multiplied, the chasm extended; the latter became more dependent; the former more haughty and unfeeling. The necessity of personal industry was, in some degree, removed. The reluctance to labour increased as the necessity diminished; and reluctancy was succeeded by contempt. Habits of indolence generated, of course, a wasteful luxury, and a proud unsocial disposition. A confused notion of distinct orders was formed; the real bands of fraternity were dissolved; the *Esprit du Corps* supplanted the genuine feelings of humanity; and as the toil of the labourer increased, his compensation and his comforts diminished.

In the mean time, however, knowledge and the useful arts would make some progress. The mere vices of the proprietor, would, in this respect, be productive of some advantage. Machines would be invented and improvements made; not, indeed, with the benevolent view of diminishing the toil of the labourer; but to furnish a cheaper substitute for manual industry, and thus encrease, at once, the dependence of the cultivator, and the wasteful enjoyments of the employer. These arts and inventions, as they threw advantages into the hands of the capitalist, would, of course, accelerate the progress of accumulation, till the labourers became so many, and their wants so urgent, that mere competition must reduce them to absolute subjection, and destroy all chances of adequate compensation.

Such was the state of society into which Athens and Rome declined, in their latter periods. Such is the state of society to which Britain is, at this time, reduced. Property is accumulated in so few hands, and the condition of the labourer has, in consequence, become so abject, that the mass of the people may, in reality, be considered as slaves; with this distinction only, that they are subject to the whole *Corporation of Employers*, instead of an individual proprietor.

II. There are, I know, among the well-meaning advocates of prevailing systems, some who speciously maintain the advantages of accumulation, on the grounds of general expediency: upholding its two-fold operation, in promoting an encreased production, and the advancement of knowledge and civilization.

1. Agricultural improvements, it is said, on account of the slow returns of profit, and the great expence with which they are attended, require large capitals. Without these, new lands could not be brought into cultivation, nor could the old be properly improved: labour could not be diminished by those machines and inventions that abound among a nation of capitalists; nor could those innumerable experiments be made, by which the productive powers of the earth are so considerably encreased.

It is somewhat extraordinary, I confess, to hear such arguments in a country which boasts (with sufficient foundation) its extensive—I might say, enormous capitals; but in which, nevertheless, a third part of the land actually remains uncultivated;[a] while the wages of the agricultural labourer will not furnish him with *more bread* and cloathing, and the product of the cultivated soil, notwithstanding its vaunted fertility, and the penury of so large a portion of the people, is inadequate to its actual consumption.[b] But in fact, in the discussion of this question, all that has been advanced in favour of the capitalist might safely be admitted, and yet the mischiefs of territorial accumulation be sufficiently demonstrated: for *Production is not, or at least ought not to be, the sole object of agricultural labour; or, indeed, of any species of industry, in civil society.* There is another object, if possible, still more important—*General and impartial distribution:* And distribution, with respect to the *common necessaries* of life, to be impartial, must be equal: for all have mouths, and all ought to be fed—the labourer, who toils, and sweats in the field, as much as the capitalist, who furnishes the land to be cultivated, and the stock to be employed in cultivation. It is privilege enough for wealth to monopolize the *luxuries* of the earth, and decide, with sickly caprice, between pheasant and ortolan[160]—Burgundy and Champagne: In the present state of society, bread and milk, and meat and beer, and those in full abundance, and warm clothing, and a well-

---

[a]See Report of the Agricultural Society, on waste lands.[157]

[b]Davies's Ca. Lab. in Husb.[158] This humane book is priced 10s. 6d. Persons who wish to be in possession of the facts at a cheaper rate, will find all that is important to the present discussion in the series of Political Lectures, beginning with No. 29 of the Tribune, vol. ii.[159] together with a great body of facts, laboriously collected from a variety of authentic documents, and brought into one point of view, in ample illustration of this important subject.

covered bed, and a winter's fire, are to be reckoned among the absolute rights of the productive labourer and his family. The indolent and the profligate, alone, should ever taste of penury.

Where this distribution is neglected, encreased production is but an insulting mockery, and aggravates the evils it should remove. Civil Society, under such circumstances, becomes a grievous yoke; and agricultural science, not a blessing but a curse: for, better is a little that is well distributed, than much that is monopolized and wasted; and small indeed would be the labour, if equally divided, (perhaps not three hours in a day, even under the rudest circumstances of cultivation) that would be necessary to furnish the individual with better subsistence than the labourer now enjoys. The fact is, that, whatever progress may be made, from accumulation, in the invaluable science of agricultural production, the waste and luxury of the proprietory will always more than keep pace with the improvement: and the mass will, accordingly, be depressed and beggared, by that very abundance which themselves produce: a statement which, with respect to this country, in particular, may be clearly demonstrated from the facts contained in "Davies's Case of Labourers in Husbandry", and the "Representation of the Lords of the Committee on Corn", quoted in p. 49 of that work.[161] Thence it plainly appears, that the efficient produce (that is to say, the proportion of the production to the consumption) has decreased, to the value of an annual million, during the last thirty years (in which almost all the small farms in the nation have been swallowed up by the vulture-maw of accumulation.) "On an average of nineteen years", says the representation, "ending in 1765, the corn exported from this country produced a clear profit of 651,000l.; but on an average of eighteen years, ending in 1788, we paid to foreigners, for a supply of corn, no less than 291,000l.; making an annual difference to this country of 942,000l." Since that time the evil has incalculably encreased. Hence the growing misery of the poor, and all the dreadful *et cetera* which make the present state of society so truly alarming.

But how happens it, my fellow citizens, that these experiments and improvements, this breaking-up of new lands, and stocking old ones, require such extraordinary capitals? Does not this very necessity arise out of the accumulation of which I complain? Of the expences incurred in these cases, how much is to be regarded as the real price of the commodity, and how much as the consequence of taxation? Alas! you are ignorant of these things: you think not of taxes, but when the collector comes to your door:

you forget that your stomachs have been gauged and your backs have been measured by rates, by customs, and excises; and that eat, drink, or wear what you will—touch what you will, for industry, or for pleasure, fifteen shillings out of every twenty must go for tythes and taxes! And how comes all this? Comes it not from accumulation? As property encreases in the hands of the few, luxury, and ostentation increase, also. But, be the luxury and ostentation of the proprietors what they will, the government will, of necessity, be still more ostentatious and luxurious. The secretary of a secretary, must vie, in his table and his equipage, with the principal landholders of the nation; and the merry-andrew who lacquies the heels of royalty, must have his lacquies also to do homage to him. And whence must all this come? From the pockets of the people. But to take it in gross sums would be an experiment too daring. Hence it is to be split, and frittered and scattered up and down, till every commodity is taxed and re-taxed, and taxed again, in fifty different ways. The enormity of the burden is, of course, disguised; not lessened.[a] Hence the enormous expence of all improvements—all production: so that great capitals are requisite, not for the actual cultivation of the earth, but for the fines that must be paid to government for permission to cultivate.

2. But it will be objected, that for the projection of these improvements and experiments—for the invention of machines, and the discovery of use-

[a] I will give but one instance—to me an interesting instance. How many times is this little pamphlet taxed before it comes into the hands of the reader? The linen from which the paper is manufactured has been taxed, in more shapes than one. The mill, and all the ingredients of which it is constructed, have been taxed also. The paper itself has been taxed at the manufacturers, and at the warehouse. The metal of which the types are constructed is also taxed. The pamphlet itself is then taxed at the stamp office, before it can be published. The house and warehouse of the publisher is likewise taxed; and all the articles necessary to the support of all the work people, &c. from the linen weaver, nay, from the cultivator of the flax, to the last retailer in the shop, whose time and attention have been necessary to its publication, all have been taxed, and all, must be taken into the account; for out of this little book they must all be paid. Nor is the account yet closed. Eight or ten pounds worth of advertisements are yet necessary to its publication; or the pamphlet will lay on the shelves of the publisher, and be never heard of. And what is this additional charge? Almost all taxation. The newspaper has been obliged to run the gainloop of taxation, in the same manner as the pamphlet, with the additional circumstance, that out of fourpence-halfpenny, the price it sells at, threepence-halfpenny is demanded by the stamp-office for every paper printed; and out of the price paid to the editors for each advertisement, the stamp-office seizes upon the largest portion also. It is obvious, that but for these circumstances, the book might be sold at a quarter of its present price; and yet the profit of the author be considerably greater. In the Tribune, vols. ii. and iii. are some similar calculations, or rather enumerations, applied to the common necessaries of life.[162] Citizens! Citizens! we toil not for ourselves, or our families—we toil for Taxation—that is to say, for placemen, pensioners, and borough-mongers!—for war and corruption!—for encreasing burthens that rivet accumulating fetters!

ful theories, considerable knowledge is requisite; and that knowledge is the fruit of leisure; and leisure of affluence. This objection immediately leads us into the second branch of the hypothesis in favour of accumulation: namely—the advantages derived from an idle class, who *may* employ their leisure in promoting useful knowledge and liberal science; by which alone, it must be granted, the real civilization of the world can be advanced.

To this argument, however, however specious, there are several serious objections. 1. "Science is not science till revealed", is a maxim not more trite than true: and certain it is, that knowledge cannot operate, to any beneficial purpose, or produce any general civilization of society, till it becomes pretty generally diffused. Like all other good things, good in themselves, it becomes, when perverted by monopoly, a source of evil: for *Knowledge is Power!* and, as such, when monopolized, is an instrument of oppression.—2. Is knowledge a good thing? I grant it is.—It is a blessing inestimable in its value: but it is a blessing multiplied by participation. And whence does it arise? Does it not grow out of the compacts and arrangements of civil society?—out of that state of laborious cultivation for which the civilized world has relinquished the idle independence of the savage and pastoral states? All must labour that knowledge may exist. Have not all, then, an equal right to its advantages?—That is to say (barring physical defects, and adventitious impediments) an equal right to the opportunities of obtaining those advantages: for *Equality of rights consists not in equality of distribution; but in equal opportunities of benefiting by the things distributed.* But, as accumulation encreases, the comparative ignorance of the multitude encreases, also; nay, it is much to be doubted, whether the incessant labour, to which they are doomed, to support the wasteful luxury and profligate ostentation of the idle class, does not sink them lower and lower in a state of *positive* ignorance. In short, it becomes, at last, a matter of state policy, among these idle classes, to keep the mass of mankind as ignorant as possible: the dull brain, as well as the strong shoulder and horn-like hoof of the ox, being regarded as a necessary attribute for the goaded, muzzled herd who are to tread out *their* harvest, and to bear the heavy yoke.—3. But the grand objection of all is, that the real improvers of society—the real cultivators of arts and sciences, even to their highest branches—the real promoters of moral and intellectual improvement, are seldom found among that idle class which the progress of accumulation has created. Bacon,[163] in England; the Medici, in Florence, and a few more illustrious exceptions might indeed be produced; but luxury and mental indolence, effeminacy, or brutal ambition, and the lethargic self-importance of ignorant pride, have been the general characteristics, in all ages, of the higher orders of society. The true lights of literature—the poets— the moralists—the genuine politicians, have generally started, like the prophet of Galilee and the philosopher of Athens, from the obscure sta- tions of mechanic life: or, at least, from the middle classes of society. Not all the Alchemy of feudalism can extract the ore of wisdom from the base metal, and false coinage of arbitrary distinction; nor was the inspiration of genius ever derived from the proud vaults and splendid charnel houses of an *illustrious* ancestry.

That the monopoly of knowledge was, however, an early consequence of the accumulation of property, is not a mere speculative opinion. It is ob- vious from all the facts of history. It was the case in the ancient world. It was the case in the dark or middle ages. It was the case on the revival of literature in the fourteenth century. It is equally obvious, that its vital influence was never properly felt in society, till it had risen above the lofty mountains of aristocracy, and the proud pinnacles of episcopal mysticism, and illuminated the vale of humble life. The heads of the towering cedars look gay, indeed, gilded by the rising or the setting sun; but its fostering beam is then most beneficent when it falls upon the lowly, but fruit-bear- ing shrub. In other words, it is not from the aristocracy, even of knowl- edge, that mankind has derived most benefit: and, with all his defects, all his grossness, and all "his ignorance"! one Thomas Paine is worth a dozen Aristotles, *and the whole race of linguists, metaphysicians, and logicians.*[164]

III. An inevitable consequence of the monopoly of knowledge, and the incessant drudgery of the multitude, would be the application of that privi- lege to the arts of force. The state of war may indeed too justly be consid- ered as a state of nature. In the simplest conditions of society we witness its barbarous ravages; and the state of cultivation and growing prosperity, however it may seem to hold out the flattering prospect of repose, is far from removing the temptations of military violence. *The Wealth of Nations*, like the honey in the hive, invites the cruel hand of rapine and murder. Nay a part, a powerful part of every nation, however, civilized, may be regarded as a band of robbers: and the polished Athenian, the austere Spar- tan, the voluptuous Roman, and the Germanic barbarian, alike, accommo- dated their different systems to this common object; and destined one por- tion of the people to toil, and one to bleed. In short, the fierce and indolent proprietors perceiving the advantages, and thirsting for the glory, of military *achievement*,[165] soon monopolized the arms, as instruments of foreign plunder, and of domestic tyranny. They reduced the use of them to a science, and disdained all other employments. This is the first grand stride towards the system of organised tyranny, as usurped and exercised by "the privileged classes, orders, distinctions, states", and since "improved, digested, and systematized" into that holy and oracular repertory of politics, liberty, and morals, "the old Germanic or Gothic custumary"! But sure a more atrocious violation of all principles of right and reason exists not in the whole hemisphere of oppression, than this appropriation. The science of arms is, in its very nature, an abuse. Other institutions, however vile corruption may have rendered them, may trace their origin, perhaps, to some just principle: but the very object of arms, from the beginning, could, in the main, be nothing but violence and oppression. The best that can be said for them, under any circumstances, is that they are a tolerated evil: and I shall proceed to shew, that unless possessed by every individual in the state, they are an evil not to be tolerated at all.

1. The only real use of arms, in any country, is the protection they may afford against the arms and violence of other states. They have indeed too frequently been considered as proper instruments to protect *the Faction of Government* against the discontents of the nation. But governments have no right to any other protection than the affections of the people for whom those governments exist: and this, if they discharge their duty, even with tolerable wisdom and honesty, will always be defence enough. Now the general protection of a country must, of necessity, be best secured, when every man in that country is a soldier, and every man is armed. Armed nations have always been invulnerable to invaders from without—But true it is, that they are equally formidable to tyrants within.

Arms fail, then, of their only justifiable object, when they are made an exclusive profession. They are calculated for the purposes of external defence, only when in the hands of the many; of internal usurpation alone, when in the hands of the few. In short, they are calculated, altogether, for the frontiers, not for the interior: and in towns and villages, the very character and accoutrements of the soldier ought never to be seen. Whatever is requisite for acquiring the art of war, should be practised in fields and on commons. In a peaceful city, the very sight of weapons is a detestable outrage. According to the original institutions of Rome, every man was a soldier, without the walls; and obliged to appear, on the first summons, with his arms and all equipments; but within the confines of the city, no one, except the lictors, who bore the fasces before the Chief Magistrate, and they were but twelve in number, was permitted to carry any weapon whatever.[a] A wise and excellent provision, to which, it is partly to be attributed, that for near six hundred years, none of the innumerable seditions, about which aristocratical declaimers make so much parade, were productive of any actual violence or bloodshed;[b] till Scipio Nassica,[168] and "a band of ruffian senators", with their slaves and clients at their heels, violated the law, attacked the unarmed people, assembled for the election of their magistrates, and after satiating their rage with plebeian massacre, extinguished Roman liberty in the blood of Gracchus.[c]

2. It is allowed, on all hands, that a main object of political institution is, the protection of the weak against the strong: in other words, the moral equalization of physical force. But to arm particular classes, is to create new

[a] Even Romulus, at the latter end of his reign, when, as we learn from Plutarch and Dionysius, that King "began to assume the Monarch to an odious degree", and to violate all the provisions of that popular constitution which himself had founded; the celeres, or guards, whom he collected about his person, to keep the people at a distance, and chastise the seditious language and wry faces of malcontents, were armed only with staves, and thongs of leather, hung around their girdles, to bind the refractory, whom they could not over-awe.[166]

[b] Unless, indeed, a boxing match, which now and then took place between the patricians and plebeians, and in which the former were, uniformly, the aggressors, (see Dion. Livy, or any Roman historians), may be regarded as an exception.[167]

[c] In a note upon my First Letter, (3rd edit. p. 21.) I have noticed a glaring misrepresentation in a farrago of forgeries, entitled, "Sketch of Democracy", written by an apostate pedagogue of the name of Bisset. Another instance of the perversion of facts, will sufficiently expose the whole character of the composition; and then Dr. B.'s six shillings-worth of Aristocracy is sufficiently answered. This fellow (to greet him in his own language—for with him every plebeian, and every advocate for the plebeians, is a fellow) having shewn his ignorance of the Agrarian Law (p. 225.) and placed Scipio Nassica (p. 229.) "at the head of an Association for defending Liberty and Property against Innovators and Levellers", proceeds to state (p. 230.) that "Tiberius (Gracchus) prepared by force, to oppose the association of men of property and patriotism. A scuffle ensued, in which Tiberius fell, &c." Now the fact is, that Tiberius, instead of preparing to effect any reformation by force, was standing upon the hustings (if I may use the term) in the Capitol, peaceably, and unarmed, as candidate for the Tribuneship: and his friends, peaceable and unarmed, also, were voting for his appointment to that office; when Scipio Nassica and his Associators, or as Hook very properly calls them (Rom. Hist.)[169] "a band of Ruffian Senators", attacked them with clubs, and swords, and daggers; murdered some, dispersed the rest, and assassinated the able and virtuous object of their terror, and their hatred.

Cassius has been called "the last of all the Romans": but the genuine Roman Character was extinct before Cassius was born. He was, indeed, the last of the Roman Aristocracy: but genuine Republican Rome expired with the Gracchi. The atrocious contests that ensued, between Sylla[170] and Marius,[171] and Caesar[172] and Pompey,[173] were mere struggles of individual ambition—or at least of Monarchic and Aristocratic factions; of which the corrupted and degenerate people were the instruments, not the objects.—As for the Agrarian Law, to which the Gracchi fell illustrious martyrs, I have long meditated a Treatise upon this subject. Suffice it here to observe, that notwithstanding the misrepresentations into which English writers have sometimes been betrayed by ignorance, and sometimes led by design, it was not a law of any man's legal hereditary estate. Spelman, in a note upon his translation of Dionysius (vol. iii p. 411.) is the only English writer I have met with, who places this subject in its true light.[174]

and still greater inequalities: to make the strong still stronger; and leave the weakness that ought to be defended still more defenceless. Property, of itself, creates a formidable influence, too often hostile to the Equality of Rights. Its tyranny is as malignant, and certainly much more extensive than that of mere animal strength. Nothing in political science is more desirable than to disarm it of its power, without violating its security. But surely, nothing can be more iniquitous than to encrease that power by privileges and exemptions; and to make the appropriated science of arms the obsequious, but ferocious vassal of superior wealth. A military government, under the capricious direction of pride and opulence, is as much a state of anarchy as any tyranny that could be exercised by the unassociated ferocity of barbarian force. Machiavel, in his "Discourses on Livy" (b.i.c.5.)[175] has sufficiently demonstrated, that arms are more likely to be abused by the wealthy and the great, than by the common people. "Freedom", says he, "is most properly committed to their custody who have least appetite to usurp. And, certainly, if the ends and designs of both be considered, it will be found, that the Nobility are ambitious of dominion, while the Commons, having less hope to usurp, have more inclination to live in freedom."—And again:—"Disturbances", he adds, "are most frequently caused by those who have large possessions, because the apprehension of losing what they have got, produces the same eagerness and passion, as desire of acquisition does in others; while, at the same time, they seldom think themselves secure in what they have, but by new accumulation. Add to which, the more wealth, or territory they have, the more power they possess of usurping as they see occasion."[176]

IV. This appropriation of arms necessarily divided the people into two distinct classes: 1. The military, or privileged order, who were to enjoy full *liberty* to plunder, riot, and *consume*;[177] and whose glory and consequences were to be proportioned to the havock they made of the human species; and, 2. The Servile class, doomed to toil for the subsistence and luxury of this sanguinary banditti, and to be despised in proportion as they were really useful and important. Such were the distinctions of which we have rude specimens in the institutions of our German and Gothic ancestors. Such also, in a more informed and cultivated age, and incorporated with a system at once rude and majestic, ferocious and refined, were the distinctions established in the Lacaedemonian state: where, though property was annihilated, as an individual distinction, it was preserved as the distinction of a class; and arms and freedom were the common privileges of the Spartan; toil and unconditional slavery, the common lot of the

Helote:—a distinction well worthy of remembrance: for in every state, however modified, *the classes that have neither land, nor wealth, nor arms, must, in effect, be slaves.* To these, under the feudal system, was added, *a third*, or intermediate class, growing out of the first, and the necessary instrument of its oppressive power.

1. The possession and use of arms thus monopolised by a combination of principal proprietors, the sequel of the feudal system follows of course. They fall upon the smaller proprietors, murder some, dispossess the remainder, and enslave the whole community. Intoxicated with power, and enflamed with the *glory* of these exploits, they then round upon the neighbouring states; repeat their ravages; extend their territories; constitute themselves, and their posterity, sole rulers over the enslaved and desolated countries, and govern by the *terror of the sword.* *[178]

But regular schemes of military violence are not to be executed without an individual leader. Some chieftain, therefore, renowned for savage deeds, becomes the director, or the instrument, of these atrocious enterprises: and thus are laid the foundations of individual tyranny. The robberies and murders are all committed in his name; large discretionary powers are vested in his hands, for the execution of the common designs: and his power, of course, is acknowledged as supreme in the first enthusiasm of success and victory. The conqueror, therefore, either of his own or a foreign country, takes possession of the conquered territory as his property. Every thing is HIS: *his* country, *his* victory, *his* people. He bought them at the common mart of feudalism: and the price was blood. He is, however, in effect, the umpire only, not the permanent possessor; and the major part of the spoil is divided among the principal leaders of the banditti, according to the dictates of his caprice, the power and number of their respective followers, or the standard of their own "bad eminence".[179] And such, according to "the venerable Gothic custumary", is *the origin of the* ORDER OF NOBILITY! If hereditary descent, therefore, were to stamp its current character upon a particular race, nobility, instead of a patent of respect, would be a title to our detestation and abhorrence. But crimes are no more hereditary than virtues: and moral attributes are not to be acquired, like legislative wisdom, by "swaddling, and rocking, and dandling."[180]

The large districts, thus allotted by the captain of the banditti to *his* great lords, are of course doled out again, in smaller parcels, to *their* inferior lordlings; who either subdivide them again, for proper compensations and services, or, compelling the mass of inhabitants to cultivate them as slaves, maintain themselves and their chieftains in riotous luxury with the produce. "Allotments, *thus acquired*", (says Blackstone) "naturally engaged such as accepted them to defend them: and as they all sprang" (to translate his legal language into plain English) "from the same *right of robbery and murder*, no part could subsist, unless the whole were preserved, by the same violence and injustice as it was obtained; wherefore all givers, as well as receivers, were mutually bound to defend each other's usurpations. But as that could not effectually be done in a tumultuous or irregular way, a chain of dependence and subordination was necessary, from the chief robber down to the meanest accessary in the plunder."[181] A regular organization was accordingly invented to secure, and a correspondent system of laws to sanctify, the usurpation. Both the robbery and the distribution were legalized with all the solemn mockery of forms and words; and it became Treason and Rebellion in the original proprietors to disobey their plunderers, or seek the restoration of their rights. "Every receiver of the stolen property was bound, when called upon by his sub-captain, or immediate commander and benefactor, to do all in his power to defend him, right or wrong. Such benefactor, or commander, was likewise subordinate to, and under the command of his immediate captain, or benefactor; and so upwards to the chief captain, or generalissimo, of the banditti himself. The several chieftains of the gang were, also, reciprocally bound, in their respective gradations, to protect the plunder they had distributed. Thus the feudal connection was established, a proper military subordination was artfully introduced; and an army of depredators was always ready enlisted, and mutually prepared to muster, not only in defence of each man's own several share of the plunder, but, also, for the defence, or enlargement, of the newly established usurpation."[a]

That this chain of reciprocal dependencies might be kept entire; that the respective links might not be broken or weakened; that the vassal might never, by looking round upon his family, forget to look up to his chief; and, above all, that every proprietor (or usurper) might be able, according to the original rank and character of his fee, to attend, with an appropriate number of vassals, upon his chief, and support the expence and preparation

---

[a]Black. Com. B.ii.c.4.[182] I have taken the liberty to make my author, though a lawyer and a judge, to speak in plain, unsophisticated language, throughout this whole quotation. The surfeit I took, in my juvenile years, of the glossing and barbarous jargon of the law, leads me to suppose that every reader will gladly be excused the personal trouble of translating its obscurities and cant phrases, into their true and intelligible meaning. If it were possible to translate the whole library of the law in the same manner, the eyes of mankind would be essentially opened; and it would then be seen how far the proud boast, &c. &c. &c.

of new conquests and incessant wars, the barbarous Law of Primogeniture was invented: and, thus, the very principles of property were violated in system, as the possession had been, before, in practice.—I repeat it—The very principles of property are violated by this law: for, if there is such a thing as a principle of descent, growing out of the nature and foundations of property, it is this—that *the property acquired by the industry of the parents, should descend to those who the passions of such parents have brought into an appropriated world.* If all, then, are, alike, the children of their parents, all, are, alike, their heirs:[a] and if this consanguinity ought not to dictate the descent of property, then is not property at all descendable; but ought either to depend entirely upon the bequest of the proprietor, or return to the bosom of the state, for the general benefit of the community. I am, however, for the relative feelings and the regular descent of property. But plunder—not property, was the principle of the feudal system: massacre and desolation—not social virtue. The ties of nature were therefore torn asunder; the relative sympathies were trampled under the iron hoof of military despotism; and (that the landholder might be able to serve the chieftain in his wars) the younger brethren were spurned, as outcasts, or retained, as servile dependents, in the paternal mansion; and the orphan daughter, in the defenceless bloom of youth and innocence, was discarded as an alien from the possessions and residence of her departed, perhaps slaughtered, father.

Such is the organization and character of the military, or privileged orders, under the boasted feudal, or Gothic system.

2. As for the useful class—the cultivators, or mass of the people—they are held, "as Sir William Temple speaks, in a condition of downright servitude, used and employed in the most servile works, and *belonging*, both they, and their children and effects, to the lord of the soil, like the rest of the cattle or stock upon it." (*Black. Com.* B. ii.c.6).[183] In other words, the plundered and disfranchised multitude, reduced to labour, like beasts of burthen, in the cultivation of the possessions wrested from them, are kept in utter ignorance, by incessant drudgery and the jealous tyranny of their masters; and are allowed only a scanty subsistence out of the produce of their own toil and property.

To fortify themselves in these usurpations, and at once debase and terrify

---

[a]I would add, "However begotten—whether in marriage, or out." But Mr. B. and the priests would call me an encourager of licentiousness, of bastardy and prostitution. O words! words! how are things abused by you. But man is man, and nature nature, and parent is parent, and child is child, whether a conjuror in a black gown mutter his spells or not.

the trampled multitude, the imperious banditti build castles upon the hills, and cathedrals and monastaries in the vallies; that thus they may enjoy *their liberty* of plundering and subjugating at pleasure; and guarantee the oppressions of one world by the terrors of another.

3. In addition to these precautions, every great proprietor maintained, in his castle, and on his estate, a sort of standing army:—a lazy, turbulent, voluptuous swarm of dependents, who *wore his livery*, bore about with them (as a sort of patent of licentiousness) the badges of his rank and family; banquetted in his hall, assisted his rapes and seductions, and robbed and murdered, at his bidding. These being held in a sort of liberal and familiar dependence, well armed, and comparatively disciplined, prided themselves in their obsequious attachment, kept the inferior vassals in due subjection, and filled the tenantry, and even the surrounding estates, with terror and consternation. This departmental banditti, or host of *liveried varlets*, was principally selected from the younger, and, of course, disfranchised and disinherited branches of the noble families (small or great): and were therefore called *Gentlemen*; as if no person was, in reality, of the race, or *generation* of man, who was not, at least in some collateral line, descended from some one of those military robbers and usurpers, who, like the *Baron de Warren*,[184] could produce their swords as titles of proprietary, and patents of distinction.

Do you wish, my fellow-citizens, for particular illustrations of this general history of the Gothic custumary? I need not refer you to the origin of the Scythian nations; or the dissolution of the Roman empire, and consequence establishment of the Goths, the Huns, the Franks, the Vandals, the Lombards, the Burgundians, and the whole swarm of heroic depredators, poured out from the northern hive. The annals of our own country furnish sufficient instances.

1. Were not the *seven kingdoms of the heptarchy*, with their Hengists,[185] and their Ellas,[186] and their Cerdics[187] at their head, thus founded, and the proprietorships, under them, thus established? Were they not afterwards melted into an individual state in the same crucible of blood and violence, under the auspices of EGBERT[188] *(or more more properly, by Athelstan),*[189] *first king of all England?* And though the Saxon institutions were deficient (if deficiency it may be called) in many of those features of deformity which characterise the feudal system, yet the general proportions were much the same. The territory was seized by murder and rapine; the proprietors were dispossessed; such as escaped the general slaughter, were either driven into the mountains of Wales, or reduced to the most abject vil-

lanage; the lands were divided among the victorious banditti; society was split into its various orders, and the main distinction between *military free-men*, and *agricultural slaves*, was ultimately established in all its rigour. Such were the boasted institutions of our Saxon ancestors.

2. In the *Norman conquest*, we have an instance completely in point.— But, perhaps, I ought to tread this ground with fear and trembling. Perhaps I ought to remember the grave looks of judges, the emphatic tone of public prosecutors, echoing the words, as they distilled (one drop of truth through a lymbic of perjury) from the lips of a hireling witness, and all the breathless wonder, which threw a deeper shade over the solemn mummery of the scene, when I was proved (upon an awful occasion) to have called our first William "a Norman robber"! But the thing is true; and I cannot tremble at the repetition. As man, I am a rational being; and I must think and speak. Circumstances—if I may adopt the language of Mr. B. on this occasion—have "made *me* (also) a *public creature*", as such I must exist, or not at all: and, if facts fall in my way, I must represent them as they appear to me.

William the Norman having collected together, by general proclamation, the nobles and assassins, the princes, and the free-booters of the continent, selected from them an army of 60,000 men, and having obtained the pope's blessing, and, of course enlisted heaven on his side, invaded England, murdered the elected prince, the nobles, and the freeholders, and seizing upon the lands of all who resisted, divided them among his followers. But as some of the proprietors, after this first victory, sided with the conqueror, and assisted his accession to the throne, he had not an immediate opportunity of seizing upon the whole territory; and many districts still continued to be held upon the Saxon tenure: one of the best properties of which was, that the estates descended to all the children, and not exclusively to the eldest son. But in the nineteenth year of his reign, *a pretence was made of an apprehended Invasion*: "upon which he brought over (another) large army of Normans and Bretons, who were quartered upon every landholder, and greatly oppressed the people." Under their auspices, "the king held a great council to enquire into the state of the nation; the immediate consequence of which was the compiling of the great survey called *Doomsday Book!*[190] which was finished in the next year: and in the latter end of that very year the king was attended by all his nobility at Sarum; where all the principal landholders *submitted their lands to the yoke* of military tenure, became king's *vassals*, and did *homage* and fealty to his person." Thus was the feudal system (with all its tyrannous

appendages, and the barbarous law of primogeniture among the rest) established in all its rigour; and "it became a fundamental maxim, *that the king is
the universal lord, and original proprietor of all the lands in his kingdom: and that
no man doth, or can possess any part of it, but what has mediately or immediately been derived as a gift from him, to be held upon feudal services*" (that is
to say upon services of robbery and murder.) *Black. Com.* b. ii. c. 4.[191] The
men of Kent, however, by a brave defence of their liberties, prevented this
territorial usurpation. The estates, through that whole district, continued
to be held in Gavel-kind (that is, they descended to all the sons alike) till
the charter of John disfranchised the lands held under the see of Canterbury, and the statute 31 Henry VIII. restricted this just and natural law
within still narrower bounds.[192]

Such, then, is the feudal system; and such the origin of landed property
under "the Gothic custumary." Do I wish then to shake this property?
Again, and again, I answer—NO. Landed property rests not upon the
metaphysical and abstract niceties of original right. It has its foundations,
broad and firm, in the principles of general expediency; and, if the proprietor oppresses not the labourer, it matters not how the property was acquired six or eight hundred years ago. But assuredly these facts will shew,
that *the property of the country is* NOT THE COUNTRY! and that *to say it
is so, is to invite the ruffian hand of plunder, and to proclaim aloud that assassins
and depredators, "murder but the proprietors, and seize their property, and you
shall have a right to dispose of the people as you see fit: you shall be Lords
Paramount, Rulers and States; and those whom you oppress and plunder shall
thenceforth *politically*[193] be nothing!*"

This conclusion, I contend, results from Mr. B.'s principles—for if the
Gothic custumary were the fountain of right, and the property of the country were the country, then property obtained according to the manner in
which, under the Gothic custumary, it was obtained, would be rightful
property; and, accordingly, would transfer the right of nationality and government. In other words, plunder and devastation would be the only legitimate title to dominion. At this rate, if the present rulers of France were
that "gang of thieves, house-breakers and assassins", which Mr. B. represents them, their right to govern the French nation would be so much the
more sacred. But I deny all this. I affirm that, *not the property, but* THE
PEOPLE ARE THE NATION. If the present government of France was
made by the French people, it is a legitimate government. If it was not
made by the people, it is an usurpation. At the same time, however, legitimacy or usurpation is nothing to us—They must settle it among them-

selves. It is more to our purpose to mark the chains upon chains that these feudalists are twisting around our limbs.

The people are nothing, it seems, "for the property of the country is the country"—talents are the bounden vassals of property, and "the revolt of enterprising talents against property, is Jacobinism": nay, even property itself is to be the obedient and "laborious slave of virtue and of public honour"—that is to say, according to Mr. B.'s mode of interpretation of "the states, privileged classes, orders and distinctions, drawn from the old Germanic or Gothic custumary!"

Into what labyrinths of tyranny would these sophists lead us? How much less than nothing, would they make that great laborious mass who are, indeed, the fountain of their prosperity—the real source of all their borrowed splendour? But it is not the barbarous cant of antiquity that can now enslave us. We, also, can appeal to the facts of history—We can appeal still further—to the first dictates of nature and the principles of eternal justice. Guided by these, we are enabled to discover, that "the Gothic custumary, with all its emanating feudal institutions", to which Mr. B. would refer as the standard of all political and moral right, was indeed the very perfection of military barbarism—the consummation of the usurping *Tyranny of Force.* By the same lights we are, also, enabled to discover, that all the existing liberties of Europe are but so many innovations upon this tyrannical system. As "in the progress of society, arts and sciences diffused *new lights*", those innovations successively arose; and, though opposed by the persecutions of power, and the senseless howl of prejudice, the growing intellect of man demanded a correspondent emancipation, and innovation triumphed over established barbarism!

Similar causes will continue to demand, and similar energies cannot fail to produce, similar effects. *Fresh innovations are again required!* We have arrived at a new and grand aera of human intellect. The press, that great luminary of the moral and political world, has dissipated, in a considerable degree, the fogs and mists of our dull atmosphere: knowledge has penetrated, as it were, the flint walls of laborious poverty; and enquiries have been awakened which no opiate can lull again into effectual slumber. In short, the altered circumstances of society, render some alterations necessary in existing systems. Such alterations must be made; and they will. In vain would fresh mounds and dams restrain the swell and progress of enquiry. The waters are rising; the fountains are inexhaustible; they demand a wider channel. Happy shall it be for those governors, who, yielding to the current of the times, shall clear the way for gradual reformations, ere the flood of popular opinion swell too high, and the congregated torrents, foaming, and bursting over their confines, spread, far and wide, the wasting inundation.

END OF PART THE SECOND.

SHOULD public countenance encourage the author to proceed, a third part of this work is intended to be published in four or five weeks; which, it is presumed, will not considerably, if at all, exceed the dimensions of the present. The materials, however, are copious; the subject important; and though compression is desirable, omissions might maim the whole. It may however be necessary, for more reasons than one, to conclude with the seventh letter. To point out the means (however benevolent) of political improvement, is not always safe and practicable: and it is not only a duty to speak the truth; but it is also a duty to speak it at such times, and in such manner, as may be most conducive to public benefit.

The heads of the remaining part are as follow:

LETTER V.   The Mercantile and Manufacturing Systems.   I. *Innovations on the Feudal System—Distinction between Slavery and Servitude—Relics of Slavery.*   II. *Origin of Merchandize—1. Barter of Natural Produce—2. Of Artificial.*   III. *Manufactures. 1. Their genuine Principle—2. Perversion—Influence on the Mass.*   IV. *Rate of Wages—Combinations of Capitalists—Laws against Combinations of Tradesmen. Tyranny of Commerce.*

LETTER VI.   The Funding System.   I. *Discordant Interests, and Common Principle of Feudalist and Capitalist.*   II. *Revenue—Commerce an Object at once of Protection and Plunder—Corporations, Patents, Monopolies.*   III. *The Funds—Paper Credit—Union of Feudal and Commercial Tyranny.*   IV. *System of Corruption—Its Progress—Ravages on Human Happiness and Virtue—Present State of Society.*   V. *Prospect of Dissolution of the Funding System— Claims of the Stockholder vindicated—Means of Indemnity.*

LETTER VII.   Causes of Popular Revolutions.   I. *Always preceded and produced by Revolutions against the People—Instances—1. From Ancient History.—2. From Modern.*   II. *Influence of Science and Philosophy in producing the*

French Revolution—Causes of the Progress and Bias of Literature. III. Causes of Excesses in France. i. State of Society and Morals—1. The Nobles—2. The Clergy—3. The Middling Orders—4. The Populace—Parallel from Dion. Hal. ii. Errors and Visionary Pride of the Literary (or Brissotine) Party—Causes of these. IV. Means of avoiding Revolutions, or lessening their Horrors.
LETTER VIII. Idea of an improved State of Society. I. Governments ought to be simple—Objects of Complexity. II. Practicability of improving the State of Man—Proved. 1. From Argument—2. From History—3. From present State of Society. III. Means of Improvement. CONCLUSION—Peace, Fraternity and intellectual Advancement (not Ambition, Wealth, and Grandeur) true Sources of National Happiness.

It may not, perhaps, be improper to subjoin, in this place, the following brief statement of facts:

At the beginning of the year 1794, several persons, active in the cause of Parliamentary Reform, wished for a place (independent of tavern-keepers and licenses) which could be used for public meetings, and other political purposes. They subscribed their names, accordingly, for annual sums, to discharge the rent; and the premises, No. 2, Beaufort Buildings, were fixed upon: it being suggested, by the first proposers, that J.T. should have the use of the house and lecture-room, without burthen or pecuniary hazard: to which it was added, that if he had the hardihood to brave the persecutions which his lectures would inevitably produce, he ought not to be exposed to the danger of any other incumbrance. In consequence of this, and upon the faith of the above subscriptions, an active patriot and zealous friend of J.T. took the lease, and made himself responsible for the rent: i.e. for £132 a year, and all taxes. The premises were used for the political purposes intended; and for that use J.T. was tried for his life: a material part of his case being that most of the meetings, by a strange abuse of terms called *treasonable*, were held at his house: i.e. at No. 2, Beaufort Buildings. But circumstances have so turned out, that J.T. has been left to the option of either paying the rent, &c. himself,[a] or throwing the burthen upon the shoulders of the friend who had rendered himself legally responsible. While the means were in his power, justice and honour forbade him to

---

[a] A part of the subscribers paid their first subscription: but to an amount scarcely exceeding the expence incurred before J.T. was, in reality, put into possession of the premises.

deliberate. He has sustained, without a murmur, the heavy burden, till every resource is exhausted. The consequences of such an incumbrance must be evident, when it is recollected that the premises have been nearly three years upon his hands; and that, during that time, for seven months, only, (the space taken up by two courses of Political Lectures) they have been productive of any emolument. But this is not the only burthen that has fallen upon his shoulders. In his zeal for diffusing political knowledge, he published his political lectures in a weekly paper (the Tribune) at so low a price that a wide circulation was necessary to defray the mere expences. It had, for a considerable time, a circulation that demanded an edition of 2,000 copies. But after the passing of the two late bills, the booksellers, in general, became afraid to execute orders for this, or any other of J.T.'s works; and thus was between £3 and 400 worth of stock thrown dead upon his hands. Over this statement aristocracy may exult, and moderatism glance with indifference: but the author appeals to that principle of Justice which ought, above all things, to actuate the friends of liberty, whether under such circumstances, he is not entitled to some countenance in the prosecution of a work by which he is struggling at once to advance the public cause, and emancipate himself from the embarrassments thus produced.

December 19, 1796.

Editor's Notes to the Texts

"The Natural and Constitutional Right of Britons . . ."

1. Francis Hargrave, ed., *A Complete Collection of State Trials, and Proceedings for High Treason*, 10 vols. (1776), 1:iii.

2. Thomas Erskine (1750–1823): Thelwall's chief counsel; MP for Portsmouth from 1790; advocate in Parliament for the Society of Friends of the People in 1792; defender of Thomas Paine at his treason trial in December 1792; later Lord Chancellor and first Baron Erskine.

3. Vicary Gibbs (1751–1820): defended William Winterbotham in 1793 and later became Solicitor-General in Pitt's last government.

4. These lectures were published in three volumes as *The Tribune* (1795–96).

5. For the earlier debate on reform in Parliament led by Pitt himself, see *The Parliamentary History of England* 22 (1814), cols. 1416–38.

6. See Edward Coke, *The First Part of the Institutes of the Laws of England*, 3 vols. (1749), vol. 2, sec. 745.

7. *State Trials for High Treason, Containing the Trial of Thomas Hardy* (Edinburgh, 1794), p. 6. Sir James Eyre (1734–99) was Chief Justice of the Common Pleas, 1793–99, and presided over the trials of Hardy, Horne Tooke, Thelwall, and others.

8. The so-called "Pop-gun plot," in which three London Corresponding Society members were imprisoned for allegedly planning to shoot a poison arrow at the King through a dart gun. They were arrested in September 1794 and finally acquitted in May 1796. See P. T. Lemaitre, *High Treason! Narrative of the Arrest, Examination, Imprisonment &c. of P. T. Lemaitre, Accused of Being a Party in the Pop-Gun Plot; or, A Pretended Plot to Kill the King!* (1795).

9. Richard II (1367–1400), King of England 1377–99; Edward II (1284–1327), King of England 1307–27; Richard III (1425–85), King of England 1483–85; Henry VIII (1491–1547), King of England 1509–47; Charles I (1600–1649), King of England 1625–49; Charles II (1630–85), King of England 1660–85; James II (1633–88), King of England 1685–88.

10. *The Trial of Mr. Thomas Hardy, for High Treason* (1793), p. 13.

11. *State Trials, Thomas Hardy*, p. 6.

12. The London Corresponding Society had discussed holding a second "British Convention" similar to that which had ended so disastrously at Edinburgh in 1793 with the arrest and transportation of several delegates.

13. *Trials for High Treason, Containing the Whole of the Proceedings at the Old Bailey, from October 28, to December 5, 1794*, 2nd ed. (1795), p. 311.

14. Part of the penalty prescribed for treason, the sentence included hanging until just short of death, then being drawn or disembowled while still alive, with the entrails then burned before the

victim, who was then decapitated, and his body divided into quarters. The penalty was inflicted on Despard and others in 1803 for conspiring to kill George III, though not fully carried out then. The sentence was last imposed in 1867, though not executed.

15. *Trials for High Treason . . . at the Old Bailey*, p. 377.

16. Louis XVI was executed on 21 January 1793.

17. The Tuilleries, where Louis XVI and his family had taken refuge, was attacked after a popular insurrection began in Paris on 10 August 1792.

18. For conspiring to permit foreign troops to invade France in order to save him, having taken an oath as constitutional monarch to uphold the new constitution, on 13 September 1791.

19. *Trials for High Treason . . . at the Old Bailey*, pp. 367–68.

20. See Shakespeare, *Macbeth* 5.5.25.

21. After the fall of Robespierre on 9 Thermidor (27 July 1794), the dictator and his supporters were executed. Following the Constitution of the Year III (1795), a Directory ruled France until 1799.

22. MS addition. The printed version is "to be."

23. *Trials for High Treason . . . at the Old Bailey*, p. 314.

24. Judicial sentence by the Inquisition, which often led to a public burning of heretics.

25. This was the sentence passed on the delegates to the British Convention at Edinburgh in 1793.

26. A national convention of Volunteers was proposed for Dublin in late 1792 but was suppressed by action of the Privy Council.

27. William Pitt (1759–1806), Chancellor of the Exchequer and Prime Minister, who had an early reputation as reformer but vigorously prosecuted war with France and repression at home.

28. A meeting took place at the Duke of Richmond's house in May 1782, at which a motion was carried requesting Pitt to put forward in Parliament various motions for parliamentary reform, curtailing the influence of the Crown, and checking bribery.

29. Supposedly the words of Anarcharsis to Solon, when writing his laws, and paraphrased by Bacon and Swift, among others.

30. See *Trials for High Treason . . . at the Old Bailey*, p. 366.

31. Sir Thomas Osborne (1631–1712), first Earl Danby, an unusually corrupt Lord Treasurer 1673–78.

32. Self-murder. Hargrave, *Complete Collection of State Trials*, 2:741.

33. Ibid., p. 752.

34. Ibid., 1:iv.

35. Ibid., 2:730.

36. Shakespeare, *Macbeth* 1.7.7–12.

37. See *The Complete Reports of the Committee of Secrecy* (1794).

38. James II was expelled, and William and Mary settled on the throne, as the result of James's efforts to engineer a Catholic succession to the throne.

39. *Trials for High Treason . . . at the Old Bailey*, p. 363.

40. Ibid., p. 375.

41. Jupiter was the Roman god of the sky, and the chief Roman and Italian god.

42. George Lynham, an ironmonger, was a government spy.

43. *State Trials for High Treason, Part Third, Containing the Trial of Mr. John Thelwall* (1795), pp. 64, 27, 29, 59. Stewart Kidd (d. 1811), a legal writer, was tried with Thelwall.

44. See Edmund Burke, "Reflections on the Revolution in France," in *The Works of the Rt. Hon. Edmund Burke*, 8 vols. (1792–1827), 3:187.

45. MS change. The original reads "never failed."

46. John Somers (1651–1716), Lord Chancellor of England 1692–1700. Somers is now, however, generally allowed not to have been the author of *The Judgement of Whole Kingdoms and*

Nations, Concerning the Rights, Power, and Prerogative of Kings, and the Rights, Privileges, and Properties of the People, a strongly Lockean tract first published as *Political Aphorisms* (1690), then reprinted as *Vox populi, vox Dei*. See Richard Ashcraft and M. M. Goldsmith, "Locke, Revolution Principles, and the Formation of Whig Ideology," *Historical Journal* 26 (1983), 773–800.

47. *Judgement of Whole Kingdoms and Nations* (see preceding note), 10th ed. (1771), p. 23.

48. Ibid., p. 24.

49. In 1780, Charles Lennox, Duke of Richmond, introduced a reform bill in Parliament that proposed annual Parliaments, manhood suffrage, and the reform of electoral districts.

50. Granville Sharp, *A Defence of the Ancient, Legal, Constitutional, Right of the People, to Elect Representatives for Every Session of Parliament* (1780), pp. 8–13.

51. William Blackstone, *Commentaries on the Laws of England*, 5th ed. 4 vols. (1773), 1:140.

52. Combinations of workers to raise wages had been prohibited by a series of statutes (a 1749 act regulated the textile industries) that were reinforced again in 1799–1800 and finally repealed in 1824.

53. *The Authentic Copy of a Petition Praying for a Reform in Parliament . . . Signed only by Members of the Society of the Friends of the People* (1793), p. 2, claimed that 70 MPs were returned by virtually no electors at all; a further 90 by 46 places with no more than 50 voters; and another 52 in elections of 200 voters or less. In total, it estimated, less than 15,000 electors returned a majority of the House.

54. See Charles Secondat, Baron de Montesquieu, *The Spirit of the Laws*, 6th ed. (1793), p. 7.

55. Literally, a boiler of a pot; applied to householders qualified by a borough vote, e.g., by having their own fireplace on which to cook.

56. Montesquieu, *Spirit of the Laws*, p. 7.

57. Ibid., p. 9.

58. Ibid.

59. Ibid., p. 115.

60. Blackstone, *Commentaries*, 1:159.

61. Members of John Reeves's Association for Preserving Liberty and Property Against Republicans and Levellers.

62. See Edward Gibbon, *The History of the Decline and Fall of the Roman Empire*, 6 vols. (1776–88), 3:290–91. The reference is to a treason law of the year 397, introduced by Arcadius.

63. MS addition.

64. See *The Second Report of the Committee of Secrecy of the House of Commons*, 4th ed. (1794), Appendix E, p. 89.

65. *First Report from the Committee of Secrecy*, 3rd ed. (1794), p. 24; *At a General Meeting of the London Corresponding Society, Held on the Green, at Chalk Farm, on Monday the 14th of April, 1794* (1794).

66. After Jean-Paul Marat (1743–93), French Jacobin leader and advocate of dictatorship.

67. Letters from Thelwall's brother-in-law were among those seized by the government.

68. *First Report from the Committee of Secrecy*, p. 24.

69. *Complete Reports of the Committee of Secrecy* p. 19.

70. *Trials for High Treason . . . at the Old Bailey*, p. 371.

71. Ibid.

72. Blackstone, *Commentaries*, 1:158.

73. A city or town tenure, where an annual rent was paid.

74. Until the 1832 reform act, the only towns to send members to Parliament were those that had received the privilege from the Crown. Because no new constituencies were created between 1677 and 1832, there was a vast overrepresentation of the more agricultural south of England, compared with the more commercial and industrial north.

75. *First Report from the Committee of Secrecy*, pp. 21, 17.

76. Ibid., p. 19.

77. Ibid., p. 22.

78. See At a General Meeting of the London Corresponding Society . . . at Chalk Farm.

79. Henry Dundas (1742–1811), first Viscount Melville: MP, Home Secretary 1791–94, then Secretary of War to 1801.

80. I.e., the practices by which the defendants at the 1793 Edinburgh treason trial were tried and convicted.

81. Complete Reports of the Committee of Secrecy, p. 34.

82. Abbé Raynal, A Philosophical and Political History of the Settlements and Trade of the Europeans in the East and West Indies, 6 vols. (1782), 6:238: "They are the first who ever made use of the expression, the majesty of the people, and that alone is sufficient to consecrate a language."

83. See Shakespeare, King Lear 3.4.29.

84. William Skirving (d. 1796), Maurice Margarot (1745–1816), Joseph Gerrald (1763–96), Thomas Muir (1765–99), and Thomas Fyshe Palmer (1747–1802)—delegates to the British Convention at Edinburgh in 1793.

85. John Clerk (1757–1832), Lord Eldin.

86. Alexander Murray (1736–95), Lord Henderland.

87. The Trial of Joseph Gerrald, Delegate from the London Corresponding Society to the British Convention (1794), p. 112.

88. The Trial of William Skirving, Secretary to the British Convention (Edinburgh, 1794), p. 55. In fact, Lord Eskgrove is speaking here.

89. MS deletion from the printed text: "and I understand from high authorities, that an act of Parliament was thought necessary, at an early period, to make even the ten commandments part of the law of England."

90. Trial of William Skirving, p. 55.

91. Trial of Joseph Gerrald, p. 104.

92. Ibid.

93. During the reign of Edward III, the royal council often sat in the Star Chamber of the Palace of Westminster. Under the Tudors, the Star Chamber became a special court dealing with offences against the state. Frequently used under the Stuarts against the Puritans, it was abolished in 1641.

94. William Laud (1573–1645), who became Archbishop of Canterbury, was notoriously intolerant of his clerical opponents.

95. Hargrave, Complete Collection of State Trials, 1:676.

96. Habeas corpus was suspended on 23 May 1794 as part of the effort to squash the reform movement.

97. Trial of Joseph Gerrald, pp. 24–25.

98. Montesquieu, Spirit of the Laws, p. 12.

99. The office of sheriff, or shire reeve, existed before the Norman Conquest but in Thelwall's time was usually appointed annually to each country by the Crown, with city and borough sheriffs appointed by corporations.

100. The Southwark Society of the Friends of the People, to which Thelwall belonged from early 1792 until late 1793.

101. Justice Ashurst's "Charge to the Grand Jury for the County of Middlesex" (19 November 1792) reiterated the government's position on seditious meetings and publications. Shortly thereafter, a Royal Proclamation, published on 1 December, authorized the use of the militia to suppress unrest.

102. Thomas Paine (1737–1809), esp. Rights of Man (1791–92); Joel Barlow (1754–1812), esp. Advice to the Privileged Orders (1792). See Trials for High Treason . . . at the Old Bailey, pp. 316–18.

103. See *Southwark Society of the Friends of the People* (1792).

104. *Second Report of the Committee of Secrecy*, p. 25.

105. A silversmith, John Baxter was chairman of the London Corresponding Society in 1793 and the author of *Resistance to Oppression, the Constitutional Right of Britons* (1795).

106. The republican Algernon Sidney (1622–83), after whom Thelwall named his eldest son, was executed for plotting against Charles II.

107. Timms was a Treasury Solicitor's messenger who testified against Thelwall at his trial.

108. Thelwall's own annotated version of the text (British Library 12270:4[2]) has this manuscript note explaining this letter: "Mentioning the subject of this letter to John Richter, some weeks after the acquittals, he exclaimed, with some astonishment, 'and did Tims swear that he found that letter in your pocket? The lying rascal! He must have found it, or rather some body else must have found it under the tyles of my house, for it was a letter sent to me, & which I had put out of the way I thought of being seen by any one."

109. MS addition by Thelwall.

110. John Richter (d. 1830) was arrested with Thelwall in May 1794.

111. *Trials for High Treason . . . at the Old Bailey*, p. 345.

112. Joseph White was the Treasury Solicitor at this time. Richard Ford was a Bow Street magistrate and spymaster. John Stuart Taylor was probably the friend Thelwall refers to here.

113. See *Trials for High Treason . . . at the Old Bailey*, p. 376.

114. Lucius Aelius Sejanus (d. 31), who attacked his enemies through a series of treason trials; Flavius Rufinus (d. 395).

115. Founder of the London Corresponding Society, the shoemaker Thomas Hardy was tried for treason and acquitted before Thelwall's trial. See *The Trials at Large of Thomas Hardy, and Others, for High Treason* (1794). For the "indecorous expressions" (a toast), see ibid., p. 93.

116. Thelwall's songs were reprinted in *The Tribune* 1 (1795):166–68, 190–92, 338–40, and in C. Boyle Thelwall, *The Life of John Thelwall* (1837), pp. 445–51.

117. James Adair (d. 1798), serjeant-at-law and recorder of London, assisted in Thelwall's prosecution.

118. The 140 members of the Convention also known as Jacobins, so-called because they sat in the highest seats of the Convention. Their principal opponents were the more moderate Girondins (who had 160 deputies), many of whom were imprisoned and executed during the Terror. Between these groups were the 749 deputies of "the marsh" or "the plain," who usually followed the Mountain.

119. *Trials for High Treason . . . at the Old Bailey*, p. 330.

120. Ibid., p. 327.

121. Ibid. Adair said that the sans-culottes were "men, who when their murdering instruments could not fall fast enough to satiate their vengeance and thirst of blood, drove hundreds of miserable victims into a church, where they were all destroyed at the same time. —These were *Sans Culottes!*"

122. John Thelwall, *Political Lectures, No. 1: On the Moral Tendency of a System of Spies and Informers* (1794).

123. Ibid., p. 34.

124. *Second Report of the Committee of Secrecy*, p. 26.

125. *Authentic Copy of a Petition Praying for a Reform in Parliament*, p. 8.

126. In 1794, Pitt made eleven new barons: Clinton, Clive, Upper-Ossony, Mulgrave, Westcot, Mendip, Bradford, Selsey, Dundas, Curzon, and Pelham.

127. Montesquieu, *Spirit of the Laws*, p. 120.

128. John Taylor.

129. Thomas Holcroft (1745–1809): radical dramatist and novelist, close friend of William Godwin; tried shortly before Thelwall.

130. *Parliamentary Register* 40 (1795), 4–12.

131. But Stanhope, at least, lauded the verdict. See ibid., pp. 26–27.

The Tribune . . . Volume 1

1. *The Tribune* 1:12–19. From the lecture "On the Proper Means of Averting National Calamities."

2. Alexander Wedderburn (1733–1805), Baron Loughborough: as Lord Chancellor, 1793–1801, vigorously prosecuted sedition trials.

3. Charles Jenkinson (1727–1808), first Earl of Liverpool: president of the Board of Trade.

4. Colonel Mack was the Austrian Quartermaster-General who came to Britain in February 1794 and thereafter promoted the Austrian Court's interests in schemes for a restoration of the monarchy in France.

5. In Greek myth, Tantalus offended the gods and was sentenced to stand up to his neck in water in Hades without being able to drink it, and to have hanging over his head fruits that the wind blew away when he tried to pluck them.

6. John Buchanan, *A General View of the Fisheries of Great Britain* (1794), pp. 62–71.

7. See 1 Kings 17.

8. Charles James Fox (1749–1806): leader of radical Whigs and Burke's chief opponent in Parliament in the mid-1790s.

9. *The Tribune* 1:34–41.

10. Thomas Walker, *A Review of Some of the Political Events Which Have Occurred in Manchester, During the Last Five Years* (1794), p. 160.

11. The stamp duty on newspapers was raised in 1796 from 2d. to 3½d. These "taxes on knowledge" prevented many of the poor from reading newspapers and pamphlets. Stamp and paper duties and the tax on advertisements were not repealed until 1855–56.

12. A meeting of some 3,000 merchants and bankers was held on 5 December 1792, at which links between British reformers and France were condemned and the loyalty to the constitution of the commercial classes was loudly proclaimed. See *The Times*, 6 December 1792, p. 3, and *Declaration of the Merchants, Bankers, Traders, and Other Inhabitants of London* (1793).

13. *The Tribune* 1:62–70.

14. Joseph Gerrald, *A Convention the Only Means of Saving Us from Ruin* (1793), p. 1.

15. Ibid., p. 2.

16. British troops commanded by the king's second son, the Duke of York, took Valenciennes on 28 July 1793.

17. Francis II (1768–1835) became the last emperor of the Holy Roman Empire in 1792.

18. Augustus, Duke of York, was compelled to retreat from Dunkirk after his defeat at Hondschoote in September 1793.

19. Gerrald, *Convention the Only Means of Saving Us*, pp. 74–75.

20. By the Manning of the Navy Act (35 Geo. 3, c. 34), e.g., justices were empowered to enlist forcibly all "able-bodied, idle, and disorderly persons, who cannot upon examination prove themselves to exercise and industriously follow some lawful trade or employment or have some substance sufficient for their support and maintenance." This remained in force until 1871.

21. Habeas corpus was suspended in May 1794.

22. Word apparently missing in printed text.

23. 33 Geo. 3 c. 4, placed aliens under supervision and gave the Secretary of State power to remove them from the kingdom if necessary.

24. Word apparently missing in printed text.

25. *The Tribune* 1:147–63.

26. A general debt here to Godwin's ideas about universal benevolence is evident. See esp. Godwin, *Enquiry Concerning Political Justice*, bk. 4, chap. 10.

27. These lectures were delivered at the Beaufort Buildings in the Strand.

28. Charles VI (1685–1740): Holy Roman Emperor from 1711.

29. Augustus Caesar (63 B.C.–A.D. 14) defeated Marcus Antonius (83–30 B.C.) at Actium (31 B.C.).

30. The reference is to a dispute over an English ship laden with furs that was seized by Spain off Vancouver Island in 1789. The affair, which nearly resulted in war between the two countries, was settled by treaty in late 1790.

31. To clapperclaw, to scold.

32. See infra, p. 96.

33. Edmund Burke (1729–97): prominent Whig MP, sympathetic to American colonists' demands but a vehement opponent of the French Revolution; best known for his *Reflections on the Revolution in France* (1790).

34. William Windham (1750–1810): MP, eventually Secretary of War; friend of Burke; leading anti-Jacobin.

35. The Bastille was stormed on 14 July 1789, when it was found to have only seven inmates. The famous prison had often been used to house opponents of the government and hence became a powerful symbol of the ancien régime.

36. The Luxembourg Palace in Paris served as a prison during the Jacobin Terror. Thomas Paine, among others, was incarcerated there.

37. Part of Thelwall's pretrial imprisonment in 1794 was in Newgate Prison.

38. Maximilien Robespierre (1758–94): prominent revolutionary and member of the Jacobin Club, best known for his defense of revolutionary dictatorship.

39. Holland was conquered by France in late 1794.

40. Under Grand Duke Ferdinand, Tuscany joined the coalition against France in 1793, but soon made peace with the French, who occupied it in 1799. See *The Annual Register . . . for the Year 1795* (1800), pp. 221–22.

41. Bertrand Barère de Vieuzac (1755–1841): member of the Committee of Public Safety arrested during the Thermidor reaction with Jacques-Nicolas Billaud-Varenne (1756–1819) and Jean-Marie Collot d'Herbois (1749–96).

42. Marc-Guillaume-Alexis Vadier (1736–1828) was president of the Committee of General Security.

43. A department south of the Loire where revolt occurred in March 1793 when authorities attempted to levy troops.

44. The Committee of Public Safety was formed in April 1793 by election from the National Convention, to root out enemies of the revolution. During the Terror (September 1793–July 1794), it exercised virtual dictatorial power.

45. Sir Michael Foster (1689–1763), eighteen years a judge on the King's bench.

46. The well-being of the people is the supreme law. Sir Michael Foster, *A Report of Some Proceedings on the Commission for the Trial of the Rebels in the Year 1746*, 3rd ed. (1792), p. 382.

47. Ibid., pp. 382–83.

48. Thelwall's mother died during his imprisonment.

49. *The Tribune* 1:222–36.

50. This doctrine was widely associated with Godwin's *Enquiry Concerning Political Justice*; see bk. 2, chap. 2.

51. The term "Whig" was originally applied to mid-seventeenth-century Scottish Presbyterians.

52. Godwin, *Enquiry Concerning Political Justice*, 1:84.

53. In this sense, both Godwin and Thelwall clearly understood gratitude as an essentially feudal

virtue that underpinned dependency and patronage. Thelwall follows Godwin's interpretation of utilitarianism closely in arguing this case.

54. Banking and mercantile center of London from the Middle Ages onward.

55. Telemon was king of Salamis, and one of the Argonauts, the lesser Ajax, son of the king of Locris.

56. John Foulkes, a Chancery Lane solicitor.

57. John Horne Tooke (1736–1812): philologist and political reformer.

58. Thomas Hardy (1752–1832): radical shoemaker, and founder of the London Corresponding Society.

59. William Bentinck (1738–1809), third Duke of Portland: Whig MP, twice Prime Minister, Home Secretary from 1749 to 1801, and hence responsible for implementing the Treason and Sedition Acts.

60. George John Spencer (1758–1834), second Earl: First Lord of the Admiralty, 1794–1800.

61. William Wentworth Fitzwilliam (1748–1833): "old Whig" who sided with Pitt after the outbreak of the French Revolution; joined the government in 1794, becoming Lord Lieutenant in Ireland.

62. See *Parliamentary History of England* 31 (1818), col. 1348.

63. William Hayley, "An Epistle on History; in Three Epistles to Edward Gibbon," in *Poems and Plays*, 6 vols. (1788), 2:43.

64. Niccolò Machiavelli (1469–1527): Italian statesman and political theorist; author most notably of *The Prince* and the *Discourses on Livy*.

65. Following its invasion by France in 1794, Holland became a republic on 16 May 1795.

66. For the initial pronouncements of the Dutch republic, see *The Times*, 30 May 1795, p. 3.

67. Doggerbank was the naval victory by Holland over Britain in 1781. The Stadholder William V (1748–1806), oft proclaimed a "traitor" for his weakness and ineptitude during a period of lengthy wars, was at least guilty of negligence toward the navy, if not worse.

68. The liberal, pro-French Patriot party was driven from office by an invading Prussian army in 1787.

69. *Annual Register . . . 1795*, pp. 213–14; on the plan of the new constitution, see *The Times*, 18 June 1795, p. 3.

70. The Brissotines, or Girondins, were the moderate faction in the early Convention (1791–93) who were purged by the Jacobins.

71. In April 1792, Prussia allied itself with the Habsburg empire against France. By the Treaty of Basel (5 April 1795), Prussia made peace with the French republic and recognized French possessions on the left bank of the Rhine and in the United Provinces.

72. Spain allied with France in 1796, while the King of Sardinia, in defeat, renounced his Austrian alliance on 28 April.

73. Friedrich Wilhelm II (1744–97), King of Prussia 1786–97.

74. Charles Stanhope (1753–1816), third Earl: radical Whig MP friendly with Pitt until the French Revolution; chairman of Revolution Society, to which Price's famous speech was delivered. Opposed suspension of habeas corpus and became known as "Citizen Stanhope."

75. On 4 April 1794, Stanhope brought forward a motion "against any interference in the internal government of France," which so incensed his fellow peers that it was ordered expunged from the journals of the House (*Parliamentary History of England*, 21 [1818], cols. 141–50, 1130–44). It was printed as *Earl Stanhope: The Speech in the House of Peers on His Motion to Prevent His Majesty's Ministers from Interfering with the Internal Government of France* (1794). Stanhope repeated the motion in 1795 (see *Parliamentary History of England* 21 [1818], cols. 141–50, 1130–44).

76. The Brunswick declaration of 25 July 1792, in name of Karl Wilhelm Ferdinand, second Duke of Brunswick and the leader of the Prussian and Austrian armies, described the allies' aims as restoring order and the monarchy in France and threatened the destruction of Paris if Louis were harmed.

77. The Duke married his English second cousin, Augusta (1737–1813), the eldest daughter of the Prince of Wales.

78. In Ben Jonson's *Every Man in His Humour*, Captain Bobadil is a braggart and coward who also takes himself too seriously.

79. Niccolò Machiavelli, *The Works of Nicholas Machiavel*, trans. Ellis Farneworth, 2nd ed., 4 vols. (1775), 2:259.

80. See infra, p. 130–31.

81. Machiavelli, *Works*, 2:259.

82. Ibid., p. 332.

83. Georges-Jacques Danton (1759–94): lawyer, prominent Jacobin, and leading member of the Committee of Public Safety.

84. Robespierre organized a revolutionary religion in order to establish the Reign of Virtue and in 1794 acted as grand pontiff at a great celebration of the Feast of the Supreme Being.

85. Shakespeare, *Henry IV, Part Two* 1.1.160.

86. See Machiavelli, *Works*, 2:413–14.

87. Ibid.

88. See Shakespeare, *Macbeth* 3.4.138.

89. Lucie-Simplice-Camille-Benoît Desmoulins (1760–94): lawyer, anticlerical republican, and revolutionary journalist.

90. Jacques-René Hébert (1757–94): anticlerical revolutionary, journalist, leader of the Paris sans-culottes.

91. Machiavelli, *Works*, 2:416.

92. Ibid., pp. 414–15.

93. Trophime-Gérard (1751–1830), Marquis de Lally-Tollendal: deputy to the Estates-General and National Assembly, fled to England in 1792.

94. Victor-François (1718–1804), Duc de Broglie: counterrevolutionary commander.

95. See *Pièces Justicatives, Contenant Différentes Motions de M. le Comte de Lally-Tollendall* (1789), p. 84; and, generally, Lally-Tollendal, *The Dream of an Englishman Faithful to His King and Country* (1793).

96. Slaughter of royalists and constitutionalists by the Commune of Paris from 2 September to 6 September 1792, instigated by the fear that the approaching Prussian army aimed to restore the monarchy.

97. Memmay, Seigneur of Quincy and a councillor at the Dijon parlement, was denounced in the Estates-General on 24 July 1789 for this deed and went into exile.

98. Gerrald was sentenced to be transported to Botany Bay for his role in the British Convention at Edinburgh in 1793.

99. Crimping was the practice of deploying impressment agents to entice the unwary into forced naval service.

100. *Parliamentary Register* 37 (1794), 325.

101. These were all agents and informers employed by the Treasury to watch the London Corresponding Society, or policemen. John Groves was a solicitor; John Taylor was a gentleman; James Walsh was a Bow Street officer; Henry Alexander was a linen-draper; George Lynham was an ironmonger; Thomas Upton was a watchmaker.

102. Antoine-Joseph Santerre (1752–1809), French general.

103. Francisco de Miranda (1750–1816), revolutionary general.

104. François-Christophe Kellermann (1735–1820), French general.

105. The Society for Constitutional Information, founded by Major John Cartwright and others in 1780.

106. The Rev. William Jackson (1737?–95), tried for treason in 1795, had been sent by Pitt on a secret mission to France prior to Louis XVI's trial. William Wentworth Fitzwilliam had been

appointed Lord Lieutenant of Ireland by Pitt but served only a few weeks because he failed to follow Pitt's instructions about leaving supporters of the government in office. Robert Watt (d. 1794), an Edinburgh wine merchant tried for treason and executed, had offered information about the Scottish reformers to the government.

107. "Rule of Three" particularly refers to Pitt's Triple Alliances—first of Britain, Prussia, and Holland, formed in 1788, then of Russia, Austria, and Britain against France, formed in 1795.

108. For the debate, see *Parliamentary Register* 41 (1795), 245ff.

109. Martinique had been captured in 1794, but Guadalupe was lost again to the French. Britain took St. Lucia, St. Vincent, and Grenada in May–June 1796.

110. See Jean-Gabriel-Maurice Rocques de Montgaillard, *State of France in May 1794* (1794), p. 9.

The Tribune . . . Volume 2

1. *The Tribune* 2:1–27.

2. "Justice," which follows in the printed version, is removed in Thelwall's ms. correction.

3. See William Fleetwood, *Chronicon Preciosum* (1745), p. 39.

4. David Hume (1711–76), Scottish historian and philosopher.

5. David Hume, *History of England*, 13 vols. (1793–94), 8:346–47.

6. Under Elizabeth, an act was passed prescribing a workday of 12 hours, with 2½ hours' rest, or 9½ hours' labor in total. Working from early morning until sunset was common.

7. William Nicholson was the author of *A Dictionary of Chemistry*, 2 vols. (1795).

8. Frederick North (1732–92), second Earl of Guildford: Chancellor of the Exchequer and subsequently First Lord of the Treasury, 1767–82, renowned for opposition to the American colonists' demands.

9. In June 1795, Britain landed a force of exiled French noblemen on the peninsula of Quiberon in Brittany; they were quickly massacred by General Hoche. The Chouans were French royalist insurgents intermittently rebellious in Brittany from 1792 to 1799.

10. Doubtless William Godwin is primarily meant.

11. William Pitt the Elder (1708–78), first Earl of Chatham, secretary of state, 1756–61.

12. Food riots were common in 1795, with stocks being frequently distributed and a "fair price" given to the seller.

13. Punchinello, or Punch, was the main character in a puppet show of Italian origin.

14. The Corn Laws regulated the import and export of grain. From 1791, corn could be imported when the domestic price rose to 54s.

15. A 10 percent tax on all produce to support the church was levied from the year 787. This became a stable charge in 1926.

16. Famous Jesuit school in northern France, often named as a center of international Catholic conspiracy. Burke was not, however, among its students.

17. William Pitt. The title of "Prime Minister" was not yet commonly in use.

18. Charles James Fox.

19. *Parliamentary History of England* 31 (1818), col. 444.

20. A dispute between Britain and the United States concerning the northern boundary of Florida was settled in 1795 by fixing the line at 31 degrees north latitude.

21. British subsidies to her allies totaled more than £2,000,000 in 1794, of which £1,226,000 was voted for Prussia in April 1794. Prussia nonetheless made peace with France in April 1795.

22. Sir Brook Watson (1735–1807): London MP; later Lord Mayor 1796–98.

23. After the new Polish constitution in May 1791, which aimed to deprive Russia of a right to interfere in her affairs, Poland was invaded by a large Russian army and in 1793 was partitioned again.

24. Catherine, Empress of Russia.

25. Izmail, in Turkey, held a fortress that was stormed by the Russian general Aleksandr Suvorov in 1790, when 38,000 Turks were massacred.

26. See *Parliamentary History of England* 31 (1818), cols. 437–42.

27. *The Tribune* 2:29–50.

28. Rachel Chiesly (d. 1745), wife of James Erskine, Lord Grange (1679–1754), who was imprisoned by her husband for seven years on St. Kilda. The story supposedly exemplifies the solidarity and secrecy of the Highland Jacobites.

29. "I have read history" is added in the printed text.

30. William Frend (1757–1841): reformer, Unitarian, and scientific writer.

31. William Frend, *Peace and Union Recommended to the Associated Bodies of Republicans and Anti-Republicans* (1793), p. 48.

32. See *The Peripatetic*, 3 vols. (1793), 1:143.

33. Shakespeare, *Hamlet* 1.4.91–92.

34. James Walsh was a Bow Street officer.

35. See Shakespeare, *Henry IV, Part Two* 4.7.25.

36. Britain's efforts to blockade France involved the seizure of ships from various nations, including the United States.

37. This is not so surprising. England was at war with France intermittently from 1740, and although a polite fiction of neutrality was sometimes maintained, undeclared acts of aggression on both sides were common. George II (1683–1760), King of England 1727–60, was not otherwise notoriously charitable.

38. *Report of the Committee, Appointed by the Board of Agriculture, to Take into Consideration the State of Waste Lands and Common Fields* (1795), p. 15.

39. Ibid.

40. From 1761 to 1801, some 2,000 acts converted 3.2 million acres of common lands to private use.

41. John of Gaunt (1340–99), Duke of Lancaster: fourth son of Edward III and an unpopular military leader who was reportedly a target in the 1381 Peasants' Revolt. See Frend, *Peace and Union*, p. 48.

42. Soame Jenyns (1704–87): political writer.

43. William Tooke (1744–1820), best known as a historian of Russia.

44. William de Grey (1719–81), first Baron Walsingham, Lord Chief Justice, 1771–80.

45. Tooke was imprisoned in the Tower at the same time as Thelwall.

46. Tooke attacked the Speaker, Sir Fletcher Norton, anonymously in the *Public Advertiser* in 1774, and succeeded in getting an enclosure bill he opposed set aside as a result.

47. James Thomson, *Spring: A Poem* (1728), p. 15.

48. *The Tribune* 2:53–82.

49. William Dodd was executed in 1778 for having forged a check in the name of his patron, the Earl of Chesterfield, to whom he had offered to repay the money. Robert and Daniel Perreau were identical twins who borrowed money with falsified bonds and were executed in 1776.

50. Mythical founder-legislator of Sparta, who made landed property more equal and sought to suppress luxury.

51. Adapted from "An Essay on the Use of Riches," in *The Works of Alexander Pope*, 9 vols. (1751), 3:155.

52. Ibid., pp. 153–54.

53. Ibid., p. 154.

54. Richard Colley Wellesley (1760–1842), Earl of Mornington: Whig MP, friend of Pitt and Burke.

55. Edmund Spenser, *The Shepherd's Callender* (1732), p. 12.

56. A journeyman printer, John Morton was tried for treason in Edinburgh in January 1793. See *Complete Collection of State Trials* (1817), 23:7–26.

57. Oliver Goldsmith, *The Deserted Village: A Poem* (1793), p. 4.

58. In some areas, such as Moreton Say, Shropshire, the farming population halved and the number of laborers increased fourfold between 1680 and 1822, as a direct result of the consolidation of farms.

59. John Reeves (1752?–1829): King's printer, legal writer, and organizer of the Association for Preserving Liberty and Property Against Republicans and Levellers in 1792. Prosecuted in 1796 for his overly absolutist *Thoughts on the English Government*.

60. Agrarian laws of this type had been proposed by, among others, James Harrington (who wanted to limit landholdings to a value of £5,000 annually), James Burgh, and William Ogilvie.

61. According to Daniel 4:25ff., the Babylonian king became insane after his many conquests and took to eating grass.

62. "Merry Andrew" was a humorous physician during the reign of Henry VIII.

63. Thomas Paine (1737–1809), the most important radical writer of his generation; the reference is to *Rights of Man, Part the Second*, 9th ed. (1792), p. 106.

64. *The Tribune* 1:1–19.

65. After the defeat of Kosciuszko, Poland was partitioned for a third time in 1795, with Russia, Prussia, and Austria sharing what remained of Poland's territory.

66. The Second Anglo-Dutch War of commercial rivalry began in 1663 and lasted until 1667. A third Dutch War (1672–74) followed.

67. In 1787, the King of Prussia sent troops to the United Provinces to overturn the pro-French party there. The new regime then joined Prussia and Britain to guarantee Dutch security against France.

68. See *Parliamentary History of England* 31 (1818), cols. 437–42.

69. Andrzei Kosciuszko (1746–1817): Polish national hero and military leader who led the unsuccessful insurrection in 1794.

70. Aleksandr Suvorov (1729–1800): Russian general, active against France.

71. George III became increasingly ill from 1788 and was intermittently *non compos mentis* until his death in 1820.

72. E.g., [John Moore], *Three Letters to His Grace the Archbishop of Canterbury, on the Prayer for His Majesty's Recovery* (1788), p. 6.

73. Thomas Wentworth (1593–1641), first Earl of Strafford: executed in 1641 for conspiracy.

74. Charles-Alexandre de Calonne (1734–1802): former Controller-General of finances; Louis-Joseph, Prince de Condé (1736–1818), Charles-Philippe, Comte d'Artois (1757–1836).

75. John Beresford (1738–1805): Irish statesman and MP; close to Pitt.

76. Grenville (Foreign Affairs), Dundas (War), and Portland (Home Department)—to whom Thelwall refers and who headed the Whig faction that joined Pitt's government in July 1794.

77. The agricultural writer Arthur Young was appointed to the newly created Board of Agriculture in 1793 at an annual salary of £400 and a house.

78. Homer, *The Iliad*, trans. Alexander Pope, 6 vols. (1770), 5:169.

79. See William Wentworth Fitzwilliam, *A Letter from Earl Fitzwilliam* (1795) and *A Letter from a Venerated Nobleman* (1795).

80. *The Tribune* 2:209–35.

81. See Plato, *The Republic* 4.445.

82. See *Trials for High Treason . . . at the Old Bailey*, p. 379.

83. See John Wilde, *An Address to the Lately Formed Society of the Friends of the People* (1793).

84. See *Trials for High Treason . . . at the Old Bailey*, p. 314.

85. John Groves, a solicitor.

86. *The Proceedings in Cases of High Treason, . . . First Opened . . . Oct. 2, 1794* (1794), p. 248.

87. William II (c. 1056–1100), King of England 1087–1100, succeeded William the Conqueror.

88. See David Hume, *Essays and Treatises on Several Subjects*, 2 vols. (1793), 1:54–59.

89. *Memoirs and Proceedings of the Manchester Literary and Philosophical Society*, 5 vols. (1785–1802), 3:31–116.

90. Augustus Toplady (1740–78), theological writer.

91. See Augustus Toplady, *Free Thoughts on the Projected Application to Parliament, for the Abolition of Ecclesiastical Subscriptions* (1771), pp. 7–8.

92. Marie Antoinette (1755–93).

93. *The Works of the Rt. Hon. Edmund Burke*, 8 vols. (1792–1827), 3:68.

94. See Shakespeare, *Hamlet* 1.4.91–92.

95. Joel Barlow, *Advice to the Privileged Orders* (1792), and *The Conspiracy of Kings* (1792); Thomas Cooper, *A Reply to Mr. Burke's Invective* (1792); James Mackintosh, *Vindiciae Gallicae* (1791).

96. A royal proclamation against sedition was published on 22 May 1792.

97. Paine's *Rights of Man* was proscribed as a "seditious libel" upon the monarchy in December 1792.

98. William Frend was expelled from the University of Cambridge for writing a supposedly seditious pamphlet, *Peace and Union Recommended to the Associated Bodies of Republicans and Anti-Republicans* (1793).

99. William Winterbotham (1763–1829), Dissenting minister.

100. See Daniel Holt, *A Vindication of the Conduct and Principles of the Printer of the "Newark Herald"* (1794).

101. See Charles Lennox, *An Authentic Copy of the Duke of Richmond's Bill for Parliamentary Reform* (1783).

102. See *The Trial of Thomas Briellat* (1794), pp. 2–7.

103. The London physician William Hodgson served two years for this offense and was fined £200; see *The Case of William Hodgson* (1796).

104. John Frost (1750–1842), secretary to and a founder of the London Corresponding Society; removed from the roll of attorneys in 1793.

105. See *A Collection of State Trials* 22 (1817): col. 482.

106. Alfred the Great (849–99), Saxon King of Wessex 871–99.

107. For their part in the "British Convention," which met at Edinburgh in 1793, Thomas Muir, Thomas Fyshe Palmer, William Skirving, and Maurice Margarot were sentenced to be transported.

108. In July 1794, the Whigs who supported Pitt agreed to merge with the government, with the Duke of Portland becoming Secretary of State for the Home Department.

109. See *An Account of the Treason and Sedition, Committed by the London Corresponding Society* (1794).

110. The son of a Putney apothecary, Sir John W. Rose became Recorder in 1782.

111. See *The Times*, 30 September 1794, p. 2.

112. Sir James Mansfield (1733–1821), MP and later judge.

113. A heavy gambler, Fox inherited an Irish clerkship of the pells, worth £2,000 a year for life, from his brother in 1774. He sold it shortly thereafter.

114. John Harrison (1738–1811), Whig MP for Great Grimsby, 1780–96, and for Thetford, 1796–1806.

115. See *Parliamentary Register* 40 (1795), 373–74.

116. Helen Maria Williams (1762–1827), novelist.

117. See Helen Maria Williams, *Letters Containing a Sketch of the Politics of France*, 3 vols. (1796).

118. Richard Brothers (1757–1824), prophet arrested for treason in 1795. See *A Revealed Knowledge of the Prophecies and Times* (1794).

119. The phrase is Paine's. See *The Age of Reason* (1795), p. 59.

120. Ornamental farms.

121. See Genesis 9:25.

122. Polyphemus to Odysseus. See Homer, *The Odyssey*, bk. 9.

123. *The Tribune* 2:281–95.

124. Royal burghs were Scottish municipal corporations created by royal charter before 1707.

125. The Beaufort Buildings were situated in the Duchy of Lancaster, which comprised the former county palatine of Lancashire and certain other lands, including parts of London. It was managed by the Chancellor of the Duchy and had its own duchy court.

126. Possibly Robert Banks Jenkinson (1770–1828), MP, a member of the Commons' Secret Committee on Sedition.

127. Ireland was conquered by England progressively from the Normans, who landed in 1167, onward.

128. Exclusive inheritance by the eldest son.

129. John Dalrymple, *Memoirs of Great Britain and Ireland*, 3 vols. (1771–88), 1 (pt. 2):156–58.

130. Passed in 1673, the Test Act required all persons holding any office under the Crown to subscribe to the dogmas of the Church of England. The Corporation Act of 1661 enforced a similar requirement on corporation officers. Both were repealed in 1828.

131. Congregationalists, Baptists, Quakers, Unitarians, and others who could not accept the Thirty-Nine Articles of Belief of the Church of England.

132. Irish Catholics were prohibited from worshiping in public, holding offices in any of the learned professions, having guardianship of their own children, and, if they had landed estates, marrying Protestants. Catholic Emancipation did not occur until 1828.

133. Fitzwilliam became Lord Lieutenant in Ireland in December 1794.

134. George Ponsonby (1755–1817), who later became Lord Chancellor of Ireland, was at the time probably the best-known member of this family.

135. At this time, Giovanni Angelo Braschi (1717–99), Pius VI (1775–99).

136. Pius VI generally pursued a moderate policy toward revolutionary France. Thelwall probably refers to Pius's brief to Louis in July 1790, which upheld the King's right to renounce his throne though not to dispense with the church's property.

137. See Shakespeare, *Sonnets* 119.3.

138. The Defenders first emerged in 1784 but were greatly revived in 1793 in response to attempts to raise militia troops. Temporarily pacified in September 1795, they merged with the wider revolutionary movement in 1798.

139. In 1795, disturbances by "Defenders" were so serious that many were arrested and sent untried to serve in the fleet, which action was covered by an indemnity act in 1796. Thelwall probably refers to the 1795 trials of James Weldon and other Defenders. See Thomas MacNevin, *The Lives and Trials of Archibald Hamilton Rowan, the Rev. William Jackson, the Defenders, William Orr, Peter Finnerty, and Other Eminent Irishmen* (1846).

140. *The Tribune* 2:321–42.

141. Edward III (1312–77), King of England 1327–77.

142. Spenser, *Shepherd's Callendar*, p. 12.

143. Geoffrey Chaucer, *Matrimonial Scenes* (1750), p. 59.

144. Samuel Butler, *Hudibras: A Poem*, 2nd ed., 3 vols. (1758), 1:22.

145. David Davies (d. c. 1819).

146. David Davies, *The Case of the Labourers in Husbandry Stated and Considered* (1795), p. 6.

147. "Tare" was waste or deterioration of goods, as well as the percentage of value deducted for wrapping. "Tret" was an allowance of 4 lb. in 104 lb. on goods sold by weight, for the deduction of tare.

148. Oliver Goldsmith, *The Deserted Village* (1793), p. 4.

149. David Hume, *History of England*, 8 vols. (1789), 3:181–82.

150. See Edmund Burke, "Reflections on the Revolution in France," in *Works of the Rt. Hon. Edmund Burke*, 3:111.

The Tribune . . . Volume 3

1. *The Tribune* 3:17–36.
2. Hume, *Essays and Treatises*, 1:54–59.
3. Daniel Peacock (1767[8]–1840), political writer. See his *Consideration on the Structure of the House of Commons, and on the Plans of Parliamentary Reform Agitated at the Present Day* (1794), e.g., p. 32.
4. Hume, *Essays and Treatises*, 1:56.
5. George, Earl Macartney (1737–1806), was sent to China with a sumptuously equipped party in 1792 to enforce the protection of British subjects; he returned in 1794.
6. The notorious constituency of Old Sarum, the property of Lord Camelford, had about 300 inhabitants and about 11 electors.
7. George Rose (1749–1818): MP, then Clerk of the Parliament; intimate friend of Pitt.
8. Thomas Paine, *Rights of Man*, Part the Second, 9th ed. (1792), pp. 123–24.
9. David Davies, *The Case of the Labourers in Husbandry Stated and Considered* (1795), pp. 18, 65, 68–69.
10. Bishop William Fleetwood, *Chronicon Precisiosum; or, An Account of English Money, the Price of Corn, and Other Commodities, the Past 600 Years* (1707); Richard Burn, *The History of the Poor Laws* (1764), pp. 13–15, 130–32; Richard Price, *Observations on Reversionary Payments* (1771).
11. *The True Briton* (1792–1803) was a government-financed newspaper.
12. *The Tribune* 3:37–52.
13. Carl Bernhard Wadstrom (1746–99), antislavery agitator and colonization projector.
14. Carl Bernhard Wadstrom, *An Essay on Colonization* (1794–95), pp. 65–72.
15. Theseus was a possibly mythical friend of Heracles and founder of the Athenian state.
16. Solon (c. 640–c. 561 B.C.), Athenian poet and legislator.
17. See, e.g., Association for Preserving Liberty and Property Against Republicans and Levellers, *Association Papers*, 2 parts (1793).
18. The former chapel of St. Stephen's became the regular meeting place of the Commons after 1550.
19. The confidence of the mercantile orders in the government was clearly vital to the war effort. See *Declaration of the Merchants, Bankers, Traders* (1793).
20. For the 1793 debate on abolishing the slave trade, see *Parliamentary History of England* 30 (1817), cols. 948–53. This was resumed in 1794 (ibid., cols. 1139–49) and in 1796 (ibid., 32: cols. 737–64).
21. France abolished slavery in May 1791.
22. In 1754, two East India Company directors were returned to Parliament. By 1768, this had risen to thirteen, and thereafter several boroughs were bought up by nabobs. By 1790, some forty-five MPs were connected to the East India interest. In 1784, Warren Hastings, who was later impeached for misconduct, for example, bought a seat at West Looe for £4,000 for his erstwhile aide-de-camp, John Scott.
23. Guy Fawkes (1570–1606) attempted to blow up the Houses of Parliament in order to aid the cause of English Catholicism.
24. One of four MPs elected in the 1796 London poll was William Lushington (1776–1868), a prominent East India merchant.
25. *The Tribune* 3:183–200.
26. Edward Hyde (1609–74), first Earl of Clarendon: statesman, trusted adviser of Charles II in exile. George Monk, first Earl of Albemarle (1608–70): general under Cromwell.
27. On 13 February 1692, British soldiers led by Archibald Campbell attacked the Macdonalds of Glencoe, ostensibly for refusing to swear allegiance to William III.
28. William III (1650–1702), King of England 1689–1702.

29. The son of Demeter, Plutus was the Greek personification of wealth.

30. Obviously ironical, this sentence may also have been inserted to forestall further prosecutions of the lectures.

31. Known as Louis XVII (1785–95).

32. Bonaparte became emperor in 1804, and Louis XVIII was restored to the throne in 1818.

33. Thelwall here regards the "Gothic" liberties of Saxon Britain more favorably than in *Rights of Nature*.

34. Oliver Cromwell (1599–1658): MP, military leader against the monarchy during the civil war; Protector, or head of state, during the Interregnum.

35. Jean-Gabriel-Maurice, Comte de Montgaillard (1761–1841): counterrevolutionary writer.

36. Emmanuel-Joseph Sieyès (1748–1836): Abbé, radical politician, author of the famous pamphlet *Qu'est que c'est le Tiers Etat?* (1789), which argued for popular sovereignty.

37. Jean-Lambert Taillon (1767–1820): moderate revolutionary politician.

38. Louis-Joseph, Prince de Condé and Duc de Bourbon (1736–1818): anti-revolutionary émigré.

39. Probably a reference to Young's *Example of France, a Warning to Britain* (1793), contrasted to, e.g., his *Political Essays* (1772).

40. E.g., Maurice Montgaillard, *Necessité de la Guerre et Dangers de la Paix* (1794).

41. Napoleon Bonaparte rose to power in 1799 after a highly successful military career.

42. See, e.g., Montesquieu, *Spirit of the Laws*, 1.2.

43. This refers to the Edinburgh treason trials of 1793, at which several prominent radicals were found guilty of treason and transported.

44. *Plutarch's Lives*, 5 vols. (1771), 3:470–71.

45. *The Tribune* 3:263–77.

46. Thelwall published a broadsheet with this title in October 1795.

47. A bill-sticker named Jobson was seized near the Royal Exchange for posting an advertisement for Thelwall's lectures.

48. Hardy was freed on the sixth day of his trial, on 3 November 1794. On the meeting of 5 November 1795, see *Memoir of Thomas Hardy* (1832), p. 55, and *Oracle and Public Advertiser*, 6 November 1795, p. 3. At the end of this meeting, most participants retired to Thelwall's lecture.

49. Because George III was frequently incapacitated by porphyria.

50. *Oracle and Public Advertiser*, 30 October 1795, p. 4.

51. On 29 October 1795, the King's carriage was struck by a stone on its way to Parliament. A large crowd had gathered, shouting "Peace, peace!" and "Down with George!"

52. The London Corresponding Society held a large meeting at Copenhagen Fields on 26 October 1795.

53. Loughborough drew this connection. See *Parliamentary History of England* 32 (1818), cols. 205–6.

54. See Thelwall, *The Speech of John Thelwall, . . . October 26, 1795* (1795).

55. Wat Tyler (d. 1381), leader of the Peasants' Revolt of 1381.

56. During the reign of Charles V (1364–80), France was repeatedly ravaged by English, Navarrese, and Breton armies.

57. See *The Times*, 31 October 1795, p. 3.

"Sober Reflections . . ."

1. The title of the work clearly plays on Thelwall's attempt to portray Burke's *Reflections* as an intemperate production. Burke's *Letter to a Noble Lord* (1795) attacks English aristocrats with revolutionary sympathies, notably the Duke of Bedford.

2. *The Political Works of William Collins* (1765), p. 82.

3. Burke was deeply upset by the death of his son, Richard Burke, in August 1794.

4. Shakespeare, *Henry IV, Part One* 4.3.34–37.

5. Presumably a reference to Burke's notorious use of the phrase "swinish multitude" (*Works of Edmund Burke*, 3:114).

6. Reference uncertain, but probably *Richard III*, acts 4–5, is misquoted.

7. The reference is partly to Godwin's rejection of gratitude in favor of universal benevolence. See William Godwin, *Enquiry Concerning Political Justice*, 2 vols. (1793; 2nd ed., 1796), bk. 2, chap. 2.

8. In the biblical story (Judges 15–16), Sampson is deprived of his great strength when the seductress Delilah cuts his hair.

9. The so-called "Two Acts" passed in December 1795 were "A Bill for the More Effectually Preventing Seditious Meetings and Assemblies" and "A Bill for the Safety and Preservation of His Majesty's Person Against Treasonable Practices and Attempts."

10. *Poetical Works of William Collins* (1794), pp. 527–28.

11. Thomas More, *Utopia* (1516; 1795 ed.), pp. 54–60.

12. Thomas Paine, *Rights of Man, Part the Second*, pp. 147–48.

13. Servius Tullius: semi-legendary Roman king, sixth in the line of succession, after Romulus.

14. Licinius Stolo helped restrict tenancy of public lands to 310 acres in 367 B.C.

15. Tiberius Sempronius Gracchus and Gaius Sempronius Gracchus passed agrarian laws in 133 B.C. limiting the amount of public land an individual could hold.

16. Godwin, *Enquiry Concerning Political Justice*, bk. 8. This is a partial retaliation for Godwin's attack on the supposedly uproarious tendency of Thelwall's lectures. See infra, p. 382.

17. Thomas Steele (1753–1823): MP and close friend of Pitt.

18. Humphrey Stafford (1402–60), first Duke of Buckingham: fought in Flanders and also acted against Jack Cade and his rebels.

19. Edmund Burke, "Reflections on the Revolution in France" (1790), in his *Works*, 3:191–208.

20. See ibid., p. 111.

21. Appius Claudius Caecus (late 4th–early 3rd century B.C.): Roman patrician who despite being a reformer was accused of wanting to reinforce the power of the older nobility (see Dionysius of Halicarnassus, *The Roman Antiquities of Dionysius Halicarnassus*, bk. 6).

22. Charles Watson Wentworth (1730–82), second Marquis of Rockingham and twice Prime Minister. He lent Burke as much as £30,000, and before his death ordered the receipts destroyed.

23. Dionysius of Halicarnassus, *Roman Antiquities*, 2:222–96.

24. This was introduced in 1788 because of George III's severe illness.

25. *The Speeches of the Rt. Hon. Edmund Burke*, 4 vols. (1816), vol. 3, p. 409.

26. *The Trial of Thomas Hardy, High Treason*, 4:238.

27. Sir John Mitford (1748–1830), first Baron Redesdale: prosecutor at many of the reformers' trials, Attorney-General after 1799.

28. Juvenal (fl. early 2nd century B.C.), the greatest Roman satirical poet.

29. Quintus Horatius Flaccus (65–8 B.C.), Roman poet.

30. George William Fitz-Hatton (1747–1823), fifth Earl of Winchelsea.

31. John Fane (1759–1841), tenth Earl of Westmorland: Lord-Lieutenant of Ireland and friend of Pitt.

32. Francis Russell (1765–1802), fifth Duke of Bedford: parliamentary reformer and friend of Fox.

33. Shakespeare, *Macbeth* 1.7.33–34.

34. Shakespeare, *Hamlet* 3.4.145.

35. John Henry Manners (1778–1857), fifth Duke of Rutland.

36. Charles Lennox (1764–1819), fourth Duke of Richmond.

37. James Lowther (1736–1802), Earl of Lonsdale.

38. Charles Jenkinson (1727–1808) was first Earl Liverpool and first Baron Hawkesbury.

39. Sir Archibald Macdonald (1747–1826) became Lord Chief Baron of the Exchequer in 1793 and was a judge at Thelwall's trial.

40. Shakespeare, *As You Like It* 3.7.144.

41. John Russell (1486?–1555), first Earl of Bedford: diplomat, soldier, and loyal servant of Henry VIII. He acquired his property partly through marriage but largely through royal grants of lands forfeited by the King's political and religious opponents.

42. William Bentinck (1649–1709), first Earl of Portland: commenced as a page to William III, Prince of Orange, and became immensely wealthy during William's English rule.

43. The House of Nassau was an independent duchy dating from the twelfth century, one member of which was William III of England.

44. Surname and dynasty founded by Henry VII in the fifteenth century.

45. Orestes, son of Agamemnon, was driven to madness by the Furies for having killed his own mother.

46. Lord William Russell (1629–83), "the patriot": country party politician.

47. In the House of Lords, Bedford and Lauderdale attacked Burke's receipt of a pension. See *Parliamentary Register* 32 (1818), col. 263.

48. See [Alain René Le Sage], *The Adventures of Gil Blas of Santillane* (1759).

49. By the Convention of Pilnitz, signed in August 1791, Emperor Leopold II and the Prussian King Friedrich Wilhelm II agreed to cooperate against France.

50. In the debate on the Alien Bill (28 December 1792), Burke threw a dagger to the floor of the House of Commons, exclaiming, "This is what you are to gain by an alliance with France."

51. William Devaynes (c. 1730–1809) was a pro-government MP active in the Society for Promoting Liberty and Property Against Republicans and Levellers. Luke Ideson was a loyalist London magistrate who assisted Devaynes at a meeting supporting the Two Acts on 14 November 1795 (*The History of Two Acts* [1796], p. 194).

52. Possibly a reference to Shakespeare, *Macbeth* 1.3.135.

53. Machiavelli, *Works*, 3:18–23.

54. On the meeting, see *The Times*, 6 December 1792, p. 4.

55. The Grocers' Hall meeting reaffirmed the loyalty of a select group of London merchants. See *The Times*, 3 December 1795, p. 4.

56. *Poetical Works of William Collins*, p. 527.

57. The bishop was Samuel Horsley (1733–1806). See his comments on the treason bill, in *The Speeches in Parliament of Samuel Horsley* (1813), pp. 167–83. Loughborough was Alexander Wedderburn (1733–1805). For his views on the treason bill, see, e.g., *Parliamentary History of England* 32 (1818), col. 256.

58. See, e.g., *Parliamentary Register* 45 (1796), 197–200.

59. Georges-Auguste Couthon (1755–94), member of the Committee of Public Safety.

60. Antoine-Quentin Fouquier-Tinville (1746–95), public prosecutor during the Terror.

61. Guislain-François-Joseph Le Bon (1765–95), member of the National Convention best known for suppression of counterrevolutionaries.

62. Marie-Jean-Antoine-Nicolas de Caritat (1743–94), Marquis de Condorcet: revolutionary philosopher and moderate deputy in the Convention.

63. Maximin Isnard (1751–1830), merchant and Girondin deputy.

64. François-Alexandre, Duke of La Rochefoucauld-Liancourt (1747–1827): reformer, philanthropist, and deputy to the National Assembly.

65. Jean-Marie Roland de la Platière (1743–93): writer and minister of the interior in the early years of the revolution.

66. Jean-Jacques Rousseau (1712–78), French philosopher and political theorist.

67. *An Appeal to Impartial Posterity, by Citizeness Roland*, pt. 2 (1795), 10–11.

68. After Claudian (d. c. 408), the last great poet of the pagan classical world, best known for his savage and extravagant panegyrics on the enemies of Emperor Honorius.

69. See, e.g., *Parliamentary Register* 43 (1796), 267–68, 499–501.

70. John Thelwall, *Political Lectures, No. 1: On the Moral Tendency of a System of Spies and Informers* (1794), p. 26.

71. See Alexander Pope, *Essay on Man* (1733), 3.103.

72. John Milton, *Paradise Lost*, 2nd ed. (1674), 1.330.

73. Publius Vergilius Maro (70–19 B.C.), Roman poet.

74. E.g., by Pitt's attempt to embargo all French commerce.

75. Influential Parisian revolutionary society, 1790–95.

76. See Robert Woolsey, *Reflections upon Reflections, Including Some Observations upon the Constitution and Laws of England* (1795), p. 76.

77. Government-supported newspapers. The *Times* did not become completely independent until 1805.

78. Milton, *Paradise Lost* 1.536.

79. John Thelwall, *Political Lectures, Volume the First* (1795), pp. xii–xiii.

80. Burke, *"Reflections on the Revolution in France,"* 3:180.

81. Francis Bacon, *Lord Bacon's Essays; or, Counsels Moral and Civil*, 2 vols. (1720), 1:82.

82. According to legend, Cadmus sowed the teeth of a serpent he had slain, from which sprang a race of men who fought each other until all were dead.

83. As a hawk, to swoop down.

84. See Milton, *Paradise Lost* 3.710.

85. *Works of the Rt. Hon. Edmund Burke*, 3:277.

86. Ibid., p. 77.

87. Arthur Young, *Travels During the Years 1787, 1788, and 1789*, 2 vols. (1793), e.g., 1:85.

88. Probably a reference to the famous "man in the iron mask," possibly Count Mattioli, who died in 1703.

89. See Machiavelli, *Works*, 3:8–9.

90. See Machiavelli, *Works* (Farneworth, 2nd ed.), 3:8–9.

91. Montesquieu, *Spirit of the Laws*, pp. 12–13.

92. Ibid., p. 120.

93. Thomas Powis (1743–1800), MP for Northamptonshire 1774–97: member of the Committee of Secrecy, which investigated the reform societies.

94. William Godwin, *Considerations on Lord Grenville's and Mr. Pitt's Bills* (1795), esp. pp. 16–22.

95. James Maitland (1759–1839), eighth Earl of Lauderdale: radical MP who strongly opposed the Treasonable Practices Bill. For the debate in both houses on these bills, see *Parliamentary History of England* 32 (1818), cols. 244–555.

96. Supra, p. 344.

97. Oliver Goldsmith, *Deserted Village* (1793), p. 14.

98. This clause was clearly chiefly directed at Thelwall himself.

99. The second edition here inserted an advertisement for Thelwall's lectures on classical history.

100. Numa Pompilius: legendary successor of Romulus as second King of Rome, who supposedly received counsel from the nymph Egeria. Socrates was inspired by his demon. Saint Dunstan (924–88) is often portrayed holding the devil's nose with a pair of tongs.

101. The other main responses were Allan Macleod, *A Warm Reply to Mr. Burke's Letter* (1796); William Miles, *A Letter to Henry Duncombe . . . on the Subject of the Very Extraordinary Pamphlet, Lately Addressed by Mr. Burke to a Noble Lord* (1796); George Neale, *A Letter to the Rt. Hon. Edmund Burke, in Answer to a Letter Respecting the Duke of Bedford* (1796); Thomas Street, *A Vindication of the Duke of Bedford's Attack on Mr. Burke's Pension* (1796); Thomas Townsend, *A*

Summary Defence of the Rt. Hon. Edmund Burke (1796); Gilbert Wakefield, *A Reply to the Letter of Edmund Burke, Esq., to a Noble Lord* (1796).

102. Erasmus Darwin, *The Botanic Garden: A Poem*, 3rd ed. (1795), p. 191.

"The Rights of Nature . . ."

1. *Sober Reflections on the Seditious and Inflammatory Letter of the Rt. Hon. Edmund Burke* (1796). The present work responds to Burke's *Letters on the Prospect of a Regicide Peace* (1796).

2. See *Letter from the Rt. Hon. Edmund Burke*, p. 3. The reference is to the Hussite leader and Bohemian general Jan Zizka (c. 1376–1424), who wanted a drum to be made from his skin, after his death, to frighten his enemies.

3. For his services to the government, Burke received an annual pension of £4,000 in 1794.

4. Heretics were burned at the stake at Smithfield under Mary Tudor.

5. Edmund Burke, *Works*, 4:402.

6. James Adair (d. 1798), serjeant-at-law and recorder of London; assisted in Thelwall's prosecution.

7. Sir John Scott (1751–1838), first Baron Eldon: MP, Attorney-General 1793–99, responsible for fashioning the Treasonable Practices and Seditious Meetings acts.

8. John Mitford (1748–1830), first Baron Redesdale: MP, judge, and Solicitor-General following Sir John Scott in 1793; played a key role in many treason prosecutions.

9. Polybius, *The General History of Polybius*, ed. [B.] Hampton, 3rd ed., 4 vols. (1772–73).

10. Dionysius of Halicarnassus, *Roman Antiquities*.

11. Thomas Paine, *Dissertation on First Principles of Government* (1795), p. 18.

12. Burke, *Works*, 1:120–34.

13. "The things, we know, are neither rich nor rare, / But wonder how the devil they got there?" (Alexander Pope, *An Epistle from Mr. Pope, to Dr. Arbuthnot* [1734], p. 9).

14. Shakespeare, *Hamlet* 2.2.211–12.

15. Edmund Burke, *Thoughts on the Prospects of a Regicide Peace* (1796); Edmund Burke, *Two Letters Addressed to a Member of the Present Parliament, on the Prospects for Peace with the Regicide Directory of France* (1796).

16. Gallant knight.

17. Here the second edition adds: "—the placemen and the pensioners; the Burkes and the Reeveses—unprincipled sophists hired with prodigal portions of the general plunder, to abuse, calumniate, and destroy the poor wretches whom this plunder reduces to starving beggary."

18. As one of the six labors imposed on him by Eurystheus in order to win immortality, Heracles was required to clean the stables of Augeas, King of Elis.

19. See Matthew 27:51.

20. Endite: indict.

21. George John Althorpe (1758–1834), second Earl Spencer, a yeomanry colonel for thirty-four years who was first Lord of the Admiralty from 1794 to 1800.

22. See Moses Mendelssohn, *Phaedon; or, The Death of Socrates*, trans. Charles Cullen (1789), appendix, p. 23.

23. During the Rule of the Thirty (401–403 B.C.E.).

24. Refusing to flee, Socrates drank the hemlock in 399 B.C.E.

25. Robert Bisset (1759–1809), Burke's first biographer, an opponent of democracy.

26. Robert Bisset, *Sketch of Democracy* (1796), p. 127.

27. A Derby physician, Peter Crompton (d. 1833) received 560 out of 2,841 votes cast. See *The Times*, 31 May 1796, p. 5.

28. Robert Smith (1752–1838), who took 1,210 votes.

29. Plural voting was permitted in some cases (e.g., where property was held in two electoral districts).

30. Bartlett Gurney (1756–1803), of the Quaker banking family.

31. Gurney, who received 1,076 out of 3,867 votes, was opposed by Henry Hobart, who received 1,622 votes, and William Windham, with 1,159. On the election, see The Times, 28 May 1796, p. 3.

32. See, e.g., The Courier, 21 November 1796, p. 3.

33. Here the second edition adds: "for distracting the world with the ravings of bedlam, and the filthy loquacity of the stews, in favour of aristocratic despotism, and beating the hide of old Zisca, 'to animate Europe to eternal battle.'"

34. Exodus 21:24.

35. Shakespeare, Macbeth 1.7.10.

36. Beaconsfield was Burke's residence.

37. See Burke, Letter to a Noble Lord, p. 18.

38. See Shakespeare, Henry IV, Part Two 2.4.160–61.

39. J. Owen, of 168 Piccadilly, a bookseller.

40. Burke, Works, 4:402.

41. Burke was partly raised as a Catholic and was often thought to hold Catholic sympathies.

42. Aeolus was the Greek god of winds who lived on the floating island of Aeolia.

43. See, e.g., Deuteronomy 28:12.

44. Burke, Letter to a Noble Lord, p. 74.

45. Burke, Works, 3:10–12.

46. Whether or not, despite; from the French malgré.

47. Denis O'Bryen, Utrum Horum? The Government, or the Country (1796), pp. 72–105.

48. Warren Hastings (1732–1818), Governor-General of India, was tried for corruption over seven years (1788–95). Burke was one of his chief opponents in Parliament.

49. See Shakespeare, Henry VI, Part Two 3.1.351.

50. "Chrononhotonthologos" was a burlesque by Henry Carey first performed in 1734. The name came to be applied to particularly bombastic speakers.

51. John Stuart Taylor was a Norwich surgeon who testified on Thelwall's behalf at his trial.

52. Robert Watt, executed for treason in 1794.

53. State Trials for High Treason, Part Third, Containing the Trial of Mr. John Thelwall (1795), p. 103.

54. South Burma, e.g., an elephant.

55. See Parliamentary Register 40 (1795), 71.

56. A creature or person, used chiefly in sport or irony.

57. John Reeves, Thoughts on the English Government (4 pts., 1796–1800).

58. See in particular Niccolò Machiavelli (1469–1527): The Discourses on the First Ten Books of Titus Livy (1531), bk. 1, chap. 13.

59. Henrico Caterino Davila, The History of the Civil Wars in France, 2 vols. (1758). See A Relation of the Barbarous and Bloody Massacre of About an Hundred Thousand Protestants . . . Collected Out of Mezeray, Thuanus, etc. (1678; 1725 ed.), pp. 33–40.

60. Gaspard II de Coligny, Seigneur de Châtillon (1519–72): Huguenot leader during the early years of the Wars of Religion (1562–98).

61. Anne, Duc de Montmorency (1493–1567): Gaspard de Coligny's uncle; fought against the Huguenots.

62. Emperor Charles V (1500–1558) began his wars against Protestantism in 1521.

63. See, e.g., 2 Samuel 5:8.

64. The Pharisees were an early Jewish religious group renowned for their piety. The Sadducees were a priestly caste.

65. The Tribune 1:89.

66. Benedict Arnold (1741–1801), traitor of the American Revolution who went over to the British in 1779.

67. Gilbert Burnet, *Bishop Burnet's History of His Own Time*, 2 vols. (1724–34), 1:14.

68. See *Parliamentary Register* 35 (1793), 428–58, 470–81.

69. Charles-Eugène de Lorraine (1751–1825), Prince de Lambesc: commander of troops in Paris.

70. See Jean-François Mallet du Pan, *Correspondance Politique pour Servir à l'Histoire du Républicanisme Français* (1796), p. xlix.

71. Tarquinius Priscus (616–579 B.C.), fifth King of Rome; later succeeded by Lucius Tarquinius Superbus, who reigned from 534 to 510 B.C. and murdered his predecessor.

72. Nero (A.D. 37–68), Roman emperor 54–68, often blamed for the fire that destroyed half of Rome in 64.

73. Caligula, or Gaius Julius Caesar Germanicus (A.D. 12–41), a particularly despotic Roman emperor, reigned 37–41.

74. Domitian (A.D. 51–96), Roman emperor 81–96.

75. Heliogabalus or Elagabalus, Roman emperor A.D. 218–22, known for his dissolute excesses.

76. *The Essays of Francis Bacon*, 2 vols. (1787), 2:58.

77. More's *Utopia* was published in 1516.

78. Hume's "Idea of a Perfect Commonwealth" first appeared in his *Political Discourses* (1750), pp. 281–304.

79. Plutarch, *The Philosophy Commonly Called the Morals* (1657), pp. 445–61.

80. Bills of attainder denied civil rights to those convicted of treason or felony, including the forfeiture of land and inheritance rights. They dated from 1459 and were wielded most notoriously against the Earl of Strafford in 1641 and against Laud. Their last use was against the Irish rebel leader Lord Edward Fitzgerald in 1798.

81. E.g., *Parliamentary History of England* 32 (1818), cols. 273–74.

82. See *The Times*, 1 November 1796, p. 2.

83. John Milton, *Paradise Lost*, 2nd ed. (1674), 1.266.

84. Alexander Pope, *Works*, 9 vols. (1752), 1:83.

85. Gaius Cilius Maecenas (c. 70–8 B.C.) was a wealthy confidant of Emperor Augustus.

86. The Medici were a Florentine banking family active in civic life from the thirteenth century. Its best-known member was Lorenzo the Magnificent (1449–92).

87. Burke, *Works*, 1:32.

88. See Judges 13–16.

89. Armed struggle against Russia began in early 1794 and ended with the Third Partition of the country in 1795.

90. Trials by fire, submersion in water, and the wager of battle were common in medieval Europe and in England until the middle of the thirteenth century.

91. Tacitus, *The Works of Cornelius Tacitus*, ed. A. Murphy, 4 vols. (1793), 4:36.

92. Reference uncertain. See, generally, *Parliamentary Register* 8 (1778), 101.

93. Marcus Tullius Cicero (106–43 B.C.), Roman orator and politician.

94. Burke, *Works*, 3:13.

95. John Locke (1632–1704), philosopher and political writer.

96. Constantine the Great (c. 285–337), emperor of Rome, baptized a Christian on his deathbed.

97. Sir Robert Filmer (d. 1653) was famous for his vindication of absolutism, *Patriarcha* (1680), which was the target of Locke's *Two Treatises on Government* (1690).

98. A leading Whig politician under Charles II, Somers was probably not, however, the author of this work. Algernon Sydney (1622–83), leading seventeenth-century republican. Thelwall named one of his sons Algernon Sydney Thelwall.

99. *The Judgement of Whole Kingdoms and Nations* (10th ed., 1771), pp. 11–19.

100. Burke, *Works*, 3:43.

101. Dr. Richard Price (1723–91), Nonconformist clergyman and moral philosopher; on 4 November 1789, preached the famous Old Jewry sermon commemorating the Revolution of 1688 and published as *A Discourse on the Love of Our Country* (1789), which provoked Burke's *Reflections* on the Revolution in France (1790).

102. Richard Price, *A Discourse on the Love of Our Country*, 2nd ed. (1790), p. 38.

103. Burke, *Works*, 3:24.

104. Woden or Odin, the ruler of heaven and earth in Nordic mythology.

105. Alaric (b. c. 370), leader of the army that sacked Rome in 410.

106. Published from 1776–83.

107. See Geoffroi, Marquis de Limon, *Manifeste Contre la Révolution Française. Déclaration que . . . le Duc de Brunswick . . . adresse aux habitans de la France, etc. Déclaration Additionelle, etc.* (1792).

108. Attila, king of the Huns 434–53, and one of the greatest barbarian enemies of Rome.

109. Gibbon, *Decline and Fall of the Roman Empire*, 6:126.

110. Gundobald (d. 516), king of the Burgundians.

111. Tacitus, *Works*, 4:187.

112. Publius Tacitus (56[57]–c.117), Roman historian much admired by Gibbon and others.

113. Gibbon, *Decline and Fall of the Roman Empire*, 5:313.

114. The Amphictyonic League was a religious association of Greek communities dedicated to protecting a particular shrine. The best known was the shrine at Delphi.

115. Hugo Grotius (1583–1645) and Samuel Pufendorf (1632–94) were the best-known natural law writers of this period.

116. E.g., Burke, *Letters to a Member*, 11th ed. (1796), p. 160.

117. The starting-point of all such discussions was Rousseau's *Discourse on the Origins of Inequality* (1755).

118. Gilbert Burnet (1643–1715), historian and Bishop of Salisbury.

119. George Louis Leclerc (1707–88), Comte de Buffon, naturalist.

120. Polybius, *General History*, 3:1–22.

121. Burke, *Works*, 1:10–15.

122. Romulus, first king of Rome, c. 753 B.C.

123. Dionysius of Halicarnassus, *Roman Antiquities*, 1:235.

124. Thelwall probably has Godwin in mind here. See William Godwin, *Enquiry Concerning Political Justice*, 2 vols. (1793), bk. 1, chap. 6.

125. This emphasis is also probably derived from Godwin, for whom it became the germ of an "anarchist" philosophy. See ibid., bk. 3, chap. 7.

126. Even Paine conceded that some original rights were ceded at the foundation of civil society, such as the right to judge in our own behalf. But the target here is clearly Burke's much stronger view that no natural rights survive in civil society, only civil rights then existing.

127. Dionysius of Halicarnassus, *Roman Antiquities*, 2:288.

128. In 1792–93 in particular, loyalist associations spread the rumor that the radicals sought to equalize property following a parliamentary reform.

129. Like Paine, in *The Decline and Fall of the English System of Finance* (1796), Thelwall here anticipates the collapse of the system of public funding or government borrowing.

130. Probably a reference to Homer's *Odyssey*, bk. 9.

131. Without a dower, portionless.

132. Jack (or John) Cade (d. 1450), an Irishman who fomented a rebellion against monarchial extortions in Kent in 1450.

133. House closely associated with the French monarchy from the fourteenth century. Louis-

Philippe Joseph, Duc d'Orléans (1747–93), known as Philippe Egalité, supported the French Revolution.

134. Notably Lucius Sergius Catilina (d. 62 B.C.), a disreputable Roman politician.

135. Christopher Columbus (1451–1506), Italian navigator.

136. Captain James Cook (1728–79), British navigator.

137. Southern African tribes.

138. The Scottish historian William Robertson (1721–93), quoted later here, is probably meant.

139. Edward Gibbon (1737–94), historian and religious skeptic.

140. See Francis Bacon, *Philosophical Works*, 3 vols. (1733), 2:345.

141. E.g., William Robertson, *The History of America*, 2 vols. (1777), 1:257.

142. Edward Gibbon, *The History of the Decline and Fall of the Roman Empire*, 6 vols. (1789), 4:275–77.

143. E.g., John White, *Journal of a Voyage to New South Wales* (1790), p. 174.

144. Tacitus, *The Works of Cornelius Tacitus*, ed. A. Murphy, 4 vols. (1793), 4: 45–46.

145. Ibid., 4, p. 27.

146. Tacitus, *Works*, 4:28.

147. G. *Julius Caesar's Commentaries*, ed. Martin Bladen, 8th ed. (1770), p. 60.

148. "To the Covetous," *A Translation of the Odes and Epodes of Horace* (1737), pp. 182–87.

149. Tacitus, *Works*, 4:23.

150. G. *Julius Caesar's Commentaries*, ed. Martin Bladen, 8th ed. (1770), p. 117.

151. Blackstone, *Commentaries*, 2:83.

152. MS correction by Thelwall; "visionary" in the published text.

153. This had been a frequent charge against Paine's *Rights of Man* in 1791–93. See my *Thomas Paine: Social and Political Thought* (London: Unwin Hyman, 1989), pp. 159–64.

154. Blackstone, *Commentaries*, 1:36.

155. For similar sentiments, see Arthur Young, *The Example of France, a Warning to Britain* (1793), pp. 33, 96.

156. "Septembrizers" refers to the September 1792 massacres of prisoners in Paris by mobs fearing counterrevolution.

157. *Report of the Committee, Appointed by the Agricultural Society, to Take into Consideration the State of the Waste Lands and Common Fields of This Kingdom* (1795), p. 15.

158. E.g., David Davies, *The Case of the Labourers in Husbandry Stated and Considered* (1795), p. 8.

159. See supra, pp. 245–83.

160. Ortolan: a small bird.

161. David Davies, *The Case of the Labourers in Husbandry Stated and Considered* (1795), p. 49.

162. See supra, pp. 255–61.

163. Francis Bacon (1561–1626), philosopher and Lord Chancellor.

164. "Or even a dozen Gibbons" in the printed text.

165. "Expeditions" in the printed text.

166. See Plutarch's *Lives*, 5 vols. (1700), 1:111–12.

167. See Dionysius of Halicarnassus, *Roman Antiquities*, bk. 6, chap. 22. This form of combat was very rare.

168. Publius Cornelius Scipio Nasica Serapio, Consul in 138 B.C., conservative aristocrat killed by his cousin, Tiberius Gracchus.

169. See Nathaniel Hooke, *The Roman History*, 4 vols. (1745), 2:526–38.

170. Lucius Cornelius Sulla (c. 138–78 B.C.), Roman general renowned for vindictive cruelty on behalf of patrician class.

171. Gaius Marius (157–86 B.C.), general who introduced volunteer army drawing from plebian classes.

172. Gaius Julius Caesar (100–44 B.C.), Roman general and dictator.

173. Gnaeus Pompeius Magnus (106–48 B.C.), Roman general and rival of Caesar.

174. Dionysius of Halicarnassus, *Roman Antiquities*, 3:411.

175. Machiavelli, *Works* (trans. Farneworth), 3:19.

176. Ibid., pp. 21–23.

177. "Destroy" in the printed text.

178. "By the sword and terror" in the printed text.

179. John Milton, *Paradise Lost*, 2nd ed. (1674), 2.6.

180. *Letter to a Noble Lord*, pp. 28–29.

181. Blackstone, *Commentaries*, 2:45–46.

182. Ibid.

183. Ibid., p. 92.

184. Probably a reference to John de Warenne (1231?–1304), a member of Henry III's council.

185. Hengist (d. 488), first recorded Saxon king in Anglo-Saxon England.

186. Aelle, fifth-century Saxon ruler who supposedly founded the kingdom of West Sussex.

187. Cerdic (d. 534), king of the West Saxons from 519.

188. Egbert (d. 839), king of Wessex; Athelstan (d. 939), son of Edward the Elder.

189. MS addition.

190. The Domesday Book was a survey of England ordered by William the Conqueror in 1086.

191. Blackstone, *Commentaries*, 2:51.

192. "An Act Changing the Custom of Gavelkind," 31 Hen. 7, c. 3, disgaveled certain Kentish landholdings.

193. MS addition.

Index

Acaia, 289
Adair, James (d. 1798), 54–56, 393
Aelle, 494
agrarian laws, xxxi, xxxiii, 1, 336, 489
Agricola, 449
agriculture, xl, xliii, xlv, xlvii, xlix, 178–79,
    181, 195, 200, 277, 467, 483–84
Aleric (b. c. 370), 449
Alexander the Great (356–323 B.C.), 313
Alfred the Great (849–99), 223
Algiers, 427
Alien Act, 86
Althorpe, George John (1758–1834), 399
America, United States of, xxiii, 55, 157,
    175, 426, 456
anarchism, xxviii
Anthony, Mark (83–30 B.C.), 93
Antoinette, Marie (1755–93), 220
Appius Claudius, 340
Arianism, 219
Aristotle (384–322 B.C.), 487
Arminianism, 219
Arnold, Benedict (1741–1801), 424
Artois, Charles Philippe, Comte d' (1757–
    1836), 206
atheism, 125, 219, 409, 422, 431
Athelstan (d. 939), 494
Attila (d. 453), 449

Bacon, Francis (1561–1626), 373, 428, 463,
    486
Barère de Vieuzac, Bertrand (1755–1841), 96
Barlow, Joel (1754–1812), 47, 221–22
Baxter, John, 50

Bedford, Duke of (Francis Russell, 1765–
    1802), lv, 348–50, 352, 354, 380
benevolence, universal, xxviii, 57, 91–92, 96,
    101, 295
Beresford, John (1738–1805), 206
Billaud-Varenne, Jacques-Nicolas (1756–
    1819), 96
Bisset, Robert (1759–1809), 401, 489
Blackstone, William (1723–1800), xlviii, liii,
    29, 35, 38, 471, 479, 492
Breillat, Thomas, 222
Brissot, Jacques-Pierre (1754–93), 308
Brissotines, xxix, xxiii, 120, 125–26, 137,
    308
Broglio, Victor-François (1718–1804), 129,
    426
Brothers, Richard (1757–1824), 229
Brunswick, Duke of (Karl Wilhelm Ferdinand,
    1735–1806), 122
Buckingham, Duke of (Humphrey Stafford,
    1402–60), 340
Buffon (Georges Louis Leclerc, Comte de,
    1707–88), 455
Burdett, Francis (1770–1844), xxxv
Burgh, James (1714–75), xl–xli
Burke, Edmund (1729–97), xvii, xxiv, xxxvii,
    li, lv, 95, 114, 156, 211–12, 218, 220,
    223, 274, 283, 309, 330–87, 390, 392,
    395–99, 402–3, 405, 407–17, 420–27,
    429–33, 435–36, 438–44, 447, 449,
    453–55, 459, 463, 474, 479, 493, 495,
    497
Burnet, Gilbert (1643–1715), 455
Butler, Samuel (1612–80), 251

Cade, Jack (d. 1450), 462
Caesar, Augustus (63 B.C.—A.D. 14), 93
Caesar, Julius (100–44 B.C.), 469–70, 479, 489
Caligula (12–41), 427
Callendar, James (d. 1803), xxvii
Calonne, Charles-Alexandre (1734–1802), 206
Calvinism, 219
capitalists, 285, 482–83, 498
Carthage, 59–60, 288, 381
Cartwright, John (1740–1824), xviii, xxxiv–xxxv
Cassius (d. 42 B.C.), 489
Cerdic (d. 534), 494
Charles I (1600–1649), 9, 206, 299, 303, 319
Charles II (1630–85), 9, 20, 51, 203, 297, 300–301, 303, 352
Charles V (1500–1558), 422
Charles VI (1685–1740), 91
Chaucer, Geoffrey (?1340–1400), 250
China, 85, 154, 426
Christ, Jesus, 423
Cicero, Marcus Tullius (106–43 B.C.), xxvii, 369, 444
Clarendon, Earl of (Edward Hyde, 1609–74), 299
Clerk, John, Lord Justice (1757–1832), 42, 190–92
Cobbett, William (1763–1835), xxvii
Coke, Edward (1552–1634), 7
Coleridge, Samuel Taylor (1772–1834), xxviii, xxxii–xxxiii
Coligny, Gaspar II de (1519–72), 421
Collot d'Herbois, Jean-Marie (1749–96), 96
Columbus, Christopher (1451–1506), 463
commerce, xl–xlvi, xlviii–xlix, 67–68, 188, 285–94, 437, 498
compact, implied, xlviii–lii, 1, 477–78
Condé, Prince de (Louis-Joseph, 1736–1818), 206, 308
Condorcet, Marie-Jean-Antoine-Nicolas Caritat, Marquis de (1743–94), 361
Constantine (?288–337), 447
Cooke, Captain James (1728–79), 463
Cooper, Thomas (1759–1839), 221
Cordeliers, Club of the, 368
corruption. See monopoly; patronage; representation; rights; taxation
Crompton, Peter (d. 1833), 402

Cromwell, Oliver (1599–1658), 303–7
Cumberland, Richard (1631–1718), liii

Dalrymple, Sir John (1726–1810), 238
Danby, Lord (Thomas Osborne, 1631–1712), 20
Danton, Georges-Jacques (1759–94), 125, 362
Darwin, Erasmus (1731–1802), 387
Dauphin (called Louis XVII, 1785–95), 301
Davies, David (d. c. 1819), 253, 278
debt, national, 74, 76
Defenderism, 243–45
deism, 125, 219
democracy, xxxviii, 209–11, 213, 216–17, 222, 225, 310, 331. See also republicanism
Demosthenes (c. 384–322 B.C.), xxvii
Desmoulins, Lucie-Simplice-Camille Benoit (1760–94), 128
Devaynes, William (c. 1730–1809), 358
Dionysius of Halicarnassus, 393, 456
Dodd, William (d. 1778), 184
Domitian (51–96), 427, 450
Dumourier, Charles-François Du Périer (1739–1823), 424
Dundas, Henry (1742–1811), xxii, 40, 45, 66, 148, 161, 181, 191, 206, 293, 366
du Pan, Jacques Mallet (1749–1800), 426

East India Company, 297–98
East Indies, Dutch, 203
Eaton, Daniel Isaac (?1751–1814), xix
Eaton, Henry, xxi
Edward II (1284–1327), 9, 99
Edward III (1312–77), 247
Egbert (d. 839), 494
Elizabeth I (1533–1603), 141, 302
employers, corporation of. See capitalists
enclosures, 175–77, 238
English Revolution of 1649, 301–2, 305, 307
equality, xli, xliii, xlv, xlvii, l–li, 118, 194, 205, 223, 288, 346, 464, 470, 472, 490
Erskine, Thomas (1750–1823), xxiv, 4, 112, 382, 407
Eyre, Sir James (1734–99), 211, 213, 418

Falkland, Lord, 44
Fawkes, Guy (1570–1606), 297
feudalism, xli, 264–65, 291, 481–98
Filmer, Sir Robert (d. 1653), 447

Fitzwilliam, William Wentworth (1748–1834), 114, 208, 241, 349, 445
Flanders, 58, 156
Florence, 288
food prices, xxxvii, 67–69, 138–59, 162–209, 230–31, 247, 252–63, 278–82, 324, 326
Ford, Richard, 53
Foster, Sir Michael (1689–1763), 99–100
Foulkes, John, 113
Fouquier-Tinville, Antoine-Quentin (1746–95), 361, 367
Fox, Charles James (1749–1806), xv, xxxiv, 73, 227, 320, 382
Frend, William (1757–1841), xxxiv, 165, 222
Frost, John (1750–1842), 223

Gaunt, John of (1340–99), 177, 350
Gavelkind, 472, 496
Genoa, 288
George II (1683–1760), 173, 270
George III (1738–1820), xvi, xix, 447
Germany, 121, 296, 449, 467, 470
Germany, Emperor of (Francis II, 1768–1835), 84
Gerrald, Joseph (1763–96), 42–43, 132
Gibbon, Edward (1737–94), 36, 449, 463, 467
Gibbs, Vicary (1751–1820), 4, 113
Girondins. See Brissotines
Glencoe, massacre at, 300, 367
Godwin, William (1756–1836), xxvii–xxx, xxxiv, xl, xlii, 109, 338, 382
Goldsmith, Oliver (1728–74), 192, 383
Gothic constitution, 398, 405, 435, 440, 442, 444, 446, 448–50, 454, 462, 473, 478, 488, 490–91, 494, 496
Gracchi, 336, 489
Grange, Lady (Rachel Chiesly, d. 1745), 163
gratitude, principle of, 109–16, 333
Greece, xl, xliv–xlv, 287–88, 400, 426, 450, 487
Grenville, Lord George (1753–1813), 348, 354, 380, 417
Grey, William de (1719–81), 179
Grotius, Hugo (1583–1645), xlviii–liii, liv, 450
Groves, John, 214, 417
Gundobald, 449
Gurney, Bartlett (1756–1803), 403

Habeas Corpus Act, 44, 47, 86
Hall, Charles (c. 1738–c. 1835), liii

Hampden, John (c. 1595–1643), 44
Hanover, Elector of, 223
Hardy, Thomas (1752–1832), xviii, xxiv–xxv, xxxv, 54, 113, 316
Harrington, James (1611–77), xxvii, xlvii
Harrison, John (1738–1811), 227
Hastings, Warren (1732–1818), 416, 433
Hawkesbury, Baron. See Jenkinson, Charles
Hébert, Jacques-René (1757–94), 128
Heliogabulus (c. 205–22), 427
Henderland, Lord (Alexander Murray, 1736–95), 42
Hengist (d. 488), 494
Henry VII (1457–1509), 215
Henry VIII (1491–1547), 9, 349
Hesse-Cassel, Prince of, 223
Hodgson, William (1745–1851), xix, 222–23
Holcroft, Thomas (1745–1809), xxxiv, 62
Holland, 58, 98, 117–18, 127, 156–57, 200, 203, 229, 288, 426, 456
Holt, Daniel (c. 1766–99), 222
Horace (65–8 b.c.), 345, 469
House of Commons, 6, 71, 73, 100, 156, 172, 179, 190, 201, 204, 209, 212, 216, 226–27, 271, 287, 291, 297, 320, 325, 339, 355, 404, 478
Howard, John (1726–90), xv
Huguenots, 421–22
Hume, David (1711–76), 141, 162, 217, 247, 265, 268–69, 271–73, 430
Hunt, Henry (1773–1835), xxxv
Hutcheson, Frances (1694–1746), l–li, liii, 1

Ideson, Luke, 358
Ireland, 206–7, 236–45

Jackson, Rev. William (?1737–95), 135
Jacobins, Jacobinism, xxiii, xxix, xxxix, lv, 47, 54, 69, 93–94, 127, 136, 141, 160, 195, 203, 268, 331, 333, 362, 366, 392, 409, 412–13, 415, 422, 435, 450, 454, 463, 479, 497
James I (1566–1625), 186
James II (1633–1701), 9, 320
Japan, 85, 426–27
Jenkinson, Charles (1727–1808), 66, 156, 349, 357, 415
Jenkinson, Robert Banks (1770–1828), 234
Jenyns, Soame (1704–87), 178
Johnson, Samuel (1709–84), 220

Julius II, Pope (1443–1513), 128
Juvenal (c. 60–140), 345

Kellermann, François-Christophe (1735–1820), 135
King, Dr. William (1786–1865), liv
Koscuisko, Andrzej (1746–1817), 204

laboring classes, xviii, xxxvii–xxxix , xlv, xlviii–xlix, li–liv, 30–33, 67, 74–80, 134, 138–50, 181–209, 229–32, 236–39, 245–66, 276–78, 324, 326, 332, 384, 392, 395, 398–401, 405–6, 493–94, 496–97
Lally-Tollendal, Trophime-Gérard (1751–1830), 129
Lamb, Charles (1775–1834), xxxiv
Lambesque, Charles-Eugène de Lorraine (1751–1825), 426
Lansdowne, Marquis of (William Petty, 1737–1805), xxvi
Laud, William (1573–1645), 43
Lauderdale, Earl of (James Maitland, 1759–1839), 361, 382
Le Bon, Guislain-François-Joseph (1765–95), 361, 367
Licinius Stolo, 336
Locke, John (1632–1704), xxvii, xlix–li, xlix, liii, 445, 448
London, 298
London Corresponding Society, xiii, xviii, xxi–xxv, xxix, xlii, xlv, 25, 36, 38–39, 135, 321–22, 354, 460
Lonsdale, Earl of (James Lowther, 1736–1802), 349
Loughborough, Baron (Alexander Wedderburn, 1733–1805), 66, 156, 349, 361
Louis XVI (1754–93), 12, 357, 426
Louis XVIII (1755–1824), 229
luxury, xl, xlii, xliv–xlv, 67, 196, 251, 264, 269, 286–87, 290, 356, 367, 379, 461, 479, 482–85, 491
Lycurgus, 185
Lynam, George, 25, 62, 417

Macartney, George (1737–1806), 270
Macdonald, Archibald (1747–1826), 349
Machiavelli, Niccolò (1469–1527), xlvii, 116, 124, 127–28, 358, 377–79, 421, 490
machinery, liv–lv, 485
Mack, Colonel, 66

Mackintosh, James (1765–1832), 221
Maecenas, Gaius Cilius (c. 70–8 B.C.), 435
Magna Charta, 21, 47, 223
Mansfield, Sir James (1733–1821), 226
manufacturing, xl, xlix, liv–lv, 437, 498
Marat, Jean-Paul (1743–93), 37, 54, 124, 308, 366–67, 394, 416
Margarot, Maurice (1745–1816), 42
Marius, Gaius (157–86 B.C.), 489
materialism, xvii
Medici, 435, 486
Memmay, M. de, 123, 130
Mexico, 274, 292
Mill, John Stuart (1806–73), liv
Miranda, Francisco de (1750–1816), 135
Mitford, Sir John (1748–1830), 343, 382, 393
Mohammed (c. 569–632), 426, 444
monarchy, xvi–xvii, 8–11, 15, 17–18, 22, 24, 36, 46, 133, 136, 195, 211–15, 242, 268–69, 311–12, 322, 440, 445, 448
Monk, George (1608–70), 299
monopoly, xliii, xlvi–xlvii, 30, 69–70, 79, 82, 99, 153, 182, 195, 207, 240, 285–86, 289–93, 296, 484
Montesquieu (Charles de Secondat, Baron de, 1689–1755), 32–33, 46, 381
Montgaillard, Jean-Gabriel-Maurice (1761–1841), 137, 308–9
Montmorency, Anne, Duc de (1493–1567), 422
moral economy, xxxvii, liii
More, Thomas (1478–1535), 336
   Utopia, 336, 430
Mornington, Lord (Richard Colley Wellesley, 1760–1842), 187, 287
Morocco, 427
Morton, John, 190
Mountain. See Jacobins
Moyle, Walter (1672–1721), xxvii, xlvii
Muir, Thomas (1765–99), 42

Napoleon Bonaparte (1769–1821), xxxv
National Convention, French, 12–14, 70, 158, 288, 479
nationality, principle of, 107
Nebuchadnezzar, 196
Nelson, Admiral Horatio (1758–1805), xxxiv
Nero (37–68), 427
New Holland, 132
Newnham, Alderman, 134
Nicholson, William (1753–1815), 144

North, Frederick Lord (1732–92), 149, 180
Northmore, Thomas (1766–1851), xxxi
Numa Pompilius, 386

O'Bryen, Denis (1755–1832), 415
Ogilvie, William (1736–1819), liii
Old Sarum, 189
Owen, Robert (1771–1858), xxxi–xxxii, liv

Paine, Thomas (1737–1809), xiii, xvii, xxvii,
    xxxvi–xxxvii, xxxviii, xl–xli, xlv–xlvii,
    1, 47, 199, 221, 276, 309, 334, 336,
    430, 487
  Rights of Man, 336, 361, 395, 441
Paley, William (1743–1805), liii
Palmer, Thomas Fyshe (1747–1802), 42
partnership, law of, li–liii
patriotism, xxviii
patronage, xxix, lv, 31, 38, 59, 71, 87, 134,
    163, 168, 187–89, 206, 217–18, 250,
    266–67, 269–76, 280–83, 287, 293,
    297, 333–34, 339, 341, 347, 349, 363,
    372, 381, 394, 402, 414–15, 417, 425,
    427
Peacock, Daniel (1767/8–1840), 269, 287–88
Perreau, Robert and Daniel (d. 1776), 184
Peru, 274, 292
Pharisees, 423
Physical Society, xx
Pilnitz, Treaty of, 357
Pitt, William (1759–1806), xxii, 17, 66, 73,
    95, 131–37, 149, 155–56, 160–61, 164,
    172, 174, 181, 187, 204, 206, 218, 222,
    226–27, 287, 297, 320, 335, 366, 380,
    404, 415, 420, 433, 454
Plato (c. 428–347 B.C.), xxvii, 210
Plutarch (c. 46–120), 431, 489
Poland, xviii, 159–60, 182, 202–5, 442
Polybius (c. 201–120 B.C.), 393, 455
Pompey (Gnaeus Pompeius Magnus, 106–48
    B.C.), 489
Ponsonby, George (1755–1817), 241
Poole, Thomas (1765–1837), xxxiii
poor rates, xxxvi, 78, 266
Pope (Giovanni Angelo Braschi, 1717–99),
    242
Pope, Alexander (1688–1744), 185
Portland, Duke of (William Bentinck, 1738–
    1809), 114, 348, 351
Powis, Thomas (1743–1800), 382
Priestley, Joseph (1733–1804), xviii
primogeniture, xlvii, 237, 474, 493, 496

property, xxxvi, xlvii, 437, 460–80
Prussia, 121, 170, 204
Prussia, King of (Friedrich Wilhelm II, 1744–
    97), 121, 157–58, 161, 172, 204
Pufendorf, Samuel (1632–94), xlix, lii–liii,
    xlviii–xlix, 450

Quakers, Quakerism, 119, 125, 403

Rapparees, 238
Reeves, John (?1752–1829), 35, 194, 225,
    234, 238, 288–89, 358, 382, 420–21,
    452
Regency Bill, 343
representation, doctrine of virtual, 27–28
representation, system of parliamentary, 6,
    27–38, 48, 59, 71, 73, 161, 187, 208,
    217, 219, 271–75, 289, 291, 405, 448,
    456
republicanism, xxxvi, xxxix, l, lii, 54, 129,
    160, 195, 204, 209, 213, 268, 287–88,
    310, 313–14, 341, 409, 440, 450
resistance, right of, 99–100
Revolution of 1688, 21, 216, 220, 224, 300,
    445
Richard II (1367–1400), 9
Richard III (1452–85), 9
Richmond, Duke of (Charles Lennox, 1735–
    1806), 207, 222, 349, 406
Richter, John (d. 1830), 51
rights, xlvi–xlviii, xlix, lv, 97, 215, 268, 316,
    336–37, 364, 381, 387, 395, 397, 400,
    404, 423, 446, 451–52, 456–59, 465,
    476–77, 486, 490
Ritson, Joseph (1752–1803), xxvii
Robertson, William (1721–93), 463, 467
Robespierre, Maximilien (1758–94), lv, 97,
    124–25, 127–28, 133–37, 204, 233, 288,
    308, 314, 366–68, 416, 454, 480
Robinson, Henry Crabb (1775–1867), xxxiv
Rochefoucauld-Liancourt, François-Alexandre,
    Duc de (1747–1827), 361
Rochester, Bishop of (Samuel Horsley, 1733–
    1806), 361
Rockingham, Marquis of (Charles Watson
    Wentworth, 1730–82), 341
Roland de la Platière, Jeanne-Manon (1754–
    93), 361, 376
Rome, xv, xl, xliv, 22–23, 33, 36, 43, 53,
    59–60, 102, 336, 341, 381, 445, 449,
    456, 459, 470, 482, 487–89, 494
Romulus, 456, 489

Rose, George (1749–1818), 275, 339
Rose, Sir John, 225
Rousseau, Jean-Jacques (1712–78), 361
Royal Exchange, 285
Rufinus, Flavius (d. 395), 53
Russel, John (First Earl of Bedford, ?1486–1555), 349–50, 352
Russel, Lord William (1629–83), 352
Russia, xviii, 160, 249
Russia, Empress of (Catherine II, 1729–96), 160, 377, 412
Rutherforth, Thomas (1712–71) l, lii
Rutland, Duke of (John Henry Manners, 1778–1857), 348

Sadducees, 423
St. Bartholomew's Day, massacre of, 123, 377, 426
St. Dunstan, 386
St. Omer's, Jesuit school at, 156
St. Peter, 444
San Marino, 289
Santerre, Antoine-Joseph (1752–1809), 135
Sardinia, 121
Saxon constitution, 21, 214, 302, 448, 494–95
Scipio Nassica, 489
Scotland, xviii, 42–43, 70–71, 107, 163, 167, 207, 232–37, 300, 312
Scott, Sir John (1751–1838), xxii, 366–67, 382, 393
Seditious Meetings and Assemblies, and Treasonable Practices Acts (1795), xxix, 44, 335, 344, 361, 380, 382–83, 404
Sejanus (d. 31), 53
sensibility, 108
Servius Tullius, 336, 342, 459–60
Sharp, Granville (1735–1813), xlvi
Sieyès, Emmanuel-Joseph (1748–1836), 308
Skirving, William (d. 1796), 42
slavery, slave trade, xvi, xxxix, 242, 253, 286, 293–94, 391, 405–8, 468, 478
Smith, Adam (1723–90), xliii, li
Smith, Robert (1752–1838), 402
socialism, xxxviii, liv
Society for Constitutional Information, xix, 135, 448
Society of Free Debate, xviii
Society of Friends of the People, xviii, 48
Socinianism, 219
Socrates (c. 469–399 B.C.), xxvii, 386, 400–401

Solon (c. 638–558 B.C.), 287
Somers, Lord John (1651–1716), 28–29, 448
Spain, 185
Sparta, xli, 59–60, 102, 151, 185, 316, 381, 468, 490
speculation, xliii, xliv, liv, 194, 230, 286, 292–93
Spence, Thomas (1750–1814), xix, xxxvii
Spencer, George John (1758–1834), 114
Spenser, Edmund (?1552–99), 247
Stanhope, Charles (1753–1816), 122, 204
Steele, Thomas (1753–1823), 339
stoicism, 1
Sulla, Lucius Cornelius (c. 138–78 B.C.), 489
Suvarov, Aleksandr (1729–1800), 205, 366, 449
Switzerland, 289, 426, 472, 482
Sydney, Algernon (1622–83), xxvii, 51, 448

Tacitus (c. 55–120), 442, 450, 463, 467–69, 479
Taillon, Jean-Lambert (1767–1820), 308
Tarquin, 342, 427
taxation, xxxix, liv, 75, 77, 79, 85, 190, 226, 270–72, 276–78, 484–85
Taylor, John, 62
Temple, Sir William (1628–99), 493
Test and Corporation Acts, 240
Thelwall, Joseph, xiv
Theseus, 287
Thompson, William (1775–1833), liv
Timms, 51–52, 417
tithes, 182, 197–99, 485
Tooke, John Horne (1736–1812), xvii, xxiv, 113, 179, 316
Tooke, William (1744–1820), 179
Toplady, Augustus (1740–78), 218
Tories, 186, 224, 226–27, 274, 383
treason, high, 7–61, 121, 132–33, 168, 221, 226, 394
Turkey, 43
Tuscany, 96, 98
Tyler, Wat (d. 1381), 244, 322

Utrecht, treaty of, 451

Vendée, La, rebellions in, 98, 150, 181, 295
Venice, 288
Virgil, 367
virtue, principle of, xl–xli, 88–116. See also benevolence, universal

Wadstrom, Carl Bernhard (1746–99), xliv, 286
Wales, xxxiii, 200
Walker, Thomas (1749–1817), 77
Walsh, James, 168
wants/needs, xliv, 67, 481. *See also* luxury
war, xli, lv, 76–78, 81–85, 87, 157, 202–3, 227, 264, 276–77, 291, 293, 347, 357
Warenne, John de (?1231–1304), 494
Warwick, Earl of, 265
waste lands, 175–76, 180, 483
Watson, Brook (1735–1807), 159
Watt, Robert (d. 1794), 135
Wentworth, Thomas (1593–1641), 206
West Indies, British, 242, 294–97, 391, 468, 478
West Indies, French, 99, 137
Westmorland, Earl of (John Fane, 1759–1841), 349
Whigs, xxix, 56, 107, 186, 224, 226–27, 274, 300, 383
White, Joseph, 53

White Boys, 238–39
Wilde, John, 212
William I (1028–87), 215, 495
William III (1650–1702), 186, 300, 351
Williams, George, xx
Williams, Helen Maria (1762–1827), 229
Winchelsea, Lord (George William Fitz-Hatton, 1747–1823), xx, 345
Windham, William (1750–1810), 95, 114, 212, 283, 333, 347–48, 356, 366, 382, 397, 417, 426
Winterbotham, William (1763–1829), 222
Woden, 448
Wollstonecraft, Mary (1759–97), xvii
women, rights of, 397
Woolsey, Robert, 369
Wordsworth, William (1770–1850), xxxii–xxxiii

Young, Arthur (1741–1820), xiii, 309, 377

Zisca, John (c. 1376–1424), 359, 391, 409